Music Therapy Supervision

Second Edition

Edited by
Michele Forinash

Barcelona PUBLISHERS

Music Therapy Supervision (Second Edition)

Copyright © 2019

Print ISBN: 9781945411427
E-ISBN: 9781945411434

Distributed throughout the world by:
Barcelona Publishers
10231 Plano Road
Dallas TX 75238

All orders are placed online as follows:

North American Orders: www.barcelonapublishers.com
Other International Orders: www.eurospanbookstore.com/barcelona

In memory of

Carolyn Kenny,

mother of qualitative research in North American music therapy;

Benedikte Barth Scheiby,

who made Mary Priestley's Analytical Music Therapy a vital part of
music therapy in the USA;

and

Al Bumanis,

director of conferences for the American Music Therapy Association, who ended
each day by saying that he had "kept music therapy safe for another day."

Indeed, they all did.

ACKNOWLEDGMENTS

Many people have been supportive of creating a second edition of this book. First and foremost, thanks go to Ken Bruscia for being such an excellent mentor and colleague and asking me in 1997 what the next book in music therapy should be. I replied "supervision," and I think that this is still true today. I've learned so much from him.

Thanks to the authors, for having the time and dedication to write and revise these chapters. I know I pushed many of you to reflect more deeply on culture, and I appreciate the work you did. Awareness of our cultural lens is so important to the work we are doing. A special thanks goes to Lisa Summer for all of our talks about supervision in the 1980s.

To my past, current, and future doctoral students at Lesley University—I have learned so much about supervision from you and look forward to learning more.

Also, my great appreciation goes to my many friends and colleagues, who probably don't know how much they helped me—Robyn Cruz, Tanya Hellman, Anita Sacks, Sally Nelson, Team Rainbow, Annette Whitehead-Pleaux, Mariagnese Cattaneo, Sandra Walker, Laura Gerhard, Angela Crawford-Ervin, Lisa Martino, CarylBeth Thomas, Marina Richie, Deborah Silverstein, Bob Brown, and Rich and Antra Borofsky—as well as to the TriCon Choir, under the leadership of Victoria Wagner, singing together twice a week is indeed good for the soul.

Thank you to my sweet fur-babies, 'Because of Winn Dixie' and 'Ms. A. Zippy': Walks and snuggles with you always made life better.

To my sweet, sweet love, Lisa Kynvi, and her amazing children, Josie and Lars: You all keep me grounded in love in a very pure form.

To my three children—Adele, Ky, and Mimi Aziz—two of whom were babies and the third who was born during the creation of the first edition of this book, 20 years ago. You are now adults, and I love who you are becoming. You remain *forever* in my heart and at the center of my world.

CONTENTS

CONTRIBUTORS

Dorit Amir, DA, CMT, associate professor, Bar Ilan University. Dr. Amir is the founder of the music therapy MA program at Bar Ilan University in Israel and headed the program for 33 years. She has taught and supervised students and professional music therapists in Israel, the USA, Europe, and Australia. She has published books, articles, and book chapters on various subjects in music therapy. Her main interests include meaningful moments in music therapy, music therapy and trauma, and music-centered supervision. Professor Amir retired in 2017 and resides in Israel and New York.

Felicity A. Baker, PhD, RMT, University of Melbourne, Australia. Professor Baker is director, International Research Partnerships, Creative Arts and Music Therapy Research Unit, at the University of Melbourne. She is known for her research on therapeutic songwriting, having recently been awarded the World Federation of Music Therapy's Research Award (2017) for her work in this area. She has secured more than AUS$8 million in research funding, including three National Health and Medical Council Research Grants and project grants funded by the Australian Research Council.

Lars Ole Bonde, PhD, DFMT, FAMI, Aalborg University, Denmark. Dr. Bonde is professor emeritus in music therapy (AAU) and in music and health (CREMAH, Norway). He is a Primary trainer in Guided Imagery and Music and clinical and academic supervisor. He has written numerous articles, book chapters, and books about music therapy, music and public health, music psychology, music education, and music history.

Darlene M. Brooks, PhD, MT-BC, LPC, FAMI, Temple University, Philadelphia, PA. Dr. Brooks is director of music therapy at Temple University and coordinator of the PhD program in music therapy. She has been a clinical and academic supervisor of music therapists for over 40 years. She has served as Council Coordinator for Education and Training, Clinical Training Committee, for NAMT and on the Education and Training Advisory Board for AMTA. Her greatest pleasure is the supervision of music therapy clinicians and future music therapists.

Kenneth Bruscia, PhD, MT-BC. Studies in music first led him to teaching and performing piano, and then studies in psychology led to practicing and teaching music therapy and participation in the professional associations. During his 35+-year tenure at Temple University, they established bachelor's and master's degrees and the first true PhD in music therapy. Founder of Barcelona Publishers. Now professor emeritus of music therapy, he resides in San Antonio, TX.

Lillian Eyre, PhD, MT-BC. Fellow of the Association for Music and Imagery. Lillian Eyre graduated from UQAM in 1997 and worked as a music therapist in psychiatry at the McGill University Hospital Center (Montreal, QC) until 2006. In 2008, she completed her PhD in music therapy at Temple University and took a faculty position at Immaculata University, where she was assistant professor and director of the music therapy program until 2018. She is currently a visiting professor at Temple University. She serves on the editorial review board of *Music Therapy Perspectives* and the *Canadian Journal of Music Therapy.* Among her many article and chapter publications is her edited book, *Guidelines to Music Therapy Practice in Mental Health,* published in 2013 by Barcelona Publishers.

Susan Feiner, MT-BC, MSW, LCAT, is an adjunct associate professor of music therapy and the internship coordinator at NYU. She has over 38 years of experience in music psychotherapy and supervision. Feiner presents at conferences and offers continuing education courses on supervision. Currently, her private practice focuses on group and individual supervision for music therapists' ongoing clinical and professional development. She has published on trauma, internship supervision, and the impact of trauma on internship.

Robyn Flaum Cruz, PhD, BC-DMT, Lesley University, Cambridge, MA. Dr. Cruz is editor-in-chief emerita of *The Arts in Psychotherapy,* and she has taught research design and statistics to doctoral students from many disciplines. She is co-author of *Feders' The Art and Science of Evaluation in the Arts Therapies* (2013) and co-editor of *Dance/Movement Therapists in Action* (2019) and has produced over 50 scholarly articles across the disciplines of dance/movement therapy, psychology, psychiatry, neurology, and communications disorders. She is a past president of American Dance Therapy Association.

Michele Forinash, DA, MT-BC, LMHC, Lesley University, Cambridge, MA. Dr. Forinash is professor and director of the PhD program in the Division of Expressive Therapies at Lesley University, and has been involved in music therapy since 1981. Michele's research and publications have focused on supervision, arts-based research, music therapy history, and LGBTQ+ topics. Michele is a former president of the American Music Therapy Association and former chair of the National Coalition of Creative Arts Therapy.

Denise Grocke, AO, PhD, FAMI, University of Melbourne, Australia. Professor Emeritus Denise Grocke is a GIM Primary Trainer and conducts her own trainings through Avalon GIM Training Australia. She is editor of *Guided Imagery and Music: The Bonny Method and Beyond,* 2nd edition (2019), co-author of *Receptive Methods in Music Therapy* (2007), and co-editor of *Guided Imagery & Music and Music Imagery Methods for Individuals and Groups* (2015). She was awarded the Order of Australia (AO) in 2016 for her pioneering contributions to music therapy.

Susan Hadley, PhD, MT-BC, Slippery Rock University, PA, is a professor of music therapy. Her books include *Experiencing Race as a Music Therapist: Personal Narratives* (2013), *Feminist Perspectives in Music Therapy* (2006), *Psychodynamic Music Therapy: Case Studies* (2003), and *Therapeutic Uses of Rap and Hip-Hop* (2012). She has published numerous scholarly articles, chapters, and reviews; serves on the editorial boards of several journals; and is co-editor-in-chief of *Voices: A World Forum for Music Therapy.*

James Hiller, PhD, MT-BC, University of Dayton, OH. James Hiller is assistant professor, coordinator of undergraduate music therapy, and clinical supervisor at the University of Dayton. Dr. Hiller received his master's and doctoral degrees from Temple University. His clinical experience includes work in institutional and private practice settings. Jim has published articles and chapters on music therapy methods, theoretical foundations of rhythm, research epistemologies, music aesthetics in emotion, and resistance in music psychotherapy. Jim is also an active performer, researcher, and student of songs.

Seung-A Kim, PhD, LCAT, MT-BC, is associate professor and coordinator of the Blended Learning Analytical Music Therapy training program at Molloy College, NY, as well as article editor of *Voices: A World Forum for Music Therapy* and past co-chair of the Diversity and Multiculturalism Committee of the American Music Therapy Association. Dr. Kim has collaborated with health professionals in the Korean immigrant community to promote music therapy and specializes in Analytical Music Therapy and supervision, culturally-informed music therapy, and stress management.

Gillian Stephens Langdon MA, MT-BC, LCAT, New York University, is an adjunct professor and former director, creative arts therapies, at the Bronx Psychiatric Center, where she practiced music therapy for over 40 years. Since her pioneering work about music therapy supervision (1984) and a chapter in the previous edition of *Supervision* (2001), her writings have included chapters in the *Music Therapy Handbook* (2015) and *Music Therapy and Trauma: Bridging Theory and Clinical Practice* (2010).

Colin Andrew Lee, PhD, MTA, Wilfrid Laurier University, Waterloo, ON. Dr. Lee is a professor of music therapy. He received a PhD from City University, London. Following piano studies at the Nordwestdeutsche Musikakademie, Germany, he earned a postgraduate diploma in music therapy from the Nordoff-Robbins Music Therapy Center, London, England. His books include *The Architecture of Aesthetic Music Therapy* (Lee & Houde, 2003), *Improvising in Styles: A Workbook for Music Therapists* (2011), *Paul Nordoff: Composer and Music Therapist* (Lee & Pun, 2014), *Song Resources for Music Therapists* (2015), and *Composition and Improvisation Resources for Music Therapists* (Lee, Pun, & Berends, 2015). In 2016, Colin completed the 2nd edition of *Music at the Edge: The Music Therapy Experiences of a Musician with AIDS*.

Kristina M. Lessard, MA, MT-BC, New York, NY. Kristina is a board-certified music therapist who has worked primarily with older adult residents of assisted living communities in the Boston area. Since graduating with her master's degree from Lesley University in 2015, Kristina has held positions as music therapist and program director in both traditional and memory care assisted living, where she has encouraged the use of a wide range of expressive arts therapies. She is currently living in New York City and working with children.

Mary-Carla MacDonald, MA, MT-BC, FAMI, Greater Boston Music Therapy. MacDonald is a founding member of Greater Boston Music Therapy, providing music therapy services, supervision, and consultations in the greater Boston area. A senior lecturer and clinical supervisor at Lesley University and a Fellow of the Association for Music and Imagery, she is known for work that is heavily influenced by faith in the music, mindfulness, developmental psychology, neurology, spirituality, and the people she is privileged to call mentors, teachers, clients, students, family, and friends.

Kathleen M. Murphy, PhD, MT-BC, State University of New York–New Paltz. Dr. Murphy is an assistant professor of music therapy. She has over 35 years of clinical experience in healthcare and educational institutions and has authored book chapters and journal articles. She is the associate editor of *Music Therapy Research* (3rd edition) and has presented nationally and internationally on topics related to music therapy clinical practice, education, and supervision. Her research interests are focused on music therapy in addiction treatment and post-traumatic stress disorder.

Marisol S. Norris, PhD, MT-BC, Lesley University, Cambridge, MA, is an assistant professor in the Expressive Therapies division. Her music therapy practice and supervisory experience have spanned medical and community health settings and have profoundly informed her cultural relational lens. Marisol's research and scholarship explore the discursive construction of race in music therapy theory and praxis, the role of cultural memory and aesthetics in mono-racial and cross-racial music therapy meaning-making processes, and pedagogical approaches to music therapy cultural responsiveness training.

Leah G. Oswanski, MA, LPC, MT-BC, Morristown Medical Center, Morristown, NJ, has been a clinician for 18 years. She is the coordinator of creative arts therapies at the Carol G. Simon Cancer Center at Morristown Medical Center and an adjunct professor at Montclair State University, as well as has a private psychotherapy practice. Leah has researched and presented both nationally and internationally on music therapy in oncology, cultural competence and bias, and LGBTQ+ topics.

Hanne Mette Ridder, PhD, DFMT, Aalborg University, Denmark. Dr. Ridder is a professor of music therapy in the Department of Communication and Psychology at Aalborg University. She is head of the doctoral program in music therapy, approved clinical supervisor, and past president of the European Music Therapy Confederation (2010–2016). Her research and publications are focused mainly on music therapy in a psychosocial understanding of dementia care.

Beth Robinson, MT-BC, Rainbow Music Therapy Services. Robinson is owner and music therapist at Rainbow Music Therapy Services, located in the Bay Area, CA, and serving the special needs and mental health communities in the Bay Area. Beth has been a practicing board-certified music therapist since 1996. Rainbow Music Therapy Services is a founding member of Team Rainbow, presenting and writing on LGBTQIA+ topics and performing, volunteering, and advocating for the LGBTQIA+ community.

Christine Anne Routhier, MA, MT-BC, LMHC, AMI Fellow, senior lecturer and clinical supervisor, Lesley University, Cambridge, MA. Routhier is a Fellow of the Association of Music and Imagery. She also provides supervision to music therapy professionals and Level 1 Supportive Music and Imagery practicum students in Asia and the United States. She also maintains a private practice, working with adolescents and adults challenged by depression, anxiety, and traumatic life experiences. Christine has presented nationally and internationally on her work in using music and imagery as a resource for self-care, inner exploration, and growth.

Benedikte B. Scheiby[1] lived, breathed, ate, drank, and dreamed music therapy. Most of her waking hours were spent practicing it, talking about it, writing about it, reflecting on it, and promoting it. She was a practitioner of Analytical Music Therapy, having trained with the originator of the approach, Mary Priestley. She also completed postgraduate trainings in Bioenergetic Psychotherapy and Mindfulness-Based Stress Reduction. Her clinical approach was eclectic and holistic, incorporating her interests in the complexities of the psyche, the material nature of our physical bodies, and modern advances in neuroscience. She was also a profound believer in the ethical necessity for all practicing music therapists to be in supervision. She was engaged in various supervision experiences throughout her career, maintaining membership in a monthly creative arts therapy supervision group run by Dr. Arthur Robbins for 26 years. In her list of competencies for supervisors, Benedikte included this one: "To love his/her work." She loved her work as she loved life.

Lisa Summer, PhD, MT-BC, AMI Fellow, Anna Maria College, Paxton, MA. Dr. Summer is a professor and the director of music therapy. She has chronicled her development of the Continuum Model of Guided Imagery and Music, including its theory, clinical applications, and use in experiential teaching and supervision, in many book chapters and articles, as well as a doctoral dissertation. She travels internationally, teaching GIM in the USA, Europe, and Asia, with ongoing trainings in China and South Korea. She received the AMTA National Presidential Award of Merit in 2017.

Sangeeta Swamy, PhD, MT-BC, Valparaiso University, Valparaiso, IN. Dr. Swamy is director of music therapy at Valparaiso. As a queer Indian-American, she specializes in socio-culturally responsive music therapy practice, supervision, and pedagogy, with an emphasis on intersectionality, mindfulness, and transpersonal approaches. A national and international presenter and speaker, she has published in peer-reviewed journals and books. She is also an advanced GIM trainee and developed *Culturally Centered Music and Imagery* through her research with Indian adults.

---

[1] Published posthumously and written by Ken Aigen.

Jessica Triana, LMHC, MT-BC, NMT, Boston, MA. Since graduating with her master's degree from Lesley University in 2015, Jessica has been practicing as a music therapist and licensed mental health counselor with young children, adolescents, and families in pediatric rehabilitation, outpatient mental health, and bereavement. She is grateful for her peers, colleagues and interns, past and present, who have been integral to her growth as a supervisor and clinician.

Alan Turry, DA, MT-BC, LCAT, Nordoff-Robbins Center for Music Therapy, New York University. As managing director of the Nordoff-Robbins Center for Music Therapy at NYU Steinhardt, Dr. Turry is responsible for the Center's overall administration, research, and clinical services and the graduate and postgraduate training programs. An expert in clinical improvisation, he has conducted funded research on the effectiveness of music therapy for a variety of neurodiverse populations, including autism and stroke rehabilitation. Dr. Turry has been instrumental in supporting the development of Nordoff-Robbins practice and training nationally and internationally.

Gwendolyn Van Baalen, MA, LMHC, MT-BC, Cambridge, MA. Gwendolyn has been practicing music therapy and mental health counseling with infants and toddlers and their caregivers since graduating with her master's degree from Lesley University in 2015. In addition to her clinical work, she orchestrates a parent mental health project and serves in a supervisory and leadership role as team leader in early intervention. Supervision, in its many forms, has been a consistent source of growth and meaning in her career.

Michael Viega, PhD, LCAT, MT-BC, Montclair State University, NJ. Dr. Viega is an assistant professor of music therapy at the John J. Cali School of Music at Montclair State University. He has published and presented internationally on a wide range of topics, such as arts-based research methodologies, therapeutic songwriting, digital music technologies, and adverse childhood experiences., He has worked extensively with children and adolescents who have experienced childhood adversity and trauma and is a Fellow in the Bonny Method of Guided Imagery and Music. He serves on the editorial boards of the *Journal of Music Therapy, Music Therapy Perspectives,* and *Voices: A World Forum for Music Therapy.*

Annette Whitehead-Pleaux, MA, MT-BC, is a music therapist who has focused on clinical practice, supervision, education, and research. Based in Massachusetts, Annette has worked with people in psychiatric, medical, school, hospice, and community music therapy settings. Annette provides supervision to music therapy clinicians internationally and serves as adjunct faculty at several universities/colleges. An active researcher, Annette is undertaking current research that focuses on cultural responsiveness in music therapy and is co-editor of *Cultural Intersections in Music Therapy: Music, Health, and the Person.*

Charlay Yates, MA, MT-BC, DBT-informed music therapist, Boston, MA. A master's-level clinician and business owner practicing since 2015, Charlay works with various populations, including adolescents with severe disabilities and complex medical health needs and adults with mental health conditions. She is also an adjunct faculty member at Lesley University and has presented and published in the field of music therapy. Charlay recognizes the challenges but also the value of supervision in her growth as a professional. She is passionate about continuing the practice of supervision with interns and colleagues.

Music Therapy Supervision

Second Edition

Chapter 1

OVERVIEW

Michele Forinash

INTRODUCTION

I began my supervision journey in 1985, and probably, like many supervisors at that time, I began supervising without having much of an idea about what I was doing. I began supervising students while working on my own identity as a supervisor. I frequently felt at a loss as a supervisor and often struggled to find the "best" way to supervise any given student. I often thought back to my own experiences as a supervisee and either emulated the way a previous supervisor had helped me or rejected the way in which an unhelpful supervisor had supervised me. At the time, this was at least a place to start.

Then I began supervising supervisors. I once again faced new territory that I did not fully understand. In the mid-1990s, I began having conversations with Dr. Lisa Summer, as we met to share ideas, philosophies, and strategies for supervising both students and supervisors. Those conversations and the many presentations we did helped me tremendously on my journey. I added another layer to my supervision journey when I began, in 2007, supervising doctoral students doing research. I turned to my colleague, dance/movement therapist Dr. Robyn Cruz, to talk about our philosophies and strategies of doctoral supervision, as we were both in relatively new territory. The complexities of doctoral research added tasks such as helping students to think like scholars and not necessarily like clinicians. While most were working as clinicians in addition to doing research, supervision also became about helping them to articulate a scholarly voice and separating that from their clinical voice.

Supervising Students and New Professionals

The focus of the supervision relationship is to address the complexities involved in helping supervisees in their ongoing, and never ending, development as compassionate and knowledgeable professionals. In the first edition of this book, I referred to "achieving competence," which is an ideal that is never really achievable. With the awareness of how intersectionality impacts all of our relationships, we find ourselves in a constant state of learning—so much so that the language we use to describe a client, student, or experience continues to evolve. Clearly, we develop into "competent enough" supervisors, but for "good" supervisors, it is an ongoing evolution. There is always something new to encounter, and we have all probably had the experience of pulling a useful supervision intervention out of our tool bag only to find it fall flat. That experience gives us an opportunity to learn.

As you will read in the following pages, our awareness of intersectionality takes priority as we begin to look at our supervisory relationships. Issues of power, privilege, and oppression can be made transparent early in the supervision process. From these beginnings we develop relationships that are unique and reflective of the individual relationships. Supervision is a relationship in which both supervisor and supervisee actively participate and interact. It is a process of unfolding, with twists and turns and missteps along the way. Hopefully, both supervisee and supervisor will leave the relationship transformed in some way. We must take care to develop a relationship that can allow and encourage questions and challenges from both participants. Both voices are critical to a good supervisory relationship.

In the first edition of this book, I referred to the concept of "dilemmas" in supervision. This was a term that Lisa Summer and I had discussed on many occasions. How do we supervise those seeking their first credential in the field? How do we supervise those who are at a more advanced level? There isn't just one way to do this! There are other dilemmas, such as how to help nurture a "competent enough" clinician when you are working on an academic timeline, how to determine the best intervention in supervision at a given moment, and how to keep track of and work on our own biases while also focusing on the supervisee and the client(s) they serve.

Supervising Doctoral Students

It was quite a learning curve for me to begin supervising doctoral students. I faced a new dilemma and found that I needed to develop a new focus. This focus had to do with helping them "put on a new hat" that was quite different from their role as a clinician or supervisor. This continues to be one of the most challenging transitions for doctoral students to make. The development of a scholarly voice, along with expertise in research, as Robyn Cruz and I often say, is like "rewiring your brain." To quote the Carnegie Institute of Doctoral Education, it is about developing the "habits of heart and mind of a scholar" (Elkana, 2006, p. 65).

Clearly, they enter with a solid understanding of themselves as clinicians and supervisors. Most have a hard time letting go of that identity as they venture into a new way of being in the world. How do we keep their clinical identity intact, while also helping them to look at clinical work from a new research perspective? How do we nurture this scholarly voice and bring it to fruition? Once again, it is about being "competent enough" as a researcher while knowing that we all grow and develop in our scholarship.

OUTLINE

Throughout this book, you will see dramatic updates, including a focus on power, privilege, and oppression; the awareness of the intersectionality of those in the supervisory relationship; an awareness of the gender-nonbinary and the use of "they" as a singular pronoun; and a new section on doctoral education.

Part One: Foundations of Supervision

This edition has an expanded first section that now focuses on emerging topics, some that were nascent in the previous edition and some that are new. Lillian Eyre (chapter 2) has written about theoretical approaches to supervision and includes approaches such as behavioral, cognitive, humanistic, psychodynamic, feminist, diversity, positive psychology, and motivational interviewing. Kathy Murphy has significantly updated chapter 3, on ethics, to include some of the more recent complexities of the therapeutic relationship. Chapter 4, by Annette Whitehead-Pleaux, is an overview of the aspects of culturally responsive supervision. Nicole Hahna and I (chapter 5) provide an update of a feminist supervision chapter that originated in Susan Hadley's book (2006). Leah Oswanski, Beth Robinson, Amy Donnenworth, and Maureen Hearns (chapter 6) provide an overview of topics involved in working in the LGBTQ+ populations, with a focus on tools and assessments for supervisors. Chapter 7, by Marisol Norris and Susan Hadley, focuses on engaging race in supervision, a topic that has not been addressed in the literature.

Part Two: Supervision Practices

This section focuses on supervision practices that are currently occurring in the field. This edition includes in this section both preprofessional (student) supervision along with the supervision of professionals in the field. Supervisors at the preprofessional level continue to be the backbone of our profession and to serve as its gatekeepers. As a greater number of new, as well as seasoned, professionals continue to seek out supervision, new developments and approaches are being forged. This section begins with an updated chapter (8) from Lisa Summer on supervising first-time practica in undergraduate students. James Hiller (chapter 9) writes about supervision in the field and how supervisors supervise in "live" situations. Susan Feiner (chapter 10) updates her chapter from the previous edition and examines the roles, dynamics, and phases of the supervisory relationship. Chapter 11, by Gillian Stephens Langdon, focuses on experiential group supervision and includes quotes from people who were in her supervision group in prior years about their experience in supervision. Dorit Amir (chapter 12) has updated her chapter about supervision for the new music therapist, including more awareness of the complexities of cross-cultural clinical treatment and supervision, specifically in the Middle East.

A newly graduated group of therapists shares their peer supervision model in chapter 13 (Charlay Yates, Kevin Kozik, Amanda Weldin, Gwen van Baalen, Kristina Lessard, and Jessica Triana). Sangeeta Swamy and Seung-A Kim write in chapter 14 about how to provide culturally responsive supervision in an academic setting. A new trend in supervision—that of "distance supervision"—is offered by Mary Carla McDonald, Christine Routhier, and Annette Whitehead-Pleaux (chapter 15). They offer the beginning of a "best practices" for distance supervision. Colin Lee and Kimberly Khare's update of chapter 16, on music-centered supervision, shares Kimberly's insights as they have developed over the past 20 years since the first edition of this book. Darlene Brook specifically looks at advanced supervision in chapter 17, as more professionals return for supervision. Kenneth Bruscia closes out this section with an update on his five levels of supervision (chapter 19).

Part Three: Institute Supervision

This section expands the three main (post-master's) institute supervision practices with many updates. Denise Grocke (chapter 20) looks at the concepts used in GIM supervision. Alan Turry (chapter 21) shares perspectives from Nordoff-Robbins Music Therapy, including NRMT as a spiritual discipline. The late Benedikte Scheiby shared her most recent thoughts about Priestley's Analytical Music Therapy (chapter 22), and Seung-A Kim brings a new chapter outlining a specific Analytical Music Therapy-oriented supervision (Chapter 23).

Part Four: Supervision of Doctoral Education

In a completely new section, Robyn Cruz and I share in chapter 24 an overview of doctoral education in the creative arts therapies based on our experiences at Lesley University, including a focus on developing "stewards of the profession." Lars Ole Bonde and Hanna Mette Ridder from Aalborg University in Denmark write about the spectrum of supervisory roles in doctoral education (chapter 25). Kenneth Bruscia, professor emeritus of Temple University, writes about the supervision of doctoral students and dissertation research (chapter 26). One thing I can say with certainty about doctoral supervision is that it can make for wonderful, long-lasting, collegial relationships.

I hope that readers find something of value in this edition. While there are no recipes offered, no protocols on how to supervise, I hope that readers are stimulated to begin discussions about supervision in all of these areas.

REFERENCE

Elkana, Y. (2006). Unmasking uncertainties and embracing contradictions: Graduate education in the sciences. In C. M. Golde & G. E. Walker (Eds.), *Envisioning the future of doctoral education: Preparing stewards of the discipline. Carnegie essays on the doctorate* (pp. 65–96). San Francisco, CA: Jossey-Bass.

Part One:
Foundations of Supervision

Chapter 2
THEORETICAL APPROACHES TO SUPERVISION

Lillian Eyre

INTRODUCTION

This chapter will present an overview of main models and approaches used in music therapy supervision. Proctor (2000) defined a model of supervision as a comprehensive approach that includes theoretical orientations, goals, methods, procedures, and techniques. The models addressed here include competency-based supervision, behavioral, cognitive, humanistic, or client-centered, and psychodynamic. We assume that both clinical and academic supervisors will have an eclectic approach to supervision, drawing from a number of models. The use of these models will depend on a number of factors, the most influential being the supervisor's education and training, her[2] individual predilection for a particular way of working, and the population with which the supervisor works. In addition, the models the supervisor uses will be determined by the supervisee's needs throughout the fieldwork and internship, his developmental level, and the task being addressed. For example, if the issue being confronted were the supervisee's music skills, then a problem-focused, competency-based model using a cognitive behavioral approach would most likely be used to address the supervisee's development. When the supervisee's personal obstacles to growth are being addressed, a humanistic or psychodynamic model would most likely be appropriate.

In addition to these primary models of supervision, as in counseling, there are a number of approaches or concepts that may be integrated into therapy or supervision. These include understanding supervision from the perspective of diversity, feminist theory, Positive Psychology Interventions (PPI), motivational interviewing (MI), and using music in supervision. This chapter will present the main models used in supervision as well as stances that may be integrated into these models.

LEVELS OF SUPERVISION: UNDERGRADUATE, GRADUATE EQUIVALENCY, AND ADVANCED

The role of the supervisor will vary according to the stage of development and needs of the supervisee. In music therapy at the current time, the undergraduate degree is the professional entry point. In many programs, an equivalency certificate or degree allows graduate students to begin their music therapy training at the graduate level. Even though most graduate equivalency students will have acquired more life experience and academic skills than undergraduates, both are involved in similar learning tasks. Therefore, these undergraduates and graduates can be considered to be at the same level of learning, which is oriented to the development and application of music therapy principles and skills to meet specific needs of various populations (Farnan, 2001).

Advanced supervision—defined here as post-professional supervision—occurs after students have completed internship and have received their CBMT credential, as well as with professional

---

[2] Please note that throughout this chapter, in the interests of presenting a clear text, feminine gender will be used to refer to the supervisor, while masculine gender will be used to refer to the supervisee. The author is aware that this is a limitation of gender and roles, and it is not intended to be taken as a literal expression or to represent the author's worldview.

music therapists who seek further supervision. Having already accomplished the process of separation-individual in the internship (Feiner, 2001, p. 111) and developed their unique approach, these upper-level master's students and professionals have different needs than preprofessional music therapists and often require different approaches. Advanced supervision is often focused on deepening one's understanding of particular client problems, managing multiple roles and relationships in the workplace, supervising students and other professionals, and self-care. The American Music Therapy Association (AMTA, 2015) classified the various tasks of a supervisor in the clinical section of the advanced competencies, focusing on the role of teaching students and helping them to increase their clinical skills and awareness.

Bruscia (2001, p. 292) described a model of apprenticeship training for graduate students in the roles of teaching and supervision; this model applies to advanced supervision, as the students in apprenticeship are professionals. In the apprenticeship model, Bruscia identified three stages of readiness in supervision, each with specific concerns. The first is the development of one's practical techniques with learning-oriented goals; the second is the development of relationships with clients (or students) while being attentive to one's conscious and preconscious internal experience; the third is concerned with internalization, countertransference, and awareness of parallel processes that take into account both conscious and unconscious influences (pp. 292–293). The processes involved in advanced supervision may involve the first level of goal-oriented learning as supervisors learn to teach skills and develop students' awareness, while in the second and third levels they develop mentoring relationships with supervisees and deepen relationships with clients. Thus, advanced supervision must take into account the internal experiences of supervisors, supervisees, and clients, while developing awareness of conscious processes and, in the third level of readiness, uncovering unconscious processes such as transference, countertransference, resistance, defenses, and parallel processes (pp. 292–294). The primary approach particularly suited to this work for advanced supervision is the psychodynamic approach (p. 290).

Advanced supervision can also be understood through the various roles the supervisor plays. Bernard (1979) developed a discrimination model of supervision in which she articulated three primary roles that a supervisor undertakes: (1) as a teacher, when providing instruction to the supervisee; (2) as a counselor, when helping the supervisee to work with client problems; and (3) as a consultant, when working collaboratively on client cases. In advanced supervision, the supervisor must discriminate which approach the supervisee needs and determine the level of readiness for a particular approach that will address the supervisee's needs (Bruscia, 2001). Barnard (1979) understands these roles to be interchangeable, in that the supervisor might perform all three roles within a single supervision session, especially when the supervisee is in the latter stages of training. Thus, every supervisor must be able to carry out a variety of roles to address the tasks of supervision. In doing so, supervisors may find that various models and approaches are applicable to specific supervisee needs at various developmental levels.

This chapter presents models and approaches commonly used in both preprofessional and advanced supervision. Keeping in mind Bernard's (1997) discrimination model that outlines the roles a supervisor may adopt, as well as Bruscia's (2001) identification of conscious and unconscious processes and the supervisee's readiness for supervision, each model and approach has unique qualities and characteristics that are suitable for the various levels of supervisee readiness.

MODELS OF SUPERVISION

Competency-Based Model

The competency-based model of supervision was developed by Farnan (2001) and is used as the basis of this section. This model is fundamental to training and supervision at the preprofessional level of fieldwork and internship supervisees. Grounded in the American Music Therapy Association (AMTA) competency guidelines, the supervisor's focus is on helping the supervisee to achieve competency in each of the areas determined by the AMTA (2013). These areas are assessed directly midway through internship and again at the end. Areas addressed are music therapy foundations, including knowledge of counseling approaches, characteristics of populations, and self-awareness; therapeutic process, including the ability to establish relationship with clients, assessment, program planning, treatment, evaluation, and documentation procedures; ability to work with groups and with individuals; ability to understand and use research materials appropriately; musical abilities, including voice, guitar, and piano, as well as basic theoretical knowledge and practice; professional competencies, including ability to present pertinent information on clients to a multidisciplinary team, ability to work constructively with others, and professional behavior; and ethics, including awareness of confidentiality and familiarity with the institutional and the AMTA code of ethics.

The competency model delineates three stages in internship—the beginning, the middle, and the final stage. This model has close parallels with the Integrated Developmental Model (IDM) developed by Stoltenberg and McNeill (2011) to sketch the stages that a supervisee goes through as he gains experience and confidence as a therapist. The supervisee's tasks are varied according to each stage of clinical training.

Supervisees in practicum experiences are considered to be in the beginning stage. Some interns, especially when working with a new population or client functioning level, may be considered to be at the beginning stage as well. In this first stage, the supervisee may be highly anxious and dependent as he is placed in a new situation, often with clients with whom he has had little or no experience. The supervisee will naturally be focused on his performance and whether what he is doing is therapeutic and appropriate for the clients. The IDM approach suggests that in this stage, supervisors need to provide specific directions on working with clients as the supervisee tests his new skills. Supervisees will benefit from a high level of structure in supervision sessions at the beginning level (Stoltenberg & McNeill, 2011). During this stage, common supervisor tasks that would fit into this model might include:

a) Defining boundaries and modeling desired workplace behaviors
b) Observing and assessing what the supervisee needs to learn
c) Determining the priorities for learning and the steps needed to acquire this knowledge
d) Assisting the supervisee in learning how to best use the supervision time

In the middle stage of clinical training (Farnan, 2001), or level two in IDM, the supervisee has gained some skill, knowledge, competence, experience, and confidence, rendering him more independent from the supervisor. The supervisee at this stage will shift his focus more to the client and understand therapy from the client's worldview (Stoltenberg & McNeill, 2011). In this stage, the supervisor may wish to use the AMTA competencies as a checklist to determine which areas of competency need further attention and which skills have been achieved. At this stage, in tandem with the supervisee's development, the supervisor will encourage more autonomy and facilitate the supervisee's reflection on their experiences with the client and the client's reactions (2011). Common supervisor tasks in this stage might include:

a) Providing the supervisee with clinical opportunities for greater independence
b) Assisting the supervisee in continuing to focus on the client and being less focused on self
c) Guiding the supervisee to a deeper understanding of client needs and the therapeutic process and the role of music in this process
d) Reviewing the supervisee's awareness of and response to client diversity and various cultures

e) Continuing to observe and evaluate the supervisee's progress

In the final stage of internship, the supervisee has become independent in much of his clinical work. During this time, he is beginning to develop his particular approach to therapy. In his interactions with clients, the supervisee often develops greater empathy for his clients as he grows in understanding and expands his worldview. This is an appropriate time to encourage the supervisee to integrate clinical experience with academic learning, theory, and research to more deeply understand the therapeutic process (Stoltenberg & McNeill, 2011). The supervisor and supervisee relationship often becomes more collaborative at this stage (2011). However, it is important to continue to assess the supervisee's progress and to address any areas of weakness before the end of internship. Often, it is in this stage, when the supervisee has developed more confidence, that difficult feedback is most easily accepted, providing opportunities for further growth (2011). At this time, it is also common to work in more depth on documentation, and particularly discharge summaries. Termination procedures also become important in this phase, particularly if the supervisee has worked with clients for a number of sessions. Supervisor tasks in this stage are similar to those in the middle stage, with the addition of the following:

a) Providing ongoing evaluation of all the competencies
b) Identifying and focusing on skills yet to be mastered
c) Assisting in planning appropriate termination procedures for each client and group
d) Assisting in reviewing client treatment plans to understand the therapeutic process over time
e) Reviewing ethical guidelines as they relate to clinical situations

When the supervisee is supervised with a competency approach, the supervisor models an approach that encourages the attainment of the following skills:

a) Awareness of the characteristics and demands of therapeutic practice in music therapy
b) Acceptance of personal responsibility to achieve basic competency in clinical practice
c) Professional competence, responsibility, and caring

Example of the Use of the Competency-Based Model
After asking the supervisee to prepare a hello song for the next group, the supervisor observes that the supervisee has chosen an inappropriate song. It is in a key that is too high for the clients to sing, and client interaction and involvement is the primary therapeutic focus in this group. The supervisor determines that one area of competency that needs to be worked on is the development of therapeutic rationale in the choice of songs and key. The supervisor discusses the clinical use of this song with the supervisee and helps to set guidelines for appropriate musical choice that the supervisee will demonstrate in the next group.

Behavioral Model

Hanser (2000, pp. 99–117) described the behavioral model as one in which the focus is on the acquisition of skills and on specific behaviors. As with the competency-based model (Farnan, 2001), the purpose of the behavioral model is to help the supervisee acquire skills that are needed to learn appropriate behaviors and to extinguish inappropriate behaviors. Thus, as in the competency-based model, it is most applicable to preprofessional training. The supervisor may intervene to directly change or adapt a supervisee's particular behavior, and, in so doing, she would be using a behavioral approach.

Common supervisor tasks that would fit into this model might include:

a) Setting learning goals and objectives for the supervisee
b) Modeling how the supervisee might achieve some of these objectives
c) Constructing and implementing strategies to achieve these goals
d) Evaluating and following up on the progress with goals
e) Providing the supervisee with information
f) Giving feedback to the supervisee regarding progress toward the goals and objectives

When the supervisee is supervised in a behavioral frame, the supervisor models an approach that encourages the supervisee to:

a) Become task-oriented
b) Acquire analytical skills to develop a therapeutic rationale in the treatment of clients
c) Develop goals, objectives, timelines, and procedures for the acquisition of competencies
d) Develop appropriate goals and objectives for clients based on client needs and functional abilities
e) Develop data collection and documentation procedures appropriate to the setting
f) Use music in a variety of methods to attain therapeutic goals
g) Develop skills related to the assessment of client culture and diversity and use of appropriate music for clients

Example of the Use of the Behavioral Model

The supervisor notes during observation of a group session that the supervisee seems to be using the same 10 songs that she has mentioned using in previous groups. Upon observation of a group, the supervisor notes that many clients seem to be lethargic and disinterested. When one client suggests a song she would like to sing, the supervisee responds "Yes," but does not sing the song or respond further to the client. After communicating with the supervisee about his response to the client and discussing how this might impact the client, the supervisor then discusses the supervisee's repertoire choices and the extent of her repertoire. The supervisor and supervisee make a list of three new songs that the supervisee will learn and memorize in the following week, including the song that the client mentioned in the group. The supervisor and supervisee review the steps involved in finding the music and learning the songs.

Competency and Behavioral Models in Advanced Supervision

While these models are admirably suited to the supervision tasks of preprofessionals in training, it would be erroneous to assume that therapists do not have any skills to learn at the advanced level. In Bruscia's (2001) apprenticeship model, advanced supervision in the first stage focused on helping professionals to develop their supervision skills as they worked with students in academic seminars and in preprofessional clinical training. Competency-based and behavioral techniques would be used in advanced supervision to assist advanced supervisors in developing their teaching skills and techniques in their supervisory roles.

Cognitive Model

The behavioral model is most often integrated with the cognitive model in supervision and is most applicable to preprofessional supervision. The cognitive model addresses thoughts and attitudes that precede, accompany, or result from the behavior (Rienecke & Freeman, 2003). Thus, in supervision, the cognitive model focuses on the thoughts and feelings that the supervisee has that inform certain perceptions or lead to specific behaviors. In the contemporary cognitive behavioral model, cognition, feelings, and behaviors are linked together, and, in each situation, these connections are explored.

An essential aspect of this approach is the belief that all behavior is maintained and modified by environmental events. The individual's unique cognitive processes or perceptions of these events will determine how he is influenced by external events. The social and environmental consequences of one's behavior in turn shape the way that others respond to the individual, and these responses influence one's cognitive perceptions of oneself, others, and one's possibilities in the world. Thus, thoughts, behaviors, and emotions are connected to one's interactions with others and linked in a neurological feedback loop of individual perception. The individual interprets the reciprocity between personal actions and environmental consequences.

The cognitive model of supervision includes behavioral interventions to address tasks to acquire competency, while maintaining an awareness of cognitive influences on the supervisee's learning experience. In supervision, this is a problem-focused, structured approach in which cognitive interventions are used to expand, where appropriate, the supervisee's cognitive perceptions. The supervisee's perceptions may be on a continuum of conscious to unconscious and include automatic thoughts, assumptions, core beliefs, and cognitive distortions. It should be noted here that the focus is not to psychoanalyze the supervisee or to change his cultural or personal values, but instead to identify and re-examine the cognitive distortions that are creating obstacles in the supervisee's work with clients. An example of this would be in helping the supervisee to understand that his anxiety resulting in negative predictions about how he will be unable to provide a good session for the group contributes to increased anxiety and decreased attentiveness for the clients and, ultimately, likely has a role to play in the success of the group.

Common supervisor tasks that would fit into this model might include:

a) Understanding how the supervisee is perceiving situations that lead to certain behaviors
b) Helping the supervisee to analyze the reciprocity between personal actions and environmental consequences
c) Helping the supervisee to analyze the relationship between thoughts and feelings about the client and the client's responses to the supervisee
d) Helping the supervisee to identify automatic thoughts, assumptions, core beliefs, cognitive distortions, and emotions that are harmful to the therapeutic process and to personal growth
e) Helping the supervisee to understand the client's mental processes from the client's perspective
f) Facilitating a greater understanding of the role of cultural norms, acculturation, diversity, and oppression as they relate to the client's therapeutic needs and responses

When the supervisee is supervised in a cognitive model, the supervisor models an approach that encourages the supervisee to:

a) Become task-oriented
b) Acquire analytical skills to develop a therapeutic rationale in the treatment of clients
c) Cultivate an attitude of reflection regarding his work
   Increase his awareness of the connections between thoughts, feelings, and behaviors

Example of the Use of the Cognitive Model

In a supervision session, the supervisor notes that the supervisee's assumptions and beliefs about people from a particular culture may have impacted her perception and her treatment of the client in a negative way. The supervisor has adopted a humanistic and feminist stance overall in the supervision, in that she has related to the supervisee with authentic interest in trying to understand his unexamined beliefs. Because the supervisee is not aware of his beliefs or the impact of them on his treatment of the client, the supervisor uses a cognitive approach and asks specific questions to facilitate the supervisee's self-reflection and bring him into a conscious awareness of those beliefs and how they pejoratively influence his approach with the client. The supervisor also asks the supervisee to research information on the culture of the client so that he has a richer understanding of the client's culture, the environmental effect of being a member of this diverse group, and how this may have an influence in the client's perceptions and responses to therapy.

Cognitive Model in Advanced Supervision

At the advanced level of supervision, the cognitive model is focused on the advanced supervisor consciously maintaining and deepening relationships with student supervisees and, where applicable, with the advanced supervisee's clients. Bruscia (2001) described this second stage of supervision readiness as a shift from the external—the acquisition of skills and techniques—to the internal: an increased awareness of one's subjective experience of relationship and empathy and an understanding the boundaries in these relationships. The cognitive model relies on conscious and preconscious experience as the supervisor and supervisee explore these relationships and their meaning from multiple perspectives of the dynamic interactions of self and other.

Humanistic or Person-Centered Model

American psychologist Carl Rogers formulated this model in 1940 (Bohart, 2013). A humanistic approach, also known as client-centered or person-centered therapy, was originally a nondirective therapy based on an authentic relationship in which the therapist offers empathy, unconditional positive regard, and genuineness (2013). In the supervision setting, empathy is based on the supervisor's interest in understanding the supervisee's feelings, thoughts, and reactions to the clients from the supervisee's perspective and communicating this understanding in an authentic manner.

Unconditional positive regard is another key component of the humanistic model (Bohart, 2013). This is expressed in supervision by the supervisor's willingness to allow the supervisee to share his experience in the way he wishes, using the words or mediums he chooses (verbal expression, role-play, improvisation, songs, art, or mandalas). The supervisor has unconditional positive regard for the uniqueness of the supervisee's perspective and, most important, holds the belief that the supervisee has the skills, knowledge, and personal capacity to resolve personal and therapeutic issues with clients, supervisor, and other professionals. Genuineness means that the supervisor is congruent in using verbal and nonverbal expressions that match her thoughts and feelings and that she communicates these thoughts and feelings in a spontaneous and authentic manner. The hypothesis of this model assumes that when the supervisee experiences empathy, unconditional positive regard, and genuineness in an authentic manner, he increases his self-esteem and self-reliance and learns to trust his ability to make decisions, thus becoming more confident with clients. These conditions, where the supervisee feels free from fear of rejection, encourage greater creativity and autonomy in working with clients. In addition, as the supervisee gains confidence, he may be more willing to accept aspects of himself that he formerly regarded as inadmissible. In integrating more aspects of the self into one's self-concept, the supervisee's mode of experiencing becomes more free, open, and spontaneous, thus preparing him to be an autonomous professional.

This model may be used in preprofessional supervision, particularly in the later stages of internship when the intern has developed functional clinical skills and is working on developing relationships with clients that foster greater therapeutic growth. It is not usually used in the preliminary stages of preprofessional training, where the acquisition of skills and techniques requires a model that can address task-oriented and functional abilities. The person-centered humanistic supervision model is best employed when the supervisor trusts that the supervisee has within himself the ability, motivation, and tools necessary to grow and explore the client–therapist situation and the self. The developmental stage of the supervisee with regard to the issue under supervision will determine whether this is the best supervision model for the supervisee with this current issue, given the supervisee's current abilities and understanding of the issue.

Common supervisor tasks that would fit into this model might include:

a) Responding with empathy and genuineness to the supervisee's experiences
b) Understanding and accepting the supervisee's beliefs, culture, developmental level, and abilities
c) Communicating authentic feelings
d) Modeling acceptance and authenticity in relations with clients, as well as with other professionals in the workplace

When the supervisee is supervised in a humanistic frame, the supervisor models an approach that encourages the attainment of the following skills:

a) Being fully present for the client in the moment
b) Feeling empathy
c) Communicating empathy and acceptance of the client
d) Understanding the client from the client's perspective, including the impact of culture and diversity on the client's therapeutic needs and perceptions
e) Knowing when to trust that the client is able to find his or her own solutions to the issues in his or her life

Example of the Use of the Person-Centered or Humanistic Model

During a supervision session, the supervisee becomes more and more agitated as he talks about his frustrations in finding the correct activities and music experiences to use with his clients. He notes that when he does one thing, the supervisor seems to suggest another, and when he does the other, that seems to be the wrong thing to do for that situation as well. The supervisor listens calmly to the supervisee, asking the occasional question to gain more clarity into the supervisee's perspective regarding his clients. The supervisor is using a humanistic model to work with the supervisee. Therefore, she does not address the supervisee's psychodynamic process, which would address past events or relationships that may be being evoked in the current supervisor/supervisee relationship. Instead, the supervisor maintains positive regard for the supervisee and accepts his feelings, while using humanistic verbal techniques such as posing questions designed to gain greater clarity and insight into the supervisee's difficulties and helping the supervisee to identify the source of his frustrations and find his own solutions in partnership with the supervisor.

Humanistic Model in Advanced Supervision

The humanistic model is most commonly used in advanced supervision, where the supervisee has mastered clinical techniques and functional skills and has developed the aptitude to engage in personal reflection. Corresponding to Bruscia's (2001) second stage of supervisory readiness, the focus is on the internal experiences of the supervisee and his clients or students. The role of the supervisor here is to help the supervisee broaden and deepen his perspective of the client or student and to clarify the thoughts, images, and emotions in his conscious and preconscious awareness. Using the verbal techniques developed by Rogers (Bohart, 2013), the supervisor models unconditional acceptance, thereby helping the supervisee to develop the confidence to sit with difficult experiences, whether with clients or students, and derive meaning from these experiences to enhance the personal growth of the supervisee and, in turn, the client and/or student.

Humanistic Model and Diversity

In supervision, it is always primordial to take into account the whole person. While we may think of various approaches in working with supervisees, the overarching and often invisible basis of all our interactions is that of culture. We are all members of various cultures. Country, ethnic heritage, locality, spiritual beliefs or lack thereof, language, gender identity, sexual orientation, race, education, and social and economic status are some of the most prevalent cultural influences in our lives. We also all have biases that are a product of unexamined unconscious beliefs related to these cultural beliefs, and it is inevitable that at some point in interactions with clients, supervisors, and supervisees, these biases will play a role in diminishing the quality of our understanding of the other. It is therefore important to keep in mind the various cultural influences that a client or supervisee may be experiencing at any time in the supervisory process. This is especially important in music therapy, where many students come from other countries to study music therapy in United States and may have different expectations about the role of therapist and client, as well as the roles of teacher or supervisor and student.

The humanistic model is particularly appropriate to work with the human challenges and opportunities that are presented to us when persons from different backgrounds work together. Within this model is embedded the obligation for us to be aware of both our shared humanity and the diversity of the presentations of our humanity as expressed through a multitude of cultures and backgrounds. The humanistic stance offers the perspective of embracing the uniqueness of each person with the authentic desire to fully comprehend the other, regardless of differences. Thus, with a spirit of cultural humility and an authentic desire to know the other, which is a primary foundation of the humanistic model, the supervisor will be positioned to better understand her supervisee, just as the supervisee will better understand his client.

Psychodynamic Model: Advanced Supervision

The psychodynamic model is the oldest therapeutic model, derived from Freud's psychoanalytical model (Bruscia, 1998). This model focuses on unconscious and preconscious processes as they are manifested in the supervisee's thoughts, feelings, images, and behaviors. This model corresponds to Bruscia's (2001) third stage of supervision readiness, which is primarily concerned with internalization—the recognition of and therapeutic work with countertransference, parallel processes, defenses, and resistance. The use of this model is usually contraindicated for the preprofessional level of supervision. In order to use the model, the supervisor must be trained in music psychotherapy or have advanced skills and knowledge in psychotherapy. In using this model, the supervisee would have to be psychologically minded as well.

This model is fundamental in advanced supervision. The psychodynamic model is well appointed to develop a deep understanding of the psyche in both conscious and unconscious manifestations through processes that occur between supervisee, client, and supervisor. With a supervisor who has knowledge and training in psychodynamics, this model would be employed in appropriate situations in advanced supervision to increase the supervisee's insight into how past events and relationship patterns are affecting his current relationships and patterns. Thus, in the supervisory situation, the model is used for three primary reasons:

a) To help the supervisee to integrate concepts such as transference, countertransference, defenses, resistance, and parallel process in clinical work where appropriate

b) To help the supervisee to understand unconscious processes that his clients or student supervisees are experiencing and how these are manifested in supervisory/therapeutic relationships

c) To help the supervisee to understand and process the relationships that occur between client and supervisee, and supervisee and supervisor, in a way that provides insight into parallel process and the interplay within these relationships

The psychodynamic model has many components; the primary concepts will be presented briefly. "Unconscious" refers to all the memories and instincts of the individual that lie completely out of awareness. Because it contains all the memories and experiences of the individual, it exerts influence over one's daily life. Thus, the past strongly influences the present, but often without the individual's awareness. The "preconscious" contains material that is out of awareness in the moment but could be called into awareness. "Consciousness" occurs in all that is within one's current awareness. Thus, anything that is not in conscious awareness (such as a rhythm or melody improvised by the client) is preconscious or unconscious (Bruscia, 1998).

"Defense mechanisms" occur when the psyche makes an effort to prevent unacceptable, that is, conflicting or threatening material from becoming conscious. Such material would pose a risk to the integrity of one's perception of the world, one's identity, or, more generally, one's ego. "Repression" is the most prevalent defense mechanism used to limit the unconscious process from becoming conscious. Other defense mechanisms include "denial," "displacement," "intellectualization," "projection," "rationalization," "reaction formation," "regression," "sublimation," and "isolation" (Vaillant, 1992). Further information on these mechanisms can be found in Bruscia (1998), Priestley (1994), and Vaillant (1992).

An understanding of the concepts of resistance, transference, and countertransference are also essential when working within the psychodynamic model. "Resistance" is any attempt that the client or supervisee makes to avoid or impede the therapeutic or supervisory process for fear that repressed material will be brought into consciousness. The individual is usually not aware of this avoidance, so the resistance may be entrenched. "Transference" occurs when the client relives significant relationships from the client's past within the therapeutic relationship. These patterns are replications of the past carried into the present, and they are transferred from one person to another. In the supervisory experience, transference occurs when the supervisee relives past patterns of relating with the supervisor or other professionals with whom he has had contact at the site or with the academic supervisor. "Countertransference" occurs when the supervisee interacts with a client in a way that resembles relationship patterns either in the client's life or in the supervisee's life. These patterns are replications of the past carried into the present, and they are transferred from one person to another. In the supervisory experience, countertransference occurs when the supervisor interacts with the supervisee in a way that resembles relationship patterns in the supervisee's life or in the supervisor's life (Bruscia, 1998, 2001).

There are essentially two kinds of countertransference: "concordant countertransference" and "complementary countertransference" (Bruscia, 1998; Priestley, 1994). A concordant countertransference may be helpful in working with a client or supervisee. This countertransference occurs when the supervisee identifies and empathizes with how the client is living out his or her relationships and feelings in therapy. In the supervisory experience, the supervisor identifies and empathizes with how the supervisee is living out his or her relationships and feelings in the supervisee's clinical work and during supervision. A complementary countertransference occurs when the supervisee has little empathy for what the client is experiencing and, instead, responds to the client with feelings and behavior patterns typical of another significant person from the client's life. Similarly, in the supervisory experience, the supervisor has little empathy for what the supervisee is experiencing and, instead, responds to the supervisee with feelings and behavior patterns typical of another significant person from the client's life. Parallel process occurs when the dynamics between the supervisee and the client have aspects similar to the dynamics between supervisor and supervisee (Bruscia, 2001).

When the supervisor is using this model to gain depth insight into the supervisee/client relationship or the supervisor/supervisee relationship, the task of this model is primarily to develop an understanding of how the supervisee perceives situations and reacts to the supervisory experience as these relate to a discernable pattern or patterns that may be based on the supervisee's past significant relationships and expectations.

Common supervisor tasks that would occur when supervising in this model might include:

a) Helping the advanced supervisee to understand the client or student supervisee from the client's or student supervisee's perspective and past history, including their culture and taking into account conscious and unconscious issues arising from economic and health status, diversity, and oppression
b) Analyzing the client's or student supervisee's thoughts and feelings toward the advanced supervisee and examining how these resemble the client's or student supervisee's patterns of relating to others and to oneself
c) Analyzing how the advanced supervisee's relationship with the client or student supervisee resembles his relationship with his supervisor
d) Helping the advanced supervisee to identify his own patterns of relating, feeling, and thinking about the client or student supervisee that may not be contributing positively to the therapeutic process and examining these to gain insight into how this way of relating resembles other patterns in the supervisee's life

It is important to note that in the psychodynamic model, even with training, the supervisor must be discreet and use good judgment in determining the boundaries between supervision and therapy with the supervisee. This is usually handled by focusing on the advanced supervisee's countertransference with and his understanding of his client or student supervisee and by recognizing parallel process in the advanced supervisee's interactions with the client or student supervisee and the advanced supervisee's interactions with his supervisor.

When using a psychodynamic frame in supervision, the supervisor models an approach that encourages the supervisee to:

a) Become process-oriented
b) Acquire analytical skills to develop an understanding of the client based on the client's history, culture, diversity, and its effects, and how past events have shaped the client's present
c) Acquire analytical skills to develop a therapeutic rationale in the treatment of clients
d) Cultivate an attitude of reflection and insight regarding his work
e) Increase his awareness of the connections between thoughts, feelings, and behaviors of the past and the present
f) Develop insight into the supervisee's own patterns of relating to others and to himself
g) Recognize occurrences of parallel process between client, supervisor, and supervisee
h) Recognize how the supervisee's unconscious may impede or assist the therapeutic process

Examples of the Use of the Psychodynamic Model

During supervision, the advanced supervisee reports fewer experiences and insights than usual to the supervisor and talks superficially about a client who does not seem to be making much progress. The supervisee sounds bored and frustrated. The supervisor has had discussions with the supervisee about this response from time to time with other clients in the past and feels that the supervisee's attitude has remained unchanged. This makes it difficult for the supervisor to know how to intervene, resulting in feelings of frustration for her. This is a parallel process. Just as the supervisee doesn't know how to intervene with the client and feels bored and frustrated, the supervisor has similar feelings of not knowing how to work with the supervisee and has similar feelings of frustration. A recognition of the fact that that there may be a parallel process occurring can give the supervisor great insight into how the supervisee is interacting with his clients and provide her with clues to the source of problems in the client/supervisee relationship.

For example, upon reflection, the supervisor recognizes that the source of some of her boredom is her feelings of inadequacy with this supervisee in this situation. The primary quality of this feeling of inadequacy is that of hopelessness. As the advanced supervisor examines her feelings more deeply and traces them back to her past experiences, she realizes that inadequacy and hopelessness are connected to her early school experiences that she had related to a learning disorder. Using this information from her own reflections, the supervisor begins to explore with the advanced supervisee the quality of his feelings toward his clients, helping the supervisee to trace back to reflect on how his feelings of boredom and disconnection have emerged at other times in his life and, finally, how these personal feelings are connected to his feelings about his client. In this scenario, the supervisor takes on a therapist role within strict boundaries to foster the supervisee's growth as a clinician, helping the supervisee to identify this issue and the impact of it in his professional life, but she does not provide personal therapy for the issue.

An example of countertransference is presented in the following scenario. The supervisee is preparing to move to another city and a new job, and the supervisor begins to talk about termination issues with current clients. The supervisee says that he doesn't really see the need for working on termination issues because the clients don't really seem to be aware of him or their environment. The supervisee's feelings about the clients are limited and do not take into consideration the whole client and thus may have a negative effect on his clients. This is an unusual attitude for the supervisee, who is normally very sensitive to the needs and internal emotional lives of his mostly nonverbal clients. The supervisor recognizes that the supervisee's difficulties with his client's termination may be connected to his feelings about leaving his clients and his current life as well as the termination of supervision. This leads the supervisor to wonder if the supervisee is experiencing countertransference issues.

Based on this, the supervisor opens a discussion related to the supervisee's feelings about the termination of their supervisory relationship and how the supervisee has dealt with major life changes and endings in the past. This discussion helps the supervisee to connect patterns of experiencing disconnection that are related to the trauma of a deep loss early in his life to the feelings of numbness and disconnection that he feels with regard to termination of his clients and his own supervision. Thus, the supervisor uses her awareness of the psychodynamic frame of countertransference to understand the supervisee, primarily to help him to become aware of the possible impact of his feelings and attitudes on his clients and to discuss the supervisee's perception of his need to seek therapy to help him process his issues related to loss.

APPROACHES AND CONCEPTS USED IN SUPERVISION

The primary models presented above provide us with schemas to address needs of supervisees from the preprofessional to the advanced level. Similar to clinical work that is focused on the developmentally sequenced needs of clients, supervision requires a fluidity of approach and techniques, based on the particular issues that emerge in supervision. A behavioral model cannot solve a deep problem related to loss, just as a psychodynamic model cannot help an intern to develop simple verbal processing skills or improvisation techniques appropriate for a particular client group.

While flexibility is required in the use of various models, there are many approaches that have been developed to work within a range of models. The approaches described here are not intended to be comprehensive; instead, they represent some of the more common current approaches used with clients. They are not specifically for preprofessional or advanced supervision but may be used to provide a framework for supervisory responses in any model.

Feminist Theory and Diversity Awareness

Feminist theory grew out of a need to understand social problems, worldviews, and existential issues from perspectives that could transcend the stronghold of dominant, patriarchal beliefs and structures in order to include the diverse perspectives of all cultures. It addressed problems of economic and power structure inequalities, oppression, and gender and sexual roles and stereotypes (Cole, 2017). Feminist therapy was grounded in these concepts and emerged in the 1980s as a response to the sexism, misogyny, and stereotyping that was common in therapeutic literature (Brown, 2017). Thus, it takes into account nondominant cultures: women, people of color, undocumented persons, people with disabilities, immigrants, refugees, people living in poverty, and people in the LGBTQ+ communities, including those with gender identities beyond the binary.

The Ethical Guidelines for Feminist Therapists (Feminist Therapy Institute Code of Ethics, 1999-Rev.) emphasize the need to take a proactive stance to eradicate oppression in the lives of clients, particularly those people, including females, who comprise nondominant cultures. Applying these tenets to supervision, the supervisor would include the feminist perspective of disempowerment and oppression in her understanding of her clients and would implement this perspective with the supervisee. Being attentive to these issues will help the supervisee to develop empathy and question his assumptions about clients by considering the environmental factors that empower or disempower clients. This perspective has much in common with one of the 14 themes that Ronnestad and Skovholt (2003) found in their analysis of counselor development: "For the practitioner, there is a realignment from self as hero to client as hero" (cited in Smith, 2009). The feminist approach can be instrumental in awakening the supervisee to the client's existential perspective and developing empathy for the client.

Structurally, in the supervisor–supervisee relationship, the feminist viewpoint would seek to establish an egalitarian approach where the responsibility for the supervision process is shared in order to empower the supervisee as much as possible (Degges White, Colon, & Borzumato Gainey, 2013). Forinash (2006) developed a perspective of feminist music therapy supervision that included eight "cornerstones" for feminist supervision: openness; honoring the supervisee and creating a process of collaboration in supervision; understanding our biases as supervisors and questioning our assumptions; being reflexive and analytical about the choices we make and the roles we assume; understanding events, clients, and supervisees from multiple perspectives; being aware of one's power as a supervisor and initiating conversations about power and equality; being an advocate and activist in order to raise consciousness; and examining the various cultures of music.

Based on Forinash's (2006) philosophical tenets, it is evident that the feminist approach can help the supervisee to expand and deepen his understanding of clients, as it is ultimately an approach that widens one's perspective. It is also important to keep in mind as supervisors that there is always a differential power relationship that is inherent within the supervision structure. While we may wish to defuse power relationships as much as possible, the pure egalitarian approach to supervision might be most applicable only in later stages of internship, when the supervisee has developed enough awareness to be able to take on the responsibility for his own learning and development.

Positive Psychology Interventions

Positive psychology interventions (PPI) are an outgrowth of humanistic counseling, which focuses on the strengths and values of human beings, as well as the cultivation of positive emotions as a means of dealing with life's problems (Csillik, 2015). Seligman (2002) chose positive interventions as his theme when he was elected president of the American Psychological Association in 1998 (Positive Psychology Center, 2017) and proposed that therapists adopt an approach to promote sound mental health as opposed to focusing merely on treating illness (Seligman, 2002). Core concepts include the facilitation of mechanisms and techniques that foster emotional, social, and psychological well-being (Kashdan & Ciarrochi, 2013). Because well-being may have different cultural interpretations, it is important to understand the individual's beliefs with regard to what constitutes subjective well-being emotionally, socially, and psychologically (Magyar-Moe, Owens, & Conoley, 2015). Counseling interventions that have been developed in the PPI framework include practicing forgiveness, keeping a gratitude journal or writing a gratitude letter, thinking about positive experiences and reliving positive events, and taking care to nurture relationships (2015).

Music therapy employs a strengths-based methodology in working with clients, meaning that the interests, motivations, preferences, and strengths of the client are taken into account when designing interventions. This therapeutic approach is an expression of key concepts in PPI. In a supervisory relationship, PPI interventions can also play a role in helping the supervisee to identify and develop his particular musical and therapeutic strengths, thereby contributing to the supervisee's growth as a professional and modeling an effective therapeutic approach.

Motivational Interviewing

Motivational interviewing (MI), like PPI, is an outgrowth of the humanistic movement in that the central concept is a belief in the human being's innate tendency toward growth and optimal functioning. Developed as a method of communication with clients, MI addresses the common therapeutic problem of ambivalence to change by using a supportive, collaborative, and empathetic counseling style that takes into account the client's strengths, aspirations and values (Csillik, 2015). MI is composed of four core concepts: partnership, acceptance, compassion, and evocation (2015). Hope and aspiration are one of the primary building blocks in MI, as clients are encouraged to envision a positive future and to determine the steps to achieve their goals (Corrigan, McCracken, & Holmes, 2001).

MI is a useful approach in helping supervisees to develop effective verbal interactions with clients. From the supervision perspective, the MI approach might also be useful in working through challenges to growth in supervisees. By modeling acceptance, compassion, and an interest in the supervisee's vision of himself as a therapist, the supervisor helps the supervisee to reflect on himself as a professional and as a person in a way that supports the development of the supervisee's identity as a therapist. Congruent with MI is the supervisor's role in assisting the supervisee to determine the steps in achieving these goals (Corrigan, McCracken, & Holmes, 2001). As in PPI, by modeling this approach in supervision, the supervisee learns through experience.

Using Music in Supervision

There are many opportunities to use music in supervision. The advantage of using music is that the supervisee can experience the client–therapist relationship nonverbally through music in addition to reflecting on the relationship verbally, which can provide new insights that stem from unconscious information about the client and the client–therapist relationship. Lee (2001) described how music improvisation is used in a music-centered approach to supervision. Stephens (1984) identified ways in which music improvisation can be used during group supervision, freely oscillating between verbal and music processes. Beginning with verbal discussion, the supervisee might improvise or use his own playing to uncover material in the client's process, which can then be further discussed. An example of this would be to have the supervisee replicate the way in which a client played to better understand the client's expression (1984). During the course of playing the role of the client, the supervisee may have access to emotions that were not experienced when observing the client in the therapist role.

Connecting to the client's emotions as well as to one's own emotions about the client and the therapeutic process is an important means of developing understanding and empathy for the client. The use of music in supervision might also provide important information about therapeutic direction. Techniques that might be helpful in achieving this in supervision can be found in Moreno's (1999) music psychodrama approach, which is based on the therapeutic modality of psychodrama. In this approach, music is improvised to express a wide variety of emotions related to a narrative of psychological significance. While this was not specifically developed for supervision purposes, Moreno described a number of music psychodrama techniques and listening perspectives that can provide rich insights into the client's psyche.

Reproducing and analyzing the client's musical expressions can help the supervisee to gain greater understanding of the client and the client–therapist relationship through the act of both *playing* the client and through the analysis of the client's music. Bruscia (1987) developed an in-depth process to analyze improvisations in his *Improvisation Assessment Profiles*. Using these in supervision, the supervisee can reproduce salient elements of the client's improvised playing and analyze them to provide fertile information about the client's psyche.

These musical techniques will provide the supervisee with the tools to explore the client's inner life and bring deeper understanding of the client's issues, emotions, and challenges. This approach would be particularly applicable to group supervision, as well as individual supervision.

CONCLUSION

The models and approaches available for use in supervision are varied in terms of goals, foci, and supervisor/supervisee roles. For the beginning supervisor, this can be daunting if one assumes that there is a correct model or approach to take at any specific time with a supervisee. This is rendered more complex by the fact that when the supervisee uses a particular approach with a client, the supervisor may use a different approach to supervise the supervisee's work. For example, in some situations where the supervisee's primary approach with the client is behavioral, a cognitive or psychodynamic model with a feminist approach might be used during supervision in order to better understand the behavioral approach that is used in the client sessions and described in clinical notes. Similarly, a humanistic approach may be the basis of the supervisee's work with his clients, while elements of psychodynamic concepts and cognitive approaches with these clients may be discussed in supervision.

In reality, flexibility is required in using the knowledge and skills that are presented in the various models and approaches. All approaches have something to offer, and the particular way in which a supervisor uses any one or combination of models is a personal choice based on the supervisor's personal therapeutic approach and the supervisee's needs. There is no correct way to go about supervision, as this is a very personal mentorship process in which the structured roles of supervisor and supervisee soon give way to professional and peer relationships and, in some situations, even lifetime friendships. The opportunity to pass on what one knows about our work with clients is a gift for both the supervisee and the supervisor, providing opportunities for growth benefiting both simultaneously. Thus, each supervisor and supervisee will develop a unique partnership of learning in the supervision process while using the many approaches and skills presented in the various approaches.

REFERENCE LIST

American Music Therapy Association. (AMTA). (2013). AMTA professional competencies. Retrieved July 10, 2017, from https://www.musictherapy.org/about/competencies/

American Music Therapy Association. (AMTA). (2015). AMTA advanced competencies. Retrieved March 9, 2018, from https://www.musictherapy.org/members/advancedcomp/

Bernard, J. M. (1979). Supervisor training: A discrimination model. *Counselor education and supervision, 19*(1), 60–68.

Bohart, A. C. (2013). The actualizing person. In M. Cooper, M. O'Hara, P. F. Schmid, & A. Bohart (Eds.), *The handbook of person-centred psychotherapy and counseling* (pp. 84–101). London, UK: Palgrave Macmillan.

Brown, L. (2017). Feminist Therapy. Retrieved July 3, 2017, from http://www.drlaurabrown.com/feminist-therapy/

Bruscia, K. E. (1987). *Improvisational models of music therapy.* Springfield, IL: Charles C Thomas Publisher.

Bruscia, K. E. (Ed.). (1988). *The dynamics of music psychotherapy.* Gilsum, NH: Barcelona Publishers.

Bruscia, K. E. (2001). A model of supervision derived from apprenticeship training. In M. Forinash (Ed.), *Music therapy supervision* (pp. 281–298). Gilsum, NH: Barcelona Publishers.

Cole, N. L. (2017). *Feminist theory in sociology.* Retrieved July 3, 2017, from https://www.thoughtco.com/feminist-theory-3026624

Corrigan, P. W., McCracken, S. G., & Holmes, E. P. (2001). Motivational interviews as goal assessment for persons with psychiatric disability. *Community Mental Health Journal, 37*(2), 113–122.

Csillik, A. (2015). Positive motivational interviewing: Activating clients' strengths and intrinsic motivation to change. *Journal of Contemporary Psychotherapy, 45*(2), 119.

Degges White, S. E., Colon, B. R., & Borzumato-Gainey, C. (2013). Counseling supervision within a feminist framework: Guidelines for intervention. *The Journal of Humanistic Counseling, 52*(1), 92–105.

Farnan, L. (2001). Competency-based approach to intern supervision. In M. Forinash (Ed.), *Music therapy supervision* (pp. 117–134). Gilsum, NH: Barcelona Publishers.

Feiner, S. (2001). A journey through internship supervision: Roles, dynamics, and phases of the supervisory relationship. In M. Forinash (Ed.), *Music therapy supervision* (pp. 99–115). Gilsum, NH: Barcelona Publishers.

Feminist Therapy Institute Code of Ethics (1999-Rev.). Retrieved July 4, 2017, from http://supp.apa.org/books/Supervision-Essentials/Appendix_D.pdf

Forinash, M. (2006). Feminist music therapy supervision. In S. Hadley (Ed.), *Feminist perspectives in music therapy* (pp. 415–428). Gilsum, NH: Barcelona Publishers.

Hanser, S. B. (2000). *The new music therapist's handbook.* Milwaukee, WI: Hal Leonard Corporation.

Kashdan, T. B., & Ciarrochi, J. V. (Eds.). (2013). *Mindfulness, acceptance, and positive psychology: The seven foundations of well-being.* Oakland, CA: New Harbinger Publications. Chapter on positive psychology retrieved July 4, 2017, from https://www.psychologytoday.com/files/attachments/101936/parksbiswasdienerinpress.pdf

Lee, C. (2001). The supervision of clinical improvisation in Aesthetic Music Therapy: A music-centered approach. In M. Forinash (Ed.), *Music therapy supervision* (pp. 247–270). Gilsum, NH: Barcelona Publishers.

Magyar-Moe, J. L., Owens, R. L., & Conoley, C. W. (2015). Positive psychological interventions in counseling: What every counseling psychologist should know. *The Counseling Psychologist, 43*(4), 508–557.

Moreno, J. J. (1999). *Acting your inner music: Music therapy and psychodrama.* St. Louis, MO: MMB Music, Inc.

Positive Psychology Center. (2017). Martin E. Seligman. Retrieved July 4, 2017, from https://ppc.sas.upenn.edu/people/martin-ep-seligman

Priestley, M. (1994). *Essays on analytical music therapy.* Gilsum, NH: Barcelona Publishers.

Proctor, I. (2000). *Group supervision: A guide to creative practice.* London, UK: SAGE Publications.

Reinecke, M. A., & Freeman, A. (2003). Cognitive therapy. In A. S. Gurman & S. B. Messer (Eds.), *Essential psychotherapies: Theory and practice* (2nd ed.; pp. 224–271). New York, NY: Guilford Press.

Rønnestad, M. H., & Skovholt, T. M. (2003). The journey of the counselor and therapist: Research findings and perspectives on professional development. *Journal of Career Development, 30*(1), 5–44.

Seligman, M. (2002). *Authentic happiness: Using the new positive psychology to realize your potential for lasting fulfillment.* New York, NY: Free Press.

Smith, K. L. (2009). *A brief summary of supervision models.* Retrieved July 4, 2017, from https://pdfs.semanticscholar.org/240f/83cb62c2bd9c84d795d6c8b8f89f2a83bb7d.pdf

Stephens, G. (1984). Group supervision in music therapy. *Music Therapy, 4*(1), 29–38.

Stoltenberg, C. D., & McNeill, B. W. (2011). *IDM supervision: An integrative developmental model for supervising counselors and therapists* (3rd ed.). New York, NY: Routledge.

Vaillant, G. E. (1992). *Ego mechanisms of defense: A guide for clinicians and researchers.* Arlington, VA: American Psychiatric Publications.

Chapter 3
ETHICAL ISSUES IN SUPERVISION[3]

Kathleen M. Murphy[4]

Music therapy supervision is the cornerstone of competent and ethical clinical practice. This is a daunting task for supervisors, who, along with music therapy educators, are the gatekeepers for professionals entering the field. While post-internship supervision is not yet required by any regulatory or legal body (the exceptions being in those states in which music therapists may become licensed as creative arts therapists, professional counselors, or mental health counselors), music therapists may supervise their colleagues who are seeking support in their clinical work. Additionally, advanced training programs such as the Bonny Method of Guided Imagery and Music, vocal psychotherapy, Analytical Music Therapy, and Nordoff-Robbins Music Therapy all require a period of supervised clinical work.

The supervisory relationship by its nature is hierarchical and evaluative; the supervisor is in a position of power over the supervisee. The supervisor in many instances determines whether the supervisee will gain entry into the profession. Supervisees often rely on recommendations from intern or other supervisors for employment or graduate school. This power differential provides an opportunity for unethical or harmful supervision, potentially putting the supervisee in a vulnerable position. Incidents of harmful and inadequate supervision have been reported in the counseling and psychology literature. A recent survey of 363 supervisees from multiple mental health professions noted that 93% of respondents reported receiving inadequate supervision and 35% reported receiving harmful supervision (Ellis et al., 2014). The editors of a recent issue of *The Clinical Supervisor* devoted to harmful clinical supervision noted that harmful supervision practices were generally the result of unethical behavior on the part of the supervisor (Ellis, Taylor, Corp, Hutman, & Kangos, 2017). A search of the music therapy and supervision literature did not reveal any cases of unethical or harmful supervision experiences. Yet, in talking with colleagues and former students, one hears that they do occur.

Ross (1930), in his seminal text *The Right and the Good*, identifies four moral principles that provide the foundation for ethical behavior, including respect for autonomy, beneficence, nonmaleficence, and justice. The American Psychological Association (2017) also includes fidelity in its ethical guidelines. These principles underlie ethical supervision and are manifest when supervisors use informed consent (autonomy), are competent to supervise (beneficence and nonmaleficence); maintain appropriate boundaries (nonmaleficence); follow guidelines for due process (justice); and agree to the guidelines set for supervision in support of the supervisee (fidelity) (Bernard & Goodyear, 2014).

Dileo (2001), in the first edition of this book, outlined specific ethical issues relevant to supervision (see Table 1). This chapter will review most of these, including (1) informed consent, (2) confidentiality, (3) competence, (4) multiple roles/relationships, (5) gatekeeping, and (6) due process.

---

[3] Cheryl Dileo wrote the chapter on ethics in the previous edition of *Music Therapy Supervision*. Her pioneering work laid the groundwork for the present chapter.

[4] The author would like to thank Michael J. Mulligan, Esq., for his expertise and review of this chapter for clarity and accuracy.

Table 1
Ethical Issues in Supervision

I. Supervisor Competence
  • Personal Functioning
  • Qualifications/Training
  • Competence in Specific Clinical Areas
  • Competence to Work with Various Types of Supervisee Needs

II. Adequacy of Supervision
  • Fulfillment of Duties/Responsibilities
  • Preparation for Supervision
  • Appropriate and Mutual Goal-Setting for Supervision
  • Adequate Discussion of Expectations and Details of Supervision
  • Consideration for Supervisee's Needs and Interests
  • Appropriate Supervisory Methods (Safeguards for Experiential Methods)
  • Awareness of Limits
  • Role-Modeling
  • Sensitivity to Multicultural and Gender Issues
  • Confidentiality of Client(s) and Supervisee Maintained
  • Adequacy of Supervision Evaluated

III. Supervisor's Behaviors
  • Gender and Other Role Stereotyping
  • Gender Discrimination
  • Negative Countertransference (Creation of Overdependence)
  • Establishment of Dual Relationship
  • Ethical Role-Modeling

IV. Misuse of Supervisor's Poser/Authority
  • Supervisee Abuse
  • Sexual Harassment
  • Imposition of Beliefs

V. Informed Consent
  • From Client
  • From Supervisee

VI. Evaluation
  • Criteria for Evaluation Clarified
  • Chance for Supervisee to Remediate Problems
  • Information on How and With Whom Supervisory Information is Shared

VII. Supervisee's Behaviors (Negative Transference)

Taken from "Ethical Issues in Supervision" by C. Dileo, in M. Forinash (Ed.), *Music Therapy Supervision* (p. 21). Copyright © 2000 Barcelona Publishers.

Code of Ethics

Mental health professions, as noted by Ladany, Lehrman-Watermn, Molinarl, and Wolgast (1991), have increased their focus on the importance of ethical standards for counseling and psychotherapy supervision by providing guidance for supervisors in their code of ethics (e.g., American Counseling Association [ACA], 2014; American Psychological Association [APA], 2017; American School Counselor Association [ASCA], 2016; Association for Counselor Education and Supervision, 1995). The ethical guidance provided in the AMTA Code of Ethics (2014a), while not as substantive as that of related professions, offers the following standards related to supervision (italics added by author):

11.2 The MT involved in education and/*or supervision* will use his/her skill to help others acquire the knowledge and skills necessary to perform with high standards of professional competence.

11.4 The MT involved in the education of students and *internship training* will ensure that clinical work performed by students is rendered under adequate supervision by other music therapists, other professionals, and/or the MT educator.

11.5 The MT involved in education and/*or supervision* will evaluate the competencies of students as required by good educational practices and will identify those students whose limitations impede performance as a competent music therapist.

11.6 The MT involved in the education of students and *internship training* will serve as an exemplary role model in regard to ethical conduct and the enforcement of the Code of Ethics.

11.7 The MT involved in education and *training* will ensure that students and interns operate under the same ethical standards that govern professionals.

In essence, these standards describe the main duties of an "ethical supervisor" as (1) helping supervisees to acquire the knowledge and skills necessary to enter the field, (2) supervising the provision of music therapy treatment, (3) providing ongoing evaluation of competencies, (4) serving as a role model, and (5) ensuring that supervisees operate under the same ethical standards as professional music therapists. Guidelines for ethical behavior on the part of the supervisor in the areas of competence, boundaries, and dual relationships are not clearly articulated and have to be translated from the AMTA (2014a) Code of Ethics as they relate to professional behavior.

Informed Consent

In the clinical setting, clients are given comprehensive information about the benefits and risks of treatment as well as alternative options. Clients then have the right to freely accept or refuse treatment based on this information. The same holds true for those seeking supervision. Supervisees have the right to clear and comprehensive information about supervision, including risks, benefits, and expectations, as well as their rights and responsibilities[5] (Bernard & Goodyear, 2014; Borders & Brown, 2005). This information should be reviewed at the beginning of the supervisory relationship. In fact, the use of informed consent is a requirement in the Code of Ethics of many related mental health disciplines (e.g., ACA, 2017; ACES, 1995; APA, 2017).

An informed consent for supervision should clearly define the supervisory relationship to ward off possible conflicts or misunderstandings (McCarthy & Sugden, 1995). Additionally, supervision is more productive when the boundaries of supervision are made explicit and both the supervisor and supervisee have a clear understanding of the relationship (Bartlett, 1983; Minnes,

---

[5] Bernard and Goodyear (2014) provide readers with an example of a Supervisee's Bill of Rights.

1987). Topics commonly included in the informed consent for supervision include the supervisor's background, beginning and end dates of the supervisory relationship, goals for supervision, method(s) of evaluation, rights and responsibilities of the supervisee and the supervisor, cancellation policies, emergency contact information, reporting requirements, conflict resolution processes, reasons for termination of the supervisory relationship, right to privacy, confidentiality, fees, and risks and benefits (Barnet & Molsen, 2014; Cobia & Boes, 2000; Thomas, 2007). It is the supervisor's responsibility to review the informed consent document with the supervisee and to answer any questions. The informed consent should be signed by both parties. Bernard and Goodyear (2014) and Ellis (2017) provide examples of consent statements and statements of supervisee rights and responsibilities that can be adapted for used in music therapy supervision. Music therapy educators, field study (practicum), and internship supervisors can look to these documents for information that they might consider, including in the syllabi for clinical training.

One area of the informed consent that needs particular attention is that of privacy and confidentiality. The supervisory relationship is not the same as a therapeutic relationship. The supervisory role is that of gatekeeper in addition to mentor and teacher (Bernard & Goodyear, 2014; Hsiao, 2014). Therefore, supervisees, whether they are students, interns, or professionals, need to know at the start of the supervisory relationship the limits of privacy and confidentiality. Supervisors should keep privacy and confidentiality in mind when documenting what was discussed in supervisory meetings. Power (2007) recommends that the following information be recorded and kept in the supervisee's file: date and beginning/end time of the supervision session, names of those in attendance, brief note of issues raised and discussed, and date and time of next supervisory meeting. Additionally, supervisors should let supervisees know the content of any documentation or evaluations that will be shared with agency staff, academic supervisors, licensing boards, or future employers (Power, 2007).

Beyond providing the supervisee with the "opportunity for informed consent" (p. 256), Bernard and Goodyear (2014) noted that supervisors must ensure that supervisees provide their clients with the opportunity to consent before starting treatment, information on the supervision procedures that will be used (e.g., recording, live observation), and what types of information will be shared with their supervisor. "Supervisees place themselves in a position to be sued for invasion of privacy and breach of confidentiality if they do not inform their clients that they will be discussing sessions with their supervisor" (Disney & Stephens, 1994, p. 50). It is recommended that supervisors meet with those clients whom practicum students and interns will treat prior to the start of therapy (Bernard & Goodyear, 2014). The supervisor can explain the parameters of supervision, including the type of information to which the supervisee will have access, the type of information the supervisee may share with the supervisor, and the number of sessions the client will receive from the supervisee. The nature of supervision (direct or indirect) should also be shared. This information will allow the client to make an informed decision as to whether to work with the supervisee.

In summary, both the supervisee and those whom the supervisee will treat have the right to informed consent. In the case where supervised practice is a requirement for degree completion, certification, or licensure, informed consent is limited to a comprehensive review of the risks and benefits of supervision, along with the rights and responsibilities of both the supervisor and the supervisee. Clients who will be treated by supervisees have the right to a comprehensive review of the risks and benefits of treatment; the limits of confidentiality and privacy, including what may be disclosed during supervisory meetings; and, most important, the right to refuse treatment from a trainee.

Confidentiality

The supervisory relationship is triadic, consisting of the supervisor, the supervisee, and the client (client group). Within that relationship, information will be disclosed about the supervisee and about the clients. The ethical principles of autonomy and fidelity explain the limits of confidentiality for the supervisee and the client(s) served (Sherry, 1991).

Confidentiality Rights of Client Information

Autonomy refers to the client's rights to make an informed decision about treatment. Fidelity requires supervisees to provide clients with a "fair and honest representation" of the therapeutic relationship, including the role of the supervisor (Sherry, 1991, p. 577). Therefore, supervisees need to seek permission from their clients before discussing their clinical work with their supervisor. Supervisees need provide their client(s) with a description of the material that will be shared, answer any questions, and reveal the name and credentials of their supervisor prior to obtaining consent. Supervisors have the responsibility to remind supervisees that anything discussed within the supervisory meeting is not to be repeated elsewhere. If the supervisor does not work in the same agency as the supervisee, pseudonyms should be used as a means of offering further protection of client information. Last, written permission must be obtained from the client if a music therapy session is going to be audio- or audio-video–recorded and shared with a supervisor.

Confidentiality Rights of Supervisee Information and Self-Disclosures

The supervisory relationship is evaluative by nature; "therefore, information received in supervision is not typically considered confidential" (Bernard & Goodyear, 2014, p. 270). Information about a supervisee's performance, including their skill level, personal functioning, and ethical behavior (Dileo, 2001), may be shared with academic institutions, certification bodies, or licensing boards. Fidelity in this instance requires that the supervisor inform the supervisee of the nature of information that may be shared with academic faculty or certification/licensing boards (Sherry, 1991). Additionally, the type of information that will be shared and with whom should be included in the consent form. That said, supervisors should strive to treat personal information "as sensitively as possible" (Bernard & Goodyear, 2014, p. 270), so as not to cause undue harm to the supervisee.

Competence

The AMTA Code of Ethics (COE) states "[t]he MT will perform only those duties for which he/she has been adequately trained, not engaging outside his/her area of competence (COE 1.1). Competence is defined as "the habitual and judicious use communication, knowledge, technical skills, clinical reason, emotions, values, and reflection in daily practice for the benefit of the individual and community being served" (Epstein & Hundert, 2002, p. 226). They further suggest that competence is built upon strong clinical skills, research knowledge, and moral development (Epstein & Hundert, 2002). Music therapy, like many other professions, focuses on the competence of the music therapist rather than the development of competence as a supervisor (Bernard & Goodyear, 2014). For example, the American Music Therapy Association requires completion only of a five-hour continuing education course offered by the Association Internship Approval Committee for internship directors (AMTA, 2014c). The Standards for Education and Training (AMTA, 2014b, 2014c) include a requirement for continuing education related to supervision, but there are no consequences if that condition is not met. Increasingly, related professionals, on the other hand, do have standards and codes of ethics for clinical supervisors (ACES, 1990; American Association of Marriage and Family Therapists [AAMFT], 2017)

Several authors have identified specific competencies for clinical supervisors (e.g., Barnett & Molzon, 2014; Borders & Brown, 2005). Common among all authors is the belief that supervisors should be competent in the "clinical area" in which they are providing supervision (Barnett & Molzon, 2014, p. 1052). In fact, the APA (2017) Code of Ethics states that psychologists may provide supervision "with populations and in areas only within the boundaries of their competence, based on their education, training, supervised experience, consultation, study or professional experience" (p. 5). It is important that supervisors identify which areas of music therapy practice they are competent to supervise. Additionally, supervisors should "realize they cannot be all things to all people" and maintain a list of colleagues who can provide supervision in areas in which they are unfamiliar (Bernard & Goodyear, 2014, p. 267). Ongoing assessment of supervisory skills and areas of competence is crucial to ethical supervision.

Supervisors also need to be competent and remain competent in supervising. They need to take responsibility for their own learning about and development of the knowledge, skills, and values related to (1) supervision, (2) developmental stages of professional growth, and (3) the clinical population of the supervisee. This also includes knowledge, understanding, and application of research and theory related to all levels of supervision (Bernard & Goodyear, 2014). Music therapists can participate in both informal and formal continuing education activities to maintain competence.

Further, Kurpius, Gibson, Leis, and Corbet (1991) recommended that supervisors disclose their training and qualifications as well as areas they are competent to supervise to their supervisees. In this way, supervisees can make an informed decision when selecting a supervisor. Falender et al. (2004) developed a competency framework for clinical supervisors. In it, the authors identify specific competencies related to knowledge, skills, values, and overarching social context issues that supervisors need to develop. Additionally, they include specific competencies related to the training supervisors should complete, as well as a checklist of skills supervisors can use to assess their readiness to be a supervisor (Falender et al., 2004, p. 778).

Ethical Competence

Supervisors are responsible for helping supervisees to become competent and ethical professionals. One way to do this is to model ethical behavior and demonstrate they value it (APA, 2015). Further, supervisors should become familiar with ethics, codes of ethics, and ethical decision-making models as they relate to clinical supervision. Supervisors should evaluate their personal knowledge of ethics, especially as it pertains to music therapy clinical work and supervision. In order to help supervisees develop self-evaluation skills (Vasquez, 1992), supervisors should reflect on and evaluate their behavior as a means of modeling reflective practice (Shöen, 1987). Finally, they should assess their ability to engage in discussions of ethical behaviors and dilemmas with supervisees as well as demonstrate and teach ethical decision-making. This will help supervisees to develop the ability to independently determine when they have crossed a competency boundary and need to know when to seek additional guidance in the form of supervision or consultation (Bernard & Goodyear, 2014).

Multicultural Competence

Competence also involves awareness and understanding of the diversity among clients and supervisees (Vasquez, 1992). Music therapists are working with more culturally diverse clients. Additionally, the cultural diversity of music therapists continues to rise. Both of these circumstances can lead to issues and problems in supervision if music therapy supervisors do not address all of the ways in which cultural differences can influence supervision and therapy (Peters, 2017). Issues related to cultural diversity that will influence both therapy and supervision include race, gender, ethnic origin, cultural beliefs and norms, values, sexual orientation, gender expression, socio-economic status, religion, and age. These cultural differences may be visible (e.g., race or gender) or invisible (e.g., cultural beliefs and values) (Burnham, 2012). Additionally, these differences will influence how clients, supervisees, and supervisors view therapy, the therapeutic relationship, health, and the role of music in healing. Supervisors, therefore, have an ethical responsibility to (1) be knowledgeable about the complexity of cultural factors in supervision and therapy and (2) create a supervisory environment in which differences in cultural identities and norms can safely be explored (Pettifor, Sinclair, & Falender, 2014). This calls for an integrative and intersectional framework for supervision (Peters, 2017). A culturally competent supervisor should "build upon a supervisee's musical strengths, acknowledge cultural differences and the acculturation process, and address supervisory expectations" (Swamy, 2011, p. 136). Supervisors also must remain vigilant so their personal values, beliefs, and worldviews do not have an undue influence on the supervisory process (Falender, Shafranske, & Falicov, 2014). They should strive create a culture in which multiple viewpoints are explored rather than one in which the dominant views are upheld (Ming-Sum, 2005). Therefore, supervisors should develop an understanding of how the intersection of social contexts and communities with multiple identities influences the supervision triad (client–supervisee–supervisor) (Inman & Ladany, 2014).

Multiple Relationships

Multiple or dual relationships occur when people have more than one role relationship with each other. These are as prevalent in music therapy as they are in other helping professions. Examples of dual relationships may include a university professor who also serves as a clinical supervisor; a supervisee in a clinical placement who is also the supervisor's research assistant; or a supervisor and supervisee who have a prior friendship or collegial relationship. These relationships in and of themselves are not harmful or unethical and in fact can be beneficial (Ammirati & Kaslow, 2017). Remembering that fidelity, or integrity, in relationships is a cornerstone of ethical behavior, the ethical supervisor will evaluate all of the relationships they have with a supervisee to ensure that there is not a risk of harm. Supervisory relationships are hierarchical by design, with the supervisor in a position of power or authority over the supervisee. Multiple relationships *may* become problematic if the person with less power (i.e., supervisee) is knowingly placed in an exploitative or harmful situation by a person with more power (i.e., supervisor) (Bernard & Goodyear, 2014). To protect the supervisee, boundaries that encapsulate expected role behavior should be put in place. Many of these boundaries are similar to those common to a client–therapist relationship and include guidelines related to self-disclosure, physical touch, intimate relationships, coercion, gift-giving, and time and place for supervision sessions. These boundaries may be violated if not doing so will result in a potential risk of harm to a supervisee or their clients (Gutheil & Gabbard, 1993).

A distinction should be made between a boundary violation and a boundary crossing. A boundary crossing occurs when a boundary is not strictly adhered to because doing so may cause harm. For example, Barnett (2007) and Vasquez (2007) noted that some boundaries, such as gift-giving, self-disclosure, or personal touch, may be crossed when working with supervisees whose cultural expectations are different from those of the supervisor. It is the supervisor's responsibility to decide when a boundary can be relaxed, always keeping the best interest of the supervisee or the client at the fore.

A review of the literature suggests that there are three types of role relationships in which caution should be exercised on the part of the supervisor so that a boundary is not violated: intimate or sexual relationships, multiple role relationships, and shifts in role relationships (Bernard & Goodyear, 2014; Pearson & Piazza, 1997).

Intimate or Sexual Relationships
Intimate or sexual relationships are the most obvious example of a boundary violation. The power differential between a supervisee and supervisor creates a risk of exploitation, even if the supervisee states they entered the relationship voluntarily (Bernard & Goodyear, 2014). Additionally, supervisors must ensure that supervisees understand that they may not enter into an intimate or sexual relationship with a client. These relationships are prohibited by the AMTA Code of Ethics (2014a) as well. It is the responsibility of the supervisor to ensure that their supervisees do not enter into inappropriate relationships with their clients. Supervisors should address the issue of sexual attraction between supervisees and clients or supervisees and their supervisors. Hamilton and Spruill (1999) suggest that the following be reviewed at the outset of supervision to minimize the risk of sexual misconduct on the part of a supervisee:

a) a discussion of the powerful effects on attraction of familiarity, similarity, self-disclosure, and physical closeness;

b) testimonials from the professor, other well-respected clinicians, or both about their encounters with their own feelings of attraction toward clients and clients' feelings of attraction toward them;

c) a discussion of specific actions to take when feelings of attraction arise, with emphasis on the importance of seeking supervision;

d) a discussion of the suspected risk factors for, and the early signs of, developing client–therapist intimacy;

e) delineation of the effects of therapist–client sexual misconduct on the client;

f) social skills–training to increase skill and decrease anxiety related to enacting ethical behavior; and

g) a very clear explanation of departmental policies regarding ethical infractions, with emphasis placed on a clear distinction between feelings that are to be expected and actions that are unacceptable. (p. 322)

Last, supervisors should be vigilant in their observations of supervisee behavior. They should look for both overt (a supervisee shares strong feelings about a client) and covert (supervisees making phone calls for clients, gift-giving) markers of boundary violations (Ladany, Friedlander, & Nelson, 2005). It is essential to address these behaviors early by engaging the supervisees in a frank discussion about their feelings, acknowledging the normalcy of the experience, and identifying ways in which the feelings can be managed without impacting the therapeutic relationship (Ladany et al., 2005).

Multiple Professional Roles

Multiple professional roles are common in music therapy, given the relatively small size of the profession and the nature of music therapy education and training. It is likely that a supervisor may serve in multiple professional roles, including educator, advisor, dissertation committee member, collaborator, employer, or mentor. Often, these roles are complementary (Kurpius et al., 1991) and can enhance the supervisory experience, as each has a prescribed function and an evaluative capacity (Gottlieb, Robinson, & Younggren, 2007). However, the nature of this relationship can change when the boundaries of the relationship change and begin to include informal meetings with supervisees, such as traveling to a conference together or meeting over lunch to discuss current professional issues (Gottlieb et al., 2007), or a personal friendship begins to develop (Borders & Brown, 2005). While these informal meetings have benefits and provide opportunities for additional mentorship, Gutheil and Gabbard (1993) suggest that the risk of harm to the supervisee increases as that nature of the relationship becomes more personal. Supervision is a complex process. Over time, feelings toward a supervisee or the level of performance may change. The additional role relationships may interfere with a supervisor's ability to objectively address these changes.

Evaluating the Potential for Harm

In the case of multiple professional role relationships, the supervisor must ensure that roles and boundaries are clarified to minimize the risk of harm to the supervisee (Bernard & Goodyear, 2014; Pearson & Piazza, 1997). Several authors offer guidance to help supervisors determine whether multiple relationships with a supervisor have the potential to cause harm. Gottlieb et al. (2007) offered the following questions for supervisors to ask themselves as they consider the roles they may have in a supervisee's training:

1. Is entering into a relationship in addition to the supervisory one necessary or should it be avoided?
2. Can the additional relationship(s) potentially cause harm?
3. If harm seems avoidable or unlikely, would the additional relationship prove beneficial?
4. Is there a risk that another relationship could disrupt the supervisory one?
5. Can the supervisor evaluate the matter objectively? (pp. 245–246)

Herlihy and Corey (1992) acknowledge that multiple relationships with supervisees may be unavoidable. It this case, they recommend that supervisors secure informed consent from the supervisee, outlining the nature of the dual relationship and potential risks; seek ongoing consultation as needed; self-monitor the relationship and document any potential issues; and, if the relationships become problematic, seek supervision. If multiple relationships are unavoidable, supervisors are advised to complete a risk-benefit assessment. If the benefits outweigh the risks, then supervisors should follow the same steps as outlined. If the risks outweigh the benefits, supervisors are advised to avoid entering in a multiple relationship (Herlihy & Corey, 1992).

Gottlieb (1993) proposed a decision-making model that supervisors can use to avoid harmful dual relationships. The model is based on the power differential between supervisor and a supervisee, duration of the supervisory relationship, and the finality of termination. The greater the power differential (e.g., an internship supervisor who can fail a music therapy intern, thereby preventing them from sitting for the board certification exam vs. a clinical supervisor who has no influence over whether a music therapist can keep their job), the longer the duration of the supervisory relationship (weekly meetings over a 6-month duration vs. occasional supervision meetings), and the lack of clear ending to the supervisory relationship put a supervisee at higher risk for harm if the supervisor is not vigilant. Figures 1 and 2 illustrate this model.

POWER

Love	**Mid-Range**	**High**
Little or no personal relationship	Clear power differential present but relationship is circumscribed	Clear power differential with profound personal influence possible
or		
Persons consider other peers (may include elements of influence)		

DURATION

Brief	**Intermediate**	**Long**
Single or free contacts over short period of time	Regular contact over a limited period of time	Continuous or episodic contact over a long period of time

TERMINATION

Specific	**Uncertain**	**Indefinite**
Relationship is limited by time externally imposed or by prior agreement of parties who are unlikely to see each other again	Professional function is completed but further contact is not ruled out	No agreement regarding when or if termination is to take place

---

Figure 1. Dimensions for ethical decision-making.

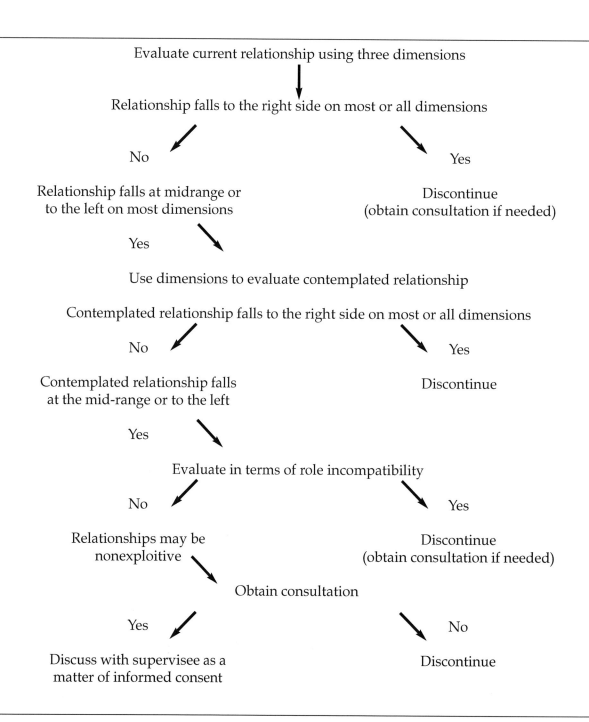

Figure 2. A decision-making model to be used to determine if a potential dual relationship with a supervisee may be harmful. Adapted from "Avoiding Exploitive Dual Relationships: A Decision-Making Model," by M. C. Gottlieb, *Psychotherapy, 30,* 45. Copyright © 1993, American Psychological Association.

Supervisor, not Therapist

The line between supervision and therapy can be a thin one and one that is easily crossed if the supervisor is not careful. Supervision often serves a dual purpose by providing: (1) the development and improvement of clinical skills and (2) insight into personal or professional limitations that may impede the therapeutic process (e.g., ACA, 2014; ACES, 1995; Herlihy & Corey, 1992). When it is apparent that a supervisee's personal issues are interfering with his/her clinical work, supervisors must be vigilant so as to not cross that line (Kurpius et al., 1991). The supervisor's role is to raise awareness of personal issues on the part of the supervisee that may have a negative influence on the therapeutic relationship or therapy process of the client (Kurpius et al., 1991), not to work through those issues. While they may encourage supervisees to examine personal issues that may interfere with clinical work or impede the therapeutic process, they need to take care that this exploration does not "approximate" personal therapy (Magnuson, Norem, & Wilcoxon, 2000, p. 180). To guard against this, supervision sessions should focus on the interactions between the client and supervisee.

Shifts in Professional Roles

Shifts in the professional role occur predominately in the workplace usually when a promotion to a supervisory role occurs from within a music therapy department. Particularly challenging is the need to separate personal feelings toward a former colleague from professional responsibilities to evaluate supervisees objectively. Prior to a promotion, relationships among coworkers are collegial. There is not a power differential, and the risk of harm is minimal. The power differential changes with the promotion to a supervisory position. Both supervisors and supervisees may have expectations based on their previous relationship. As coworkers, music therapists have an ethical obligation to act in a supportive and collegial manner toward each other (AMTA Code of Ethics, 2014). A supervisor's responsibilities may seemingly come in conflict with those obligations. This is especially true when a close personal relationship exists between a supervisor and their supervisees. The relationship needs to evolve for both, but it is the supervisor's responsibility to guarantee that the shift in power differential does not compromise professionalism.

An open dialogue in which the "limits, boundaries, and power structure" that will be in place is the first step in maintaining an ethical supervisory relationship (Pearson & Piazza, 1997, para. 21). Second, supervisors must be self-analytic and critical. Self-evaluation of personal motives for making decisions, especially in relation to former coworkers' job performances is important. For example, was an inappropriate action or rule violation overlooked because of a previous friendship between a supervisor and a supervisee? Conversely, was a minor infraction dealt with harshly due to a previous contentious relationship? Participation in a supervision group for supervisors can help explore motivations for actions taken in support of or against a supervisee who was a coworker.

Promoting Ethical Behavior

Supervisors have an obligation to model and demonstrate that they value ethical behavior if they expect their supervisees to do the same (APA, 2015). To do this, supervisors should become familiar with ethical principles, codes of ethics, and ethical decision-making. Additionally, supervisors should evaluate their personal knowledge of ethics, especially as it pertains to music therapy clinical work and supervision. Further, they should reflect on and evaluate their behavior in terms of the ethical standards set by the American Music Therapy Association. Finally, they should assess their ability to engage in discussions of ethical behaviors and dilemmas with supervisees as well as demonstrate and teach ethical decision-making.

Supervisors also have the responsibility to help supervises "develop expertise in ethical decision-making" (Bernard & Goodyear, 2014, p. 277). While there is a dearth of literature on ethics training in mental health professions (Self, Wise, Beauvais, & Molinari, 2017), Narvea and Lapsley (2005) suggest the first step is for supervisors to model ethical decision-making. In addition, they suggest the following strategies:

1. **Explicitly focusing on personal values.** Most professionals are influenced by personal values (Hanson & Goldberg, 1999). Therefore, supervisors should help supervisees to explore their personal values and attitudes. Bashe, Anderson, Handelsman, and Klevansky (2007) recommend the use of an ethics autobiography in which supervisees are challenged to consider how their values, traditions, and backgrounds may influence or conflict with ethical principles. The authors also recommend the use of reflection papers and evaluations of personal strengths and weaknesses in terms of ethical behavior.
2. **Mastering the content of ethical codes.** Music therapy supervisors should ensure that supervisees know and understand the expectations of the AMTA Code of Ethics and CBMT Code of Professional of Professional Practice.
3. **Opportunities to apply ethical knowledge.** Bernard (1981) was one of the first to suggest that ethical mistakes typically are not the result of malicious intent, but instead acts of omission. Subsequently, Plante (1995) noted that while trainees were aware of their professional codes of ethics, they did not know how to apply them to resolve ethical dilemmas. Case studies and experiential learning can be useful in helping supervisees to explore and then discuss ramifications of various responses to ethical dilemmas.
4. **Teaching ethical decision-making.** Dileo (2001) developed a model for ethical decision-making that is appropriate for use by music therapists. Supervisors should include training in the use of this model or similar models for their supervisees (see Cottone & Clause's 2000 review of ethical decision-making models).

Gatekeeping

Gatekeeping, the process of safeguarding access to a profession to ensure the quality of clinical services to the public, is an ethical imperative. The AMTA (2014a) Code of Ethics,[6] as well as those of related helping professions, include standards relating to gatekeeping. Supervisors have an ethical obligation to both the supervisee and, more important, the public to take this responsibility seriously (e.g., Kitchener, 1992; Pearson & Piazza, 1997). Music therapy educators, practicum supervisors, and internship supervisors are the primary gatekeepers for entry into the music therapy profession. Ambivalence or neglect toward this responsibility risks harm to the public. Care must be taken to avoid the "hot potato game" in which problematic students and interns get passed along without remediation or advisement that music therapy may not be the profession for them (Johnson, 2008).

Monitoring professional competence to ensure the safe and high-quality delivery of services is a defining characteristic of most helping professions (Sinclair, Simon, & Pettifor, 1996). Therefore, the gatekeeper must have the integrity to enforce the profession's competency standards as well as assess personal fitness. To do this, evaluations should be reliable and valid measures of competency that are applied objectively. As of this writing, reliable and valid measures for evaluating a supervisee's competence have not been adopted by the music therapy profession. Therefore, supervisors have only their observations and personal standards for evaluating supervisees. A danger

---

[6] From the AMTA Code of Ethics, Standard 11.5: The MT involved in education and/or *supervision* will evaluate the competencies of students as required by good educational practices and will identify those students whose limitations impede performance as a competent music therapist. The MT will recommend only those students for internship or membership whom he/she feels will perform as competent music therapists and who meet the academic, clinical, and ethical expectations of the American Music Therapy Association, Inc.

here is that subjectivity will influence evaluations. It is interesting to note that in a survey of academic psychologists that has not yet been replicated, 60% reported occasionally allowing likability to influence their evaluations (Tabachnick, Keith-Spiegel, & Pope, 1991).

Second, and much more difficult to evaluate, is a supervisee's fitness to be a music therapist. In a recent survey, 98.3% of academic programs and 66.2% of internships reported having students with severe professional competency problems (Hsiao, 2014). Unfortunately, there are not any reliable or valid measures to evaluate personal fitness. This is a common issue in the helping professions, and professional associations continue to develop ways of identifying and working with impaired trainees and professionals (see Johnson et al., 2008). In the meantime, supervisors who have concerns about their supervisees' personal fitness for music therapy should seek consultation to validate observations before making conclusions. Regardless of the area of difficulty—competency to deliver quality music therapy or personal fitness to be a music therapist—it is a supervisor's responsibility to provide honest feedback to the supervisee and to develop a plan for remediation, which may include a recommendation for personal therapy, dismissal from the program, or leaving the field. These latter two options may be difficult for a supervisor to exercise, as they "require social assertiveness, integrity, moral commitment, and ego strength" (Vasquez, 1992, p. 200). Supervisors cannot let their loyalty to a supervisee conflict with their ethical responsibility to protect the public (Bernard & Goodyear, 2014; Vasquez, 1992). Further, Vasquez (1992) reminds supervisors that they …

… must guard against a tendency to collude or avoid these important ethical responsibilities that exist to protect the trainee, clients, and the profession. At times, responsibilities and loyalties to the supervisee will seemingly conflict with the ethical responsibility to protect clients and the profession. This dilemma is a challenging one for supervisors, but one which supervisors must be willing to address. The client's welfare must be primary. (p. 200)

Due Process

Due process is an ethical responsibility for supervisees and a legal right of supervisees. The 14th Amendment to the U.S. Constitution guarantees the right of due process for citizens in all matters involving the government. Courts have generally extended this right to any and all institutions that are controlled and run by states or the federal government or that receive funding from governmental entities (personal communication from M. J. Mulligan, Esq., December 27, 2017). Due process aspires to ensure that supervisees' rights are not violated and that objective criteria are used before a negative consequence is administered.

Due process attempts to ensure not only that fair standards are created and applied but also that disputes on whether those standards have been met are fully and fairly noticed, investigated, and decided upon. Substantive due process refers to the fair and consistent application of criteria and procedures that are followed the supervisor. Procedural due process refers to the process by which supervisees are notified of requirements, evaluated on their performance, notified of any performance deficiencies, and given remedial opportunities. Procedural due process also includes an opportunity for supervisees to challenge decisions made based on their performance to an objective body (per institutional standards) to ensure the evaluation of the supervisee's performance has been done fully and fairly (personal communication from M. J. Mulligan, Esq., December 27, 2017; see Forrest, Elman, Gizara, & Vacha-Haase, 1999; Gilfoyle, 2008).

Supervisors are responsible for articulating training objectives, assessment and evaluation procedures, guidelines for supervision, and expectations for personal growth and self-reflection on the part of the supervisee (Borders & Brown, 2005). In order to protect supervisees' due process rights, both informal and formal evaluations should be provided on a regular basis. Any deficiencies should be identified and reviewed with the supervisee. A corrective action should be developed with input from both parties. This plan should have specific measurable outcome objectives and allow sufficient time for remediation of any deficiencies. The corrective action plan should also include the date for review and consequences if deficiencies are not addressed. Both parties should sign the document as well. The results of all evaluations should be documented in the supervisor's notes (informal) or in an evaluation report (formal).

CONCLUSION

Supervisors have an ethical obligation to their supervisees and the public. In order to fulfill those obligations, supervisors need to remain competent in their area of clinical practice, supervision, and ethics. Additionally, they have a responsibility to model ethical behavior for their supervisees. This chapter has provided an overview of the main issues that if not fully understood and implemented can lead to ethical breaches. Supervisors are encouraged to continue to develop their ethical competence and include a focus on ethical behavior in their supervisory sessions.

REFERENCE LIST

American Association for Marriage and Family Therapists. (2017). *Becoming an approved supervisor.* Alexandria, VA: Author. Retrieved from https://www.aamft.org/iMIS15/AAMFT/Content/supervision/Becoming_Supervisor.aspx

American Counseling Association. (2014). *Code of ethics.* Alexandra, VA: Author. Retrieved from https://www.counseling.org/resources/aca-code-of-ethics.pdf

American Music Therapy Association. (2014a). *Code of ethics.* Silver Spring, MD: Author. Retrieved from https://www.musictherapy.org/about/ethics/

American Music Therapy Association. (2014b). *National roster internship guidelines.* Silver Spring, MD: Author. Retrieved from https://www.musictherapy.org/careers/national_roster_internship_guidelines/

American Music Therapy Association. (2014c). *Standards for education and clinical training.* Silver Spring, MD: Author. Retrieved from https://www.musictherapy.org/members/edctstan/

American Psychological Association. (2015). Guidelines for clinical supervision in health service psychology. *American Psychologist, 70,* 33–46. doi:10.1017/a0038112

American Psychological Association. (2017). *Ethical principles of psychologists and code of conduct.* Washington, DC: Author. Retrieved from http://www.apa.org/ethics/code/

American School Counselor Association. (2016). *ASCA ethical standards for school counselors.* Alexandria, VA: Author. Retrieved from https://www.schoolcounselor.org/asca/media/asca/Ethics/EthicalStandards2016.pdf

Ammirati, R. J., & Kaslow, N. J. (2017). All supervisors have the potential to be harmful. *The Clinical Supervisor, 36,* 116–123. doi:10.1080/07325223.2047.1298071

Association for Counselor Education and Supervision. (1995). Ethical guidelines for counseling supervisors. *Counselor Education and Supervision, 34*(3), 270–276.

Barnett, J. E. (2007). Whose boundaries are they, anyway? *Professional Psychology: Research and Practice, 38,* 401–405.

Barnett, J. E., & Molzon, C. H. (2014). Clinical supervision of psychotherapy: Essential ethics issues for supervisors and supervisees. *Journal of Clinical Psychology: In Session, 70,* 1051–1061. doi:10.1002/jclp22126

Bartlett, W. (1983). Multidimensional framework for the analysis of counseling. *The Counseling Psychologist, 11,* 9–17.

Bashe, A., Anderson, S. K., Handelsman, M. M., & Klevansky, R. (2007). An acculturation model for ethics training: The ethics autobiography and beyond. *Professional Psychology: Research and Practice, 38*(1), 60–67. doi:10.1037/0735-7028.38.1.60

Bernard, J. M. (1981). In-service training for clinical supervisors. *Counselor Education & Supervision, 19*, 60–68.

Bernard, J. M., & Goodyear, R. K. (2014). *Fundamentals of clinical supervision* (5th ed.). Boston, MA: Pearson.

Borders, L. D., & Brown, L. L. (2005). *The new handbook of counseling supervision.* Mahwah, NJ: Lawrence Erlbaum Associates.

Burham, J. (2012). Developments in social GRRRAAACCEEESSS: Visible-invisible and voiced-unvoiced. In L. B. Krause (Ed.), *Multiple perspectives: Culture and reflexivity in contemporary systemic psychotherapy.* London, UK: Karnec.

Cobia, D. C., & Boes, S. R. (2000). Professional disclosure statements and formal plans for supervision: Two strategies for minimizing the risk of ethical conflicts in post-master's supervision. *Journal of Counseling & Development, 78*, 293–296.

Cottone, R. R., & Clause, R. E. (2000). Ethical decision-making models: A review of the literature. *Journal of Counseling & Development, 78*, 275–283.

Dileo, C. (2001). *Ethical thinking in music therapy.* Cherry Hill, NJ: Jeffrey Books.

Disney, M. J., & Stephens, A. M. (1994). *Legal issues in clinical supervision.* Alexandria, VA: ACA Press.

Ellis, M. V. (2017). Clinical supervision contract & consent statement and supervisee rights and responsibilities. *The Clinical Supervisor, 36*, 145–159. doi:10.1080/07325223.2017.1321885

Ellis, M. V., Berger, L., Hanus, A. E., Ayala, E. E., Swords, B. A., & Siembor, M. (2014). Inadequate and harmful clinical supervision: Testing a revised framework and assessing occurrence. *The Counseling Psychologist, 47*, 434–472. doi:10.1177/0011000013508656

Ellis, M. V., Taylor, E. J., Corp, D. A., Hutman, H., & Kangos, K. A. (2017). Narratives of harmful clinical supervision: Introduction to the special issue. *The Clinical Supervisor, 36*(1), 4-19. doi:10.1080/07325223.2017.1297753

Epstein, R. M., & Hundert, E. M. (2002). Defining and assessing professional competence. *Journal of the American Medical Association, 287*, 226–235.

Falender, C. A., Cornish, J. A., Goodyear, R., Hatcher, R., Kaslow, N. J., Leventhal, G., Shafranske, E., Sigmon, S. T., Stoltenberg, C., & Grus, C. (2004). Defining competencies in psychology supervision: A consensus statement. *Journal of Clinical Psychology, 60*, 771–785.

Falender, C. A., Shafranske, E. P., & Falicov, C. P. (Eds.). (2014). *Diversity and multiculturalism in clinical supervision: Foundations and praxis.* Washington, DC: American Psychological Association.

Forrest, L., Elman, N., Gizara, S., & Vacha-Haase, T. (1999). Trainee impairment: A review of identification, remediation, dismissal, and legal issues. *The Counseling Psychologist, 27*, 627–686.

Gilfoyle, N. (2008). The legal exosystem: Risk management in addressing student competence problems in professional psychology training. *Training & Education in Professional Psychology, 2*, 202–209.

Gottlieb, M. C. (1993). Avoiding exploitive dual relationships: A decision-making model. *Psychotherapy, 30*, 41–48.

Gottlieb, M. C., Robinson, K., & Yonggren, J. N. (2007). Multiple relations in supervision: Guidance for administrators, supervisor, and students. *Professional Psychology: Research and Practice, 38*, 241–247. doi:10.1037/0735-7028.38.3.241

Gutheil, T. G., & Gabbard, G. O. (1993). The concept of boundaries in clinical practice: Theoretical and risk-management dimensions. *Journal of Psychiatry, 150*, 188–196.

Hamilton, J. C., & Spruill, J. (1999). Identifying and reducing risk factors related to trainee–client sexual misconduct. *Professional Psychology: Research and Practice, 30,* 318–327.

Hansen, N. D., & Goldberg, S. C. (1999). Navigating the nuances: A matrix of considerations ethical-legal dilemmas. *Professional Psychology: Research and Practice, 30,* 66–74.

Hsiao, F. (2014). Gatekeeping practices of music therapy academic programs and internships: A national survey. *Journal of Music Therapy, 51,* 186–206. doi:10.1093/hnt/thu010

Herlihy, B., & Corey, G. (1992). *Dual relationships in counseling.* Alexandria, VA: American Association for Counseling and Development.

Inman, A. G., & Ladany, N. (2014). Multicultural competencies in psychotherapy supervision. In T. T. L. Leong, L. Comas-Diaz, G. C. Nagayama Hall, V. C. McLoyd, & U. J. S. Trimble (Eds.), *APA handbook of multicultural psychology* (Vol. 2, pp. 643–658). Washington, DC: American Psychological Association.

Johnson, W. B. (2008). Can psychologists find a way to stop the hot potato game? In W. B. Johnson, N. S. Elman, L. Forrest, W. N. Robiner, E. Rodolfa, & J. B. Schaffer, Addressing professional competence problems in trainees: Some ethical considerations (pp. 589–593). *Professional Psychology: Research and Practice, 39,* 589–599. doi:10/1037/a0014264

Johnson, W. B., Elman, N. S., Forrest, L., Robiner, W. N., Rodolfa, E., & Schaffer, J. B. (2008). Addressing professional competence problems in trainees: Some ethical considerations. *Professional Psychology: Research and Practice, 39,* 589–599. doi:10/1037/a0014264

Kitchener, K. S. (1992). Psychologist as teacher and mentor: Affirming ethical values throughout the curriculum. *Professional Psychology: Research and Practice, 23,* 190–195.

Kurpius, D., Gibson, G., Lewis, J., & Corbet, M. (1991). Ethical issues in supervising counseling practitioners. *Counselor Education & Supervision, 31,* 48–57. doi:10.1002/j.1556-6978.1991.tb00370.x

Ladany, N., Friedlander, M. L., & Nelson, M. L. (2005). *Critical events in psychotherapy supervision: An interpersonal approach.* Washington, DC: American Psychological Association.

Ladany, N., Lehrman-Watermen, D., Molinaro, M., & Wolgast, B. (1991). Psychotherapy supervisor ethical practices: Adherence to guidelines, the supervisory working alliance, and supervisee satisfaction. *The Counseling Psychologist, 27,* 443–475.

Magnuson, S., Norem, K., & Wilcoxon, A. (2000). Clinical supervision of prelicensed counselors: Recommendations for consideration and practice. *Journal of Mental Health Counseling, 23,* 176–188.

McCarthy, R., & Sugden, S. (1995). A practical guide to informed consent in clinical supervision. *Counselor Education & Supervision, 35*(2), 130–138.

Ming-sum, T. (2005). The nature, culture, and future of supervision. In L. Beddoe, J. Worrall, & F. Howard (Eds.), *Weaving together the strands of supervision* (pp. 25–32). Auckland, New Zealand: Auckland University Press.

Minnes, P. M. (1987). Ethical issues in supervision. *Canadian Psychology, 28,* 285–290.

Narvaez, D., & Lapsley, D. K. (2005). The psychological foundations of everyday morality and moral expertise. In C. Lapsley & D. Power (Eds.), *Character psychology and character education* (pp. 140–165). South Bend, IN: University of Notre Dame Press.

Patterson, J. B. (1989). Ethics and rehabilitation supervision. *Journal of Rehabilitation, 55*(4), 44–49.

Pearson, B., & Piazza, N. (1997). Classification of dual relationships in the helping professions. *Counselor Education & Supervision, 37,* 89–99.

Peters, H. C. (2017). Multicultural complexity: An intersectional lens for clinical supervision. *International Journal for the Advancement of Counselling, 39,* 176–187. doi:10.1007/s10447-01709290-2

Pettifor, J., Sinclair, C., & Falender, C. A. (2014). Ethical supervision: Harmonizing rules and ideals in a globalizing world. *Training and Education in Professional Psychology, 8,* 201–210. doi:10.1037/tep0000046

Plante, T. G. (1995). Training child clinical predoctoral interns and postdoctoral fellows in ethics and professional issues: An experiential model. *Professional Psychology: Research and Practice, 26,* 616–619.

Power, S. (2007). Boundaries and responsibilities in clinical supervision. In J. Driscoll (Ed.), *Practising clinical supervision: A reflective approach for healthcare professionals* (2nd ed., pp. 53–71). New York, NY: Elsevier.

Ross, W. D. (1930). *The right and the good.* Oxford, UK: Oxford University Press.

Self, M. M., Wise, E. H., Beauvais, J., & Molinari, V. (2017, November 30). Ethics in Training and Training in Ethics: Special Considerations for Postdoctoral Fellowships in Health Service Psychology. *Training and Education in Professional Psychology.* Advance online publication. doi:10.1037/tep0000178

Sherry, P. (1991). Ethical issues in the conduct of supervision. *The Counseling Psychologist, 19,* 566–584.

Shöen, D. A. (1987). *Educating a reflexive practitioner.* San Francisco, CA: Jossey-Bass.

Sinclair, C., Simon, N., & Pettifor, J. (1996). The history of ethical codes and licensure. In L. J. Bass, D. T. DeMers, J. R. Ogloff, C. Peterson, J. L. Pettifor, R. P. Reaves, T. Rétfalvi, N. P. Simon, C. Sinclair, & R. M. Tipton (Eds.), Professional conduct and discipline in psychology (pp. 1–15). Washington, DC: American Psychological Association.

Swamy, S. (2011). "No, she doesn't seem to know anything about cultural differences!": Culturally centered music therapy supervision. *Music Therapy Perspectives, 29,* 133–137. doi:10.1093/mtp/29.2.133

Tabachnick, B. G., Keith-Spiegel, P., & Pope, K. S. (1991). Ethics of teaching: Beliefs and behaviors of psychologists as educators. *American Psychologist, 46,* 505–515.

Thomas, J. T. (2007). Informed consent through contracting for supervision: Minimizing risks, enhancing benefits. *Professional Psychology: Research and Practice, 38,* 221–231. doi:10.1037/0735-7028.38.3.221

Vasquez, M. J. T. (1992). Psychologist as clinical supervisor: Promoting ethical practice. *Professional Psychology: Research and Practice, 23,* 196–202.

Vasquez, M. J. T. (2007). Sometimes a taco is just a taco! In J. D. Barnett, A. E. Lazarus, M. J. T. Vasquez, O. Moorehead-Slaughter, & W. B. Johnson, Boundary issues and multiple relationships: Fantasy and reality. *Professional Psychology: Research & Practice, 38,* 401–410. doi:10.1037/0735-7028.38.4.401

Chapter 4

CULTURALLY RESPONSIVE MUSIC THERAPY SUPERVISION

Annette Whitehead-Pleaux

INTRODUCTION

What is culturally responsive music therapy, and why is it important to music therapy supervisors? To understand this, it is best to start with understanding what the different terms mean and to explore the connections between music therapy and culture. Through the examination of definitions of different terms, the reasons why culturally responsive music therapy supervision is vital for music therapy supervisors to understand and practice will become clear.

To begin to understand this practice, it is best to begin at culture. Dileo (2000) defined culture as the "beliefs, actions, and behaviors associated with sex, age, location of residence, educational status, social economic status, history, formal and informal affiliations, nationality, ethnic group, language, race, religion, disability, illness, developmental handicap, lifestyle, and sexual orientation" (p. 149). There are many important factors within this definition. Culture is belief, actions, and behaviors. It tells us what is true and right, what we are to do, and how we are to behave. Another important factor to explore is how cultural behaviors are interacting with different identities, including heritage, religion, ability, wellness, gender, and affiliations. Culture may dictate one's role or behavior based on these different identities. An example is that gender can determine someone's dress, occupation, speaking manner, and so forth within a culture.

The American Sociological Association views culture from a different vantage point, exploring the different features that are expressions of culture. They have stated that culture is "the languages, customs, beliefs, rules, arts, knowledge, and collective identities and memories developed by members of all social groups that make their social environments meaningful" (American Sociological Association, 2017). Cultures are learned and shared between members of a common community. Not static, cultures are dynamic and always changing and growing. In contemplating this definition, it is important to see that art is part of culture and that contained within art is music; music is a cultural artifact.

Over the past 20 years, there has been a greater focus on culture in music therapy. Music therapists have begun to explore the interactions between music therapy and culture (Brown, 2002; Chase, 2003; Donley, 2018; Dos Santos, 2004; Elwafi, 2011; Forrest, 2001; Gonzalez, 2011; Hadley, 2006; Hadley & Norris, 2016; Kim, 2008; Kim & Whitehead-Pleaux, 2015; Shapiro, 2002; Steig, 2002; Swamy, 2011, 2014, 2017; Wheeler, 2002; Whitehead-Pleaux, 2009; Whitehead-Pleaux, Donnenwerth, Robinson, Hardy, Oswanski, Forinash, Hearns, Anderson, & Tan, 2013; Whitehead-Pleaux, Donnenwerth, Robinson, Hardy, Oswanski, Forinash, Hearns, Anderson, & York, 2012; Whitehead-Pleaux & Tan, 2017; Young, 2009, 2016.). In these writings, many terms have been used to describe this work, including "multicultural," "cultural competence," and "cultural responsiveness." Although these terms sometimes are used interchangeably, their meanings are quite different. Understanding these and how they differ from each other is key.

"Multicultural" is one of the first terms used in this wave of music therapy scholarship. According to the Merriam-Webster dictionary (n.d.), multicultural is "of, relating to, reflecting, or adapted to diverse cultures." Often this term is used when discussing pluralistic societies that have a dominant culture as well as many other cultures that center around heritage, religion, ability, gender, sexual orientation, affiliations, and so on. Multiculturalism acknowledges the dynamics of power and oppression within these societies. Music therapy scholars (Chase, 2003; Donley, 2018; Dos Santos, 2005; Mahoney, 2015; Shapiro, 2002; Vaillancourt, 2015; Yehuda, 2002) who explored multicultural music therapy discussed the differences between dominant and marginalized cultures. These writings often focused on cultural norms and practices and what to do or not do when working with someone from a particular culture.

Another term that is used by music therapists is "culture-centered." According to Steig (2002), "culture-centered music therapy may be understood as awareness about music therapy as culture" and is culture-specific (p. 42). Several music therapists have written about culture-centered music therapy (Brown, 2002; Elwafi, 2010; Kim, 2008; Steig, 2002; Swamy, 2011, 2014, 2018; Whitehead-Pleaux, 2009).

A term explored here that is used often with multiculturalism is "cultural competence." Cultural competence is defined by the *McGraw-Hill Concise Dictionary of Modern Medicine* (2002) as "the ability to understand, appreciate, and interact with persons from cultures and/or belief systems other than one's own." The Substance Abuse and Mental Health Services Administration (2016) defined cultural competence slightly differently, saying that cultural competence is "the ability to interact effectively with people of different cultures, [which] helps to ensure [that] the needs of all community members are addressed." These definitions differ from that of multiculturalism by not only recognizing that there are many cultures present beyond the dominant culture, but also extending that knowledge to acts of understanding, appreciating, and interacting with people from different cultures for the benefit of all. There is reluctance toward using this term, for the word "competence" implies that this work has a definitive end point where one gains a level of competence and does not need to work anymore. This is far from the truth. Cultural competence is a reflexive practice upon which one continues to work as if one is an eternal beginner. It is impossible for one person to become competent at all cultures across the globe and remain updated upon the changes within these cultures. The more knowledge and expertise each person gains, the more they see there is even more to learn. Many music therapy scholars have explored cultural competence in music therapy practice (Hadley & Norris, 2016; Kim & Whitehead-Pleaux, 2015; Whitehead-Pleaux, Donnenwerth, Robinson, Hardy, Oswanski, Forinash, Hearns, Anderson, & York, 2012; Whitehead-Pleaux & Tan, 2017; Young, 2016).

The final term to be defined is "culturally responsive." According to the Cambridge dictionary (n.d.), being culturally responsive is being "able to understand and consider the different cultural backgrounds of the people one teaches, offers services to, etc." Within music therapy, cultural responsiveness is understanding the different cultures and musics of the people with whom we work as well as considering how these different intersecting cultures operate within a person's self-identity and what they bring to the therapeutic process. It is, in essence, the ability to respond to and incorporate when appropriate the cultures of people with whom one works (Whitehead-Pleaux & Tan, 2017).

SUPERVISION ACROSS CULTURES

The majority of music therapists in the United States are white, straight, cisgender women. According to the American Music Therapy Association (2018), the racial identity of music therapists is 87.4% white/Caucasian/European, 4.7% Asian/Asian-American, 2.4% Hispanic/Latino/Spanish, 1.9% African-American/black, 0.5% American Indian/Alaskan Native, 0.9% other race or origin not specified, and 2.3% multiracial. However, the United States demographics are much different, with 72.4% being white, 12.6% African-American/black, 4.8% Asian, 0.9% Native American/Alaska Native, 0.2% Native Hawaiian/Pacific Islander, 2.9% multiracial, and 6.2% some other race (U.S. Census, 2013). When comparing the music therapist population in the United States with the national data, the dominance of white people in the field is apparent. At this time, there are no studies that survey the racial makeup of music therapy clients. However, one can assume that clients may reflect some of the racial diversity of the country. Given this homogeneity of our field, it is likely that music therapists are working transculturally, that is, across cultures. It is important for the supervisor to be aware that their supervisees are working transculturally. The supervisor needs to understand the impact of the supervisees' racial identities on the sessions as well as understand the client's intersectional identities and experiences. It is equally important for the supervisor to be careful to refrain from viewing the client's experiences and actions through the music therapist's biases or their own intersectional identities. Finally, the supervisor must work with the supervisee to improve the transcultural music therapy services provided by the music therapist. When a supervisor is working with music therapy clinicians or students who have minority identities, it is imperative for the supervisor to have the skills to work in a culturally responsive manner, so that supervisors are aware of the differences in cultures and are able to be supportive of the unique experiences of these supervisees.

In 2018, Whitehead-Pleaux, Oswanski, and Tan explored the cultural competence of music therapists in the United States. As they surveyed nearly 700 music therapists (approximately 10% of the population of music therapists in the United States at that time), the authors asked them to identify their sexual orientation. The majority of respondents, 81.68%, identified their sexual orientation as heterosexual. The other sexual orientations were as follows: 8.11% bi+, 2.85% lesbian, 2.7% gay, 1.9% queer, 0.9% asexual, and 1.8% other. According to the 2017 Gallup Poll, overall, 5.1% of women and 3.9% of men identified as LGBT, with an overall percentage of 4.5% of the U.S. population identifying as LGBT (Newport, 2018).

As the field of music therapy is dominated by cisgender women, cross-gender music therapy clinical and supervision practices occur regularly. According to the AMTA (2018), 88.12% of music therapists identify as female, 10.58% as male, .82% as genderqueer, .21% as transgender, and .27% as a different identifier. The 2010 U.S. Census states that 50.9% of the U.S. population is female and 49.1% is male (Howden & Meyer, 2011). The U.S. Census did not include other genders in its survey. However, the Williams Institute estimated the "trans" population to be 0.58% (Flores, Herman, Gates, & Taylor, 2016). Given the homogeneity of the field, much of our work with clients is transcultural with gender. When supervising music therapists, the supervisor must be aware of the differences of the cultures of gender within the supervisee's clinical practice as well as between the supervisor and supervisee.

Within my practice as a music therapy clinician, educator, and supervisor, I have come to embrace the term "culturally responsive" music therapy. It is my experience that with each new client, student, or supervisee, I find new cultures or different groupings of cultures within each person's intersecting identities. Because of this ever-shifting landscape of the cultures of the people with whom I work, instead of being competent at each new person's culture(s) (which would be impossible), I am responsive to the endless variations in human cultural identities. I am open to these variations, curious to learn more, willing to say "I don't understand, please tell me more," and creative in designing ways to address their clinical, educational, or supervisory needs in a way that is relevant to and incorporates their cultural beliefs, norms, music, and identity.

Becoming a Culturally Responsive Music Therapy Supervisor

The greatest enemy of knowledge is not ignorance but the illusion of knowledge.
–Daniel J. Boorstin

There are several steps to take to become a culturally responsive music therapy supervisor. The foundation of these steps is to have clinical music therapy experience in working with people from different cultures, including cultures of heritage, religion, gender, sexual orientation, ability, socio-economic status, age, and others. Before supervising music therapists, a supervisor needs to understand the complexities of working with people who have different cultural identifies. Given the pluralistic societies we live in, it is quite improbable that a music therapy supervisor will supervise a music therapist who has the same intersectional identities as the supervisor or that the caseload of said music therapist will all be clients with the same intersectional identities. Without this firsthand knowledge of working across cultures, how can a supervisor relate to the supervisee's experiences, emotions, struggles, and successes?

Once the supervisor gains significant experience in cross-cultural music therapy, then they can begin the steps to becoming a culturally responsive music therapy supervisor. These steps are examining oneself, exposure to other cultures, and evaluating and modifying one's supervision practice (Whitehead-Pleaux & Tan, 2017). Within each step, there are many tasks. Like any reflexive practice, culturally responsive music therapy supervision is not something one studies and accomplishes but is something in which one engages in steps, every day through one's career.

Examining Oneself

The first step in culturally responsive music therapy supervision is examining oneself. This step must be completed prior to working with supervisory clients from other cultures and before engaging in any of the culturally responsive music therapy supervision interventions. Music therapy supervisors must know themselves as fully as possible before they can enter into these cultural spaces with others. Otherwise, their privileges and unconscious biases will deeply impact their work, often damaging the supervisory relationship.

Knowing ourselves starts with understanding our intersectional identities and, specifically, where we have power and privilege and where we are oppressed. To accomplish this, music therapy supervisors need to engage in supervision with a culturally responsive music therapy supervisor, attend trainings, and engage in learning about the cultures of the clients in their clinical caseload and their supervision caseload. Knowing oneself through supervision is a vital component in becoming a culturally responsive music therapy supervisor. Through this supervision, music therapists will learn more both about themselves and about how to supervise in a culturally responsive manner. Through talk, working with different tools, music therapy interventions, and other arts interventions, the supervisor will guide the music therapist in exploring their intersectional identities and the privilege they have. If music therapy supervisors do not know themselves, they cannot know others and understand the power dynamic that exists between supervision clients and themselves. If the music therapy supervisor has undiscovered biases and unchecked privileges, the minority music therapist will not feel comfortable in discussing the experiences they have in the intersections of their cultural identities with their music therapy identity.

Another component of growing in understanding of themselves is to attend trainings within music therapy and outside of music therapy around privilege, bias, oppression, culturally competent supervision, and culturally responsive supervision. Learning with a group brings unique experiences and opportunities to interact and learn with people of different intersectional identities and different skills. Often in group trainings, members are challenged to grow and discover in ways that do not happen in one-on-one supervision. Hearing the experiences of the others in the group as well as working together in the learning experientials with diverse people will bring new awareness of self and others.

A third component of growing to understand oneself is taking an ally training. No matter what one's intersecting identities are, everyone has identities where they are part of the majority and have power and privilege over others. Engaging in an ally training will help one to learn how to use the privileges they have in order to work with the marginalized communities on their agendas for civil rights and social justice. Learning about the developmental steps of being an ally can help the music therapy supervisor identify where they are and how they need to grow to become a better ally to the supervisees with whom they will be working.

Learning About Cultures

The second step in preparing to become a culturally responsive music therapy supervisor is to engage in learning about the cultures of the communities one serves as a clinician, educator, and supervisor. This can be through reading, studying music, taking classes, reaching out to cultural centers/organizations, ethnomusicology departments, and so forth. Self-study is important, but when learning about cultures, it is best if one engages with people from that culture. If we read and learn only by ourselves, we run the risk of creating our own constructs of the culture from the conscious and unconscious biases and preconceived notions we hold. We are likely to be influenced by popular myths and stereotypes of that culture. When we engage in learning with people from that culture, our understanding of the culture is more likely to be accurate to the experiences of our clients, students, and supervisees. To accurately see and hear other cultures, we need to do all we can to remove our biases and cultural lenses.

The cultures that music therapists need to learn about are not just cultures of heritage. In considering culture, music therapists' learning needs to include cultures of religion, gender, sexual orientation, age, ability, socio-economic status, and region, as well as smaller specific cultures, such as cultures of survivors, uniformed persons cultures, and occupational cultures. By expanding our understanding and vision of cultures to include these, we have a greater opportunity to understand ourselves and our clients.

Modifying Supervisory Practice

The final step is to evaluate and modify one's music therapy supervisory practice to reflect on culturally responsive practices. There are many different tasks within this step. A central task is to embody the different aspects of cultural humility. Cultural humility was defined by Hook, Davis, Owen, Worthington, and Utsey (2013) as the "ability to maintain an interpersonal stance that is other-oriented (or open to the other) in relation to aspects of cultural identity that are most important to the [person]" (p. 2). Tervalon and Murray-Garcia (1998) define three components of cultural humility. The first is a commitment to self-review and exploration about privilege, power, and cultural identities. This self-evaluation is not a one-and-done but a reflexive practice that the therapist employs across their career and lifetime.

The second and third aspects of cultural humility that Tervalon and Murray-Garcia (1998) discussed are directly related to using one's power and privilege to bring social justice to places of oppression. This is central to being an ally. The second aspect is working to rectify power imbalances where they exist (Tervalon & Murray-Garcia, 1998). Within music therapy supervision, the supervisor can develop ways to illuminate power imbalances within the supervisee's practice and help them to explore ways to rectify these. The third aspect of cultural humility according to Tervalon and Murray-Garcia (1998) is developing partnerships and working groups with people who advocate for marginalized individuals and groups. Through networking and developing resource lists, the music therapy supervisor can develop these relationships and work toward civil rights and social justice for oppressed groups.

Foronda, Baptiste, Reinholdt, and Ousman (2015) further developed the understanding of cultural humility through an analysis of articles that discussed cultural humility. They identified five aspects: openness; self-awareness; egolessness; supportive interactions; and self-reflection and critique (pp. 211–212). Openness relates to having an "open mind or to be open to interactions with a culturally diverse individual" (p. 211). For music therapy supervisors, this extends not only to being open in verbal interactions but also to being open to cross-cultural music and the values assigned to music that is brought to the supervision session. The second aspect is a self-awareness in the supervisor, including appreciation of their "strengths, limitations, values, beliefs, behaviors, and appearance to others" (p. 211). The third aspect is being egoless. Within this aspect, the supervisor is humble and able to say, "I don't know." The supervisor recognizes the supervisee's expertise and acknowledges their naïveté within the supervisory relationship, for it is impossible for anyone to be adequately knowledgeable about cultures other than their own. The supervisor must believe in equality and work to level any hierarchical power systems, including the supervisory power system. The fourth aspect that Foronda, Baptiste, Reinholdt, and Ousman (2015) discuss is supportive interactions. The supervisor is willing to enter the supervisee's worldview and set aside their own worldview and biases. The supervisor is supportive of the supervisee's experiences, and especially those with which the supervisor has no experience. Along with a willingness to enter the supervisee's world, supportive interactions include taking responsibility for the interactions between the supervisor and the supervisee, the supervisee and clients, and the supervisee and coworkers/stakeholders. It is upon the supervisor to engage the supervisee. The final aspect is self-reflection and critique. The supervisor must be willing to engage in "a critical process of reflecting on one's thoughts, feelings, and actions" within the supervisory sessions (p. 212). These aspects constitute cultural humility and are ways to modify the music therapy supervision practice to be more culturally responsive.

The music therapy supervisor will need to explore and become adept with different tools for examining power and privilege, intersectional identities, cultural identities, cultural competence, and so on. Within this and other chapters of this book, the reader will find many different tools that can be used within music therapy supervision sessions. These tools can be incorporated into any music therapy supervision practice, as the supervisor becomes not only familiar with but adept at using the tools. It is recommended that the music therapy supervisor not use any tool with a supervisee that they have not used on themselves. To use a tool accurately and effectively, the supervisor must have personal knowledge of and a deep familiarity with the tool.

The music therapy supervisor and supervisee need to be comfortable in talking about topics such as race, discrimination, religious views, sexual orientation, unconscious bias, gender identity, privilege, and so forth. The words and probing questions about these sensitive topics must not be halting or awkwardly delivered. Instead, the supervisor needs to speak these words and questions with ease and with comfort. This comfort will help the supervisee to open up and talk about the intersections of their cultural identities and their music therapy practice. Not only must the supervisor be good at speaking these words, but also the supervisor must be ready to hear the answer by having their own cultural lenses removed. This allows the supervisor to hear the supervisee's experiences as told and not interpreted through the supervisor's experiences, biases, and expectations.

Finally, the music therapist needs to examine the environment where supervision takes place. If a new supervision client walked into the office, what would they see? Is the office inviting and comfortable for people from other cultures? It is important for the office environment to strike a balance between being inviting to others and reflecting the supervisor's personality through photos, displayed items, and music instruments available for use in the sessions. While displaying instruments from other cultures can feel like creating an open and inviting environment, it may strike some supervisees as an appropriation of artifacts from other cultures. As the supervisor modifies the meeting space, they should attempt to look at the room and decorations with fresh eyes in order to more accurately assess the office space for comfort.

Once music therapy supervisors have done these steps of examining themselves, learning about cultures, and modifying their music therapy supervision practice, they can begin to practice from this theoretical orientation. The next section of this chapter explores tools and interventions a music therapy supervisor can use to explore culture, power, oppression, and cross-cultural concerns in supervision with a music therapy clinician and/or student.

Culturally Responsive Music Therapy Supervision

Supervision is a professional relationship that focuses on enhancing one's music therapy services and improving outcomes for clients. It is a place of reflection, increased self-awareness, and emotional support where a music therapist can discuss their questions and concerns about music therapy practice, best practices, and ethics as well as examine and strengthen their therapeutic relationships. It can provide frameworks to better understand clients, systems, and oneself. Supervision is a way to enhance one's competence and confidence. It is a time to be in community with like-minded music therapists who have similar experiences and concerns. It is a supportive environment for self-examination, empowerment, and improving confidence in clinical and musical skills.

Culturally responsive supervision is all of this, with the addition of a culturally responsive practices and a focus on seeing and understanding the transcultural interactions, systems of privilege and oppression, and processes of enhancing the music therapist's cultural responsiveness. In my culturally responsive music therapy supervision practice, I use verbal, written, music, and arts interventions to foster understanding, growth, and change in the supervisee. I rely upon a variety of tools and interventions, tailoring them to the specifics of each supervisee's needs, situation, and development.

I use several different tools to explore the similarities and differences between the music therapists whom I supervise. I use each of these tools personally prior to ever using them in a session. This personal exploration is necessary both to understand how to use the tool and to understand the cognitive and emotional components and challenges of it. Preparation is vital to supervision.

Intersecting Identities

The first tool I want to explore is the diagram shared by Oswanski and Donnenwerth (2017). It is a way to identify one's intersectional identities and where one has power/privilege and where one is oppressed.

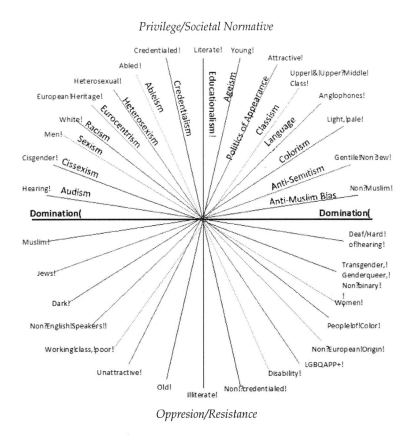

Figure 1. Intersecting identities.

In supervision, I use this tool regularly when introducing the concepts of power, privilege, discrimination, and oppression. Within this figure, there are many lines. There is a dark line through the middle of the identity lines, which is the line of social justice. Above this line are those identities that have privilege and power. Below it are identities that are oppressed. Each of the other lines represents an identity and is labeled with the "ism" of those opposing identities. For example, the colorism line has the identities of light skin tone and dark skin tone at either end of the line. These lines are not binary but continuums. One can identify oneself anywhere along that continuum by how much one is a part of that identity. For example, on the racism line, I am at the top, as I am white and experience the privileges and power of that identity. On the genderism line, I am at the bottom, for I identify as nonbinary and do not have cisgender privileges. On the ableism line, I identify somewhere between the top of the line and the line of social justice, as I have dyslexia. For me, this is a disability that has had some impact upon my privilege and power within our society but does not, in my experience, qualify as something where I have no power.

This tool is one way to view someone's intersecting identities. Through utilizing this tool, they will see not only their different identities, but also where they have power and privilege and where they are oppressed. It helps therapists to start to identify where they have biases. It helps therapists to see where their power and privileges lie and how others may perceive their power. If a supervisor wants supervisees to open up to them about their cultural identifies, then the supervisor must have an awareness of their own power and privilege. Otherwise, the supervisee will not open up fully and supervision will remain on the surface.

To this end, I share my diagram with my supervisee when they complete theirs. I open up the discussion by pointing out where we are similar and where we are different. I invite the supervisee to share their thoughts and observations about their diagram, as well as about my diagram. We discuss similarities as well as differences. These are important discussions and explorations that help the supervisor and supervisee to understand each other. It is through open conversations and explorations that trust and depth of process develop. Similarly, the supervisee can explore their diagram with a diagram of what they know about a client with whom they work. Comparing where the therapist has privilege and oppression to where the client has privilege and oppression can be illuminating in understanding the dynamics within the music therapy sessions.

To explore the concepts within this tool further, I often will incorporate music and art interventions. To dive deeper into the concepts of different identities that are explored, I will turn to musical collage, songwriting, improvisation, and drawing to music with a prompt about expressing their different identities. This may be in the session or as an assignment to do on their own in between supervision sessions. One of my favorite interventions is to instruct the supervisee to create a musical collage using precomposed or original music that relates to 3 to 5 identities to which they most relate. To examine their privileges and oppression, I may ask the supervisee to write a song, improvise, or draw. The prompt will encourage them to explore something in the diagram that may have been a surprise in terms of their privileges or oppression. With groups or with individual supervisees, I have used improvisations that explore the dynamics of privilege and oppression. With an individual session, the supervisor and supervisee can improvise together, taking opposite roles (privileged or oppressed) or the same roles to explore these experiences via music. In groups, the supervisor can split the group in half and direct each half to take one role (privileged or oppressed) and play separately or together. Another option for groups is for each supervisee to orchestrate a referential piece/improvisation that relates to their insights related to the chart. They will direct the different group members to play specific instruments, directing rhythms and melodies. Finally, the supervisee and supervisors can explore their similarities and differences through improvisation. With the supervisor's creativity, there are many ways to incorporate music and arts into the supervisory experiences.

Interlocking Systems of Oppression

Another tool I use for understanding someone's power, privilege, and oppression is the Interlocking Systems of Oppression grid developed by Collins (1990). I use one that has more categories than Collins originally created, as it is important to separate out things like sexism, cissexism, and heterosexism and not have them contained within one category. On the x-axis is different forms of oppression. The y-axis shows different ways in which those oppressions are expressed or experienced.

	Institutional	Interpersonal	Internalized
Sexism			
Racism			
Classism			
Heterosexism			
Ableism			
Ageism			
Genderism			
Imperialism			
Protestantism			

Figure 2. Matrix of Domination/Interlocking Systems of Oppression Theory

To use the Interlocking Systems of Oppression, one marks in the corresponding box where they oppress others, where they experience oppression, where they are complacent with the oppression of themselves and others, and where they resist the oppression of themselves and others. This exercise requires brutal honesty about our actions, beliefs, and nonactions. From this grid, one can then see where they stand with many different minority groups and the corresponding "isms."

After completing this grid, the supervisor can share their own grid to talk about the similarities and differences. It can feel uneasy for the supervisor to enter into this level of transparency with the supervisee. Letting the supervisee know where the supervisor may falter can feel like the supervisory power and boundaries are challenged. However, being up front about who we are and our experiences with different "isms" will facilitate open and honest communication, which will continue to build the trust and depth.

As the supervisee and supervisor explore the supervisee's grid, the discussion can turn to the supervisee's clients. By looking at the supervisee's areas of oppressing, oppression, complacency, and resistance and comparing them to the identities of their clients, understanding of interpersonal dynamics will emerge.

Once completed, the supervisor can again use improvisation, songwriting, and other arts. These can be conducted in the supervision session or by the supervisee in between supervision sessions. The supervisor can direct the supervisee to explore the feelings and thoughts associated with oppression, oppressing, complacency, and resistance through songwriting, improvisations, drawing, writing poems or narratives, and/or dance/movement. Moving to the arts can help to further deepen the supervisee's expressions, understanding, and exploration of these concepts in their music therapy practice.

Personal and Theoretical Ecological Niche

Another tool that is useful in understanding oneself is conducting a personal and theoretical ecological niche (Falicov, 2014b). To use this tool, one identifies first one's identities, "groups of belonging, participation, and identification" (p. 39), which make up the personal ecological niche. Next, one identifies one's theoretical and professional identities, which make up the theoretical niche.

This tool opens up exploration of the identities that music therapists carry. In supervision, the exploration of these different identities may be illuminating. Going deeper, the conversation can move to how these different identities interact—which get along or which are in conflict. The supervisor can share their personal and theoretical ecological niche with the supervisee. By comparing the similar and different identities, much can be learned about each other. When examining the music therapist's relationships with their clients, the ecological niche can be used to explore which identities are in line with, complementary to, or in conflict with their client's identities. Similarly, the supervisor and supervisee can explore the triad of the supervisor's, supervisee's, and client's identities, focusing on shared and disparate identifies. Finally, this model can also be used to examine music therapy interventions, narratives, and understandings that "integrate culture and social locations for the client's presenting problem" (Falicov, 2014b, p. 53).

The supervisor can also incorporate music and arts supervisory interventions to deepen this exercise—for example, writing a song that explores the primary identities or the identities that are in conflict, with a verse dedicated to each identity and the chorus that unifies these identities. This can be done as when exploring any combination of the identities of the client, supervisee, and supervisor. Through a music and drawing intervention, the supervisee can draw the conflict between the opposing roles within the ecological niche. When examining the drawing together, the supervisor can ask the supervisee to give sound/music to the different parts of the drawing of the conflict. By combining arts modalities to explore the ethnography, the supervisor and supervisee can examine these relationships in greater depth.

Migration-Related Supervision

When the music therapist being supervised or their client is an immigrant or has an immigrant heritage, there are several steps the music therapy supervisor can take to provide meaningful and quality supervision around issues of migration/immigration. There are many different tools in psychology that focus on exploring immigrant/migration within supervision. The goals of this focus in music therapy supervision are to identify the strengths and stressors of immigration and immigration heritage, help the music therapist to select roles according to the patterns exhibited, develop interventions that support the client's or supervisee's stage of immigration and/or acculturation, engage in self-discovery, become aware of errors in assessment and treatment due to lack of understanding of immigration/acculturation, and integrate immigration into understanding of the identities of the client or music therapist (Falicov, 2014a).

One intervention is to construct the migration/immigration narrative (Falicov, 2014a). This is a narrative about the music therapist's or client's or family's experiences. Within music therapy supervision, the supervisor could have the music therapy supervisee complete this narrative prior to the supervision session or work on it in the session. The music therapy supervisor needs to plan on taking time in supervision to explore the supervisee's migration/immigration narrative fully. In addition to talking and writing, incorporating music into this exploration can be quite powerful. Using pre-existing music, composition, or improvisation, the supervisee can construct a musical narrative of their identity and experiences in being an immigrant/having an immigration heritage.

When the supervisee is working with a client who is an immigrant or who has an immigrant heritage, the supervisor can direct the supervisee to work with the client or their family to construct an immigration/migration narrative. The supervisor can also assist the supervisee in developing music interventions to further explore these identities through music. Once the supervisee has learned the client's narrative, the supervisor can work with the supervisee to explore the differences between the supervisee and client as well as to foster understanding and learning about immigration.

Socio-economic Status and Class

There is very little written on music therapy and socio-economic status. While many music therapists assume the profession is middle- to upper middle-class as a whole, there are no studies that investigate the actual status. Similarly, there are no demographic studies on the clients that music therapists serve as a whole population. However, it can be assumed that music therapists work with clients who both share and do not share the socio-economic status and class of the music therapist. As cultures of socio-economic status and class can impact clinical and supervisory sessions, supervisors must be aware of their own identities in this realm as well as bring awareness to their supervisees of its impact on sessions (Fouad & Chavez-Korell, 2014). The music therapy supervisor can initiate and facilitate open and personal conversations in supervision about the supervisee's understanding of socio-economic status and class, how they identify, how their clients identify, how socio-economic status and class impact different intersectional identities, and the interplay of socio-economic status and class in the music therapy session (Fouad & Chavez-Korell, 2014).

Bringing music and arts into these discussions can deepen the exploration and understanding of the supervisee. The supervisor can use musical collage intervention to explore the supervisee's, supervisor's, and/or clients' socio-economic status and class. Similarly, songwriting, improvisation, and lyric analysis can be used to explore these issues in the supervisee's identity, in the clinical sessions, and in the supervisory sessions.

Religion and Spirituality

Religion and spirituality are often present in music therapy sessions, whether we realize it or not. Music has been a part of religion possibly since its inception. Religious and spiritual beliefs have been expressed through music, and music is used in many religious and spiritual ceremonies and rituals. It is important that supervisors discuss religion and spirituality with supervisees (Shafranske, 2014). Supervisors need to explore with supervisees their beliefs about religion and spirituality. This can include direct questions about religion and spirituality, including the role of spirituality and religion in clinical work in general, the role of spirituality and religion in the supervisee's clinical practice and their personal life, and how much religion and spirituality play a part in decision-making in their professional work and private life. The supervisor can also explore through indirect questions about the supervisee's beliefs about meaning or fulfillment in life and where it comes from, the purpose of life, the role of science and psychology in understanding life, and so on (Shafranske, 2014). Open discussions about the supervisee's religion and spirituality maybe enhanced through the supervisor sharing their own beliefs. This can lead to discussions about similarities and differences. The discussions about differences can help to develop tolerance and open-mindedness in the supervisee as well as to explore the supervisee's reactions to opposing beliefs. In these discussions, the supervisor investigates the biases from the supervisee's religions and/or spiritual beliefs that impact the music therapy session. These impacts can range from music selection to interpretation of the client's behaviors, music, experiences, or beliefs through the lenses of the supervisee's religious/spiritual beliefs. In addition to exploring the supervisee's and supervisor's beliefs and their interactions, the supervisor must lead discussions on the intersections of the clients' beliefs with the supervisee's beliefs.

These discussions can be held verbally or facilitated through music therapy supervision interventions. A prerecorded music collage of different aspects of the supervisee's religions and spiritual beliefs and experiences is an excellent way to start this exploration. Songwriting, drawing to music, improvisations, and lyric analysis are other interventions that can be used to explore the discussions listed above.

CONCLUSION

This chapter and the ideas shared here are just the starting place for music therapy supervisors. I again caution anyone reading this chapter against implementing any of the suggested interventions in supervision sessions without doing the personal work first. Each supervisor must undergo a deep and honest self-examination prior to anything else, and then engage in education about cultures and change their practice. Only after completing these three steps can the reader start to use these interventions. We cannot help others to work in a culturally responsive manner if we are not working in that way. Working in a culturally responsive manner is not just about our jobs—it is about how we view the world and the systems around us. It is how we interact with people throughout our days, at work, at home, in the grocery store, at the PTG meeting, and so forth.

Cultural responsiveness is a reflexive practice in which one engages throughout a lifetime. For music therapy supervisors, this practice needs to be ever present. Music therapy supervisors must continue to explore themselves, learn about others, and modify their practice as they learn new information. This is the key to remaining responsive to the cultures in this pluralistic society.

REFERENCE LIST

American Music Therapy Association. (2018). *2017 AMTA membership survey and workforce analysis.* Retrieved on September 25, 2018, from https://www.musictherapy.org/assets/1/7/17WorkforceAnalysis.pdf

American Sociological Association. (2018). *Culture.* Retrieved on September 25, 2018, from http://www.asanet.org/topics/culture

Brown, J. M. (2002). Towards a culturally centered music therapy practice. *Voices: A World Forum for Music Therapy, 2*(1).

Chase, K. M. (2003). Multicultural music therapy: A review of literature. *Music Therapy Perspectives, 21*(2), 84–88. doi:10.1093/mtp/21.2.84

Collins, P. H. (1990). *Black feminist thought: Knowledge, consciousness, and the politics of empowerment.* Boston, MA: Unwin Human.

cultural competence. (n.d.). *McGraw-Hill Concise Dictionary of Modern Medicine.* (2002). Retrieved September 25, 2018, from https://medical-dictionary.thefreedictionary.com/cultural+competence

culturally responsive. (n.d.). *Cambridge Dictionary.* (2018). Retrieved September 25, 2018, from https://dictionary.cambridge.org/dictionary/english/culturally-responsive

Dileo, C. (2000). *Ethical thinking in music therapy.* Cherry Hills, NJ: Jeffrey Books.

Donley, J. (2018). Multicultural Experiential Learning: An Approach to Learning, Developing, and Maintaining Multicultural Skills. *Voices: A World Forum for Music Therapy, 18*(2). doi:10.15845/voices.v18i2.985

Dos Santos, A. (2005). The Role of Culture in Group Music Therapy in South Africa. *Voices: A World Forum for Music Therapy, 5*(2). doi:10.15845/voices.v5i2.225

Elwafi, P. (2010). The impact of music therapists' religious beliefs on clinical identity and professional practice. *Qualitative Inquiries in Music Therapy, 6,* 155–191.

Falicov, C. J. (2014a). Immigrant clients, supervisees, and supervisors. In C. A. Falender, E. P. Shafranske, & C. J. Falicov (Eds.), *Multiculturalism and diversity in clinical supervision: A competency-based approach* (pp. 111–143). Washington, DC: American Psychological Association.

Falicov, C. J. (2014b). Psychotherapy and supervision as cultural encounters: The multidimensional ecological comparative approach framework. In C. A. Falender, E. P. Shafranske, & C. J.

Falicov (Eds.), *Multiculturalism and diversity in clinical supervision: A competency-based approach* (pp. 29–58). Washington, DC: American Psychological Association.

Flores, A. R., Herman, J. L., Gates, G. J., & Brown, T N. T. (2016). *How many adults identify as transgender in the United States?* Retrieved on September 25, 2018, from https://williamsinstitute.law.ucla.edu/wp-content/uploads/How-Many-Adults-Identify-as-Transgender-in-the-United-States.pdf

Foronda, C. L., Baptiste, D., Reinholdt, M., & Ousman, K. (2015). Cultural humility: A concept analysis. *Journal of Transcultural Nursing, 27*(3), 210–217.

Fouad, N. A., & Chavez-Korell, S. (2014). Considering social class and socio-economic status in the context of multiple identities: An integrative clinical supervision approach. In C. A. Falender, E. P. Shafranske, & C. J. Falicov (Eds.), *Multiculturalism and diversity in clinical supervision: A competency-based approach* (pp. 145–162). Washington, DC: American Psychological Association.

Gonzalez, P. (2011). The impact of music therapists' music cultures on the development of their professional identities. *Qualitative Inquiries in Music Therapy, 6,* 1–33.

Hadley, S. (Ed.). (2006). *Feminist perspectives in music therapy.* Gilsum, NH: Barcelona.

Hadley, S., & Norris, M. S. (2016). Musical multicultural competency in music therapy: The first step. *Music Therapy Perspectives, 34*(2), 129–137. doi:10.1093/mtp/miv045

Hook, J. N., Davis, D. E., Owen, J., Worthington, E. L., Jr., & Utsey, S. O. (2013). Cultural humility: Measuring openness to culturally diverse clients. *Journal of Counseling Psychology, 60*(3), 53–66.

Howden, L. M., & Meyer, J. A. (2011). Age and sex composition: 2010. *2010 Census Briefs.* Retrieved on September 28, 2018, from https://www.census.gov/prod/cen2010/briefs/c2010br-03.pdf

Humes, K. R., Jones, N. A., & Ramirez, R. R. (2011). *Overview of Race and Hispanic Origin: 2010.* United States Census Bureau. Retrieved on September 25, 2018, from https://www.census.gov/prod/cen2010/briefs/c2010br-02.pdf

Kim, S. A. (2008). The supervisee's experience in cross-cultural music therapy supervision. *Qualitative Inquiries in Music Therapy, 4,* 1–44.

Kim, S. A., & Whitehead-Pleaux, A. (2015). Music therapy and cultural diversity. In B. Wheeler (Ed.), *Music Therapy Handbook.* New York, NY: Guilford Press.

Mahoney, E. (2015). Multicultural Music Therapy: An Exploration. *Voices: A World Forum for Music Therapy, 15*(2). doi:10.15845/voices.v15i2.844

multiculturalism. (n.d.). *Cambridge Dictionary.* (2018). Retrieved January 8, 2019, from https://dictionary.cambridge.org/us/dictionary/english/multicultural

Newport, F. (2018). *In U.S., Estimate of LGBT Population Rises to 4.5%.* Retrieved from https://news.gallup.com/poll/234863/estimate-lgbt-population-rises.aspx

Oswanski, L., & Donnenwerth, A. (2017). Social Justice Allies. In A. Whitehead-Pleaux & X. Tan (Eds.), *Cultural Intersections in Music Therapy: Music, Health, and the Person.* Philadelphia, PA: Barcelona Publishers.

SAMHSA. (2016). *Cultural Competence.* Retrieved September 25, 2018, from https://www.samhsa.gov/capt/applying-strategic-prevention/cultural-competence

Shafranske, E. P. (2014). Addressing religiousness and spirituality as clinically relevant cultural features in supervision. In C. A. Falender, E. P. Shafranske, & C. J. Falicov (Eds.), *Multiculturalism and diversity in clinical supervision: A competency-based approach* (pp. 181–207). Washington, DC: American Psychological Association.

Shapiro, N. (2002). Sounds in the world: Multicultural influences in music therapy in clinical practice and training. *Music Therapy Perspectives, 23*(1), 29–35.

Steig, B. (2002). *Culture-Centered Music Therapy.* Gilsum, NH: Barcelona Publishers.

Swamy, S. (2011). "No, she doesn't seem to know anything about cultural differences!": Culturally centered music therapy supervision. *Music Therapy Perspectives, 29*(2), 133–137.

Swamy, S. (2014). Music therapy in the global age: Three keys to successful culturally centred practice. *New Zealand Journal of Music Therapy, 12*, 34–57.

Swamy, S. (2018). Music, myth, and motherland: Culturally centered music and imagery with Indian Adults. *Qualitative Inquiries in Music Therapy.* Dallas, TX: Barcelona Publishers.

Tervalon, M., & Murray-Garcia, J. (1998). Cultural humility versus cultural competence: A critical distinction in defining physician training outcomes in multicultural education. *Journal of Health Care for the Poor and Undeserved, 9,* 117–125.

Vaillancourt, G. (2007). Multicultural Music Therapy as an Instrument for Leadership: Listening–Vision–Process. *Voices: A World Forum for Music Therapy, 7*(2). doi:10.15845/voices.v7i2.493

Wheeler, B. L. (2002). Experiences and concerns of students during music therapy practica. *Journal of Music Therapy, 39*(4), 274–304.

Whitehead-Pleaux, A. (2009). *Ismaee il musika*—listen to the music. *Voices: A World Forum for Music Therapy, 9*(3). http://www.voices.no/mainissues/mi4000999049.php

Whitehead-Pleaux, A., Donnenwerth, A., Robinson, B., Hardy, S., Oswanski, L., Forinash, M., Hearns, M., Anderson, N., & Tan, X. (2013). Serving the LGBTQ community: Exploring attitudes and education within the music therapy profession: Preliminary report. *The Arts in Psychotherapy, 40,* 409–414.

Whitehead-Pleaux, A., Donnenwerth, A., Robinson, B., Hardy, S., Oswanski, L., Forinash, M., Hearns, M., Anderson, N., & York, E. (2012). Lesbian, gay, bisexual, transgender, and questioning: Best practices in music therapy. *Music Therapy Perspectives, 2,* 158–166.

Whitehead-Pleaux, A., Oswanski, L., & Tan, X. (2018). *Surveying cultural competence in of music therapist in the United States.* Manuscript submitted for publication.

Whitehead-Pleaux, A., & Tan, X. (Eds). (2017). *Cultural Intersections in Music Therapy: Music, Health, and the Person.* Philadelphia, PA: Barcelona Publishers.

Yehuda, N. (2002). Multicultural encounters in music therapy: A qualitative research. *Voices: A World Forum for Music Therapy, 2*(3). doi:10.15845/voices.v2i3.100

Young, L. (2009). Multicultural issues encountered in the supervision of music therapy internships in the United States and Canada. *The Arts in Psychotherapy, 36*(4), 191–201.

Young, L. (2016). Multicultural musical competence in music therapy. *Music Therapy Perspectives, 34.* doi:10.1093/mtp/miw016

Chapter 5

FEMINIST APPROACHES TO SUPERVISION

Nicole Hahna
Michele Forinash

INTRODUCTION

Supervision is a central component in the training of music therapists as well as an important tool used throughout a music therapist's career. It can be understood as part of a continuum of development—from a requirement during certain aspects of clinical training, such as pre-internship clinical development, to a self-initiated process of engagement over the course of one's professional career. It involves a combination of self-assessment, reflexivity, and feedback that can vary in terms of styles based upon the philosophical foundations of the supervisor and the structure of the supervision group. While the reasons we seek supervision may differ over our careers, we hope that in reading this chapter you will develop a better understanding of the lens of feminist supervision as an aspirational process of engagement between the supervisee and supervisor as well as of how feminist supervision can be used within the field of music therapy. Finally, we hope that reading this chapter will encourage us all to seek supervision throughout our careers and to think deeply about how the philosophies we each hold as foundational to our clinical practice might also impact our giving and receiving of supervision.

Feminist supervision can be defined as "the application of feminist theory and values to the supervisory process, content, and relationship" (Degges-White, Colon, & Borzumato-Gainey, 2013, p. 92). It can be best understood within the context of feminist theory as it applies to clinical supervision (Worrell & Remer, 1992), with the philosophy of feminist therapy serving as a container for the process of supervision. In clinical practice, we often frame our clinical decision-making process within a foundational theory or theories, and to date there has been little music therapy literature describing the relationship between theoretical foundations and supervision. In this chapter, we hope to help bridge this gap and encourage the teaching of theory, as it relates to supervision, as we train each new generation of music therapists. We hope that in reading this chapter, more supervisors will reflect on their personal philosophies and the impacts that these have on the supervision process, as it is important to have a theoretical grounding which serves as a basis for decision-making in the supervision process (Burnes, Wood, Inman, & Welikson, 2013). Counseling and psychology have emerging literature that examines the difference between feminist supervision and "good supervision," and we also hope that this chapter helps to differentiate the dimensions of feminist supervision from other forms of supervision that may or may not be grounded in a specific theoretical orientation in music therapy. While it may be the case that feminist supervision is "good supervision," depending on own's personal experience, it is not always the case that good supervision is feminist supervision. In the next section, we will explore the importance of feminist perspectives in supervision for both authors, given the fact that a small percentage of music therapists in North America identifies as feminist music therapists (7%), according to a survey conducted by Sandra Curtis (2015).

Personal Reflections on the Importance of Feminism

From Michele

So much has happened since I first wrote the chapter on feminist music therapy supervision for Susan Hadley's book *Feminist Perspectives in Music Therapy* (2006). There have been some increases in awareness of and support for feminism, and strides have been made for women's rights in some areas. In 2013, the 80-year-old definition of rape was expanded to include any kind of nonconsensual penetration by one person of another. In 2015, marriage equality was passed, allowing the LGBTQIA+ community to marry. In 2016, women were permitted to serve in combat positions in the military. At the same time, there has been little progress in other areas. While women have served as representatives and senators since 1917, women of color only began to serve in Congress in 1964. While the 2018 U.S. House elections saw an increase in women elected to it, still, women hold only 24% of seats there and 25% of seats in the U.S. Senate (Center for American Women and Politics, 2019a). "Of the 127 women serving in the 116th U.S. Congress, 47, or 37.0%, are women of color, four in the Senate and 43 in the House" (Center for American Women and Politics, 2019b, para. 1). Economically, women are still behind. The National Women's Law Center reported that Hispanic women make 54 cents for every dollar a white man makes. Black women make 63 cents, Native women make between 45 and 64 cents, white women make 80 cents, and Asian women make 87 cents on that same dollar.

Unfortunately, there have been major setbacks to women's rights in other areas. We have returned to a culture that devalues women and sees sexual oppression and violence as acceptable. The National Organization for Women (NOW) has deemed sexual violence a hate crime as a way of combatting this attitude (Jacoby, 2017). While it was an honor to march with nearly 500,000 people in Washington on January 21, 2017, including my three children, to protest and to advocate for women's rights, reproductive rights, and rights to healthcare, among other issues, it was discouraging that these basic rights have been and are being threatened. There are estimates that there were between 4 million and 5 million people around the world marching that day to protest and advocate for these rights.

In examining well-developed theories about the developmental stages in multicultural awareness and feminism (Estrella, 2001; Porter & Vasquez, 1997; Priest, 1994), we see that while apparently we are not in stage 1 of denying or ignoring gender and cultural differences, we are actually experiencing direct oppression for being female, and even more so for being women of color. We have work to do to get back on track for recognizing and appreciating differences and integrating a solid understanding of how gender and cultural differences influence us in life and in the process of supervision.

When we look at gender and ethnicity in music therapy, we can see that there has been very little change over the past 10 years. In 2004, the membership of the American Music Therapy Association was 88% female, 10% male, 1.3% transgender, and 90% white. In 2018, 87% identified as women, 12% as men, and 1% as transgender/gender-nonconforming/other. In terms of diversity, the 2018 membership of the AMTA was 88% white, 2% African-American, 3% Hispanic, 4% Asian, and 2% multiracial (American Music Therapy Association, 2018).

From Nicole

I remember the first time I heard a teacher identify as feminist, while I was taking a counseling class in graduate school. He was so passionate about feminism and how it applied to the therapeutic setting. I remember feeling exhilarated, fearful (of backlash he might receive), and confused, all at the same time. The transformation of that classroom space and self-disclosure of that teacher served as a springboard for my own exploration of feminist music therapy. It was the catalyst I needed to learn more about feminist therapy and apply these theories to the clinical space. After graduation, I was mentored by many feminist therapists from a variety of diverse backgrounds throughout my clinical work, which helped me to expand and grow in my continually evolving personal embodiment of feminist music therapy. The mentoring process provided me with a safe space in which to explore, question, and be vulnerable as I attempted to infuse the transformational aspects of feminist music therapy from the clinical setting to the educational setting—both the classroom and within supervision groups. My clinical work in three IPV (intimate partner violence) shelters helped me to see how feminist perspectives and a focus on the need for systemic change can be integrated throughout an organization (from meetings to sessions). From within academe, I realized just how difficult it is to maintain a feminist stance, and I feel like I am starting anew each day as I aspire to incorporate this philosophy into practice.

I wanted to expand my understanding of how to apply feminist principles within academe, so I enrolled in a graduate gender studies course on feminist pedagogy in between my master's and doctoral work. This class inspired my doctoral work on the topic of feminist pedagogy, mentored by Michele, where I had a chance to learn from music therapy educators who were finding their own paths in practicing feminist pedagogy in music therapy classrooms. Again, as soon as I thought I understood what it meant to "teach music therapy" and teach using "feminist perspectives," I was confronted with things such as the looming deadline of a semester coming to an end, competency-based education and assessment requirements for accreditation agencies, and student resistance to a more collaborative classroom space. Am I doing this right? Am I using too much self-disclosure? Am I too product-oriented? And, where do the boundaries between teaching, mentoring, and supervising begin and end?

I am still searching deeply to better understand my personal definition of feminist music therapy. Currently, I am interested in how feminist theory can be expanded to this liminal space of undergraduate supervision. It's not a clinical space, and yet we are talking about applying clinical skills. It's not a classroom, and yet I evaluate student progress. It's not a mentoring relationship, and yet I ask students to look within and encourage them to trust the process, the music, and themselves and collaborate in peer supervision. How can I best integrate the components of feminist supervision with my undergraduate students? Again, feeling the artificial pull of the seemingly forced binary choice of process vs. product (client outcomes, safety, etc.), as well as the role of the gatekeeper meshed with the role of facilitator of consciousness raising, I am consistently adjusting my approach. I have so much to learn, and I am grateful to read of others' journeys incorporating feminist supervision (Fickling & Tangen, 2017).

FEMINIST SUPERVISION

To best understand feminist supervision, we will begin with an overview of feminist therapy. Feminist theory continues to have a diversity of definitions. Russell and Carey (2003) stated "what [is] very clear is that feminism means very different things to different people." Hahna (2013), who wrote about feminist pedagogy in the creative arts therapies (2013), also voiced this. "It should be noted that feminist pedagogy, as with feminist theory, does not have one singular definition or meaning, as it is an approach to teaching that values the diversity and complexity of multiple voices" (p. 437). Counseling and psychology have examined concepts such a feminist supervision identity and the creation of a feminist supervision scale to assess feminist supervision practice (Burnes, Wood, Inman, & Welikson, 2013; Degges-White, Colon, & Borzumato-Gainey; Fickling & Tangen, 2017; Prouty, Thomas, Johnson, & Long, 2001; Szymanski, 2003, 2005). This chapter is our attempt to create an emerging feminist supervision identity for ourselves and within music therapy.

In this edition, the definition of supervision will be modified from the one articulated in 2004 to incorporate feminist values as they apply to supervision (Forinash, 2004). Supervision is a relationship, one in which both supervisor and supervisee actively participate and interact. It is a process of unfolding—not simply following a recipe but engaging in a rich and dynamic relationship. Supervision, then, is also a journey, or odyssey, of sorts, in which supervisor and supervisee learn and grow and from which both will likely leave transformed in some way. Supervision holds an awareness of issues of power and oppression. Feminist supervision is based upon an egalitarian model, with an understanding that there is an inherent power differential, each person's lived experience is valued, and growth and reflexivity are encouraged for all participants.

In reading the above definition, you may wonder, What is the difference between "good supervision" and feminist supervision? This question has been explored by a variety of authors and, due to the multiplicity of voices in feminist theory, there are different voices highlighting the distinction between these constructs. Some important distinctions include "practicing ... within the feminist framework" (Degges-White, Colon, & Borzumato-Gainey, 2013, p. 103), as well as focusing on systemic or intrapsychic issues (Szymanski, 2005). To better understand the nuances of feminist supervision, Szymanski (2003) created and tested a Feminist Supervision Scale (FSS) and found four core dimensions for feminist supervision: "(a) collaborative relationships, (b) power analysis, (c) diversity and social context, and (d) feminist advocacy and activism" (p. 226). While good supervision may incorporate some of these dimensions, it does not use all four as the core aspects of the supervisory relationship. Additionally, feminist supervision is based upon the feminist therapy principle that the personal is political, with an emphasis on social justice and especially on how we both model these concepts and "train emerging professionals using certain competency benchmarks related to diversity and cultural competence in supervision practice" (Burnes, Wood, Inman, & Welikson, 2013, p. 103). Now that we have distinguished feminist supervision from "good supervision," we will examine the theories and philosophies that serve as a foundation for the practice.

Philosophies of Feminist Supervision

What Makes Feminist Supervision Unique?
Judith Worell and Pamela Remer (1992), building on the work of Natalie Porter (1985), discussed what they consider to be unique aspects of feminist supervision: "In particular, feminist supervision is sensitive to power differentials between trainee and supervisor, as well as to broadly valued philosophical goals" (p. 333). They go on to list nine essential components of feminist supervision: (a) a focus on process, (b) awareness and analysis of gender and sex-role, (c) relationship between one's theoretical orientation and feminist principles, (d) analysis of goals of therapy, (e) openness to a redefinition of health and pathology, (f) awareness of both external and internal issues in therapy, (g) supervision process providing ongoing feedback for client, (h) focus on creating women's groups, and (i) respect for the supervisee's experience and strengths (pp. 333–334).

Feminist Supervision Is a Process
Porter (1995) offered a four-stage developmental model of feminist supervision. In stage one, there is a focus on developing a perspective that is anti-racist, feminist, and multicultural. In this stage, supervisees are exposed to "alternative explanations to traditional formulations" (p. 167) of their clients' presenting issues. Supervisors not only teach about cultural differences but also challenge basic assumptions made on the part of the supervisee. While stage one is concrete and directive, stage two is a more philosophical perspective of "exploring the roots of racism, sexism, and ethnocentrism in society" (p. 168). The third stage focuses on the supervisee's own internalized feelings and attitudes, especially those of a racist and sexist nature. Stage four focuses on "adopting a social action, collective perspective" (p. 170), where the emphasis is on systems and collective action (pp. 167–171).

Feminist Supervision Is Collaborative

In a later publication, Natalie Porter and Norine Vasquez (1997) coined the term "covision" to describe feminist supervision that focuses on process and collaboration. They offered nine principles of feminist supervision: (a) the need to analyze power differentials and use power only in the "service of the supervisee" (p. 162); (b) the need for a mutually respectful and collaborative relationship; (c) a focus on self-reflection and self-examination; (d) respect for diversity of women's lives; (e) awareness of "social construction of gender and the role of language" (p. 165); (f) a call for activism; (g) maintaining ethical standards; (h) awareness and respect for the growth and development of the supervisee and how this changes the supervisory relationship; and (i) a need for supervisors to advocate for supervisees and clients (pp. 162–167). They go on to offer a definition of feminist supervision as …

> … a collaborative, respectful process, personal but unintrusive, balanced between supervisory responsibility and supervisee autonomy. Feminist supervision emphasizes an open discussion and analysis of power dynamics and targets the best interests of the supervisee. It is a process that remains focused on the social context of the lives of the client, supervisee, and supervisor. (p. 169)

Feminist Supervision Addressed Power Differentials

Daphne Hewson (1999) focused on the issues of power in the supervisory relationship. She wrote about differences between having "power over" someone and having the "power to." She argues that some feminists see power as something "bad and destructive" (p. 407) and attempt to have total equality in the supervisory relationship. This equality is essentially false, as there is a power differential in the supervisory relationship. She seeks to make power structures explicit, for only when they are explicit can they be negotiated. Talking about this power differential in feminist supervision is essential.

Anne Prouty, Volker Thomas, Scott Johnson, and Janie Long (2001) engaged in a grounded theory research study analyzing the processes that feminist supervisors used in supervision. They reported three types of methods: contracting methods, collaborative methods, and hierarchical methods. They also provided an analysis of when these different methods are used and what the supervisor's process was in determining which method to use. They found that supervisors used "contracts to minimize hierarchy and to promote clarity" (p. 93). Supervisors used "collaborative techniques not only to teach but to create a collaborative learning environment" (p. 94), and they only used "hierarchical methods when they felt that collaborative methods would not be sufficient" (p. 94).

The Culture of Music in Supervision

Karen Estrella (2001) wrote specifically about multicultural issues in music therapy supervision and stressed the need to examine the culture of music in addition to many of the topics discussed above. In particular, she emphasized the need to understand the role of music in the different cultures of clients, therapists, and supervisors, as "music in particular becomes a form of cultural legacy for families … [and] music may be one way that clients retain, regain, or remember their cultural identities" (Estrella, 2017, p. 46). As supervisors, it is important to model and facilitate a process through which all participants have an opportunity to reflect on the cultural implications of music. Hahna (2017) reflected on the need, when using classical music as part of the Bonny Method of Guided Imagery and Music (GIM), to "analyze not only the music/score, but also the cultural context of the piece and composer. Otherwise, I may be passing on cultural messages that perpetuate systems of privilege and oppression" (p. 29). Stige (2002) cautioned that "classical music is not different from any other tradition of music; it is embedded in culture(s) and it carries certain cultural values" (p.

93). The same considerations for music within a cultural context apply to popular music as well, and the feminist music therapy supervisor strives to facilitate discussion of the cultural contexts of music.

To fully understand the meaning of music in different cultures, we must become sensitive to our own cultural encapsulation. We must recognize the ways in which we take music-making and music listening for granted as normal and universal. While music certainly exists as a universal phenomenon, it is by no means a singular universal construct (Stevens & Byron, 2016). The meanings and functions of church music for a working-class African-American woman and of pop rock-and-roll for an upper-class white adolescent [girl] are different. How culture defines, contextualizes, and prioritizes the experience of music is essential knowledge for music therapists and an important issue to discuss in supervision (p. 54).

From these rich resources, how might we begin to articulate a feminist perspective of music therapy supervision? What, then, are the cornerstones of feminist music therapy supervision? We will review important concepts of feminist music therapy in the next section.

CORNERSTONES OF FEMINIST MUSIC THERAPY SUPERVISION

Below, we have updated Forinash's (2006) "cornerstones" of music therapy supervision to now offer these principles of feminist music therapy supervision built upon more recent publications. These principles include mutually respectful, collaborative relationships in which supervisor and supervisee autonomy are encouraged and diverse perspectives valued; attention to and validation of the diversity of women's lives and context; attention to the social construction of gender and the role of language in maintaining a gendered society; facilitation of the understanding of diversity, oppression, societal expectations and roles; encouragement of the development of personal cultural identities; identification of power differentials within therapy, within supervision, and within society, with the goal of client empowerment, including taking responsibility for one's actions; assisting the supervisee in seeing their own privilege (e.g., white, heterosexual) and in using their greater power inappropriately; and assisting supervisee self-reflection and examination by supervisor modeling of openness, authenticity, reflexivity, and self- monitoring.

Open, Authentic, Respectful, and Collaborative

As supervisors, we first must model an openness to our own experiences and the experiences of our supervisees. We must engage in an authentic manner and be respectful of the experiences of our supervisees. Supervisees who are different from their supervisors—in terms of gender, race, religion, culture, and/or socio-economic status—will likely have different experiences in the world, in supervision, and in the clinic. We need to value and validate the diverse experiences that they report to us. We must recognize that we live in an ableist, heteronormative, racist, and sexist world and use the supervisory space to inspire social change and social justice (Gentile, Ballou, Roffman, & Ritchie, 2010).

Supervision is seen as a collaborative "safe and support[ive]" relationship process in feminist supervision (Fickling & Tangen, 2017, p. 215). Supervisors and supervisees working from a feminist lens co-construct a supervisory relationship based on the values, goals, client needs, and cultural awareness that are shared and discussed. Supervision is built from the bottom up, and it is likely that each supervisory relationship will be different. There is no one way to supervise. Each supervisee may need something specific and different from the supervisor. It is the supervisor's job to collaborate with the supervisee, with an understanding of the supervisee's personal learning style, and to co-construct a supervisory environment that encourages reflexivity and insight. It is also important for the feminist supervisor to be aware of power differentials, privilege, and oppression as summarized below:

> We can accept and acknowledge our power as supervisors while also critiquing the knower-known dichotomy, which can be easily exaggerated in a supervisory context. We have not found a way to be supervisors without power but believe we can use it positively without the diminishing the power of the supervisee, who also brings her subjectivity to the relationship. (Flickling & Tangen, 2017, p. 216)

Understanding Privilege

The feminist principles of making explicit the sociocultural, gender, and historical issues we bring to the supervisory relationship have been well documented in feminist theory (Prouty, 2001). In particular, we have to understand areas where we as supervisors have privilege and where our supervisees have privilege. This can be quite difficult for all of us.

From Michele

When I have had discussions about unearned privilege with colleagues and students, I sometimes have gotten push-back, as people tend to want to believe they got where they are due to hard work and not that they got there, at least partially, due to unacknowledged privilege. Exploring the intersectionality of race, class, and gender, among other attributes, can be challenging, but it is necessary in order to see clearly in what areas we are privileged and in what areas we are marginalized. I am a white, cisgender, lesbian/queer, academic, middle-class, Christian with Buddhist leanings, mother of Arab-American children. My white, academic, middle-class, and Christian identities provide me with certain privileges that I need to acknowledge and understand. I belong to a dominant religion, I am respected for my educational background where I live, my race is dominant, and people aren't suspicious or afraid of me when I walk down the street. On the flip side, though, my female, queer/lesbian, mother of Arab-American children identities provide me with experiences of being marginalized. I am a white parent to Arab-American children, thus making this aspect of my identity invisible. Since 9/11, I have had people talk disparagingly to me about Arabs, not knowing my children are Arab-American. My children, now grown, have experienced microaggressions and have been questioned by strangers and new acquaintances about their country of origin and their race. This is especially true now that we have proposed immigration bans for countries with large Muslim populations. Although born in Concord, MA, they are frequently exotified and asked by people—"Where are you *really* from?" "What kind of Latino are you?" As a queer/lesbian woman, there are places in this country where I do not feel safe. While I do not try to pass as straight, I am well aware of the risk that I am taking by not doing so.

As supervisors, we need to understand that our intersectional identities and thus our privileges and marginalizations help our students to understand their identities and their privileges, as this will impact our supervisory relationship and the therapy relationship.

From Nicole

As an able-bodied, college-educated, white, cisgender woman, I supervise undergraduate music therapy students' clinical work in my role as a music therapy educator. One topic students often discuss early on in supervision is the process of determining objectives. Many times, this is the first time students have had an opportunity for consciousness-raising regarding the power differentials that exist within the therapeutic setting, including issues surrounding assessment and ableism. In working with a client in the music therapy clinic who communicates nonverbally, inevitably students voice concerns about writing an objective analysis without client input. I try to use these student-initiated opportunities to process ways to show how the system is set up in such a way that it is all too easy for therapists to write an objective *for* a client, instead of *with* a client.

Before having a child with developmental delays, as an able-bodied person I may have approached this supervision in a more matter-of-fact way. I never considered all of the ways in which an ableist society decides for others (the first doctor to diagnose my child started by telling me what my child could not do when he became older). I had the privilege of not having to address my ableism until that moment. At that first doctor's appointment and all of the appointments that have come since, I realized how easy it is for the medical system to decide for others (the doctor decided which therapies to order, which tests to order, etc.) and that it takes every bit of my being to find the strength to advocate for alternatives.

During an IFSP meeting, I remember refusing to approve an objective for my child, telling the OT "that's society's problem, not my child's problem"—and yet in feminist supervision, I sit with this paradox every day. Even in my role as a supervisor, where I also grade student's clinical writing, I am in some ways approving or condoning goals. Who am I to decide what is best for another person? This semester in supervision, it was only when a client did not communicate verbally that the supervisee noticed how often we decide for clients. And yet, this is often the case. I wonder, what is the "best" way to process such power differentials and issues of privilege? As they organically emerge? In a systematic way? Both/and? I need to use reflexivity to work through my personal bias as well as the pitfalls of being an ally as part of my practice of feminist supervision to help make the invisible visible and raise consciousness within the therapeutic relationship (Edwards, 2006). I need to acknowledge my privilege and power in the therapeutic setting and in the supervisory setting.

Reflexivity

Staying open to the supervisee's experience requires reflexivity. We must demonstrate a willingness to challenge our assumptions as well as the assumptions of our supervisees. We must be open to an alternative—perhaps even paradoxical—understanding of a situation, whether it is in supervision or in society at large. For us, reflexivity is a thread that is woven throughout our feminist supervisory experiences. This is not a reflexivity that derails us into a constant questioning and paralyzes our ability to make decisions. It is a reflexivity that calls us to be responsible for the choices we make and to analyze what we are doing and why. This is not a one-time event, but an ongoing process of being willing to examine one's own process. As Brynjulf Stige (2001) wrote:

> Reflexivity also needs to be part of the [supervision] process. … (Self)-reflexivity then could be understood as both the supervisor's and the supervisee's exploration of their own roles in the supervision process, and as their exploration of their own role in the community and society they are living in. (p. 172)

Reflexivity requires that both supervisor and supervisee "take responsibility for their actions, feelings, and beliefs" (Porter & Vasquez, 1997, p. 164). As stated throughout feminist literature, supervisors have an important opportunity to model reflexivity for their supervisees. As Stige indicated above, this reflexivity includes not only the supervisory relationship, but also one's role in both community and society. One must be vigilant and always question assumptions as bias. Discrimination based on gender is often both subtle and pervasive. It is also important to keep in mind that our assumptions become more complicated when gender biases intersect with biases based on race, class, ability, and so forth. Reflexivity also calls on us to acknowledge the biases that we bring to the supervisory experience. It is only by recognizing and naming these that we are able to create change.

Multiple Perspectives

Yet another cornerstone of feminist supervision is the valuing of multiple perspectives, which expands upon phenomenological concepts. For instance, in seeking to embrace alternative meanings, we take into account issues of culture and power from a feminist stance. Let's go back for a moment to our initial query about whether feminist perspectives are inherent in music therapy supervision literature and just need to be named. In terms of this tenet of multiple perspectives, music therapy literature comes up short. Feminist theory has a focus on understanding women's experience in society. This is often overlooked in the music therapy literature. As we supervise, do we honor that women's experience of society is often different from what is perceived in traditional patriarchal models? Given that our field is made up largely of women, do we just assume an understanding of women's experience (Curtis, 1990)? A feminist perspective would challenge us to take what may be a quiet assumption and make it a much more articulate and vocal point of view. How do our women supervisees experience the society and the clinical world? How can we help our men supervisees develop an appreciation and awareness of women's experience, whether they are fellow colleagues, bosses, subordinates, or clients? As we supervise someone, how can we embrace the multiple perspectives that our supervisees and their clients bring to supervision?

We may use another phenomenological idea—"free phantasie variation" (Kenny, 1996, p. 61)—as another way to embrace multiple perspectives that incorporates feminist theory with phenomenology in feminist supervision. For example, free phantasie variation refers to the idea of uncovering essences of an event or experience through reflective thinking during which one imagines the experience being studied in different forms (Forinash & Grocke, 2005). In feminist supervision, we would not necessarily be looking for essential structures of the experience. We would use this concept to allow us to imagine a variety of meanings of the event.

Likewise, in transcendental phenomenology, multiple perspectives are embraced. "Experiences are viewed from two perspectives: what was experienced (the textural description, or noema) and how it was experienced (the structural description, or noesis)" (Forinash & Grocke, 2005, p. 323).

To embrace multiple perspectives, we must ask questions such as: How might this supervision process be understood differently? How might we find an alternative way of looking and understanding the client's issue or the supervisee's conceptualization of it? Valuing the lived experience of the supervisee and being open to learning are essential components of feminist supervision.

Awareness of Power

Another important area for consideration in feminist supervision is the ongoing analysis of power differentials. Therefore, issues of power and equality must be discussed. Prouty, Thomas, Johnson, and Long (2001) wrote about feminist family therapy supervision. In their article, they discuss various methods of supervision. They highlight three basic methods of feminist supervision that reflect a balanced use of power. One method is that of "contracting." In this method, a verbal understanding of what is to be accomplished in supervision is created. This includes the supervisee sharing her goals for supervision and having the option to change or discard them as supervision progresses. Power is also equalized in the contracting process through "mutual evaluation" (p. 89), in which both supervisee and supervisor evaluate each other. Supervisees have the power to challenge evaluations and "make additions to their evaluations before they became part of their record" (p. 89). They go on to discuss collaborative methods in feminist supervision, which include fostering competence, offering multiple perspectives, providing various options from which the supervisee can choose, and providing ongoing mutual feedback (pp. 90–91). Finally, they discuss hierarchical methods, which were used much less frequently and usually only when the client was not safe or the clinical "situation was beyond the therapist's current therapeutic abilities" (p. 91). These methods include behavioral directives, where the supervisee is told how to act or what to say in the session, and reading directives, where the supervisor suggests certain readings for the supervisee. Modeling is also discussed as a hierarchical method and is described as role-play or when the supervisor takes part in the therapy session and models a way of interacting.

In all of these methods, it is clear that the supervisee has the ability to influence the direction of supervision; that there is respect for a variety of ways of looking at the issues in supervision; and that the supervisee is given options from which to choose whenever possible. The supervisor only assumes the traditional, more powerful role when there are issues of safety. We are encouraged to see the AMTA's shift from a more traditional ethics code to the new, aspirational *Code of Ethics*, a shift that includes recommendations related to supervision. This new, aspirational code highlights the importance of the understanding of culture and as well as the use of peer or collaborative supervision groups for music therapists. Two specific parts of the new *Code of Ethics* that address supervision are:

- 1.8. Acquire knowledge and information about the specific cultural group(s) with whom they work, seeking supervision and education as needed.
...
- 4.2. Use resources available to them to enhance and better their practice (e.g., peer/professional supervision).

As we stated earlier, Porter and Vasquez (1997) have called supervision "covision" (p. 155) as a way of equalizing issues of power. We are interested in seeing how music therapists utilize this concept in feminist supervision. Sue Hadley (personal communication, July 14, 2005) sees covision not as meaning equal vision but instead as a way for supervisor and supervisee to gain understanding together. She went on to say that:

Although we view it together, this doesn't mean that we don't have specific roles or differential levels of experience or even power. It does seem to suggest that we each may have "expertise" that the other does not, whether in music therapy, life, music, etc. It also seems to support the notion that because we are sharing our views together, it can lead to greater understanding—for all of us, supervisor and supervisee. What I like about it is that this viewing together or understanding together allows for "dissensus," which, when worked through, can lead to expanded vision for all involved. (personal communication, July 14, 2005)

We would argue that, as supervisors, we do have tremendous power over supervisees in terms of gatekeeping, how we focus supervision, and how we make sense of what issues come up in supervision. While our supervisees may indeed have more expertise in certain areas, such as foreign language, musical styles, and so on, in terms of the clinical awareness, the supervisor is likely to have the expertise. Of course, we should always question our use of power and strive to use power in service of the supervisee and their clients. As we have seen in previous discussions, pretending not to have power and expertise as a supervisor can be seen as condescending and may lead to unintended and potentially harmful consequences. Finding a way to use our power in an appropriate balance of support and challenge is essential.

Social Change

Feminist theory implies a desire for social change. Hahna (2011) stated:

> A key difference between feminist pedagogy and other pedagogies is its investment in social change. … Its goal is to create an emancipatory space so that all of the stakeholders in the classroom—teachers and learners—can be transformed. It is hoped that through this transformation, dismantling systems of power, privilege, and oppression too can change society. (p. 438)

The same holds true for feminist supervision. At the heart of feminist ideals is embracing the concept of the intersectionality of our identities (Villaverde, 2008). We are not simply male/female straight/queer/trans and so forth. These binary concepts no longer apply. Humans are complex. Feminist theory emphasizes the concept that helping an individual adjust to their environment is not the focus of therapy and thus not the focus of supervision. We should not encourage our supervisees to adjust to the absurd sexist and racist encounters that are perpetuated by our culture, but instead we should question each instance of sexism and racism that we encounter inherent in patriarchy. This applies not only to supervision and the supervisory relationship, but also to our encounters in the world. The personal is indeed political (Curtis, 2012).

Of course, once one takes such a position of activism, it opens us up to further criticism and marginalization. By confronting ableism, sexism, and racism, we risk being excluded by those who are reluctant to take such an activist stance. In working with a supervisee, it is important to identify the ableist, heteronormative, sexist, and racist ideas that exist in the world, while remaining open to all voices and allowing supervisees to develop their own feminist consciousness.

A favorite bumper sticker says, "If you aren't outraged, then you aren't paying attention." While we believe this was meant as a statement about the current political situation, it certainly applies to owning a feminist perspective. Essentially, as we acknowledge these systemic issues in supervision and in society, we experience a sense of outrage. With the awareness of systemic oppression, the importance of social justice allows for the supervisory relationship to become a transformative space.

As feminist supervisors, then, we need to take an activist stance and confront these situations that are ableist, ageist, classist, heterosexist, racist, sexist, and so on. This activism takes the form of consciousness-raising and grassroots activism. How are we working toward our social justice aims within and outside of the systems with which we interact? Baines (2013) encourages music therapists working from an anti-oppressive stance to begin …

> … recognizing that the power imbalances in our society affect us all. It is a way of addressing the "problems" that our clients present within the context of their social-political reality and resourcing both ourselves and persons we serve to address social inequity toward the goal of creating a socially just future. (p. 4)

Through questioning, challenging, and confronting inequalities, we can begin to effect change, which is important not only for our supervisees and their clients, but also for all of those who are impacted by implicit ableism, sexism, and racism.

The Cultures of Music

A final cornerstone of feminist music therapy supervision is an examination of the cultures of music. Our tool as music therapists is quite complex. Music has a multitude of forms and uses and defies generalization. Yet, much of music therapy is founded in western music. As music therapy begins to find a more truly international voice (see, for example, www.voices.no), we must continue to examine not only different forms of music, but also how music is used and understood by different cultures. How do women in various cultures experience music? As Sue Hadley also emphasized:

> [W]hat is being communicated in the music that we use? Are we upholding patriarchal values by using certain types of music? Are we supporting gender and cultural stereotypes? We and our supervisees need to analyze song choices based on the patriarchal, white, middle-class, heterosexual values they are supporting. (personal communication, July 14, 2005)

Feminist Supervision Methods

While there is no single way to incorporate feminist theory into music therapy supervision, we acknowledge that it can be helpful at times to see how other feminist supervisors have incorporated feminist philosophy into the supervision process. The following suggestions come from Degges-White, Colon, and Borzumato-Gainey (2013):

- Group Supervision: Group supervision allows for peer-to-peer interactions and opportunities for supervisees to find their voice, encourage consciousness-raising, and provide an opportunity for supervisees to hear "multiple perspectives" (p. 100) when a feminist framework is incorporated.
- Tag Team Supervision: This occurs when "different group members take turns playing the counselor" and allows "mutual feedback with one another and the supervisor" (p. 101).
- Live Supervision: This includes the incorporation of a "consultation break" that the supervisee requests of the supervisor and can be "empowering" for the supervisee (p. 102).

Just as making changes to the classroom space, such as moving desks into a circle, does not in-and-of-itself create a feminist classroom, the incorporation of any of the above methods does not necessarily create a feminist supervisory co-created relationship. It is the incorporation and practice of these techniques as a foundational principle and core belief that transform the supervisory relationship—not the application of techniques. This grounding in feminist theory is the difference between "good supervision" and feminist supervision.

CONCLUSION

As we provide a description of feminist supervision, first and foremost, a feminist supervisor must help to articulate and examine the many concepts shared above, for if these concepts are left unspoken, then it is not feminist supervision. Naming, claiming, and giving voice is essential and often a process. As I (Nicole) wrote in my dissertation on feminist pedagogy, "It took me a long time before I could own the label 'feminist' and I now understand this identity formation to be a journey" (Hahna, 2011, p. 239). Feminist concepts do not exist in isolation. One cannot pick one or two of these concepts to embrace. Similarly, adding a concept without understanding feminist theory is not recommended, as feminist theory should be the foundation for the supervisory relationship for feminist supervision. They exist in relationship and build on each other. They are entwined and intermingled. Feminist supervision is a way of thinking and of seeing the world. It is a practice. While how one uses the elements of feminist supervision may be quite individual, the ideas discussed above are basic and essential principles of feminist supervision.

In this chapter, we described key components of feminist therapy as it serves as a foundation for feminist supervision. These components included an emphasis on diversity, acknowledgement of power differentials, collaboration, egalitarianism, and an emphasis on the personal as political. We then explored the need to understand the music, supervisor, and supervisee within a cultural context. We concluded by describing dimensions of feminist supervision, which included concepts such as addressing power and privilege, reflexivity, holding multiple perspectives, and using the supervisory space as a catalyst for social change. Given this overview, we will take a moment to reflect upon the definition of supervision offered previously in this chapter.

Earlier in the chapter, we offered a definition of supervision that is not expressly feminist. Having reviewed the cornerstones of feminist supervision, we would now describe feminist supervision as a rich and dynamic relationship that is a collaborative process in which both supervisor and supervisee are open to self-examination and reflection. Assumptions about our worldview are challenged, and multiple perspectives on a situation are actively sought and embraced. Power differentials are discussed, and power is always used in service of the supervisee and their client(s). Supervision is collaboratively pursued, with the idea of challenging sexism, racism, ableism, and other forms of oppression.

The music therapy literature does have ideas that are essential to feminist theory. These include ideas such as multiple perspectives, respect, and embracing a not-knowing approach. What is missing, however, is the articulation of these ideas as essentially feminist. To just "assume" them only further denies a true feminist perspective. We must embrace these ideas and articulate them as essentially feminist rather than put them under the umbrella of traditional patriarchal thought. While we acknowledge that not all music therapists reading this chapter will resonate with feminist theory as a foundation for their supervisory work, we encourage music therapists to mindfully base their supervisory relationships in a theory that supports the supervisor and supervisee. We ourselves aspire to practice supervision from the basis of our values in feminist theory. We acknowledge the emancipatory elements of a theory when used for social justice in feminist music therapy supervision. As bell hooks reminds us, "theory is not inherently healing, liberatory, or revolutionary. It fulfills this function only when we ask that it do so and direct our theorizing towards this end" (1994, p. 61).

REFERENCE LIST

American Music Therapy Association. (2018). *2018 AMTA Member Survey & Workforce Analysis.* Silver Spring, MD: Author.

Amir, D. (2001). The journey of two: Supervision for the new music therapist working in an educational setting. In M. Forinash (Ed.), *Music Therapy Supervision.* Gilsum, NH: Barcelona Publishers.

Baines, S. (2013). Music therapy as an anti-oppressive practice. *The Arts in Psychotherapy, 40,* 1–5. doi:10.1016/j.aip.2012.09.003

Burnes, T. R., Wood, J. M., Inman, J. L., & Welikson, G. A. (2013). An investigation of process variables in feminist group clinical supervision. *The Counseling Psychologist, 41,* 86–109. doi:10.1177/001100002442653

The Center for American Women and Politics. (2019a). *Women in the U.S. Congress 2019.* Rutgers University, Eagleton Institute of Politics. Retrieved from http://www.cawp.rutgers.edu/women-us-congress-2019

The Center for American Women and Politics (2019b). *Facts on women of color in office.* Rutgers University, Eagleton Institute of Politics. Retrieved from https://www.cawp.rutgers.edu/fact-sheets-women-color

Curtis, S. (1990). Women's issues and music therapists. *Music Therapy Perspectives, 8,* 61–66. doi:10.1093/mtp/8.1.61

Curtis, S. (2012). Music therapy and social justice. *The Arts in Psychotherapy, 39*(2), 209–213. doi:10.1016/j.aip.2011.12.004

Curtis, S. (2015). Feminist music therapists in North American: Their lives and their practices. *Voices: A World Forum for Music Therapy, 15*(2). doi:10.15845/voices.v15i2.812

Degges-White, S. E., Colon, B. R., & Borzumato-Gainey, C. (2013). Counseling supervision within a feminist framework: Guidelines for intervention. *Journal of Humanistic Counseling, 52,* 92–105. doi:10.1002/j.2161-1939.2013.00035.x

Edwards, K. E. (2006). Aspiring social justice ally identity development: A conceptual model. *NASPA Journal, 43*(4), 39–60.

Estrella, K. (2001). Multicultural approaches to music therapy supervision. In M. Forinash (Ed.), *Music Therapy Supervision.* Gilsum, NH: Barcelona Publishers.

Estrella, K. (2017). Music therapy with Hispanic/latino clients. In A. Whitehead-Pleaux & X. Tan (Eds.), *Cultural intersections in music therapy: Music, health, and the person* (pp. 35–49). Dallas, TX: Barcelona Publishers.

Falender, C. A., & Shafranske, E. P. (2008). *Casebook for Clinical Supervision: A Competency-Based Approach.* Washington, DC: American Psychological Association. doi:10.1037/11792-006

Fickling, M. J., & Tangen, J. L. (2017). A journey toward feminist supervision: A dual autoethnographic inquiry. *Journal of Counselor Preparation and Supervision, 9,* 206–232.

Forinash, M. (1995). Phenomenological research. In B. Wheeler (Ed.), *Music Therapy Research: Quantitative and Qualitative Perspectives.* Gilsum, NH: Barcelona Publishers.

Forinash, M. (2001). *Music Therapy Supervision.* Gilsum, NH: Barcelona Publishers.

Forinash, M., & Grocke, D. (2005). Phenomenological inquiry. In B. Wheeler (Ed.), *Music Therapy Research* (2nd ed.). Gilsum, NH: Barcelona Publishers.

Gentile, L., Ballou, M., Roffman, E., & Ritchie, J. (2010). Supervision for social change: A feminist ecological perspective. *Women & Therapy, 33*(1/2), 140–151. doi:10.1080/02703140903404929

Hahna, N. D. (2011). *Conversations from the classroom: Reflections on feminist music therapy pedagogy in teaching music therapy* (Doctoral dissertation). Retrieved from ProQuest Dissertations & Thesis database. (UMI No. 3453869).

Hahna, N. D. (2013). Towards an emancipatory practice: Incorporating feminist pedagogy in the creative arts therapies. *The Arts in Psychotherapy, 40,* 436–440.

Hahna, N. D. (2017). Reflecting on personal bias. In A. Whitehead-Pleaux & X. Tan (Eds.), *Cultural intersections in music therapy: Music, health, and the person* (pp. 23–33). Dallas, TX: Barcelona Publishers.

Hewson, D. (1999). Empowerment in supervision. *Feminism & Psychology, 9,* 406–409.

hooks, bell. (1994). *Teaching to transgress: Education as the practice of freedom.* New York, NY: Routledge.

Jacoby, J. (2017). *Sexual violence is a hate crime.* [Web log post]. Retrieved from https://now.org/blog/sexual-violence-is-a-hate-crime/

Kenny, C. B. (1996). The story of the field of play. In M. Langenberg, K. Aigen, & J. Frommer (Eds.), *Qualitative Music Therapy Research: Beginning Dialogues.* Gilsum, NH: Barcelona Publishers.

Porter, N. (1985). New perspectives on therapy supervision. In L. B. Rosewater & L. E. A. Walker (Eds.), *Handbook of Feminist Therapy: Women's Issues in Psychotherapy* (pp. 332–343). New York, NY: Springer.

Porter, N. (1995). Supervision of psychotherapists: Integrating anti-racist, feminist, and multicultural perspectives. In H. Landrine (Ed.), *Bringing Cultural Diversity to Feminist Psychology: Theory, Research, and Practice.* Washington, DC: American Psychological Association.

Porter, N. (2009). Feminist and Multicultural Underpinnings to Supervision: An Overview. *Women & Therapy, 33*(1–2), 1–6. doi:10.1080/02703140903404622

Porter, N., & Vasquez, N. (1997). Covision: Feminist supervision, process, and collaboration. In J. Worell & N. G. Johnson (Eds.), *Shaping the Future of Feminist Psychology: Education, Research, and Practice.* Washington, DC: American Psychological Association.

Priest, R. (1994). Minority supervisor and majority supervisee: Another perspective of clinical reality. *Counselor Education and Supervision, 34,* 152–158.

Prouty, A. (2001). Experiencing feminist family therapy supervision. *Journal of Feminist Family Therapy, 12*(4), 171–203. doi:10.1300/J086v12n04_01

Prouty, A. M., Thomas, V., Johnson, S., & Long, J. K. (2001). Methods of feminist family therapy supervision. *Journal of Marital and Family Therapy, 27,* 85–97.

Rosewater, L. B., & Walker, L. E. A. (Eds.). (1985). *Handbook of Feminist Therapy: Women's Issues in Psychotherapy.* New York, NY: Springer.

Russell, S., & Carey, M. (2003). Feminism, therapy, and narrative ideas: Exploring some not so commonly asked questions. *International Journal of Narrative Therapy and Community Work, 2.* http://www.dulwichcentre.com.au/feminism.htm

Stevens, C. J., & Byron, T. (2016). Universals in music processing: Entrainment, acquiring expectations, and learning. In S. Hallam, I. Cross, & M. Thaut (Eds.), *The Oxford Handbook of Music Psychology* (2nd ed., pp. 19–31). Oxford, UK: Oxford University Press.

Stige, B. (2001). The fostering of not-knowing barefoot supervisors. In M. Forinash (Ed.), *Music Therapy Supervision.* Gilsum, NH: Barcelona Publishers.

Stige, B. (2002). *Culture-centered music therapy.* Gilsum, NH: Barcelona Publishers.

Summer, L. (2001). Group supervision in first-time music therapy practicum. In M. Forinash (Ed.), *Music Therapy Supervision.* Gilsum, NH: Barcelona Publishers.

Szymanski, D. M. (2003). The feminist supervision scale: A rational/theoretical approach. *Psychology of Women Quarterly, 27*(3), 221–232. doi:10.1111/1471-6402.00102

Szymanski, D. M. (2005). Feminist identity and theories as correlates of feminist supervision practices. *The Counseling Psychologist, 33,* 729–747.

Thomas, C. (2001). Student-centered internship supervision. In M. Forinash (Ed.), *Music Therapy Supervision.* Gilsum, NH: Barcelona Publishers.

Villaverde, L. E. (2008). *Feminist theories and education.* New York, NY: Peter Lang.

Worell, J., & Remer, P. (1992). *Feminist Perspectives in Therapy: An Empowerment Model for Women.* Oxford, UK: John Wiley and Sons.

Chapter 6

EQUALITY FOR ALL: THE INTERSECTION OF SUPERVISION AND LGBTQ+ TOPICS

Leah Oswanski
Beth Robinson
Amy Donnenwerth
Maureen Hearns

INTRODUCTION

Gender identity and sexual orientation are potential issues that can either facilitate or disrupt a supervisory dynamic due to power issues, minority status, and the intersectionality of other minority statuses. (Sand, 2017, p. 1541)

In music therapy literature, little attention has been given to LGBTQ+ education or training (Whitehead-Pleaux et al., 2013), which may be perceived as unnecessary due to other resources being available for students (York, 2015). In this chapter, the authors are addressing specific considerations related to gender identity, sexual orientation, and supervision. Topics will include LGBTQ+ 101, types of bias, self-assessment tools, transgender-specific issues, conflicting religious/personal beliefs, ethical considerations, and support resources. The authors wish to note that some of the literature highlighted in this chapter, as well as each author's lived perspective, comes from the standpoints of four white people, three female and one genderqueer, some of whom are members of the LGBTQ+ community and some of whom are allies. It is important to communicate that the intersectional identities of an LGBTQ+ person shift levels of power, privilege, and social inequity within an already marginalized group. For further reading on intersectionality, the authors suggest Patricia Hill Collins (2000) and Kimberlé Crenshaw (1995) to deepen understanding of how your identity, as well as your clients' and supervisees' identities, intersect and impact our biases and lived experiences.

While the focus of this chapter is concentrated on considerations for heterosexual (sometimes identified with the term "straight") music therapy supervisors supervising LGBTQ+-identified music therapists and students, this information is also pertinent for a heterosexual supervisor supervising music therapists and students where sexual identity is unknown or presumed heterosexual. LGBTQ+ people, whether self-identified or not, are present within every population with which music therapists work. The assumption that a music therapist or student who works with a population such as a neonatal intensive care unit (NICU) or in eldercare does not need training in LGBTQ+ issues for their job is false. A music therapist in a NICU could be working with an LGBTQ+ parent or couple, as LGBTQ+ people are present in all populations at any age.

A critical examination of our biases, assumptions, values, and intersectional identity related, but not limited, to race, ethnicity, religion, gender identity, gender expression, political affiliation, age, sexual orientation, and socio-economic status is imperative for both the supervisor/educator and the supervisee (Dileo, 2000). According to O'Brien, Kosoko-Lasaki, Cook, Kissell, Peak, and Williams (2006) and Sue (1990), an in-depth self-review may include:

1. Recognizing and acknowledging personal biases and prejudices.

2. Examining biases, privilege, beliefs, and values.
3. Acknowledging differences that we have with others.
4. Developing cultural competence and humility.
5. Identifying resources available within our own institutions or workplace.
6. Recognizing the influence of our own religious, sociocultural, and political environments.
7. Identifying and taking responsibility for personal discomforts, limitations, and challenges.
8. Engaging in dialogue to educate others concerning oppression and inequality.
9. Seeking supervision and continuing education on these issues.

Falender and Shafranske (2004) defined supervision as a "collaborative interpersonal process" and wrote that an effective relationship between supervisor and supervisee was built on integrity and a shared alliance. When the supervisory alliance is compromised due to a lack of integrity, trust, and appreciation of diversity, supervisees may experience an increase in personal vulnerability, self-doubt, anxiety, and self-criticism (Norcross & Guy, 2007; Orlinsky & Ronnestad, 2005). Counseling and social work research show that discussion of sexual orientation in supervision is seldom addressed (Gatmon, Jackson, Koshkarian, Martos-Perry, Molina, Patel, & Rodolfa, 2001), possibly due to the struggle of how to bring these issues up without seeming uncomfortable or appearing overly concerned (Messinger, 2007). Messinger (2013) witnessed that LGBT students were characterized as "problems to be addressed or accommodated" (p. 9). The consistent practice of openly discussing the topics of discrimination, oppression, sexuality, gender identity and expression with *all* students can make the discussions easier for the supervisor (Messinger, 2007, 2013; Newman, Bodo, & Daley, 2008; Newman, Daley, & Bogo, 2009). In schools of social work, there has been a direct correlation between the relationship of the LGBTQ+ competence of the organization, departmental LGBTQ+ competence, and increased perception of competency of students to work with LGBTQ+ people (Craig, Dentato, Messinger, & McInroy, 2016; McCarty-Caplan, 2018). Some ways in which competency can be promoted through a program level are through the recruitment and retention of LGBTQ+ faculty and students and creating research and clinical opportunities to work with LGBTQ+ issues (Chui, McGann, Ziemer, Hoffman, & Stahl, 2018; Hope & Chappell, 2015).

Although not specifically related to supervisors, in a 2013 study, Whitehead-Pleaux et al. discovered that 57.9% of music therapists reported having no training in LGBTQ+ issues; of those who did have training, 59.2% still felt that they were not prepared to work with people in the LGBTQ+ community, suggesting that our education and training in this area is woefully inadequate. Perhaps even more concerning is that 63.4% of music therapists felt that their level of comfort in working with LGBTQ+ populations was "very comfortable" and 18.6% felt "somewhat comfortable" (Whitehead-Pleaux et al., 2013). The dichotomy between reported lack of education and training and the perception of comfort in clinical practice is problematic. How can we feel comfortable clinically with something for which we have no education or training?

LGBTQ+: THE BASICS

Before exploring LGBTQ+ topics in depth, it is important to lay the foundation for what the acronym stands for. Keep in mind that there are an infinite number of ways for someone to express their sexuality, sex, or gender; not all people identify with the letters of this acronym, but they still are a part of or connected to the LGBTQ+ community. A person might also identify with one of the letters in the acronym but subscribe to a meaning or variation of it that might differ from that of another person who identifies as the same letter. Language is fluid and always changing, and the individual is the only person who can decide what their identity is.

Another consideration for music therapy supervision is the generational differences that exist within the LGBTQ+ community itself. In a 2005 report, the Institute for Gay and Lesbian Strategic

Studies determined that LGBTQ+ people from diverse age groups have dissimilar beliefs and experiences regarding the evolving treatment of LGBTQ+ people in families, in the workplace, in schools, and in communities. Mitchell (2010) affirmed that clinical supervisors consider that the individual LGBTQ+ client, the intern, and the supervisor may possess cultural concepts that vacillate between the dreadful and closeted 1950s and a more hopeful and advantageous modern time.

It is important to point out that the T (transgender) is a gender identity and the LGBQ (and many of the + words) are related to sexual orientation. This is sometimes confusing, as these are very different concepts, and someone who is transgender may identify as straight, queer, lesbian, and so forth. Gender identity is separate from sexuality and will be detailed later in this chapter. Historically, the LGBTQ+ community became a "catchall" for many marginalized groups of people who were disenfranchised due to their sexual orientation, gender identity, and biological sex. The letters of the acronym, modified from https://www.pflag.org/glossary (2018), stand for:

> **L: Lesbian.** A woman who is emotionally, romantically, and/or physically attracted to other women. People who are lesbians need not have had any sexual experience; it is the attraction that helps to determine orientation.
>
> **G: Gay.** Used to describe people who are emotionally, romantically, or physically attracted to people of the same gender or someone who is under the transgender umbrella (e.g., gay man, gay people). People who are gay need not have had any sexual experience; it is the attraction that helps to determine orientation.
>
> **B: Bisexual.** An individual who is emotionally, romantically, and/or physically attracted to the same gender and different genders. People who are bisexual need not have had equal sexual experience with people of the same or different genders and, in fact, need not have had any sexual experience at all; it is the attraction that helps to determine orientation. Bisexuality, as it is frequently used today, can act as an umbrella term that encapsulates many identities—for example, pansexual. Sometimes referred to as bi or bi+.
>
> **T: Transgender.** This is sometime shortened to "trans." A term describing a person's gender identity that does not necessarily match their assigned sex at birth. This word is also used as a broad umbrella term to describe those who transcend conventional expectations of gender identity or expression. As with any umbrella term, many different groups of people with different histories and experiences are often included within the greater transgender community—such groups include, but are certainly not limited to, people who identify as nonbinary, genderqueer, gender creative, gender diverse, and androgynous.
>
> **Q: Queer or Questioning.** "Queer" is a term used by some people to describe themselves and/or their community. Reclaimed from its earlier negative use, the term is valued by some for its defiance, by some because it can be inclusive of the entire community, and by others who find it to be an appropriate term to describe their more fluid identities. Traditionally a negative or pejorative term for people who are gay, "queer" is still sometimes disliked within the LGBTQ+ community. Due to its varying meanings, this word should be used only when self-identified. Questioning is a term used to describe those who are in a process of discovery and exploration about their sexual orientation, gender identity, gender expression, or a combination thereof.
>
> **+: Plus.** Encompasses identities such as intersex, ally, two-spirit, pansexual, asexual, and so on.

There is a comprehensive list of LGBTQ+ clinical resources, online trainings, civil rights and legal organizations, support and social organizations, and news and media websites at the end of this chapter.

Heterosexism, Heteronormativity, Homophobia, Microaggressions, Biphobia, and Transphobia—Enemies of the Supervisory Relationship

The sexual orientation of the patient, supervisee, or supervisor will enter the room unconsciously, if not consciously and openly (Sand, 2017, p. 1541).

Dynamics extremely disruptive to the supervisory relationship include heterosexism, homophobia, biphobia, and transphobia, both internal and external. Externalized versions of these phobias are an irrational hatred or negative perception of LGBTQ+ people. Internalized versions of these phobias mean that the LGBTQ+ person has negative attitudes toward the self, due to minority stress processes (Frost & Meyer, 2009). Minority stress, born from explanatory frameworks of sexual minority health risk, is a construct that looks at the social environment of minority group members, and specifically the conflictual relationship between dominant and minority values that causes intense stress (Dentato, 2012; Meyer, 1995; Mirowsky & Ross, 1989; Pearlin, 1989). Because the word "phobia" implies that this process is a phobic reaction and not an external minority stress process, alternative terms such as "internalized heterosexism" and "internalized cissexism" (prejudice or discrimination against transgender people) are favored, although still not the terminology used (Frost & Meyer, 2009). According to Mitchell (2010):

> Since the early days of feminist therapy (Rawlings & Carter, 1977), clinicians have realized that we must all look unsparingly at the ways we carry sexism and other oppressive biases, as members of our culture, class, and time. Only by becoming conscious of our attitudes, including our own homophobia = heterocentrism and transphobia, can we begin to consider how they impact our therapy with LGBT clients. However, this is delicate work. Discovering and "unpacking" these beliefs, their roots, and their potential impact requires a capacity to tolerate unwanted aspects of oneself. Exposing these attitudes in front of one's supervisor (or oneself) may feel embarrassing, even shameful; fears of disapproving judgment, or even of rejection or exclusion, may loom. (p. 13)

This process of "unpacking" is important not only for the supervisee who is working with LGBTQ+ clients but also for any supervisor offering clinical supervision. Without exploring their own issues and lack of awareness, supervisors are ill-equipped in their capacity to assist LGBTQ+ clinicians in managing the issues of identity and oppression within the therapeutic milieu (Satterly & Dyson, 2008). As Perlstein (2010) pointed out, "supervisor helps supervisee help client" (p. 85). If the supervisor has not done their own work in "unpacking" their own issues, they will not be as effective and have potential to do great harm to both their supervisees and the clients of their supervisees, LGBTQ+ or not.

Heterosexism is the belief that opposite-sex attraction is superior to LGBTQ+ attraction, while heteronormativity is the presumption that opposite-sex attraction is the norm for everyone. These terms can be related and often overlap. According to Dudley (2013), there is a tendency to assume heterosexuality in clinical supervision unless specifically defined otherwise. This is problematic for the supervisory relationship because heterosexism can be an unconscious or conscious privileging of heterosexual normativity, which may lead to incorrect pathological assumptions of LGBTQ+ people and the expression of microaggressions that serve to diminish the LGBTQ+ person (Sand, 2017). Heterosexism and heteronormativity are building blocks for homophobia, which is negative feelings or dislike for people who identify or are perceived as identifying as LGBTQ+. In music therapy research, Whitehead-Pleaux et al. (2013) discovered that only 34.8% of music therapists studied were familiar with the term "heteronormativity," indicating that this is an area of potential bias in clinical practice and supervision from lack of awareness on this topic.

Microaggressions

"Microaggressions are the brief and commonplace daily verbal, behavioral, and environmental indignities, whether intentional or unintentional, that communicate hostile, derogatory, or negative racial, gender, sexual-orientation, and religious slights and insults to the target person or group" (Sue, 2010; Sue et al., 2007, p. 5). Although originally discussed within the context of race, any marginalized group including LGBTQ+ people can experience microaggressions. The role of microaggressions is part of a larger oppressive system in place to maintain cultural imperialism (Sterzing, Gartner, Woodford, & Fisher, 2017). Commonly, the person who delivers the microaggression does not realize that they have said anything that demeans the person with whom they are communicating (Sue, 2010). Microaggressions are subtle rather than overt statements of bias or discrimination, but the impact is just as damaging for the supervisory/clinical relationship.

Microaggression themes have been identified in relation to the oppression of gender and sexual minorities and continue to validate the construct that hetero- and gender-normative cultures are superior (Sterzing, Gartner, Woodford, & Fisher, 2017). Four themes found were the assumptions of sexual abnormality or pathology, discomfort/disapproval of nonheterosexual and noncisgender experiences, assumption of a universal experience, and exoticization (Nadal et al., 2010; Sterzing, Gartner, Woodford, & Fisher, 2017).

It is critical to examine ways that you deliver microaggressions to create a solid foundation for change no matter how small or insignificant you feel the interaction was. If you are not part of a marginalized group, it is often difficult to *truly comprehend* the impact of a lifetime of microaggressions and the levels of stress that this causes. A common example of a heteronormative microaggression that LGBTQ+-identified people may have dealt with is the sentiment that "I don't have any problem with gay people at all—what they do in the privacy of their own homes is not my business" or "Gay people should tone down any physical displays of affection in public." These continual messages contribute to the minority stress process for LGBTQ+ people and the process of internalized homophobia, as they indicate that their love or affection for their partner should be hidden because it makes people uncomfortable.

An example of a microaggression toward LGBTQ+ people in music therapy supervision would be a that a female supervisee comes out to you as queer and is married to a woman and your response is: "Oh, that isn't a problem for me at all—you could love a rabbit and it wouldn't make a difference in how I treat you." Another example would be a supervisee disclosing that they are a trans woman and saying "Wow—you look amazing, I had no idea that you were not born female." The supervisor may believe that these statements show support and acceptance, but the hidden message in both of these exchanges is that there is something abnormal about the LGBTQ+ person. By comparing an LGBTQ+ person's relationship to a relationship between a human and an animal or highlighting that the trans person's sex assigned at birth is different than their gender identity does not create a foundation of support and respect. A better option for both of these scenarios is responding with "Thank you for trusting me enough to share this important information. Please let me know if there is anything I can do to support you."

Biphobia

What immediately comes to your mind if a person identifies themselves as bisexual to you? According to a 2011 Williams Institute summary, people identifying as bisexual comprise 52% of the LGB population and are also six times more likely to hide their orientation than people who identify as gay and lesbian (Gates, 2011). Biphobia, or bi-negativity, is prevalent in both the heterosexual and the LGBTQ+ communities. Negative stereotypes about bisexual people include that bisexuals are promiscuous, that bisexuals are actually gay or lesbian people in denial or are afraid to fully "come out," and that bisexuals don't actually exist (Fox, 2006; Satterly & Dyson, 2008). Mullick and Wright (2002) developed a 30-item instrument, the Biphobia Scale, to measure negative behavior, cognition, and affect toward bisexual people and bisexuality. This instrument has supported the theory that bisexual people are subject to "double discrimination" (Mullick & Wright, 2008). A supervisor looking at a person through the lens of heteronormativity often cannot understand that a person in an opposite-sex relationship can identify as bisexual. The exploration and careful dismantling of our own bi-negativity and a deeper understanding of why so many people feel they need to hide this orientation will positively impact supervisory relationships.

Transphobia

While homophobia and biphobia are minority stress issues related to sexual orientation, transphobia is focused on gender identity and can pertain to transgender (trans) individuals as well as gender-nonbinary individuals. The term "transgender," which is described in more detail in another section of this chapter, is an umbrella word that can encompass binary trans identities (male/female) as well as people who identify as gender-nonbinary, genderqueer, gender-fluid, transmasculine, and so on. Transgender people, like bisexual people, often are subjected to discrimination from both the heterosexual and the LGBTQ+ communities (Alexander & Yescavage, 2003; Satterly & Dyson, 2008). At the time this chapter was being written, there had been very little published on the supervision of trans-identified supervisees. Related to counseling transgender clients, Burnes et al. (2010) pointed out the importance of acknowledging that transgender people have been historically marginalized and pathologized by the medical and psychological communities. The authors recommend reviewing the 2010 document titled "American Counseling Association Competencies for Counseling with Transgender Clients" listed in the reference section to familiarize yourself with these competencies, which can be translatable and adaptable to the supervision of transgender supervisees.

ASSESSMENT TOOLS

Supervision and self-assessment are critical in the process of developing competence with LGBTQ+ people and increasing awareness of a therapist's own values and biases (ALGBTIC LGBQQIA Competencies Task Force, 2013; Dillon et al., 2004; Moe, Perera-Diltz, & Sepulveda, 2017). The development of a therapeutic self, a person who has access within themselves to personal capacities that they use in addition to empathy and understanding to work toward therapeutic change, is part of the supervision process (Mitchell, 2010).

As music therapy supervisors working with and for the LGBTQ+ community, ethical requirements motivate us to work toward increasing our self-awareness, education, training, and direct practice. Part of the self-awareness process is introspectively assessing our own personal beliefs related to LGBTQ+ issues. This assessment includes asking questions about the earliest messages we received about LGBTQ+ people, where those messages came from, whether those messages were positive or negative, and whether we still find them to be true. Understanding the first messages we received can help us to identify our own beliefs and biases, which we can then challenge. The authors recommend that all music therapy supervisors engage in this assessment process in order to work beyond any personal biases that can be disruptive and harmful to the supervisory relationship.

In 2004, Long and Lindsey developed the Sexual Orientation Matrix for Supervision (SOMS) in order to assist supervisors in preparing supervisees to work with lesbian, gay, and bisexual clients. This tool was expanded in 2006 to include sexual identities, sexual orientations, and gender identities

(Long & Bonomo, 2006). The development of the SOMS was based on two core issues: the degree of heterosexual bias and the degree of acceptance of LGBTQ+ orientations and behavior. The matrix can be used to explore their own and their supervisees' levels of knowledge, comfort, and experience in working with LGBTQ+ clients including same-sex couples (Long & Lindsay, 2004).

Long and Lindsay (2004) found that pseudo-accepting attitudes are problematic in the supervisory relationship because it is inherently dismissive of a person's sexual or gender orientation and minimizes the minority stress faced by LGBTQ+ people. Examples of a pseudo-accepting attitude would be "I can provide therapy/supervision for LGBTQ+ people as long as it is not the focus of our work" and statements such as "You're not a lesbian to me, you are a person" (Long & Lindsay, 2004, p. 25).

A validated and reliable resource specific to LGB awareness, knowledge, and skills (not Transgender) is the Sexual Orientation Counselor Competency Scale (SOCCS) (Bidell, 2005). The SOCCS contains 29 items split into three sections—attitudes, knowledge, and skill—that are rated on a 1–7 Likert scale (1 = not at all true, 7 = totally true). The SOCCS was developed for mental health practitioners and trainees and has been used extensively among counseling and psychology trainees, practitioners, supervisors, and educators (Bidell, 2015, p. 3). The scale and scoring information can be downloaded at https://www.mededportal.org/publication/10040/.

The authors recommend utilizing this scale as a means to explore your LGB awareness, attitudes, and skill levels as a starting point for "unpacking" and self-exploration. Honest reflection is the starting point for this work. Without it, you are not giving yourself an accurate picture of the issues at hand. Be mindful to answer the questions honestly and not how you think you would be answering them if another professional or client were going to read it.

Another resource for self-assessment is "Check Yourself: Understanding Your Own Beliefs," which is contained in the Gay, Lesbian, and Straight Education Network (GLSEN) Safe Space Kit available free online in PDF form at https://www.glsen.org/safespace. Although the Safe Space Kit is designed for educators supporting LGBTQ+ youth in schools, it is full of applicable information for all music therapy supervisors. As GLSEN (2016) detailed:

> All of us, LGBT and non-LGBT, have learned messages about LGBT people. What were the earliest messages you received about LGBT people, and where did they come from? Were they positive, negative, or neutral? Understanding the messages that we receive can help us to identify our own beliefs and biases that we can then challenge, helping to make us stronger allies. (p. 7)

Only when you uncover your own biases can you begin to honestly look at them and how they affect your work. Some questions included are: How would you feel if your child came out to you as LGBT? If you do not identify as LGBT, how would you feel if people thought you were LGBT? (GLSEN, 2016, p. 7). The authors strongly recommend attending an LGBTQ+ ally training and seeking training on ally development as a step toward competency as supervisors.

SUPERVISING MUSIC THERAPY SUPERVISEES WHO IDENTIFY AS TRANSGENDER OR GENDER-NONBINARY

According to the statistics cited in a Williams Institute article in June 2016, there are approximately 0.6% adult Americans who identify as transgender, which is estimated to be 1.4 million Americans (Flores et al., 2016). This is an increase from data that was taken five years before, which estimated that 0.3% of adults in United States identified as transgender. In tandem with the increase in numbers in the general American population, there is a growing community of transgender and gender-nonbinary music therapists and music therapy students in America.

This section addresses language, terms, and information specific to transgender and gender-nonbinary people. The authors wish to acknowledge that this is far from a comprehensive list of best practices or competencies and more a starting point, with hope that readers continue to educate themselves on transgender and nonbinary culture, issues, terms, and resources and affirming, strength-based approaches.

Language and Terms

Language is alive and continuously changing and evolving. Depending on your current knowledge, the words defined in this section might be familiar words you know or present new vocabulary and understanding for you. In the LGBTQ+ culture, and particularly in the transgender and gender-nonbinary communities and culture, language is still evolving. Terms and definitions can vary from person to person, in different communities and cultures, and with age groups. It is important to stay informed and up-to-date with terms and definitions and their significance. As music therapists, we should understand how moving, powerful, and emotionally charged words can be. We observe not only how words can affect us in wounding and painful ways, but also how words can be used to affirm and empower as well. When thinking about language, it's important to clearly understand the words unique to transgender and gender-nonbinary issues.

Gender vs. Biological Sex

It is often presumed that gender is interchangeable with biological sex, but gender is a multidimensional social construct that is different from biological sex. As explained by GenderSpectrum.org (n.d.) …

> While our gender may begin with the assignment of our sex, it doesn't end there. A person's gender is the complex interrelationship between three dimensions: body—our body, our experience of our own body, how society genders bodies, and how others interact with us based on our body; identity—our deeply held, internal sense of self as male, female, a blend of both, or neither, or who we internally know ourselves to be; and expression—how we present our gender in the world and how society, culture, community, and family perceive, interact with, and try to shape our gender. Gender expression is also related to gender roles and how society uses those roles to try to enforce conformity to current gender norms.

Biological sex includes physical attributes such as external genitalia, sex chromosomes, gonads, sex hormones, and internal reproductive structures (GenderSpectrum.org, n.d.). These reproductive and sexual anatomies are used to assign a sex as male or female at birth. Many people will be born and grow up to feel their gender aligns with their biological sex; however, some people will not. Transgender and gender-nonbinary people grow up with their gender not matching their assigned sex.

In the naturally occurring case of intersex, genitalia and sex chromosomes do not fit the typical definition of male or female. According to the United States affiliate of the organization Intersex International, intersex people make up roughly 1.7% of our population (Intersex Campaign for Equality, 2017). This is about as common has having red hair. Often in America, medically unnecessary sex assignment surgery is performed on infants and minors in order to align their sex characteristics to a gender-binary system.

Gender is the complex interrelationship between an individual's biological sex; one's internal sense of self as male, female, both, or neither (gender identity); and one's outward presentations, appearance, mannerisms, and behaviors (gender expression) related to that perception, including their gender role. Gender roles are socially constructed mannerisms, activities, and behaviors a society considers to be appropriate for men and women (American Psychological Association, 2017). Together, the intersection of these three dimensions produces one's authentic sense of gender, both in how people experience their own gender and in how others perceive it. Gender is independent of one's sexual orientation. Sexual orientation is about attraction, or to whom we are physically, emotionally, and romantically drawn.

The Gender Spectrum

The gender spectrum is a nonbinary approach to thinking about gender. From a binary perspective, there two genders, male and female. From a gender spectrum perspective, there are many genders on a continuum. This allows for inclusion of other and all genders, including intersex, nonbinary, gender-nonconforming, transgender, two-spirit, and others (GenderSpectrum.org, n.d.). Many people identify their gender with the biological sex that they were assigned at birth, which is called being cisgender. A transgender person has a gender identity that does not match their assigned biological sex. Transgender people may identify as male, female, or elsewhere on the gender spectrum. Transgender is an umbrella term that can include nonbinary, genderqueer, gender-nonconforming, gender-fluid, agender, bigender, pangender, and third gender.

There is no one-way to be transgender. Some transgender people seek to bring their body in alignment with their gender while others do not. Transitioning is the active process of changing one's external gender expression and aligning one's body and appearance with one's internal gender identity. This can include choices in clothing, hairstyles, accessories, and outward appearances. Some transgender people chose medical treatments such as hormone replacement therapy and/or gender affirmation surgeries. What transitioning means for each person is unique to that person. Not all transgender people transition the same way, and not all transgender people transition. Transitioning is a process and can take months to years, and each transition is a journey unique to the person in it. For some people who identify outside of the gender-binary (genderqueer, gender-nonbinary, gender-fluid), transitioning can be a lifelong process of defining and redefining their gender and may not have a set ending point.

Pronouns

In many languages, pronouns are used to identify and gender people. Most pronouns are binary in gender—he/him/his and she/her/hers. To become aware of how often pronouns are used in casual conversation, try having a five-minute pronoun-free conversation with a friend. It can be eye-opening to become aware of how often we use binary pronouns. Imagine that your gender identity did not match the pronouns being used to refer to you. Consider how it might feel to be misgendered. It is important to learn and respect the pronouns someone uses or prefers vs. just assuming. With pronouns and other identity terms, trust and respect the person using the term and their definition or description of it over all other resources.

Frequently Asked Questions About Pronouns

Q: How do I ask someone what pronouns they use?
A: Try asking, "What pronouns do you use?" or "Can you remind me what pronouns you use?" It can feel awkward at first, but it is not half as awkward as making a hurtful assumption (University of Wisconsin–Milwaukee—Lesbian Gay Bisexual Transgender Resource Center, 2017).

Q: What are the most commonly used pronouns, including gender-neutral ones?
A: Binary pronouns—she/her/hers/herself, he/him/his/himself. gender-neutral pronouns—they/them/theirs/themselves, ze/hir/hirs/hirself, ze/zir/zirs/zirself, xe/xem/xyr/xemself (Gender Neutral Pronoun Blog, 2010).

Q: How can I incorporate more gender-neutral language to be more inclusive when speaking to a group of people?
A: Instead of "ladies" and "gentlemen," "boys" and "girls," use "folks," "friends," "everyone," or "everybody." Instead of "wife" or "husband," use "spouse" or "partner." Instead of "sister" or "brother," use "sibling." Instead of "mother" or "father," use "parent."

Q: What are some ways to create inclusivity in my practice regarding pronouns?
A: Come from a respectful and affirming place when asking, learning, and using pronouns or other identifying language. State your name and pronouns first before asking others. Create and use forms/intake documents that include inclusive language when asking about gender and pronouns. Honor and use the person's name, pronouns and, other identifying language and hold other team and staff members accountable for the same. Use the least restrictive and assuming language if you are not informed (e.g., use the person's name or "they," as opposed to an assumed pronoun in cases where the pronoun is unknown).

Environment, Policies, and Resources

The safety and inclusivity of the environment that houses the supervision is also an important question to consider when supervising transgender or gender-nonbinary supervisees. Frequently asked questions about how to create an inclusive and safe environment for transgender and gender-nonbinary people include:

Q: What are the most inclusive bathrooms?
A: Gender-neutral bathrooms are the most inclusive bathrooms. These bathrooms are for everyone.

Q: What policies should my workplace have in place to protect the rights of transgender and nonbinary people?
A: Nondiscrimination policies that include prohibiting discrimination on the basis of gender identity and gender expression.

Q: What can I do in my workspace to show I am an ally for transgender and nonbinary people?
A: One of ways to quickly show you are an ally and safe person is to visibly display Safe Space stickers, posters, or flyers in your workspace and/or on your badge or outfit. However, make sure you have done the work and feel prepared, trained, and educated to effectively be an ally or safe person if you are going to display these signs.

Q: How can I make my forms more inclusive of transgender and nonbinary people?
A: Offer a fill-in-the-blank option for gender vs. checking a box with only male or female as an option. Provide an area for writing in pronouns.

Q: What transgender- and nonbinary-affirming resources should I have readily available?
A: Affirming and supportive resources for transgender and nonbinary people can include but are not limited to local and national LGBTQ+ transgender and gender nonbinary websites;

local brochures and flyers, which often include social group events as well as support groups; and lists of LGBTQ+-identified therapists and supervisors. See our references at the end of this chapter.

CONFLICTING RELIGIOUS/PERSONAL BELIEFS

One person's religious freedom ends where another person's discrimination begins (Dessel, Jacobsen, Levy, McCarty-Caplan, Lewis, & Kaplan, 2017, p. 16).

Religion is a deeply personal cultural experience that shapes not only the belief system of an individual, but often also the belief system of a community. Religious beliefs are often cited as the point for discrimination directed at LGBTQ+ people and may be an incredibly sensitive topic for some supervisors and supervisees to address. Although this section of the chapter could be an entire book unto itself, the authors would like to highlight some of the issues and a process for working with identified conflicts.

In the counseling literature, evidence has emerged that counselors' higher frequency of church attendance, political conservatism, heterosexist, and rigid and authoritarian orientations of religious identity exhibit more negative attitudes and prejudice toward LGBTQ+ people (Balkin et al., 2009; Bidell, 2014; Farmer, 2017; Rainey & Trusty, 2007; Sanbria, 2012; Satcher & Schumacker, 2009). On the opposite side of the spectrum, spirituality has been connected to empathy and compassion for others (Farmer, 2017; Morrison & Borgen, 2010; Saslow et al., 2013). Farmer (2017) found that while counselor religiosity had a negative relationship with LGB-affirmative counselor competence, counselor spirituality had a positive one. In this chapter, we are addressing organized religion(s) because spirituality is a human process and motivation that may exist apart from religion (Farmer, 2017; Pargamet, 2013).

Several authors have suggested that the supervisory relationship will be mirrored in the relationship between future therapist and client (Burkhard et al., 2009; Kaiser, 1992; Perry, 1998; Murphy, Rawlings, & Howe, 2002). An intolerance of differences, including those based in religious beliefs held by supervisors who condemn LGBTQ+ culture and identity, may result not only in poor supervision (Magnuson, Wilcoxon, & Norem, 2000) but also in discriminatory practices toward LGBTQ+ students (Burkward et al., 2009). For example, one participant in the Burkward et al. (2009) study reported that they were "treated differently than other practicum students because [one individual's] ultraconservative religious values would not allow her to be affirming" (p. 12).

Dessel, Bolen, and Shepardson (2011) examined the complex dynamic between respect for religious belief systems that condemn LGBTQ+ identities and practices and professional standards that advocate for affirming practices in supervision and education. The authors challenged the often-accepted practice of "referring out" clients and supervisees with conflicting beliefs, suggesting that this further marginalized the individual. Instead, the authors advocated for the development of and adherence to ethical best practices for LGBTQ+ clients and students. Cole and Harris (2017) pointed out that helping professionals have historically worked with clients who have different values/views about drinking alcohol and sex outside of marriage. They pose the question, "What would keep practitioners from applying those same skills for managing work with clients who have different value positions and cultural experiences?" (Cole & Harris, 2017, p. 49).

In recent years, there has been more attention paid to the legal aspects of First Amendment rights involved in counseling graduate students, related to remediation requirements placed by schools surrounding LGBTQ+ competency. Courts often support the counseling educator's considerable authority to place limitations on student speech in curricular/instructional settings and often defer to colleges and universities when reviewing academic decisions. At the same time, they recognize that First Amendment rights do intersect with these decisions in a public university setting

(Hutchens, Block, & Young, 2013). As Hancock (2014) pointed out in her article looking at recent court cases in this vein, "Student Beliefs, Multiculturalism, and Client Welfare" …

> Professions and the institutions that educate and train professionals cannot afford to fashion their ethics and curriculum around the individual personal beliefs of professionals or students in the profession. … Certainly, personal beliefs can and do inform the lives of practitioners; however, they cannot trump the ethical principles and standards of the profession—not when serving the welfare of the client. Educational and training institutions must not be taken to task for upholding these principles and standards. They must not be penalized for helping students acquire the knowledge, attitudes, and skills needed to provide multiculturally competent mental health services. (p. 8)

Music therapists providing clinical supervision for students and colleagues should be familiar with and support the codes of ethics of our professional organizations. An international organization representing music therapy associations and individuals throughout the world, the World Federation of Music Therapy (WFMT) includes within its core values (2018) an inclusivity statement supportive of sexual orientation and gender identity. The American Music Therapy Association (AMTA) provides ethical guidance for its members who work with the LGBTQ+ community through its Code of Ethics (2018) and Standards of Clinical Practice (2013). Regarding sexual orientation, gender identity, and gender expression, the AMTA's code of ethics is similar in nature to those in other related fields such as counseling, social work, and art and drama therapy. The language is clear: It is not ethical to discriminate.

A major concern for LGBTQ+ people at the time of this writing is the current political climate. In 30 states, Religious Freedom Restoration Act bills have been proposed to place religious-based exemptions in every state law (HRC, 2017). These bills are targeted at individuals and businesses that deny services to LGBTQ+ people under the guise of religious freedom (NASW, 2016). Related national organizations such as the American Counseling Association (ACA, 2017), the National Organization of Social Workers (NASW), and the American Psychiatric Association (APA) (NASW, 2016) have created strong position statements against these bills. In 2016, in view of the initial passage of SB1556/HB1840 in Tennessee, "which is a discriminatory law that clearly targets the LGBTQ community" (para. 1), the American Counseling Association (ACA) relocated its 2017 Conference & Expo from Nashville, TN, to San Francisco, CA (ACA, May 10, 2016). As 2016 ACA president Richard Yep reported:

> This law directly targets the counseling profession, would deny services to those most in need, and constitutes a dilemma for ACA members because it allows for violation of ACA's Code of Ethics. By relocating from Tennessee, ACA is standing up to this discriminatory law, and we remain committed in the battle to ensure that this law does not become the national standard. (ACA, June 13, 2016, para. 4)

With these complex religious, legal, and political issues influencing practice, it is incredibly important for music therapists to address their own value-based conflicts within the therapeutic or supervisory relationship to provide ethical services.

To address value-based conflicts within the counseling or supervisory relationship, Kocet and Herlihy (2014) proposed a process, derived from qualitative research procedures, called ethical bracketing (EB).

Ethical bracketing is defined as the intentional separating of a counselor's personal values from his or her professional values or the intentional setting aside of the counselor's personal values in order to provide ethical and appropriate counseling to all clients, especially those whose worldviews, values, belief systems, and decisions differ significantly from those of the counselor. (Kocet & Herlihy, 2014, p. 182)

Although this process can be applicable to many value-based conflicts, the authors believe that this is a crucial process in which to engage if you have conflicting religious/personal beliefs related to LGBTQ+ people/issues. The steps in the ethical bracketing process are immersion, education, consultation, supervision, and personal counseling. Two of the steps, immersion and education, can be done on an individual basis through some of the tools and references included in this chapter. The other three need to be a collaborative effort on the music therapist's part. Ensuring that you are seeking consultation/supervision and/or personal counseling with someone or a group that has done extensive self-immersion and training on LGBTQ+ topics is paramount to the process.

At the time of this writing, there are several faith-based organizations that directly address LGBTQ+ issues within a religious framework to increase acceptance and inclusion, which may be a helpful resource for supervisor or supervisee. Some of these organizations are Affirm United, Affirmation LGBTQ Mormons Families & Friends, Affirmation United Methodist, Association of Welcoming & Affirming Baptists, Believe Out Loud (Welcoming Christian-based churches across the country), Brethren Mennonite Council for LGBT Interests, Church Within a Church Movement (Methodist), Covenant Network of Presbyterians, Dignity USA (Catholic), Queer Asian Spirit, Seventh-Day Adventist Kinship International, The Evangelical Network (TEN), The Gay and Lesbian Vaishnava Association (Hindu), The World Congress: Keshet Ga'avah (Jewish), UCC LBTQ Ministries, Muslims for Progressive Values, Reconciling Works, Room for All, Unitarian Universalist Association LGBTQ Ministries, and Welcoming Community Network.

It is important to note that there are some religious organizations that outwardly appear welcoming and accepting to LGBTQ+ people at first glance but actually ascribe to overt or covert conversion (sometimes called "reparative") therapies/thought processes. Reparative/conversion therapies, which are detrimental to the health and well-being of LGBTQ+ people, despite being strictly prohibited and admonished by all major medical and psychological organizations, are still commonplace in certain religious counseling contexts (Whitehead-Pleaux et al., 2012). Please use caution and scrutinize any potential religious/LGBTQ+ website for potential harm.

SPECIFIC CONSIDERATIONS FOR SUPERVISION OF LGBTQ+ SUPERVISEES

Models of LGBTQ+ affirmative supervision include Halpert, Reinhardt, and Toohey's (2007) Integrative Affirmative Supervision (IAS), Singh and Chun's (2010) Queer People of Color (QPOC) Resilience-Based Model of Supervision, and Pett's (2000) Gay-Affirmative Model of Supervision. The cornerstone of all of the LGBTQ+ affirmative approaches to supervision is the belief that "all gender identities and sexual orientations are equally valid" (Halpert, Reinhardt, & Toohey, 2007, p. 341). Singh and Chun (2010) highlighted the importance of exploring intersecting identities related to being both queer (nonheterosexual) and people of color and propose that supervisor development is an essential component in supervision. In this model, resilience is the cornerstone of six domains: supervisor-focused personal development, supervisee-focused personal development, conceptualization, skills, process, and outcome (Singh & Chun, 2010, p. 40).

Chui, McGann, Ziemer, Hoffman, and Stahl (2018) noted that heterosexual and nonheterosexual supervisees could have different supervision needs when working with LGBTQ+ clients due to caveats of guilt/shame of the privileged group (heterosexual) or overidentification of the marginalized group (nonheterosexual). The researchers also noted that disclosure of the supervisor's sexual identity may actually not be necessary in LGBTQ+ affirmative supervision, but that exploration of countertransference is critical (Chui, McGann, Ziemer, Hoffman, & Stahl, 2018).

Although there has not been any research on this topic specifically related to LGBTQ+ music therapy supervisees and their experiences of fieldwork, internship, and professional supervision, there are several indicators from which to draw in social work and counseling literature. Messinger (2004) described 11 categories of sexual orientation–related issues defined by LGBTQ+ supervisees, grouped into three different system levels: individual, interpersonal, and institutional. The individual level includes the managing of disclosure of sexual orientation, identity development concerns, pressures in hiding one's sexual orientation, professionalism as a gay or lesbian person, and general feelings of lack of safety or anxiety. The interpersonal and institutional levels include (many are similar): homophobic and heterosexist behaviors and attitudes, unfriendly climate of placement, conflicts in intimate relationships, conflicts with field instructors, absence of gay and lesbian topics, and general feelings of lack of safety or anxiety (Messinger, 2004, 2007). Music therapy supervisors should be aware of these issues and check in with their LGBTQ+-identified supervisees to offer support and available resources.

Messinger also described supports and resources desired by LGBTQ+ supervisees as being faculty support and mentoring, supportive field education staff, LGBTQ+ professionals as mentors, educated field instructors, out LGBTQ+ agency staff, educated and supportive heterosexual coworkers, resource information for LGBTQ+ students, information about sexual orientation issues in placement, list of LGBTQ+ friendly agencies, and resources for LGBTQ+ clients (2004). Positive affirmation and carefully connecting LGBTQ+ music therapy supervisees with any or all of the resources above have the potential to make a profound impact on their professional development. Messinger highlighted that "silencing LGB students about their sexual orientation and sexual orientation–related experiences out of some professional notion of sexuality as 'private' clearly limits field instructors' understanding of and discussions about their students' experiences, and thus inhibits the students' learning" (2007, p. 219).

In their research with graduate-level human service professionals, Satterly and Dyson (2008) identified the following needs for sexual minority clinical trainees: to work through identity issues related to their role as a sexual minority clinical professional; to develop skills for navigating disclosure to clients, colleagues, and supervisors; to have sexual minority–specific experiences within their programs where they can develop and explore free from the phobias and "-isms" listed above"; and to have supportive sexual minority professional mentors. One way to meet these needs is through the offering of LGBTQ+ supervision groups facilitated by LGBTQ+-identified professionals (Satterly & Dyson, 2008).

ETHICAL CONSIDERATIONS

The AMTA Standards of Clinical Practice (2013) address LGBTQ+ individuals in relation to culturally competent assessment practices and require the process to include the exploration of the client's culture. In recent developments, mental health professions have benefited from expert, intellectual, clinical writing about gay men and lesbians and, to a reduced but noteworthy degree, about bisexual and transgender people and their culture (Mitchell, 2010). However, Bain, Grzanka, and Crowe (2016) noted that the documentation of music therapy with LGBTQ+ populations within community settings is sparse. Despite the limited amount of music therapy literature addressing work with and for the LGBTQ+ community, there are strides being made toward LGBTQ+-inclusive music therapy practices.

While the AMTA Standards of Clinical Practice do not specifically define best practices for working with LGBTQ+ individuals, Whitehead-Pleaux et al. (2012) identified "Best Practices" when working with and for LGBTQ+ community members in the work environment, recommending that "the music therapist [supervisor] will … be open and affirming to LGBTQ+ [individuals] … react respectfully when a coworker [supervisee] discloses her/his gender and/or sexual identity … [and] create a safe space for all" (p. 161). Creating such a space would require the intentional use of nondiscriminatory language, the integration of LGBTQ+ issues into the learning process, and the opportunity for open, ongoing communication between supervisor and supervisee.

With the goal of providing inclusive thoughtful, and comprehensive care, there are numerous ethical considerations in working with and for the LGBTQ+ community. Some of these are …

- There are many LGBTQ+ stereotypes and myths that are inaccurately supported by the popular culture. Television shows, movies, magazines, and books, to name a few, promote these dishonest portrayals.
- There is great diversity within the LGBTQ+ culture. LGBTQ+ people span all ages, races, ethnicities, classes, genders, gender identities, religions, and abilities.
- Older adult LGBTQ+-identified people are driven or often choose to go back into hiding their sexual orientation. Due to a vulnerable status in their health, some individuals become fearful that their caretakers will not be sensitive to or accepting of their LGBTQ+ identification and practices.
- Homelessness in LGBTQ+ youth is significantly higher vs. in the general youth population. Statistics indicate that 20% to 40% of homeless youth are LGBTQ+-identified vs. 10% of the general population (Quintana, Rosenthal, & Krehely, 2010).
- Job termination and the ability to be hired are concerns for the LGBTQ+ community. At the time of this writing, there are many states with no job protection policies for the LGBTQ+ community.
- Persons in the LGBTQ+ community face a high incidence of hate crimes and police violence. In 2016, FBI data showed that there was an increase of reported incidents of anti-LGBTQ+ hate crimes, with a combined (sexual orientation and gender identity) increase of 11% (HRC.org, 2017).
- LGB youth are five times more likely to have attempted suicide and three times more likely to contemplate suicide than heterosexual youth (CDC, 2016).
- LGBTQ+ individuals are subjected to abusive practices such as conversion/reparative therapy. At the time of this writing, there are a handful of states that have laws preventing this practice with minors. Additionally, there are concerted efforts being made by the Human Rights Campaign (2016) to have similar laws passed in all states.

Ethically Addressing Discrimination

Knowing that the AMTA Code of Ethics (2018) requires MTs to protect the individual's (including music therapy students and clients) right to dignity and respect, the music therapy supervisor has the responsibility of understanding that anti-LGBTQ+ bias is pervasive. It is witnessed in a variety of ways through heterosexism, heteronormativity, microaggressions, biphobia, and transphobia. A few specific examples include exposure to anti-LGBTQ+ jokes, the exclusion of LGBTQ+-related themes in curricula, and anti-LGBTQ+ name-calling. Music therapy supervisors can model nondiscrimination practices in the workplace by educating staff/colleagues on the fact that these practices are harmful, hurtful, and discriminatory. They can recommend and help to provide LGBTQ+ inclusivity practices. The authors recognize that some issues related to facility-specific policies may hinder the level of action taken (having client moved to another unit, etc.) but suggest that the music therapist advocate for policy changes to support institutional inclusivity. Below are specific, real-life examples of music therapy scenarios of LGBTQ+ discrimination:

- Anti-LGBTQ+ joke scenario: A music therapy supervisor, along with a music therapy intern, were in the staff office of an outpatient behavioral health program and overheard one staff member say to another, "Hey, you aren't Cindy. Where did Cindy go? She was just sitting in that chair a minute ago?" The staff member sitting in the chair laughed and stated, "Do I look like a female to you? Do I look like I went and changed my sex? What is wrong with you? Can't you see I'm a man? I am not Cindy!" The music therapy supervisor intervened and said to the staff member sitting in the chair, "It would be absolutely fine if you did come out as transgender or genderqueer or gender-fluid. That would be acceptable, and I would support you and would educate others to support you, too." This led to a lengthy conversation with the staff members in the office about inclusivity and what it means to professionally, authentically, and ethically support LGBTQ+ colleagues, students, and clients. While the music therapy supervisor could have walked away shaking their head and yet fuming inside about the anti-LGBTQ+ remark, they took the opportunity to address the discriminatory remarks and educate the staff about the importance of LGBTQ+ inclusivity. The worst-case scenario would be a music therapy supervisor who laughed with the staff and thereby marginalizing any LGBTQ+-identified staff and/or students in the room.

- Exclusion of LGBTQ+ curricula in a music therapy setting: A self-identified LGBTQ+ music therapy intern brought in a set of songs for the clients to hear and discuss around the topic of self-esteem and self-expression. One of the selections was a well-known song with self-empowerment lyrics for minorities, including the LGBTQ+ community. The music therapy supervisor reviewed the session plan and then said to the music therapy intern, "I don't think it is a good idea for you to include this particular song in the play list. It is too controversial, and the clients might get upset by it." The music therapy intern felt defeated both personally and professionally as the music therapy supervisor diminished the importance of positive expressions for the LGBTQ+ community. Believing they were in a position of vulnerability, the music therapy intern did not say anything to the music therapy supervisor about these insensitive, discriminatory remarks. A best-case scenario would be for a music therapy supervisor who was actively working on LGBTQ+ culture competence and nondiscriminatory practices to support the inclusion of the song, inviting the music therapy intern into a discussion about LGBTQ+ inclusivity and offering support and guidelines for navigating a productive discussion during group sessions.

- Anti-LGBTQ+ name-calling scenario: The music therapy supervisor and music therapy intern were leading a music therapy group session with a song sung by a band with a well-known LGBTQ+-identified member. One of the clients started loudly talking about the musician/singer in a derogatory, bigoted manner stating, "Well, he sure was a great singer for being such a fruit loop!" Several of the clients started to laugh, and one of the clients looked visibly upset. As the music therapy supervisor approached the client to address the comment, the client looked at the music therapy supervisor and said, "What? I can't help it if he was a fruity tooty. It's the truth!" The music therapy supervisor spoke calmly to the client and group, letting them know that their words were not acceptable. The supervisor then explained that although they may have grown up hearing those words, the words were harmful and would not be tolerated, and then referred back to the ground rules of respect, safety, and empathy that were identified at the beginning of the group. Furthermore, the music therapy supervisor checked in with the visibly upset client after the session. The client was upset and scared and told the music therapy supervisor, "I don't feel safe on this unit. That person has said too many things that make me feel like I am not safe here." The music therapy supervisor spoke with the administrative staff about the concerns, and the distraught, fearful client was moved to another unit where they felt safe and secure to move forward with treatment. A music therapy supervisor not following the ethical guidelines for nondiscrimination against the LGBTQ+ community could have ignored the entire situation and done nothing. The worst-case response would have been a music therapy supervisor who laughed with the other clients.

CONCLUSION

Unless we can think and talk openly about our different backgrounds and experiences within a multiethnic, mixed racial, global frame, then white, Eurocentric, middle-class, heterosexual assumptions and stereotypes will continue within supervision settings where we practice. (Dudley, 2013, p. 492)

It is our hope that this chapter has provided readers with useful information and considerations related to sexual orientation, gender identity, and supervision. Beginning at a place of honest introspection is the first step in providing quality supervision to LGBTQ+ supervisees and their clients. Using the assessment tools suggested in our chapter can help the supervisor to gain awareness of their LGBTQ+ knowledge, attitudes, and beliefs. Learning and understanding terms connected to the LGBTQ+ culture, understanding the gender spectrum and gender expression, as well as assessment of the environment, forms, and policies for creating a safe space, are all pieces of this puzzle.

A vital step toward ethical practices with and for the LGBTQ+ community is for music therapy supervisors to make a concerted effort toward deconstructing and evaluating how their personal values and beliefs will inevitably influence their music therapy practice. Reaching beyond competence toward comprehensive LGBTQ+ inclusivity is the ultimate goal for ethically relevant and meaningful music therapy supervision practices. Through ongoing, high-quality LGBTQ+ education and training, music therapy supervisors can provide much needed support and advocacy with and for the LGBTQ+ community.

REFERENCE LIST

Alexander, J., & Yescavage, K. (2003). Bisexuality and transgenderism: InterSEX-ions of the others. *Journal of Bisexuality, 3*(3–4), 1–23.

ALGBTIC LGBQQIA Competencies Task Force. (2013). Association for lesbian, gay, bisexual, and transgender issues in counseling competencies for counseling with lesbian, gay, bisexual, queer, questioning, intersex, and ally individuals. *Journal of LGBT in Counseling, 7*(1), 2–43. doi:10.1080/15538605.2013.755444

Allen, G. J., Szollos, S. J., & Williams, B. E. (1986). Doctoral students' comparative evaluations of best and worst psychotherapy supervision. *Professional Psychology Research and Practice, 17*(2), 91–99.

American Counseling Association. (2016, May 10). *The American Counseling Association will not hold its annual conference and expo in Tennessee.* Retrieved from https://www.counseling.org/news/updates/2016/05/10/the-american-counseling-association-will-not-hold-its-annual-conference-expo-in-tennessee

American Counseling Association. (2016, June 13). *ACA 2017 Conference and expo will be held in San Francisco.* Retrieved from https://www.counseling.org/news/news-release-archives/by-year/2016/2016/06/13/aca-2017-conference-expo-will-be-held-in-san-francisco

American Music Therapy Association. (2014). *Code of ethics.* Retrieved from https://www.musictherapy.org/about/ethics/

American Music Therapy Association. (2013). *AMTA standards of clinical practice.* Retrieved from https://www.musictherapy.org/about/standards/

American Psychological Association. (2017). *Transgender people, gender identity, and gender expression.* Retrieved from http://www.apa.org/topics/lgbt/transgender.aspx

Bain, C., Grzanka, P. R., & Crowe, B. J., (2016). Toward a queer music therapy: The implications of queer theory for radically inclusive music therapy. *The Arts in Psychotherapy, 50,* 22–33.

Balkin, R. S., Schlosser, L. Z., & Levi , D. H. (2009). Religious identity and cultural diversity: Exploring the relationships between religious identity, sexism, homophobia, and multicultural competence. *Journal of Counseling & Development, 87,* 420–427. doi:10.1002/j.1556-6678.2009.tb00126.x

Betancourt, R. J., Green, A. R., & Ananeth-Firempong II, O. (2003). Defining cultural competence: A practical framework for addressing racial/ethnic disparities in health and health-care. *Public Health Reports, 118,* 293–302.

Bidell, M. (2015). *Using the Sexual Orientation Counselor Competency Scale (SOCCS) in Mental Health and Healthcare Settings: An Instructor's Guide.* MedEdPORTAL Publications.

Bidell, M. P. (2005). The sexual orientation counselor competency scale: Assessing attitudes, skills, and knowledge of counselors working with lesbian, gay, and bisexual clients. *Counselor Education and Supervision, 44,* 267–279.

Bidell, M. P. (2014). Personal and professional discord: Examining religious conservatism and lesbian-, gay-, and bisexual-affirmative counselor competence. *Journal of Counseling & Development, 92,* 170–179. doi:10.1002/j.1556-6676.2014.00145

Burkard, A. W., Knox, S., Hess, S. A., & Schultz, J. (2009). Lesbian, gay, and bisexual supervisees' experiences of LGB-affirmative and nonaffirmative supervision. *Journal of Counseling Psychology, 56*(1), 176–188.

Burnes, T. R., Singh, A. A., Harper, A. J., Harper, B., Maxon-Kann, W., Pickering, D. L., & Hosea, J. (2010). American counseling association competencies for counseling with transgender clients. *Journal of LGBT Issues in Counseling, 4*(3–4), 135–159.

CDC. (2016). *Sexual Identity, Sex of Sexual Contacts, and Health-Risk Behaviors Among Students in Grades 9–12: Youth Risk Behavior Surveillance.* Atlanta, GA: U.S. Department of Health and Human Services.

Chui, H., McGann, K. J., Ziemer, K. S., Hoffman, M. A., & Stahl, J. (2018). Trainees' use of supervision for therapy with sexual minority clients: A qualitative study. *Journal of Counseling Psychology, 65*(1), 36–50. doi:10.1037/cou0000232

Cole, C., & Harris, H. W. (2017). The lived experiences of people who identify as LGBT Christians: Considerations for social work helping. *Social Work & Christianity, 44*(1/2), 11.

Collins, P. H. (2000). *Black feminist thought: Knowledge, consciousness, and the politics of empowerment* (2nd ed.). New York, NY, & London, UK: Routledge.

Craig, S. L., Dentato, M. P., Messinger, L., & McInroy, L. B. (2016). Educational determinants of readiness to practice with LGBTQ clients: Social work students speak out. *British Journal of Social Work, 46,* 115–134.

Crenshaw, K. W. (1995). Mapping the margins: Intersectionality, identity politics, and violence against women of color. In K. Crenshaw, N. Gotanda, G. Peller, & K. Thomas (Eds.), *Critical race theory: The key writings that formed the movement* (pp. 357–383). New York, NY: New Press.

Cullen, M. (2008). *35 dumb things well-intended people say.* Garden City, NY: Morgan James.

Dentato, M. (2012, April). *The minority stress perspective.* Psychology and AIDS Exchange Newsletter. Retrieved from http://www.apa.org/pi/aids/resources/exchange/2012/04/minority-stress.aspx

Dessel, A., Bolen, R., & Shepardson, C. (2011). Can religious expression and sexual orientation affirmation coexist in social work? A critique of Hodge's theoretical, theological, and conceptual frameworks. *Journal of Social Work Education, 47*(2), 213–234.

Dessel, A. B., Jacobsen, J., Levy, D. L., McCarty-Caplan, D., Lewis, T. O., & Kaplan, L. E. (2017). LGBTQ Topics and Christianity in Social Work: Tackling the Tough Questions. *Social Work & Christianity, 44*(1/2), 11.

Dileo, C. (2000). *Ethical thinking in music therapy.* Cherry Hill, NJ: Jeffrey Books.

Dillon, F., Worthington, R., Savoy, H., Rooney, S., Becker-Schutte, A., & Guerra, R. (2004). On becoming allies: A qualitative study of lesbian-, gay-, and bisexual-affirmative counselor training. *Counselor Education & Supervision, 43*(3), 162–178. doi:10.1002/j.1556-6978.2004.tb01840.x

Dudley, J. (2013). The assumption of heterosexuality in supervision. *The Arts in Psychotherapy, 40*(5), 486–494. doi:10.1016/j.aip.2013.07.003

Falender, C. A., & Shafranske, E. P. (2004). *Clinical supervision: A competency-based approach* (pp. 37–58). Washington, DC: American Psychological Association.

Farmer, L. B. (2017). An examination of counselors' religiosity, spirituality, and lesbian-, gay-, and bisexual- affirmative counselor competence. *Professional Counselor, 7*(2), 114–128. doi:10.15241/lbf.7.2.114

Fausto-Sterling, A. (2000). *Sexing the body: Gender politics and the construction of sexuality.* New York, NY: Basic Books.

Flores, A. R., Herman, J. L., Gates, G. J., & Brown, T. N. T. (2016). *How many adults identify as transgender in the United States?* Los Angeles, CA: The Williams Institute.

Fox, R. C. (2006). Affirmative psychotherapy with bisexual women and bisexual men: An introduction. *Journal of Bisexuality, 6*(2), 1–11.

Friedlander, M. L., & Ward, L. G. (1984). Development and validation of the supervisory styles inventory. *Journal of Counseling Psychology, 31*(4), 541–557.

Frost, D. M., & Meyer, I. H. (2009). Internalized homophobia and relationship quality among lesbians, gay men, and bisexuals. *Journal of Counseling Psychology, 56*(1), 97–109. doi:10.1037/a0012844

Gates, G. (2011, April). *How many people are lesbian, gay, bisexual, and transgender?* The Williams Institute. Retrieved from http://williamsinstitute.law.ucla.edu/wp-content/uploads/Gates-How-Many-People-LGBT-Apr-2011.pdf

Gatmon, D., Jackson, D., Koshkarian, L., Martos-Perry, N., Molina, A., Patel, N., & Rodolfa, E. (2001). Exploring ethnic, gender, and sexual orientation variables in supervision: Do they really matter? *Journal of Multicultural Counseling and Development, 29,* 102–113.

Gay, Lesbian, & Straight Education Network. (2016). *Safe space kit.* Retrieved from https://www.glsen.org/sites/default/files/GLSEN Safe Space Kit.pdf

Gender Neutral Pronoun Blog: Or the Search for a Polite Specific Gender-Neutral Third-Person Singular Pronoun. (2010, January 24). *The need for a gender-neutral pronoun.* Retrieved from https://genderneutralpronoun.wordpress.com

Gender Spectrum. (2017). Understanding gender. Retrieved from https://www.genderspectrum.org/quick-links/understanding-gender/

Halpert, S. C., Reinhardt, B., & Toohey, M. J. (2007). Affirmative clinical supervision. In K. Bieschke, R. Perez, & K. DeBord (Eds.), *Handbook of counseling and psychotherapy with lesbian, gay, bisexual, and transgender clients* (2nd ed., pp. 341–358). Washington, DC: American Psychological Association. doi:10.1037/11482-014

Hancock, K. A. (2014). Student beliefs, multiculturalism, and client welfare. *Psychology of Sexual Orientation and Gender Diversity, 1*(1), 4–9.

Hope, D. A., & Chappell, C. L. (2015). Extending training in multicultural competencies to include individuals identifying as lesbian, gay, and bisexual: Key choice points for clinical psychology training programs. *Clinical Psychology: Science and Practice, 22,* 105–118.

Human Rights Campaign. (2016). *The lies and dangers of reparative therapy.* Retrieved from https://www.hrc.org/resources/the-lies-and-dangers-of-reparative-therapy/

Human Rights Campaign. (2017). *New FBI data shows increase of anti-LGBTQ hate crimes.* Retrieved from https://www.hrc.org/blog/new-fbi-data-shows-increased-reported-incidents-of-anti-lgbtq-hate-crimes-i

Hutchens, N., Block, J., & Young, M. (2013), Counselor educators' gatekeeping responsibilities and students' first amendment rights. *Counselor Education and Supervision, 52,* 82–95. doi:10.1002/j.1556-6978.2013.00030.x

Intersex Campaign for Equality. (2017). *What is intersex?* Retrieved from http://www.intersexequality.com/intersex/

Kaiser, T. (1992). The supervisory relationship: An identification of the primary elements in the relationship and an application of two theories of ethical relationship. *Journal of Marital and Family Therapy, 18,* 283–296.

Kocet, M. M., & Herlihy, B. J. (2014), Addressing value based conflicts within the counseling relationship: A decision making model. *Journal of Counseling & Development, 92,* 180–186. doi:10.1002/j.1556-6676.2014.00146.x

Long, B. J. K., & Bonomo, J. (2008). Revisiting the Sexual Orientation Matrix for Supervision. *Journal of GLBT Family Studies, 2*(3–4), 151–166.

Long, J., & Lindsey, E. (2004). The sexual orientation matrix for supervision: A tool for training therapists to work with same-sex couples. *Journal of Couple and Relationship Therapy, 3*(2/3), 123–135.

Magnuson, S., Wilcoxon, S. A., & Norem, K. (2000). A profile of lousy supervision. Experienced counselors' perspectives. *Counselor Education and Supervision, 39*(3), 189–204.

McCarty-Caplan, D. (2018). LGBT-competence in social work education: The relationship of school contexts to student sexual minority competence. *Journal of Homosexuality, 65*(1), 19–41. doi:10.1080/00918369.2017.1310547

Messinger, L. (2004). Special Section: Field education in social work out in the field: Gay and lesbian social work students' experiences in field placement. *Social Work, 40*(2), 187–205. doi:10.1080/10437797.2004.10778489

Messinger, L. (2007). Supervision of lesbian, gay, and bisexual social work students by heterosexual field instructors: A qualitative dyad analysis. *The Clinical Supervisor, 26*(1/2), 195–222. doi:10.1300/ J001v26n01_13

Messinger, L. (2013). *Reflections on LGBT students in social work field education.* Field Scholar, 3.1. Retrieved from http://fieldeducator.simmons.edu

Meyer, I. H. (1995). Minority stress and mental health in gay men. *Journal of Health and Social Behavior, 36,* 38–56.

Mirowsky, J., & Ross, C. E. (1989). *Social causes of psychological distress.* Hawthorne, NY: Aldine de Gruyter.

Mitchell, V. (2010). Developing the therapeutic self: Supervising therapists with lesbian, gay, bisexual, and transgender clients in the 21st century. *Women and Therapy, 33*(1–2), 7–21. doi:10.1080/02703140903404671

Moe, J. L., Perera-Diltz, D., & Sepulveda, V. (2014). Beyond competence: Fostering LGBTQ+QI ally development through supervision. *Journal of LGBT Issues in Counseling, 8*(4), 389–401. doi:10.1080/15538605.2014.960129

Morrison, M., & Borgen, W. A. (2010). How Christian spiritual and religious beliefs help and hinder counselors' empathy toward clients. *Counseling and Values, 55,* 25–45.

Mulick, P. S., & Wright, L.W., Jr. (2002). Examining the existence of biphobia in the heterosexual and homosexual populations. *Journal of Bisexuality, 2*(4), 45–64. doi:10.1300/J159v02n04_03

Murphy, J. A., Rawlings, E. I., & Howe, S. R. (2002). A survey of clinical psychologists on treating lesbian, gay, and bisexual clients. *Professional Psychology: Research and Practice, 33,* 183–189.

Nadal, K. L., Rivera, D. P., & Corpus, M. J. (2010). Sexual orientation and transgender microaggressions: Implications for mental health and counseling. In D. W. Sue (Ed.), *Microaggressions and marginality: Manifestation, dynamics, and impact* (pp. 217–240). Hoboken, NJ: John Wiley & Sons, Inc.

National Association of Social Workers. (2016, April 20). *NASW joins other mental health organizations to protest so-called "Religious Freedom" laws.* Retrieved from https://www.socialworkers.org/News/News-Releases/ID/96/NASW-joins-other-mental-health-organizations-to-protest-so-called-Religious-Freedom-laws

Newman, P., Bogo, M., & Daley, A. (2008). Self-disclosure of sexual orientation in social work field education: Field instructor and lesbian and gay student perspectives. *The Clinical Supervisor, 27*(2), 215–237. doi:10.1080/07325220802487881

Newman, P., Daley, A., & Bogo, M. (2009). Breaking the silence: Sexual orientation in the social work field education. *Journal of Social Work Education, 45*(1), 7–27.

Norcross , J. C., & Guy, J. D. (2007). *Leaving it at the office: A guide to psychotherapist self-care.* New York, NY: Guilford Press.

O'Brien, R. L., Kosoko-Lasaki, O., Cook, C. T., Kissell, J., Peak F., & Williams, E. H. (2006). Self-assessment of cultural attitudes and competence of clinical investigators to enhance recruitment and participation of minority populations in research. *Journal of National Medical Association, 98*(5), 674–682.

Orlinsky, D. E., Rønnestad, M. H., & Collaborative Research Network of the Society for Psychotherapy Research. (2005). *How psychotherapists develop: A study of therapeutic work and professional growth.* Washington, DC: American Psychological Association. doi:10.1037/11157-000

Pargament, K. I. (2013). Spirituality as an irreducible human motivation and process. *The International Journal for the Psychology of Religion, 23,* 271–281.

Pearlin, L. I. (1989). The sociological study of stress. *Journal of Health and Social Behavior, 30,* 241–256.

Perlstein, M. (2010). Virgins and Veterans: Culturally Sensitive Supervision in the LGBT Community. *Women and Therapy, 33*(1–2), 85–100. doi:10.1080/02703140903404887

Perry, G. F. (1998). The relationship between faith and well-being. *Journal of Religion and Health, 37*(2), 125–136.

Pett, J. (2000). Gay, lesbian, and bisexual therapy and its supervision. In D. Davies & C. Neal (Eds.), *Therapeutic perspectives on working with lesbian, gay, and bisexual clients* (pp. 54–72). Philadelphia, PA: Open University Press.

PFLAG. (2018). *National glossary of terms.* Retrieved from https://www.pflag.org/glossary

Quintana, N. S., Rosenthal, J., & Krehely, J. (2010). *On the streets: The federal response to gay and transgender homeless youth. Center for American Progress.* Retrieved from https://cdn.americanprogress.org/wp-content/uploads/issues/2010/06/pdf/lgbtyouthhomelessness.pdf

Rainey, J. S., & Trusty, J. (2007). Attitudes of master's-level counseling students toward gay men and lesbians. *Counseling and Values, 52,* 12–24.

Rawlings, E. J., & Carter, D. K. (Eds.). (1977). *Psychotherapy for women: Treatment toward equality.* Springfield, IL: Charles C Thomas Publisher.

Sanabria, S. (2012). Religious orientation and prejudice: Predictors of homoprejudice. *Journal of LGBT Issues in Counseling, 6*(3), 183–201. doi:10.1080/15538605.2012.708894

Sand, S. (2017). Sexual Orientation Dynamics in Clinical Supervision. In K. Nadal (Ed.), *The SAGE Encyclopedia of Psychology and Gender* (pp. 1539–1541). Thousand Oaks, CA: SAGE Publications.

Saslow, L. R., John, O. P., Pi, P. K., Willer, R., Wong, E., Impe, E. A., & Saturn, S. R. (2013). The social significance of spirituality: New perspectives on the compassion-altruism relationship. *Psychology of Religion and Spirituality, 5,* 201–218. doi:10.1037/a0031870

Satcher, J., & Schumacker, R. (2009). Predictors of modern homonegativity among professional school counselors. *Journal of LGBT Issues in Counseling, 3,* 21–36. doi:10.1080/15538600902754452

Satterly, B. A., & Dyson, D. (2008). Sexual minority supervision. *Clinical Supervisor, 27*(1), 17–38. doi:10.1080/07325220802221462

Shiu-Thornton, S. (2003). Addressing cultural competency in research: Integrating a community-based participatory research approach. *Alcoholism, Clinical, and Experimental Research, 27*(8), 1361–1364.

Singh, A., & Chun, K. Y. S. (2010). "From the margins to the center": Moving towards a resilience-based model of supervision for queer people of color supervisors. *Training and Education in Professional Psychology, 4,* 36–46. doi:10.1037/a0017373

Sterzing, P. R., Gartner, R. E., Woodford, M. R., & Fisher, C. M. (2017). Sexual orientation, gender, and gender identity microaggressions: Toward an intersectional framework for social work research. *Journal of Ethnic and Cultural Diversity in Social Work, 26*(1–2), 81–94. doi:10.1080/15313204.2016.1263819

Sue, D. W. (1990). *Counseling the culturally different: Theory and practice.* New York, NY: John Wiley.

Sue, D. W. (2010). Microaggressions, Marginality, and Oppression. In D. W. Sue (Ed.), *Microaggressions and Marginality* (pp. 3–22). Hoboken, NJ: Wiley.

Sue, D. W., Capodilupo, C. M, Torino, G. C., Bucceri, J. M., Holder, A. M. B., Nadal, K. L., & Esquilin, M. (2007). Racial microaggressions in everyday life: Implications for clinical practice. *American Psychologist, 6*(4), 271–286.

University of Wisconsin–Milwaukee Lesbian Gay Bisexual Transgender Resource Center. (2017). *Gender pronouns.* Retrieved from https://uwm.edu/lgbtrc/support/gender-pronouns/

Vanderbilt University Center for Teaching. (2017). Teaching beyond the gender binary in the university classroom. Retrieved from https://cft.vanderbilt.edu/teaching-beyond-the-gender-binary-in-the-university-classroom/

Whitehead-Pleaux, A., Donnenwerth, A., Robinson, B., Hardy, S., Oswanski, L., Forinash, M., & York, E. (2012). Lesbian, gay, bisexual, transgender, and questioning: Best practices in music therapy. *Music Therapy Perspectives, 30*(2).

Whitehead-Pleaux, A., Donnenwerth, A. M., Robinson, B., Hardy, S., Oswanski, L. G., Forinash, M., Tan, X. (2013). Music therapists' attitudes and actions regarding the LGBTQ+ community: A preliminary report. *The Arts in Psychotherapy, 40*(4). doi:10.1016/j.aip.2013.05.006

World Federation of Music Therapy. (2018). *Values.* Retrieved from https://www.wfmt.info

York, E. (2015). Inclusion of Lesbian, Gay, Bisexual, Transgender, Questioning content into the music therapy curriculum: Resources for the educator. In K. D. Goodman (Ed.), *International Perspectives in Music Therapy Education and Training* (pp. 241–266). Springfield, IL: Charles C Thomas Publisher.

APPENDIX 1

Resource List Compiled by the Members of Team Rainbow

Clinical Resources
1. **Team Rainbow**
2. Whitehead-Pleaux, A., Donnenwerth, A., Robinson, B., Hardy, S., Oswanski, L., Forinash, M., & York, E. (2012). Lesbian, gay, bisexual, transgender, and questioning: Best practices in music therapy. *Music Therapy Perspectives, 30*(2).
3. Whitehead-Pleaux, A., Donnenwerth, A. M., Robinson, B., Hardy, S., Oswanski, L. G., Forinash, M., & Tan, X. (2013). Music therapists' attitudes and actions regarding the LGBTQ+ community: A preliminary report. *The Arts in Psychotherapy, 40*(4). doi:10.1016/j.aip.2013.05.006
4. York, E. (2015). Inclusion of Lesbian, Gay, Bisexual, Transgender, Questioning content into the music therapy curriculum: Resources for the educator. In K. D. Goodman (Ed.), *International Perspectives in Music Therapy Education and Training* (pp. 241–266). Springfield, IL: Charles C Thomas Publisher.
5. **Association for Lesbian, Gay, Bisexual, & Transgender Issues in Counseling:** competencies for counseling LGBTQ clients, http://www.algbtic.org/
6. **American Psychological Association:** APA Division 44—Society for the Study of Lesbian, Gay, Bisexual, and Transgender Issues, http://www.apadivision44.org/; guidelines for working with LGBTQAI+ individuals, http://www.apadivisions.org/division-44/resources/guidelines.aspx

Online Training
1. Healthcare (over 50 available trainings): https://www.lgbthealtheducation.org
2. Coming out as a supporter: http://www.hrc.org/resources/straight-guide-to-lgbt-americans
3. GLSEN's Safe Space Kit—Guide to Being an Ally to LGBT Students: https://www.glsen.org/sites/default/files/GLSEN Safe Space Kit.pdf
4. APA LGBT resources and publications: http://www.apa.org/pi/lgbt/resources/index.aspx

LGBTQAI+ Civil Rights and Legal Organizations
1. **American Civil Liberties Union:** National civil rights organization that guards liberty, working in courts, legislatures, and communities to defend and preserve the individual rights and liberties that the Constitution and the laws of the United States guarantee to everyone in this country; http://www.aclu.org
2. **Astraea Lesbian Foundation for Justice:** The Astraea Lesbian Foundation for Justice is the only philanthropic organization working exclusively to advance LGBTQI human rights around the globe; https://www.astraeafoundation.org/
3. **Human Rights Campaign:** National lesbian, gay, bisexual, transgender, and queer civil rights organization; http://www.HRC.org
4. **GLAAD:** A media watch group that advocates for and researches LGBTQAi+ visibility and representation in the media; http://www.GLAAD.org
5. **National GLBTQ Task Force:** The National LGBTQ Task Force advances full freedom, justice, and equality for LGBTQ people; http://www.thetaskforce.org/
6. **National Center for Lesbian Rights:** The National Center for Lesbian Rights (NCLR) has been advancing the civil and human rights of lesbian, gay, bisexual, and transgender people and their families through litigation, legislation, policy, and public education since its founding in 1977; http://www.nclrights.org/

7. **National Center for Transgender Equality:** The National Center for Transgender Equality is the nation's leading social justice advocacy organization, winning life-saving change for transgender people; http://www.transequality.org
8. **National Coalition of Anti-Violence Programs:** AVP empowers lesbian, gay, bisexual, transgender, queer, and HIV-affected communities and allies to end all forms of violence through organizing and education and supports survivors through counseling and advocacy; http://www.avp.org
9. **Out and Equal Workplace Advocates:** Out and Equal Workplace Advocates is the world's premier nonprofit organization dedicated to achieving lesbian, gay, bisexual, and transgender workplace equality; http://outandequal.org/
10. **Pride@Work:** Pride@Work is a nonprofit organization that represents LGBTQ union members and their allies. They are an officially recognized constituency group of the AFL-CIO (American Federation of Labor & Congress of Industrial Organizations) that organizes mutual support between the organized labor movement and the LGBTQ community to further social and economic justice; http://www.prideatwork.org
11. **Service and Advocacy for Gay, Lesbian, Bisexual, and Transgender Elders:** Services and Advocacy for GLBT Elders (SAGE) is the country's largest and oldest organization dedicated to improving the lives of lesbian, gay, bisexual, and transgender (LGBT) older adults; http://www.sageusa.org
12. **Transgender Law Center:** Transgender Law Center works to change law, policy, and attitudes so that all people can live safely, authentically, and free from discrimination regardless of their gender identity or expression; http://www.transgenderlawcenter.org
13. **Transgender Legal Defense and Education Fund:** A nonprofit that works to end discrimination and achieve equality for transgender people, particularly those in our most vulnerable communities; http://www.tldef.org
14. **Lambda Legal:** Lambda Legal is a national legal organization whose mission is to achieve full recognition of the civil rights of lesbians, gay men, bisexuals, transgender people, and those with HIV, through impact litigation, education, and public policy work; http://www.lambdalegal.org/
15. **GLBTQ Legal Advocates and Defenders:** Through strategic litigation, public policy advocacy, and education, GLBTQ Legal Advocates and Defenders works in New England and nationally to create a just society free of discrimination based on gender identity and expression, HIV status, and sexual orientation; http://www.GLAD.org

Support and Social Organizations
1. **Team Rainbow** on Facebook: Music Therapy LGBTQ/Allies Connection
2. **Parents and Friends of Lesbians and Gays:** National organization with local chapters across the country that provides support and education to loved ones of LGBTQAI+ individuals as well as members of those communities; http://www.PFLAG.org
3. **BiNET USA:** A 501(c)(3) nonprofit advocating for bisexual communities in the U.S.; http://www.binetusa.org
4. **GLSEN:** National organization with local chapters that create safe and affirming schools for all, regardless of sexual orientation, gender identity, or gender expression; http://www.GLSEN.org
5. **American Institute of Bisexuality:** The American Institute of Bisexuality encourages, supports, and assists research and education about bisexuality, through programs likely to make a material difference and enhance public knowledge, awareness, and understanding about bisexuality; http://www.americaninstituteofbisexuality.org
6. **American Military Partner Association:** The American Military Partner Association is the nation's largest resource and support network for the partners, spouses, families, and allies of

America's lesbian, gay, bisexual, and transgender (LGBT) service members and veterans; http://www.militarypartners.org

7. **American Unity Fund:** The mission of American Unity Fund is freedom. They are dedicated to advancing the cause of freedom for LGBTQ Americans by making the conservative case that freedom truly means freedom for everyone; http://www.americanunityfund.com

8. **Bisexual Resource Center:** The BRC continues to raise awareness and build bridges within the LGBT and ally communities and fosters bi-supportive social and political space wherever it can; http://www.biresource.net

9. **Black Transmen:** Black Transmen Inc. is the first national nonprofit organization of African-American transmen solely focused on acknowledgment, social advocacy, and empowering transmen with resources to aid in a healthy female-to-male transition; http://www.blacktransmen.org

10. **CenterLink—The Community of LGBT Centers:** CenterLink was founded in 1994 as a member-based coalition to support the development of strong, sustainable LGBT community centers. The organization plays an important role in supporting the growth of LGBT centers and addressing the challenges that they face by helping them to improve their organizational and service delivery capacity and increase access to public resources; http://www.lgbtcenters.org

11. **Erasing 76 Crimes:** The "Erasing 76 Crimes" blog focuses on the human toll of 76+ countries' anti-LGBTI laws and the struggle to repeal them; http://www.76crimes.com

12. **Freedom for All Americans:** Freedom for All Americans is the bipartisan campaign to secure full nondiscrimination protections for LGBT people nationwide; http://www.freedomforallamericans.org

13. **Funders for LGBTQ Issues:** Working side-by-side with funders and their movement's organizations through three decades, Funders for LGBTQ Issues remains the sole organization dedicated exclusively to increasing institutional giving to LGBTQ communities; https://lgbtfunders.org/

14. **Gay & Lesbian Victory Fund:** The Gay & Lesbian Victory Fund works to elect LGBT leaders to public office for one simple reason—they change America's politics; http://www.victoryfund.org

15. **Gender Spectrum:** Gender Spectrum's mission is to create a gender-inclusive world for all children and youth. To accomplish this, they help families, organizations, and institutions increase understandings of gender and consider the implications that evolving views have for each of us; http://www.genderspectrum.org

16. **Gay Straight Alliance Network:** Their overall strategy for fighting for educational justice is to work with grassroots, youth-led groups and GSAs, empowering them to educate their schools and communities, advocate for just policies that protect LGBTQ youth from harassment and violence, and organize in coalition with other youth groups across identity lines to address broader issues of oppression; http://www.gsanetwork.org

17. **Human Dignity Trust:** The Human Dignity Trust is a legal charity that supports those who want to challenge anti-gay laws wherever they exist in the world; http://www.humandignitytrust.org

18. **International Lesbian, Gay, Bisexual, Trans, and Intersex Association:** The International Lesbian, Gay, Bisexual, Trans and Intersex Association is the world federation of national and local organizations dedicated to achieving equal rights for lesbian, gay, bisexual, trans, and intersex (LGBTI) people; http://www.ilga.org

19. **It Gets Better Project:** The It Gets Better Project's mission is to communicate to lesbian, gay, bisexual, and transgender youth around the world that it gets better and to create and inspire the changes needed to make it better for them; http://www.itgetsbetter.org

20. **Lambda Literary:** Lambda Literary believes that lesbian, gay, bisexual, transgender, and queer literature is fundamental to the preservation of their culture and that LGBTQ lives are affirmed when their stories are written, published and read. http://www.lambdaliterary.org
21. **LGBT Science:** LGBT Science is an ongoing project of Truth Wins Out (TWO), exploring the latest research and interviewing key scientists who have studied human sexuality; http://www.lgbtscience.org
22. **Movement Advancement Project:** MAP's mission is to provide independent and rigorous research, insight, and analysis that can help to speed full equality for LGBT people; http://www.lgbtmap.org
23. **National Black Justice Coalition:** The National Black Justice Coalition (NBJC) is a civil rights organization dedicated to empowering black lesbian, gay, bisexual, and transgender (LGBT) people. NBJC's mission is to end racism and homophobia; http://www.nbjc.org
24. **Point Foundation—The National LGBTQ Scholarship Foundation:** Point Foundation empowers promising lesbian, gay, bisexual, transgender, and queer students to achieve their full academic and leadership potential—despite the obstacles often put before them—to make a significant impact on society; http://www.pointfoundation.org
25. **Trans Women of Color Collective:** To uplift the narratives, lived experiences, and leadership of trans and gender-nonconforming people of color and their families and comrades as they build toward collective liberation for all oppressed people; http://www.twocc.us
26. **Trans Youth Equality Foundation:** The Trans Youth Equality Foundation provides education, advocacy, and support for transgender and gender-nonconforming children and youth and their families. Their mission is to share information about the unique needs of this community, partnering with families, educators, and service providers to help to foster a healthy, caring, and safe environment for all transgender children; http://www.transyouthequality.org
27. **The Trevor Project:** The Trevor Project is the leading national organization providing crisis intervention and suicide prevention services to lesbian, gay, bisexual, transgender, and questioning (LGBTQ) young people of ages 13–24; http://www.thetrevorproject.org
28. **World Professional Association for Transgender Health:** WPATH is a nonprofit, interdisciplinary professional and educational organization devoted to transgender health. Their professional, supporting, and student members engage in clinical and academic research to develop evidence-based medicine and strive to promote a high quality of care for transsexual, transgender, and gender-nonconforming individuals internationally; http://www.wpath.org
29. **The Williams Institute:** The Williams Institute is dedicated to conducting rigorous, independent research on sexual orientation and gender identity law and public policy. A think tank at UCLA Law, the Williams Institute produces high-quality research with real-world relevance and disseminates it to judges, legislators, policymakers, media, and the public; https://williamsinstitute.law.ucla.edu/
30. **COLAGE:** COLAGE unites people with lesbian, gay, bisexual, transgender, and/or queer parents into a network of peers and supports them as they nurture and empower each other to be skilled, self-confident, and just leaders in our collective communities; http://www.Colage.org

Chapter 7

ENGAGING RACE IN MUSIC THERAPY SUPERVISION

Marisol Norris
Susan Hadley

LOCATION OF SELVES

Marisol: I am a Black, nondisabled, heterosexual, middle-class, Christian, immigrant, cis woman of Jamaican descent. The intersection of these multiple social locations contributes to my social identity, personhood, and evolving worldview and ultimately shapes each supervisory relationship I enter. While honoring and celebrating its beauty and multiplicity, I recognize my social identity also marks my existence within an oppressive social system of what bell hooks refers to as *imperialist white-supremacist capitalist patriarchy* (hooks, 2003). Recognizing music therapy as dually existent within the complexity and pervasiveness of these "political systems," I am continually beholden to the process of examining and challenging the perpetuation of social injustices within music therapy supervision. This includes (1) fostering social curiosity of supervisees by co-examining the multiple ways in which music therapy, in theory and praxis, may perpetuate injustices and function as a system of oppression for the clients served, and (2) tending to the social locations of both myself and my supervisees and the ways in which our interactions may dually serve as a microcosm of larger structures of social oppression. In so doing, my effectiveness as a racially responsive supervisor is dependent on the commitment to examine the nexus of my sociocultural location as an *outsider within* the white-dominant disciplinary practice of music therapy. I must be simultaneously mindful of the influence of internalized racism and caretaker roles, both of which are historically indexical of women of color working within white-dominant cultures, in cross-racial and mono-racial supervisory relationships. To do this work demands professional agency and courage that all music therapy supervisors must access or muster in order to walk firmly through a path of most resistance in service to our clients, our students, and our profession.

    Susan: I come to the supervisory relationship as a white,[7] Australian-American, enabled (or nondisabled), educated, heterosexual, middle-age, middle-class, cis woman. My consciousness of my racialized identity as white is constantly present, given that I am in a cross-racial marriage and am the mother of a Black stepson and four biracial sons. For this chapter, I will focus directly on my white racialized identity, yet it is important to acknowledge how my racialized white identity intersects with my other sociocultural identities and how this locates me socially in a way different from those of others whose identities intersect in other ways. Furthermore, I acknowledge that I benefit from unearned advantages as a result of systemic white privilege, and although I have witnessed racism in many forms, I have not personally experienced it. I have also unknowingly perpetrated racism to the detriment of people of color, and even though I'm well intentioned and knowledgeable about racism, I am sure that at different times I will continue to perpetrate it. As a white person in a white supremacist system, I have taken my racialized identity for granted. I have learned values and beliefs and attitudes that shape how I assign meaning to what I hear and see. This must be acknowledged

---

[7] Early Black thinkers fought to capitalize the word "Negro," as that was a significant marker of political identity. Capitalizing "Black" continues this political identity. Leaving "white" in lowercase is one form of resistance that recognizes the hegemony of whiteness.

and continually challenged within myself, as I believe that our humanity is connected not only to our self-awareness, but also to what we choose to do after gaining greater awareness. I believe that in order to forge a strong working alliance in supervision, it is important to be transparent about our respective social locations (in terms of race, disability, gender, sexuality, socio-economic class, etc.) and how this impacts our values, beliefs, actions, and, therefore, therapeutic and supervisory relationships.

DISTINCTIONS BETWEEN MULTICULTURAL, CROSS-CULTURAL, CROSS-RACIAL, AND MONO-RACIAL SUPERVISION

The discipline of multicultural supervision has been brought under severe critique due to the cultural complexity of all human interactions. The "multicultural" identifier, as with the concept of multiculturalism, often presumes colonial sentiments of cultural assimilation and integration in dominant society and assumes that some human interactions, notably those involving people of color, are more cultural than others, notably those of white people. Multicultural and cross-cultural supervision more aptly denote supervisory relationships in which the supervisor, supervisee, or client hold differing social locations of one or more cultural markers (Constantine, 1997; Estrada, Frame, & Williams, 2004; Schroeder, Andrews, & Hindes, 2009; Toporek, Ortega-Villalobos, & Pope-Davis, 2004). It indexes the multiplicity of supervisor and supervisee interactions and the primacy of multiple cultural influences within the supervisory relationship. Cross-racial supervision, on the other hand, denotes the supervisory relationship in which supervisor and supervisee come from different racial locations (Daniels, D'Andrea, & Kyung Kim, 1999; Schroeder, Andrews, & Hindes, 2009). Supervision deemed cross-racial or mono-racial (i.e., relationships in which the supervisor and supervisee are of the same race) assumes racial social location as an inherent focus amidst intersecting identities of gender, class, sexual orientation, ability, and/or religion, and so on. In this chapter, we will discuss ways to engage race in cross-racial as well as mono-racial supervisory relationships.

WHY RACIALIZED IDENTITY MATTERS

In our society, we often pride ourselves on our uniqueness, with no one being quite like we are. At the same time, we are categorized into various groups (either self-nominated or assigned by others) from which we derive our identities. In terms of our social identities, Jun (2010) described how we tend to favor those who are perceived to be members of our social groups (in-group favoritism), believe that they are like us (social projection), and attribute the behavior of those in the out-group to be because of a fundamental disposition of members of that group (attribution error) rather than taking into account situational factors (pp. 107–109). Furthermore, we tend to believe that those in the out-group are more homogeneous than those in our in-group, whom we perceive to have more individuality (Jun, 2010, p. 108). The multiple sociocultural identities and subsequent social locations of a person indicate the significant presence of intragroup variability among all humans, and yet those in dominant groups, in particular, often minimize this heterogeneity in nondominant groups, a function of the values and beliefs taught by our Eurocentric culture.

One of the major social groups to which we are assigned is a racial group. It was in the context of European colonial expansion that categorizing the colonized as not just different but inferior was a way of justifying domination over the colonized. This was later solidified through "scientific" explanations of distinct "races" of people who were said to have stable, inherited characteristics, with Caucasians, native inhabitants of the Caucasus region (DeGruy, 2005), being said to have innate biological superiority over other races and Africans being "nearer the apes than other men" (Fredrickson, 2002, p. 57). While it is now widely accepted that there is no biological basis for racial categorization, the historical weight of such hierarchicalized race-based societies has deeply affected how racial identity is experienced.

In the majority of countries in which music therapy as a "discipline" is practiced, "perceived and assigned racial group membership continues to have profound sociopolitical and interpersonal implications with respect to everyday life experiences, power, and privilege" (Harrell, 2014, p. 84). Around the globe, white people have reaped the benefits of a racial system that has disproportionately privileged white people socially, politically, and legally and has subjugated people of color in differential ways. Understanding the historical contexts of different racialized groups in relationship to white social, political, and legal discriminatory practices is vital in terms of understanding the impact of such systemic oppression on current cross-racial interactions. Racial identity socialization begins from birth and takes hold before conscious memory. Early and continued experiences of white privilege and the internalization of oppression for people of color lead to prejudices and stereotypes being activated automatically, having a profound impact on in-group and out-group perception and judgment (Jun, 2010).

Given the reality of structural racism and white privilege and power in our society and hence its impact on our racial identity formation (Harrell, 2014; Jernigan, Green, Helms, Perez-Gualdron, & Henze, 2010; Jun, 2010; Kohl, 2006; Tummala-Narra, 2004), one would expect the thematization of race to play a more prominent role in clinical supervision. However, racial issues have been largely avoided in clinical supervision across disciplines (Harrell, 2014; Kim, 2008; Kleintjes & Swartz, 1996; Kohl, 2006; Millán, 2010; Swamy, 2011; Tummala-Narra, 2004; White-Davis, Stein, & Karasz, 2016). So, even though race impacts so much of our everyday life and our interpersonal interactions, we tend not to acknowledge its impact openly. This is most likely because discussing issues of race can feel risky and/or shameful and can lead to feelings of discomfort, anxiety, fear, and narcissistic vulnerability (Tummala-Narra, 2004; White-Davis et al., 2016).

Our identities and relationships and how we make sense of our experiences are shaped by personal, familial, cultural, and dominant societal narratives (Hadley, 2013b). Accordingly, our sociocultural locations impact how we make sense of our clinical experiences. What we hear, what we see, and thus what we narrate are influenced by dynamics of power and privilege. Given this dynamic, "some narratives are silenced, whereas others are amplified" (Harrell, 2014, p. 92). It is important to give attention to narratives that have historically been silenced.

Many clinicians and supervisors adopt a color-evasive racial ideology, ignoring race and power dynamics as areas to explore. Research indicates, however, that avoiding dialogues about racial dynamics in therapeutic relationships and supervisory relationships leads to adverse outcomes (Burkard, Edwards, & Adams, 2016). Conversely, adopting a relational ideology—one that incorporates race consciousness and oppression consciousness—leads to positive outcomes. When racial issues are openly addressed, clients of color and supervisees of color as well as white supervisees perceive their counselor/supervisor positively (Burkard et al., 2016) and build a strong working alliance (Kim, 2008). In such situations, supervisees felt that the supervisor was more attentive and responsive to their needs (Jernigan et al., 2010), and they felt more understood (Kim, 2008). This provides a strong rationale for supervisors to introduce race as a relational dynamic to explore within supervision. Interestingly, though, Jernigan et al. (2010) found that supervisees perceived that they introduced race and culture more than their supervisors, although White-Davis et al. (2016) found that this may vary according to the racial identity of the supervisor. Unlike white supervisors, most supervisors of color actively initiated race-related dialogues in supervision.

POSSIBLE REASONS WHY ISSUES OF RACE ARE AVOIDED IN MUSIC THERAPY SUPERVISION

Music therapy is a predominantly white Eurocentric discipline (Hadley, 2013a). Consequently, race has often been excluded from music therapy discourses on theory and praxis. This monocultural and color-evasive stance has been exhibited by (1) alluding to the nature of music as a cultural phenomenon that circumvents issues of race, (2) exploring racialized groups with the aim of conforming them to a dominant culture, (3) avoiding processes that explore the racialized selves of both client and therapist, (4) neglecting the effects of racial sameness and difference on the therapeutic relationship, and (5) failing to consider the ways in which various micro and macro systems impact clients' presenting concerns. The inherent lack of racial discourse in music therapy practice contributes to limitations in effectively exploring race in music therapy training and supervision. Further compounded by the significant lack of music therapists of color in the field, dominant white narratives are reiterated in music therapy training coursework and supervision. Although it has been found that supervisors and supervisees of color tend to attribute greater importance to racial issues than white supervisors and supervisees (Harrell, 2014), this white Euro-dominant perspective from which all music therapists are taught influences the supervisors and supervisees, both of color and white, to adequately explore and gain insight into their own racialized identity and the influence of race upon their work.

In recent years, more emphasis has been placed on culture and ethnicity in the context of music therapy supervision (Estrella, 2001; Kim, 2008; Swamy, 2011; Young, 2009), but not specifically on racial issues as a distinct area of exploration. When exploring ethnicity, the focus is more on ancestry, history, values, customs, and worldview, whereas when exploring racial issues, the focus is on power, privilege, oppression, racism, and in-group/out-group dynamics. Of course, focusing on both race and ethnicity in addition to other cultural identities is necessary in supervision. However, even when therapists are aware of how they are culturally located and challenge their racial biases, they may not know how to effectively work with racial issues that arise within their clinical work or in supervision. As Kohl (2006) stated, "Social identity awareness and social justice consciousness are necessary, but not sufficient, conditions for successful clinical intervention" (p. 175).

Tummala-Narra (2004) suggested that the supervisory relationship encourages the supervisor to adopt an expert role, encouraged by the needs of the supervisee for an all-knowing supervisor, which has the potential to lead to a desire of the supervisor to be omniscient (perhaps a parallel process with the supervisee in relationship to the client). This may prevent explorations of racial issues due to the white supervisor's or supervisee's inability to tolerate the anxiety, fear, and narcissistic vulnerability that accompany such explorations (p. 304). Supervisors of color adopting an expert stance may refrain from discussing race in favor of more notably accepted approaches to music therapy supervision that hold dominant white perspectives of music therapy practice or lack race-based features. Additionally, supervisees of color may also avoid bringing up race due to minimal insights into how race impacts practice, perceived expectations of supervision to limit exploration of race, or fear of being accused of using race as an excuse for poor clinical outcomes, of using race as a defense against exploring other clinical issues, or of being persistently preoccupied with issues of race and discrimination (Kleintjes & Swartz, 1996). Another possible factor for not engaging race in music therapy supervision is that supervisors tend to be more senior clinicians, and it has been found that older supervisors of all races may have had less experience in addressing issues of race and culture in therapy or supervision due to a lack of multicultural training (Jernigan et al., 2010). In fact, in many cases, the supervisees may have had more training in terms of social and cultural awareness than their supervisors.

Since clinical work and supervision that engage racial issues have been found to lead to more positive outcomes for both people of color and white people, it is our view that as music therapists we have an ethical obligation to address race in supervision.

PHILOSOPHY OF SUPERVISION

Given the ways in which our racialized identities fundamentally influence our perceptions and judgments, we hold the assumption that race is a critical dimension of therapy relationships and thus should be explored in *all* clinical supervision relationships. Furthermore, we believe that race should be brought up in the very first session in order to make clear that race matters and to normalize it as a topic (Watson, 2016, p. 45). Our philosophy of supervision grows out of a worldview that we are relational beings and we develop in relational contexts (Hardy, 2016; Stige, 2017). Further, we believe that we must create a space for mutuality in the supervisory relationship and that a strong working alliance is founded on trust, fairness, and reciprocity (Arczynski & Morrow, 2017). We hold to a worldview that each of us has a complex, multifaceted, cultural identity (Hadley & Norris, 2016) and that music therapists must become aware of how our relational dynamics are tied into the ways that our respective complex, multifaceted cultural identities intersect with those of the *other*. Ours is an ecological worldview, one that emphasizes relationships between the person "and the various situations, contexts, structures, values, and environments in which the person lives" (Bruscia, 2014, p. 162).

Our philosophy has an emphasis on personal awareness and is in line with what Hardy (2016) referred to as a multicultural relational perspective (pp. 4–10) and what Aponte referred to as the Person-of-the-Therapist model (Aponte & Carlsen, 2009; Aponte, Powell, Brooks, Watson, Litzke, Lawless, & Johnson, 2009). Hardy emphasized multicultural awareness. Rather than a set of skills that one performs or a set of competencies that one achieves, a multicultural relational perspective is "a worldview that recognizes how the nuances of culture and all of its appendages are contaminants, informants, and meaning-makers throughout virtually all aspects of our lives" (Hardy, 2016, p. 4). A multicultural relational perspective is one which understands culture to be multidimensional; simultaneously dynamic, fluid, and static; pervasive and influential; serving many varied functions; and transcending the past, present, and future (Hardy, 2016). Aponte emphasized personal awareness (self-knowledge), access to the self (memories, emotions, and values), and the ability to purposefully use the self therapeutically in a therapeutic relationship (Aponte & Carlsen, 2009). He defined this pursuit as a mastery of self, one in which the supervisee experiences increased clinical freedom through the familiarity, comfort, and command of central issues (*signature themes*) within their personal and social selves (Aponte & Carlsen, 2009). Through this process, their personal vulnerabilities are transformed into clinical assets.

Our philosophy is in contrast to multicultural approaches to race that are frequently adopted in music therapy training programs, in which the focus is more on a "static transfer of information" about different racial groups (as if fairly homogeneous) and specific techniques for addressing these race-based traits/attributes (Millán, 2010, p. 8). Millán (2010) rightly pointed out that this latter kind of training focuses on "descriptions of characteristics of the group with whom the clinician [is working] rather than on establishing interpersonal, therapeutic relationships with members of the group" (p. 8).

Our approach integrates principles of feminism and critical theory. It recognizes the importance of addressing the complexities of power in supervision, addressing each party's social location and exploring their history of privilege and oppression. We engage with supervisees in collaborative processes, cultivating critical reflexivity, analyzing the influence of context, and finding ways of addressing harmful contexts. In this way, we maintain a commitment to social justice and antiracism, which aligns with our critical pedagogical approach (Arczynski & Morrow, 2017; Freire, 2012; Porter, 2014).

Finally, our approach to supervision incorporates elements from psychodynamic models such as exploring resistance, transference, countertransference, and parallel processes. We see these as phenomena within human exchange that readily influence the supervisory relationship and the ego-resourcefulness of music therapists within clinical work. We also understand our work within the framework of systems theory, where both supervisor and supervisee exist within multiple interconnecting systems and a holistic approach is necessary to enact systematic change.

The Racialized Supervisor

Music therapy supervisors are called to the critical role of teaching, guiding, and modeling cultural humility amidst emergent music therapy cultural competency standards and cultural frameworks. In order to effectively facilitate the racial responsivity of the supervisee, the supervisor must be able to effectively locate both themselves and the trainees within the continuum of racial identity. Racial identity refers to an individual's psychological experience of the social construct of race and sense of belonging assigned to racial categories (Hadley & Norris, 2016; Jernigan et al., 2010). There are multiple racial identity models (see Table 1) that offer conceptual understandings of the racial dynamics that manifest within clinical spaces and between members of the supervision dyad (Cross, 1971; Cross & Fhagen-Smith, 2001; Gallegos & Ferdman, 2012; Hardiman, 1982; Helms, 1984, 1990, 1995; Horse, 2012; Jackson, 2012; Kim, 1981, 2012; Poston, 1990; Rockquemore & Laszloffy, 2003; Wijeyesinghe & Jackson, 2012). Most often they share two common assumptions: (1) individuals are influenced by multiple interacting social systems and respond based upon levels of social awareness, and (2) in the presence of a model of racial identity development, individuals may begin to track their level of racial awareness and foster a *liberated or antiracist social identity* (Wijeyesinghe & Jackson, 2012). Following a step-wise approach, they depict a progressive yet fluid process of exploration and commitment to anti-racist ideology and the racial functioning of both white people and people of color.

Building on models of Black identity development (Cross, 1971; Cross & Fhagen-Smith, 2001; Jackson, 1976), Atkinson, Morten, and Sue (1998) created five-stage models to denote the general process of minority identity development that was later revamped by Sue and Sue (2003) to depict racial and cultural identity development. Although intragroup variation may exist across racial categories, racially minoritized group development includes: (1) *conformity* to dominant white culture, the belief of its superiority to one's own racial culture, and the internalization of negative racial stereotypes of one's own racial group; (2) *dissonance* between self-deprecating messages of white culture and self-appreciating messages of one's own racial culture and an increased awareness of the existence of racism and its impact on all racially minoritized groups; (3) *resistance* to white cultural values and norms and uninhibited *immersion* in one's assumed racial culture; (4) *introspection* on one's racial autonomy and the variability of all racial groups, marked by proactive rather than reactive response to white culture; and (5) *synergistic articulation and awareness* of the individual's own cultural intersectionality and an increased sense of autonomy and racial pride in addition to selective appreciation of white cultural values and selective trust toward members of the white-dominant group.

Models of white racial identity development similarly recognize the existence of systems of racial oppression. In addition, they make the underlying assumption of white people's socialization toward white superiority and progression toward the acceptance of the individual's whiteness. Sue and Sue (2016) proposed a seven-step process built upon Hardiman's (1982) and Helms's (1984, 1990, 1995) white racial identity development. Although these models have been widely used as a conceptual foundation of white identity, they have been criticized for replicating oppression-adaptive models of minority identity development and focusing on attitudes toward racially subjugated groups rather than affinities toward white supremacy (Rowe, Bennett, & Atkinson, 1994; Sue & Sue, 2016).

Nonetheless, these models offer important parallels for white racial identity construction. The phases of this process include: (1) *naïveté* and neutrality toward racial difference with limited accurate knowledge of racial minorities; (2) *conformity* toward the norms of dominant white culture and uncontested belief in its universality; (3) *dissonance* between socialized norms and information or experiences of subjugated racial groups; (4) *resistance* to the dominant messages of white culture that is accompanied by feelings of shame, anger, guilt, and racial self-hatred and *immersion* into nonwhite cultures often marked by white liberal syndrome, by which white members participate in paternalistic protection or overidentification with nonwhite groups; (5) *introspective* integration of whiteness in an individual's own identity construction, less defensive and motivated by guilt; (6) *integrative awareness* and development of a nonracist white Euro-American identity with the appreciation of cultural diversity and commitment to the eradication of racism; and, (7) *commitment to anti-racist action* defined as moral fortitude and direct objection to racism in daily life.

Table 1
Racial Identity Models

Asian American Racial Identity Development (Jean Kim, 1981, 2012)
1. ETHNIC AWARENESS: neutral or positive feelings toward ethnic groups, depending on ethnic exposure
2. WHITE IDENTIFICATION: absorbs dominant views of whiteness with increased contact with white culture; begins to develop negative views toward racial heritage and other marginalized racial groups; attempts to identify with white society
3. SOCIOPOLITICAL CONSCIOUSNESS: experiences an event or series of events that challenges white dominant views and contributes to a growing social conscious; abandons identification with white culture and positive toward other racial groups
4. REDIRECTION: renewed connection to Asian American heritage and culture (pan-ethnic Asian American consciousness); begin to develop more positive self-concept; increased anger toward white racism
5. INCORPORATION: develops positive self-concept; clear identification with Asian identity; increased respect for other cultural and racial identities

---

Black American Racial Identity (William E. Cross, Jr., 1971,1991)
1. PRE-ENCOUNTER: absorbs anti-Black beliefs and values of the dominant white culture; consciously or unconsciously devalues Black racial group; de-emphasizes membership in Black racial group with strong desire to assimilate to white dominant culture
2. ENCOUNTER: experiences an event or series of events that encourages the reinterpretation of white dominant views of Black racial group and the impact of racism in their life; begins to explore identity as a member of a group targeted by racism
3. IMMERSION/EMERSION: active withdrawal from dominant culture and symbols of whiteness; desire to actively immerse self with symbols of Black culture; actively seeks opportunities to explore Black narratives, histories, and cultures; seeks support of Black peers; early development of Black pride
4. INTERNALIZATION: becomes more secure in racial identity as conflicts between old and new perceptions of Black identity are resolved; anti-white feelings lessen; pro-Black attitudes become more expansive and open and less defensive; increased willingness to establish meaningful relationships with white people who acknowledge and respect Black personhood
5. INTERNALIZATION-COMMITMENT: inner and outer commitment to concerns of Black people as a group and social justice

---

Biracial/Mixed Race/ Multiracial Racial Identity Development (Walker S. Carlos Poston, 1990)
1. PERSONAL IDENTITY: sense of self is not linked to racial consciousness
2. CHOICE OF GROUP/CATEGORIZATION: pressure to choose one racial or ethnic group identity over another due to multiple factors (e.g., parental influence, status of racial groups, physical appearance, early experiences and racial socialization, cultural knowledge and attachment, political orientations)
3. ENMESHMENT/ DENIAL: guilt and confusion for selecting one racial group that is not fully expressive of their multiple racial influences; denial of differences between the racial groupings that results in a pseudo-identification with multiple racial identities not selected in previous stage
4. APPRECIATION: exploration of the racial identities not selected in previous stages or previously ignored
5. INTEGRATION: self-concept demonstrates an integration of multiple racial identities; this may result in choosing (1) a singular racial identity, (2) primary and secondary racial identities, or (3) two (or more) blended racial identities with equal emphasis

Latinx Ethno-racial Identity Orientation(Placida V. Gallegos & Bernardo M. Ferdman, 2012)
1. WHITE-IDENTIFIED: assimilation into dominant white ideology of race and white Euro-American culture; avoids situations that highlight racial difference
2. UNDIFFERENTIATED/DENIAL: "Color-evasive stance" and deviation from connection with Latinx[8] ethnic groups
3. LATINO AS OTHER: distinguish self as "not white" without awareness of intragroup variability amongst Latinx groups
4. SUBGROUP-IDENTIFIED: recognize self by one's own country of national origin with low appreciation of members from group outside of own
5. LATINO-IDENTIFIED: unified conceptualization of and advocacy for Latinx population without the distinction of ingroup variability
6. LATINO-INTEGRATED: clear and fluid sense of Latinx identity as an important part of intersectional identity

Native American/ Indigenous Identity Development(Perry G. Horse, 2012)
1. ERAS OF CHANGE IN INDIAN CONSCIOUSNESS: consciousness influenced by tribal histories and cultures as well as multiple eras of thought: (1) free indigenous people before European colonization, (2) U.S. Declaration of Independence and Western expansion, (3) U.S. declared natives as domestic dependent nations, (4) Native movement for independence from U.S. government
2. ORIENTATION TO RACE CONSCIOUSNESS: contact with Eurocentric notion of race and systems of racism
3. ORIENTATION TOWARD POLITICAL CONSCIOUSNESS: greater awareness and understanding of current political events and struggles tribes experience and general mistrust of U.S. government
4. ORIENTATION TOWARD LINGUISTIC CONSCIOUSNESS: increased tribal identity and desire to preserve native language
5. ORIENTATION TOWARD CULTURAL CONSCIOUSNESS: responsibility and pride in learning and maintaining cultural elements (old, renewed, and new)

---

[8] Latinx is "used as a gender-neutral alternative to Latino or Latina" (Merriam Webster, n.d.)

White Identity (Janet Helms, 1990)
1. CONTACT: uncritical acceptance of white supremacist beliefs that marginalized groups are inferior; adheres to a "color-evasive" stance; minimally aware of racial difference and/or do not find it a salient factor of identity
2. DISINTEGRATION: new experiences which challenge prior conception of the race and marginalized racial groups; increased awareness of own whiteness; experience cognitive dissonance that often results in feelings of guilt and shame
3. REINTEGRATION: retreat to dominant belief in white superiority and marginalized groups' inferiority in attempt to resolve cognitive dissonance
4. PSEUDO-INDEPENDENCE: acknowledgment of racism's existence but struggles to see how they may be both white and nonracist; unintentionally perpetuates racism by (1) supporting the conformity of marginalized groups to white cultural ideals, (2) overidentifying with marginalized racial groups, (3) relegating the task of addressing racism to people of color; or (4) attempting to comfort person of color in efforts to validate their own desire to be nonracist
5. IMMERSION/EMERSION: genuine attempt to connect to his/her own white identity and to be antiracist; increased willingness to confront own racial bias; seeks other white people who actively challenge racism6. AUTONOMY: develops a nonracist white identity; increased awareness of own whiteness and role in perpetuating racism; reduced feelings of guilt and shame; actively pursuing social justice

Although research widely supports the use of racial identity development models, there are less investigated alternative models that offer nondirectional, typological approaches to racial identity and mono- and cross-racial interaction styles. Rowe, Bennett, and Atkinson's (1994) white racial consciousness statuses denote the fluid nature of racial identity being often influenced by past histories and present environment and circumstances. White racial consciousness is grouped into two states: achieved and unachieved. Achieved white racial consciousness indexes an individual's exploration of racial concerns and commitment to detailed beliefs that have been integrated within a personal worldview. Alternately, an individual may experience an unachieved white racial consciousness in which exploration, commitment, or the combination of the two is absent from the individual's personal identity construction. The three *types* exhibited in this unachieved status are *avoidant* (attitudes are avoidant of concern for racial minority issues), *dependent* (superficial commitment to a set of attitudes with minimal exploration of alternatives), and *dissonant* (open to an informed sense of whiteness, but lack commitment to the attitudes expressed). Achieved statuses include *dominative type* (exhibits white-centric beliefs that are used to justify white supremacy and racial dominance), *conflictive type* (opposed to discriminatory practices yet also hold to prejudices toward minority groups and oppose procedures that would eliminate discrimination), *reactive type* (aware of the significance of racism in the U.S. and may align themselves with issues of the oppressed in ways that are often infantilizing, romanticizing, or idealizing of a minority group), and *integrative type* (develops a complex understanding of the sociopolitical factors of race as it pertains to themselves and racial minorities and often take a pragmatic approach in which individual behaviors toward social change may vary from passive to active). Similarly, Johnson and Quaye (2017) have encouraged queering racial identity to provide a nonlinear, stage-wise model or directional modes moving toward nonracist or integrated levels of awareness, as well as an intersectional approach of integrating racial identity within multiple social locations.

Although existing models demonstrate multiple requirements for effective supervision, racial location is emphasized as a core influence within supervisory relationships (Helms, 1984, 1995; Helms & Cook, 1999; Jernigan et al., 2010). The supervisors' racial identification often indicates their willingness to engage in the supervisee's racial reflexivity. For example, supervisors of color are often noted to have more awareness than white counterparts of racial factors that influence the therapeutic space as well as the capacity to engage in racial discourse (Goode-Cross, 2011). This willingness is primarily attributed to the acquired knowledge and lived experience as subjugated members in a white-dominant society. Being a racial minority, however, is not an adequate alternative to knowledge and expertise in facilitating the racial awareness, sensitivity, and responsiveness of supervisees (Jernigan et al., 2010). The quality of social interaction and level of increased racial responsiveness is more readily determined by the supervisor's level of racial identity development (Helms, 1984). As with their white counterparts, supervisors of color exhibit varying levels of racial identity development and need to be dually equipped to enhance supervisees' professional functioning as it pertains to race and navigate the racial dynamics of the supervisory relationship (Constantine & Sue, 2007).

Supervisory racial locations denote the primacy of racial development in effective racial training. The congruency between the supervisor and supervisee directly influences the level of effectiveness the dyad will experience. Helms's (1990) Social Interaction Model (SIM) has been applied to supervisory relationships to explore the embedded power associated with the supervisor role and how this may impact racial training (Cook, 1994; Helms & Cook, 1999). Three possible interaction styles relevant to the supervisee's racial identity development and responsiveness are proposed: regressive, progressive, and parallel (see Table 2). Supervisory pairings in which the supervisor and supervisee share similar racial worldviews and concordant racial identity statuses (e.g., conformity and conformity or committed and committed) are perceived as parallel in nature. Both supervisor and supervisee will respond to racial stimuli in similar ways and will ultimately seek shared homeostasis that is less contentious. Crossed interactions denote relationships that do not share similar worldviews or racial identity development statuses (e.g., resistant and committed or dissonant and synergistic articulation and awareness). Crossed interactions are defined as regressive, in which the supervisee is comparatively more advanced in racial identity development than the supervisor.

Table 2
Social Interaction Model for Supervision

Interaction Style	Description	Supervisor Roles	Outcome
Parallel	Supervisor and supervisee share concordant racial identity statuses and similar racial worldviews (e.g., conformity and conformity)	Most Agreeable. If racial conflict or perspectives clash, dyad quickly resolves conflict and returns to a level of homeostasis	Growth toward cultural sensitivity and responsiveness of trainee is sustainable but often minimal
Crossed: Regressive	Supervisee is more advanced in racial identity development than supervisor	Potential for frequent opposition. Both experience multiple affective responses that present as oppositional	Relationship is socially conflictual (level of conflict dependent upon disparity between statuses)

Crossed: Progressive	Supervisor is more advanced in racial identity development than supervisee	Supervisor models and guides supervisee toward increased racial awareness leading to a growth-promoting environment	Supervisee's racial and cultural exploration is deepened and racial competence is increased

RACIAL CONFIGURATIONS OF SUPERVISORY RELATIONSHIPS: UTILIZING TRANSFERENTIAL RELATIONSHIPS AND SOCIAL PROJECTIONS

In order to effectively guide the supervisee toward deeper cultural sensitivity and responsiveness, the supervisor must be aware of the racial narratives that contribute to the social dynamics of the clinical and supervisory relationships. In so doing, they must keep account of the many levels of racial defensiveness as well as affinities that might threaten constructive engagement in the supervisory relationship. These experiences are evident for both white supervisors and supervisors of color within cross-racial and mono-racial supervision dyads.

Supervisors of Color

In multiple healthcare settings, supervisors of color notably tend to offer more cultural responsiveness than white supervisors. They are reported to spend more time discussing the sociocultural foundations of therapy and the specific influence of race on the therapeutic milieu (White-Davis et al., 2016). While deemed as having increased cultural competence by supervisees, they are perceived as less generally competent than their white counterparts and at increased risk of stereotype threat. This noted challenge is often compounded by inequities found at individual, environmental, and institutional levels and the experience of tokenism, marginalization, overt and covert racism, and microaggressions toward people of color within various professional settings. Music therapy supervision resources often neglect to discuss racial location and intersectionality of supervisors of color. When addressed, it is typically presented from a singular white lens and minimally highlights cross-racial and mono-racial conflicts or in-group tensions. To broaden cultural competency within supervision, music therapy supervisors of color most often draw upon personal knowledge, peer supervision and mentorship, or literature and training provided from outside the music therapy discipline.

The Supervisor of Color and Mono-racial Supervision Dyad

Supervisors of color report relationships with mono-racial supervision dyads as "qualitatively different" than cross-racial pairings (Field, Chavel-Korell, & Domenech Rodriguez, 2010; Goode-Cross, 2011; Kelly & Boyd-Franklin, 2005; Reynaga-Abiko, 2010; Tummala-Narra, 2004; Watts-Jones, Ali, Alfaro, & Frederick, 2007). Same-race supervisors, often drawing from shared cultural knowledge inclusive of common race-based histories and narratives, are noted to provide a greater sense of safety for the supervisee, leading to increased authenticity within the supervisory relationship (Goode-Cross, 2011). In so doing, supervisors of color engage in greater use of self, more readily discuss culturally congruent treatment interventions, debunk myths and address experience of social projections of same-race clients, explore supervisee's race-based transference and countertransference with clients as well as with supervisor, and function in multiple personal and professional roles (Goode-Cross, 2011; Reynag-Abiko, 2010). Black supervisors, for example, are noted to enter into collaborative mentorship with Black supervisees. They dually provide supervision to enhance clinical functioning and frequently assist in the supervisee's professional development by providing networking opportunities and sponsorship in which the supervisee takes on the role of protégé/mentee and quickly develops a long-lasting collegial friendship (Goode-Cross, 2011). Relationships were also sometimes described as familial and embedded in "kinship," and often the supervisor felt a sense of duty to the development of Black trainees into competent therapists (Goode-Cross, 2011). Supervisors in mono-racial supervision dyads, across racial groups, provide a sense of normalization to supervisees' experiences within the discipline, and supervisees are noted to feel a more substantial degree of self-efficacy (Goode-Cross, 2011; Watts-Jones, Ali, Alfaro, & Frederick, 2007). Although these attributes are reported to strengthen the therapeutic alliance, these dyads are also hampered by multiple factors that influence their level of effectiveness.

Mono-racial supervision dyads are at an increased potential for experiencing race-based overidentification, shame, resistance, and complex power dynamics between the supervisor and supervisee (Goode-Cross, 2011; Tummala-Narra, 2004). Field, Chavez-Korell, and Domenech Rodriguez (2010), exploring supervisory relationships between Latina-identified supervisors and supervisees, described how the desire for same-ethnic support could lead to difficulty regarding boundary negotiations, unmet expectations as a result of idealization and overidentification, and cultural misunderstandings based on social projections of sameness. Furthermore, both individuals may experience in-group tensions attributed to dimensions of color, ethnicity, nationality, socio-economic class, gender, and sexual orientation (Cook & Hargrove, 1997). Supervisors may dually minimize and invalidate supervisees' multiple identities and inflict microaggressions upon supervisees based upon personal biases or unprocessed internalized oppression (Murphy-Shigematsu, 2010). When a same-race supervisor exhibits a racial identity status that is less developed than that of the supervisee, they may commit microaggressions against supervisees of color (Goode-Cross, 2011; Butler-Boyd, 2010; Jernigan et al., 2010; Murphy-Shigematsu, 2010). Within these regressive dyads, trainees report receiving a lack of support accompanied by feelings of anger, frustration, resentment, discomfort, discouragement, and confusion (Jernigan et al., 2010). Jernigan et al. (2010) reported supervisees consciously and unconsciously withdrawing from the supervision process, "passively accommodating the supervision 'to just get through it,'" engaging in inner dialogue as a means of resolving conflicts regarding racial supervisory tensions, experiencing hypervigilance, and sometimes being burdened with the responsibility of educating supervisors regarding the centrality of racial issues or integrating knowledge of culture independently (p. 65).

The Supervisor of Color and Cross-racial Minority Supervisee Dyad

As with mono-racial dyads, limited research exists in the area of cross-racial minority supervision, yet, these supervisory relationships are becoming increasingly common and are laden with opportunities and challenges that denote their complexity (Jernigan et al., 2010). Relational similarities and differences are often seen between racially minoritized groups that are often deemed as markers of cross-racial minority supervision pairings. Cultural distinctions include variations among cultural norms (e.g., giving and receiving hugs or gifts, attending supervisees' graduations, meeting family members), communication styles (e.g., direct and indirect speech, use of silence, pace of speech, tone of voice, facial expression, or body language), understandings of time, and the centrality of spirituality as a supportive factor in minority sense of personhood (Reynaga-Abiko, 2010). Furthermore, cross-racial minority dyads are dually contextualized by complementary and pejorative social images seen across racial minorities that yield an array of projective identifications. As in cross-racial minority therapeutic relationships, supervisors and supervisees may both exhibit overcompliance or racial mistrust, suspicion, and hostility (Comas-Diaz & Jacobsen, 1991). Both supervisors and supervisees may unwillingly draw upon stereotypic ideas or behaviors that lead to racial dissent within the dyad. These are often based upon the hierarchy of racial belonging between minority groups. In these instances, supervisees of color frequently report "an internalization of self-doubt and incompetence" (Jernigan et al., 2010, p. 70). Supervisors of color within cross-racial minority dyads, however, notably raise supervisees' awareness to these issues and educate through the multiplicity of marginalized and agented experiences.

Supervisors of color must be willing to (1) recognize supervising practices as Eurocentric in nature, (2) evaluate their own cultural competence/responsiveness and self-efficacy with respect to racial dynamics within cross-racial minority supervision, (3) initiate conversations about race, (4) acknowledge potential conflict in the dyad, (5) seek out racially progressive professional relationships, and (6) offer extra positive regard to supervisees of color who are courageous enough to initiate such conversations (Jernigan et al., 2010; Nelson, Gizara, Hope, Phelps, Steward, & Weitzman, 2006). By exploring supervisees' unchecked biases and modeling and supporting racial vulnerability, supervisors can facilitate a healthy development of supervisees' cultural responsiveness and the supervision alliance.

The Supervisor of Color and White Supervisee Dyad

Within cross-racial dyads, supervisors of color are said to experience higher risk of negative outcomes when working with white supervisees (Burkard, Knox, Clark, Phelps, & Inman, 2014). They often experience higher levels of resistance by white supervisees and are a target of racist microaggressions. For example, Geneva Reynaga-Abiko (2010), in her reflections as a Mexican-American supervisor working with white supervisees, noted that "European-American supervisees typically take time to determine if I am intelligent, adequately trained, have experience in the field, and am generally competent to act as their supervisor. This can involve everything from asking where I went to school [to] how long I have been supervising professionals in training, or if I am licensed to practice" (p. 20). Given this, supervisors of color are reported to experience increased cognitive and emotional stress as a result of their attempts to dispel or avoid negative perceptions or stereotypes. White supervisees are noted to sometimes become avoidant when discussing racially stereotypic client behaviors out of fear of being perceived as holding and condoning "stereotyped associations" (Remington & DaCosta, 1989, p. 400). White supervisees are also noted to become hyperfocused on race as a reactionary defense of masking personal biases, as a means of mitigating guilt, or as a means of aligning with supervisors who are considered more culturally competent. Supervisees are also noted to experience increased defensiveness or denial of racial factors in client interactions.

White Supervisors

The White Supervisor and White Supervisee Dyad

In all white supervision dyads or groups, it can be easy to ignore race as a factor influencing the supervisory relationship, in much the same way that it can be easy to ignore race as a factor in the therapeutic relationship when white therapists are working with white clients. Perhaps because of this, it is rarely noted in the literature. However, we feel that bringing this into supervision is important because how we are racialized shapes our values, beliefs, and interactions, both in cross-racial and in mono-racial relationships. To explore race in these relationships requires one to attend to the ways in which we do not understand race as permeating that space, how we see it as nonconsequential. It takes effort to attend to racialized values and beliefs and interactions that are being communicated in these spaces. This becomes easier as one becomes more aware of one's everyday forms of enacting whiteness. For example, the more that one interrogates whiteness in everyday interactions, such as noticing how whiteness is performed in the news, in textbooks, in movies, one will begin to notice how it is performed between white individuals in multiple ways. One way to do this is through the practice of mindfulness. Just as a person might regularly take an inventory of one's body to monitor and adapt their body tension, a white person can take note of how they are interacting in ways that might reinforce whiteness as the norm or as superior. By bringing this awareness into one's everyday practice, it becomes more natural to make note of this also within supervision.

The White Supervisor and Supervisee of Color Dyad

The majority of models address the cross-racial supervision with an emphasis on white and person of color dyads (Chang, Hays, & Shoffner, 2003; Constantine & Sue, 2007; Duan & Roehlke, 2001; Falendar & Shafranske, 2004; Gatmon, Jackson, Koshkarian, Martos-Perry, Molina, Patel & Rodolfa, 2001). White supervisors often reported having less cultural competence than their counterparts of minoritized races. Research on Black supervisees' perceptions of their cross-racial supervision dyad tended to note difficulties in language and communication styles (Gardner, 2002). Constantine and Sue (2007), in their study of racial perceptions of cross-racial dyads, noted that white supervisors were reported to often minimize, dismiss, invalidate, or avoid racial issues; they projected stereotypical assumptions onto Black clients and supervisees; provided insufficient performance feedback so as to not appear pejorative or racist; painted an unbalanced picture of supervisees' strengths and weaknesses, focusing on weaknesses and often trying to alter supervisees behavior to fit Eurocentric models or blaming supervisees for undue assumptions of the role of racism in clients' presentation/lived experience; and offered treatment recommendations that were culturally insensitive. Although the relationship offers increased opportunity to aid in the supervisee's cross-racial understanding of therapy and cross-racial narratives and behaviors/tendencies, this potential is hampered if the supervisor is ill-equipped. When white supervisors take on a color-evasive approach to supervision or are ill-equipped to engage in racial dialogues, the experience can result in negative outcomes. Lack of personal racial awareness, lack of awareness of racial biases and prejudices, anxiety about racial discourse, limited multicultural knowledge, and limited experiences of the white supervisor often lead to the cultural instability of the relationship and a preponderance of racial microaggressions and ineffective supervision (Constantine & Sue, 2007).

There has been limited exploration of the quality of supervision for supervisees of color. For supervisees of color, learning has often been a product of trial-and-error and of the supervisee's agency—personal research and commitment to their own racial development and pursuit of mentee relationships with therapists of color.

STRATEGIES IN SUPERVISION

In order to help music therapists develop supervisory practices that are racially responsive, we have provided the following strategies as examples.

Supervision Informed Consent Agreement

When we create a supervision informed consent agreement, we are transparent about our philosophy of supervision and our multicultural relational approach (Campbell, 2006). Being open about this at the outset indicates to the supervisee that this is foundational to the supervision approach and not brought up as a consequence of the supervisee being inadequate. Normalizing multiple dimensions of culture that must be engaged in supervision in order to practice ethically helps to minimize the supervisees' feelings that they must be doing something wrong when the topics are raised.

Social Location/Location of Self

As we did at the beginning of this chapter, we believe that as a supervisor it is important from the beginning of the relationship to be transparent and to disclose our various identities—gender, racialization, ethnicity, sexuality, socio-economic status, disability, language, religious/spiritual beliefs/values, and more. In this way, we are bringing attention to our understanding of a multidimensional view of the self. As we do this, we also bring attention to how each of these selves has a certain place in the social hierarchy, depending on varying degrees of power, privilege, and subjugation. By sharing this information and encouraging supervisees to do the same, we are opening a space where we can see ourselves and others more comprehensively, which can lead to greater degrees of compassion, understanding, and humility for each other (Hardy, 2016; Watts-Jones, 2010).

Cultural Genograms

As part of the supervision model, we often utilize the cultural genogram as a means of exploring and deepening the awareness of the supervisee's cultural heritage. Hardy and Laszloffy (1995) built this educational model on the premise that by understanding one's own cultural identities, the trainee increases accessibility and sensitivity toward individuals who are both similar and dissimilar. This step-based model provides instructions for the trainee's detailed mapping of their culture of origin. This includes an identification of constructs that organize the trainee's heritage and the specific pride and shame narratives embedded in the cultures referenced. The trainee is asked to consider migratory patterns and conditions, experiences of discrimination, intergroup tensions, and the intersectionality of targeted and agented social locations within the trainee's assumed cultural identity.

The supervisor, playing a central role in facilitating the trainee's engagement in the critical analysis of their cultural narrative, further assists the trainee in exploring various factors that contribute to their cultural identity and situates the trainee's process within the clinical context. The supervisor highlights any disproportionate attention made by the supervisee on pride or shame issues and familial or cultural issues. For example, the supervisee may focus on the positive aspects of their culture of origin that warrant a sense of pride, such as educational achievement, within their racial group, but minimally discuss the shamefulness the supervisee may feel with regard to members of their culture of origin who do not exhibit the same level or value in academic success and the economic leverage it offers. The supervisor's role would be to encourage the supervisee to explore the imbalanced focus on pride or shame issues. The supervisor would help to reveal the supervisee's biases as they pertain to race and class as well as the ways in which they may manifest (e.g., within a politic of respectability) with clients at a practicum or internship site. Additionally, the supervisor assists in identifying the multiple ways in which the cultural narrative influences the supervisee's clinical interactions and produces inherent biases that impact clinical decision-making. Additional variations of this model have been created to further situate individuals' individual and family identities within sociopolitical macrosystems and historical contexts.

Kosiutic, Gracia, Graves, Barnett, Hall, Haley, Rock, Bathon, and Kaiser's (2009) critical genogram similarly aids in mapping social location. Although not specifically created for clinical training, the critical emphasis on race, gender, and sexual orientation decontextualized from ethnicity serves as an additional resource to facilitate verbal processing. The authors provide guiding questions that explore markers of oppression/privilege associated with social location (such as the exploration of colorism within various contexts or the intersectional performance of race, gender, or sexuality across multiple generations), as well as explore insights from the experience of marginalization.

Modeling Vulnerability

As a way of reducing the hierarchical dynamics in supervision, we believe in the supervisor using a healthy amount of self-disclosure. This includes sharing stories of their experiences and openly sharing mistakes they have made and continue to make (Hadley, 2013a). We have found that by being vulnerable ourselves, a space for greater risk-taking by our supervisees is opened up. As a white supervisor, supervisees seem more prepared to share their experiences if they perceive the supervisor as also still working to dismantle their own racist habits of responding. Furthermore, in groups when supervisees of color feel able to challenge their white supervisor on something they say or do, and when the supervisor is able to hear them nondefensively and take ownership of their mistake, white supervisees have a model in terms of ways of responding when a mistake is made. In addition, it is important for supervisees of color to be acknowledged for their courage in calling out the supervisor, in order for them to feel more comfortable to continue to speak up when they recognize something as racist in the supervision or clinical context. Due to racist socialization that has rendered voices of people of color as threatening or irrelevant, supervisees of color often do not speak in the face of a stereotype threat. The role of the supervisor, therefore, is to model vulnerability as a means of building a healthy supervisory alliance and deepening the supervisee's authentic therapist self.

Reflexive Journaling

An incredibly difficult and yet essential process for both supervisors and supervisees is to become aware of their values, beliefs, and biases in relationship to race. This can be especially difficult for white supervisors and supervisees because many of their values, beliefs, and biases in relation to race are imperceptible to them, taken as givens. Of course, we are not born with our sociocultural values and beliefs, but we learn to cherish them very early on. They are already forming and taking hold long before our ability to self-reflect develops (Jun, 2010). These sociocultural values and beliefs shape our understandings of ourselves and of others. Given that our values and beliefs are so entrenched, it is difficult to bring these into awareness and to challenge them.

One approach is to have the supervisees maintain a reflexive journal during the entire supervision relationship about things they notice in their clinical practice that are related to race and racism. This approach is modeled after one that is outlined by Barry and O'Callaghan (2008). In this approach, there are "four steps which [alternate] in a back-and-forth manner: descriptive journal writing, extending self-critiquing and understanding, integration of new insights into practice, and reflexive evaluation" (p. 58). Thus, the supervisee first describes the encounters or experience. They then bring a critical lens to the experience, including reflections on how they did or did not respond and exploring why they may or may not have responded. They explore the thoughts, emotions, and even bodily responses they had at the time and then reflect on them. Once they have explored these thoughts and feelings, they may explore ways that they would have ideally responded, providing them with options in the future when they are likely to have similar encounters or experiences. Sharing their journal with the supervisor in a shared document (e.g., Google Doc) allows the supervisor to add comments and ask questions to help the supervisee to be more reflexive. Sometimes these reflexive journals can lead supervisees to feel that their sense of themselves as "good" is shaken. This is an opportune moment to explore the systemic nature of racism and to challenge the dichotomous thinking that leads to characterizations of good and bad.

Given that our interpersonal communications grow out of our intrapersonal communication, it is imperative to begin to take more notice of our inner dialogue because that is a way to understand our values and beliefs more clearly. Jun (2010) stated that "[i]ntrapersonal communication is a mirror image of one's own cultural values, beliefs, and biases" (p. 19). One of the challenges with our internal dialogue is that unless we are mindful of this, "there is no feedback loop for a reality check because the sender and the receiver are the same person, the self" (p. 21). Because of this, there is no challenge to our thoughts because the sender and the receiver are in agreement. Depending on how often these messages are repeated to oneself, they become automatic thoughts, often the result of cognitive distortions that have grown out of negative messages received as children. So, an important practice is to externalize the inner dialogue and write it down uncensored in a stream of consciousness. This is important to include in the reflexive journal. The externalization of inner dialogue may take multiple forms. It may include written journaling as stated above or may also utilize musical journaling and sharing within a process of musical reflexivity as described in the following.

Cross-Cultural Music Listening Log

This exercise was first introduced by Paul Nolan in his Multicultural Perspectives in Music Therapy course. It has been adapted to meet supervisory needs. The supervisee prepares a listening log of a musical genre or style that is cross-cultural in nature or deemed culturally new as a form of musical immersion. Active and passive listening is encouraged for a minimum of six weeks. The supervisee is tasked to explore the sociocultural context and musical iconicity of the genre or style and identify personal musical associations, biases, and reflections that arise through music listening. Moreover, the supervisee explores changes in affective or subjective responses, understandings, and attitudes about the ethnic group or culture from which this music originates and personal biases or associations that manifest throughout the process. The supervisor serves as a mirror, reflecting unconscious bias as revealed in the supervisee's narratives.

Musical Presentations

Amir (2012) utilized musical presentations as a therapeutic tool for developing the supervisee's self-knowledge and for exploration and sharing of their musical identity. The process includes preparing a musical collage that reflects aspects of the supervisee's life (e.g., their relationship with music during early adolescence, their experience of self-growth/self-realization, an important discovery, a meaningful relationship, a geographical move, or a significant life event). Expanding on this model, one can explore musical identity at the intersection of sociocultural influences. The supervisee may develop musical presentations to denote musical culture throughout their life span and the relational aspects of racial identity on the supervisee's perception of self and relationship with clients, supervisors, or peers.

Artistic Racial Self-reflexivity

We also have supervisees engage in an introspective process of *artistic racial self-reflexivity*, in which various aspects of racial identity and discourse are explored through art mediums as a means of deepening self-awareness and engendering greater levels of cultural responsiveness. The supervisor and supervisee, both individually or jointly, can center music-making and reflection on race-based narratives (e.g., internalized racism, antiracist development or functioning), social projections, transferential/ countertransferential material, resistance, or aggression (e.g., racial microinsults, microinvalidations, microassaults) found within the supervisory relationship or therapeutic milieu. The exploratory process may include externalizing the following questions adapted and expanded from Hardy and Bobes' (2017) *Promoting cultural sensitivity in supervision: A manual for practitioners* (p.23; pp.107-109). Exploring these questions can serve as an introduction into a personal process of artistic racial self-reflexivity.

- How do I perceive myself as a racial being?
- What meaning do I attach to who I am as a racial being?
- What meaning do I imagine others attach to who I am racially within a sociocultural context?
- What realities/perceptions do I have that are informed by racial identification?
- How does my racial identity inform my personal relationships?
- How does my racial identity inform my professional relationships?

- How do these relationships inform my views about various systems I inhabit? Society? The music therapy field? Academic spaces? Practicum/internship spaces?
- How does my racial identification (assumed and assigned) facilitate interactions with members of another target/agent group?
- What dimensions of my racial identity are easy to own or embrace? Which are not easy to own or embrace?
- What has my experience been in having others witness my responses to these questions?
- What themes manifest within my musical process as I explore various aspects race and racial oppression/privilege?
- In what ways has my artistic process deepened my understanding of the ways in which I navigate personal, therapeutic, and supervisory relationships and the various systems I inhabit?
- As I share my artistic process with others, are they any consistencies or inconsistencies between how I perceive myself and my artistic reflections and how others perceive me and my artistic reflections?
- What has my experience been having others witness my responses to these questions?

Although musical responses may provide deeper levels of personal insight, greater potential will be achieved in supervisory pairings that are progressive in style, in which the supervisor has more developed racial awareness, knowledge, and skill and can acutely assess raced-based material.

Both/And Thinking

It is important to go back over inner dialogues externalized through the reflexive journals and identify one's thinking style: hierarchical, dichotomous, linear, or holistic (Jun, 2010, pp. 27–29). Hierarchical thinking is closely tied to dichotomous thinking in that individuals and groups learn to see themselves as superior or inferior to others, better or worse, more or less. Dichotomous thinking is thinking in two extremes, such as good and bad, right and wrong, us and them. This kind of thinking leads to feelings of superiority and inferiority, inclusion and exclusion. Linear thinking projects and generalizes based on past events or experiences. While this can sometimes be useful, it is very damaging when it comes to discrimination, stereotyping, and marginalizing others based on one experience or based on beliefs passed from generation to generation. Holistic thinking, in contrast, is multilayered and multidimensional. It requires a nonjudgmental attitude, a nondefensive stance. It requires really listening to others and trying to understand and appreciate multiple perspectives. It requires mindful practice. In many Western societies, there is a tendency to utilize hierarchical, dichotomous, and linear thinking over more holistic both/and thinking. It is not that there are not appropriate ways of utilizing each of these thinking styles, but it is necessary to understand problematic thinking styles and to learn ways to disrupt automatic thinking patterns which contribute to ethnocentric, racist beliefs and values.

Recognizing and Working to Eliminate Racial Microaggressions

In the early 1970s, African-American psychiatrist and Harvard University professor Chester M. Pierce first described what he named as microaggressions. More recently, cross-cultural counselor Derald Wing Sue has described these as the "everyday verbal, nonverbal, and environmental slights, snubs, or insults, whether intentional or unintentional, that communicate hostile, derogatory, or negative messages to target persons based solely upon their marginalized group membership" (Sue, 2003, p. 10). These comments, tones of voice, looks, gestures, actions, and/or inactions leave recipients feeling invalidated, demeaned, overlooked, devalued, excluded, undesirable, inferior, dangerous, or even abnormal, purely because of their race, class, gender, sexuality, disability, religion, ethnicity, and so on. Microaggressions imply that all people of a particular group are the same and that if not from that group, one does not belong. Because these behaviors are so widespread, they are often unrecognized or dismissed as innocent and harmless. Yet continually being on the receiving end of these can be very damaging psychologically (in terms of self-esteem), emotionally (in terms of the anger and frustration they foster), and physically (in terms of health and well-being).

Overt discrimination and hate crimes, in contrast, are defined as macroaggressions. These overt messages and behaviors are deliberate. While they are no doubt threatening and harmful, the intentions behind them are more openly expressed and thus easier to navigate. Microaggressions, however, are most often unconscious, unintentional, and automatic. Because microaggressions are largely fueled by unconscious biases, they are often perpetuated by well-intentioned people and therefore more difficult to navigate. Because in our society our values and beliefs are structured within the oppressive system of white supremacy, and because perpetrators of microaggressions are members of groups that historically have had power and privilege over those not in the dominant group, racist microaggressions are perpetuated by well-intentioned white people on people of color.

Microaggressions can occur at multiple levels: the individual (from one person to another); the institutional (in terms of policies, practices, procedures, and structures which are in place in different institutions); and the cultural (where one group sees itself as superior and has the power to impose their values and standards on other groups). Furthermore, microaggressions can be expressed verbally (as direct or indirect comments to targets); nonverbally/behaviorally (through the use of body language or other more direct physical actions); or environmentally (the physical surroundings, including physical structures, numerical imbalance of one's own group, inaccurate media portrayals, inclusion or exclusion in educational curriculum, signs, symbols, and even mascots).

It is important that white supervisors and white supervisees become very aware of racist microaggressions toward people of color. In order for supervisees to understand the concept of microaggressions, it is beneficial to begin with their own standpoint. For music therapy supervisees who are not cis men, you can begin by exploring gender microaggressions. If the supervisor begins by sharing some experiences of gender microaggressions, supervisees will generally start to share theirs. Exploring these microaggressions and their impact on each of us personally, along with sharing stories of how our experiences of microaggressions are often minimized and negated by the dominant group, provides a bridge for becoming more aware of how we perpetuate, minimize, and negate racial microaggressions toward people of color.

As our supervisees learn more about racist microaggressions toward people of color, they are able to recognize instances of these in their clinical contexts and to include these in their reflexive journals. It is easier, of course, to recognize when these are committed by others than when supervisees themselves commit them. In time, however, they are more able to recognize ways in which they unwittingly commit racist microaggressions toward people of color, and they can then listen more nondefensively to the experiences and accusations of people of color regarding racist microaggressions. Once this level of awareness is reached, there is a greater chance to reduce the frequency and intensity of racist microaggressions and to make amends when they commit racist microaggressions.

Practicing Mindfulness to Navigate Difficult Dialogues Regarding Race

One of the most challenging situations in which both supervisors and supervisees find themselves is navigating difficult dialogues (Hardy & Bobes, 2016). For white supervisees, this happens as they become more aware of everyday racism. At this point in their process of transformative learning, they realize that by staying silent, they are remaining part of the problem. However, as they begin to speak out about racist comments, racist jokes, and racist microaggressions, they become the target of scorn.

As they speak out, they are trivialized and accused of being overly sensitive, being overly reactive, lacking a sense of humor, or even being aggressive. This parallels the kind of experience that supervisees of color have experienced throughout their experiences. As they are made to feel bad about themselves, as if they are the ones with the problem, white supervisees may begin to second-guess themselves. So, it is important for supervisors to discuss ways of staying with the conversations and using "I" statements instead of statements that are perceived as more accusatory.

Another technique that can be useful is a mindfulness exercise that encourages softening around discomfort. Supervisors can have the supervisee(s) sit in a comfortable position with their eyes shut and instruct them to stay in this position without moving throughout a music and meditation experience. The supervisor invites the supervisee(s) to notice any desire to move and anything that provides them with discomfort but reminds them that they must remain still. When they notice feelings of discomfort, it is important that they allow themselves to soften around it, to relax any muscles that may tighten in response, but to remain still. Supervisees should focus on the sensation of discomfort as it emerges and to stay with it without trying to move away from it. It is important to continue to prompt them to allow themselves to soften around the discomfort, to relax any muscle tension that occurs in response to the discomfort. Once the music and meditation experience have ended, the supervisees can move into whatever position they have been wanting to sit in, and they are asked to focus on the sensations as they do this. Does it provide relief? Is the relief immediate or gradual? In what way does their body feel better? And to release any remaining tension they may feel.

After this experience, it can be very helpful to discuss how people usually respond to discomfort by trying to build a solid wall of tightness around it, attempting to block off the feeling or avoid it. It is helpful to talk about the alternative strategy of sitting in the discomfort, acknowledging its presence, being mindful, sitting with oneself compassionately, and softening around the feelings of discomfort. By doing this, the supervisee can focus on the discomfort without all of the resistance that they usually add to it. It is important for supervisees to remember this exercise in mindfulness and softening around the discomfort and to find ways of practicing the strategies that we used in this experience as they encounter feelings of discomfort and the wall of resistance with which they want to protect themselves as they work on becoming more aware of how power and privilege permeates their everyday encounters and their therapeutic relationships.

Response/Ability

According to Nisha Sajnani (2012), as creative arts therapists we need to encourage *response-ability* in our practice—that is, the *ability* to *respond* amidst suffering and against oppression. She stated that we need to form "collaborative relationships based on respect for our clients' wisdom about their own lived experiences" and that we need to be willing "to make our values and assumptions transparent" (Sajnani, 2012, p. 189). She also encourages us to think about the politics of representation, that is, how bodies and histories are signified in various arts media. Sajnani emphasized the politics of witnessing, that is, how we honor the experiences of those who have experienced personal and social trauma.

A critical race feminist paradigm also challenges us to think through the politics of representation and witnessing. Through our various modalities, we are able to provide a platform and an artform through which human experience can be communicated and heard. However, art is never neutral. Representation refers to how bodies and histories are signified in print, on canvas, on stage, [in music], and on video. Witnessing, in this context, refers to how we support our audiences, especially those who may feel emotionally or socially alienated by what they are presented with to respond to, and possibly even enter into alliance with those performing (or exhibiting, etc.). (Sajnani, 2012, p. 190)

Thus, it is important to explore with supervisees that to be authentic in their work as music therapists, it is important to act upon their ability to respond to issues of racial oppression and suffering within their practice. Music therapists must explore the implicit and explicit messages in the music that we use and how they reinforce or challenge racial oppression. The supervisor and supervisee can explore ways of creating music with clients that bear witness to their experiences of racial oppression and that support expressions of outrage and resistance and provide vehicles for empowerment.

Furthermore, we believe, given the predominance of whiteness in our profession, that it is the response/ability of white supervisors and supervisees to explore the impact of race on therapeutic relationships. Therefore, as stated above, we bring race to the foreground in our supervision sessions, not just when it is seen as "getting in the way" of the therapeutic relationship, but as an aspect of all therapeutic and supervisory relationships. Indeed, it is our response/ability to discuss this aspect of our supervisory relationship. And it is the response/ability of supervisees to explore these issues in their supervision sessions; in clinical journals; in their clinical assessment, treatment, and evaluation practices; and in clinical research.

Finally, even when we do not see a direct connection between our own actions and the root causes of racial injustice, supervisors must stress the importance of making it our response/ability to work together in an effort to dismantle power structures that continue to oppress and privilege groups based on racialization.

CONCLUSION

Music therapy cultural competency calls for a contextual understanding of the multiple ways in which race plays a role in the broader societal structures that impact our clients' lived experiences and the multiple ways in which it influences therapeutic processes. Despite the growing literature denoting the contribution of supervision in the trainee's racial awareness and responsivity, race is not often enough discussed as a significant self-identifier in music therapy supervision. Many music therapy supervisors struggle with understanding and navigating the complexities of racial identities and narratives in the supervisory relationship. The process of constructively deepening supervisee racial responsiveness demands the active location of self within the sociopolitical landscape in which both supervisor and supervisee exist. These experiences are qualitatively different in mono-racial and cross-racial supervisory pairings. Nonetheless, it is vital that supervisors foster a racially safe environment that normalizes conversations of race and encourages the exploration and critique of personal racial assumptions and the racial tension encountered in music therapy supervision.

REFERENCE LIST

Amir, D. (2012). "My music is me": Musical presentation as a way of forming and sharing identity in music therapy group. *Nordic Journal of Music Therapy, 21*(2), 176–193.

Aponte, H. J., & Carol Carlsen, J. (2009). An Instrument for Person-of-the-Therapist Supervision. *Journal of Marital and Family Therapy, 35*(4), 395–405.

Aponte, H. J., Powell, F. D., Brooks, S., Watson, M. F., Litzke, C., Lawless, J., & Johnson, E. (2009). Training the person of the therapist in an academic setting. *Journal of Marital and Family Therapy, 35*(4), 381–394.

Arczynski, A. V., & Morrow, S. L. (2017). The complexities of power in feminist multicultural psychotherapy supervision. *Journal of Counseling Psychology, 64*(2), 192–205.

Atkinson, D. R., Morten, G., & Sue, D. W. (1998). Addressing the mental health needs of racial/ethnic minorities. In D. R. Atkinson et al. (Eds.), *Counseling American Minorities* (5th ed., pp. 51–80). Boston, MA: McGraw-Hill.

Barry, P., & O'Callaghan, C. (2008). "Reflexive journal writing: A tool for music therapy student clinical practice development." *Nordic Journal of Music Therapy, 17*(1), 55–66.

Bruscia, K. E. (2014). *Defining music therapy* (3rd ed.). University Park, IL: Barcelona Publishers.

Burkard, A. W., Edwards, L. M., & Adams, H. A. (2016). Racial color blindness in counseling, therapy, and supervision. In H. A. Neville, M. E. Gallardo, & D. W. Sue (Eds.), *The myth of racial color blindness: Manifestations, dynamics, and impact* (pp. 294–311). Washington, DC: American Psychological Association.

Burkard, A. W., Knox, S., Clark, R., Phelps, D., & Inman, A. (2014). Easy and difficult feedback in cross-cultural supervision. *The Counseling Psychologist, 42*, 314–344.

Butler-Boyd, N. M. (2010). An African-American supervisor's reflections on multicultural supervision. *Training and Education in Professional Psychology, 4*, 11–15. doi:10.1037/a0018351

Campbell, J. M. (2011). *Essentials of clinical supervision* (Vol. 28). Chichester, UK: John Wiley & Sons.

Chang, C. Y., Hays, D. G., & Shoffner, M. F. (2003). Cross-racial supervision: A developmental approach for White supervisors working with supervisees of Color. *The Clinical Supervisor, 22*(2), 121–138. doi:10.1300/j001v22n02_08

Comas–Diaz, L., & Jacobsen, F. M. (1991). Ethnocultural transference and countertransference in the therapeutic dyad. *American Journal of Orthopsychiatry, 61*, 392–402. doi:10.1037/h0079267

Constantine, M. G. (1997). Facilitating multicultural competency in counseling supervision: Operationalizing a practical framework. In D. B. Pope-Davis & H. L. K. Coleman (Eds.), *Multicultural counseling competencies: Assessment, education and training, and supervision* (pp. 310–324). Thousand Oaks, CA: SAGE.

Constantine, M. G., & Sue, D. W. (2007). Perceptions of racial microaggressions among Black supervisees in cross-racial dyads. *Journal of Counseling Psychology, 54*, 142–153.

Cook, D. A. (1994). Racial identity in supervision. *Counselor Education & Supervision, 34*, 132–141.

Cook, D. A., & Hargrove, L. P. (1997). The supervisory experience. In C. E. Thompson & R. T. Carter (Eds.), *Racial identity theory: Applications to individual, group, and organizational interventions* (pp. 83–96). Mahwah, NJ: Erlbaum.

Cross, W. E. (1971). The Negro-to-Black conversion experience. *Black World, 20*(9), 13–27.

Cross, W. E. (1991). *Shades of Black: Diversity in African-American identity*. Philadelphia, PA: Temple University Press.

Cross, W. E., Jr., & Fhagen-Smith, P. (2001). Patterns of African-American identity development: A life span perspective. In C. Wijeyesinghe & B. Jackson (Eds.), *New perspectives on racial identity development: A theoretical and practical anthology* (pp. 243–270). New York, NY: New York University Press.

Daniels, J., D'Andrea, M., & Kyung Kim, B. S. (1999). Assessing the barriers and challenges of cross-cultural supervision: A case study. *Counselor Education and Supervision, 38*, 191–204.

DeGruy, J. (2005). *Post-traumatic slave syndrome: America's legacy of enduring injury and healing*. Portland, OR: Joy DeGruy Publications Inc.

Duan, C., & Roehlke, H. (2001). A descriptive "snapshot" of cross-racial supervision in university counseling center internships. *Journal of Multicultural Counseling & Development, 29*(2), 131–146.

Estrada, D., Frame, M. W., & Williams, C. B. (2004). Cross-cultural supervision: Guiding the conversation toward race and ethnicity. *Journal of Multicultural Counseling & Development, 32*, 307–319.

Estrella, K. (2001). Multicultural approaches to music therapy supervision. In M. Forinash (Ed.), *Music therapy supervision* (pp. 39–66). Gilsum, NH: Barcelona Publishers.

Falendar, C. A., & Shafranske, E. P. (2004). *Clinical supervision: A competency-based approach.* Washington, DC: American Psychological Association.

Field, L. D., Chavel-Korell, S., & Domenech Rodriguez, M. M. (2010). No hay rosas sin espinas: Conceptualizing Latina-Latina supervision from a multicultural developmental supervisory model. *Training and Education in Professional Psychology, 4,* 47–54. doi:10.1037/a0018521

Fredrickson, G. M. (2002). *Racism: A short history.* Princeton, NJ: Princeton University Press.

Freire, P. (2012). *Pedagogy of the oppressed.* New York, NY: Bloomsbury.

Gallegos, P., & Ferdman, B. (2012). Latina and Latino Ethnoracial Identity Orientations: A Dynamic and Developmental Perspective. In C. Wijeyesinghe & B. Jackson (Eds.), *New perspectives on racial identity development: Integrating emerging frameworks* (2nd ed., pp. 51–80). New York, NY: NYU Press. Retrieved from http://www.jstor.org/stable/j.ctt9qg2qt.8

Gardner, R., M.D. (2002). Cross-cultural perspectives in supervision. *The Western Journal of Black Studies, 26*(2), 98–106.

Gatmon, D., Jackson, D., Koshkarian, L., Martos-Perry, N., Molina, A., Patel, N., & Rodolfa, E. (2001). Exploring ethnic, gender, and sexual orientation variables in supervision: Do they really matter? *Journal of Multicultural Counseling and Development, 29*(2), 102–113.

Goode-Cross, D. T. (2011). "Those who learn have a responsibility to teach": Black therapists' experiences supervising Black therapist trainees. *Training and Education in Professional Psychology, 5*(2), 73–80. doi:10.1037/a0023187

Hadley, S. (2013a). *Experiencing race as a music therapist: Personal narratives.* Gilsum, NH: Barcelona Publishers.

Hadley, S. (2013b). Dominant narratives: Complicity and the need for vigilance in the Creative Arts Therapies. *The Arts in Psychotherapy, 40*(4), 373–381.

Hadley, S., & Norris, M. S. (2016). Musical multicultural competency in music therapy: The first step. *Music Therapy Perspectives, 34*(2), 129–137.

Hardiman, R. (1982). *White identity development: A process-oriented model for describing the racial consciousness of White Americans.* Unpublished doctoral dissertation, University of Massachusetts, Amherst, MA.

Hardy, K. V. (2016). Toward the development of a multicultural relational perspective in training and supervision. In K. V. Hardy & T. Bobes (Eds.), *Culturally sensitive supervision and training: Diverse perspectives and practical applications.* New York, NY: Routledge.

Hardy, K. V., & Bobes, T. (Eds.). (2017). *Promoting cultural sensitivity in supervision: A manual for practitioners.* New York, NY: Taylor & Francis.

Hardy, K. V., & Laszloffy, T. A. (1995). The cultural genogram: Key to training culturally competent family therapists. *Journal of marital and family therapy, 21*(3), 227–237.

Harrell, S. P. (2014). Compassionate confrontation and empathic exploration: The integration of race-related narratives in clinical supervision. In C. A. Falender, E. P. Shafranske, & C. J. Falicov (Eds.), *Multiculturalism and diversity in clinical supervision: A competency-based approach* (pp. 83–110). Washington, DC: American Psychological Association.

Helms, J. E. (1984). Toward a theoretical explanation of the effects of race on counseling: A Black and White model. *Counseling Psychologist, 12,* 153–165.

Helms, J. E. (Ed.). (1990). *Black and White racial identity: Theory, research, and practice.* Westport, CT: Greenwood.

Helms, J. E. (1995). An update of Helms's white and people of color racial identity models. In J. G. Ponterotto, J. M. Casas, L. A. Suzuki, & C. M. Alexander (Eds.), *Handbook of multicultural counseling* (pp. 181–198). Thousand Oaks, CA: SAGE.

Helms, J. E., & Cook, D. A. (1999). *Using race and culture in counseling and psychotherapy: Theory and process.* Boston, MA: Allyn & Bacon.

hooks, b. (2003). *Teaching community: A pedagogy of hope.* New York, NY: Routledge.

Horse, P. (2012). Twenty-First Century Native American Consciousness: A Thematic Model of Indian Identity. In C. Wijeyesinghe & B. Jackson (Eds.), *New Perspectives on Racial Identity Development: Integrating Emerging Framework* (2nd ed., 108–120). New York, NY: NYU Press. Retrieved from http://www.jstor.org/stable/j.ctt9qg2qt.10

Jackson, B. (2012). Black Identity Development: Influences of Culture and Social Oppression. In C. Wijeyesinghe & B. Jackson (Eds.), *New Perspectives on Racial Identity Development: Integrating Emerging Frameworks* (2nd ed., pp. 33–50). New York, NY: NYU Press. Retrieved from http://www.jstor.org/stable/j.ctt9qg2qt.7

Jernigan, M. M., Green, C. E., Helms, J. E., Perez-Gualdron, L., & Henze, K. (2010). An examination of people of color supervision dyads: Racial identity matters as much as race. *Training and Education in Professional Psychology, 4*(1), 62–73.

Johnson, A. A., & Quaye, S. J. (2017). Queering Black Racial Identity Development. *Journal of College Student Development, 58*(8), 1135–1148.

Jun, H. (2010). *Social justice, multicultural counseling, and practice: Beyond a conventional approach.* Thousand Oaks, CA: SAGE.

Kelly, S., & Boyd-Franklin, N. (2005). African-American women in client, therapist, and supervisory relationships: The parallel processes of race, culture, and family. In M. Rostagi & E. Wieling (Eds.), *Voices of color: First-person accounts of ethnic minority therapists* (pp. 67–90). Thousand Oaks, CA: SAGE.

Kim, J. (1981). *The process of Asian-American identity development: A study of Japanese-American women's perceptions of their struggle to achieve positive identities* (Doctoral dissertation). University of Massachusetts, Amherst, MA.

Kim, J. (2012). Asian-American racial identity development theory. . In C. Wijeyesinghe & B. Jackson (Eds.), *New Perspectives on Racial Identity Development: Integrating Emerging Frameworks* (2nd ed., pp. 138–160). New York, NY: NYU Press. Retrieved from http://www.jstor.org/stable/j.ctt9qg2qt.12

Kim, S. A. (2008). The supervisee's experience in cross-cultural music therapy supervision. *Qualitative Inquiries in Music Therapy, 4,* 1–44.

Kleintjes, S., & Swartz, L. (1996). Black clinical psychology trainees at a "White" South African university: Issues for clinical supervision. *The Clinical Supervisor, 14*(1), 87–109.

Kohl, B. G. (2006). Can you feel me now? Worldview, empathy, and racial identity in a therapy dyad. *Journal of Emotional Abuse, 6*(2–3), 173–196.

Kosutic, I., Garcia, M., Graves, T., Barnett, F., Hall, J., Haley, E., Rock, J., Bathon, A., & Kaiser, B. (2009). The critical genogram: A tool for promoting critical consciousness. *Journal of Feminist Family Therapy, 21*(3), 151–176. doi:10.1080/08952830903079037

Millán, F. (2010). On supervision: Reflections of a Latino psychologist. *Training and Education in Professional Psychology, 4*(1), 7–10.

Murphy-Shigematsu, S. (2010). Microaggressions by supervisors of color. *Training and Education in Professional Psychology, 4*(1), 16–18. doi:10.1037/a0017472

Nelson, M. L., Gizara, S., Hope, A. C., Phelps, R., Steward, R., & Weitzman, L. (2006). A feminist multicultural perspective on supervision. *Journal of Multicultural Counseling and Development, 34,* 105–115.

Porter, N. (2014). Women, culture, and social justice: Supervision across the intersections. In C. A. Falender, E. P. Shafranske, & C. J. Falicov (Eds.), *Multiculturalism and diversity in clinical supervision: A competency-based approach* (pp. 59–82). Washington, DC: American Psychological Association.

Poston, W. S. C. (1990). The biracial identity development model: A needed addition. *Journal of Counseling & Development, 69*(2), 152–155. doi:10.1002/j.1556-6676.1990.tb01477.x

Remington, G., & DaCosta, G. (1989). Ethnocultural factors in resident supervision: Black supervisor and white supervisees. *American Journal of Psychotherapy, 43*(3), 398–404.

Reynaga-Abiko, G. (2010). Opportunity amidst challenge: Reflections of a Latina supervisor. *Training and Education in Professional Psychology, 4*, 19–25. doi:10.1037/a0017052

Rockquemore, K. A., & Laszloffy, T. A. (2003). Multiple realities: A relational narrative approach in therapy with black-white mixed-race clients. *Family Relations, 52*(2), 119–128. doi:10.1111/j.1741-3729.2003.00119.x

Rowe, W., Bennett, S., & Atkinson, D. R. (1994). White racial identity models: A critique and alternative proposal. *Counseling Psychologist, 22*, 120–146.

Sajnani, N. (2012). Response/ability: Imagining a critical race feminist paradigm for the creative arts therapies. *The Arts in Psychotherapy, 39*(3), 186–191.

Schroeder, M., Andrews, J. J. W., & Hindes, Y. L. (2009). Cross-Racial Supervision: Critical Issues in the Supervisory Relationship. *Canadian Journal of Counselling, 43*(4), 295–310.

Stige, B. (2017). Foreword: Actual families, possible practices. In S. L. Jacobsen & G. Thompson (Eds.), *Music therapy with families: Therapeutic approaches and theoretical perspectives.* Philadelphia, PA: Jessica Kingsley Press.

Sue, D. W., & Sue, D. (2003). *Counseling the culturally diverse: Theory and practice* (4th ed.). New York, NY: Wiley.

Sue, D. W., & Sue, D. (2016). *Counseling the culturally diverse: Theory and practice* (7th ed.). Hoboken, NJ: John Wiley & Sons, Inc.

Swamy, S. (2011). "No, she doesn't seem to know anything about cultural differences!": Culturally centered music therapy supervision. *Music Therapy Perspectives, 29*(2), 133–137.

Toporek, R. L., Ortega-Villalobos, L., & Pope-Davis, D. B. (2004). Critical incidents in multi-cultural supervision: Exploring students' and supervisors' experiences. *Journal of Multicultural Counseling and Development, 32*, 66–83.

Tummala-Narra, P. (2004). Dynamics of race and culture in the supervisory encounter. *Psychoanalytic Psychology, 21*(2), 300–311.

Watson, M. F. (2016). Supervision in black and white: Navigating cross-racial interactions in the supervisory process. In K. V. Hardy & T. Bobes (Eds.), *Culturally sensitive supervision and training: Diverse perspectives and practical applications.* New York, NY: Routledge.

Watts-Jones, D., Ali, R., Alfaro, J., & Frederick, A. (2007). The role of a mentoring group for family therapy trainees and therapists of color. *Family Process, 46*, 437–450.

White-Davis, T., Stein, E., & Karasz, A. (2016). The elephant in the room: Dialogues about race within cross-cultural supervisory relationships. *The International Journal of Psychiatry in Medicine, 51*(4), 347–356.

Wijeyesinghe, C., & Jackson, B. (Eds.). (2012). *New perspectives on racial identity development: Integrating emerging frameworks* (2nd ed.). New York, NY: NYU Press. Retrieved from http://www.jstor.org/stable/j.ctt9qg2qt

Young, L. (2009). Multicultural issues encountered in the supervision of music therapy internships in the United States and Canada. *The Arts in Psychotherapy, 36*(4), 191–201.

Part Two:
Supervision Practices

Chapter 8

SUPERVISION OF FIRST-TIME PRACTICA

Lisa Summer

INTRODUCTION

The practicum is the crucible in which music therapists are forged. No classroom work can compare to the intensity of face-to-face engagement with real individuals—real individuals with real needs, disabilities, and emotions. Like other "first" experiences, the first practicum is emotionally charged and transformative. I will address the principal obstacles confronting all first-year practicum students as they acquire the clinical skills, theoretical knowledge, musical abilities, and personal growth to prepare them to enter the profession (Summer, 2014a), and I will share my supervisory strategy for guiding students through them. Even though the specific methods of my supervision may differ from yours (e.g., I work most effectively in group supervision, while you may favor individual supervision), I hope you will find herein a useful summary of the most common first-year practicum issues.

Supervision should take into account differences in gender, gender identity, age, sex, ethnicity, sexual orientation, religion, socio-economic status, geography, and language. An approach to supervision that recognizes and appreciates the differences with which each student enters her training will foster the development of a natural therapeutic style built upon the strengths of each trainee, rather than create a simulacrum, a pale imitation of the supervisor. The beginning music therapy student should not be treated as a tabula rasa upon which the supervisor impresses her style. Music therapy students should not be trained uniformly as if they emerged from some prototypical music therapy student template, nor should they become imitations of their supervisors. Preferably, the practicum will cultivate within the student the ability to utilize the unique and individual attributes already present within her so that she might best actualize her latent potential to benefit music therapy clients.

An effective therapist must be "present" for her client, ready to react spontaneously and unassumingly to difficult clinical situations, not tentatively struggling to recall what her supervisor would do under the circumstances. We, as supervisors, have a responsibility to countenance independence of thought and action in our charges, not tie them to an artificial dependence on pedantic formulas of our own devices (Forinash & Summer; 1998, 1999). The educational goal of the first-time practicum is to create a reflective, independent student, not one dependent upon the supervisor. This is the first developmental step toward creating music therapists who are individuals, with a naturally therapeutic style instead of one inculcated in them by teachers and supervisors.

The goals of the first-time practicum course are to gain basic knowledge and skills in (1) therapeutic presence, (2) musical skills, and (3) working with resistance, in order to develop an effective, therapeutic relationship in music over time with a disabled client.[9]

---

[9] I have limited myself to discussing group supervision (as opposed to individual supervision) with students who are working with an individual client (as opposed to students who are working with a therapy group).

VIGNETTE: CHELSEA

When a music therapy student visits her first clinical setting, she does not yet know how to make therapeutic contact with a person with significant disabilities. Chelsea, a first-time practicum student, had already visited her first clinical site, a nursing home, several times to observe and informally interact with the older adult residents. In the first music therapy session with her individual client, Linda, Chelsea initiated contact. Asking loudly, she inquired, "Hello, what's your name?" Although the client lifted her head and made eye contact with her, she did not answer Chelsea's question. Chelsea continued, without a pause, more loudly, "What a nice dress—it's such a pretty color and it looks so nice with the color of your hair!" The client looked inquisitively at Chelsea, looked down at her dress and rearranged it, but gave no verbal response. Chelsea continued, "I have my guitar right here in this case. Maybe you'd like to hear a song. I'll play one for you and you tell me if you know it. I bet you'll like this song …."

Discussion

Chelsea has unknowingly rejected the client's attempt to connect with her because she does not yet understand how to be therapeutically present with a client. Chelsea was sincere in her attempt to make contact with her client, but an examination of her interaction with Linda shows that she approached her with a specific response in mind. She wanted her to respond verbally: "My name is Linda." When she did not get the response she desired, she ignored Linda's actual response to her. Linda's eye contact was her form of response. Chelsea's next interventions actually cut off Linda's response by directing Linda's eye contact to her clothes, to her guitar, everywhere but to Chelsea's eyes. Linda's eye contact *is* personal contact with Chelsea, but Chelsea did not observe and identify it as such. Instead, she rejected her eye contact and looked for her to verbalize. After Chelsea realized that Linda was not going to be verbally responsive to her, she should have let go of her expectation and made a transition to a mode of nonverbal communication.

Chelsea needs to learn to receive contact from a client in the form in which the client is able and willing to give it. This means that Chelsea needs to give up her own expectations and/or preferences about how a client will respond. Rather than go into a session with a narrowed view of what will or should happen, she needs to cultivate an open state of mind. The client's responses, not the therapist's expectations, must dictate how the therapeutic relationship will unfold.

Entering a therapeutic relationship with a client must be accomplished in an open state of awareness and observation. The therapist interacts with the client by using "evenly suspended attention" (Freud, 1912), a state of mind in which the therapist globally observes the client. In this state, the therapist gives equal and impartial recognition to the verbal and nonverbal aspects of the client. Such a state of consciousness will diminish the chances that the student will circumvent honest communication from a client in favor of what the student perceives as "appropriate."

Chelsea attended a one-hour group supervision session with nine other first-time practicum students, fresh and excited from their first clinical observation session. The class began with Chelsea recounting her interaction with Linda. "I asked her her name, but she didn't respond. I tried to be friendly and talked about her clothes. I don't know why she didn't answer me, but then I played a song for her, hoping that I could help to make her feel more comfortable with me." (As I did not take notes during the class or record the proceedings, this is not a verbatim transcript. After the group supervision sessions recounted here and below, I reconstructed as accurately as I could recall the pertinent dialogue. Although much of the discussion is omitted, I believe that the salient material is accurate.) Chelsea was asked to conjecture why Linda did not answer her. She ventured her opinion that Linda might have felt anxious or nervous at seeing a new face at the nursing home.

With further prompting, Chelsea reflected more deeply upon her interaction with Linda. She recalled two important subtleties of the encounter. She remembered that Linda seemed neither anxious nor nervous. She recollected clearly how Linda had made direct eye contact with her. Chelsea said that, at the time, she had a sense that Linda had really wanted to respond. Second, Chelsea realized that she herself was anxious and nervous and had become more so when Linda did not readily "respond" to her. (By "respond," Chelsea means there was no verbal response.) This is Chelsea's first step toward recognizing her own state of mind in therapeutic interactions and in observing the subtle responsiveness of disabled clients. This reflection yields two insights which I, as supervisor, could now reinforce to Chelsea and the supervision class: first, the negative impact of one's expectations upon observing clients, and second, the tendency to project one's own feelings upon the client and how one's own feelings affect client observations.

Chelsea was asked to re-enact her interaction with Linda through role-playing with another student volunteer; Chelsea played Linda while another student, Jennifer, assumed Chelsea's part as the therapist. They re-enacted the encounter as Chelsea had described it. After the role-play, each student was asked to reflect on their experience in character. Chelsea, as Linda, reported that she felt Jennifer's good intentions, but that she felt rejected by her. She felt that Jennifer (in the role of Chelsea) just wanted to play her song—that this was what she was there to do. Chelsea said, "It was like you had an assignment, something you were supposed to do … oh, now I get it! When I was with Linda, I *did* think that this was what I was supposed to do—to do music therapy, I was supposed to play my guitar. I didn't realize that I skipped over the most important part—I missed the human contact with Linda."

Many of the students recognized Chelsea's experience as similar to their own. Chelsea was then asked to reverse roles and to approach Linda anew, with greater openness. Chelsea and the class were given enough freedom to discover on their own, through role-playing, different strategies for approaching a client with therapeutic openness. This role-playing constituted a rehearsal for the students' next session with their clients.

In order to address this issue further, the practicum class was given an assignment to prepare them for visits to their clinical sites for the rest of the semester. They were given guidelines for developing a relaxation or centering technique that they would utilize before each clinic visit to put them in an optimal state of consciousness in which they could better observe and respond to their client. This stratagem for improving observation skills and the class discussion and role-playing preceding it are a part of my own pedagogical method. Other teachers and supervisors utilize their own styles and methods, but all first-time practicum supervisors will confront the problem exemplified in Chelsea's situation.

In this practicum supervision session, the students learned, through reflection, role-playing and centering, the first step in developing "therapeutic presence" with the client: observing the client's verbal and nonverbal expression in a state of evenly suspended attention, as opposed to the highly self-critical, judgmental state of mind that all music therapy students have cultivated from years of producing polished musical performances. Practicum students may be confused because the narrowed state of mind so beneficial for music practice (and for which they received reinforcement from their music teachers) is precisely the worst state of mind for the proper practice of music therapy (Summer, 1997). When a therapist is in a state of narrowed expectations, this fosters an inflexible relationship that is based upon the client's compliance with the therapist. The student therapist looks for the client to respond in an "appropriate" way. This kind of expectation is counterproductive to the global perception of the client's behavior and to the unfolding of a basic therapeutic relationship. Because music students are so used to playing music in a performance-oriented state, unless they are taught to shift their state of mind for therapy sessions to one which is open and nonjudgmental, their observation skills and their general responsiveness to clients will be diminished.

Diminished observation skills and responsiveness are not the only limitations in the establishment of an empathic therapeutic relationship. Sometimes a student's inability to empathize with a client is rooted more deeply in unconscious cultural biases, especially when a when a client's age, gender, ethnicity, religion, sexual orientation, gender identity, socio-economic status, geography, language, and/or musical preference are different from her own. Most students are aware of the fact that society, in general, negatively judges old age, and, consequently, that older adults are marginalized by American culture. But there is a significant difference between this kind of intellectual, conceptual understanding of age bias and a true empathic acceptance of one's own personal bias against older adults. Unfortunately, it is the nature of unconscious cultural biases that they are readily projected onto others, yet they remain unseen within oneself. Whereas a conceptual understanding of cultural bias is easily achieved, a personal, unconscious bias cannot be known without forcibly pressing it into conscious awareness. The remedy for an unconscious bias cannot occur within a short supervision hour. Therefore, experiential exercises and group discussions that take considerable time and effort are typically included in course meetings.

I cannot stress strongly enough that students' implicit biases regarding their clients must be consciously addressed. If aspects of a client's cultural identity are overlooked as a variable in the therapeutic relationship, this constitutes a rejection of essential aspects of the client. Furthermore, unexamined cultural differences become the central impetus for the impulse to "fix" the client. Essentially, ignoring cultural biases results in a severely restricted therapist/client relationship in which the student unintentionally requires her client to conform to the student's own idea of what is right and wrong or "good" and "bad" (Mahoney, 2015). For example, one student—after examining her personal biases through classroom discussion and experiential exercises—shared her new perspective: "Instead of being fixated on 'repairing,' we need to celebrate the strengths of [the client] and use these strengths to form an effective therapeutic relationship."

VIGNETTE: PAULA

Paula's first practicum was with Kenny, who was nine years old, developmentally delayed, and enrolled in a special education classroom in a public school. Paula spent the first three music therapy sessions in assessing Kenny's strengths and limitations. By the fourth session, she had designed Kenny's treatment plan, which began by singing precomposed and improvised songs designed to improve contact with Kenny.

Prior to working with Kenny, Paula learned from her client's special education teacher Kenny's favorite song. In her fourth session, Paula sang "It's a Small World After All," accompanying herself on guitar. She kept eye contact with Kenny throughout the piece, performing with unwavering tempo, dynamic, timbre, and phrasing. Kenny began to jump up and down in his chair with excitement, continuing sporadically during the entire song—at times in tempo with the song, at other times, not. At one point in the song, he clapped loudly in a sporadic rhythm. For parts of the song, he had his eyes closed with a smile on his face. At the first chorus, "It's a small world," Kenny said the word "world" in exact time with the music.

Discussion

Kenny's responses during the song demonstrate that this technique was not working toward the development of their relationship. Kenny's excitement showed that Paula has the potential to make excellent therapeutic contact with him through the song. However, despite the fact that Kenny enjoyed Paula's performance, contact between them was not made. Kenny's body responses—jumping and clapping—were, for the most part, not related to the tempo or rhythms of the song, and closing his eyes was a sign that he was more internally stimulated by this song than stimulated to make contact with Paula. In addition, Kenny's one verbal response was at the beginning of the song, but he attempted no others after that. As the song progressed, Kenny's responses did not grow more responsive to the music. His movements never accommodated to the rhythm of the music. His responses were more from stimulation and excitement about the music. This indicates that Kenny was not able to use Paula's music as a vehicle for contact; instead, he used the song as a medium for self-stimulation. Had Paula's therapeutic goal in playing this song been to increase Kenny's engagement in the session, then her approach to this song would have been valid. However, there being no issue with Kenny's level of engagement, Paula did not further her treatment plan in this session.

Paula cannot engender within Kenny a sense of trust and therapeutic connection simply by playing Kenny's favorite song, once or repeatedly. "It's a Small World After All" is an excellent context within which to develop their connection, but Kenny needs more than this. Kenny is exhibiting engagement, but not interpersonal engagement. Paula must not only observe Kenny's reactions to the music, but also respond immediately to them. She needs to utilize Kenny's nonverbal responses as a means to make interpersonal contact with him throughout the length of the music. Paula's task is to seek contact with Kenny by spontaneously adapting the song to his responses.

Musicians realize songs by being responsive to the song's lyrics. The musician realizes the meaning of the song and takes stylistic liberties with the elements of music (e.g., dynamics, timbre, tempo, attack, phrasing) in order to communicate its meaning to listeners. Whereas the musician is responsive to the meaning of the song's lyrics, the therapeutic realization of a song is primarily dependent upon the client's behavior and the meaning behind the behaviors. "It's a Small World" is a musical structure—a musical container—which should be interpreted by the music therapist not in relation to the song's text but, instead, in relation to the client's in-the-moment responses. Therapists must be accommodating, incorporating the client's responses into the constantly metamorphosizing musical container of the therapeutic relationship.

Altering the tempo of the piece through the use of ritardandi, accelerandi, and pauses would permit Paula to mirror musically the rhythm and intensity of Kenny's physical responses. The tempo, phrasing, and attacks should match Kenny's jumping and clapping; the dynamic intensity should be matched to the size of Kenny's gestures, by the look on his face. In order to focus Kenny's attention on Paula, Kenny should become aware, consciously or unconsciously, that his responses are shaping his song. Paula should not be performing "It's a Small World After All," copyright © Wonderland Music Co., Inc., but instead "It's Kenny's World, After All," with the copyright equally shared by Kenny and Paula.

Music therapy students must learn to make more intimate moment-by-moment contact with clients than they have ever done before in ordinary music-making situations (such as singing in chorus, playing in ensembles, and even playing guitar and singing in social situations).

Paula's rendition of the song was actually unresponsive to the song's lyrics as well as to her client. Her unwavering use of tempo, dynamic, timbre, rhythms, and phrasing is common in beginning music therapy students who are just learning how to play the guitar. Before she can gain enough musical creativity to respond to Kenny, she must first develop musical flexibility on guitar and voice. Most children's songs provide ample opportunities to "play" stylistically because of their simple phrasing and predictable chord changes. Differences in the song's verses can be exaggerated to create different means of contact. Repetition of the chorus can be emphasized, creating a sense of security and trust within which the therapist can musically prompt the client to sing a simple verbal response. Simple, popular songs are flexible musical containers ripe with possibilities for accommodation to make contact with clients. Although precomposed, they must be significantly altered to become interpersonal experiences with therapeutic significance.

Some students come with an innate ability to realize a piece of music with sensitivity to the lyrics, and some have an innate ability to interpret the client's responses musically. For effective therapy, all students must develop a strategic balance of attention between the client and musical responsiveness. Since the therapist acts as the bridge between the client and the music, she should not focus on the client to the exclusion of the music, nor exaggerate the musical interpretation of a piece in a way that excludes the client from influencing the piece.

In group supervision, Paula was asked to describe her session with Kenny to the class. "I was so happy that I had asked his teacher for his favorite song—he loved it. When I started the song, he was distant at first. During the song, we had such a good time and I felt so good afterwards." She described Kenny as extremely responsive, engaged and enjoying the music, and characterized the experience as very therapeutic. Paula was very pleased with this experience.

I questioned her further about her own experience during the music. "Where was your attention? What were you thinking about? Did any specific moments during the song stand out to you?" Paula was able to clearly remember and describe in detail Kenny's responses. In supervision, it is important to first hear Paula's perception of this experience, because I need to know whether she is aware of the problems I have noticed. Paula and another student, Hillary, were asked to role-play Paula's session with Kenny. Hillary was asked to take on the role of Kenny and to adopt the emotionally distant stance in which Paula had described him to be before she began the song. For purposes of learning, Hillary's portrayal was exaggerated. Paula was asked to re-create "It's a Small World" for Hillary in the same way she had for Kenny the day before.

Hillary began the role-play by taking a withdrawn stance in relation to Paula. She portrayed Kenny as feeling mistrustful of Paula, unmotivated, and undesirous of any contact. Paula played with strong, mechanical, rhythmic strokes; a rigid tempo; and a consistent dynamic through two verses and two repetitions of the chorus. She played with good technical skills on guitar and sang with a clear, but unchanging, voice quality. She kept eye contact with Hillary throughout the song. As she played, Hillary re-enacted Kenny as he became activated in the music. Then, Hillary was asked to report what she had experienced from the client's point of view. Hillary reported that she had indeed felt cared for by Paula as she began to play her favorite song. The song had called her out of her withdrawn state and activated her. However, as the song progressed, she reported feeling connected to the song, but not to Paula. She reported that as the song progressed, she had an impulse to close her eyes in order to enjoy the music even more. She said that the connection with the music seemed to take her inside herself and away from Paula. I directed Paula back to her original therapeutic intent. "What was your goal in playing his favorite song?" Immediately, she responded, "Oh, no, I think I really messed up—but it seemed so therapeutic!"

Moments of soul-searching and remorse should be treasured by the supervisor, not immediately assuaged to reduce anxiety in the student and class. Uncomfortable insights are fertile ground for student growth. The first-time student needs to struggle with the recognition that there is much that she does not yet know. True learning is derived from allowing this tension. Students will feel defeated when they have done something wrong—especially when the wrong is perceived to have been committed on a client—but a supervisor is obliged to place students in this awkward position because there is no way to adequately prepare a first-time clinical student for all possible contingencies. Students have to be willing to use their instincts, to take what they perceive as therapeutic action with a client, even when such action may be questioned in the subsequent supervision session. Students will make mistakes—especially first-time practicum students—but these errors need to be handled with sensitivity and an appreciation of their utility in the learning process. Of course, the supervisor must take precautions to place students in settings which contribute to the learning environment and to match the student with a particular client where they can achieve a good amount of immediate success. When this is accomplished, the damage will be only to their egos and only fleetingly.

Such was the case with Paula and Chelsea. Their errors will help them and their classmates who experience them vicariously through the group supervision session in a twofold manner. First, examining the error in the clinical practice itself will be turned into new learning and skill development; second, and just as important, the students learn to accept the criticism and correction necessary to facilitate their professional growth. My strategy of allowing self-evaluation and peer evaluation to function as the predominant methods of correction, I believe, lessens the deleterious blows to the student's self-esteem that can occur when criticism is directed at them by the supervisor herself. When a student receives too much criticism from a supervisor, she can become unwilling to trust her own instincts and to take reasonable risks. A student afraid of stretching herself during the clinical experience, fearful of thinking on her own, perpetually concerned about displeasing her supervisor, is not going to succeed as a music therapist.

By having been given the opportunity to direct her own correction through the group process, Paula became an educational leader of the group, not merely a student who had "messed up." I directed a question to Paula: "Remembering that your goal is to make more contact with Kenny, what could you do with 'It's a Small World' in your next session?" I encouraged her not to censor any ideas that came immediately to her mind. When she had generated several ideas, I suggested that she also ask the supervision group to contribute their ideas. Once Paula and the class had generated many ideas, Paula chose one suggestion given by a classmate to try in a role-play. In this second role-play, Paula adjusted the music to follow "Kenny's" body responses—jumping and clapping. "Kenny" felt her alterations in tempo and dynamics as a game. The changeable tempo encouraged "Kenny" to pay attention to Paula. She felt a kind of playful contact with Paula and enjoyment of the song itself.

Through this role-play, Paula discovered that choosing a client's favorite song was only the beginning of developing a trustful therapeutic relationship through music and that "performing" music is not quality therapeutic contact. The class learned the concept of flexible responsiveness to the client in the music. A homework assignment was given. Divided into dyads, the students were given a four-part assignment to (1) play and sing a specific song to their dyad partner, with a *focus upon the music,* in as musical a manner as possible; (2) play and sing the song with their dyad partner, with *a focus upon the partner,* accommodating the song to the partner; (3) play and sing the song with the dyad partner, practicing *a balance between client (partner) and musical responsiveness;* and (4) practice free improvisation as a vehicle for developing a relationship with the partner through music.

Students come to their first practicum with the idea that therapy contains recipes. The concept of singing a song with no consideration to accommodating it musically to the client's responses connotes that the therapy is solely in the music—it neglects the heart of the therapeutic process: the development of the relationship. Although music therapy sessions (especially with undergraduate students) are, in part, preplanned and task-oriented, focusing too exclusively on the preplanned musical task creates the erroneous impression that music-making in the clinic is an external task rather than a container within which the therapeutic relationship develops.

Even when students understand the difference between being task-oriented and relationship-oriented, there can still be a misunderstanding about the role of enjoyment in therapy. First-time students may become stuck in the idea that music therapy should be fun and pleasurable for the client. They feel a need to be liked by the client, to be a provider of fun. They find it difficult to understand the concept that therapy is not built upon being happy. Musical contact can be light and fun, but it is also at times serious and difficult. However, students may continue to hold on to the concept of music therapy as fun, to the detriment of their learning. One reason students confuse the practice of music therapy with the purveyance of pleasure is that they themselves have lost some personal pleasure in their own performing due to the workload of a college music curriculum. When student music therapists experience a client's unbridled enjoyment of music, it helps them to regain their own joy. The student may then become unduly and unconsciously motivated toward focusing on the simple enjoyment of music as the quintessential goal of the therapeutic intervention. Although enjoyment may, at times, be a therapeutic goal, it should not be mistaken for the basis of the therapeutic process.

Once the student has developed her first simple treatment plan and has worked with the client for several weeks, she will have developed rudimentary skills and understanding in developing the therapeutic relationship through music. Once this prerequisite is accomplished, the beginning music therapy student is ready to take the next developmental step in learning: identifying and working with client resistance.

VIGNETTE: MONICA

Monica's older adult client, Vince, had been in the nursing home for approximately four years. He was depressed and constantly asked to be taken back to his home. He had little relief from his depression, except for visits from his children. Most days when Monica arrived, Vince was happy to go to music therapy. He engaged easily and developed good contact with Monica through music.

After several weeks of sessions, Vince changed. He was hesitant to begin the music therapy session, and once Monica began the session, he quickly showed resistance. He complained about the nursing home, the room, and Monica, and asked to be taken back to his room. He refused most music, saying that it "wasn't real music," that simple rhythm instruments "weren't real instruments," songs were "boring," and that music therapy was "boring." He questioned, "Why should I have music therapy?" and "How did you choose me—why not anyone else?" Finally, he declared the session to be over.

Monica listened to Vince and tried to answer his questions honestly. To the best of her ability, she tried to help Vince understand what music therapy was and why he had been chosen for music therapy. With sincerity, Monica expressed her concern and caring for Vince. Next, Monica tried to get Vince to sing their usual greeting and engage in their usual music therapy session. Vince rejected this. Next, Monica offered him activity after activity, hoping that she would find something that wasn't "boring" to Vince or something that he considered "real": singing familiar songs, improvising on simple rhythm instruments, playing autoharp together, playing guitar, movement with scarves, and so forth. Through her many offerings, Monica found one activity that Vince felt was "real": singing his favorite song, "Irish Eyes," on the piano. Monica happily fulfilled this request, feeling that she had found the formula to hold Vince's interest in the session and, hence, to hold the session together. But after Vince and Monica sang his song at the piano, he again asked to be taken back to his room. Monica tried again, suggesting other activities, offering to sing "Irish Eyes" again, but Vince refused any song or activity and sat with his head down and arms crossed, making no contact whatsoever with Monica. Monica decided to give up and end the session.

Discussion

Naturally, Monica does not yet understand how to deal with a client's resistance. Because of this, Vince's resistance escalated quickly and took over the session. Monica's problem is multilevel. Monica had a natural emotional response to Vince's characterization of her and her session as boring. She felt hurt and defeated, and by the time she had finished the session, she also felt angry, since she had tried so hard to accommodate Vince's preferences. Because of her emotional response (and also because she is inexperienced), Monica got stuck in trying to "normalize" Vince and the session instead of accepting and accommodating to the significant difference in Vince's state in the music therapy session. Monica's strategy was to try to concentrate on what Vince was saying (his specific complaints). She was unable to be open to examine and understand Vince's expressed boredom to find out why he was resistant. She was attempting to find an activity—a formula—to combat Vince's resistance.

Resistance must be dealt with by addressing the feelings underlying the client's rejection and by adapting one's style of nurturance to meet the client's resistance. The solution to resistance is found in the adjustment of the therapeutic relationship in the moment, not in an activity or a task. Through supervision, students can arrive at this conclusion on their own.

In group supervision, Monica brought up her session for discussion. At first, she minimized the situation, describing it tentatively and in an embarrassed manner. With support, she was able to describe in detail, and with feeling, the exact circumstances of the session and how terrible it was for her. Monica reported that after her session, she had left the nursing home in tears. She felt angry from her attempts to deal with Vince's resistance, depressed because of her failure to find a way to re-engage Vince, and inadequate from Vince's harsh insults upon her. She questioned whether she could ever become a music therapist. This is one of the hardest challenges for supervision because first-time students are just getting on their feet and developing confidence. Confronting resistance means acknowledging rejection from the client, which brings up the student's feelings of inadequacy.

At anxious moments like this, it is tempting for the supervisor to reduce the high level of tension by solving the dilemma for the student. I could say, for example, "Monica, Vince was not really bored with your session. He was simply acting out a typical client behavior known as 'resistance.' This is your fourth week of therapy with him, and this is what happens at this point in the therapeutic process." I believe that answering Monica's dilemma would deprive her and the supervision class of the educational value derived from working together to honestly confront their feelings of inadequacy while acquiring a better understanding of Vince.

Although it may seem reasonable that Monica's classmates would be sympathetic to her situation, it is not uncommon for a usually supportive supervision group to distance themselves from a clinical situation that involves rejection from a client and feelings of inadequacy because these are such emotionally challenging issues. Comments such as, "Oh, that must have been so hard for you; I don't have such a difficult client" and "I don't know what I would do if my client ever did that to me!" are evidence that first-time students tend to deny that they have experienced any resistance from their clients. For beginning students, it is much easier to overlook moments of client resistance, especially when they are fleeting, in favor of focusing upon the exciting gains that a client is making in therapy. This common group response threatens the class's integrity as an educational support system and requires an approach to supervision that will aid the student in crisis, as well as help the other students to uncover their own experiences with client resistance. Although dealing with the student's emotional responses to the client's rejection is an important component of addressing resistance, the beginning practicum student first needs to be able to clearly identify resistance, without denial, before tackling her own feelings of inadequacy. Supervisory techniques that are experiential and expressive in nature, rather than verbal techniques, are helpful in allowing students to examine more fully conscious and unconscious aspects of resistance. Role-playing through improvisation is perhaps the most common experiential technique used in music therapy supervision; however, group music and imagery is also an effective technique (Summer, 1996, 2014). The supervision session with Monica utilized music and imagery with a component of art to examine resistant contact in contrast to engaged, quality musical contact with the client.

Sitting comfortably on the floor with eyes closed, focused on their breath, the students were given the following instructions: "Take this time to reflect on your therapy sessions so far with your client … let yourself remember a time when you felt very connected to your client in the music … you may remember many times, but bring forward the moment in time when you felt *most strongly connected* to your client and also to the music you were playing … now, open your eyes and let the music that is playing help you to draw that moment of connection on your paper … be as expressive as you can be to show how the connection felt …." As the Dvořák *String Serenade*, op. 22, 1st movement, played, the students drew with oil and chalk pastels. Subsequently, this exercise was repeated with the same instructions, except that the students were asked to draw the experience in which they felt the *most disconnected* and distanced from their client during music. For this exercise, I substituted Brahms's *Third Symphony*, 3rd movement, for the Dvořák. These two pieces of music were chosen to structure and reflect the respective tasks of drawing "connection" and "disconnection" and to support their imagery expression through art (Summer, 2014b).

Monica's first drawing was pastel and mostly abstract. She drew the therapy room which, Monica explained, was filled half with purple for Vince, half with blue for herself. Between these two equal-size areas was a yellow area where she and Vince "connected" in the music. Each color was clear but blended together with the other, and the drawing was yellow at the point of connection. In addition, Monica had drawn lines which radiated from and around the room to illustrate the feeling of expansiveness and expressivity she felt was present in their music. Monica said that her sessions usually felt like this drawing—smooth, flowing, and natural, like the Dvoák serenade. In her picture of resistant contact, two-thirds of the page—drawn in black and red with harsh, disconnected lines, circling around each other—represented Vince, according to Monica. Monica depicted herself in the remaining space with blue, purple, and yellow pastels. The two unequal portions merged at the point of connection. Monica was asked to describe both pictures fully. Regarding the second picture, she said, "This is Vince in the session yesterday. He is disoriented. He is paying no attention to me. All these lines are going nowhere, they're all over the place; he's really confused. I can see here that he is really disoriented, and he feels very angry. As the Brahms played, I heard the dissonance in the music, and it sounded like how Vince's anger must feel to him. I drew the disjointed lines with the strongly accented rhythms of the music. In the session yesterday, I didn't notice that he was confused. I know that he always *says* he is angry about being in the nursing home, but I have never *felt* his anger before."

Monica was asked to describe how she characterized herself in the picture. She said, "I'm trying to reach him, but he is bigger than usual, and my pretty smooth colors are so ineffective next to his sharp lines." I asked, "What is your strategy in trying to reach Vince in this picture?" She responded, "I can see how different he is in this session from in my other sessions, but I'm trying to approach him in the same way I always do. It's like I'm trying to get him back to his usual self. I can see why he kept rejecting me. I'm not really paying attention to *him*."

Putting her session with Vince into the medium of art gave Monica the ability to examine Vince's state and to examine her interaction with Vince from a new perspective, a perspective that led her to understand that Vince was not really bored during their session together. To reinforce Monica's change of perception, I reminded her of Vince's previous delight with her music therapy sessions. When Monica said, "If Vince wasn't really bored, then it's certainly not helpful to be spending all of my time looking for something that wouldn't be boring to him," I believed that she was ready to identify a new strategy for dealing with Vince's resistance. I drew her attention to her second drawing and asked, "Look at this drawing again. Can you see from this visual representation what kind of contact would be helpful for Vince?"

Monica responded immediately. "I can see visually that he needs colors and shapes as strong as his, not my soft pastels. If I were to draw another picture, I would make myself more complementary to him—I would draw myself in the same colors, with more shape and definition, maybe the same shapes as he is."

Resistance is a form of emotional communication, and Monica had learned that in order to hear Vince's confused and angry feelings over his stated objections to playing music, she needed to become emotionally open herself (Summer, 2014b). In order to practice this skill, I assigned Monica the task of choosing a piece of music that was personally very nurturing and, using the music as support, of drawing at least one new picture that would represent a new therapeutic approach to Vince: one that uses music to meet, match, and contain Vince's confusion and anger.

That Monica's dynamic work and her new insights impressed the group became obvious during the ensuing discussion. Using their drawings, Monica's classmates also began to identify their own clients' resistances in past sessions that had not been exposed during previous supervision classes. As closure, Monica was asked to summarize what she had learned. "I can see that I was trying to change Vince's confusion, to just take it away and make him happy with his favorite song, but that's obviously not possible because the reality is that he is very depressed and angry about being in the nursing home. I have to accept that I can't save him from that."

CONCLUSION

Students come to music therapy unaware of the amount of intellectual and emotional effort it takes to be a therapist, and sometimes it must be admitted that some students, even some academically proficient students, will not be able—or they may be unwilling—to develop the empathetic and nurturing skills necessary to become music therapists. Often, it is during the first practica that this becomes evident. It is tempting to give a student a passing grade in practicum, especially a student who produces good academic work, but it is of no real value to the student or to the field to camouflage their deficiencies as a therapist. Practicum supervisors must be careful not to adopt an attitude that is too "therapeutic." Unlike therapy in which a client's growth proceeds at his own pace and without deadlines, music therapy education is time restricted, since there is a standard of competence to be acquired before graduation.

In a real sense, the practicum is the crucible in which our future music therapists must learn to thrive. We cannot turn down the heat for individuals whom we respect intellectually or for those we care about in our role as therapists without sacrificing the transformative energy needed to change the student into a professional.

REFERENCE LIST

Forinash, M., & Summer, L. (1998, April). *Supervision in music therapy.* Lecture delivered at the Conference of the New England Region of the American Music Therapy Association, Hartford, CT.

Forinash, M., & Summer, L. (1999, March). *Continued explorations into music therapy supervision.* Lecture delivered at the Conference of the New England Region of the American Music Therapy Association, Meredith, NH.

Freud, S. (1912). *Recommendations to physicians practicing psychoanalysis* (Vol. 12, pp. 109–120). Standard edition of the complete psychological works of Sigmund Freud. London, UK: Hogarth Press.

Mahoney, E. (2015). Multicultural Music Therapy: An Exploration. *Voices: A World Forum for Music Therapy, 15*(2). doi:10.15845/voices.v15i2.844

Summer, L. (1996, March). *Music as mother.* Lecture delivered at the Conference of the New England Region of the American Music Therapy Association, Springfield, MA.

Summer, L. (1997, December). *The music therapist's relationship with music.* Lecture delivered at the Lesley College Expressive Therapies Brown Bag Lecture Series, Boston, MA.

Summer, L. (2014a). Foreword. In L. T. Chen, *Music therapy clinical practice* (p. 2). (Chinese language). Taipei City, Taiwan: Chuan Hwa Book Co, Ltd.

Summer, L. (2014b). Case vignettes demonstrating experiential learning in Guided Imagery and Music seminars. In K. Bruscia (Ed.), *Self-experiences in music therapy education, training, and supervision* (pp. 837–869). Gilsum, NH: Barcelona Publishers.

Chapter 9

SUPERVISION IN THE FIELD

James Hiller

INTRODUCTION

The focus of this chapter is supervision provided in the field for undergraduate student music therapists (SMTs) moving through five developmentally sequenced levels of practicum. Accordingly, each level of practicum poses new challenges, but also provides opportunities for SMTs to hone already evolving competencies. Supervising in the field means being keenly present in the unfolding moments as SMTs engage with clients and learn from each encounter about themselves, their clients, treatment processes, and the potential impacts of music and music experiences in therapy. Field supervision is, therefore, exciting and often spontaneous work, but it is also a delicate business. SMTs, it is assumed, are doing the best they can in the clinical moment to relate to their clients and address their clinical needs, yet to do so they draw from what is at first a rather shallow pool of knowledge, skills, and experiences. This is a pool that will take considerable time and effort on both SMTs' and supervisors' parts to adequately fill prior to internship and entrance into professional life. Along the way, supervisors must provide careful guidance toward helping the SMT develop facilitation skills, while at the same time attending to the needs of volunteer clients and seeing that their clinical needs are adequately addressed.[10] SMTs and their clients are both in vulnerable positions in these somewhat contrived therapeutic situations—contrived in the sense that practica are, by necessity, relationships of convenience created between a healthcare facility or school and a university training program and undertaken between vulnerable clients and novice music therapists. Thus, an essential role of a supervisor in the field is seeing that both SMTs and clients have mutually beneficial experiences during the times that they share and that each comes away having gained in some fashion—not just the SMT in training. Following sessions, SMTs will have the benefit of ongoing supervisory interactions during practicum labs and one-on-one supervision meetings, whereas volunteer clients continue on into their daily milieu, hopefully carrying over any benefits gained from music therapy. It is thus important that field supervisors are alert to the nature of the unfolding interactions, particularly during early practicum experiences, in order to offer relevant support so that clinically beneficial and satisfactory experiences are had.

DEVELOPMENTAL ISSUES IN FIELD SUPERVISION

The five levels of practicum in the program with which I am involved are developmentally sequenced such that competencies developed in earlier experiences support the work of latter practica. Naturally, the SMT also continues to face new challenges with each subsequent clinical group, and these challenges must be assimilated within the SMT's level of development both as a therapist and as a person. Undergraduate SMTs are generally identified as being in the developmental stage of *self-*

---

[10] Clients with whom our SMTs work in most practicum sites outside of the on-campus clinic have not sought music therapy services on their own and are, in essence, volunteered *by* the facilities in which they are clientele, residents, students, or program participants. It is in this sense that I use the term *volunteer clients*. This is also why, from an ethical standpoint, a supervisor's efforts must include attending carefully to these clients' welfare during music therapy practica.

definition or that which Kegan (1982) refers to as the *institutional self* (pp. 221–254). This is a time when an individual "determines one's own identity, formulates one's life goals, invests in the future, and sacrifices various things to achieve one's own personal dreams" (Bruscia, 1991, p. 8). Through eventual navigation of the challenges in this developmental stage, an individual comes to express their sense of self as structurally organized and balanced, and they are able to hold fast to opinions and beliefs regarding their roles within organizations and in relationships. The path to becoming a therapist clearly mirrors the challenges of this developmental period. Also, during this stage, an individual is said to develop their "musical personality" as they come to understand and embrace their distinctive relationship with music and how they use music to meet their own personal/psychological needs (p. 9). Hence, one can conceive of SMTs as traveling parallel paths of personal and professional development, awareness of which is helpful to supervisors as they consider ways of intervening, guiding, and supporting supervisees. For instance, supervisors might encourage SMTs to go to their preferred music as support for and accompaniment to difficult growth processes and to practice careful reflection about their experiences of and relationship with music. Such reflection not only is beneficial to an SMT but also may inform their clinical decisions about music's potential for clients' therapy processes.

Each SMT's maturity, consequently, is taken into account not only in the process of determining practicum placements, but also when providing supervision in the field. Each SMT's level and path of development is unique across the knowledge and skills areas relevant to music therapy. Some SMTs possess a surprisingly high level of personal, interpersonal, and musical maturity, some seem to be only at the beginning stages of forming and embracing a stable sense of musical and personal identity, and still others fall somewhere in between. Due to the challenges placed on SMTs at this particular stage of human development and the practical necessities and demands of undergraduate music therapy education and training, carefully sequenced exposure to informational materials, therapy processes, theoretical concepts, and clinical responsibilities in practica (and in the classroom, for that matter) is essential. Supervision in the field and in practicum labs serves to help SMTs integrate learning from these various avenues into a cohesive understanding of themselves, of the potentials of music therapy as a treatment modality, and of their own evolving role in it.

Decisions regarding the clinical placement sequence for each SMT are complex and are accomplished through consultation between music therapy faculty and field supervisors. Multiple layers of considerations are taken into account throughout the five-level sequence relative to each SMT's personal development, musical and interpersonal readiness, demands of the clientele in various clinical sites, and available supervisors. In our program, undergraduate SMTs become eligible to begin practicum following three semesters of course work that includes passing courses or competency examinations in introductory music therapy and music therapy treatment processes, music theory and aural skills, guitar and keyboard skills, and development of a song repertoire that is relevant across clinical groups, along with the vocal skills required to re-create that material. These preparatory semesters allow music therapy faculty to gain a sense of each SMT's personality, music and interpersonal skills, and work ethic, as well as already present foundational competencies, and the relative rate at which each SMT develops new competencies.

The first level of practicum in our program always involves work with nursing facility residents with Alzheimer's disease and related dementias (ADRD) and other complications of aging. This decision in no way reflects a perception that these individuals' needs are less significant than, say, individuals in a psychiatric setting, or that the work is in some way easier or potentially less intense. Rather, this decision is based largely on the complementary nature of the needs of older adults with ADRD and the early training needs of SMTs. Hence, three pre-established, overarching aims for the work during this first practicum are for the SMT to (1) provide music and music experiences in which that residents can engage as deeply as possible, given their challenged resources; (2) create opportunities within music experiences for intermusical responding between residents and the SMT and/or other residents; and (3) forge an interpersonal connection with each resident. These aims touch simultaneously on a broad range of competencies related to music, clinical, and music therapy foundations (AMTA, 2013). Yet, just as important is the point that addressing these three aims helps to focus SMTs' in-session efforts primarily on musicing (Elliot, 1998) and relating, rather than on extramusical endeavors such as observing and accounting for specific predetermined resident responses/actions. The emphasis here is for the SMT to develop skills for entering into and staying as fully as possible in the music with and for the residents. At the same time, residents—whose expectations while attending a "music group" are to somehow be involved musically—can experience the satisfactions and benefits of engaging with the music and with others (Aigen, 2005).

The second and third practicum placements vary according to the areas of competence that each SMT demonstrates during the first level as well as programmatic needs, availability of training sites, and availability of supervisors during a given semester. Competency issues surrounding musical and interpersonal skill development are primary considerations, along with an SMT's evolving facilitation style. Facilitation style at this level has to do with an SMT's evolving ability to act fluidly in both directive and nondirective ways as warranted and to consciously "… use oneself effectively in the therapist role …" toward forging and deepening a therapeutic relationship (AMTA Competency 9.3). SMTs invariably demonstrate different levels of competence in these areas and are therefore positioned to benefit from the second level of practicum in different ways. Given supervisors' evaluations of the pool of SMTs moving to the second level, each will be placed in a school situation where they will work with students in an early intervention, elementary, or middle school classroom, in the on-campus clinic with a child, or in an adult psychiatric facility. The third level of practicum entails redistributing these same SMTs among the sites just described. With regard to placement in adult psychiatric settings for SMTs who might not have been ready the previous semester, it is assumed that, for most students, potential success is enhanced due to ongoing development during the previous two terms. In rare cases, an SMT may be redirected away from psychiatric work until a later semester due to ongoing personal and academic developmental concerns.

SMTs in the final two levels of practicum are placed in the on-campus clinic, a children's hospital, a short-term adolescent treatment facility, a high school classroom, or a hospice setting. These decisions are made with SMTs' expressed preferences in mind as well as supervisors' input, with the caveat that an SMT's preference is not necessarily the top priority, depending on the student's overall competence to date. An additional consideration for practicum placement that is brought to bear at this point in training has to do with theoretically striving to help *round* an SMT's experience and skills sets, regardless of the nature of prior placements. For instance, an SMT who demonstrates inadequately developed verbal skills may be placed in a setting where they are challenged to use their verbal techniques to a significant degree. A student whose abilities with regard to re-creating live song material with guitar or keyboard will be placed where those skills are consistently in demand. An SMT who has yet to work one-on-one with a client will be placed in this type of situation. All told, determination of practicum placements requires careful consideration of many variables that are influenced by each SMT's ongoing developmental processes.

COMPETENCIES, PROGRAMMATIC, AND PRACTICUM STRUCTURES

Given the nature of music therapy education and training as competency-driven, evaluation of an SMT's growth relative to the AMTA Professional Competencies (2013) occurs at every level of practicum. Competencies relative to actual facilitation of therapeutic encounters are of particular focus for undergraduate supervision in the field as SMTs are in the process of shaping their conceptualizations of the practice of music therapy with varied clinical groups. As articulated, the somewhat vague nature of many of the AMTA Professional Competencies poses a challenge for supervisors in that they require careful interpretation. Yet interpretations must also be malleable in that they may need to be adapted according to the precise level and focus of the clinical work at hand.

For example, interpretation of competencies relative to the nature of therapeutic relationships (e.g., competencies 8.1 and 9.1) and use of one's self (e.g., competency 9.3) will vary between the contexts of music psychotherapy and neurological rehabilitation or activity level therapy (Wheeler, 1983).

Student enrollment in our program is typically approximately 90% Caucasian and 90% female, which is not atypical for undergraduate programs in the midwestern United States. We have had students with African-American, Chinese, Indonesian, Korean, Latina, and Nigerian racial and ethnic identities in our program. While present in our practica, there is currently not a great amount of identified racial and ethnic diversity among the clients whom we typically serve. As a program, we continually strive to expand the range of persons with whom our SMTs work (and thereby learn from), including individuals with varied ethnic, religious, gender, social, and generational identities and so forth, as well as those who are racially different from the predominantly white population of our geographic area and our university. Admittedly, we as a program are in the early stages of incorporating across our curriculum and supervision concepts related to culture as significant factors in therapeutic processes. Topics related to cultural differences were only minimally an aspect of music therapy training during the 1980s, 1990s, and even early 2000s, when the two longest-term instructors completed their degrees. Historically, therefore, concerns related to culture have only periodically been a part of our undergraduate supervision processes. As a program, we are really just entering the territory where faculty and supervisors possess useful language and modern conceptualizations of culture in order to be/feel qualified to meaningfully and knowledgably address culture-related issues with students. Interestingly, I personally believe that many of the current generation of our students have, in a general and perhaps unconscious way, already gained considerable exposure to contemporary language and concepts relative to the significance of culture and cultural identities. But now, with a strong emphasis on cultural awareness in the mass media and regular training opportunities available on and off campus, faculty have initiated a fundamental shift to bring issues of culture to all aspects of the program. Looking to the AMTA Competencies, we recognize the following specific competencies related to culture that serve as a basic grounding for supervision around issues of culture in music therapy:

1.2 Identify the elemental, structural, and stylistic characteristics of music from various periods and cultures.
11.1 Select and implement effective culturally-based methods for assessing the client's strengths, needs, musical preferences, level of musical functioning, and development.
13.12 Develop and maintain a repertoire of music for age, culture, and stylistic differences.
17.9 Demonstrate knowledge of and respect for diverse cultural backgrounds.
17.11 Demonstrate skill in working with culturally diverse populations.

With these competencies in mind, supervisors endeavor to include foci on cultural diversity and understanding of the concept of *cultural humility* (Hook, 2017) into their supervisory repertoire and to increase their sensitivity to the challenges encountered by SMTs as they learn to recognize and address various aspects of culture that might impact treatment.

Supervision in our program is currently provided by one of three full-time instructional/supervision faculty (two doctoral and one master's-level MT-BCs) and we also draw on the expertise of seven MT-BCs who work in varied facilities or private practices throughout our community (four are master's-level, two are in graduate programs, and one is in a PhD program). Supervisors are paid employees of our university (i.e., adjunct faculty) during the semesters that they provide supervision. While we seek to diversify our supervisors, all current supervisors are Caucasian and all but one are women. Three of our current practicum sites have an MT-BC on staff who provides supervision; these individuals are included among the adjunct faculty just mentioned. For the remaining sites, supervisors must travel to and from sessions. The range in years of clinical experience among all available supervisors is from 3 to 25+ years. Areas of clinical expertise among the supervisors include child, adolescent, adult, and geriatric psychiatry; addictions; ID/DD (early intervention through midlife adults); geriatric; hospice; medical; and neurological disorders. We strive to capitalize on the strengths and experiences of each supervisor as assignments are considered, but at times programmatic needs take precedence as schedules are coordinated between supervisors and SMTs. Supervisory assignments are primarily made through initial consultations among the full-time faculty followed by further coordination with available supervisors. One full-time faculty member serves as Clinical Coordinator. This person manages many aspects of practica each semester including, for example, the process of assigning supervision responsibilities, tracking document processes related to background checks, confidentiality, video or audio releases, and other requisite documentation required of the various clinical sites.

The first level of practicum is supervised by at least one of the full-time faculty who know the entering students from at least one academic course. This faculty member also facilitates the first-level supervision lab, thereby providing initial consistency between feedback and guidance provided in the field and during labs. We believe that this arrangement helps new SMTs to develop a sense of security in the supervisory relationship and in laying a strong foundation within the culture of our program. Responsibilities for subsequent practica and lab supervision are distributed among available full-time and adjunct faculty.

In our program, each level of practicum has its own competency evaluation form populated with AMTA Professional Competencies that faculty supervisors have determined are the most relevant to account for, given the characteristics of the specific client or group with whom an SMT is assigned. Given the obvious developmental nature of any competency attainment process, SMTs are evaluated on the ongoing progression of growth that they demonstrate and not on total achievement or mastery of competencies—as there is always room for growth and nuanced development, even among seasoned professionals. Hence, supervisors and SMTs at every level of practicum are aware of the specific competencies for which evaluation will occur during any semester. This knowledge helps SMTs to understand the types of demands that they will face during their practicum. Isolating the most relevant competencies per practicum placement also helps to focus the field supervisor's attention on the most important clinical actions and interactions believed applicable in each setting. A supervisor's efforts can therefore be maximized toward helping SMTs advance toward competence at their developmentally appropriate level.

The organization of our five levels of practicum has evolved over the past 20 or so years and is now fairly stable in its structure. Practica typically occur two days per week for 45 minutes of hands-on client engagement each day. Each level of practicum has an associated weekly group supervision lab facilitated by a full-time or adjunct MT-BC faculty member. During the first three levels of practicum (which I refer to here as *early levels*), SMTs typically co-lead in teams of two, the work is conducted with client groups in varied facilities (typically from 2 to 15 participants per group), and an assigned supervisor is present at each and every session throughout the semester. Also, during the early levels of practicum, at least 10 to 15 minutes of debriefing time occurs directly following each session, giving SMTs and supervisors the opportunity to bring immediate concerns to light or to celebrate successes. Debriefing time is, therefore, precious time. It is sometimes the case that supervisors and SMTs ride together to and from practicum sites, and these times are also often used for aspects of supervision. Examples of topics addressed in transit might include revisiting salient events from the previous session, discussing specific clients and their needs and strengths, and talking through session plans and roles to be taken during the day's session by SMTs and the supervisor. Procedural issues for discrete music experiences are also sometimes reviewed, such as speaking out loud any verbal instructions that one of the SMTs will be required to offer toward facilitating certain music experiences. We have also often engaged in singing through song material that is planned for the session. While perhaps considered informal supervision, this time can be essential for troubleshooting a session plan by identifying uncertainties on an SMT's part and thereby enhancing their potential for successful engagement with clients. The ride back to campus is often used for further debriefing following sessions and considering potential aims for the next session.

An on-campus music therapy clinic is also available for practica. Assignments for the clinic are typically made for senior-level SMTs, but earlier-level students may work in the clinic as well. A supervisor is present at all sessions regardless of the level of SMT due to legal implications related to running an on-campus clinic. Structurally, supervision of SMTs in the clinic differs in a variety of ways from how it is carried out in the field. Sessions are most typically conducted with individual clients. These might include, for example, persons with organic neurologic disorders, such as children on the autism spectrum; children with Down syndrome or another form of intellectual disability; or an adult who has experienced a stroke. The supervisor observes sessions from an adjacent observation room through a one-way mirror. The supervisor's presence, therefore, is less visually obvious during sessions, yet they can speak into a microphone to offer suggestions that are audible to the SMT in the clinic space. A microphone in the clinic space ceiling continuously picks up the sounds of each session, which are audible to the supervisor in the observation room. This technology allows for immediate interactions to occur between the SMT and the supervisor in the clinical moment. Guidance regarding the music, instruments, procedures, facilitation techniques, or how the SMT might use the space differently can be made with little to no distraction to the client's experience. Sessions in the clinic are videotaped, which provides yet another extremely useful tool for supervision following sessions. With the convenience of being on campus, supervisor and SMT engage in debriefing time immediately following all sessions.

It should be noted that our program does not include a semester of student observation in the field. This is based on a belief that, regardless of the amount of prior observation, actually engaging and interacting with clients musically is a truly unique experience that each SMT must undergo in order to begin to understand the processes and challenges involved in providing music therapy. We therefore believe that SMTs benefit more from a practicum schedule that maximizes hands-on clinical work rather than observation. It can be argued, however, that an adequate amount of observation experiences does, in fact, take place within this model, but these occur within the context of seeing a supervisor facilitate or co-facilitate as well as when sharing leadership responsibilities with peer SMTs.

During the latter two levels (i.e., *senior-level* practica), SMTs might be on their own as facilitators or may still work with a partner. During senior levels of practicum, a supervisor will accompany the SMT to the clinical site, provide at least two sessions of modeling or co-facilitating, and then withdraw for a few weeks while the SMT, who now has a considerably deeper pool of knowledge, skills, and experiences from which to draw, works independently. (Our policy for psychiatric and hospice work, however, is that a supervisor must be present at all sessions, regardless of practicum level.[11]) The supervisor then returns to observe the SMT typically from three to five more times during the semester. As a consistent touch point, upper-level SMTs provide a required "phone update" to the supervisor within two hours of completing each session. During phone updates, SMTs report on which clients were in attendance, session aims, salient musical and nonmusical events that

---

[11] Our policy insisting that a supervisor be present at all sessions when an undergraduate SMT works with hospice patients is based on our belief that the end of life is a potentially deeply transformative time for each patient (and often as well for the patient's family) and that therapeutic encounters must therefore reflect that potential depth of experience. Hospice is not an appropriate time for activity-level therapy. Therefore, only SMTs who demonstrate strong musical and verbal skills, suitable clinical intuition, and adequate psycho-emotional maturity are permitted to work in hospice—with constant supervision. This policy not only protects patients and families by ensuring that therapeutic encounters are need-based and meaningful, but also protects SMTs from emotional harm as they provide treatment and comfort to a dying patient. Both of these intentions align with ethical code 3.11 of the AMTA Code of Ethics: "In those emerging areas of practice for which generally recognized standards are not yet defined, the MT will nevertheless utilize cautious judgment and will take reasonable steps to ensure the competence of his/her work, as well as to protect clients, students, and research subjects from harm" (AMTA, 2014).

occurred during the session, and statements regarding what the SMT learned from the day's experiences. All SMTs across levels submit a session plan for every outing, a session evaluation afterward, and a reflexive journal for each session. These documents are evaluated and commented upon by assigned supervisors, who may address a wide range of topics, from writing style and use of clinical terminology and nomenclature to exploring SMTs' awareness of countertransference issues as they manifest in various ways. Thus, exchanges that occur between SMTs and supervisors via clinical documentation play a critical role in the overall supervision process. All told, the amount and variety of interactions between SMTs and supervisors on a weekly basis across all practicum levels is extensive. But whereas the demands placed on supervisors in our program is great, we also have long enjoyed a 100% success rate for SMTs securing excellent internships, passing the Board Certification examination the first time taking it, and obtaining satisfactory employment.

CLINICAL ORIENTATION ISSUES AND INTEGRAL THINKING

Our program has fully embraced the notion of *Integral Thinking* articulated by Bruscia in his William Sears Distinguished Lecture at the AMTA Annual Conference in Atlanta, Georgia (2011), expounded in the third edition of *Defining Music Therapy* (2014), and also described by Lee in the *Journal of Music and Human Behavior* (2015). Since the Sears lecture, these concepts have become foundational to the way that I personally provide supervision. Briefly, integral thinking advocates for a therapist to understand and be as fluent as possible in a variety of theoretical orientations that support music therapy and to access and apply a particular theoretical stance based on clients' needs, rather than practicing from a predetermined orientation. The basic rationale is that different clients and their changing needs often call for a different approach to therapy than that used earlier in treatment or even earlier in a session. Therapists, therefore, are called upon to flexibly shift their perspective along with their application of music therapy methods and techniques to accommodate a client's emerging needs. In clarifying concepts related to integral thinking, Bruscia also described three ways of thinking that undergird music therapy practice and between which a therapist may think and act integrally: outcome-oriented, experience-oriented, and context-oriented (2011). Each way of thinking is a viable and important way to approach and individualize treatment for clients and their clinical concerns. Working knowledge of the attributes of these ways of thinking is therefore important within the various forms of supervision that SMTs receive.

In an outcome orientation, clinical outcomes (i.e., client responses) are predetermined and music experiences are used in various ways to elicit these responses. Outcome-oriented thinking is beneficial when therapeutically beneficial client responses that are observable and/or measurable have been clearly identified. Examples include particular movement schemes for physical or neurological habilitation or rehabilitation or when pain management or alteration of physiological functions (e.g., heart or respiration rate) is called for in a medical setting. In an experience orientation, on the other hand, broad clinical aims are kept firmly in a therapist's mind going into treatment, but specific client responses toward those aims are not predetermined. Rather, music experiences are brought to bear in order to identify and work with clients' specific needs as they emerge in the moment. Here, a client's agency in determining and enacting relevant sorts of therapeutic responses is encouraged and supported. Experience-oriented thinking is beneficial when specific responses toward addressing clinical change are not clearly identified or identifiable, for instance, when working psychotherapeutically with adult clients with issues related to depression or addiction. Finally, a context orientation, simply considered, has to do with treating the contexts in which our clients live and interact (rather than just the client alone) and might include, for example, a client's familial or social contexts or the broader community in which they live. A fundamental rationale for context-oriented work is that we are products of the different contexts in which we develop and live. Health and nonhealth, therefore, are related and potentially reflected in those contexts as well as in the client.

It therefore makes sense to work to enhance the health of both the client and their particular context or community. Music therapy for context-oriented aims is, for our program, not a focus at the undergraduate level and therefore is not further addressed in this chapter.

The needs of the volunteer clients with whom our SMTs work are amenable to both outcome- and experience-oriented approaches. SMTs learn through course work and supervision in clinical settings and labs when each orientation might be indicated for a client or group, as well as how to adopt each orientation during session planning, designing, facilitating, and evaluating processes. Whereas SMTs in the early levels of practicum are not yet versed in a range of theoretical positions from which to enact decisions related to these orientations, the supervisor will use their own expertise and judgment to provide relevant guidance appropriate to the clients and clinical setting. Therefore, when working from an outcome orientation, clinical practice concepts such as those from medical, behavioral, or cognitive-behavioral approaches are encouraged and supported by the field supervisor. In contrast, when working from an experience orientation, concepts from humanistic, psychodynamic, existential, gestalt, or music-centered approaches are encouraged and supported. A similar supervisory approach is also used for senior levels of practicum. Here, however, senior-level SMTs will have a stronger understanding of the various theoretical perspectives available from course work and prior clinical experiences and supervision. These SMTs may therefore begin making their own decisions regarding the most relevant or useful perspective to assume and related techniques to enact in a certain instance for a client's benefit.

SUPERVISOR ROLES

While supervising in the field, each session poses different types and levels of challenges for SMTs, and supervisors may, therefore, position themselves differently in order to provide the most useful guidance and support. Particularly during the early levels of practicum, a field supervisor may choose from a variety of roles as they observe and provide requisite supervisory assistance, including as a model, a co-facilitator (aka, co-leader or co-therapist), a group member, or an observer. Each role offers potentially different "positions" from which to experience, observe, comprehend, and respond to the nature of an SMT's clinical facilitation. The decision regarding which role might be most beneficial for any given session is based on a host of factors that may include, for example, the SMT's (1) level of readiness for independent leadership, (2) musical and conceptual preparedness relative to the types of experiences that are planned and designed for the session, (3) ability to effectively use musical or verbal techniques, (4) emotional and interpersonal maturity, and (5) ability to handle the intensity of psychological demands that one might experience given the acute nature of a particular clinical group. For example, there are clearly different psychological/emotional demands placed on an SMT when providing habilitative services for children with IDD in a school setting vs. when providing rehabilitative services for adult males in a substance use disorders treatment program. During senior-level practica in our program, a supervisor typically takes a co-facilitator role for a few sessions at the start of each semester and an observer role later in the term. Yet, such decisions are flexibly made in accordance with the needs of the clinical group and the particular competency development needs of the SMT. Explanations of the various supervisory roles follow.

In taking the role of *model,* the supervisor is directly involved with clients, demonstrating for SMTs one way of working with the particular client group, while the SMTs place themselves among the clients and participate as the clients do. SMTs in the group are also available to assist clients as they see the need arise or as suggested by the supervisor. In the modeling role, a good deal of teaching may take place as the supervisor explains their actions to the SMTs before, during, and/or after the session. Supervisors also share their perspectives regarding client responses, actions, and interactions that are witnessed. In my approach, prior to a session, I share with my supervisees my session plan and the decision processes that I underwent to create the plan, design the specific music experiences, and select the relevant musical resources to be used. I may also share my speculations about adaptations that may need to occur as the session unfolds, depending on client responses. SMTs may have witnessed their supervisor's approach to facilitating music experiences via classroom demonstrations, as mine have, but in the actual context of work with clients, the type of modeling described here takes on new meaning due to the authenticity of the client–therapist–music interactions. The goal from this role is not to present "the way" to facilitate music therapy, but rather "one way" from which SMTs might draw ideas and inspiration as they prepare to facilitate their own sessions. Gradually, SMTs will take supervisors' modeling and their own experiences to reconceptualize and form their own approach to engaging clients based on their own strengths, proclivities, and personality. In my work during the first three practicum levels, I model two or three sessions and then co-facilitate at least one time with each SMT prior to the teams beginning to co-facilitate together. In latter levels of practicum, I provide modeling within the context of co-facilitation. I share session leadership during at least two sessions at the start of a semester, thereby providing support and modeling toward helping the SMTs to establish themselves in the setting and in relationship with the clients whom they will serve.

As *co-facilitator*, a supervisor shares with an SMT the responsibilities of planning a session, designing the music experiences to be carried out, engaging clients through musicing, and processing clients' experiences. Supervisor co-facilitation, in this conceptualization, is part teaching, part modeling, and part supporting. In that responsibilities for the session events are shared, the co-facilitating SMT can take as strong a leadership stance as possible, with the knowledge that full and immediate assistance is at the ready. Co-facilitation in the field can be structured in a variety of ways. For example, in early levels of practicum, supervisor and SMT might take turns engaging clients in discrete music experiences throughout the session. Here, the SMT shifts from leadership to observation and back, learning from each position. For the insecure SMT, this format provides brief episodes of breathing room as they prepare to facilitate the next music encounter. Alternatively, during early practica, supervisor and SMT might split a session into first and second halves, with each taking responsibility for one or the other. In this situation, the SMT experiences sustained but time-limited engagement with clients, with the challenges of creating a cohesive flow of interactions while also observing the supervisor's approach during a sustained period. Another co-facilitation variation is for the SMT to take the leading role as facilitator of the entire session while the supervisor acts as assistant. In this case, the supervisor may take responsibility for structural aspects of the session, such as arranging the space and instrumentarium required for different music experiences and setting up, testing, and monitoring technology/sound equipment. The SMT thus maintains their focus and efforts on interacting with clients musically and interpersonally or preparing them for subsequent music encounters. Throughout the co-facilitation process, the supervisor can offer the SMT in-the-moment instructions, suggestions, and/or affirmations as the work unfolds. Care is taken not to overwhelm the SMT with facilitation guidance, but to offer a level of support that can be quickly processed and acted upon by the SMT as necessary for the client/group to have a clinically beneficial experience. As in the role of modeling, the point is never to dictate a way to work but to provide nuanced guidance that may help the SMT's individualized efforts to unfold in a successful way for both the SMT and their clients.

When a supervisor takes the role of *group member*, they have the opportunity to experience the SMT's techniques of engagement from the same perspective as that of the volunteer clients.[12] From this position, one can engage in the various musical and nonmusical encounters that occur along with the actual group members, while also being ready to offer suggestions to the SMT as needed. One can choose to simply be a group member and respond authentically, while at the same time meta-processing regarding salient techniques and related client responses that will be important to address following the session. The perspective of group member can be quite informative in considering both interpersonal and intermusical interactions that occur between the SMT and the client(s). With regard to interpersonal interactions, the supervisor may attend to the relative effectiveness of the SMT's use of physical space (i.e., proximity), touch, gestures, affect, and verbalizations as they attempt to forge trusting relationships with individuals or the group. Concerning intermusical interactions, particularly when considering experiences wherein clients improvise or re-create musical sounds, the supervisor can experience firsthand the nature of the group's musicing and how its processes unfold, as well as the aesthetic appeal of the music for the group, as this may relate to the SMT's facilitation techniques. Here the supervisor may attend to the SMT's effective modeling and facilitating of the music, such as vocally demonstrating an accurate melody and lyrics for a song re-creation, playing a clearly recognizable rhythm pattern to be imitated or for which clients are to synchronize instrumentally, offering strong rhythmic and/or harmonic grounding, conducting dynamic shifts, and so on, along with the use of verbal and gestural guidance as needed. Participating as a group member during musicing also allows for the supervisor to subtly bring their own musical techniques to bear, if warranted, to help support the group's musical efforts.

Finally, a supervisor may take the role of *observer*, witnessing events of the session from outside of the group. As an observer, the supervisor can assume a wider and potentially more objective perspective on the session processes, observing the SMT's and group members' actions and interactions free from the supervisor's own direct influence. As observer, the supervisor may choose to remain entirely removed from the session events and withhold all opinions and suggestions until after the session. Or they may verbally or gesturally interpose these as they see a necessity in the clinical moment.

Different supervisory roles allow the supervisor to experience different phenomena related to the SMT's efforts and the clients' processes. These varied forms of information become useful during debriefing times that follow sessions.

PROCESSING CLINICAL EXPERIENCES

Debriefing between SMTs and the supervisor that occurs immediately following each session during the early levels of practicum is an important opportunity for SMTs to bring to light the clinically salient events and interactions that they experienced. Processing the myriad events and interactions that happen within a music therapy session is often daunting due to the complexity of accounting for nearly an hour's worth of musical and nonmusical engagement with 2 to 15 volunteer clients but is nonetheless an essential aspect of field supervision. Having a structure within which SMTs can organize their recollections and immediate reflections about a session is also essential to ascertaining that significant musical and interpersonal events and interactions receive attention. An effective model

---

[12] To be clear, we subscribe to Bruscia's (2014) definitions of *technique, procedure,* and *method* toward carefully discerning and communicating about an SMT's actions within a session. "A technique is a single operation or interaction that a therapist uses to elicit an immediate reaction from a client or to shape the ongoing, immediate experience of the client" (pp. 128–129). Techniques can be musical, verbal, or gestural. Procedures are "the organized sequence of operations and interactions that a therapist uses in taking the client through an entire music experience" (p. 128); a method is "a particular type of music experience used for assessment, treatment, and/or evaluation" (p. 128) and includes improvisation, re-creation, composition, and receptive or listening experiences and their myriad variations.

for observation and processing of experiences from practica is one developed by Gardstrom (2002), which focuses on three aspects relevant in all music therapy sessions regardless of model practiced or approach taken: structural, musical, and relational. Addressing one of these aspects at a time helps to narrow the focus during debriefing, making for an efficient use of precious processing time. Issues brought forth during debriefing are often subsequently given attention in the SMT's clinical journals, in one-on-one supervision meetings, and in the weekly supervision lab.

Structural aspects are those having to do with the environment as well as the organization and sequencing of an SMT's facilitation procedures as they were enacted throughout a session. Environmental aspects have to do with the clinical space and how its use benefits or detracts from session events. The most basic example of an environmental aspect is consideration of the arrangement of the contents in the room, or of the group itself, for maximum engagement and interaction. Other examples include placement of instruments in the space so that their distribution to group members can be accomplished quickly and efficiently and/or placement of instruments relative to each client's physical capabilities or challenges (i.e., proximity and positioning), toward maximizing the potential for successful music engagement and expression. The environment can function to enhance or inhibit intermusical and interpersonal interactions. In my experience, however, once environmental concerns are recognized by an SMT and examined relative to their beneficial or deleterious impact on session events, they infrequently reappear in subsequent sessions. This is because solutions for environmental issues are often concrete and easily managed.

Facilitation procedures, on the other hand, are structural aspects of sessions that are more challenging to address because they are situation-dependent. This is in part because there exist no inviolate protocols for how any given music experience *should* be facilitated with any particular client or group. But it is also the case that facilitation procedures are gradually shaped by each SMT's particular personality and interaction style, the process of which should be not only critically considered but also nurtured as appropriate by the supervisor (Summer, 2001). And whereas there may be a few fundamental steps that any therapist must enact to engage clients in a given type of music experience, procedures must be flexibly brought to bear during a session, depending on the nature of clients' cognitive, physical, and psychological functioning and readiness. Procedures and their facilitation, therefore, are often idiocentric in character (i.e., uniquely carried out by each SMT), as they are performed in response to particular clients' functioning and proclivities, which are interpreted by the SMT in the moment. For example, the way that verbal instructions are articulated toward engaging a group in a referential or nonreferential improvisation must account for the clients' cognitive and receptive language skills, past experiences that they may or may not have had with improvising, and current level of receptiveness or resistance.

I recall a female SMT who was working with men with substance use disorders and who sought to introduce referential improvisation. The choice of method was intended as an opportunity for the group to explore feelings surrounding establishing and maintaining healthy boundaries relative to friends and family members, some of whom were themselves substance users and others of whom were inimical or "toxic" in other ways. We had learned that many in the group came from economically depressed parts of Appalachia, where education was not necessarily emphasized or encouraged in families or within the coal-mining communities in which they lived. The typical vocabulary used among most of the men seemed to evidence this particular cultural characteristic. The SMT eagerly began the introduction by using terms that she had learned in the classroom relative to clinical improvisation methods, such as "referential," "programmatic," "extemporaneous," and "interpretation." These words, however, did not fit into the group members' vocabularies and seemed to elicit confusion and resistance to the intended process, potentially evoking an unintentional resentment of elitism aimed at the SMT by the group members. Intervening following a question from a group member about the term "referential," as well as reading the look of confusion on some of the men's faces, I quickly provided an alternate description of the intended process of "playing an instrument with a specific feeling in mind" and "play with the energy of that feeling," and the group was able to engage meaningfully in the process. The SMT learned the importance of considering language as a cultural attribute and meeting the group at a linguistically functional and helpful level in order to communicate successfully. A manualized way of describing the experience and inviting clients into it, therefore, would not be able to account for the different abilities and attitudes that often exist in client groups. Therefore, it is the SMT's challenge to match their procedures and how they are carried out to the needs of the client or group. In my experience, next to meaningful client musical or verbal responses during a session, facilitation procedures are often the first aspects that SMTs wish to discuss during debriefing as they reflect on what felt to them to be successful interactions or missteps in the process. Evaluating each SMT's progress in developing various facilitation competencies, therefore, means that supervisors must be careful not to impose their own preferences on the SMT's facilitation style/approach but rather to support them in critically discerning the most useful options for shaping their own repertoire of procedural actions.

Musical aspects are those related to the specific music experiences (i.e., method variations) selected and designed toward particular clinical aims and the musical materials selected and/or sounded during the session. Musical materials might include, for example, live or recorded renderings of songs or pieces used within discrete music experiences; salient music elements performed, improvised, composed, or heard; intermusical events that occur between clients or between clients and the SMT (i.e., interactions during musicing episodes); and instruments or playback devices. With the supervisor's understanding of each SMT's maturity and musical and clinical acumen at a given point in time, reflection on musical aspects of the session is encouraged at varying levels. For instance, on a practical level, the SMT might reflect first on whether the music experiences and related musical materials were at all beneficial to the therapy process, that is, whether they met the clients' needs during that particular session. Another practical musical concern might be evaluation of the key, tempo, and dynamics of a live rendering of a song and how these features functioned toward the session aims and helped or hindered clients' engagement. In this regard, I recall supervising an SMT while working with a group of older adults in a dementia unit in a religiously affiliated facility where the clear majority of residents were Caucasian women. These group members, whose ages ranged from their 70s into their 90s, had lived most of their lives in the immediate area where we were located in the northern Midwest of the United States. As part of the session plan, the SMT had prepared to engage the residents in singing together "Over the Rainbow" (by Harold Arlen and E. Y. Harburg)— typically an excellent song choice for this particular group to stimulate reminiscences to be shared verbally. With this song, the SMT surmised that the residents would more than likely recall many of the musical features as well as the lyrics, the film from which the song gained its popularity, and perhaps the film's starring actors as well. However, the live rendition that the student provided was not based on the original arrangement sung by Judy Garland in *The Wizard of Oz*. Instead, the SMT chose a version that was, at the time, receiving considerable airplay on radio stations geared toward youth and young adults and used in advertising. This version was recorded by a male Hawaiian artist named Israel Ka ano i Kamakawiwo ole and featured a male singer, ukulele played in a quasi-Reggae rhythmic style, and altered melody and lyrics sung in a sequence of lines that deviated from the Garland performance. While this song was pleasant to listen to, the residents were largely nonresponsive to it due to their lack of familiarity with most of the musical features of the SMT's rendition. The experience seemed to leave the residents somewhat perplexed, and the energy in the room, which had been rather lively and ebullient prior to this song, had dissipated by the time the song had concluded. Not aware of why the mood had changed and the residents had struggled to remark in accordance with the SMT's probes about the song and the film, the SMT eventually moved forward by introducing another Tin Pan Alley song in its original and overlearned style and arrangement, thereby regrounding the group in the music therapy session and helping the SMT to follow through with the aim of evoking reminiscences among the residents. In subsequent processing during supervision, the SMT was asked to recount the thought processes that had led to her decision to learn and use the alternate arrangement of "Over the Rainbow." The SMT recognized that it was her own enjoyment of and enthusiasm over the newer rendition that guided her decision to use it rather than a careful accounting of the residents' cultural contexts and experiences. She was able to connect the residents' lack of responsiveness to the musical mismatching that occurred between the residents' expectancies regarding the *definitive* recording they had grown accustomed to hearing and the newer version.

Concerns more peripheral to the sounded music might include the SMT's use of proximity, affect, and musical, verbal, and/or gestural cues/guidance during musicing episodes. A concern more immediately related to an SMT's specific musical competencies is reflecting on how and when various musical techniques were initiated and what their impact was on clients' musicing experiences. Last, an example of a theoretical concern relative to clients' musicing might be the SMT's ability to construct in-the-moment interpretations of a client's musical contributions (i.e., meanings that the SMT might ascribe to the client's music) and discerning how an interpretation may have influenced the SMT's decision-making as the music or the session unfolded.

Finally, *relational* aspects have to do with interpersonal and intermusical relating between clients and between clients and the SMT and how those experiences inhibit or help to facilitate and perhaps deepen the therapy process. Reflecting on how clients relate to each other involves the SMT interpreting observations of group members' interactions during and between discrete music experiences. On the other hand, the SMT has direct access to their own experiences regarding the nature of interactions with clients, how these felt at the time, and whether and how an experience influenced further decision-making or the client's experience. With regard to both beneficial or detrimental episodes of relating, the SMT might be encouraged to reflect on the precise nature of a salient interaction, noting who initiated the contact and through which modality (e.g., gesture, words, or music), precise words used, affect/feelings evoked, how long the interaction occurred and how it ended, and how the interaction may compare to previous ones. Reflection on relational aspects are informative on many levels, as an SMT learns about their developing use of self in the treatment process as well as how music and music experiences have great potential to elicit and deepen connections in therapy.

An episode was shared with me regarding an SMT's work in the psychiatric unit of a local hospital where she encountered a Caucasian adolescent female who had been admitted following a suicide attempt two days previously. The young woman suggested listening to a rap song together but warned that the lyrics were rather explicit and included liberal use of the n-word among other potentially offensive words/phrases. The SMT, who identified as Asian-American, considered her options to honor the patient's choice of song, find a "clean version" of the song, or suggest an alternate song. The SMT decided to honor the patient's choice and, while listening, consciously focused her attention on the underlying massages of the song lyrics and then chose to not bring further attention to the potentially offensive words. The SMT reported that there was some palpable tension between the SMT and the patient while listening to the song. Yet the session continued in a positive way and the therapeutic relationship seemed to the SMT to have been strong and beneficial to the patient, as she freely discussed aspects of her life experiences. However, the SMT also described wondering in the clinical moment as she made what she considered to be a crucial decision (as well as later in her reflective journal) how the session events might have been different had she been either black or white. The SMT and the patient did not share the same racial background. Might the patient's song choice have been different had the SMT been white? Was the patient's warning about offensive language offered as a common courtesy or would the warning itself have been different or perhaps not issued at all had the SMT been black? This SMT believed that issues related to race were clearly influential during the session and were related to the choice of music and how the music was shared.

The SMT went on to explore how the sharing of music has potential for impacting the development of a therapeutic relationship between persons with disparate cultural characteristics and histories.

As indicated, field supervision during senior-level practica occurs less frequently than at earlier levels. Most SMTs at this point have presumably developed suitable functionality with regard to competencies relevant for more independent clinical work. At the senior level, SMTs have accumulated three semesters' worth of experiences in facilitating music therapy with different clinical groups (some in which the clients and SMTs did not share the same cultural backgrounds), are generally more advanced in their musicianship and understandings regarding music in therapy processes, and have continued to grow in their personal maturity. At this level, then, SMTs are encouraged to reflect more critically about the nature of structural, musical, and relational aspects of music therapy sessions and discrete music experiences and to begin couching their reflections within theoretical perspectives and concepts. Commensurate with these levels of practicum in our program, students' course work includes focus on myriad theories that support music therapy and concepts relative to music psychotherapy and also engage in authentic, process-oriented group work with peers in a closely monitored, student-led learning/support music therapy group. Thus, as noted in the introduction to this chapter, a key focus of supervision at this level is on helping students to integrate these diverse streams of knowledge and experiences into a firm conceptualization of music therapy and the SMT's potential roles in it.

An additional point is made here regarding supervisors' experiences related to processing therapeutic encounters, particularly when the supervisor is in the role of co-facilitator as described previously and as occurs in some work at the senior level. I noted that supervisor co-facilitation is part teaching, part modeling, and part supporting. In the following vignette, we see that in the role of co-facilitator, the supervisor must also exercise a high level of reflexivity and internal meta-processing as they consider not only how to most usefully respond to clients but also how their supervisee might perceive their processing techniques. An example of group work, created from an aggregate of supervisory encounters, is the following having to do with practicum at a substance abuse treatment facility.

During her first session, the only African-American person in a women's group began the session with arms folded, legs crossed, and a flat affect which we interpreted as displaying a closed body posture and indifference to the process. Later in the session, while listening to a peer's song choice, she seemed to be deeply moved, she smiled and began to interact with the group and shared her story and insights. This event was recognized and discussed in debriefing by the supervisor and the white female SMT co-facilitator as important for the woman and for the group. In subsequent sessions, and from our cultural perspective, we began to perceive this woman as dominating, to the potential detriment of the group therapy process and to relationships with her peers. The supervisor (also white) struggled during a later session with how to intervene in order to bring more balanced attention and focus on all of the group members. The supervisor's typical response would be to act in a fairly direct manner to work with the woman's actions and bring awareness of the need for equal time for all members, but she hesitated due to concern that her limiting of the woman's verbal contributions might be perceived either by the woman or by the SMT as diminishing of the woman's voice and agency on racial grounds. The conflict was perceived by the supervisor in the moment as protecting the group as a whole without being perceived as thwarting the woman's agency.

In a subsequent debriefing, it came to light that the SMT co-facilitator had reservations similar to the supervisor's. She wondered about the implications of drawing too firm a line when it comes to what we assess from our perspective as overactive client participation, especially when the client might already feel somewhat isolated due to racial differences among the group members. The supervision discussion brought to awareness the challenges of balancing group members' voices while carefully considering the contexts within which those voices have developed and been used effectively or ineffectively to communicate one's self and one's needs in life. The supervisor's self-disclosure of her own reflexive processes and struggle with this client in the moment and afterward provided a thoughtful model for the student to witness and perhaps emulate in their own way in future encounters.

CONCLUSION

Described above are what I hope is a helpful variety of concepts relative to supervision in the field with undergraduate student music therapists (SMTs). The concepts presented stem from field supervision provided for SMTs in five levels of practica through a university program in the midwestern Unites States and have evolved over an approximately 20-year period. Premises that undergird the approaches described were provided with an emphasis on the perception of students as actively developing both as persons and as music therapists. It was noted that one of the unique concerns of a field supervisor is to carefully attend to and balance the needs of both SMTs and their volunteer clients in the moments of clinical–musical interaction. SMTs consistently progress in developing the many requisite facilitation competencies articulated by AMTA (2013) through varied practicum experiences, and the developmental structure of the program's practicum sequence and the various types of supervision experiences provided assist in this process. SMTs and supervisors begin each term with awareness of the relevant competencies to be practiced and evaluated, thereby focusing the work of each. A brief description of the program's reliance on concepts related to integral thinking (Bruscia, 2011, 2014), including the utility of outcome- and experience-oriented perspectives with their relevance for training and supervision, was provided. Four useful roles that a field supervisor may take within any given music therapy session were described: model, co-facilitator, group member, and observer. These roles provide a supervisor with different sorts of opportunities with which to teach, model, guide, and support SMTs as they in turn learn from their facilitation experiences. The significance of engaging in debriefing immediately following sessions to process SMTs' experiences was stressed. Last, a model that focuses SMTs' and a supervisor's attention during debriefing on structural, musical, and relational aspects of therapy sessions was presented, along with explanations of potential benefits associated with use of this observation model for both SMTs and supervisors.

Just as supervision processes are not intended to impose an approach on a supervisee as "the way" to practice, the concepts presented above are intended to show just "one way" that field supervision may be conceptualized and conducted for undergraduate trainees. In fact, looking back at this chapter, I realize that there remains a wide range of important concepts at work across our various practica that were not even mentioned here, let alone explained. Given careful reflection on all that was articulated above, however, I realize also that supervision at the undergraduate level is, to a large degree, similar to a music improvisation process. It draws on myriad nuances of observation, listening, and action. Due to the multiplicity of constituent facets that interact during the practicum process, such as the personalities of clients, SMTs, and the supervisor, the time of day, the weather, the broken guitar string, the emotionally moving song, and so on, supervision in the field is, in its inspiring way, never the same way twice.

REFERENCE LIST

American Music Therapy Association (AMTA). (2013). *AMTA professional competencies*. Retrieved March 26, 2017, from https://www.musictherapy.org/about/competencies/

American Music Therapy Association (AMTA). (2014). *AMTA code of ethics*. Retrieved September 13, 2017, from https://www.musictherapy.org/about/ethics/

Bruscia, K. (1991). Musical origins: Developmental foundations for therapy. *Proceedings of the 18th Annual Conference of the Canadian Association for Music Therapy* (pp. 2–10). Regina, SK: Canadian Association for Music Therapy.

Bruscia, K. (2011). *Ways of thinking in music therapy.* Paper presented at the 2011 conference of the American Music Therapy Association, Atlanta, GA. Podcast available at musictherapy.org

Bruscia, K. (2014). *Defining music therapy* (3rd ed.). University Park, IL: Barcelona Publishers.

Elliot, D. (1995). *Music Matters.* Oxford, UK: Oxford University Press.

Gardstrom, S. C. (2002). *Observation model: Structural, musical, relational aspects.* Unpublished manuscript, Department of Music, University of Dayton, Dayton, OH.

Hook, J. (2017). *Cultural humility: Engaging diverse identities in therapy.* Washington, DC: American Psychological Association.

Kegan, R. (1982). *The evolving self: Problem and process in human development.* Cambridge, MA: Harvard University.

Lee, J. H. (2015). Integral thinking in music therapy. *Journal of Music and Human Behavior, 12*(1), 65–94.

Summer, L. (2001). Group supervision in first-time music therapy practicum. In M. Forinash (Ed.), *Music therapy supervision* (pp. 69–86). Gilsum, NH: Barcelona Publishers.

Wheeler, B. (1983). A psychotherapeutic classification of music therapy practices. *Music Therapy Perspectives, 1*(2), 8–12.

Chapter 10

A JOURNEY THROUGH INTERNSHIP SUPERVISION REVISITED: ROLES, DYNAMICS, AND PHASES OF THE SUPERVISORY RELATIONSHIP

Susan Feiner

INTRODUCTION

Embarking on internship, for both supervisor and intern, is like boarding a small, intimate vessel that cannot sail without the full involvement of two barely acquainted travelers. Waves come from all directions. Every turn brings new territories that can be explored and learned from. Each traveler is dependent upon the other, for if one leans forward, lets out the sail, or changes direction, the other will feel this and will need to decide how to respond. Each journey is unique, and the ocean is full of challenges, from within and without.

My experience has taught me that this metaphor still rings true today, 19 years later, as I update this chapter, but with the caveat that this is an extremely crowded vessel, filled not only with supervisor and supervisee, but also with their varied cultural and personal history and identities. A chorus of voices sings out, filling every inch of space and commanding varying directions as the waves buffet and propel this journey along.

The potential for both travelers on this journey is rich, full of exploration, accomplishment, and self-knowledge. At the end of this journey, the intern, now a professional, feels ready to embark upon a career with a foundation of knowledge and experience necessary to meet the challenges that will come. The supervisor feels gratified by having met the challenge to pass this knowledge to another, enriched by having participated in such an unfolding. Hopefully, both feel honored to have shared this journey together, pleased they have navigated these waters in spite of the times when there may have been obstacles that were difficult or even scary to traverse.

Many students have spoken of how their internships and relationships with their supervisors have been a time not only of professional growth, but also of personal growth and even transformation. Their relationship with their supervisors brought about major changes in who they were and how they felt about themselves. I am continually awed by what transpires in this relationship, much of which goes well beyond what appears as the explicit tasks at hand.

This chapter examines some of the dynamics of the supervisor–intern relationship in order to illuminate the challenges and potential of this period. I will focus on supervision issues that arise for supervisor and intern as well as the relationship between them as they journey through the phases of this training experience: the marvelous potential of this relationship; what makes it unique; developmental phases of internship and how roles change; the issues and challenges that arise for both supervisor and intern; and possible supervisory interventions. Additions to this updated chapter include increased emphasis upon cultural awareness and responsiveness and the impact of cultural diversity on the supervisory relationship. This topic warrants more attention than the parameters of this chapter allow but is referred to as one important aspect of the supervisory process. Supervisee trauma, both past and current, and its impact on internship and the internship/supervisor relationship, will also be referred to and likewise deserves more discussion (for more a detailed discussion of trauma and internship, see Feiner, 2010).

DYNAMICS WITHIN THE SUPERVISORY RELATIONSHIP

Assumptions and Expectations

What are some of the dynamics that contribute to the complexity and intensity of the supervisor–intern relationship? As a way to begin to understand these dynamics, let us start with some of the unrealistic assumptions that both supervisor and supervisee may bring. Looking at dictionary definitions is a remarkably accurate way of describing common preconceptions regarding supervision. If we break supervision into "super" and "vision," "super" is: of a higher kind; having greater influence, capacity, etc., than another of its kind" (Stevenson & Lindberg, 2010) and "to a degree greater than normal" (Webster, 2016). "Vision" is: unusual discernment or foresight (Merriam-Webster.com, 2018) and "something seen by other than normal sight … or supernaturally revealed" (Stevenson & Lindberg, 2010). Students' expectations are usually not far off from these. They often idealize their supervisors, at least at first, believing that they can see and know all. Interns may assume that because a supervisor is an expert, the supervisor will understand their differing cultural backgrounds or identity and therefore know best how to guide them through internship, without needing explanation. Or perhaps the opposite: Interns might feel, based upon experience as a marginalized person, that there was no way to be heard or understood, so that the best way to survive successfully would be to do what is expected and keep one's feelings private.

Supervisors' expectations of themselves, especially those of new supervisors, are often not far off from these as well. Not only must a supervisor know all clinically and be the perfect model, but also the supervisor must have a divine understanding of what the supervisee needs. Quite a torch for the supervisor to bear!

As seen above, when the words are broken into "super" and "vision," this connotes an almost omnipotent being. This being is not only superior and greater, but also one who knows all and sees all and has the powers of divination. Now, if we combine "super" and "vision" into one word and look at the dictionary definition of "supervision," we find that it means: "a critical watching and directing" (Merriam-Webster.com, 2018). As one word, "supervision" takes on an added dimension, portraying a criticizing and controlling supervisor. Beginning interns are insecure about their abilities, even their sense of self and identity, as they enter this new and demanding role. Compounding this, if the intern is from a marginalized community, then the anticipation of judgment might further intensify insecurity or lack of safety. Supervisors must be extremely sensitive to these expectations and to their power (Forinash, 2001; Porter, 2014; Sue et al., 2007), not only in their role as supervisor, but also when there is cultural or economic disparity. They need to remain open to "not knowing" and able to empower their intern to educate them (Estrella, 2001; Hahna, 2014). Supervisors must also watch for unrealistic expectations they might put upon themselves to be perfect, to have all the answers.

Given all of these superhuman expectations, in reality, the potential of the supervisory relationship is both humble and grand. For the supervisor, it becomes a professional challenge to refine and pass on knowledge and to learn with the intern what one does not know. Supervision is an opportunity to challenge one's assumptions, broaden one's cultural lens, and be humble enough to learn from differences.

Fears and Uncertainty

For many students, internship is the culmination of their academic studies; others are engaged simultaneously with course work while in their internship. Both are in a position to be responsible for a caseload with on-site supervision. When starting a new career, the student looks at him- or herself anew and is challenged to develop a new identity as a professional music therapist. By being intimately observed by another, the supervisor is equally challenged to look at him- or herself anew, for each intern brings out another part of one's self for further acquaintance. Interns are often overwhelmed with excitement and fear, as well as unbounded expectations, when they first begin. They are usually full of questions. Of themselves they may be asking: Can I really do this work (Wheeler & Williams, 2012)? Will I really like or love this work as much as I imagined? They watch their supervisors keenly and with trepidation. You will see me inept and vulnerable. I will be so exposed—how will you be? How will you react to my mistakes? I depend upon you to guide and teach me—will you be able to do this? Can I fulfill your expectations of me? Can I trust you? Will I be safe with you? How much can I share about myself with you? Will you appreciate and respect me even though I am of a different race, younger, older, LGBTQ, a foreign student, a different religion, socio-economic class, and so on? Will you understand me? Will you like me? When these feelings are not there, I am often on the alert for problems. Phenomenological research that examined students' experiences and concerns during their clinical placements found that they often began their placements with tremendous fear and anxiety, as well as fear of critique and ridicule by their supervisor (Wheeler, 2002; Wheeler & Williams, 2012). Their sense of self is often dependent on how the supervisor views and interacts with them as they go through this transition.

Supervisors also begin with similar concerns: Will you respect my work and want to learn from me? How will you react to my mistakes? Will I be able to work well with you? Can I understand you or you me? Will you respect me if I am younger than you or from a marginalized community? Can I trust you? Can I trust you to represent the music therapy program and to represent *me* in this setting? Will you like me? Through the intern and supervisor getting to know each other, these questions gradually are answered. This leads to a foundation of mutual trust and respect in most cases—and difficulties when trust is not developed. Kadushin and Harkness (2014) discussed how new supervisors' feelings of well-being are dependent upon supervisees' affirmation and approval as they establish their new identity as supervisors.

Self-Disclosure and Vulnerability

Issues related to self-disclosure and vulnerability also compound the complexity of the supervisory relationship. The amount of time spent together, the intern not being able to control the pace and timing of self-disclosure, ongoing observation of the intern by the supervisor, cultural differences, and vulnerability inherent in the process of music itself are all significant factors.

At times, internship can feel even more threatening or deeply challenging than one's own therapy. In therapy, the client usually sets one's own pace, opening up and addressing what one is ready to explore (except during crises). The intern, in contrast, is often at some level of crisis, faced with a constant barrage of challenges and issues from the setting, the supervisor, and clients, whether ready or not. There is no place to wait, hide, or rest until ready, because the intern must respond to internship demands and clients' needs as they arise. For example, an intern may have difficulty with feelings of anger or loss (is there anyone who doesn't?). In personal therapy, these types of emotions may be triggered by internal stressors, life events, or experiences in therapy. The individual can then address them in weekly therapy and/or on-and-off between sessions at their own pace. Within internship, however, a client's anger or fear of death, or even death itself, may come up suddenly.

The intern will need to address this immediately, not necessarily aligning with the intern's own personal readiness. This poses a challenge for the student and can be quite overwhelming. It is a given that this occurs for all therapists, for we are always responsible for learning about ourselves in the treatment process, but this can be especially difficult for a new intern, intensifying feelings of inadequacy or vulnerability. This also poses a challenge for the supervisor: how to handle these issues without crossing the line and becoming the intern's therapist (this will be addressed later).

Differences in cultural identity can further complicate feelings of vulnerability and comfort with the challenges inherent in self-disclosure (Estrella, 2001; Hahna, 2014; Milville, Rosa, & Constantine, 2005; Sue, 2015; Sue et al., 2007). Interns from different cultures adjusting to unfamiliar cultural norms at their site might feel more vulnerable and fearful, as well as confused (Sue et al., 2007). An intern may feel it totally inappropriate to share with their supervisor feelings of insecurity or being overwhelmed or feel unable to reflect on feelings that are felt as unsafe or culturally not an option to share or express. A supervisor might incorrectly interpret this as being resistant or avoidant.

Another source of vulnerability for the intern is the format of supervision. In many music therapy settings, the intern not only has supervisory meetings but also is regularly observed actually doing the music therapy sessions. Again, there is a lack of control for the intern, who is not able to pick and choose what to discuss or what vignettes or recordings to review in a supervision hour. The intern is fully exposed in the moment and does not have the option to consciously or unconsciously edit what the supervisor is observing. Because the medium of treatment is music, the intern often feels vulnerable and anxious about being observed. What will the supervisor think of my skills, my repertory, my musical sensitivity? How does the music make me feel, and can I show this to my supervisor? What will it be like if my supervisor wants to work with me in music? The task for the supervisor is to create space for these concerns to be shared and discussed, as well as to pace supervision and feedback appropriately to the intern's learning process while remaining cognizant of these vulnerability issues.

But with this greater exposure and risk also comes greater potential for support and learning. Once the initial fears and vulnerability are overcome and a trusting environment is established, the student now has the potential to plunge and explore, knowing that the supervisor is there for their journey together. The supervisor also feels free to share and explore and learn from the intern. A fruitful parallel process can take place—between the student and supervisor and between the student and clients. The intern's self-awareness grows as dynamics or issues with clients will often be mirrored in the relationship with the supervisor (Feiner, 2010; Young & Aigen, 2010).

The following is a quote from an intern's final summary at the end of her internship that eloquently illustrates this:

> In my interaction with the many therapists at the clinic, I have felt respected and revered, accepted and understood. Speaking about them collectively, they each take the time to stop, look and listen, to me, with me, and for me. It is as if I am a seed that has been planted in this garden we call music therapy, and because of their way of being, I am never without sunlight, their warmth, or consideration. This has genuinely affected and subtly guided my process as an intern. I've been able to face issues that I was not comfortable with because of this guidance and support, and actually see them through, see myself grow, and allow myself their years of experience to comfort me. This in turn has been bestowed upon the children I work with each week. It's a bit like passing the torch. I daresay there is no other way to learn this technique but through personal experience as the recipient of such gifts.

THE ROLE OF THE SUPERVISOR

As supervisor, what is our role? Are we educators? Mentors? Therapists? Administrators? Determining our role not only is a challenge but also can be downright confusing. How do we manage all of these roles? What happens when they conflict? What does a supervisor do with the intern's personal material or personality issues that become exposed? Where do supervisors ethically draw the line in the use of their therapy skills when working with interns? How does one sensitively explore together cultural differences inherent in both supervisor and supervisee?

Kadushin (1992) and Kadushin and Harkness (2014), from the field of social work, break down the supervisory role into categories that help to clarify these questions. They pose that as supervisor we wear three hats and therefore must juggle the roles of: educator, administrator, and supporter. These different roles impact each other and work together.

Educator

As educator, the supervisor is responsible for teaching. Interns must learn a vast body of knowledge by the end of their internship in order to be clinically qualified for graduation. This challenges supervisors to expand their expertise to encompass a new role as educator, one for which most music therapists have received little training in spite of their many years of study and practice as therapists.

Mordock (1990) described this as a new and challenging role for supervisors. As therapists, we are trained to react to what a client brings to treatment, but as educators we are challenged to shift from this reactive stance to a proactive stance, focusing on what a student must learn. Supervisors must feel comfortable in initiating and more actively giving and modeling information rather than waiting until a student brings it up. Supervisors need to initiate the discussion of expectations, of areas of tension, and of differing cultural perspectives, expectations, and customs and how they impact client treatment as well as the supervisory relationship (Hadley, 2017).

The good news is that interns want to be taught and they want feedback. If interns are not given sufficient information and feedback (Wheeler, 2002), if they do not get the opportunity to regularly observe their supervisor's work, they often flounder unproductively. They become extremely anxious, struggling to meet elusive expectations. If overly vigilant for reassurance from their supervisor that they are doing well, interns may consequently have fewer resources available to focus on their work with clients. Being proactive with teaching can lessen anxiety (McClain, 2001), as students want to know what their supervisor does, how they do it, and why they do it. They also want a clear understanding of what is expected of them. The educator role is markedly different from a therapist's role.

This poses an interesting challenge for supervisors. How do we offer our work as a model, articulate what our expectations are of our interns, and at the same time help interns develop their own "way" according to their unique qualities, strengths, and skills? The answer is that once interns have a solid foundation in the understanding and practice of their supervisor's work, they can use it as a safe home base from which to explore as they progress in their internship. Supervisors can teach their "way" and still support an intern's development of their own unique qualities.

Excellent therapists often need support to understand how important it is to "teach" when supervising interns. They often fear they would be hampering their intern's creativity and individuality if they taught. What can happen instead are misunderstandings, confusion, and paralyzing anxiety. I usually make this explicit and tell my intern: "I'll show you my way, my methods, my understanding of clients, and my rationale for interventions. Imitate as much as you'd like, and when ready, you can develop more and more of your own. Don't burden yourself now with 'originality' for the sake of originality before you have a basis to work from. Then take it and fly."

It is enormously helpful and important to teach the intern how to use supervision. Be clear about what an intern's responsibilities entail: paperwork requirements, what to expect from you during observations and supervision time, how important it is for you to know what the intern is experiencing—and this means keeping informed of personal reactions. Make it your agenda to hear these feelings, fears, and excitements. Make it your agenda as supervisor to initiate and explore the differences and similarities in each other's cultures and how these might impact understanding each other and the client population, as well as the supervisory process, (Hahna, 2014; Kim, 2008, 2014; Porter, 2014; Stige, 2002; Sue, 2015). Details are important, too—organizing and prioritizing daily responsibilities, avenues of communication and decision-making, and whom to contact when a crisis occurs.

Administrator

As administrator, we must juggle: the university's requirements—caseload, size of groups, logs, and so forth; the site's requirements—numbers of clients, which clients, allocation of supervisor's time; the student's needs—variety of caseload, student's learning style, their special interests; and, most important, the clients' needs—which clients need services and how these needs fit with your intern's abilities. Kadushin and Harkness (2014) go into detail about the challenges of the administrative role in supervising in the field of social work for both supervisor and supervisee, with detailed recommendations and examples of how to do so effectively.

A situation I have seen many times in the field of music therapy occurs when a supervisor may be caught in a struggle between the caseload and the size of groups usually seen at the site and the smaller groups or individual sessions required by the university. A supervisor might want a student to be assigned a varied caseload, but the site has assigned music therapy to only a particular subset of clients. A site might have a music therapist do only group work and not the individual work required by the internship. To advocate for change can provide a professional challenge and a new role, particularly for the new supervisor who has not had the authority in the past to challenge the structure of how the music therapy program is set up. I encourage supervisors to use the support of the university (and its authority in the field) to advocate and bring about changes in or growth of the music therapy program that might not have been previously possible. When setting up a new internship, I often will ask the music therapist what changes they see would strengthen the program and the training of an intern and then talk over with them how this fits into the music therapy program's requirements. Most institutions are eager to affiliate with universities and reap the expanded services that interns can provide. Supervisors can use the support of the university to educate and advocate for a music therapy program that is more responsive to clients' needs. I have seen program growth and refinement happen a multitude of times through the supervisor's advocacy with the university's support.

The supervisor's varying responsibilities can also cause confusion and stress for both supervisor and intern. A student can perceive conflict between the supervisor's varying roles, given the power the supervisor holds: "This is an educator who judges me and an administrator who is my boss. How open can I be during supervision? Will I be penalized for my weaknesses and vulnerabilities? This person can fail me!" Successfully negotiating such potential role conflicts and confusion requires clarity and self-awareness on the part of supervisor and a foundation of goodwill and trust between supervisor and intern (Kadushin & Harkness, 2014). For this to occur, it is the supervisor's responsibility to initiate the discussion of role conflicts and the confusion and vulnerability they can cause, providing the necessary support (Kim, 2008; Sue et al., 2007).

Supporter

One of the important functions of the third role, "supporter" (Kadushin, 1992), is to build a foundation of support for the intern that facilitates successful learning, navigation of internship challenges, and the development of a capable and inspired professional. "A supervisor, by implementing the responsibilities of supportive supervision, not only relieves, restores, confronts, and replenishes, but more positively inspires, animates, exhilarates, and increases job satisfaction" (Kadushin & Harkness, 2014, p. 202).

Keeping in mind an intern's fears and vulnerabilities, the supportive role includes the supervisor communicating belief in the intern's special abilities and enthusiasm at being part of the process and undertakes actions to reassure the student's self-worth.

This process may be challenged by differing cultural identities and norms among client, intern, and supervisor. As supervisor and supporter, setting the groundwork for a collaboration of trust means bringing out into the open these similarities and differences (Estrella, 2001; Forinash, 2006: Hahna, 2014; Kim, 2008; Milville et al., 2005). Appreciating differing cultural norms, as well as acknowledging how this may be challenging within the context of the internship and supervisory relationship, is an important way to create safety, awareness, and open communication. Agree to navigate these challenges together, with the awareness that this may feel uncomfortable for both of you. Talk about the discomfort that this may cause as a normal part of the process for both supervisor and supervisee. Regularly check in for feedback about how each other's words and actions are understood. Interns from abroad have reported to me that they often are fearful that their intentions or their actions are misunderstood and therefore could cause confusion or harm in their relationships with clients, supervisor, and staff.

Another area to be ready to explore is the intern's past trauma and how this trauma might impact working with specific clients, the supervisory relationship, or maybe even the intern's relationship with the internship institution due to past experiences in a similar setting (e.g., a former school or hospitalization). Students may block out their past trauma, be shameful of it, feel it a weakness, or be unaware of how it can impact client and supervisory relationships, sense of self, and the learning process. It is the supervisor's responsibility to help the intern to understand the importance of past or present trauma and see it as an asset to be handled responsibly, as well as its potential for activation and interference in the successful internship experience (Feiner, 2010).

In order to create a supportive foundation for the intern, it is also important to resist the temptation to focus solely on what the student still has to learn, being sure to regularly acknowledge progress and appreciate the intern's strengths as they develop. Interns need reassurance and acknowledgement. They are often unable to hear the positive and only hear feedback as criticism. They can be overwhelmed by what there is still to learn and not see what they have accomplished or their special qualities and strengths. Sometimes I ask students to report back to me the positive feedback they have taken in, or we might pause and just sit and reflect together on how much the intern has grown over the past period of time. It is remarkable how difficult it is for an intern to "remember" because of their focus on what they did not "do right" or do not know. I often have to remind supervisors, and myself, to resist getting carried away with enthusiasm about what there is yet to learn, without balancing this with what has been accomplished—otherwise, an intern can become easily overwhelmed. I warn interns of my tendency to get so enthused that I can get carried away and ask them to please stop me if they cannot absorb more.

The experience of internship and supervision goes beyond supporting an intern's progress. It *challenges* an intern to stretch and grow, to re-evaluate basic assumptions about themselves and others—clients, peers, teachers, or supervisors. It is the push to meet one's potential in the clinical work—the work on oneself, personally and professionally—that drives an intern to grow. The supervisor–intern relationship also provides the "ground" or experience for this development, challenging the intern's and supervisor's personality structure and cultural biases (Hadley, 2017; Porter, 2014). The internship can thus create a new experience that will change an intern's self-image and sense of self, their place in society and relationships with others. This can have a significant impact on a student's life, both professionally and personally.

The same applies to the supervisor. The supervisor has the wonderful challenge of learning from the supervisee, stretching and honing their clinical work, evaluating basic assumptions and cultural perspectives. This process is not easy; it is a challenge to be open and vulnerable in this process with the intern as the shared journey unfolds.

To Teach or Treat?

As supervisors, we learn a great deal about our supervisees. We learn from their interactions with their clients, fellow staff, and the setting. We learn about them from their music. We learn from their interactions and relationship with us and listen to their reflections. What might we learn? We often learn about their past experiences with authority. We learn about their sense of self, how their cultural identity and their history of trauma impact their sense of self, and how they experience the world. We learn their basic assumptions about living life fully, how they view illness, health and growth, and maybe even about how they view death. We learn about their developmental challenges in their current stage of life and how important life events unfold and impact them from day to day. We learn about their passions and fears. We learn about their relationship with music, where they are comfortable and uncomfortable in the music, and how they interact in the music. These are just a few examples of what we learn, but certainly we learn a lot about their personal strengths, their personality, their history, and their cultural norms, as well as their challenges.

What do we do with what we learn? What do we do with these challenges as they come up? This brings us to the teach/treat dilemma. What is our responsibility to address an intern's personal issues as they arise? Their cultural differences? Their past history? When are we overstepping our boundaries as supervisor? What are our boundaries? My answer is that we are not the student's therapists, yet it is our responsibility to identify and address any issues that interfere with the student's work as an intern and developing therapist. This does not mean we take on the role of the intern's therapist.

Sarnat (1992), a psychoanalytic psychotherapist, raises this question: How much should a supervisor allow a supervisee's personality to become a focus in supervision? Sarnat suggested that it is the supervisor's responsibility to address the supervisee's personality problems that interfere in the clinical work. It has been my experience that interns, if feeling safe enough, are often motivated to bear with the discomfort of exploring what interferes in their work with a client for the sake of their learning and for the sake of the client. I have found them willing to traverse areas they would otherwise have found too frightening or painful. This is not unlike my experiences in working with clients who will reflect and make changes for the sake of their children or loved ones that they might not have done for themselves.

So, when should these issues be addressed?

1. When these issues interfere with the intern's understanding or treatment of clients;
2. When issues interfere with the intern's relationship with the supervisor, thereby impeding the learning process;
3. When issues interfere with the intern's relationship with staff on-site.

Once an intern is not able to respond to feedback or develop in certain areas in spite of challenges having been pointed out several times, this usually means that "something" is in the way, regardless of what students may consider to be their best efforts. What is this something? Personal issues or countertransference issues? Learning issues? Cultural differences? Past trauma (Feiner, 2010)? Students are often eager to work on identifying this "something" if safe enough in the supervisory relationship. It often helps for me to reassure them that this is the life of being a therapist; clients challenge us to learn more about ourselves in order to ethically carry out our role. I often find that my interns laugh with some relief when I congratulate them on getting to "a golden moment," welcoming them to the life of a therapist that we all go through regularly. By doing this, I generalize this experience and, if appropriate, share a relevant challenge that I might have gone through.

It is at this point, this "golden" opportunity, when careful interventions are called for so that the issues can be clarified and explored, allowing the intern's learning to progress. This is also a time for supervisors to resist the temptation to go beyond the boundaries of the supervisor and venture into the role of the therapist. Often the identification of the challenge is enough to cause it to subside, but sometimes more work needs to be done, on which the intern can follow up in therapy or with other support systems.

The following are some examples of when an intern's countertransference issues interfere with understanding or treatment of clients: A particular member in an intern's therapy group is avoided or overlooked repeatedly, even after both supervisor and intern have discussed the client's dynamics and what his behavior may be communicating. It may be the intern's revulsion to something as simple as drooling, or perhaps there is something about this client that evokes emotions that the intern is avoiding. I find that if I make it clear that we all have countertransference reactions in our work, that they are a given to be embraced, explored, and learned from, rather than that we are bad therapists for having them, interns may then feel comfortable in taking the next step in exploring with me what may be going on for them. Sometimes just acknowledging that it is OK to have "negative reactions" to our clients is enough to clear up the resistance.

We are then able to explore the origin of these countertransference reactions. Are they in response to dynamics or transferences that originate from the client—what I call a "working countertransference" that teaches us something about the client? For example, is the client evoking the intern's feelings of anger because of subtle provocations this client always directs toward anyone in an important relationship to them? Or is the intern feeling or reacting in such a way because of the intern's own personal past or present experiences that are being triggered—what I call a "personal countertransference" from one's own past or present, not stemming from the client? Or perhaps these are not countertransference reactions at all but overlapping differences in culture that have created obstacles to understanding that need to be addressed?

It is important to give time for an intern's countertransference feelings to "blossom" so the intern can reflect back with you over time and really see what you are addressing. For example, I may point out a client who has been avoided a number of times before examining why with the intern. Then I can observe with the intern how this has come up a repeatedly and explore the origin of these feelings. This can be frightening or painful, and it is very important to be clear with the student that this happens to everyone. Supervisors giving examples of their own countertransference feelings and the resulting interference in the treatment process can often be helpful at these times.

An important way to lay the groundwork for this is to make self-reflection a part of the process from the beginning of internship (Milville et al., 2005; Porter, 2014; Sue, 2015). This sets the stage for future self-inquiry, making it a natural aspect of the treatment and supervision process rather than one that is used only when there are problems. For example, at the very beginning of their internship, I may ask interns to pick out which clients they are attracted to and which they would rather avoid. We then explore what triggers these feelings. This may be a way to approach countertransference issues, cultural challenges, or a history of trauma that can become an integrated and useful part of the treatment and supervisory process. Why are you attracted to the timid child? What is it about you that is attracted to her (e.g., "I like drawing out people"; "I like this kind of challenge because it moves at a slow pace"; "she is from my country of origin, so I will better understand her and she, me"; "I am more comfortable with clients who are [female/older/LGBTQ]"; "I have had a similar trauma in my life")? What is it about the active child that is not appealing (e.g., "I get scared when I feel out of control")? What is it about this child that you feel inside of you when you see her? Is this her sadness that you are feeling or yours? What about sadness intrigues you? Let's explore musically and improvise how you feel about this client. We begin to tease out which reactions we have that are due to what we are picking up about the client and which are due to our own personal experiences and issues. This sets a precedent so that when problems come up, the process of self-examination is already an integral part of the work and a given in our work together. The intern begins to see self-reflection, cultural awareness, and countertransference as useful clinical tools for learning about the client and about themselves.

One example of a common issue that can interfere in the treatment process occurs when a particular mood of music is absent from an intern's vocabulary and cannot be accessed when a client needs it. Sometimes a quality of voice when singing or a touch on the piano is too narrow in range. I once had an intern who could not bear to play music that expressed sadness. To explore this, we played music together. First, I had her try to improvise a musical portrait of the client and then the child's sadness. When this was too difficult, we just explored sadness musically. Over and over, we played until the intern could finally approach the feeling of "sad." Eventually, she began to see what she was avoiding and how this particular mood in the music was extremely threatening to her, given her past experiences. This new awareness set her free to be more responsive to the client, and she was able to further process the origins of these feelings in her own therapy. Only through musical exploration and then our processing was she able to identify her own unresolved issues and the impact that these were having on the child whom was treating.

Another common example of when feelings may be aroused due to countertransference or cultural differences can be seen when limits need to be set or authority initiated. It can be difficult for beginning interns to be clear and supportive in setting limits due to their own discomfort in doing so. For example, they may say, "I don't want to be a boss, to be punishing or punitive"; "I was like him as a child and I am concerned that he may no longer see me as his friend"; or "I could never say no to an elder—in my culture, that would show such disrespect." This can stem from lack of understanding of how some clients need limits in order to feel safe and how to have authority and not be authoritarian. One can also see the other extreme, where an intern easily becomes angry, punitive, and authoritarian when limits need to be set. This may reflect the intern's own past unresolved authority issues, feelings of anger at having to set limits, or feelings of anger provoked by the client's behavior. In such a case, an intern learns to use their own feelings of anger to explore whether these feelings stem from past personal experiences or indeed are a working countertransference evoked by the client that can be used to better understand who this client is in the world.

The following is an example of when there is interference in the relationship between the supervisor and supervisee: I remember a student, once so eager to work with me, who began to withdraw and even looked pained as I would enter the room for our supervision time. She was still doing everything required of her, and her work with clients was excellent, but I decided I had to talk with her about how she seemed with me. There was no way I could work with her when I felt so shut out and unwelcome. Gone was the positive spirit of us working together. I saw myself "dancing" in order to "get her back" (more of my countertransference). When I finally caught on to what was happening, I pointed it out. After hearing how I felt, she realized that she was dreading her time with me, feeling uncomfortable at how I saw things about her before she saw them. Exploring together further, she realized this originated from her past experiences of being intruded upon and abused by an important authority. My way of working with her at that time felt intrusive when earlier, when she had been more dependent upon me during her early stages as intern, it had felt supportive. I had to evaluate my own countertransference feelings and reevaluate and adjust my supervision style. She was in a different phase of her training now that necessitated my providing more space and independence. I had to reflect on how I felt with her not needing me—was I needing her to depend upon me? She was amazed at having her feelings accepted and responded to without retaliation. She also became clear on what she needed to work on in her own personal therapy.

Sarnat (1992) wrote of how some supervisors are resistant to this type of exploration because of reluctance to see humanness as a contributor to the impasse with a supervisee. He says that the way to overcome this is through acceptance of one's fallibility. Rather than see personality as flawed when these events occur, he suggests that they be seen as ordinary, inevitable, and "subject to analytic curiosity." Again, if we keep our reflective "curiosity" alive throughout, then it will be more comfortably used when there are difficulties for both supervisor and intern.

Another arena for exploration and support is when challenges arise that interfere with the intern's interactions with other staff. The following are a few examples to look out for: lack of communication and teamwork or even avoidance; competition with other staff; lack of assertiveness when needed for the client's best interests; feelings of disempowerment or lack of value when music therapy is not understood. These areas need to be understood and addressed. I remember the relief one intern felt when able to sit down with a teacher and plan some treatment strategies rather than feel continually thwarted by the teacher's intrusions. This intern took personally the teacher's overwhelmed behavior, thinking she was disliked. This accomplishment gave her the confidence to initiate other contacts with staff and helped her to realize that she did indeed have a voice and the respect of fellow team members.

But perhaps an intern's difficulties in the setting are due not to countertransference or other personal issues but to the power structure in the setting? Might there be a power hierarchy in the clinical team, and does this impact how team members view music therapy and possibly intimidate the intern? Or perhaps the intern feels less entitled to speak up because they are from a foreign culture or are part of a marginalized population or maybe even have heard disparaging remarks or microaggressions (Sue et al., 2007) that have occurred and silenced them (Porter, 2014)?

Many settings, particularly hospitals, have a hierarchical power structure that can intimidate the intern and the supervisor. Estrella (2001) talked about how music therapy can be a culture in and of itself and, given this, the importance for the music therapist to constructively find a way to have a voice and not see ourselves and our field as defined or limited by the culture of the setting. When it is safe for the supervisor and supervisee to discuss these vicissitudes of power (Amir, 2006; Estrella, 2001; Forinash, 2006), then the intern and supervisor can work together toward the intern feeling safe and empowered to assert the music therapist's role in patient care.

When an intern's countertransference issues, cultural differences, or history of trauma arise, we can then talk about what comes up to the extent that it is appropriate for both of us to become sensitized and united on what needs to be done next (Forinash, 2006; Whitehead-Pleaux et al., 2012). Support systems for following through on the issues can be discussed. It is hoped that the student is in therapy, where the issues can be worked with in depth. It is important for the student to have additional supports if there are overwhelming cultural challenges arising, through their own therapy or other resources. It can be tempting to take on the role of therapist if the intern does not have one, but it is best at this time for the intern to enter outside treatment and support so that roles and transferences do not become confused.

It is equally important for supervisors to be continually responsible for their own countertransference, their own cultural biases (Hahna, 2014; Sue, 2015), and any past trauma so that they can be effective and supportive supervisors. An important area related to this is the supervisor's own experiences in supervision. What was your music therapy intern supervisor like? Was it a good experience? Why? Was there anything traumatic in your training? How might what was helpful to you not be helpful for your intern because of your differences? If a past supervisory relationship was negative or traumatic, are you trying so hard not to replicate your negative experience that you are avoidant of areas of discomfort? Is the culture of your setting and/or your current supervisor authoritarian? If so, are you transmitting this institutional culture to your supervisee?

INTERNSHIP PHASES

The intern–supervisor relationship, like all relationships, is not static but continually evolves over time. This evolution can be organized into developmental phases. How do these phases evolve and what are the dynamics of each phase? How does the relationship unfold and how can we, as supervisors and interns, be most effective? Chazan (1990) has divided the supervisory relationship into three phases of development that I have found to be a helpful framework. Her use of different theorists to capture the essence of each phase can be both illuminating and helpful to supervisors.

Phase 1: The "Creation of Space"

Chazan (1990) described the first phase between the supervisor and supervisee as the "creation of space." This "safe space" must be created for the supervisory relationship to develop productively and forms the safe home base to which the supervisee can return for exploration and experimentation. It is a space where work and play are fused as one, as personal and professional identity become closely bonded. Chazan uses the term "play" as Winnicott (1971) did—a special form of communication and interaction between the two individuals that contributes toward growth and health. It is a transitional space similar to the special relationship space between mother and child, where through explorative play the supervisee can work, grow, and communicate, processing experiences from the outside world and trying out new ways of being.

Both supervisor and supervisee, according to Chazan (1990), begin this relationship, which is both uncertain and full of promise, with the same questions posed earlier in this chapter: Will I be liked? Can we work together? Can I trust this supervisor? Can I reveal my doubts? Will I be understood? Will I be appreciated?

How can supervisors create a safe space where interns feel comfortable being just who they are, safe enough to be open and exposed, to take risks without fear of condemnation? How can this relationship be a place where a supervisor will feel listened to and appreciated, allowed to be partner in this journey? Much of this has already been discussed in the section on roles, but a few additional points are merited.

A sacrosanct supervision weekly place and time must be set up, with interruptions not allowed. By setting aside this time, interns will immediately feel respected, valued, and listened to. This becomes a sacred joint time of exploration. In supervision, be sure to solicit, listen to, and respect the intern's feelings and questions. Help interns to value their own feelings and their clinical intuition. Be sure to include exploration of their feelings as part of the written assignments, weekly logs, musical explorations, and discussions.

Make playing music together part of the supervision process right from the beginning. This provides a way to connect (Levinge, 2002) and deepen the relationship between supervisor and supervisee and a means for the supervisee to feel listened to and respected (Feiner, 2010). Aside from relationship-building, by playing music together, interns can use it to ground and focus as well as to bring awareness to the resources that they bring with them (Amir, 2001; Feiner, 2001; Langdon, (2001). Using music is a means for self-exploration as well as accessing feelings that were not apparent to the intern before playing (Scheiby, 2001; Turry, 2001) and can become a process that parallels the work they do with their clients (Young & Aigen, 2010).

It is important to help interns to feel as safe as possible in this new setting. Educate them about the proper communication structures and decision-making processes. Discuss the power structure and the status and challenges of music therapy within this structure. Educate them about some of the challenges with which they may be confronted so that they not only know what to expect, but also know that you are sensitized to what it is like for them. An example might be preparing a student for interruptions in the medical setting or from a particular unsupportive staff member, with choices on how best to handle these interruptions. In this way, your vulnerable student will not take such actions personally but instead understand it as part of the package. Identify and connect the intern to staff who are especially supportive and rewarding to work with. Have a backup person available to the student accessible if needed when you are not around.

As discussed earlier, help your intern to understand how much you value communication and need feedback. Communicate this with your words and actions. Structure a space for this type of communication from the beginning: checking in on feelings, being matter-of-fact in assuming that there will be feelings (e.g., about starting, about being in a new role, about clients that are elicited during observations and interactions, about the setting, about supervision). Try to really carve out the space to really listen to the intern, even if it is hard to make this time or the intern defers. To make it safe, perhaps even share your own difficult experiences as a new intern. Be sure to read your intern's written journals or logs and give them back promptly with feedback that values their perspective while expanding their knowledge. As discussed earlier, it is important to promptly provide feedback that appreciates strengths (Turry, 2001; Wheeler, 2012). Make sure that a section on personal reactions is included, conveying how important it is for you to know how they react to things and what is on their mind. Explore when this is resisted. Explore how it feels to report feelings and any discomfort involved in doing so rather than making assumptions, for example, of lack of self-awareness or lack of caring.

As described earlier, it is the supervisor's responsibility to initiate and facilitate the discussion of diversity differences early in the internship (Kim, 2008), making it a part of ongoing dialogue while acknowledging the potential difficulty of doing so for both supervisor and supervisee. Nilsson's (2004) research shows that a strong working alliance is more likely to develop from addressing cultural differences and the acculturation process and placing importance on the intern feeling accepted by the supervisor. Nilsson stressed that interns from different cultures may need to be more dependent upon the supervisor "for advice, support, training, and validation" needed for "self-efficacy, understanding the process of supervision, and examining cultural-related concerns" (p. 311). He points out how these discussions, although difficult for both, "may increase not only the supervisee's cultural competence but the supervisor's as well" (p. 311).

I always tell my intern that I will try to do my best but at times I will get things wrong, misunderstand, or say something hurtful. I make mistakes. I really need them to let me know when this happens so that I can learn from them and about them. I need them to educate me about their culture, their upbringing, and therefore their perspectives. I need to hear about challenges that come up for them in our relationship or their work with clients (Kim, 2008). I want them to know that I need their feedback.

Phase 2: "Structure Building"

The second phase Chazan (1990) describes is "structure building," using as a model Margaret Mahler's steps in the separation-individuation process.

Twinning
The first step she describes in this phase of the supervisor–supervisee relationship is "twinning." The supervisee "twins" with the supervisor, learns the supervisor's way of working and being with clients, learns the music as a stepping-stone toward developing one's own way. An intern can then eventually accept and integrate or reject the supervisor's material and methods as part of the learning process.

The supervisor functions as an alter ego, adjusts to the supervisee's individual style, and blends and enhances rather than negating pre-existing patterns. The supervisee will feel this as affirming and supportive, will feel competent in learning, and will be brave enough to try out new approaches and techniques.

Interns often place unrealistic pressure on themselves to be spontaneously and prolifically creative. As mentioned previously, alleviate the pressure new interns feel to immediately develop their own greeting songs, their own repertoire, their own improvisational styles. Let them take yours and then go from there, using your methods and activities as a foundation. (Some students will need to immediately develop their own.)

Develop an understanding of their learning style. Some students feel it is supportive for the supervisor to make suggestions while they are leading a session, while others cannot handle this and may throw up their hands and give up their leadership. How much information or feedback can they absorb before feeling overwhelmed? Do they like to work themselves slowly into the leadership position or do they work best by plunging in fully? Learn how to go at their speed and respond to their questions, observations, and interests as a guide for what to teach next.

It is also important to learn where they are developmentally in their lives. Are they right out of college and on their own for the first time, still separating from their parents? This brings developmental needs different from those of someone re-entering the workforce or changing careers and experiencing the narcissistic blow of being a beginner again. For example, I find that those with a professional identity and sense of competence from their previous professions have an especially difficult time in not being proficient and excellent in their own eyes immediately. I need to do a lot of reassuring that their experiences of disorientation and/or negative feelings about themselves or abilities are common. They may have to leave their expertise at the door and not be able to integrate it into their new professional identity right away. At the same time, it is important at this time to help them to stay in touch with the experiences and skills they possess that apply to this new work. Reassure them that their expertise can indeed be integrated and explore with them how to do so.

If your intern is from another country or even another culture within the same country, continue the process of understanding each other's culture. It is important to come to a mutual understanding of differing social norms and communication patterns and how these differences may be considered in your work together. As supervisors, we must be aware of our own assumptions and worldview and how these impact our understanding of an intern (Sue, 2015; Sue et al., 2007). For example, some cultures have a clear boundary between teacher and student, where divulging personal feelings are taboo, and an individual would not consider developing in one's own way. This must be openly addressed.

Separation-Individuation

After the period of "twinning," after feeling secure, interns are ready to begin to separate-individuate, to develop their own way, as Mahler would say (Mahler, Pine, & Bergman, 1975). Interns become less dependent upon imitation of their supervisors. The supervisee continues to venture into clinical forays of exploration, and Chazan (1990) described how they then return to home base for feedback and support in the process of constructing their own therapy model and techniques. The supervisee survives making mistakes, and criticism is appreciated and accepted better when each little growth step is supported and acknowledged (Wheeler, 2012).

During this period, differences of opinion and power struggles typical to the challenge of establishing a separate identity can occur. The honeymoon is over; the supervisor is no longer so idealized. Part of the individuation process is having issues come up. Expect them to emerge as a result of the intern's past experiences and as a push for separation in the present. As a supervisor, you might feel that you are being pushed away. It is normal that challenges arise at this point. Interns are no longer as comfortable feeling dependent, nor do they need to be, so there are a host of ways they may use to break away. At this time, students might finally feel more comfortable with the population and how to manage getting through a session with challenging clients but may become angry or "tired" when challenged to go deeper in the work. "I am finally comfortable … don't make me see how much more I have to learn … I do not want to feel so insecure again and be so dependent upon you!"

A supervisor's task is to continue to supportively address issues that interfere with a student's work or relationship with you, even when the intern "rebels." Be aware of your own countertransference to these changes, reevaluate your supervisory style, and determine whether it needs to be modified. Be willing to appreciate the strengths your intern demonstrates and acknowledge what you learn from your intern (Wheeler, 2012).

Support and encourage further independence. For example, during the latter part of the internship, when they are ready, I may shift in my role as educator and teach less explicitly, focusing on helping the intern to learn how to learn. I am explicit about this. As we evaluate where we have come and what is ahead, I put forward how my expectations have changed. For example, after a session that I observe, I may ask the intern to process the session for me and organize where input is most needed. I might hold back with suggestions and wait for the intern to come up with options to try out and then evaluate. It is time to help interns to identify and further develop their special qualities and strengths. Support them in developing further their own methods and music therapy materials, their areas of strength, and their individual interests.

Phase 3: "Reciprocity and Well-being"

Chazan (1990) borrowed from Erikson's identity formation stage of "intimacy, generativity, and integrity" (p. 27) to describe this last phase, called "reciprocity and well-being." In this phase, the intern has developed a professional identity and personal identity with an emerging inner experience of "well-being" (fragile as it may be). There is a greater feeling of mutuality and reciprocity between supervisor and supervisee. She states that not all relationships progress to this point, but this is the goal.

During this stage, the termination period in internship, an intern's tasks are to be aware of what was learned, of their special strengths, and of what still needs to be learned. The intern is able to communicate clearly about the field and articulate clients' goals and clinical intent and has become a professional with much to offer clients and fellow staff.

I make a point of relating differently to an intern at this stage. For example, in discussing my work, I will seek out impressions and feedback in a more collegial way. I often ask the intern to hypothesize other ways in which I may have worked with clients during my sessions that they have observed. I want interns to see that there are other options for working with clients that they may think of that are equally good or even better than what I chose. I have to be careful to be open and not dismiss their suggestions due to my own countertransference feelings, but rather to appreciate what I have learned from the intern. I want them to feel a shift in their role with me. I want to stimulate professional interchanges and reinforce the intern's new professional identity. This might be the time to help the international student think about and share with you how they can apply what they've learned from their internship to the cultural norms of the culture to which they are returning. Not only has the intern established a secure professional identity, but also the supervisor feels the rewards of launching a new professional into the field.

Additional Considerations

This final section presents some common "issues" or challenges that often come up for supervisor and supervisee in addition to those already discussed. This is by no means a complete list but instead a selection of examples from my experience.

1. A supervisor—especially a new supervisor or a supervisor starting a new job—can become concerned about the repercussions an inexperienced intern will have on the status of the music therapy program and as a result not be able to fully support the learning process. These feelings can create unrealistic expectations of the student's work and perhaps as a result impede the freedom an intern needs to learn by exploring and making mistakes. The supervisor may become tense, overbearing, and critical. My experience has been that in most cases, other staff can be more comfortable with a student's mistakes than a new supervisor may be. I've also noticed that if, as supervisor, I am open to hearing staff's concerns and feedback about a student, appreciating their feedback and suggestions, they will often align with me to help an intern rather be accusatory or judgmental.

2. Contributing to the above, supervisors can be confronted with their own control issues as they supervise. At times, it may be difficult to let students learn from their own efforts and even make mistakes. It can be difficult to watch the therapy proceed in a slower manner than what you would have done or have a client with whom you have worked not be understood in the way you might. The tendency may be then to jump in too soon, sabotaging the relationship and the intern's leadership.

3. Supervisors should be aware of their own countertransference around the issue of being an authority. The potential exists for the supervisor to become an authority from the supervisor's past or reenact an intern's earlier experience with authority. If these authority experiences were problematic, then this may lead to difficulties. Sometimes the new supervisor is uncomfortable in taking on authority and power. The new supervisor is giving up old identity and, in some ways, starting all over (Kadushin, 2014). It can be difficult to assert oneself in this role for many reasons—for example, for fear of the intern's anger, wanting to be liked or looked up to, or confusion due to cultural norms. It is extremely important for the new supervisor to examine their own feelings about authority. Equally important, as stressed previously, is the need for feedback to be integrated into the supervision process not only for the supervisee, but also to fulfill the new supervisor's need for confirmation of effectiveness in this new role (Kadushin, 2014).

4. Feelings about dependency can be a difficult issue for both supervisor and supervisee. As supervisor, how does it feel to be depended upon, in the way an intern may need you, especially at the beginning of internship? Does it make you uncomfortable in any way? Are any feelings stirred up by being in this role? This leads to the question of how much dependence upon the supervisor is healthy. Norman (1987) discussed this issue in some detail. The amount of dependence is not the question, but instead why it is occurring. She framed this in terms of the "transitional relationship" that I discussed earlier, saying that some supervisees really need to have everything spelled out for them and supported in the beginning in order to feel safe. What is key is how the intern progresses over time. The dependency usually dissipates as the intern becomes more secure. When it does not, it is time to explore with the student what may be interfering. She also gave an interesting case example of a supervisee whom she had had who had not become dependent at all and had been resistant to the supervisor's support and feedback. She had to explore with

the supervisee what was getting in the way of the relationship, and only after this was done could the supervisee move on and commit to the supervision process.

5. It is important to understand the intern's phases of individuation in the supervisor–intern relationship and how they relate to the ways in which independence is asserted. When students are learning their own way or exploring other ways, this shift may cause a supervisor to experience feelings of rejection or loss of control. Again, watch out that as supervisor you do not feel challenged by this exploration in such a way as to feel tempted to squash it or "best" it. It is also important to be aware of when the intern shows signs that there is difficulty with the individuation process. Examples may be when a student becomes provocative or belligerent. All of a sudden, a supervisor is left out of important decisions. A student might "forget" to check with the supervisor about changes or events or find other indirect ways to assert and challenge. It is then time to explore your student's feelings and of course any of your feelings or actions that may be contributing to this dynamic. This may be a time to adjust your supervision style or expand autonomy.

6. Related to dependence is how it feels to be "separated from," to no longer be needed after all of the work invested in an intern. In my own experience, I have had to watch myself to not expect unrealistic amounts of gratitude just at the time when an intern is separating.

7. There can be a sense of loss when a supervisor gives up some of their own caseload and the intimacy of that client contact. This may be especially pertinent to part-time clinicians who no longer have a large caseload when they start supervising. There can be a backlash of feelings when an especially interesting client is assigned or transferred to a supervisee. Don't pass on cases that you find so rewarding that you then resent the intern. Watch out for competition.

8. A supervisor must sort through which countertransference the intern induces and which is due to their own personal issues. As described earlier, in a very short amount of time we learn, by an intern's responses to us, what their previous experiences have been with parental figures and authorities. The intensity of this relationship fosters this dynamic. An obvious example of this is a supervisor who comes to me and says that she feels more like a policewoman than a supervisor because she must constantly be on top of her intern to oversee that he gets things done. When the supervisor explored this with the intern in a supportive way, the intern, who was at first oblivious, was able to identify how this is what he expected from her based upon his past experiences with authority figures. From this experience, the intern saw a pattern of how this dynamic occurred even outside of internship. He could then bring it to his personal therapy and explore it and then be able to move on and act more responsibly.

9. Another interesting dynamic of which the supervisor should be aware is feelings of competition. This can arise especially when an intern is more skilled musically in some area or "has a way" with a particular type of client. What do you find yourself doing in response? Do you go home and feel less adequate as a therapist? Do you feel the urge to show off your great therapy skills and put this intern "in her place"? Or perhaps your intern starts to get feedback from other team members who appreciate her work or the intern is having success with a client that you did not have. How do you subtly—or not so subtly—respond to this? Do you put greater demands on the student so that you are still the authority? Do you withdraw? Do you put your student down? Does your own sense of esteem suddenly dip?

Conclusion

The journey that intern and supervisor together embark upon during internship is both rich and complex, as well as risky and not always predictable. Both partners who join in navigating the various roles and phases share an enormous potential for professional growth, self-knowledge, even transformation. This chapter endeavored to provide a "map" highlighting important features throughout the internship journey. Using this map, the supervisor can develop greater understanding of the demands and dynamics that, at any time, could capsize the fragile vessel that supervisor and intern pilot together. With a broader understanding and perspective regarding the evolution of roles, phases, and issues, a supervisor will become increasingly sensitized to the significance of what takes place and empowered to respond effectively.

Acknowledgments

I would like to thank all of my supervisors and colleagues who have given to me what I am now so eager to share with others. I am so grateful to the supervisors and interns with whom I have worked who have taught me so much as they allowed me to accompany them on their most wondrous journeys through internship and beyond. I also thank my devoted friend and husband, Dr. Marc Goloff, for his tireless support and belief in my work, as well as superb editing skills that I used to full advantage.

Reference List

Amir, D. (2001). The journey of two: Supervision for the new music therapist working in an educational Setting. In M. Forinash (Ed.), *Music therapy supervision.* Gilsum, NH: Barcelona Publishers.

Amir, D. (2006). Awaking the "Wild Woman": Feminist music therapy and with Israeli women who suffered trauma in their lives. In S. Hadley (Ed.), *Feminist perspectives in music therapy* (pp. 267–290). Gilsum, NH: Barcelona Publishers.

Chazan, S. E. (1990). On being supervised and supervision. In R. Lane (Ed.), *Psychoanalytic approaches to supervision* (pp. 25–28). Philadelphia, PA: Bruner/Mazel.

Erikson, E. (1959). *Identity and the life cycle.* New York, NY: International Universities Press.

Estrella, K. (2001). Multicultural approaches to music therapy supervision. In M. Forinash (Ed.), *Music therapy supervision.* Gilsum, NH: Barcelona Publishers.

Feiner, S. (2001). A journey through internship supervision: Roles, dynamics, and phases of the supervisory relationship. In M. Forinash (Ed.), *Music therapy supervision.* Gilsum, NH: Barcelona Publishers.

Feiner, S. (2010). What is happening to me? The potential for activation of trauma during music therapy internship. In K. Stewart (Ed.), *Music therapy & trauma: Bridging theory and clinical practice.* New York, NY: Satchnote Press.

Forinash, M. (2001). Overview. In M. Forinash (Ed.), *Music therapy supervision.* Gilsum, NH: Barcelona Publishers.

Forinash, M. (2006). Feminist music therapy supervision. In S. Hadley (Ed.), *Feminist perspectives in music therapy.* Gilsum, NH: Barcelona Publishers.

Hadley, S. (2017). I don't see you as black/gay/disabled/Muslim/etc.: Microaggressions in everyday encounters. In A. Whitehead-Pleaux & X. Tan (Eds.), *Cultural intersections in music therapy: Music, health, and the person.* Dallas, TX: Barcelona Publishers.

Hahna, N. (2014). Reflecting on personal bias. In A. Whitehead-Pleaux & X. Tan, (Eds.) *Cultural intersections in music therapy: Music, health, and the person.* Dallas, TX: Barcelona Publishers.

Kadushin, A. (1992). *Supervision in social work*. New York, NY: Columbia University Press.

Kadushin, A., & Harkness, D. (2014). *Supervision in social work*. New York, NY: Columbia University Press.

Kim, S. A. (2008). The Supervisee's Experience in Cross-Cultural Music Therapy Supervision. *Qualitative Inquiries in Music Therapy: A Monograph Series, 24*, 1–44.

Langdon, G. S. (2001) Experiential music therapy group as a method of professional supervision. In M. Forinash (Ed.), *Music therapy supervision*. Gilsum, NH: Barcelona Publishers.

Levinge, A. (2002). Supervision or double vision: An exploration of the task of music therapy supervision. *British Journal of Music Therapy, 16*(2), 83–89.

Mahler, M., Pine, F., & Bergman, A. (1975). *The psychological birth of the human infant*. New York, NY: Basic Books.

McClain, F. J. (2001). Music therapy supervision: A review of the literature. In M. Forinash (Ed.), *Music therapy supervision* (pp. 9–18). Gilsum, NH: Barcelona Publishers.

Merriam-Webster.com. (2018). Retrieved April 9, 2018, from https://www.merriam-webster.com/dictionary/

Milville, M. L., Rosa, D., & Constantine, M. (2005). Building multicultural competence in clinical supervision. In. M. Constantine & D. W. Sue (Eds.), *Strategies for building multicultural competence in mental health and educational settings*. Hoboken, NJ: John Wiley & Sons, Inc.

Mordock, J. B. (1990). The new supervisor: Awareness of problems experienced and some suggestions for problem resolution through supervisory training. *The Clinical Supervisor, 8*(1), 81–92.

Nilsson, J. E., & Anderson, M. Z. (2004). Supervising international students: the role of acculturation, role ambiguity, and multicultural discussions. *Professional Psychology: Research and Practice, 35*(3), 306–312.

Norman, J. S. (1987). Supervision: The affective process. *Social Casework: The Journal of Contemporary Social Work, 68*(6), 374–379.

Porter, N. (2014). Women, culture, and social justice: Supervision across the intersections. In C. Falender, E. Shafranske, & C. Falicov (Eds.), *Multiculturalism and diversity in clinical supervision: A competency-based approach*. Washington, DC: American Psychological Association.

Sarnat, J. E. (1992). Supervision in relationship: Resolving the teach–treat controversy in psychoanalytic supervision. *Psychoanalytic Psychology, 9*(3), 387–403.

Scheiby, B. B. (2001). Forming an identity as a music psychotherapist through Analytical Music Therapy supervision. In M. Forinash (Ed.), *Music therapy supervision*. Gilsum, NH: Barcelona Publishers.

Stevenson, A., & Lindberg, C. A. (Eds.). (2010). *New Oxford American Dictionary* (3rd ed.). New York, NY: Oxford University Press.

Stige, B. (2002). *Culture-Centered Music Therapy*. Gilsum, NH: Barcelona Publishers.

Sue, D. W. (2015). *Race talk*. Hoboken, NJ: John Wiley & Sons, Inc.

Sue, D. W., Capodilupo, C. M., Torino, G. C., Bucceri, J. M., Holder, A. M., Nadal, K. L., & Esquilin, M. (2007). Racial microaggressions in everyday Life: Implications for Clinical Practice. *American Psychologist, 62*(4), 271–286.

Turry, A. (2001). Supervision in Nordoff-Robbins Music Therapy Training Program. In M. Forinash (Ed.), *Music therapy supervision*. Gilsum, NH: Barcelona Publishers.

Webster's New World College Dictionary (5th ed.). (2016). New York, NY: Houghton Mifflin Harcourt.

Wheeler, B. (2002). Experiences and concerns of students during music therapy practica. *Journal of Music Therapy, 39*(4), 274–304.

Wheeler, B. L., & Williams, C. (2012). Students' thoughts and feelings about music therapy practicum supervision. *Nordic Journal of Music Therapy, 2*, 111–132.

Whitehead-Pleaux, A., Donnenwerth, A., Robinson, B., Hardy, S., Oswanski, L., Forinash, M., Hearns, M., Anderson N., & York, E. (2012). Lesbian, gay, bisexual, transgender, and questioning: Best practices in music therapy. *Music Therapy Perspectives, 30,* 158–166.

Winnicott, D. W. (1971). *Playing and reality.* London, UK: Tavistock.

Young, L., & Aigen, K. (2010). Supervising the supervisor: The use of live music and identification of parallel processes. *The Arts in Psychotherapy, 37*(2), 125–134.

Chapter 11

EXPERIENTIAL MUSIC THERAPY GROUP AS A METHOD OF PROFESSIONAL SUPERVISION

Gillian Stephens Langdon

INTRODUCTION

I am honored to have the opportunity to contribute this revised chapter to *Music Therapy Supervision*. Based on my original writing in 1984 and adapted for the earlier version of this book in 2001, it appears that the content is still timely.

There continues to be increased focus on the importance of the music in music therapy and in music therapy supervision. As Julie Sutton and Jos De Backer (2010) point out, "To develop our musical skills as music therapists, it is important that musical improvisation is part of our supervision work. It is important that our supervisors have the capacity to work both verbally and musically. This recognizes that our identity is as musician therapists and that we have and continue to work to integrate both aspects of who we are" (p. 315). Kennelly, Daveson, and Baker (2016) "identified the role of music within supervision which could be experienced further in order to draw out the uniqueness of what a music therapy supervisor could bring to supervision" (p. 201). Kenneth Aigen and Laurel Young (2010) stated that "the authors conclude that the practice of live music-making in a supervisory context is beneficial on many levels" (p. 125).

As I wrote in the chapter for the 2001 edition of this book, "The current world of the music therapist is rich and engaging as new knowledge of music and the brain is uncovered daily. The field of practice for the music therapist is also changing daily. Music therapists need support in designing innovative programs and navigating the systems of changeable institutions. One of the most important needs for support is in nurturing the way of thinking that allows us to move back and forth between words and music and, particularly, being able to nurture what can be called the 'musical mind'" (Langdon, 2001, p. 211).

It is not within the scope of this chapter to delineate the ways in which music therapy supervision is used to address psychodynamic issues such as transference and countertransference. Among others, Kenneth Bruscia's edited book *The Dynamics of Music Psychotherapy* (1998) contains valuable descriptions of these processes. In this chapter, I focus on looking at the use of the different characteristics of words and music and how they can interplay within the process of a professional supervision group. It is necessary to understand where the music is key and where words may be vital in deepening understanding during the supervision process. We will look at how music therapy group supervision can address specific needs and issues in the early stages of professional development (post-internship) as well as in the supervision of mature professionals.

In a new section, I present responses to a recent survey of the original group members from my first music therapy supervision groups to uncover in what ways this music-centered model of supervision has influenced their work over the years.

THE MUSIC

The group always engaged in music-making, which was a major joy and draw
(I traveled from out of state) that always made an impact on me.[13]

Music is the foundation of the experiential music therapy supervision group. We ground ourselves in music. We seek to understand the music in the groups that we are running. We use the power of music to untangle puzzles and to strengthen our work. We affirm our identities as musician therapists.

We are surrounded by ideas and words. As clinicians, we are constantly being called upon to verbalize descriptions of musical events and regularly produce written records of our work. And yet, I'm sure most music therapists have struggled as I have in trying to explain to the treatment team a pivotal moment in a session, only to find ourselves at a loss for words.

For a long while, I thought it was my inability to articulate what had occurred—or worse, that the event was not so important after all—that made me uncomfortable as I listened to the neatly verbalized group dynamics set forth by the psychologists, psychiatrists, and social workers where I worked. Yet when I co-led a group with one of these psychologists who was particularly articulate, I saw an interesting thing happen. She had been playing music in the group and was excited about a few pivotal moments that had occurred through the music-making process. She was eager to share this progress in our supervision group, where we met regularly with other group leaders. When it became time to report on the session, she was unable to bring forth the words. She stopped in the middle, exclaiming, "This is really hard! It's hard doing the switch to words." She had a vast clinical knowledge, and yet when she remembered the music therapy session, it was with her musical mind. She had to work to cross over into her rich verbal realm.

Most of us need practice in this quick back-and-forth between immersion in music in our groups to the verbal and analytic mode. Music therapists need a forum where we can practice this and nurture both modes equally. It is interesting that without a conscious effort, even in the music therapy supervision group we can find ourselves getting stuck in the verbal mode. The group members begin to report their groups, analyze them, and find verbal solutions. Yet, just as we would lose the specific, the analytic, and the didactic by avoiding words, by avoiding music in supervision we lose the dynamic, the intuitive, and the integral healing of music. "The concrete aspects of language help us to articulate our rational, intellectual thoughts, and the abstract nature of music allows for a deep expression of the emotional and transpersonal aspects of life" (Hesser, 1995, p. 46). What we are looking for is a synthesis of both modes.

THE EXPERIENTIAL MUSIC THERAPY SUPERVISION GROUP

I tried to think about how to obtain the environment of [the] supervision group
in my music therapy groups.

The experiential music therapy supervision group has a framework and flow similar to that of many music therapy groups, having a beginning warm-up, a middle section of working on issues, and closure. If one is sensitized to this experience, one is more likely, in the immediacy of the music therapy group, to grab the moment—the foot that is already tapping, the segment of a melody already being sung by a group member—rather than start with that "perfect" treatment intervention that had been planned.

---

[13] All quotes are from various members of music therapy supervision groups.

Warm-up

The warm-up, or "gathering music," allows for the group members to "arrive" and to renew or develop a feeling of connection and trust with one another. The group members arrive after a long day of work, working in hospitals, clinics, schools, and so on. Perhaps having had a long train ride during rush hour. Group members need to "arrive" and to ground themselves. We are able to do this through stretching, breathing, and, when practical, lying on the floor. Soon a sound emerges—a sigh or a tone or an instrument being plucked or tapped. Sometimes the music is subdued. Sometimes it is explosive. This is an important time for its release of the tensions and burdens of the week, as well as for bringing the group to an aware present. This may crystalize for the individual group member what the core concerns are for this supervisory session.

Sometimes there is a feeling that the music can go on forever. As a leader, I need to be aware of making room for group members to identify their issues or topics. This is not a therapy group where I might let the music continue to the end. Sometimes I ask the group to find an ending to this preliminary improvisation.

Middle Section

Following the warm-up, we may talk a little about our improvisation. At certain times, we can explore our interactions as a group and even work with music to address certain issues that arise. Usually, however, there is a verbal sharing of how the week has gone and who wants to present a topic or an issue of concern. As group members present, the group leader observes their movements, facial expressions, and tone of voice. This may help the group leader to decide whether to work within the music or in words.

The issues of the group members may be worked through in many ways: through verbally shared group discussions, didactic information, verbal or musical role-playing, musical improvisation, and so forth. Throughout the group, the supervisor listens for possible musical interventions. Whatever is most useful is chosen. Because we get so easily "stuck" in the verbal mode, it is important to keep musical possibilities in mind. But, of course, we should never use the music just for the sake of using it. In the next section, an in-depth discussion of the various modes of intervention is presented.

Closure

It is helpful to end the music therapy supervision group with a musical improvisation. This affirms again the music as the root and inspiration for the work of the participants as therapists and group members. It also affirms the group support and renewal. "Using live, improvised music in supervision can release playfulness and spontaneity. … It continues to be a vital way of keeping her clinical work 'fresh and music-centered'" (Scheiby, 2015, p. 215).

MODES OF INTERVENTION

I came for the supervision because I was having a very difficult time with [a group] that I was leading— so obviously I came because of a problematic situation—perhaps you went to the music when I might have found it more useful to use words—or perhaps [you might] have had more directed music toward whatever I was feeling.

Each person is unique, and each has different needs regarding supervision. It is important to find what is needed—to not only match the mode of what the supervisor observes but also to use the mode that meets the needs of the supervisee. It is important to provide a welcoming space where the supervisee can present the issues in the mode in which they are most comfortable. If the supervisor feels that the supervisee needs to enter into a more musical mode to express feelings or intuitive expression, this must not cut off the verbalizing of a specific issue that may be important.

It is important to be aware of the processes available in the supervision group, although in one sense these are obvious. In another sense, it is important to think through how we are addressing issues and what tools are available to us. When do we just use words in a music therapy supervision group? When do we just use music? When do we start with words and move into music? When do we start with music and move into words? Although there should be a fluid intermingling of verbal and musical modes and combinations, for the purpose of studying them and bringing them to awareness it is useful to look at the discreet modes to observe what differences there are and what can be gained by each pattern.

Verbal—Verbal

What does it actually mean to verbalize? In the *Merriam-Webster Dictionary* (2017), the synonyms are: "bring out, enunciate, pass, speak, state, talk, tell, utter, say, vocalize." In the music therapy supervision group, we use the verbal—verbal mode when we are seeking the specific or the analytic or need clarification. Questions such as these arise:

a) The specific: What did you see? Where was the group held? How was the room set up? Who was present? What was happening? What happened before?
b) The analytic: What do you make of this? When did your feelings change? What were you thinking of then?
c) For clarification: Did I understand you correctly? Are you OK with this intervention? Is there something else you would like to add?

In this mode, the exploration continues with words. Using the example for the quote above, there was apparently a need for the supervisee to be asked to describe the situation more fully. For example: What is the issue that concerns you? At what levels of training are the group members? What have you tried? What results have you had? Where was the group held? The group might respond with examples from their own work: I have had a similar situation. When I tried this, it seemed to help. After reassuring the supervisee of the support of the group and coming up with concrete suggestions, it is possible to expand the mode to verbal—verbal—music.

Verbal—verbal also allows for important discussions of ethics and cultural awareness. Although these are covered during basic music therapy course work, these discussions continue to be essential throughout the career of all music therapists.

Verbal—Music

In this mode, we are attempting to take the analytic, the evident, the words into the level of feeling, physicality, intuition. In the quote at the beginning of this section, there is an example of the need for the supervisee to be heard fully and the specific issue to be explored verbally, perhaps with input from the group. After this, there is an opportunity to explore the feelings that arise about what was going on in the therapy and or the supervision. The music might be used as a vent and a release of feelings.

In another situation, the supervisor may notice that although the supervisee observes well and gives a good verbal account of the dynamics of a session, as she speaks, she seems distant or impersonal in relation to the action—showing an inability to be truly present as a leader in the moment. The therapist's work reveals a lack of spontaneity and a rigidity of style. In this case, the therapist can be encouraged to explore musically her feelings about being a leader and to notice where she feels cut off. Movement and breathing might be used to strengthen the therapist's musical expression.

In another way, after a verbal presentation, the music may be a way to uncover deep feelings about a client or interaction. I had a powerful and surprising experience of this when I attended a supervision group composed primarily of creative arts therapists.

The work was mostly on a verbal level, and on this day I was the only music therapist present. I presented the case of a young man of mixed race who created beautiful, rapped lyrics that reflected his personal struggles. In contrast to many stereotypes of rappers as tough street kids, he was gentle, polite, and eager to contribute. He would take out his phone to set up the tones that he had found to go with the words that he had written down in a notebook, and he would begin. Through supervision, I wanted to find how I could address his issues and whether there were ways through which could bring him more into this group of older adults. I was surprised when the supervision group leader for the first time asked me what I would sing to him. Voice is not my main instrument and I felt embarrassed to sing in front of the group, but he pushed me. I began, tentatively at first. My mind was racing, wondering what I would uncover that I was suppressing. Would I find a hidden anger? Or an area I would be embarrassed to show to the group? I was worried about my limited vocal technique. But part of me worked to push away these thoughts, and soon I was able to free myself, letting my voice go where it wished. My voice took me way up high and swooped down again. Thoughts would come. "What am I hiding?" "Where is the negative feeling I have been suppressing?" "Dig into it! This is the moment to find what I really feel!"

As I set my voice and my mind free, the music transformed into an honoring of this young man as an artist in a multicultural world of artists. I became aware of my music creating a blessing from my deep Welsh roots to a fellow poet of music. By now, unconsciously, my hand had become raised as one sees in a gospel congregation when a person becomes filled with the spirit. I lost track of time, letting my voice go where it wanted to. Finally, I ended the music and sat in silence, along with the supervision group members. Several people shared that what happened looked like an experience of prayer. It was truly beyond words and something on which I have since reflected with a sense of reverence and wonder. Without this free improvisation, there is no way I would have allowed myself to enter into this honoring experience. I was able to take with me the importance of being a listener, a witness, and a validator of the artistic endeavors of my clients.

Music—Verbal

When we start with music, we have the opportunity to immerse ourselves in our own experience to gain a fuller sense of what we are experiencing. Referring again to the quote at the beginning of this section, one way to focus on this would be to start with the music, encouraging the supervisee to play what they are feeling about their situation and for the group members to provide musical support. Following this, the verbal mode can be used to strategize and to share common experiences.

Music—verbal is also a mode where we can role-play a client and afterward engage in discussion. For example, a supervisee might present a session where they are unsure of the full meaning of a particular improvisation and how to develop the material in future sessions. The supervisee can be encouraged to play their remembrance of the music of the client, shaping their body posture and movement to the remembered image of the client. The muscles, the arms, and the fingers re-create the client's melodies, rhythms, dynamics, and phrasing. After this music, the supervisor might ask, "What did you discover by playing?" "What specific needs did you become aware of?" "Is there something you discovered about yourself?" "Are there aspects of this exploration that bring you closer to an understanding of this client's history?" A discussion can expand to a teaching moment about, for example, how these patterns and needs are exemplary of a client with a trauma history and the need to establish safety and containment. Group members can be encouraged to share similar patterns they have experienced with their own clients.

Music—Music

This mode is useful when one needs to immerse oneself in the music either as a solution to a problem or to more fully experience an interaction. "Improvised music reflects conscious and unconscious feelings, both of which feed the wellspring of creativity. And the music therapist's process is deeply related to the core creative process, the inner self, which comes with a host of unconscious feelings, associations, and images that can never be completely specified or quantified" (Turry, 1998, p. 209).

In immersing oneself in the musical realm, beginning with music and moving deeper into music there is a rich exploration available as one trusts the music to find the solutions. In the above example of role-play, if the supervisor decides to encourage the supervisee to explore the musical material though music instead of a verbal discussion of what it felt like to play as the client played, the supervisee might be encouraged to keep playing as the client played and let the music be the guide to what needs to come next. Is it a loud crescendo? A lyrical phrase? An invitation to others to join in?

The music allows for a deep understanding of process and transitions. Another supervisee might present the case of a client who plays in a very rigid style. He or she wants to encourage more freedom of expression in seeking techniques to help the client move forward. As the supervisee is encouraged to re-create this rigid style of playing and transition into a freer style, the supervisee can feel in a very real way what is involved. Perhaps they will moderate their expectations of a quick transition, discovering that it takes time to make this transition into freedom of expression. This understanding may lead to respecting where the client is, supporting the need to take time to trust a move to another way of expression.

Another salient aspect of the use of the music—music mode is in developing cultural awareness. Seung-A Kim stated that culturally informed music therapy goals, among others, "include therapists' development of increased cultural awareness; acknowledgement of own cultural identity; resolution of cultural conflicts within the context of the client's culture …" (Kim, 2015, p. 58). Although these aspects can be addressed in any of the modes, the music—music mode provides a real immersion. In playing music and developing an improvisation, supervisees can delve into their full experience, discover habits and preferences, and uncover hidden prejudices that arise in the creation of music. This can follow in an extended mode to be music—music—verbal, allowing for a discussion of the discoveries and shared experiences of other group members.

For example, a young therapist brings into supervision the problem of how to incorporate an older adult, a Spanish-speaking man, into a younger, English-speaking group in a psychiatric outpatient program. The client is unable to communicate to the therapist or to the group, none of whom speak Spanish. His rhythms are described as erratic, and when he is not playing music, he is quite withdrawn. As the supervisee describes the client's music, it is unclear how it sounds. The supervisor asks if the supervisee might get permission to record a session and bring it into the music therapy supervision group.

By the next week, she has succeeded in getting the permission and has a fairly good recording of the session. As the group listens, one of the members' eyes light up and, tapping into his Cuban heritage, he starts to play along in a rough, polyrhythmic style, saying, "Viva la musica Cubana!" The recording is faded out, and the supervisor encourages the group to follow along with this group member as the supervisor attempts to find a basic "clave" beat. After the music comes to a close, everyone cheers. A discussion follows as the group listens to the recording again, discovering that—although his rhythm is somewhat irregular—the client's point of reference is the clave, not a 4/4 beat. Strategies for supporting the client's music are presented, including encouraging the client to name his music with a few simple words in Spanish. "Que es?" ("What is it?") "Salsa?" Perhaps the client can be encouraged to initiate the music, with the supervisor attempting to help the group follow. The therapist is encouraged to listen to Cuban music from the '40s to get a feel for the rhythmic intricacies, to practice finding the clave beat, and to learn a few basic phrases in Spanish.

WORKING WITH THE ISSUES OF THE PROFESSIONAL MUSIC THERAPIST: EARLY STAGES

I felt that attending the music therapy supervision group in the beginning of my career led to many exciting experiences because of my experiences in supervision.

In the early stages, professional music therapists are continuing the work they had begun during their student years. "During … the termination period in internship, an intern's tasks are to be aware of what was learned, one's special strengths, and what still needs to be learned. The intern is able to communicate clearly about the field and the work that they do and has established themselves as a professional who has much to offer to clients and fellow staff" (Feiner, 2001, p. 112). There are many tasks that lie ahead in the early stages as music therapists move into their professional roles. In joining a professional music therapy supervision group, they have the opportunity to continue their work of self-discovery. They may need to expand their musical knowledge to meet the needs of the specific clients in their new setting. New challenges appear in relation to cultural competence and gender issues in a new population. Among staff or clients in their new setting, they may encounter an ethnic group with which they are unfamiliar. They may discover that although they articulate being fully accepting of the LGBTQ community, a transgender client seems to arouse uncomfortable feelings that they can explore in the supervisory group.

Music therapy professionals need to continue what Cheryl Dileo (2000) described as "the acquisition of ethical thinking" to be unafraid to address new challenges in the workplace. "I've learned how necessary training in the process of ethical thinking is for music therapy students and professionals. Whereas ethical dilemmas that arise in our profession may often be similar to those of professionals in related fields, they are sometimes quite different, due to the medium of our intervention, the intensity of the music therapy process, the diverse and multicultural nature of our work, and the level and types of training we receive" (Dileo, 2000, p. xi). All of these aspects can be addressed in the experiential music therapy supervision group, either through conversations, role-plays, teaching, or improvisation.

Although there is increasing recognition of music therapy as a field, there are at the same time challenges in the many roles that may be required of a new therapist. The music therapist needs to be able to weigh what compromises are acceptable and also how to work within a system to maximize the important use of music therapy. In other words, it is important for the music therapist starting out to be able to "improvise." The experiential music therapy supervision group provides just such a forum in which to use music to find their way. In the early stages of a music therapist's career, there are four primary needs that can be met in the experiential music therapy group. These are (1) the need for creativity in dealing with the challenges of a new career; (2) support for their emerging identity as a music therapist; (3) the need for continuing development of the ability to move between the musical and verbal modes as the verbal challenge grows with professional reporting and documentation; and (4) a place to share music freely with a community of understanding peers.

An example of the first need is where the music therapist is faced with a programming site that has just moved to a new model. The groups must be designed as "courses" as part of a "core curriculum." The administration requires the new therapist to lead these as verbal groups. The therapist brings her frustration into the music therapy supervision group. As the musical improvisation begins, the rhythm is subdued and the therapist uses a small amount of space to move in. With the group support, the therapist finds room for her sound within the larger sound of the group. She gradually becomes more assertive and free, able to fill the space available with her own drumming. Following a verbal discussion of the improvisation, a way of designing a "course" emerges that complies with the new model yet provides the resources of music to her clients. She decides to propose to her supervisor a series of skills development music therapy groups, such as anger management through music therapy and problem-solving through improvisation.

The second need, supporting the music therapist's emerging identity, is important to address as the music therapist works within a verbal setting consisting of meetings, case conferences, written documentation, and so on. There are two pitfalls at this early stage. As one becomes more adept in reporting and documenting without support, it is easy to begin to feel that the musical realm is secondary. Another pitfall is to begin to simply "translate" verbal concepts into musical activities. This can have great value but can also be limiting. As the music therapists expand their knowledge of psychological issues and group dynamics, they need to continue to deepen their awareness of the basic power of music itself to heal. With a continued self-exploration through regular musical experiences and through accompanying others in their explorations using music, supervisees can continue to develop their deep sense of this music therapy work. They are able to delve into a deeper understanding of group dynamics and transferences as they are expressed and felt through music. The group members voice their dilemmas, all sharing the common goal of using music therapy to the full and continuing their growth as music therapists.

The third need is supported throughout the supervisory sessions. The supervisor looks for openings for introducing music wherever this makes sense. The supervisor is always aware of the need of the new professional to continue developing the fluidity of movement between the verbal and musical realms.

Above all at the early stages of a music therapist's career is the fourth need, that of peer support. The music therapy experiential supervision group can be a haven to which to return, providing a community of peers who understand one's ideals and aspirations and who love to play music together.

ISSUES OF THE PROFESSIONAL MUSIC THERAPIST: ADVANCED STAGES

The group created a protest chant to air out my anger/resistance to the job change. … This experience later was greatly helpful for me as a supervisor to help staff adjust to major institutional changes.

Many of the issues of the music therapist at the early stages continue throughout one's career. Music therapists are constantly pioneering programs, educating other professionals and the public about music therapy, and carving out a place for music therapy. As paradigms change under each new administration, the relevance of music therapy needs to be fought for all over again. In the later stages of the professional music therapist's career, other roles emerge: the music therapist as intern supervisor, the music therapist as administrator, the music therapist in private practice, the music therapist as writer, and the music therapist as active participant in the professional music therapy organization. The music therapy supervision group provides a forum for verbal sharing of different music therapy settings; ongoing restructuring within facilities; city, state, and federal laws and changes in the laws; clinical opportunities and the development of private practice. It is a place to try out new possibilities with other professionals with similar ideals. It is a place to keep up with the latest techniques and ideas in the music therapy field. It is also a place to delve into ethical dilemmas and to develop strategies to encourage cultural competence.

New issues of transference and countertransference occur as the music therapist takes on the role of supervisor of music therapy interns and perhaps that of administrator for a department, becoming a supervisor to other rehabilitation staff. Work on boundaries can take on fresh meanings. Support from the group may be especially valuable at this time, as individual supervision may be unavailable and caring attitudes in the workplace may be rare as the music therapist discovers that colleagues are preoccupied with attempting to survive the increasing demands of the facility. In this later stage, the music therapist may embark on developing new programs or opening a private practice. The group is a place to use music to release tensions and renew oneself. The group also provides a place to brainstorm solutions and review ethical dilemmas, in addition to networking with other music therapists, becoming informed about conferences, and exploring the possibility of taking positions in the music therapy and related professional associations.

The group is also the place to keep nurturing the musical mind. In this stage, sometimes the music is used to solve dilemmas that are about systems in addition to clinical issues. The music therapist can improvise the feeling of being overwhelmed with multiple responsibilities and difficult choices in programming, staffing, and hiring. The intense strategizing and working and reworking of systems in the mind and on paper can be played out through music into a creative solution that might not emerge in the verbal mode. Staff conflicts can be broken up into their affective components through music to deepen the understanding of the music therapist's transference and countertransference as a supervisor and/or through musical role-playing a variety of interactions.

A music therapist/administrator may present the overwhelming pressure at work of complying with shifting administrative paradigms and the continuous changes in institutional survey standards accompanied by low staff morale. They can be encouraged to improvise their feelings of being in the midst of these pressures. The music may evolve from a quiet sound to a loud, cathartic release. As the music progresses, the therapist might be encouraged to find a sound that reflects an inner strength or sense of purpose while the group plays a supportive improvisation. In a further development, the group may create sounds reflecting the pressures surrounding the therapist. The therapist can travel through this maelstrom, experimenting with attempting to maintain a centered feeling. Discussion can follow to uncover in words what has occurred: Was it possible to maintain a centered feeling? What got in the way of maintaining it? What concrete changes might need to be made to allow room for this to occur? The group can share their feelings of "being" the pressure instead of having to "survive" it themselves.

As the music therapist continues on day by day, the isolation and the seeming repetitiveness of the work may lead to burnout. With a group of peers, one can improvise and receive healing that is necessary to continue on. Perhaps one captures a new perspective, listening to another music therapist's solution. Perhaps a free musical improvisation revitalizes the sense of the healing power of music and renews one's sense of creativity. We are all growing and changing as human beings, traversing different stages of our lives. The experiential music therapy supervision group helps to keep a sense of balance of our needs, whether musical, intellectual, or spiritual.

Reflections

As part of this revised chapter, I decided to contact the original members of my music therapy supervision groups from the 1980s to find out what effects this experience had on their present work. I wanted to know how the music therapy supervision group influenced them, how the music worked, and what they are still able to take from the experience, if anything.

At the time of my original group, there were no supervision groups using music in the New York area or in the United States of which I was aware. I was participating in a verbal supervision group with a Gestalt therapist, which proved quite effective in bringing me into the experience of the here-and-now and understanding boundaries. However, after listening to colleagues of mine, I felt we weren't trusting enough in our own music to uncover our feelings, reactions, transferences, and countertransferences. We were working with music, and we needed to support one another to understand, uncover, and experience the joy of this discovery through the unique power of music.

The following is based on a survey of some of the original members of my music therapy supervision group. (As can be seen, I have also used quotes from this survey throughout this chapter.) The music therapists who joined the group were an amazing group of people—creative, eager, and original. Most members had had some professional experience by the time they joined. Some had been in the field for many years. They loved music, and we experimented with many memorable techniques. We always began the group with improvisation, often adding movement and awareness of breathing, sometimes lying on the floor. At times, we experimented with "toning" from Laurel Keyes's work (Keyes, 1979). After intense days in clinics, psychiatric hospitals, developmental centers, and schools, we worked toward "arriving," grounding, and release. Each group member of this culturally diverse group of men and women brought new ideas and techniques. We experimented with breathing techniques, bodywork, and improvisations using percussion, melodic percussion, guitar, keyboard, and voice. We delved into topics ranging from working to understand the dynamics of a session, sharing and overcoming feelings of discouragement and burnout, negotiating music therapy identities in institutions that were not familiar with music therapy, taking on new roles as intern supervisors, working with the oversight of music therapy training programs and administration, to sharing the joy of being together in music. And, most important, we shared the moments that confirmed in our work the healing power of music.

In returning to this writing, I was curious to know what effects this experience had had on their work over the years. The questions I asked were: What is remembered? What may have been helpful? What was not helpful? In follow-up discussions, I asked whether there were anything that the participants embody today that might have stemmed from the group.

It has been a pleasure to reconnect with some of participants and hear their experiences. My great thanks go to Janice Dvorkin, David Gonzalez, Gary Hara, Joseph Piccinnini, Noah Shapiro, Barbara Wheeler, and Alan Wittenberg for spending the time with me in this reflection. As I went through their responses, several categories emerged: being present, entering into the music, and daring.

Being Present

In receiving the responses about members' experiences in the music therapy experiential group, I am struck by the recurrence of the aspect of being present:

[T]he important thing I learned was about being totally concerned with the patient's responses and how that begins the process of the work.

… encouraged attention to unfolding process, I became more willing to suspend judgment, more able to "be" with what was presented …

Encouraged me to pay attention to clients in detail, step-by-step, methodically: physical movements (micro check); emotional expression (not just "happy," what did you see?).

We used to play and simulate a session. This experience was invaluable for me to experience how my presenting, reacting, feeling during the music-playing can influence how I relate, play, and therapeutically work with patients.

We had fun with it, even though at times I was challenged by the depths of perception as we addressed specific details rather than generalized.

The thing that stands out to me … was the focus on being present in the music and the musical interactions while playing. Regardless of the character of the music itself, the intention was clear and focused on the importance and "sacredness" of playing the music together. This seems timely, as this aspect of being present with clients, especially in music, may be the essence of the treatment, whether meeting the person once or over a period of time. It seems more and more so to me and reminds me that playing music together has this ability to focus on being present and receiving the being present of another. I value this in my own life, further reinforcing the importance of that quality when I think about the impact on the people we work with.

Music Therapy Process

Music therapy process appears to be very important in the feedback I received.

I think the way that you helped us use music to work through our music therapy "issues" was the most valuable thing. I don't think I had been in this kind of situation before, so that was very helpful. Thinking about it now, I STILL believe that words are important for working things out—probably more than you did or do (or than I think that you did or do), but it was very useful to do so much without them.

I became more conscious of my motivations, and thereby more able to choose interventions with greater clarity and less messy transference.

I became more observant to the organic unfolding of the music and the group dynamics.

One thing I remember is not trying to repeat an experience, not relying on a technique to make the same experience happen, since it is often the timing and context, rather than the technique or activity, that matters.

It was very important in terms of feedback, peer support, experimentation, and acquiring ideas, approaches, and the perspectives of others. … It helped me to experiment with structure and freedom in musical experiences. It also put me more in touch with areas in which I was both weak and strong.

I was able to explore what's possible and what's real. Grounding the possibility with reality. "Being grounded in the body." Going "from playing to cognitive understanding to emotion."

… a good model of … approaches to use with a variety of patients at the state hospital. … I learned how to go beyond what I was doing, so I always felt my work was relevant.

I recall supervision provided the safety of trying out musical interventions. I think I became more comfortable and knowledgeable about letting the music develop and listening more clinically to what sound may represent and working spontaneously in the moment.

Music-making and processing on the experience were the most helpful.

It was the first time I was asked to look at the effect of sound on a group I was running.

Daring

… encouraged creative daring, I became more willing to take creative risks, to trust my creative impulses, to take an artistic stand in my music therapy identity.

It … stopped me from quitting, after working awhile. This happened to several music therapists in my class. I learned how to go beyond what I was doing, so I always felt my work was relevant.

The supervision experience helped me to have more confidence in music and myself. Once again, it was and is something of value every time I work or present music therapy.

[Helped me to] create a more clinical, professional way of doing things, a better presentation at the workplace to medical doctors, social workers, psychiatrists, and administrators. [I remember one group when] I had adolescents lying on the floor with the lights down. The director came in and asked me what I was doing. I was able to explain clearly about grounding and breathing and about music therapy. In the next few weeks, he gave me a raise!

CONCLUSION

I present in this chapter many ways to use music and words to enrich the experience of supervision for music therapists. In a general way, there can be a deepening of therapists' connection with music. Therapists are able to expand their appreciation of moving and ability to move back and forth between words and music. This can come from the persistent search to find ways to use music as a primary mode, rather than just an adjunct to the verbal mode.

The purpose of an experiential music therapy group is to provide shared experiences, a forum for experimenting with new ideas and exploring cultural differences, a musical support, and, most of all, a music therapy support. The group can provide a sounding board for feelings that arise from unexpected turns in the road and a nurturing place in which music therapy ideals can flourish and tools develop. As music therapists share struggles, they feel less isolated. As they compare strategies in handling difficult situations, they can feel strengthened. Having exposure to the healing of music in each group session supports the difficult mission of educating others of its effects. Because music is used extensively, the musical mode is encouraged and the sense of identity as musician therapists is supported.

Gathering with other music therapists provides not only a forum for support of music therapists' issues but also a tangible community that is able to affirm the mission that we all share in creating opportunities for people to benefit from the healing power of music.

It is my hope that by looking back over this work and by sharing the reflections of these first group members of my music therapy professional experiential supervision group, I am able to support the continuing importance of music in music therapy supervision. I hope that by studying the music and verbal elements (or "modes," as I have called them here), a better understanding and clarity of use may emerge. It has been exciting to reflect on the intensity of exploration possible in this type of music-oriented professional supervision group. As can be seen in the reflections, it is evident that the group allows for an intense exploration of material and deepens the supervisees' understanding of the music therapy experience.

Acknowledgments

Special thanks go to:

Janice Dvorkin, PhD, coordinator of the music therapy program at the University of the Incarnate Word in San Antonio, Texas, and a licensed psychologist in Texas and New York State.

David Gonzalez, DA music therapy, musician, poet, storyteller, and Joseph Campbell Foundation Fellow.

Gary Hara, MA, LCAT, MT-BC, director of therapeutic activities, Jacobi Medical Center in the Bronx, New York.

Joseph Piccinnini, MA, CMT, LCAT, music therapy supervisor, clinical music therapist, and president of the Richmond Music Center; consultant and site supervisor of New York University music therapy program; consultant, Nordoff-Robbins Center for Music Therapy at NYU.

Noah Shapiro, MA, NRMT, LCAT, MT-BC, adjunct professor at New York University and supervisor of activities therapies, Bellevue Hospital, New York City.

Barbara Wheeler, PhD, MT-BC, professor emeritus, Montclair State (NJ) University and prolific writer on music therapy and music therapy research.

Alan Wittenberg, MA, CMT, music therapist and founder of the Surry Music Therapy Center, Surry, Maine.

REFERENCE LIST

Aigen, K., & Young, L. (2010). Supervising the supervisor: the use of live music and identification of parallel processes. *The Arts in Psychotherapy, 37*, 125.

Bruscia, K. (1998). *The dynamics of music psychotherapy.* Gilsum, NH: Barcelona Publishers.

De Backer, J., & Sutton, J. (2014). Supervision in music therapy: the jumping-off point. In J. De Backer & J. Sutton (Eds.), *The music in music therapy: psychodynamic music therapy in Europe—clinical, theoretical, and research approaches.* London, UK: Jessica Kingsley.

Dileo, C. (2000). *Ethical thinking in music therapy.* Cherry Hill, NJ: Jeffrey Books.

Feiner, S. (2001). A journey through internship supervision: roles, dynamics, and phases of the supervisory relationship. In M. Forinash (Ed.), *Music therapy supervision.* Gilsum, NH: Barcelona Publishers.

Hesser, B. (1995). The power of sound and music in therapy and healing. In C. B. Kenny (Ed.), *Listening, playing, creating essays on the power of sound.* Albany, NY: State University of New York Press.

Kennelly, J., Daveson, B., & Baker, F. (2016). Effects of professional music therapy supervision on clinical outcomes and therapist competency: a systematic review involving narrative synthesis. *Nordic Journal of Music Therapy, 25*(2), 201.

Keyes, L. E. (1979). *Toning: the creative power of the voice.* Camarillo, CA: DeVorss & Co.

Kim, S. A. (2015). Music therapy and cultural diversity. In B. Wheeler (Ed.), *Music therapy handbook.* New York, NY: Guilford Press.

Langdon, G. S. (2001). Experiential music therapy group as a method of professional supervision. In M. Forinash (Ed.), *Music therapy supervision.* Gilsum, NH: Barcelona Publishers.

Scheiby, B. (2015). Analytical music therapy. In B. Wheeler (Ed.), *Music therapy handbook.* New York, NY: Guilford Press.

Stephens, G. (1984). Group supervision in music therapy. *Music therapy, 4,* 29–38.

Stephens, G. (1987). The experiential music therapy group as a method of training and supervision. In C. D. Maranto & K. Bruscia (Eds.), *Perspectives on music therapy education and training.* Philadelphia, PA: Temple University, Esther Boyer College of Music.

Turry, A. (1998). Transference and countertransference in Nordoff-Robbins music therapy. In K. Bruscia (Ed.), *The dynamics of music therapy.* Gilsum, NH: Barcelona Publishers.

verbalize. (2017). At Merriam-Webster.com. Retrieved September 29, 2017, from https://www.merriam-webster.com/dictionary/verbalize

Chapter 12

THE JOURNEY OF TWO:
SUPERVISION FOR THE NEW MUSIC THERAPIST

Dorit Amir

INTRODUCTION

When this chapter was published in this book's first edition, my focus was on supervision for the new music therapist who works in an educational setting. During the almost 20 years that have passed, I have continued to give individual and group supervision in Israel to Israeli, Arab, and Jewish students, new and advanced music therapists, and supervision on supervision for advanced music therapists who want to become supervisors. I have been working mainly in Israel, but also have provided supervision to Greek and American music therapists. During these years, the number of music therapists has grown, the number of places that offer music therapy services has expanded, and I have gained more experience as a supervisor. When I was asked to rewrite for the second edition, I decided to focus on individual supervision for the new music therapist who works in various settings with various populations. By "new music therapist," I mean one who has been working less than four years. I also put more focus on cultural and ethical issues.

New music therapists face many difficulties at the beginning of their professional journey even before they start focusing on understanding their work with clients. The jobs they find are usually in places such as schools, hospitals, mental health clinics, homes for older adults, centers for abused women, and so forth. They have to get to know the physical setting; the staff; the setting's philosophy, regulations and hierarchy; and obviously, the clients. While some places have suitable rooms equipped with musical instruments, others do not, and the music therapist has to work in someone else's room. Many places have some musical instruments but not a lot, and usually there is only a small budget to buy more. As a result, many music therapists need to carry their own musical instruments to work. Most of the music therapy rooms are not soundproof, and loud sounds might disturb people who work in a classroom or an office nearby. Often people come into the room and ask therapists to reduce the volume. These are a few of the difficulties new music therapists face at the beginning of their journey. These difficulties often cause confusion, frustration, and anger that might bring them to be disillusioned about the profession, and some of them may even consider quitting.

This is why supervision is essential for the new music therapist. It is a safe place where the supervisor accompanies and supports the supervisee and, together, they continue to further the supervisee's education and empower her[14] in facing and dealing with the obstacles.

In a survey that was done by Jackson (2008), music therapists in the USA were asked if they had participated in supervision and how important they thought supervision was for them as professional music therapists. The results indicated that for various reasons, almost two-thirds of professional music therapists had not participated in supervision. Those who had been getting supervision gave it a higher importance rating than those who had not participated in supervision as professionals.

---

[14] Throughout this chapter, I generally refer to the supervisee as a female (she, her) and to the client as a male (he, his).

These results surprised me. During the past 20 years since this chapter was first published (Amir, 2001), supervision has become an integral part of the music therapist's professional development in many countries. In Israel, it is mandated by the ministry of education, and music therapists who are at the beginning of their careers are required by the professional association to participate in supervision in order to get jobs in health and education.

In this chapter, I describe aims of supervision and my role as a supervisor for the beginning music therapist, supervision approaches, and areas to focus on. I discuss the supervisory relationship and explain the role of music in supervision. A special attention is given to multicultural and ethical issues that come up in supervising new music therapists.

AIMS OF SUPERVISION AND MY ROLE AS A SUPERVISOR

I believe that supervision has to be experienced as a positive experience of personal growth. I aim for the supervisee to gain confidence and to believe in herself. Only then will the knowledge and the emotional maturity that she earned be manifested in clinical work.

Sloan (2005) wrote about clinical supervision in nursing and explained that the ultimate function of supervision is improving the quality of care, safety, and protection for patients. This is also true for music therapy supervision: The ultimate goal is to educate and empower the supervisee in order to improve the quality of her work so that she can empower her clients and improve their life quality. The more empowered the supervisee, the more empowered her clients will become.

More Specific Goals of the Role of Supervisor

- Supporting and helping the supervisee to settle into her new job.
- Educating:
  - Exploring and understanding multicultural and ethical issues;
  - Exploring and understanding verbal and musical therapeutic techniques, interventions, and activities suitable for her clients;
  - Exploring and trying to understand clients' certain behaviors and musical material;
  - Suggesting technical means and procedures such as what to look for while observing the client, how to approach parents whose child is in music therapy, and what questions to ask them.
- Exploring feelings:
  - Dealing with the supervisee's feelings concerning the client, the setting, the staff, the therapeutic process;
  - Dealing with the supervisee's feelings concerning her own being and her intervention during the therapeutic session;
  - Dealing with the supervisee's feelings with regard to me, the supervisor, and the supervision process;
  - Dealing, to a certain degree, with her personal feelings around her own private life that come up in the supervision process.
  - Exploring the interpersonal dynamics in the supervision session in order to better understand what is going on in the interpersonal dynamics in the therapy room.

Supervision Approaches and Areas on Which to Focus in Music Therapy Supervision

Music therapists who are just starting to work as professionals often feel tension and confusion. Many of them come to a supervision session and say something like, "There are so many things I want to talk about … I don't know where to start … am not sure what to focus on." Being aware of various supervision approaches might help me and my supervisee have a clearer idea what to focus on.

In the first edition, I mentioned Alonso (1985) and Grinberg (1990), who wrote about supervision approaches in psychotherapy. Alonso (1985) perceives three major supervision approaches: cognitive-didactic approaches; approaches that are based on the experience of personal-emotional growth; and approaches that emphasize the interpersonal process that is based on empathic connection. Grinberg (1990) sees two main approaches: approaches that are based on the client and approaches that are based on the supervisee.

Music therapy supervision differs from these two approaches since music is a very important component that needs special attention in supervision. Brown (2009) describes major areas for music therapy supervision: musical relationship in the therapy room; practical management in the therapy room and workplace; interpersonal dynamics in the therapy room; interpersonal dynamics in the workplace; and interpersonal dynamics in the supervision room.

I find myself moving from one approach to another according to my supervisee's needs and stage of professional development and maturity as a person and according to my own inner listening to myself. I might be didactic and deal with the issues that are brought up cognitively; I might focus on the supervisee's feelings and explore them with her; I can share with her my own feelings, images, and sensations I have concerning her client musically and/or verbally; and I can also bring up the relationship between her and me in case she is ready to look at and deal with that. There are times when I share with my supervisee my own personal experiences from being a therapist, and there can be times when I share with her some things from my private, personal life if I believe that this can contribute to her understanding. I try to listen to my physiological, cognitive, emotional, intuitive, and spiritual selves.

In general, I have found that using a cognitive-didactic approach with music therapists who have just started working can be very helpful, especially at the beginning stage of supervision. Many supervisees ask me to help them to settle into the new workplace: offer them musical activities which are suitable to the populations they work with, refer them to relevant articles and books, and give practical advice concerning practical things ("I don't have a room"; "I hardly have musical instruments"; "how do I chose whom to work with?"; "the principal wants to come and observe me"; "there is invasion of privacy/noise"; "people come and go during therapy"; etc.). At a later stage, when the supervisee has settled into her workplace, I can focus on the emotional growth of the supervisee, help her to understand what is going on in her inner world during her therapeutic work, encourage her to get insight with regard to her feelings, and understand the reasons for these feelings. This is true in theory, but in reality, I change approaches according to the supervisee's needs, wishes, and maturity. Often, we focus on the client in order to understand his being—his behavior, inner world, and feelings. We try to understand the client's cultural background and his musical experiences. At other times, we focus on the supervisee. We try to understand her behavior and feelings, her musical and verbal responses, and examine their connections to her personal history and cultural background. We also look at the interpersonal process and the dynamics between us in order to identify parallel processes between client and therapist (Brown, 1997).

Supervision has to include the application of music therapy to the specific client population with whom the supervisee works. Therefore, I believe that I have to be knowledgeable about the populations with which my supervisees work and share my knowledge with them. Centering on the supervisee's feelings is important, but it cannot come at the expense of making sure that she learns to do music therapy with a particular population. For example, supervisees who work with clients who suffer from PTSD need supervisors who have experience in working with PTSD clients and who are knowledgeable about and familiar with literature on trauma so they can refer the supervisees to specific literature on PTSD.

Supervision has to include culture. Clients, supervisors, and supervisees do not live in an empty space. Factors such as music, life experiences, culture, community, and society play an important role in keeping and maintaining good health and quality of life. I have to understand the cultures with which my supervisees and their clients identify and acknowledge how all of us are defined and shaped by the culture with which we identify. A cultural focus can help me and my supervisees to understand how individuals function in society and view our work with greater empathy, self-awareness, and acceptance (Mahoney, 2015).

THE SUPERVISORY RELATIONSHIP

The supervisory relationship has an important influence on clinical supervision (Bond & Holland, 1998; Kilminster & Jolly, 2000). Once the supervisees (especially new therapists) feel supported in a safe place by someone who listens empathically, they experience less stress, increase their confidence, and develop their clinical competence and knowledge (Sloan, 2005). As stated earlier, there are times when the supervisory relationship needs to be dealt with.

The beginning stages can cause anxiety to the supervisee (Bond & Holland, 1998), especially if they are new professionals. Some are aware of it and able to acknowledge it and work it through in supervision or in personal therapy. Others are not aware of their anxiety, are disabled by it, and use various defenses in order to protect themselves. They get stuck in denying their anxiety and are unable to gain important insights and to grow. Another response to an unconscious anxiety can be talking in cliché in order to feel part of the established psychiatry club so they can hide their lack of knowledge and confidence (De la Torre & Appelbaum, 1974). I try to bring up these issues when I feel that my supervisee is ready to explore them and that it can be a growth experience. Doing it at the wrong time can cause distrust in the supervisory relationship. The supervisor can also experience anxiety due to a belief that she is responsible for resolving the supervisee's stress and improving her emotional well-being (Sloan, 2005). According to Power (1999), in the first session it is important to find out the supervisee's expectations from the supervisor and to get to know each other a bit before signing the contract.

As a supervisor, I want to be empathic and sensitive and have the ability to tune in and listen to my supervisees (Feiner, 2010). These qualities contribute to fruitful dialogue that strengthens the supervisee and helps her to learn and grow.

THE ROLE OF MUSIC IN SUPERVISION

Theoretically, there are three kinds of dialogues in supervision: (1) The dialogue is only verbal—reporting, describing, analyzing, and interpreting, and addressing topics that are processed verbally. (2) The dialogue is based on listening to music that was recorded in the therapy room played solely by the client, by client and therapist, and by the therapist—her musical interventions. In the supervision session, the supervisor and supervisee listen to the music and analyze it musically and psychologically. There are many benefits in bringing recorded music from the therapy sessions to supervision: Listening helps the supervisee to remember interventions, responses, and processes; analyzing the music helps in understanding musical and psychological intrapersonal and interpersonal processes. Listening allows reflecting on the meaning of music in the therapeutic process. (3) The dialogue is based on creating live music in supervision. Stephens (2001) described three directions: from music to words—the supervisee plays in order to expose unconscious material that might be the focus of verbal processing; from music to music—the supervisee plays and allows the music to bring insights; from words to music—music is being created in order to deepen the understanding of the supervisee with regard to issues that she brought up at the beginning of the session. All three kinds take place intuitively in the supervision process according to the issue, the supervisee's wishes and needs, and the supervisor's opinion and intuition.

The main goals of the use of live music in supervision are to examine and process topics such as transference and countertransference (Austin & Dvorkin, 2001; Young & Aigen, 2010); to develop professional musical skills (Turry, 2001); to deepen the connection between supervisee and supervisor (Austin & Dvorkin, 2001; Scheiby, 2001); to explore topics that are related to the client (Scheiby, 2001(; to explore topics that are related to the supervisee that come up during the therapy session, such as how she perceives the client and how she feels toward him (Amir, 2001); to understand the influence of music on the therapeutic process, on the client, and on the therapist (Amir, 2001); to release blocks and resistance to exploring certain issues (Amir, 2001); and to find the supervisee's blind spots and strengthen her professional identity (Scheiby, 2001). Creating music in supervision helps to develop the musical intuition of both supervisor and supervisee and encourages spontaneity and playfulness. For new music therapists, the use of live music can help to develop musical interventions, to better understand the client, and to start understanding transference and countertransference issues.

Music-centered supervision is a model I created (Amir, 2010) in which musicking (Small, 1998) is at the heart of supervision. Obviously, I talk in supervision, but throughout the years I have found that musicking (Small, 1998) has been the main and most meaningful factor for a deeper understanding of certain processes in music therapy. Musicking includes listening to musical excerpts that were recorded in the therapeutic session and creating live music in the supervision session either by the supervisee alone or by both supervisee and supervisor. It can be improvising, musical role-playing, singing, and/or playing songs that are relevant to the issues brought up in supervision. We can imagine music-centered supervision as a musical structure or composition: there are sessions that have a clear A-B structure, meaning starting or ending with music; A-B-A (rondo structure), meaning starting or ending with music, while in the middle there is verbal discussion; or vice versa, meaning starting and ending with words and making music in the middle. There are group supervision sessions that can be imagined as a concerto where the soloist (the member who brings something to work on) interacts with the orchestra (group members).

In music-centered supervision, the musical experience and its connections are at the heart of supervision: the connection between the supervisee and the music she creates in the supervision session; the connection between the supervisee and her client's music; and the connection between the supervisee and the supervisor to the music they create in supervision. The last can be looked at and examined as a process parallel to the supervisee and her client's joint music-making. There are supervision sessions without a specific and clear structure, where the sounds come as needed, and there are sessions where the music has a clear role in the structure of the session, such as musicking always at the beginning of the session.

There are sessions with no music. Over the years, there have been sessions in which I have suggested playing music, but my supervisees have refused and wanted to work only verbally. There have been times that even when the actual music is missing, it is very present since we talk about it and try to understand the reasons for its absence. This can be a delicate issue. On one hand, I feel that it is my responsibility as the supervisor to bring up the issue of not having music in the supervision sessions and explore it. On the other hand, it is the supervisee who brings issues to work on and not me. How do I bring it up? What is the right timing? The answers to these questions vary, depending on the reasons for the absence of music.

This example illustrates these points. David[15] is a 24-year-old Israeli Jewish music therapist who has been working almost two years as a music therapist in a special school for children with autism. The children come from various backgrounds: Most of them were born in Israel to parents who came to Israel from Russia, Georgia, Ukraine, and Ethiopia. Many of the parents do not speak

---

[15] All names of supervisees and clients have been changed to pseudonyms.

Hebrew well. The school's philosophy is based on behavior modification, and each child has a chart with weekly points that he gets for "good behavior" and demerits for "bad behavior." David feels frustrated because he hates this approach and does not know what to do. He has struggled with it since the beginning of his work. Also, the principal of the school expects him to conduct the "end of the year" performance and to be in charge of the musical part of the holiday celebrations. David does not get extra hours for these additional responsibilities, and he needs to do rehearsals during therapy hours. Also, the principal wants David to create a choir and an orchestra in the school and to devote two weekly hours to rehearsals.

David has been coming to me for supervision every other week since he started working in this school, and these were the issues he brought to supervision. David felt frustrated and angry. He felt that the principal was very demanding and controlling and did not understand him and his work. David felt that he was not succeeding in standing up for what he believes in. On the other hand, he enjoys working with the children and felt that his work was productive. Overall, he felt trapped and told me that since he could not do his work properly, he was thinking of quitting his job.

During the first six months of supervision, I listened to David and acknowledged his difficulties with a lot of empathy. I said that it is hard to work in a place that forces you to be part of a philosophy in which you don't believe and that is quite the opposite of your belief system. At this initial stage, I let David ventilate his feelings and release his frustrations and anger verbally. When I suggested trying to express his feelings musically, he refused. When I asked him why, he said that he was afraid that the sound would be so big and frightening that he wouldn't be able to tolerate it.

I had a dilemma: Is this something I should focus on with David? He is a music therapist, and if he cannot express his anger and frustration musically, how can he ask his clients to do it? I also wondered why he was so afraid of a big sound. Another dilemma had to do with the timing—is it the right timing for me to bring this issue up in supervision? Is David ready to deal with these issues? I decided to wait. The rationale for waiting was that David was dealing with a tough situation, and I thought that maybe I could wait until some of the issues he brought in were resolved, and then he would feel less tense and frustrated at work. Together, we tried to look for ways to deal with the situation, to see how David could be part of the system and go along with the school philosophy yet allow himself the freedom to work according to his own philosophy inside the therapy room.

We discussed what this required from him, and he said that he needed to be more flexible and try not to see things in black and white. When I asked him if there were a price that he had to pay for this kind of flexibility, he said that he needed to give up total control and that this was hard for him. Also, he had to give up "being right" and being the only one who knows what is good for the children in this school.

We had discussions about performances, celebrations, choirs, and orchestras in the context of his work. Again, we found out that David's anger had a lot to do with his rigidity about what is right and what is wrong, with what he sees as his job description, and what is not part of his job. We talked about the therapeutic potential of performances in front of others, as well as its potential damage. We could slowly see together that with some of the kids this can be a wonderful thing to do, while with others it would be counterproductive. Slowly I started to see a shift in David's way of approaching things. He went from the general to the individual, and he started to look at the uniqueness of each situation instead of following his principles in a rigid way.

Only after this shift occurred did we move to a more personal area. Throughout the supervision process, I had a feeling that the school's principal represented a harsh father figure to David, and that David's reactions to him are transferential. I suggested musical role-playing, but David was still afraid of it. My dilemma arose again, but I still felt that this was not the right time for bringing up the issue of not being able to music. We did verbal role-playing. I asked David to close his eyes, to see the principal and talk to him. When he did that, it became obvious to me and to him that he was talking to his father, who was a very harsh and dominant figure in David's life. In this role-playing, David told the principal that whenever he was talking to him, he felt like a child—small, helpless, and hurt, that he could not be himself. This realization opened the way to looking at the transference and to separating the two figures. David took this issue to his own therapy, and in our supervision, we were able to look at things with more clarity.

Later on, when David started to feel more relaxed at his work, he agreed to add music to our sessions. Now David was willing to try expressing his anger on the piano. His piano improvisations expressed a lot of anger at the beginning, but soon they changed and both of us heard sadness. David realized that it was easier for him to get angry than to feel sad in his life. Exposing the sadness through musicking gave way to acknowledging it, and he took this to his therapy and processed it there.

David continued working in the school. He no longer thought of quitting his job. He started bringing other issues to supervision, issues from the therapy room. We continued to work on all levels now, the personal and the professional: understanding the child's cultural background, music, actions, and behaviors; understanding David's reactions; analyzing the dynamics between him and the child in the therapy room and comparing it to the dynamics between him and me in the supervision room or between him and another significant person in his life. We did this through words and music.

MULTICULTURAL ISSUES IN SUPERVISION

I have been supervising Israeli, American, and Greek music therapists. Working in a multicultural society in Israel, with clients and supervisees from various and sometimes diverse ethnic, cultural, and religious groups—some of them in conflict with each other—required me to pay more attention to cultural issues. In my work with supervisees, I often see the uneasy feelings that they have when they work with clients from a different culture. Jewish music therapists who work with Arab clients (two nationalities in conflict with one another), Arab music therapists who work with Arab populations in Israel, nonreligious music therapists who work with extremely religious children whose parents have strong constrictions on the kinds of music they are allowed to listen to, music therapists who are sabras[16] and work with Ethiopian clients—all of these often experience strong feelings of inadequacy and confusion as to how to approach the other, how to make a connection and build trust between them. Some of them deal with this difficulty by trying to focus on the purely clinical aspects of their work and ignoring cultural ones. By doing so, however, "they fragment themselves and leave aspects of their own identities behind" (Stige & Kenny, 2002, p. 26).

Overall, I believe that my supervisees who are working with clients who come from diverse cultural backgrounds want to encourage their clients to become part of the community and enhance their sense of belonging to society in order to feel less isolated. I have supervisees who themselves emigrated to Israel from other countries, and part of my work is to help them to become part of the community. The key question is often what the right balance is between preserving the "old culture" and assimilating into the "new culture."

The Balance Between Preserving the Past and Adopting the New Culture

There are supervisees and clients who tend to preserve their traditions. Their parents' traditions become a source of comfort, pride, and confidence. In times of discomfort, pressure, or personal crisis, the natural thing for supervisees and clients who have immigrated from countries such as Russia, Ukraine, Georgia, the USA, England, and Australia to do is to go back to their native language and to sing songs from their childhood. There are others, who have rejected their tradition, who will not speak their native language or sing childhood songs because they do not want to emphasize feelings

---

[16] Born in Israel.

of being an outsider. Some of them are ashamed of their foreign accent. They want to erase any sign of their past in order to become "assimilated" into the Israeli culture.

Here is an example of a therapist working with this issue. Adel is a 25-year-old music therapist with two years of experience who comes to me for supervision. She had immigrated from Russia seven years before becoming a professional music therapist. Her Hebrew is quite good. She started working as a music therapist in a nursing home. Most of the residents were Russian immigrants, and some of them had lived in Israel many years. All of them loved to sing old Russian and Hebrew songs. She told me that she feels uncomfortable in singing Russian songs and that she also feels uncomfortable in singing old Hebrew songs because she is not familiar with these.

We tried to understand why she feels uncomfortable in singing Russian songs. She told me that since she had come to Israel, she had been trying to speak only Hebrew because she felt that this was the only way for her to be accepted by Israeli society. She also told me that she speaks Russian with her parents, since they do not speak Hebrew. She believes that unlike her, her parents live in their past and cannot be part of the new culture. Both she and I assumed that in order to become "assimilated" into being an Israeli, she had made an unconscious decision to erase her past and not to speak Russian outside of her home.

We talked about her decision to work in a place where the residents are older Russian adults, a place where it was obvious that she needs to speak Russian with certain clients. I felt that Adel needed to re-examine her beliefs about erasing any signs of her past. In supervision, I asked her to play a Russian song that she likes. She chose a song that was Russian but had a Hebrew translation. I was familiar with the song and we both sang it together: She sang it in Russian and I sang it in Hebrew. She started singing Russian songs with her Russian-speaking clients and also learned Israeli songs that her native clients wanted her to sing and play with them. Her work as a music therapist helped her to find the right balance between her past traditions and present life. Having to learn a big repertoire of Israeli songs sped up her process of becoming an integral part of the Israeli culture.

Dealing with Cultural Barriers

Barriers appear in various shapes and forms with regard to ethnicity, race, religion, age, gender, status, musical taste, sexual orientation, geographical location, political beliefs, education, and so forth. To us music therapists, the barriers we face in our work are more obvious when we work with clients from a different ethnic group (cultural-political barriers, religious barriers), gender, or age. Barriers often cause tension, frustration, intimidation, anger, distance, uneasiness, misunderstanding, and even helplessness.

Here is an example of dealing with cultural barriers. Shira, a young Jewish Israeli sabra of Ashkenazi origin and a beginner music therapist, came to me for supervision. Shira brought her work with Samuel, a 5-year-old Ethiopian boy who is extremely shy and hardly talks. When he talks, he talks in Amharic, not in Hebrew. He lives with his mother and four sisters. His father left the country and is not in touch with his wife and children. Samuel feels very insecure. He has no real sense of home. Shira was told that he likes Ethiopian music, and this is why the kindergarten teacher referred him to music therapy.

In the first session, he made few vocal sounds (*ah-ah-ah-ah-oooooooooo*, in a rhythmic pattern of four eights and a long *ohh* sound). Shira imitated the sounds Samuel was producing. Shira explained that she wanted to establish a connection with Samuel and interact with him, but Samuel kept producing these sounds without acknowledging her effort to make contact with him. She felt frustrated. While listening to the recording, both Shira and I felt that the interaction was not playful and somewhat mechanical. When we analyzed her musical intervention, we noticed that Shira imitated Samuel's sounds in an exact manner: She produced the same sounds that he did—the same color, rhythm, duration, and dynamics, in the same form. She focused only on the musical parameters of her client's music and completely shut out her own creativity and playfulness.

Yehuda (2002), who studied multicultural encounters in music therapy, explains that by focusing only on the musical parameters, music therapists miss the human elements. Music is human and was born out of human needs. Therefore, Yehuda says, music therapists are encouraged to be authentic and not to ignore their own musical tastes, creativity, and playfulness. Shira had accepted her client's music, but her own identity was totally shut down, as if she did not exist in the room. By doing so, she had fragmented herself and left aspects of her own identity behind (Stige & Kenny, 2002).

In this supervision session, Shira realized that she did not know how to relate to Samuel. She did not speak Amharic and did not know his culture. We discussed possible ways to establish a connection with Samuel. Since we knew that Samuel likes Ethiopian music, we discussed the possibility of bringing a disc of Ethiopian music to the session to see if Shira and Samuel could make a connection while listening to music that he is familiar with and likes. Since Shira had never listened to Ethiopian music before, I encouraged her to get familiar with it and suggested borrowing the disc that Samuel likes listening to and listen to it.

In our next supervision session, Shira told me that she had listened to the disc she borrowed from the teacher, but she felt that it was hard for her to relate to it. She did not like the music and hesitated to play it for Samuel. We tried to understand why she did not like the music. She thought that maybe the fact that the songs were sung in Amharic, a language she does not understand, was the reason for not liking the disc. She also did not like the instrumental pieces on the disc—"too much drumming." While we experimented with drumming, Shira felt frustrated and stopped. She realized that she felt incompetent and tense since she could play these complicated rhythms, and thus she distanced herself. These feelings became a barrier that prevented her from playing music from Samuel's culture. Working on it in supervision made her understand that she needs to overcome this barrier. In our next supervision session, we listened to the disc and experimented with various drumming responses to the music we heard. Shira realized that she could accompany the music by playing simple rhythmic patterns and did not need to play complicated rhythms. She also told me that she listened to more Ethiopian music at home and improvised with her flute while listening to the music.

Shira brought the disc to her next session with Samuel. They listened to several pieces, and Samuel hummed, sang a few words in Amharic, and smiled at her. She also felt freer to improvise along with the drumming. Shira brought to supervision a vocal improvisation they did together. It was a very different improvisation. Shira added something from her own creative and understanding mind, and I felt her intention to interact with Samuel. Samuel responded by expanding his vocal sounds, and later on he started making eye contact with her and smiling at her more often.

Working through the issues of incompetence and not liking Ethiopian music brought a change. Shira found a way to improvise that was more congruent with Samuel's being. Samuel felt empathically understood, and both a sense of connectedness and a validation and expansion of his self were achieved. By listening more deeply and empathically to Samuel, Shira was able to create a shared space between them. He most likely felt that she was listening to him and seeing him.

Here is another example of the role (and absence) of musicking in supervision and dealing with cultural barriers. Alison is a 28-year-old Jewish music therapist who studied music therapy in the USA and immigrated to Israel when she was 25 years old. She had had one year of experience when she came to me for supervision. Alison worked in an Arab school in one of the Arab villages in Israel. At the beginning of her supervision process, she told me about Fahid, a 10-year-old child. Alison told me that Fahid sits quietly but refuses to play, and she does not know what to do. Alison knows a few words in Arabic, but she cannot speak the language and therefore cannot communicate verbally with Fahid. I asked her whether she had tried to initiate a musical dialogue with him, and she said that she had played and sung a few American children songs, but he had not joined her. I asked her if she had tried improvising with him, and she said no. We tried to understand why he did not want to communicate with her through playing, but we got nowhere. I suggested that she play him instead of talking about him. This is something I do quite often when I feel that I am not getting a clear picture, and many times I find that the impressions and images I get from the musical improvisation are clearer. Alison said that she couldn't play, and she was not sure why. She said that it would be difficult for her to improvise him and that it was easier for her to talk about him. I mentioned to her that every time I suggested playing, she refused. I wondered if there might be a parallel process: Could her client's refusal to play in the therapy sessions be parallel to her refusal to play in her supervision sessions? This question helped Alison to gain a deeper understanding concerning her refusal to play. It turned out that Alison was very judgmental toward her own improvisations and feared that I would judge her, too. She said that she feels panic when it comes to improvising and, in fact, that she did not know how to improvise. She admitted that it was easier for her to talk instead of play. She told me that she had studied classical piano in the music academy and had never improvised during her studies. During her music therapy studies, she had participated in improvisation courses but had never felt comfortable in improvising. We discussed the possibility that her client might have felt the same way—maybe he was afraid that since he does not know how to play, she will judge him and not be able to accept him.

We also talked about the gap between her culture and Fahid's culture. She was a young American woman who had immigrated to Israel and had to adjust to the Israeli culture. We talked about her playing English children songs that belonged to another culture. Playing and singing songs with which Fahid was unfamiliar could have sent a message that Alison did not understand Fahid and that he might not be able to trust her. I encouraged her to become familiar with Arabic music and songs in order to try to make a connection via improvising musical patterns with which he might be familiar.

I asked her if she wanted to work on her improvisations in supervision, and once she agreed, we decided to start every session with a short improvisation. She started with very simple improvisations, her alone and us together, and gradually we began improvising with more freedom. She started to take risks and enjoyed it. After a few more sessions, she told me that she was starting to feel more comfortable in improvising. She also brought this issue to her private music therapy sessions. Interestingly enough, after she started playing in her supervision sessions, her client started playing in the therapy sessions.

In this example, I focused on two issues: the role of musicking (and the absence of it) in the supervision process, as well as looking at cultural issues. Although there was no concrete music during the first sessions, the music was at the center of supervision. We worked on identifying the issue and presenting it verbally, arriving at a decision by the supervisee that she wanted to work on this issue and finding the right way of working on it—by starting every supervision session with improvising. The words in this first session paved the way to musicking in the following supervision sessions. It was an intersubjective session, where the verbal dialogue between two partners, with conscious (no music) and unconscious (the reasons for no music—fear of being judged by me) parts, allowed for relevant content to come up and be dealt with in supervision. Focusing on cultural issues encouraged Alison to examine the gap between the two cultures and to learn music that belongs to her client's culture so he could feel more accepted.

ETHICAL CONCERNS

Music therapists who are at the start of their professional journey deal with many specific ethical concerns in their supervision. Here are some examples.

The Issue of Boundaries—Working in the Same Neighborhood

I have had several supervisees who have been working in the same area where they live and happened to know the client and his family from the neighborhood. The concern is over how the therapist can keep confidentiality and clear boundaries when meeting the client in the grocery store or when the supervisee's child goes to the same kindergarten as her client.

Here is an example of working with boundaries. Doreen is a new music therapist who lives in Greece. Occasionally, we have supervision sessions via Skype. She lives in a small village and pretty much knows all of the people who live in the community. Doreen works as a music therapist in a kindergarten for special children in the neighborhood. Danny, one of her clients, is a five-year-old Greek boy who lives with his family two houses away from where Doreen lives. In her very first supervision session, Doreen talked about her concern with regard to working with Danny: Whenever she meets Danny's mother in the neighborhood, the mother asks Doreen how Danny is doing and wants to know what has been going on in therapy. Doreen feels uncomfortable in discussing Danny with his mother whenever she meets her in the neighborhood.

Working in the neighborhood where the music therapist lives can be problematic and forces the therapist to pay attention to and be more flexible with the issue of boundaries. Zur (2001) believes that boundaries in psychotherapy should be flexible and explains that there are two types of boundary issues: boundary violations and boundary crossings. Boundary crossing can be ethical and unethical. Zur talks about accidental encounters and avoidable or unavoidable encounters outside of therapy. Unavoidable encounters have to be dealt with sensitively. In supervision, we faced Doreen's concerns. We raised the ethical issues that usually come up when working with people whom she sees almost every day outside therapy and worked musically with Doreen's feelings. It was obvious to Doreen that it was not ethical to tell the mother what was happening behind closed doors with her son every time she sees Doreen and wants this information. We talked about the need for making clear boundaries with the mother.

Understanding the Scope of Responsibility and the Need to Share Information

Some of my new supervisees feel confused concerning their responsibilities. They do not know exactly what the scope of their responsibilities is as music therapists. Some of them take too much responsibility and do not share important and sometimes crucial information with other professionals, such as social workers, psychologists, counselors, or health services providers, who know better how to deal with certain issues. The issue of confidentiality can be confusing for the new music therapists. On one hand, they are committed to the client and promise not to share what the client does not want them to share. On the other hand, there are issues that need to be shared, especially when the client is minor.

What follows is an example of this issue. Luna is a 26-year-old Jewish Israeli woman who immigrated from Russia when she was 10 years old. While she adjusted well to Israeli society, her parents had difficulties in learning Hebrew and adjusting to the Israeli culture. Luna is a new music therapist who works in the child and adolescent ward in a psychiatric hospital. She has been working with Eliana, a 14-year-old-girl who had immigrated from Russia only two years before she was admitted to the hospital. She had difficulties in adjusting to the Israeli culture and did not speak Hebrew very well. She told Luna that she is going to hurt herself and asked Luna not to tell anybody. Luna felt that if she told this secret to the psychologist, she would betray the girl's trust in her and therefore promised Eliana that she would keep it between them. Luna felt uncomfortable about this decision. She did not know if she had made the right choice in promising not to tell anybody and brought this issue to supervision. Luna explained that since she promised Eliana that she would keep her secret, it would have been unethical to betray the girl's trust. We discussed the danger of not sharing such information with the girl's psychologist. We also talked about making promises that she cannot keep. We discussed Luna's responsibility to her client—would it benefit her client if she did not tell the right person about it and kept it to herself? If this girl had hurt herself badly, Luna would not have been able to forgive herself.

Another issue over information-sharing comes up when working in a school setting. Many times, people who belong to the educational staff, such as teachers, want to get information from the music therapist, ask the wrong questions, sometimes in front of the child ("Was he a good boy today?" "Did she behave nicely?"), and demand an answer. Supervisees who are beginning their professional journey often wonder how much confidential information needs to be shared with the client's teacher.

The following is an example of this issue. Brian is a 30-year-old Jewish Israeli who works as a music therapist in a Jewish religious school with children who need special attention. Although Brian is not religious himself, he respects the school and behaves accordingly (puts a yamaka on his head, respects musical restrictions such as not listening to female singers, etc.). One of his clients is Benny, a 7-year-old-boy who exhibits aggressive behavior toward his classmates. The teacher wants to know everything that goes on in the music therapy sessions and even tells Brian how to deal with Benny ("You need to set up clear boundaries with him and punish him if he does not obey you"). He also wants to come and observe a session. In supervision, we discussed the need for Brian to set up clear boundaries yet show respect to the teacher. We did role-playing and tried various ways of dealing with this teacher. We talked about expectations—what this teacher can and cannot expect in terms of getting information (for instance: "I will be happy to meet with you every month and tell you about Benny, but you cannot come to the room and observe us working, since the music therapy room is a sacred place that only Benny and I share, in order to gain his trust"). Brian had negative feelings toward the teacher, and we worked on expressing and dealing with these feelings musically. Brian realized that it might be a good idea to keep the teacher informed about certain things and try working with the teacher to gain his trust so he could change his attitude toward Benny.

We also talked about Brian's feelings with regard to working in a religious school. Brian talked about his difficulties in working in a different cultural environment and accepting some of the religious restrictions he had to take upon himself. Together we tried to understand what he likes about working there and how he can deal with the difficulties he experienced. Brian told me that he liked the children with whom he worked and enjoyed Hasidic songs[17] a lot. Hasidic songs became a bridge between Brian's culture and his clients' culture.

CONCLUSION

In this chapter, I focused mainly on the role of musicking in supervision and paid attention to cultural as well as ethical issues. I have to say that for me, the absence of musicking in supervision is unethical. Musicking is at the core of the music therapy profession and needs to be present in therapy and supervision. Supervision processes that do not include musical experiences, such as playing and listening, harm our professional identity and damage our integrity. I also believe that not being aware of personal and cultural biases and ignoring their impact on our work is unethical, specifically when working with clients who identify with other cultures. It is my responsibility as a supervisor to make

---

[17] Hasidic songs are considered to be the richest among all Jewish folk songs. The Hasidim are a mystic Jewish sect which flourished in Eastern Europe, originally in the eastern Carpathians, in the middle of the 18th century. Like the Biblical prophets, the Hasidim resort to singing to exalt their mood to the state of ecstasy. The Hasidic leaders believed that vocal music is one of the best vehicles to achieve salvation. The Hasidim believe that song is the soul of the universe. Some gates in the high spheres can be opened through songs only (Teitelbaum, in Idelsohn, 1929).

The Hasidic songs are unique in character and form. "Niggun" is the Hasidic term for a tune. "Most niggunim are sung without any words, with the frequent use of carrier syllables such as Ah, Ay, Oy, Hey, Ya-ba-bam, etc." (Hajdu & Mazor, 1972, p. 1423). The tunes are mystical in character and usually have a prayerful mood.

sure that my supervisees respect their clients and do not let their own personal and cultural values and beliefs disregard those who identify with other personal and cultural values and beliefs.

Supervising music therapists who are at the beginning of their professional journey has been very rewarding yet challenging. In my own journey as a supervisor, I take risks by challenging myself and my supervisees to see both the visible and the invisible. I try to find the suitable approach for each one of my supervisees and change it according to their needs and growth. During a supervision session, I try to pay attention to my mind, body, and soul. Usually, my mind is very busy with lots of questions and dilemmas that come up for me: what to bring to the center and what to put aside; what to say and what to notice but not say; when to let the music speak and when to let my supervisee keep talking; when is the right time for particular interventions and responses. My body "speaks." Sometimes it aches or becomes stiff, tense, or numb; at other times, I notice that my heart beats faster or slower. And there are times when my soul takes me to a different direction—I find myself day-dreaming, alert like I am in a different cosmos or in a very quiet, sleeping mode. I try to let my intuition decide where to go, when to change focus, and how to intervene. I try to pay attention to the way I talk and play in supervision. I find that suggestions and questions are better than clear sentences that are said with confidence, such as "You might want to work on it in your own therapy" instead of "You should pay attention to it" or "Would you like to explore this issue musically?" instead of "I want you to play music in order to explore this."

As in therapy, I need to tune myself before the session. I remind myself that each supervisee is unique, and I try to look for the things that I like and appreciate in each and every one in order to create a positive and welcoming atmosphere. I need to tune myself during the session, to listen and try to understand what is going on in the session. I also need to stay a few minutes after the session to listen to myself and to reflect and process my thoughts, feelings, and reactions, sometimes musically, at other times by writing. Every once in a while, I have to go to supervision myself, in order to share my feelings and thoughts and talk things over with another supervisor. Supervision is a journey of two. It is like an improvised song: It creates itself in the here-and-now, out of material from the past. It starts from a specific title, a word, or a sentence and travels to the unknown.

REFERENCE LIST

Alonso, A. (1985). *The Quiet Profession: Supervisors of Psychotherapy.* New York, NY: Macmillan.

Amir, D. (2001). The Journey of Two: Supervision for the New Music Therapist Working in an Educational Setting. In M. Forinash (Ed.), *Music Therapy Supervision* (pp. 163–178). Gilsum, NH: Barcelona Publishers.

Amir, D. (2010). Music-centered supervision: the role and meaning of music in music therapy supervision. (In Hebrew). *Mifgash, 32,* 9–29.

Austin, D., & Dvorkin, J. (2001). Peer supervision in music therapy. In M. Forinash (Ed.), *Music Therapy Supervision* (pp. 219–230). Gilsum, NH: Barcelona Publishers.

Bond, M., & Holland, S. (1998). *Skills of Clinical Supervision: A Practical Guide for Supervisees, Clinical Supervisors and Managers.* Buckingham, UK: Open University Press.

Brown, S. (1997). Supervision in context: a balancing act. *British Journal of Music Therapy, 11*(1), 4–12.

Brown, S. (2009). Supervision in context: a balancing act. In H. Odell-Miller & E. Richards (Eds.), *Supervision of music therapy* (pp. 119–134). London, UK: Routledge.

De la Torre, J., & Appelbaum, A. (1974). Use and misuse of clichés in clinical supervision. *Arch Gen Psych, 31*(9), 302–306.

Feiner, S. (2010). What is Happening to Me? The Potential for Activation of Trauma During Music Therapy Internship. In K. Stewart (Ed.), *Music Therapy & Trauma: Bridging Theory and Clinical Practice.* New York, NY: Satchnote Press.

Grinberg, L. (1990). *The Goals of Psychoanalysis: Identification, Identity, and Supervision.* London, UK: Karnac Books.

Idelsohn, A. Z. (1929). *Jewish Music and its Historical Development.* New York, NY: Tudor Publishing Company.

Hajdu, A., & Mazor, Y. (1972) The musical tradition of Hasidism. *Encyclopedia Judaica,* (Vol. 7, pp. 1421–1432). Jerusalem: Keter Publishing Company.

Jackson, N. A. (2008). Professional music therapy supervision: a survey. *Journal of Music Therapy, 45*(2), 192–216. doi:10.1093/jmt/45.2.192

Kilminster, S. M., & Jolly, B. C. (2000). Effective supervision in clinical practice settings: a literature review. *Med Educ, 34*(10), 827–840.

Mahoney, E. R. (2015). Multicultural Music Therapy: An Exploration. *Voices: A World Forum for Music Therapy, 15*(2). doi:10.15845/voices.v15i2.844

Power, S. (1999). *Nursing supervision.* Thousand Oaks, CA: SAGE.

Scheiby, B. B. (2001). Forming an identity as a music psychotherapist through analytical music therapy. In M. Forinash (Ed.), *Music therapy supervision* (pp. 299–334). Gilsum, NH: Barcelona Publishers.

Sloan, G. (2005). Clinical supervision: beginning the supervisory relationship. *British Journal of Nursing, 14*(17).

Small, C. (1998). *Musicking: the meanings of performing and listening.* Hanover, NH, & London, UK: University Press of New England.

Stephens, G. (1984). Group Supervision in Music Therapy. *Music Therapy, 4*(1), 29–38.

Stige, B., & Kenny, C. (2002). Introduction—The Turn to Culture. In C. Kenny & B. Stige (Eds.), *Contemporary Voices in Music Therapy* (pp. 13–31). Oslo, Norway: Unipub Forlag.

Young, L., & Aigen, K. (2010). Supervising the supervisor: the use of live music and identification of parallel processes. *The Arts in Psychotherapy, 37*(2), 125–134.

Turry, A. (2001). Supervision in Nordoff-Robbins training program. In M. Forinash (Ed.), *Music therapy supervision* (pp. 351–378). Gilsum, NH: Barcelona Publishers.

Zur, O. (2001). Out-of-Office Experience: When crossing office boundaries and engaging in dual relationships are clinically beneficial and ethically sound. *The Independent Practitioner, 21*(1), 96–100.

Chapter 13

PEER SUPERVISION FOR NEW PROFESSIONALS

Charlay Yates
Kevin Kozik
Jessica Triana
Gwendolyn Van Baalen
Amanda Weldin
Kristina Lessard

INTRODUCTION

The transition from "student intern" to "certified professional" can leave new therapists feeling overwhelmed, as they may receive little academic, socio-emotional, professional, or supervisory support as compared to the supervision and mentorship received throughout education or certification programs. Research on the effects of peer supervision for music therapists is uncommon, as is that on the effects of supervision for new professional music therapists.

In the spring of 2015, the authors formed a peer supervision group for music therapists in transition to provide mutual support and guidance as they transitioned from their graduate studies in music therapy and mental health counseling to careers in the field. This framework will be identified as Peer Supervision for New Professionals or PSNP. Its creation grew organically out of discussions between graduate-level courses that often led the authors to offer resources and share experiences.

As the authors transitioned into the professional world and left behind many of the organized supports offered by school, a space for continuing supervision, support, and resource sharing was needed. The authors are aware of similar collaborations, such as the group described by Baratta et al. in the first edition of this book (2000). However, the authors of this chapter questioned why continuing peer supervision is not a typical experience in the field, seemingly leaving a portion of new clinicians to navigate transitional challenges alone.

This group was formed from members of the same cohort from a clinical mental health counseling and music therapy graduate program. The members of PSNP worked in a variety of settings, including medical, psychiatric, educational, outpatient mental health, in-home therapy, and memory care, with individuals across the life span, and addressed a multitude of diagnoses and goals. The racial, gender, and age makeup of the group was largely homogenous. Five members identified as Caucasian and one identified as African-American. Five members identified as female and one identified as male. There was a difference of four years between the youngest and oldest members of the group. Additionally, members of the group identified differences in geographic regions of origin within the United States, with five members originating from the East Coast and one from the Mountain West. In terms of other markers of religious and cultural background, one member identified as ethnically and culturally Jewish, one member identified as a practicing Catholic, one member identified as a nonpracticing Catholic with a strong history of involvement in the Catholic Church, and three members identified as secular. All members identified as cis-gendered, heterosexual individuals.

This chapter will address the existence and necessity of peer supervision, present the structure of a peer supervision group for music therapists in transition, and share themes and experiences that arrived during the PSNP group as well as the major benefits group members received from participation in the group.

WHAT IS PEER SUPERVISION?

Wilkerson (2006) defined peer supervision as a "structured, supportive process in which counselor colleagues (or trainees), in pairs or in groups, use their professional knowledge and relationship expertise to monitor practice and effectiveness on a regular basis for the purpose of improving specific counseling, conceptualizations, and theoretical skills" (p. 6). Various definitions of peer supervision "highlight the establishment of ongoing and regular relationships that focus on the enhancement of professional skills" (p. 5).

According to Mastoras (2011), group supervision may provide "unique opportunities for obtaining multiple perspectives, peer-to-peer learning, [and] exposure to a greater number of clients and may reduce the experience of supervisee anxiety" (p. 102). For new professionals still in the early stages of learning, these benefits can be invaluable.

SUPERVISION FOR NEW HELPING PROFESSIONALS
CURRENT SUPERVISION PRACTICES

The term "new professional" suggests that an individual will be experiencing certain situations for the first time and will therefore be in need of guidance from a more seasoned professional. Supervision provides avenues for inquiry and vicarious learning through mentorships with professionals. According to O'Keefe (2014), "the overall aim of professional supervision is to develop the competence, creativity, confidence, and compassion of the participants" (p. 994).

The content of supervision hours is largely left up to the individual supervisors and supervisees. Several studies examined characteristics and trends in supervision for new professions. Barham and Winston (2006) proposed that a significant amount of supervision content for new professional school counselors focused on administrative issues, rather than clinical or professional growth. Furthermore, new professionals reported that their supervision was not meeting their needs and there seemed to be a lack of understanding regarding the content of supervision, evaluation, and mentorship (2006).

Barham and Winston (2006) similarly identified several trends and potential problems with the quality of supervision for new professionals in student affairs. Researchers found that new professionals often experience difficulty in identifying and communicating their needs in supervision, and supervisors with less supervision experience struggle to identify the needs of new professionals. Additionally, researchers found a disconnection between the new professionals' and supervisors' perspectives on the needs being addressed in supervision. Furthermore, researchers propose that the supervision needs of new professionals are frequently not addressed by continuing professional development. The researchers concluded by calling for increased education of qualified supervisors of new professionals. These studies suggest that new professionals' experiences in supervision vary widely based on the structure of supervision in their individual workplace and on their supervisor (2006). Notably, research in this area has focused on supervision for new professionals in the fields of education and nursing.

THE TRANSITION PROCESS

The authors believed that their experiences of transition had parallels to the transition that new nurses experience. In order to provide the appropriate support for new music therapists, it is important to assess the challenges an individual faces when transitioning from student to new professional.

Duchscher (2009) defined the experience of moving from the known role of a student to a relatively less familiar role of professional nurse as "transition shock" (p. 1013). This experience highlights the contrast between the academic setting and the professional practice setting.

Duchscher (2009) identified stages that new nurses go through when transitioning from students to professionals. During the initial stage of transition, or "doing" stage, she highlighted the range, overwhelming intensity, and labile nature of the emotions expressed, but also identified them as being relatively predictable. Duchscher (2009) noted that participants felt ill-prepared for the toll the transition would take on their personal energy and time and on their evolving professional self-concepts. While anticipating some adjustment would be necessary, they assumed their choice of career would be affirmed through a positive work experience (2009).

Bridges (1991) claimed that young nursing professionals generally have limited practical experience, lack social and developmental maturity, and struggle with basic clinical and work management skills (e.g., communicating with and delegating to others and balancing time with responsibilities and tasks). Dearmun (2000) and Duchscher (2001) claimed that the initial three months of newly graduated nurses' transition is consumed by an adjustment to new roles and responsibilities, an acceptance of the differences between the theoretical orientation of their education and the practical focus of their professional work, and their integration into an environment that emphasizes teamwork as opposed to individually based care provision. Many of these challenges translate to challenges the authors faced during transition and needed to address in supervision.

WHY IS PEER SUPERVISION BENEFICIAL?

Although infrequently mentioned in the literature, benefits of group peer supervision for music therapists can be linked to greater job satisfaction, improved self-care, career longevity, and burnout prevention (Oppenheim, 1987; Salmon & Stewart, 2005). The following factors have been correlated with positive job satisfaction: longevity in the field, client progress, peer support, and engagement in personal and professional development (Cohen & Behring, 2002; Stewart, 2000; Vega, 2010). Furthermore, Smith and Steindler (1983) recommended that professionals who encounter highly challenging patients regularly collaborate with other professionals. Peers may offer comments and insight into client progress and working with "difficult patients" that may be overlooked by clinicians when working alone. Leon, Altholz, and Dziegielewski (1999) cautioned that countertransference issues may be contributors to stress and burnout. Their work supported professional and group supervision as effective practices for identifying, addressing, decreasing, and preventing threats to career longevity.

In a national survey investigating self-care practices and awareness of self-care needs among music therapists, 95% of participants reported consistently practicing self-care and using music outside of the workplace and cited the following benefits of musical self-care: support of general coping mechanisms, enhancement of relaxation, rejuvenation of energy, release of stress, ability to use music as an emotional outlet and distraction, facilitation of self-expression, and stabilization of the individual (Salmon & Stewart, 2005). Norman (2009) also found that music therapists who participate in deliberate musical self-care generally have higher levels of engagement in their work when compared to those who do not. Music can be incorporated to process common issues that arise during supervision.

There exists a multitude of issues that affect when and how music therapists leave the field. Music therapy clinicians may choose to leave the field based on problems or pressures in personal life, unrealistic workloads, boredom or lack of motivation, insufficient pay, the absence of adequate support networks or outside interests, the limited job market, lack of staff recognition, limited opportunities for advancement, lack of autonomy, adjustments due to crisis intervention, micromanagement, lack of administrative support, having to perform activities outside of the field, lack of respect and direction, and/or compromising ideals (Clements-Cortes, 2013; Green, Albanese, Shapiro, & Aarons, 2014; Kennelly, Daveson, & Baker, 2016).

Salmon and Stewart (2005) identified common and frequent coping strategies within the data they collected, including creative expression, spiritual practice, exercise, collegial support, and social interactions outside of work. Self-care is also recurrently mentioned in the literature in the form of professional or peer supervision and consultation. Supervision is more valued by music therapists who participate in supervision, although the majority of music therapists feel that it is "at least moderately important" (Jackson, 2008). Oppenheim (1987) suggested preventative measures to burnout, including professional counseling, in-service health training, nutrition and stress management, daily exercise, hobbies, sleep, continued learning, maintenance of unscheduled leisure hours, termination of unhealthy relationships, goal-setting, and peer support and discussion.

Specifically planned self-care maintenance is necessary for all practicing music therapy clinicians. Swezey (2013) recommended that music therapy professionals take the time to assess work stressors and strategies (in a variety of self-care domains, including psychological, physical, and spiritual) to promote professional well-being. Knoll, Reuer, and Henry (1988) also argued for specific steps toward stress management. They suggested clearly defining the specific problem, listing all alternative solutions, evaluating each option, and then moving forward to resolve the situation. Supervision provides an opportunity to navigate these steps.

FOUNDATION FOR FRAMEWORK

The authors, members of PSNP, discovered the need for an organizing framework early in the life of the group. As others have done, the authors noted that peer supervision groups have the potential to be unproductive and unhelpful if they lack structure or goals. Additionally, groups deteriorate if there is an inability to maintain a common focus. Most models of peer or group supervision, including both scholarly articles and models practiced by training programs and universities, acknowledge the importance of providing a structure to organize and optimize the functioning of these groups.

Borders (1991) emphasized the importance of providing a structure for peer supervision groups in order to maximize the benefits of peer feedback. Borders (1991) offered a specific procedure in her framework, including identifying questions about clinical practice, assigning roles in processing clinical material, providing feedback, further discussion, and summary. Borders (1991) also identified the importance of considering mutual goals in designing a framework.

Malchiodi (1996) offered guidelines for providing a structure for peer supervision and suggested determining a set meeting time and the interval of meetings. Additionally, the author advocated for the selection of group members who are similar in caliber, professional stature, and level of training. Finally, she suggested designing a consistent strategy of allocating time in meetings and designating leadership for each meeting. Additionally, she observed, the structure of groups is most effective when based on mutual goals.

PSNP FRAMEWORK

The framework developed by PSNP provides structure around membership, length and frequency of meetings, assignment of roles and leadership, and the content of meetings. The membership of the group formed organically to include members of similar professional caliber from the same cohort in a graduate training program. Further deliberation was needed only to decide on limitations on the size of the group, which was determined to be a maximum of six members. The authors considered their schedules, the level of content to be covered in meetings, and the base level of support needed to facilitate professional growth. The group established a flexible biweekly (twice-monthly) frequency of meetings that would allow for regular continued support without overwhelming the authors with an overly demanding schedule. In order to allow sufficient time for the intended content of these meetings, 1.5 to 2 hours was allotted for each.

In order to provide for the clear definition of roles in each meeting, it was determined that a leader and secretary would be assigned on a rotating basis. This allowed each member to regularly serve in both roles. This strategy attempted to ensure that responsibility is vested in members equitably and provides opportunity for richer, more diverse subject matter to emerge under the guidance of rotating leaders. Influenced by Malchiodi's (1996) description, the leader was assigned the role of moderating the group, keeping everyone on track, designing an agenda for the meeting, ensuring that everyone was heard, timekeeping, and summarizing feedback. The role of secretary involved taking minutes and providing snacks. Additionally, the secretary would become the leader at the following meeting. This pattern of role succession allowed for advanced preparation in the leadership role.

CONTENT OF MEETINGS/ MEETING AGENDA

A structure for the content of each meeting was developed to address the most salient topics in each meeting and to optimize continuity between meetings. These components include professional membership, professional competencies, and supervision. The goal of each meeting was to offer support in each of the three components, moving from a broad view of music therapy as a profession to a specific personal view of the group members as music therapists and people.

Professional Membership

As defined by this framework, the professional membership component provided an opportunity to discuss important changes, updates, shifts, and opportunities in governing bodies and the profession in its entirety (globally, internationally, nationally, regionally, and locally). Group members shared information related to upcoming conferences, dues, and resources from conferences and other pertinent trainings. This may have included the presentation or discussion of information relevant to the group's professional organizations.

Professional Competencies

Professional competencies are designed to support and enrich the knowledge and skills necessary to be a professional music therapist and offer the highest level of care to present and future clients. This includes sharing resources that keep group members up to date in their practice, including interventions and directives. This element of the framework has proven to be particularly valuable, as members of PSNP often do not work closely with other colleagues of their discipline.

To address professional competencies, the meeting's leader prepared to share resources or techniques or to facilitate discussion around a particular topic that would contribute to the group's level of knowledge and clinical skill. Examples of topics addressed in meetings include useful chord progressions or drumming techniques, as well as new research around a relevant topic such as self-care or trauma-informed practices. The members of PSNP each work in dissimilar settings and with unique populations and thus able to provide a variety of resources and techniques that are relevant at their respective sites and that other members may not have yet encountered. This directly addresses the need for members to continue to deepen and further their understanding of the field and to practice and build clinical skills.

Check-ins/Crises

The final component of the meeting, supervision, is where the authors examined and offered support in professional issues and development and is usually the bulk of discussion during the meeting. Areas that are often discussed include self-care, burnout, employer pressures, difficult clients or cases, and isolation. This component allows each member to "check in" by sharing with the group current struggles or "crises" or accomplishments or requesting feedback about a specific issue encountered at work. This component often serves as a launching point for discussions based on ethical questions, case studies, and/or requests for specific resources.

RE-EVALUATIONS OF GROUP NEEDS

As Borders (1991) suggested, the group considered mutual goals in the process of designing a framework for the group. These goals focused on professional priorities and emphasized areas of support needed to supplement professional supervision and development. As the group has grown and progressed, it has also become necessary to structure ongoing evaluations of the effectiveness of the model. This is accomplished by considering the present professional goals and priorities of group members and discussing the extent to which the framework is accommodating them. To articulate how this framework was effective for the members involved, the authors worked together to document personal/professional challenges and stressors in the transition period from student to new professional and if/how they were supported by PSNP inside and outside of the bimonthly meetings.

FORMATION AND EARLY STAGES

The members of PSNP specifically note several ways in which participation in the group has been helpful since its formation in 2015. One primary benefit the authors have unanimously noted is support in identifying and pursuing the next steps of professional development. The members of PSNP began meeting before the culmination of graduate study and originally convened to support the successful completion of each participant's thesis, a requirement for graduation in this program of study. Next, PSNP members studied together for the music therapy certification test and supported one another as each participant signed up for and took the exam. Once that step had been completed, the focus of the group shifted toward seeking employment in the field. The authors of this chapter were able to consult with one another regarding whether potential job placements would ultimately support larger career goals and compare notes about logistics such as job specifications, salary, and benefits.

Now that the authors of this chapter have been out of school and working for over two years, focus has again shifted for some members of the group to the pursuit of licensure and support around taking the Massachusetts Mental Health Counselors Association Licensed Mental Health Counseling examination and the specific requirements of applying for the LMHC. Due to the diversity in workplace and career goals among the participants of PSNP, not all members are currently pursuing licensure, but participants do note that it is helpful to have the support of a team when trying to keep track of various deadlines and requirements and that participation in the group is helpful for accountability.

IDENTITY AND ISOLATION

In addition to support around navigating the logistical requirements of becoming a new professional, PSNP members also use the group to address issues associated with forming and solidifying a professional identity. Most members of PSNP are the sole music therapist present at their work site(s).

Some do not work with any other expressive therapists at all and are the only representative of expressive therapies at their workplace. This experience is not unique among music therapists or other expressive therapists, and the feelings of isolation as well as the felt responsibility to constantly educate coworkers are both reasons cited by music therapists as contributors to burnout (Clements-Cortes, 2013). One member of PSNP has continually had to advocate for increased funding and the presence of music therapy at the setting where she is employed. Another, as the only music therapist at her site, struggles to respond to the high volume of referrals for music therapy evaluations she receives while also balancing her own established caseload. Almost every member of PSNP has shared stories of feeling pressured to pick up clients even when schedules do not allow because a specific client has expressed interest in music, even though interest in music does not necessarily indicate that music therapy would be the most effective treatment option.

Bringing these experiences to PSNP allowed members to reconnect to the community of music therapists they lack at their respective workplaces. Sharing these and other similar anecdotes with each other was validating. Group members were able to work together to brainstorm how to navigate each of the above situations in ways that took into account workplace politics but that were ultimately focused on advocacy for both self and the field in general.

Another issue that PSNP needed to address, as members began to get jobs in the field, was the issue of supervision. While some members had supervision provided for them at job sites, about half of the group needed to find outside supervision. PSNP shared resources and recommendations in order to assist members in trying to connect to outside supervisors and pored over LMHC supervision requirements to ensure that all criteria were being met. Some of the members who did not have to find outside supervision are being supervised by social workers or clinicians with totally different theoretical underpinnings. It has occasionally been a struggle to communicate the relevancy of the expressive arts in a clinical setting, making effective supervision around music therapy interventions difficult.

INCORPORATING THE ARTS

PSNP has proven to be an essential resource for connection to the arts and music in clinical practice for the authors of this chapter. Most courses in the music therapy graduate program at Lesley University incorporated some kind of music or art experiential in every class, so the members of the group were constantly engaging in music and the arts during school. Since graduation, it has required more of an effort to maintain a practice of music-making and artistic expression, both in self-care and in a clinical context. Group members are encouraged to bring arts interventions to PSNP meetings and share strategies that have been working in practice to share with the group. The "clinical competencies" portion of meetings has focused on increasing instrumental proficiencies, including work on drumming patterns and guitar chords. When members of PSNP gather socially, active music-making for fun and enjoyment is often engaged in to encourage connection to personal use of music for self-care.

SELF-CARE

Self-care practice was frequently addressed in meetings as well, as it has been established that a practice of self-care is essential for new professionals in order to prevent burnout and vicarious trauma (Killian, 2008). Members of PSNP bring resources connected to this issue to meetings to encourage discussion of self-care practice and to increase awareness of signs of burnout. One member of PSNP attended an event focused on vicarious trauma and provided handouts to the group. These handouts prompted a discussion about ways that vicarious trauma impact functioning both in and out of work, and each member reflected on ways this new material resonated with personal experience. Group members then assigned self-care "homework" to each other and followed up about it at the next meeting. One member of PSNP noted that it is beneficial not only to have a place to share work-related challenges and experiences, but also "when the other group members reflect back to you that you seem stressed; it makes it easier to acknowledge it and do something about it."

PSNP members also make it a point to gather specifically for socializing and doing fun things just for the sake of having fun, with no discussion of work-related topics whatsoever. For example, three members of the group have birthdays within a week of each other, and it has become a tradition to celebrate together. PSNP members also participate in "secret snowflake" gift-giving during the holiday season and make an effort to go out to eat or go bowling at other points during the year. While these activities are first and foremost fun self-care activities unrelated to work, this time together also strengthens the relationships between PSNP members. These strong relationships and knowledge of one another's likes, dislikes, strengths, and needs, in both a clinical setting and a personal setting, improves the quality of the supervision offered in PSNP meetings. When a member presents a case or asks for supervision around an issue, they receive individualized feedback that takes into account their specific skill set and style, making it more likely that it will be helpful and effective.

EXPOSURE TO DIFFERENT PROFESSIONAL/PERSONAL POINTS OF VIEW

The authors of this chapter also report the benefit of receiving supervision from a group of individuals working with different populations and doing different types of clinical work. The participants in PSNP work in medical, psychiatric, educational, memory-care, and community mental health settings with clients at all stages in the life span and at different levels of acuity. When one member brings a case to share in the group, the other participants are able to provide a wide variety of resources, clinical formulations, and ideas for treatment due to each participant's unique experience in the field. The supervision provided in PSNP is comprehensive and inclusive, allowing each member to expand their "clinical toolbox" at a time in their career when it is essential to do so.

ETHICS

PSNP has also proven to be a valuable space where members can present and receive support around ethical quandaries. For example, establishing appropriate clinical and personal boundaries when you are providing outreach services in someone's home is an issue that has been brought to the group. How do you balance maintaining an appropriate clinical relationship while also establishing rapport in the intimate setting of someone's home? One member who does such work described the challenge of working with an interpreter who did not have the same understanding of appropriate clinical boundaries and the challenge of maintaining a professional relationship without seeming cold and damaging rapport with the client. PSNP was able to brainstorm approaches to handling this complicated situation, and ultimately that member was able to address it in a way that felt comfortable to her.

Another issue that has come up is the issue of working with coworkers who play music and do therapy but are not music therapists. How do you address this in a way that protects the profession and the clients who may be negatively impacted by misuse of music in therapy while also being mindful of professional relationships? Also, there is the challenge of running into clients or former clients in the community who ask for clinical support on the fly. How do you manage a situation when you feel obligated to help the person standing in front of you, but it is outside of your role and inappropriate to get involved? PSNP discusses these issues in meetings and is a valuable resource when members are facing complicated clinical situations.

MULTICULTURAL ISSUES

At least one course specific to multicultural issues is often a requirement for preparation for licensure as a mental health professional. Every individual involved in the therapeutic process possesses a unique culture, composed of a myriad of components from skin color and religion to political affiliation and communication style. Additionally, these "cultural, racial-ethnic aspects shape core assumptions, attitudes, and values of the persons involved and may enhance or impede counselor effectiveness" (Fong, 1994, p. 13). As mentioned earlier, the demographic of this group was largely homogeneous in terms of identified race, gender, sexual orientation, and age. It is possible that Bernard and Goodyear's (1992) concept "myth of sameness" was prevalent during peer supervision sessions. This concept claims that the majority cultural patterns held by group members are accepted by the group without pause or thought. The group members did frequently acknowledge differences in the personal experiences, worldviews, and philosophies of music therapy and counseling. During peer supervision meetings, the group members presented and addressed multicultural issues within their clinical practice, including:

- difficulty with differences in language and communication styles
- learning how to manage interpreter involvement in the therapeutic process
- navigating in-home therapy sessions with clients of a different culture
- expanding musical repertoire and understanding appropriateness and implications of song use
- identifying the influence of the therapist's culture in professional and clinical relationships
- recovering from accidentally insulting or offending a client due to the therapist's lack of cultural awareness (microaggression)

This PSNP model allowed space and time to generate awareness, discussion, and analysis of multicultural issues. Being new professionals, the group members had clinical experiences that were limited, impacting the breadth and quality of peer supervision around these issues and perpetuating the "myth of sameness." It is critical that the group members continue to seek education, consultation, and supervision opportunities with a multicultural emphasis to address gaps in current knowledge and experience.

CONCLUSION

As students, the authors all experienced anxiety over completing a thesis and attempting to meet requirements for clinical internships with the additional pressure of finding a job. The social support and encouragement received from peers in PSNP provided the authors with motivation. Similarly, setting goals from meeting to meeting kept the authors accountable to both the group and their own growth in the profession. Assigning the authors certain articles to read, or certain "assignments" to complete, has motivated us to develop professionally because others were depending on our doing so.

On many occasions, the authors have all needed to ask the advice of the group, regarding both professional and personal choices. If any of the authors is undecided or challenged by the next step necessary in a client's course of treatment, the resource of five other people with different perspectives and experience in working with different populations is available. If the authors are challenged by personal choices regarding the next step in their career, such as whether to leave or take a certain job, the advice of five other people who are in a similar situation of trying to develop their new professional identities is available. Once the authors have secured a professional position and passed the national board certification exam, the group supported members through the challenges that come with transitioning into a novel, demanding job; navigating licensing requirements and ethical issues in practice; balancing work and self-care; exploring multiple aspects of changing professional identities; and advancing clinical knowledge and skills.

Additionally, the authors kept each other informed about professional growth opportunities that otherwise would have gone undiscovered. The post-graduation job search experience can feel overwhelming because of the whole process of searching, applying, and interviewing for jobs and studying for the music therapy boards. Each new, challenging case brought to a meeting is an opportunity to hear from five capable individuals with a diverse set of skills, strengths, and experiences with different populations and to brainstorm new solutions that the individual would not have previously considered. This process also helped to develop the ability to diagnose and create a treatment plan.

Meetings often dealt with high-stress topics, but the humor, lightness, and refreshments helped to alleviate some of the anxious atmosphere surrounding these issues. In a period of transition, when graduate school comes to an end and a professional career begins, it has been grounding to be involved in something consistent.

REFERENCE LIST

Baratta, E., Bertolami, M., Hubbard, A., MacDonald, M. C., & Spragg, D. (2001). Peer supervision in the development of the new music and expressive therapist. In M. Forinash (Ed.), *Music therapy supervision*. Gilsum, NH: Barcelona Publishers.

Barham, J. D., & Winston, R. B., Jr. (2006). Supervision of new professionals in student affairs: Assessing and addressing needs. *The College Student Affairs Journal, 26*(1), 64–89.

Bernard, J. M., & Goodyear, R. K. (1992). Fundamentals of clinical supervision. Boston, MA: Allyn and Bacon.

Bitcon, C. (1981). Guest editorial. *Journal of Music Therapy, 18*, 2–6.

Borders, L. D. (1991). A Systematic Approach to Peer Group Supervision. *Journal of Counseling & Development, 69*, 248–252.

Bridges, W. (1991). *Managing transitions: Making the most of change*. Reading, MA: Addison-Wesley.

Chopra, T. (2013). All supervision is multicultural: A review of literature on the need for multicultural supervision in counseling. *Psychological Studies, 58*(3), 335–338.

Clements-Cortes, A. (2013). Burnout in music therapists: Work, individual, and social factors. *Music Therapy Perspectives, 31*(2), 166–174.

Cohen, N., & Behrens. G. A. (2002). The relationship between type of degree and professional status in clinical music therapists. *Journal of Music Therapy, 39*, 188–208.

Dearmun, A. (2000). Supporting newly qualified staff nurses: the Lecturer Practitioner contribution. *Journal of Nursing Management, 8*(3), 159–165.

Duchscher, J. B. (2009). Transition shock: The initial stage or role adaptation for newly graduated registered nurses. *Journal of Advanced Nursing, 65*(5), 1103–1113.

Duchscher, J. E. B. (2001). Out in the real world: newly graduated nurses in acute care speak out. *Journal of Nursing Administration, 31*(9), 426–439.

Fong, M. L. (1994). *Multicultural issues in supervision*. ERIC Digest. Greensboro, NC: ERIC Clearinghouse on Counseling and Student Services.

Green, A. E., Albanese, B. J., Shapiro, N. M., & Aarons, G. A. (2014). The roles of individual and organizational factors in burnout among community-based mental health service providers. *Psychological Services, 11*(1), 41–49. doi:10.1037/a0035299

Jackson, N. A. (2008). Professional music therapy supervision: A survey. *Journal of Music Therapy*, *45*(2), 192–215.

Killian, K. D. (2008). Helping till it hurts? A multimethod study of compassion fatigue, burnout, and self-care in clinicians working with trauma survivors. *Traumatology*, *14*(2), 32–44. doi:10.1177/1534765608319083

Knoll, C., Reuer, B., & Henry, D. (1988). Working ways: Tips for job success. *Music Therapy Perspectives*, *5*, 119–120.

Leon, A. M., Altholz, J. A., & Dziegielewski, S. F. (1999). Compassion fatigue: Considerations for working with the elderly. *Journal of Gerontological Social Work*, *32*(1), 43–62.

Malchiodi, C. (1996). *Peer supervision. Supervision and related issues: A handbook for professionals.* Chicago, IL: Magnolia Street.

Mastoras, S. M., & Andrews, J. W. (2011). The supervisee experience of group supervision: Implications for research and practice. *Training and Education in Professional Psychology*, *5*(2), 102–111. doi:10.1037/a0023567

Norman, R. (2009). *The relationship between music therapists' personal use of music and work engagement.* Unpublished master's thesis, Saint Mary-of-the-Woods College, Saint Mary-of-the-Woods, IN.

O'Keeffe, M., & James, F. (2014). Facilitated group supervision: Harnessing the power of peers. *Journal of Paediatrics & Child Health*, *50*(12), 944–948. doi:10.1111/jpc.12638

Oppenheim, L. (1987). Factors related to occupational stress or burnout among music therapists. *Journal of Music Therapy*, *24*, 97–106.

Salmon, D., & Stewart, K.. (2005). The role of music therapy in care for the caregivers of the terminally ill. In C. Dileo & J. V. Loewy (Eds.), *Music therapy at the end of life* (pp. 239–250). Cherry Hill, NJ: Jeffrey Books.

Smith, R. J., & Steindler, E. M. (1983). The impact of difficult patients upon treaters: Consequences and remedies. *Bulletin of the Menninger Clinic, 47*(2), 107–116.

Stewart, D. (2000). The state of the UK music therapy profession: personal qualities, working models, support networks, and job satisfaction. *British Journal of Music Therapy, 14*(1), 13–31.

Swezey, S. C. (2013). *What keeps us well? Professional quality of life and career-sustaining behaviors of music therapy professionals.* Theses and Dissertations—Music. 17. Master's thesis, University of Kentucky, Lexington, KY. https://uknowledge.uky.edu/music_etds/17

Vega, V. (2010). Personality, burnout, and longevity among professional music therapists. *Journal of Music Therapy, 47*(2), 155–179.

Wilkerson, K. (2006). Peer Supervision for the Professional Development of School Counselors: Toward an Understanding of Terms and Findings. *Counselor Education and Supervision, 46*(1), 59.

Chapter 14

CULTURALLY RESPONSIVE ACADEMIC SUPERVISION IN MUSIC THERAPY

Sangeeta Swamy
Seung-A Kim

We are all in the human condition. Who would deny that?
This condition can be used as we choose.
It brings us home to paradox (Kenny, 2006, p. 98).

As academic supervisors of music therapy fieldwork students and interns, we play many roles. At a minimum, we provide a safe place for students to share their fears, vulnerabilities, and reflections, take risks, and explore new musical and preprofessional identities. We also are responsible for balancing this support with challenge and growth, evaluating and grading student supervisees' progress and competence. In many programs, academic supervisors are also responsible for curriculum and education, assigning related readings, papers, and projects. In addition, academic supervisors serve as advocates and liaisons between universities and internship or practicum sites and often provide necessary resources for students.

However, as the student body in the United States increasingly grows to include international music therapy students as well as students from a variety of sociocultural backgrounds, many questions arise from academic supervisors (Kim, 2013a; Kim, Sairam, Shapiro, & Swamy, 2012). How do we evaluate student supervisees in a way that is sensitive and responsive to their own sociocultural backgrounds? How can we adequately support minority supervisees at an individual as well as a systemic level? How do we keep supervision discussions safe from racism, sexism, and homophobia and facilitate awareness and learning around these topics? How do social forces of isolationism, anti-immigrant policies, xenophobia, Islamophobia, and an increase in racism and white supremacy affect our supervisees and their clients, and what is our responsibility to address this in supervision? In internship and fieldwork settings, how do we distinguish supervisees' personal and clinical deficiencies from culturally different expectations and communication styles? In addition, how can we best support supervisees for whom English is a second or third language, and what are reasonable expectations for these supervisees? What is our responsibility to adjust existing supervision approaches and curricula to meet the needs of international students and cultural and ethnic minorities? How should we teach and guide supervisees who may not ultimately practice music therapy in the United States? While these questions are relevant for all academic supervisors, this chapter may be particularly beneficial for supervisors from privileged sociocultural backgrounds who are working with minority student supervisees.

Many of these questions do not necessarily have simple or easy answers. However, in this chapter, we will share important concepts, issues, and suggestions that we have found helpful regarding the academic supervisory relationship, illustrated by personal and case examples,[18] literature, and research. This includes important qualities for academic supervisors to develop, such

---

[18] In some instances, names and identifying information in case examples have been changed in order to protect the identity of supervisors and supervisees.

as cultural sensitivity, cultural competence, cultural humility, cultural empathy, cultural self-reflexivity, and cultural responsiveness. We also address the importance of understanding power and privilege dynamics and responsively facilitating sociocultural discussions in academic supervision groups. In addition, we provide practical and systemic suggestions for supporting international supervisees and cultural and ethnic minorities in academic settings and discuss the role of ethnic identity in the supervisory process. Last, we offer suggestions and recommendations from our own experiences as academic supervisors and educators. We draw from our own personal and professional experiences as a first-generation, Korean-American, immigrant, music therapy educator (Seung-A Kim) and a second generation, Indian-American, middle-class, able-bodied, queer and gender-nonconforming music therapy educator (Sangeeta Swamy).

OVERVIEW

Sometimes the terms "race," "culture," and "ethnicity" are used interchangeably. However, they are distinct concepts. The term *culture* has historically referred to patterns of meaning-making, shared beliefs, customs, and behaviors by a specific group. "We tend to think of culture as fixed entities defined by ethnic or geographical borders: Maasai culture, Hispanic culture, Asian culture, etc." (Stige, 2002, p. 1). However, it is important to note that cultural identity is not necessarily the same as national identity, nor is culture quite the same as ethnicity. *Ethnicity* has historically been defined more essentially, referring to common membership from a shared genetic or specific ancestral connection (Jenkins, 2008). *Race* has been historically defined according to shared biological characteristics, such as skin color and physical features. However, these concepts are not fixed or concrete and cannot necessarily be measured or defined by geographic, biological, or ancestral boundaries. In this chapter, therefore, race, ethnicity, and culture are considered social constructions (Hoshmand, 2006; Kenny & Stige, 2002). In other words, each supervisee will experience their race, culture, and ethnicity uniquely. For example, a student supervisee may identify culturally as American, ethnically with a regional, caste or religious identity and racially as white, Asian, black or another race.

We also use the terms *students of color* and *ethnic and cultural minorities* to represent various nonwhite student supervisee groups who not only may be minorities numerically, but also face discrimination and racism in mainstream society. In addition, race, culture, and ethnicity intersect with and cannot be separated from other social identities such as gender identity, sexual orientation, socio-economic status, religion and spirituality, age, ability, and neurodiversity (Swamy, 2011b). This also includes other identities or locations such as "indigenous heritage, national origin, [...] as well as vocation, body size, health, experiences of colonization, and choices concerning partnering and parenting" (Curtis, 2013, p. 268). For this reason, the term *sociocultural* is also used in this chapter as an umbrella term to encompass these intersecting identities.

The AMTA Code of Ethics (2015) does not explicitly discuss discrimination or ethical issues related to supervision, except to say that music therapy educators are expected to "serve as an exemplary role model in regard to ethical conduct and the enforcement of the Code of Ethics" (section 11.6). It is safe to assume, then, that discrimination in academic supervision "based upon race, ethnicity, language, religion, marital status, gender, gender identity or expression, sexual orientation, age, ability, socio-economic status, or political affiliation" (section 2.3.2) is prohibited. In addition, academic supervisors are expected "to eliminate the effect of biases based on these factors on his or her work" (AMTA, 2015). Unfortunately, despite these statements in our code of ethics, overt, subtle, covert, and unconscious bias and discrimination still exists within music therapy programs (Beer, 2015; Kim, 2008; Swamy, 2011a; Young, 2009).

For example, qualitative research and case studies investigating music therapy supervision with international students found that some minority supervisees experienced their majority supervisors as unsupportive and uncaring (Kim, 2008; Swamy, 2011a). Research by Beer (2015) found that, at times, international supervisees felt "discouragement and doubt" (p. 165) at the lack of cultural empathy and understanding from their music therapy educators and supervisors. In addition, others reported experiencing discrimination, "misunderstanding and neglect from classmates, staff at internship sites, and even supervisors," leading to self-blame and anxiety (Zhang, Shi, & Hsu, 2016, p. 28). A study by Young (2009) also highlighted experiences of cross-cultural tension, with minority music therapy supervisees reporting difficulty in "establishing trust" with supervisors from more privileged backgrounds (p. 197), due to differing beliefs and values, as well as trouble reconciling their cultural beliefs around mental illness with their supervisors' beliefs.

While literature and training on culture-centered music therapy supervision is slowly growing (Dileo, 2001; Estrella, 2001; Kim, 2008, 2011; Swamy, 2011a, 2017; Young, 2009), sociocultural issues in academic music therapy supervision have not been explicitly addressed in the literature. Given that a safe and supportive working alliance is essential for student supervisees to learn and grow, these are crucial issues for music therapy academic supervision in the United States and other related countries (Dileo, 2001; Kim, 2008; Ramos-Sanchez et al., 2002; Toporek, Ortega-Villalobos, & Pope-Davis, 2004).

QUALITIES OF CULTURALLY RESPONSIVE ACADEMIC SUPERVISORS

Sangeeta: When I was a student music therapy intern many years ago, I found myself struggling with my ethnic identity as a second-generation Indian-American woman. After pushing away my own heritage for years, for the first time in my life, I began to wake up to the decades of racism and discrimination that I had experienced. As a result, it was quite painful for me at that time to be taught primarily European psychological theories, Western harmonies, and American models of music therapy. I longed for an approach that would help me to understand the internal confusion I felt, validate my perspective, and respect the cultural norms with which I had grown up.

At the beginning of the semester, my academic supervisor, who was white and male, asked the class for feedback about the syllabus. Was there anything else that we wanted to cover? Did we have any suggestions? The thought of openly critiquing a teacher—which, according to traditional Indian norms, was considered disrespectful—created a fair amount of anxiety for me at that time. After a few minutes of procrastinating, I gathered the courage to challenge him and spoke up. "I looked at the syllabus and I noticed there are no classes addressing multicultural issues," I said. "I'd like for that to be included." He responded that there were too many marginalized groups to discuss, and since he could not include them all, he was not going to include any. He immediately went on to the next topic. I was in complete shock, trying to sort out what had just happened and not at all prepared for his response.

I do not think that my professor intended harm, but I felt humiliated and angry, nonetheless. Perhaps he was afraid that he did not know enough. Maybe he thought he would be judged and found lacking. However, he could have showed a sense of cultural humility and acknowledged that my request was legitimate, but that he was not sure how to implement it. He could have offered to meet with me afterward or asked the class for suggestions on how he might facilitate more culturally inclusive discussions. He might have sought to be more culturally informed and consulted with colleagues, supervisors who were knowledgeable about these issues. He could have read literature about sociocultural issues in supervision. However, his lack of cultural sensitivity, cultural awareness, and self-reflexivity around his underlying feelings and actions prevented him from demonstrating cultural empathy and responsiveness (see below for more detail). Although it was likely not his intention, his power dismissed my comment and excluded me, as well as other marginalized groups, from the entire curriculum. He was speaking from a position of privilege not only as my professor, but as a Caucasian, heterosexual, middle-class, able-bodied, cisgender male, which gave him a world of invisible resources to which many other groups did not have access. He was not aware of the social and cultural power he had inherited and that he could use it either to do further psychological harm or to elicit change and benefit both his supervisees as well as their clients.

Cultural Sensitivity

The first step in meeting the needs of our minority student supervisees is to acknowledge that the majority of the music therapy programs and academic supervision courses, as well as many music therapy supervision models in the United States and Europe, are ethnocentric (Curtis, 2013; Hadley, 2013; Kim, 2008; Toppozada, 1995). Ng described how the university classroom is situated within a larger sociocultural context.

> The classroom, especially the university classroom, is not a neutral place. It is a site where knowledge is constructed and contested. It is here that a complex of power relations based on class, gender, race, age, social position, and so on is animated, struggled over, inscribed, and reinscribed. (Ng, 2005, p. 2)

In other words, what is often seen as a universal or neutral approach to supervision, education, and music therapy training is actually based on white, North American and European norms and values. Hadley (2013) wrote that this perspective "permeates our theories, our musical practices, our research practices, our educational practices, and so on" (p. 8). However, in reality, our students embody many different worldviews, belief systems, communication styles, and values from various cultures around the world, and these have a profound impact upon the academic supervisory relationship.

For example, in a supervisory case study (Swamy, 2011), "Wei," a Taiwanese graduate music therapy student, expressed confusion in an individual supervision meeting one day. Her supervisor had assigned students to write a song in the style of the blues, saying, "Let's start with something that everyone is familiar with, the blues" (p. 134). However, Wei had never heard of the blues before and was anxious and unsure about how to begin. Also, she was enculturated to defer to authority figures and was not comfortable in approaching her professor. Her instructor assumed that the blues was a universal musical form, insensitive to the fact that it has a very specific national as well as cultural context with which every student may not be familiar.

In an interview for a qualitative research study (2007), Participant A described her struggle with emulating her supervisor's style of empathic and emotional expression.

> When she was modeling her facial expression in the class to me, it felt too intrusive, the way that she was modeling being empathetic to someone in pain. That was something that I would not have done back home. Sometimes I think that I would like to go back home some days, and I think about how effective some music therapy techniques would be.

Once we understand that sociocultural context impacts our student supervisees as well as their clients, it is our responsibility as academic supervisors to be sensitive and respectful of these differences. Karen Estrella (2001) described this as a stage where "cultural differences are recognized, but the supervisor doesn't know what to do with this awareness, and he or she is likely to feel overwhelmed with learning about new cultures" (p. 59). In this early stage, we run the risk of rejecting or pathologizing the differences that we notice, as well as being defensive and minimizing the differences we notice (Oswanski & Donnenwerth, 2017). Estrella (2001) suggested that white supervisors who are unaware of cultural differences may not only misinterpret basic verbal and nonverbal cues, but also:

> ... misinterpret minimal eye contact, quiet deferent verbalizing, or an indirect approach as fear, resistance, incompetence, or low self-esteem. In fact, these behaviors may

represent different cultural values, such as respect for or deference to authority, or the value of avoiding conflict in the service of sustaining interpersonal contact, or of being self-effacing in the service of belonging. (p. 59)

While cultural sensitivity is an important first step, many consider it to be insufficient to meet the needs of academic supervisees (Foronda, 2008; Rice & O'Donohue, 2002; Ridley et al., 1994).

Cultural Competence

Cultural competence in music therapy goes beyond sensitivity and focuses on mastering knowledge, skills, and awareness in the supervisory and therapeutic relationship (Coleman, 1997; Hadley & Norris, 2016; Rapp, 2000; Sue, 2004; Sue, Arredondo, & McDavis, 1992). This includes not just being open-minded when exposed to various sociocultural traditions, but also familiarizing ourselves with the cultural backgrounds, norms, worldviews, gender roles, behaviors, communication styles, and sociopolitical history of different racial or ethnic groups. For example, one research participant described the cultural differences she experienced in her classes after coming to the United States from abroad:

Personally, I am quite a discreet person to begin with, and partly because of my Asian background, we always believe that we shouldn't be too explicit with our emotions, and we shouldn't air our problems like dirty laundry in public, and things like that. (Beer, 2015, p. 147)

While it is beyond of the scope of this chapter to discuss the sociocultural norms of specific groups in detail, readers are referred to "Cultural Intersections in Music Therapy: Music, Health and the Individual" (Whitehead-Pleaux & Tan, 2017) and "Ethnicity and Family Therapy" (McGoldrick, Giordano, & Garcia-Preto, 2005) for more information. These resources are primarily centered on the therapist–client relationship; however, the basic information surrounding cultural norms relayed in this literature is also relevant to academic supervision. Seeking continuing sociocultural education, attending workshops, and pursuing other resources will also help supervisors to develop the knowledge to effectively work with supervisees, and particularly those who are from different sociocultural backgrounds than they are. Estrella described this information-gathering stage as one where "the supervisor attempts to identify the differences and similarities between and among cultures and to identify the way these cultures impact the supervisory relationship" (2001, p. 59). As we gain knowledge and understanding about how various sociocultural norms differ from each other and from our own, this can help us to differentiate between a supervisee's personal strengths and weaknesses, their clinical skills, culturally influenced behaviors, and natural human responses.

The Student Supervisee's Sociocultural Identity

While gaining sociocultural information and knowledge is important, it can be difficult to define what constitutes cultural competence. How much knowledge, awareness, and skill is sufficient for culturally competent academic supervision? How would this be evaluated? Is there an end point? In addition, there are risks to focusing exclusively on intellectual information, including stereotyping supervisees according to cultural norms, overlooking the diversity of sociocultural groups, and misunderstanding how supervisees may manifest their sociocultural identity in unique ways (Hoskins, 1999; Swamy, 2011b). For instance, at a music therapy event, two music therapy student supervisees shared very different experiences of being black. "I am so lucky to have an internship instructor who totally supports me," said one student. "She told me, 'You're a black woman! Be proud of that!' She really helped me to embrace who I am." Shortly afterward, however, another black student said, "As a gay man who is also black, I'm struggling with how to embrace being African-American. I want to, but I'm having to choose between my sexual orientation and my race because my community isn't generally okay with gay people. How do I do that?"

Racial and ethnic identity developmental models (Cross, 1991; Helms, 1990; Parham, 1989; Phinney, 1990, 2005) were created in the 1990s to explain this type of diversity within racial and ethnic groups. These maps can help supervisors to better understand supervisees' experiences. In other words, all black supervisees do not necessarily have the same experience of being black. Simply encouraging or expecting black supervisees to embrace their ethnicity or race will not necessarily be helpful. Like the supervisee in the example above, students may be struggling with their relationship to their race or ethnicity and need more guidance, support, and room for exploration. In particular, they will need to acknowledge and sort out their own feelings while working with clients from a similar sociocultural background. This example also highlights the complexity of how other identities, such as sexual orientation, socio-economic status, religion, ability, age, gender identity, education level, and others, can impact and intersect with one's sense of racial or ethnic identity (Gatmon, 2001; Kim, 2013b; Swamy, 2011b).

Student supervisees may also reject the norms of their own cultural group(s), depending on their sociocultural identification as well as their own personal and family history. Supervisees in this stage of ethnic and racial identity development may distance themselves from their own ethnicity or race due to the pain of internalized oppression. They may experience their race as not salient for them and primarily identify with white values and norms. They may consciously or unconsciously adopt white American values and norms in hope of fitting in and finding a sense of belonging or acceptance (Cross, 1991; Phinney, 1989; Phinney & Ong, 2007). In one example, Carolyn Kenny wrote about how her mother had denied her own Native American heritage in dramatic ways.

> Abandoned by her own Native mother at the age of 3, she spent most of her life just wanting to make life easier by being White. She bleached her skin. She broke and reset her nose. She put aside all things "Indian." Never mind that her father also had an Indian mother, a fact that most of the family tried to ignore or deny. (Kenny, 2006, p. 550)

Other student supervisees from abroad described the pressure to be as American as possible:

> I used to wish that I were an American. We had all become frustrated by problems that were caused by not understanding our changing identities. [...] We made our best efforts to speak like Americans, think like Americans, and even act like Americans. (Zhang, Shi, & Hsu, 2016, p. 50)

In contrast, some supervisees may be in a stage where they express anti-white sentiments and feelings of rage, anxiety, and guilt (Vandiver et al., 2001). They may be experiencing overt racism and discrimination in their daily lives, socialize primarily with their own sociocultural group, and need support in developing a sense of racial or ethnic pride. Instead of reacting defensively to anger or accusations of racism, academic supervisors can best support supervisees in this stage by acknowledging the reality of racism, listening to and believing their students' experiences, and expressing empathy and taking appropriate action to support students as needed. Supervisors should also be careful not to judge or penalize supervisees who openly express anger about racism and favor supervisees who don't "rock the boat."

However, sometimes the process of ethnic identity is more complex than traditional models. The example of the black student above particularly shows the complexity of how other identities such as sexual orientation can impact one's sense of racial or ethnic identity. In addition, some students may be negotiating a hybrid or reconstructed identity (Bhabha, 2004; Gilroy, 1993; Hall, 1996; Radhakrishnan, 2001), attempting to re-create or reinvent themselves and being unsure of who they are in the moment. Academic supervisors may also witness students expressing their identities in fluid ways. For example, some may negotiate and adopt various identities depending on context and place (Rattansi & Phoenix, 1997; Swamy, 2011b), such as showing allegiance to one identity one week and another identity the next week. Alternatively, students may express one aspect of their identity in one context and another facet of their identity in another context. For example, a student supervisee from Japan described having two different identities after finishing her music therapy degree.

> When I came back, I was pretty much Americanized. [...] I wanted to talk more about problems and discuss them. [...] But I learned that this way doesn't work with my family, or with my friends, or coworkers, or anything. So, yes, I started adjusting, and I have two different identities. [...] When I work with the Japanese community that really focuses only on the Japanese way, I become very Japanese. (Beer, 2015, p. 158)

In addition to gaining knowledge about culturally specific groups, as academic supervisors, we should recognize that understanding ethnic and racial identity is a process. We should seek to understand and respect the various ways that our students' identities may manifest in class, as well as at their fieldwork and internship sites. We should support and empathize with our supervisees' experiences and provide appropriate resources for them to explore their identities and address any confusion or ethnic identity conflict. This may include referrals to university support groups, peer groups, or clubs, community organizations, mentoring relationships, counseling centers, or individual therapy. Last, it is our responsibility to help student supervisees understand how their identities interface with their clinical work.

Cultural Humility

Instead of focusing on competence, cultural humility emphasizes that learning about culture is a process rather than a skill that can be mastered. The intent is a lifelong commitment to self-reflection and awareness, open-mindedness, mutual empowerment, and humility (Curtis, 2013; Foronda, 2016; Tervalon & Murray-Garcia, 1998). Cultural humility can help academic music therapy supervisors to begin what can often feel like an overwhelming task. With so many different cultural norms, musical genres, styles, idioms, and worldviews on the planet, it can sometimes feel impossible to be well versed in all of them (Swamy, 2014).

Cultural humility helps us to recognize that although we may have traveled abroad and learned about cultural characteristics or customs from living in another country, there is always more to learn. Hoskyns (2007) described this realization upon arriving to teach in New Zealand for the first time. She was initially unsure of how to respond when a M ori student introduced himself in class with a lengthy, traditional welcome speech, describing his *whakapapa*, or background and heritage. "Dennis's introduction to us of an aspect of M ori custom, and its potential to influence music therapy practice in New Zealand, was a significant pointer to me about the ways in which I might need to keep my eyes and ears open (and perhaps mouth shut) as a new professional here" (para. 11).

In addition, cultural humility involves accepting our limitations and admitting what we do not know about various sociocultural groups or individuals, including our supervisees and their clients. Instead of viewing mistakes or cultural missteps as experiences to avoid, supervisors can benefit by seeing errors as a natural part of the learning process. Music therapists Leah Oswanski and Amy Donnenwerth (2017) described this process of being a social justice ally, with one sharing how, after growing up in several different countries, she still makes mistakes: "I am nowhere near a social justice ally expert. Not even close. I, like all of us, am just a work in progress. I make mistakes all the time, sometimes big mistakes. I apologize. I ask for feedback. I learn. I grow" (p. 257). By accepting what we do not know, we open ourselves to learning more, giving ourselves permission to ask questions and challenge our existing approaches. "Am I doing all I can to teach international students what they need to know to facilitate reentry to their home country? ... I intuit there is indeed something more I could be doing to bridge the two worlds" (Beer, 2015, p. 131).

Perhaps most important, cultural humility involves decentering our own position and perspective in order to make room for other voices to be heard:

> In order to be truly humble, a person must make him- or herself vulnerable by reaching forward into the space between self and other and to be mindful of the fact that such "reaching toward" may not be well received by those who have been marginalized by the dominant culture. This reaching toward without a guarantee of reciprocity takes courage and a willingness to abandon the need for social comfort. Within this move toward connection, there is a sense of surrender, a sense of acquiescing to another. Furthermore, to acquiesce to another is to surrender cultural perspectives, biases, and expectations for "correct behavior." This often feels frightening, like being lost at sea without a tether, especially for those of us who are acutely aware of the dominant culture's norms for behavior. (Hoskins, 1999, p. 79)

Cultural Empathy

In addition to cultural sensitivity, knowledge, and humility, the concept of cultural empathy provides us with an opportunity to connect from the heart. Used across disciplines such as counseling, healthcare, and intercultural communication (Cundiff, Nadler, & Swan, 2009; Garcia, Lu, & Maurer, 2012; Hoskins, 1999; Pederson & Pope, 2010; Ridley & Lingle, 1996), cultural empathy goes beyond gaining intellectual knowledge about other cultures into "affective connection and interpersonal relatedness" (Dyche & Zayas, 2001, p. 247). In academic supervision, cultural empathy helps us to understand the socio-emotional world of our supervisee and their clients, helping us to connect in a shared human experience. It helps us to "see the world through another's eyes," (p. 247), imagining what it might feel like to experience racism or discrimination in the classroom, survive and learn in a completely foreign environment, or fear for our lives on a daily basis because of the color of our skin. It helps us to have an idea of what it might be like for students beginning their internship or fieldwork placement in a new country.

Given that empathy is already considered an essential quality for ethical music therapy, it may seem that developing cultural empathy is unnecessary. Brown (2002) pointed out, however, that a generic sense of empathy is not sufficient and may lead to misunderstandings of behavior and gestures if our empathy is not made explicit. Kenny added that sometimes our empathy may be conditional, centered on our interaction with certain supervisees and their client populations with whom we can immediately relate. "Sometimes we assume that we have empathy for others only when we have had similar experiences" (Kenny, 2003, para. 23). It is much easier to empathize with those who share common life experiences and identities with us. However, cultural empathy toward those who are from different sociocultural backgrounds from ourselves is essential if we are to meet the needs of our supervisees.

In particular, a lack of cultural empathy can affect our evaluation process. If we evaluate supervisees according to ethnocentric curriculum requirements, we are likely to see their cultural differences as divergent from the "norm" of our program. In addition, when student supervisees do not feel validated or supported enough to create a positive supervisory alliance, they are unlikely to share thoughts, reflections, and questions that are critical to their growth into professional music therapists. "I felt frustrated that I was ignored or brushed off," said one minority student supervisee.

"I began to blame myself and become more nervous and anxious when talking to others. Consequently, I rarely shared my thoughts, experiences, and feelings during internship seminars and interdisciplinary meetings" (Zhang, Shi, & Hsu, 2016, p. 28). Supervisees who are not supported may feel anger and resistance, while supervisors may respond with irritation, judgment, rejection, defensiveness, countertransference, and attempts to control the process (Garrett et al., 2001; Kim, 2008).

Academic supervisors showing cultural empathy express openness, acceptance, receptivity, and genuine curiosity in response to sociocultural conflicts or dissonance. A phenomenological study of supervisees from a variety of cultural backgrounds described characteristics of cultural empathy that supervisees found helpful in developing an effective supervisory relationship (Kim, 2008). These included validating supervisees' thoughts and experiences, "being a good listener, accepting, normalizing the issues brought by the supervisee, and having a nonjudgmental attitude" (p. 19). Participants felt that these supervisors had their interests at heart and did not make generalizations about their culture, despite the fact that some supervisors were from different cultural backgrounds than they were. Culturally empathetic supervisors were also encouraging and inclusive and verbally acknowledged the cultural differences between themselves and their supervisees in a supportive and open-minded way. "I can see where you are coming from and how you are trying to negotiate who you are and who they [the clients] are, [...] that's quite a different perception than mine" (p. 21).

Cultural Self-Reflexivity

As the Korean saying goes, "Knowing [self-awareness] is power." Music therapy supervisors and educators have long stressed how increasing self-awareness, self-inquiry, and self-reflexivity is an essential part of music therapy training (Bruscia, 2012; Hadley & Norris, 2016; Priestley, 1994; Stige, 2001). However, cultural self-reflexivity in music therapy academic supervision has not been thoroughly discussed. Cultural self-reflexivity goes beyond an awareness of individual countertransference and involves a deep and ongoing exploration of our sociocultural identities, acknowledgement of our privileges and biases, recognition of our vulnerabilities and fears, and examination of our resistance and defenses.

The Supervisor's Sociocultural Identity
In "The Courage to Teach," transformative educator Parker Palmer (2007) asked, "Who is the self that teaches?" (p. 4). Palmer pointed out that we spend copious amounts of energy on what and how we teach, but rarely focus on who is doing the teaching. Similarly, in music therapy supervision, there is a significant amount of literature written about how we should supervise fieldwork students and interns and what we should include in the process (AMTA, 2013; Farnan, 2001; Feiner, 2001; Forinash, 2001; Hanser, 2001; Odell-Miller & Krueckeberg, 2009; Shulman-Fagen, 2001; Stige, 2001; Summer, 2001; Wheeler, 2005). However, as academic supervisors, we rarely ask the question, Who is doing the teaching and supervising? What are our own sociocultural backgrounds, and how do we identify? What is our racial and ethnic background? How do white supervisors understand "whiteness" as a racial identity (Hadley, 2013, p. 377)? What is our socio-economic status? How do we define or experience our gender, sexual orientation, religion, abilities, or other identities? How do these affect our values, belief systems, expectations, communication styles, behaviors, and attitudes, and how do these impact the supervision process?

Self-reflexivity about our sociocultural identities allows us to recognize the privileges and unearned advantages we have in relation to our supervisees that are often taken for granted, such as "class oppression, sexism, racism, ableism, or heterosexism" (Hadley, 2013, p. 375). In a seminal paper first published in the late '90s, Peggy McIntosh (2010) listed specific ways that she experienced her white privilege, such as going to the store and not having to worry about being suspected of stealing or not having to fear being stopped by the police for no reason. Academic supervisors would benefit from reading McIntosh's paper and making a similar list of all of the ways in which they have sociocultural advantages over their students. Hadley (2013) described this recognition as a crucial step in dismantling these oppressive systems and narratives by which we are unconsciously influenced. In other words, in addition to having the power to grade, evaluate, and decide whether student supervisees will meet competencies, our sociocultural privileges add an additional layer of power that can adversely affect the supervisory relationship if left unexamined. If we do not challenge these existing narratives and systems, we risk being complicit and participating in them.

Examining our own sociocultural backgrounds routinely will help us, as academic supervisors, to have a clear understanding of culture-related interactions with our supervisees. This also includes academic supervisors who appear to share a similar background as their supervisees, as both supervisor and supervisee may have other hidden or invisible identities that differ or conflict. This should be an ongoing process, as our sociocultural beings are continually developing. Our attitudes toward sociocultural issues must be thoroughly examined, as a rigid and biased attitude on the part of the supervisor will only prevent the supervisory process from achieving effective outcomes.

Bias, Discrimination, and Microaggressions

Since music therapy is a profession that involves empathy, service, and helping people, it may seem difficult to imagine that academic music therapy supervisors, including ourselves, are capable of discrimination, bias, or oppression. However, discrimination does not always involve hate crimes and can take many forms. Differential treatment in admitting students, awarding scholarships and graduate assistantships, assigning grades, evaluating supervisees' readiness for internship, requiring remedial work, and other areas may also be problematic. For instance, negative comments about a student's accent, race, national origin, or other identity combined with treating supervisees differently than others may be considered illegal discrimination by inference or pretext, according to a court of law (Civil Rights Act, 1964; U.S. Department of Education, 2015).

In addition, there are many subtle, covert, and unconscious forms of oppression, including microaggressions, or slights and insults, that can affect both our students and their clients (Beer, 2015; Hadley, 2013). These might include telling ethnic minorities for whom English is their native language, "Your English is so good!" or calling a Lakota student who misses classes for Indian holidays "not invested enough." Over time, the cumulative effect of these comments can send an oppressive message to minority students, contributing to feelings of "defeat, fatigue, anger, and fear" (Beer, 2015, p. 133). It is important to remember that although we may not intend psychological harm, we are all capable of conscious or unconscious bias. Tatum (2007) pointed out how we are all influenced by the racist, sexist, homophobic, ableist, and transphobic narratives and actions around us:

> We all have prejudices, not because we want them but because we are so continually exposed to misinformation about others. [...] If we live in an environment in which we are bombarded with stereotypical images in the media, are frequently exposed to the ethnic jokes of friends and family members, and are rarely informed of the accomplishments of oppressed groups, we will develop the negative categorizations of those groups that form the basis of prejudice. (2007, p. 126)

It is only when we deny or are silent about our biases that they have the power to influence our behaviors and actions and perpetuate systems of oppression.

Without an awareness of and sensitivity to their own identities, biases, and worldviews, supervisors are at risk for engaging in microaggressions and other acts of racism and discrimination in relation to their culturally different supervisees or their supervisees' clients (e.g., stereotyping and pathologizing trainee/client behaviors), and providing culturally insensitive treatment recommendations. (Inman et al., 2014, p. 75)

In addition, when supervisors neglect to examine their own knowledge, assumptions, attitudes, perceptions, and feelings, they may prematurely judge supervisees, be insensitive to supervisees' nonverbal communication, and show an inability to understand the strengths and competencies of the minority supervisee (Garrett et al., 2001).

Acknowledging that we are indeed biased takes courage. It takes courage to be vulnerable and to recognize the fears that interfere with becoming the highest possible versions of ourselves as academic supervisors. Palmer (2007) described the surface-level fears that get in the way of self-reflexivity for faculty members, including university grading systems, professional competition, and administrative assessments, as well as the fears of losing one's job or status. However, he suggested that deeper fears are at play, that we are "fearful that I am not just a bad teacher [supervisor] but a bad person, so closely is my sense of self tied to the work I do" (p. 37). He also proposed that in our passion to connect to our students, "we make ourselves, as well as our subjects, vulnerable to indifference, judgment, ridicule" (p. 18). Last, he asserted that we fear diversity and a "live encounter with otherness" (p. 39), that "as soon as we admit pluralism, we are forced to admit that ours is not the only standpoint, the only experience, the only way, and the truths we have built our lives on begin to feel fragile" (p. 38).

Exposing our vulnerabilities and questioning the very foundations of our approach can be uncomfortable and anxiety-provoking. In fact, given the sensitive and personal nature of these topics, it is recommended that academic supervisors discuss challenges around bias and privilege with trusted colleagues, in their own supervision, or in personal therapy. This is especially important if supervisors are feeling particularly reactive, defensive, or frustrated with minority supervisees. This level of cultural self-reflexivity is essential in order to fully support student supervisees of color, as well as their clients. Michele Forinash (2002) suggests that one way to do this is to step out of our comfort zones and challenge ourselves to learn about new perspectives.

I (and others, I am sure) tend to get "comfortable" in our roles and traditions in music therapy. […] It is very much like belonging to a club. However, the world of music therapy is much bigger than my personal and professional interests and the field is expanding every day. […] What would it take for all of us to stop for a moment, look up from our theoretical perspectives, look away from our prescribed roles, look beyond our favored models and approaches to see and hear the diverse landscape of music therapy? What would it take for us to move from a position of defending "our way" of doing music therapy to one of appreciating and accepting a radically different way of working? What would it take to let go of how we think music therapy should sound and rather listen for new and different ways of being in music? (Forinash, 2002, paras. 3-4)

Discussing Sociocultural Issues in Academic Supervision

Another tenet of cultural self-reflexivity is being willing to openly discuss power, privilege, and bias with student supervisees. Kenny and her colleagues (2006) surveyed 33 music therapy educators around the world and found that while some programs did include required courses on multicultural issues and world musics, many found discussions about culture to be a "delicate topic" and did not see cultural issues as significant for music therapy education. Others reported that discussing "ethnic" issues was taboo (p. 208). While this survey was taken over 20 years ago, unfortunately, many of the same problems exist in some music therapy programs today. In fact, in her study, Laurel Young (2009) found that numerous programs "still consider the development of multicultural competence in music therapy practice and supervision to be an optional endeavor" (p. 199).

As academic supervisors, it is our responsibility to lead discussions around these issues in a mindful way (Kim, 2008). When we neglect to take a leadership role around sociocultural topics, students are often afraid to share their concerns and questions. In one example, a white music therapy student raised in a predominantly white community started his internship in a juvenile detention center with black, Latinx, and racially mixed adolescents. "I feel like I'm not supposed to say this," he said, "but I feel strange being white there, I mean is that okay to say?" Beverly Tatum explains how this taboo, along with "self-consciousness," "trepidation," denial, and questioning the reality of racism are forms of resistance (1992, p. 5). In supervision, this may take the form of supervisors trivializing or discounting the validity of supervisees' experiences of discrimination, denying that they themselves are capable of racism, accusing supervisees who share experiences of discrimination of being "wrong, too sensitive, or being unfair," or downplaying the importance of sociocultural issues (Hadley, 2013, p. 375).

Because there is so much political and social tension and violence in the United States today (as well as in many other countries), in some ways, discussions about race and culture have become even more fraught with tension and volatility and require sensitive facilitation. Tatum (1992, 2001) recommended establishing a safe environment by asking all students to agree to confidentiality, communicate in "I" statements, and recognize that we are all affected by racism as a systemic and institutional problem. She also seeks to reduce feelings of blame and defensiveness by defining racism (and other forms of oppression) as learned behavior that is not our fault, but that we have a responsibility to address.

> Because of the prejudice and racism inherent in our environments when we were children, I assume that we cannot be blamed for learning what we were taught (intentionally or unintentionally). Yet, as adults, we have a responsibility to try to identify and interrupt the cycle of oppression. When we recognize that we have been misinformed, we have a responsibility to seek out more accurate information and to adjust our behavior accordingly. (Tatum, 1992, p. 4)

In addition, we should make it clear that hate speech, name-calling, and racial and social slurs will not be tolerated.

As academic supervisors, we have a responsibility not only to interrupt the cycle of oppression that we have been exposed to but also to challenge our student supervisees to do the same. Finally, we should openly discuss the differences in verbal and nonverbal interactions that supervisees experience and observe with clients and inquire about their sociocultural views around music, health, therapy, and emotional expression, as well as ask about their general values and belief systems (Kim, 2008). Although discussing topics surrounding race, culture, and ethnicity may feel uncomfortable, in academic supervision, it is critical.

Cultural Responsiveness

In addition to developing individual qualities as an academic supervisor, cultural responsiveness encourages a systemic approach to pedagogy (Gay, 2000) and supervision. This includes supporting minority students not just individually, but also systemically, through examining our curricula, pedagogical styles and expectations, and student support systems. It is important for academic supervisors to realize that academic success is not based purely on individual motivation and effort but is a result of the interaction between the individual and the environment (Bronfenbrenner & Morris, 1998).

For example, ethnic minority students, such as those from Latin American, African-American, First Nations, Asian-American, Arab, or multiracial backgrounds, face additional barriers when compared to their Caucasian peers. In addition, minority students who are the first members of their families to attend college often struggle with academic performance, taking longer to finish their degrees. They may lack basic knowledge about how the university system works, as well as misunderstand general expectations about college (Dennis, Phinney, & Chuateco, 2005). From the individualistic perspective of most universities in the United States, minority students who struggle can often be stereotyped as unmotivated, uncommitted, lazy, or not serious enough.

These systemic problems can manifest in many ways for music therapy student supervisees. Students who come from families that emphasize interdependence may be expected to fulfill obligations to their family even if they conflict with student or clinical obligations (Tseng, 2004). For example, a Latinx music therapy student preparing for fieldwork was at risk for failing a required class, missing homework assignments, advising appointments, and arriving late to class. Once her advisor was able to arrange a meeting, however, faculty discovered that she was expected to help her family take care of her younger sibling. Her family was struggling financially and could not afford childcare. As a result, she was feeling torn between her family obligations and completing pre-fieldwork requirements. A study by Phinney and Haas (2003) found that students who were having trouble coping shared that they needed someone to provide help, guidance, or emotional support. Academic supervisors can play this important role, providing systemic and practical resources in addition to serving as confidant and mentor.

Systemically, university multicultural and international student centers and support groups provide important sources of support for international and ethnic minority student supervisees. These resources are designed to empower and support marginalized communities by providing a space where students can feel included, be heard, and be encouraged toward social, cultural, academic, and professional growth. In addition, they provide opportunities for international students to learn about unspoken expectations and norms for thinking, writing, behaving, and learning at American universities, as well as understanding the "individualistic learning paradigm" prevalent in the United States (Wang & Machado, 2015, p. 153). Minority students can often benefit from separate orientations; practical support for visas, finances, and housing; support groups consisting of students from similar backgrounds; discussions and roundtables around sociocultural issues; and other systemic resources to help them survive in environments that are predominantly white, able-bodied, cisgender, heterosexual, and English-speaking. In addition, supervisors should refer supervisees to online, regional, national, and international support networks and associations such as the Black Music Therapy Network, Music Therapists with Disabilities, Team Rainbow, and The Latin American Music Therapy Network, as well as others. Overall, these important resources can help minority students to be supported at a basic level so that they can focus on their clinical and academic work.

A culturally responsive approach is also strength-based or resource-oriented. It "affirms students' cultures, viewing them as transformative and emancipatory strengths (rather than deficits)" (Santamaria, 2009, p. 226). As academic supervisors, we should help supervisees who are ethnic minorities to see themselves in a positive light, encouraging and acknowledging their innate and natural strengths. Given that minorities face increasing amounts of discrimination, racism, and anti-immigrant laws and policies, "they are in need of assistance to remind them where they do have power, competence, and capability" (Swamy, 2011a, p. 136). For example, in working with "Wei," a music therapy student supervisee from Taiwan, Swamy (2011a) affirmed Wei's strengths rather than focusing on what her instructors labeled as her deficits. A music-centered approach using piano improvisation, her primary instrument, helped to supervise her without shaming her for her lack of English skills. Instead, it supported her growth as a music therapist in training, honoring her own "culturally based wisdom and knowledge" (p. 136). As a result, she felt less anxiety, learned more about relationships in a clinical context, and was able to openly explore her own Taiwanese-American identity.

In addition, instead of expecting students to assimilate and adopt all of the communication styles, learning approaches, and worldviews of their university program, culturally responsive pedagogy uses the cultural experiences, perspectives, and characteristics of students to enhance the learning process (Kim, 2013). It "incorporates students' cultures in the teaching process, thus empowering them to take ownership of their learning, and leads to their increased participation in societal activities" (Santamaria, 2009, p. 227).

Culturally responsive academic supervision also necessitates a systematic re-evaluation of general program philosophy and curriculum content. While a full discussion of music therapy pedagogy is beyond the scope of this chapter, academic supervisors are challenged to assess their programs from a systemic perspective. Does the music therapy curriculum reflect the needs of minority populations in musical and nonmusical terms? Is the program philosophy and vision inclusive of a variety of sociocultural values and norms? Do academic supervisors respectfully challenge peers, colleagues, and coworkers to uphold culturally responsive supervision and hold themselves accountable (Hadley & Norris, 2016)? Ultimately, supervision that is culturally sensitive, informed, humble, self-reflexive, and responsive is essential in supporting student supervisee development and minimizing misunderstandings and miscommunication.

INTERNATIONAL STUDENTS

Because international student enrollment at higher education institutions in the United States has been continuously growing (The Power of International Education, 2017), international students and English-language learners require specialized understanding and resources. To date, we have not been able to find information about the number of the international students who are currently enrolled in music therapy degree programs in the United States. However, based on the workforce study conducted by AMTA (2017), the highest numbers of minority music therapists are Asian. Important concerns that affect academic supervision with international students include financial stresses, culture shock, lack of social support, difficulties in learning to speak and write English, trouble in understanding American cultural norms, and specific needs in assigning fieldwork and internship populations (Nisson, 2007; Sandhu, 1995).

One challenge that international music therapy supervisees face is that they must obtain an F1 visa while studying in the United States and maintain a full-time course load. More and more so, American immigration policies have made it difficult for international students to remain in the United States unless they are full-time college students. Financially, international students also rely heavily on their own resources due to limited opportunities to apply for local scholarships. Therefore, in addition to academic pressure, international students often feel pressure to complete their education as quickly as possible.

International students also often experience culture shock during their education and training in the States as they acculturate, or become adjusted to a new environment (Kim, 2011). This acculturation process can be defined as "the process of acquiring cultural characteristics of the new country one migrates to" (Berry, 1997, p. 34).

Berry (1997) identified four strategies that immigrants use in their acculturation process. In terms of academic supervision, *integration* is used when student supervisees maintain their own culture during interactions with others, as well as adapt to American culture as necessary. One supervisee described an integration experience in this way: "My self-identity gradually changed to accept that I am a foreigner. I realized that adapting to this culture was necessary, and that I could do so without giving up my own culture" (Zhang, Shi, & Hsu, 2016, p. 50). Some supervisees, however, use the opposite approach, actively adopting white, mainstream, American culture and moving away from their own culture of origin. This is known as an *assimilation* strategy. Others may resist learning English and isolate themselves out of fear of losing their own culture. This is known as *separation*, when supervisees hold on to their own traditions and avoid interaction with others from the dominant culture. This can include a reluctance to learn English. Last, when students show interest in neither their own culture nor their new culture, this is known as *marginalization*. Several supervisees described this strategy as a period of time when they felt forced to give up their own cultures in order to succeed in their music therapy programs. "Eventually, we became a strange group of people who felt somewhat out of place among our native people, and foreign in the new society to which we were trying to get accustomed" (p. 50). According to Berry (1997), people who use separation and marginalization strategies tend to experience more stress than others who use assimilation and integration.

Some scholars (Rudmin 2003, 2006) have criticized this theory, however, due to its psychometric problems: "Because the four constructs are mutually exclusive, agreement to items about one construct should impede agreement to the corresponding items about the other three" (Rudmin, 2006, p. 5). Moreover, there have been inconsistent results in various studies as to whether the acculturation process is stressful. Furthermore, it is questionable whether people who use the integration strategy experience the least amount of stress (Rudmin, 2006). As acculturation theory has developed over time, however, various views on acculturation have been proposed. For example, acculturation can be understood as a process that people experience developmentally: Oppedal et al. (2004) stated that "acculturation, rather than being a process that runs parallel to life span development, is an integral part of it, and that acculturation changes, by nature, are developmental processes toward adaption and gaining competence within more than one cultural setting" (p. 482). Therefore, this process takes place over time, while the individual is adapting and restructuring their values and behaviors. Physical, social, and psychological consequences may appear throughout the process.

While acculturation can "enhance one's life chances and mental health" (Berry, Kim, Minde, & Mok, 1987, p. 493), it can also be detrimental to one's well-being. While all international students experience acculturation, some will positively and successfully integrate into their new culture. Others who are unable to adjust may be negatively affected and experience more chronic acculturative stress (Fuertes & Westbrook, 1996; Kim, 2011; Misra, Crist, & Burant, 2003). This can include anxiety, depression, post- traumatic stress, and other symptoms that may mimic mental health problems. Even though acculturative stress may cause physical, somatic, cognitive, and psychological symptoms, the majority of music therapy programs have not adequately addressed this phenomenon (Young, 2009). Consequently, more resources and support systems to supervise international music therapy students in a culturally responsive way are needed.

Acculturative Stress Management

It is believed that all student supervisees who come from abroad undergo the process of acculturation and thereby experience some degree of acculturative stress; however, the type and degree of acculturative stress may vary. For instance, research by Seung-A Kim (2011) showed that European international music therapy students experience less acculturative stress than other ethnic groups of international students in the United States. In addition, the greater the cultural gap between mainstream, white, American culture and one's own culture, the greater the acculturative stress that students experience (Schwartz, Zamboanga, Rodriguez, & Wang, 2007).

Although learning to read, write, and speak English as a second language is challenging for many international students, in some ways, difficulties surrounding cultural differences may be more significant than language barriers. For instance, culture is closely related to one's worldview, values, and attitudes. International student supervisees may need to shift their worldview and values, which may influence them in supervision. Since one's worldview may affect client assessment and treatment, international supervisees may need more time in understanding and responding to their clients. Culturally responsive supervisors should be sensitive to international supervisees' emotional well-being and actively help them to develop strategies to deal with existing stress. In addition, improvisation or other creative modalities can be used to reduce the stress level of students (Gilboa, Bodner, & Amir, 2006; Kim, 2011).

Although clinical training has been identified as a general source of stress for music therapy supervisees (Wheeler, 2002), clinical training can exacerbate the stress levels of international students (Kim, 2011). This may be intensified by required course work being completed simultaneously with their internship. For other international supervisees, the process of clinical training can be a mildly traumatic experience. For example, according to the participants in Kim's study (2008), due to cultural differences, the "interview" for fieldwork placement was a stressful event. Another international student said, "At the beginning of my internship, I felt I could not handle clinical training and schoolwork anymore. On my way home, I cried many times. 'If I am alive, at least I can cry'" (Zhang, Shi, & Hsu, 2016, p. 38).

During training, international supervisees are also required to actively participate in the community, interacting with people living in the United States. These and other components of clinical training can be particularly anxiety-provoking for individuals who are less proficient in English and may be struggling with their own neuroticism (Kim, 2011). Moreover, "nuances of U.S. culture may be especially difficult to grasp, for example, those associated with ethnic and racial relations" (Nilsson & Dodds, 2006, p. 51). In addition, many international students will return to their country of origin when they complete their studies. Therefore, international student supervisees may need additional support due to their workload or acculturative needs during their training. Observant supervisors can help students to identify existing acculturative stress and develop coping strategies (Kim, 2011).

Finally, international students' anxiety may increase depending on their fieldwork and internship setting and population. For example, placements with acute psychiatric populations and at-risk adolescents may be more difficult due to these clients' complex diagnostic needs. In addition, client use of slang and need for sophisticated verbal interventions can add an additional layer of difficulty for international students (Zhang, Sri, & Hsu, 2016). Thus, academic supervisors should assess international students' acculturation level, acculturative stress level, English proficiency, and personality traits when placing international music therapy students in any kind of fieldwork (Kim, 2011).

English-Language Learners

While the content of academic supervision varies between music therapy undergraduate and graduate programs, at a minimum, student supervisees are expected to complete clinical documentation, such as logs and progress notes. Other course work may include writing research papers related to one's fieldwork or internship populations, self-reflection papers, or other written work. This also often includes reading literature about supervision, related clinical populations, and other relevant clinical and music therapy readings. While many programs require international students to pass exams to show English proficiency, it is ultimately our responsibility as academic supervisors to support international students who are English-language learners, as well as help them to expand their English comprehension and language skills.

However, by the time students reach fieldwork and internship, it is often too late to begin this process. Support should be provided at the beginning stages of a student's education as well as throughout their program. For instance, Wang and Machado (2015) suggested that English-language-learner students be given reading material in their native language if at all possible. While it may seem counterintuitive, research has shown that learning material in the student's first language, and then in English, actually helps their English comprehension and writing skills (Wang & Machado, 2015; Zhang, 2008). However, Wang and Machado (2015) recommended that this be used only in the early stages of a student's education. They also recommended English tutors from the student's cultural background, who can help them to navigate differences and cultural expectations in American colleges and classrooms (Kobayashi & Rinnert, 1992). Last, as students gain more proficiency, researchers encourage graduate students, as well as those writing at a high level, to eventually write directly in English, rather than translating from their native language.

It is important to note that some researchers and theorists question whether students should be writing and speaking only in English. Marginson (1999) suggested that the process of international students coming to the United States to learn in English is a form of "soft imperialism which imposes 'Western' ways of thinking" (p. 19). Marginson proposed that by letting English-language and Americanized practices dominate education, "global education markets colonize national cultures and identities and sustain imbalance in the power relationship between developed and developing nations" (Marginson, 2003, p. 25). This is especially relevant for international music therapy students who may not stay in the United States. For instance, New Zealand (known as Aotearoa in M ori) is an example of a bicultural country, where both English and M ori are official languages. University buildings are labeled in both English and M ori. The music therapy program at the New Zealand School of Music is also a bicultural program, with professors and music therapists answering the phone in M ori. In addition, local music therapists such as Morva Croxson have focused on bicultural approaches by "speaking fluently in M ori, consulting widely with local elders, and ensuring M ori interests have been represented as the profession has developed" (Hoskyns, 2007, para. 16). As a result, M ori students are given a voice, and p keh (white European, non-M ori) students are given the opportunity to learn more about M ori culture and language. This is especially significant, given the history of displacement and oppression of the M ori people.

CONCLUSION

Adjusting our approaches, curricula, and supervision styles in an already rapidly changing world is an ongoing task. Perhaps even more difficult is acknowledging how much we do not know, especially when we are expected to be the experts, guiding and mentoring our student supervisees. Kenny likened this dilemma to old mapmakers pondering what was beyond the edges of their maps, with wise old captains warning, "Beyond this point there be dragons" (Kenny, 2006, p. 138). Remaining within our familiar methods, supervision approaches and curricula may seem like the easier path. However, it is our responsibility to stretch beyond our sociocultural comfort zone in order to grow and learn. We owe it to our supervisees and their clients to travel beyond the edges of our old maps. We owe it to ourselves and the field of music therapy to confront the dragons awaiting us.

Culturally responsive academic supervision means going beyond neutral ideas about what we perceive music therapy to be and challenging our limitations, habitual perceptions, and worldviews. It means delving into self-examination and being willing to learn and listen, both as individuals and as a music therapy community. It means accepting that we are not perfect, acknowledging our privileges, and being transparent about our sociocultural identities. Meeting the needs of our minority supervisees means acknowledging, discussing, and re-evaluating the sociocultural qualities of the invisible "field" (p. 104) created between supervisor, supervisee, client, university program, and community. Perhaps most important, culturally responsive supervision means opening our hearts and responding to our student supervisees with cultural humility and empathy. In the words of Carolyn Kenny, "Leave your theories outside the door. […] First, be a human being with heart" (2006, p. 74).

REFERENCE LIST

American Music Therapy Association. (2013). *Professional Competencies.* https:// www.musictherapy.org/ about/competencies/

American Music Therapy Association. (2015). *Code of Ethics.* https://www.musictherapy.org/ about/ethics/

American Music Therapy Association. (2017). *2017 AMTA member survey and workforce analysis.* Retrieved from www.musictherapy.org

Beer, L. E. (2015). Crisscrossing cultural divides: Experiences of U.S.-trained Asian music therapists. *Qualitative inquiries in music therapy: A monograph series, 10*(1), 127–173.

Berry, J. W. (1997). Immigration, acculturation, and adaptation. *Applied Psychology, 46*(1), 5–34.

Berry, J. W., Kim, U., Minde, T., & Mok, D. (1987). Comparative studies of acculturative stress. *International migration review, 21*(3), 491–511.

Bhabha, H. (2004). *The Location of Culture.* New York, NY: Routledge.

Bronfenbrenner, U., & Morris, P. A. (1998). The ecology of developmental processes. In W. Damon & R. E. Lerner (Eds.), *Handbook of Child Psychology, Vol. 1, Theoretical Models of Human Development* (5th ed.). New York, NY: Wiley.

Brown, J. M. (2002). Towards a culturally centered music therapy practice. *Voices: A World Forum for Music Therapy, 2*(1).

Bruscia, K. E. (Ed.). (2012). *Self-experiences in music therapy education, training, and supervision.* Gilsum, NH: Barcelona Publishers.

Civil Rights Act of 1964. (1964). *Public Law 88-352, 78 Stat. 241.*

Coleman, H. L. K. (1997). Portfolio assessment of multicultural counseling competence. In D. B. Pope-Davis & H. L. K. Coleman (Eds.), *Multicultural aspects of counseling series, Vol. 7. Multicultural counseling competencies: Assessment, education and training, and supervision* (pp. 43–59). Thousand Oaks, CA: SAGE Publications, Inc.

Cross, W. E., Jr. (1991). *Shades of black: Diversity in African-American identity.* Philadelphia, PA: Temple University Press.

Cross, W. E., Jr., & Fhagen-Smith, P. (2001). Patterns of African-American identity development: A life span perspective. *New perspectives on racial identity development: A theoretical and practical anthology* (pp. 243–270). New York, NY: New York University Press.

Cundiff, N., Nadler, J., & Swan, A. (2009). The Influence of Cultural Empathy and Gender on Perceptions of Diversity Programs. *Journal of Leadership & Organizational Studies, 16*(1), 97–110.

Curtis, S. L. (2013). Women survivors of abuse and developmental trauma. In L. Eyre (Ed.), *Guidelines for music therapy practice: Mental health* (pp. 263–288). Philadelphia, PA: Barcelona Publishers.

Dennis, J. M., Phinney, J. S., & Chuateco, L. I. (2005). The role of motivation, parental support, and peer support in the academic success of ethnic minority first-generation college students. *Journal of college student development, 46*(3), 223–236.

Dileo, C. (2001). Ethical issues in supervision. In M. Forinash (Ed.), *Music therapy supervision* (pp. 19–38). Gilsum, NH: Barcelona Publishers.

Dyche, L., & Zayas, L. (2001). Cross-Cultural Empathy and Training the Contemporary Psychotherapist. *Clinical Social Work Journal, 29*(3), 245–258.

Estrella, K. (2001). Multicultural approaches to music therapy supervision. In M. Forinash (Ed.), *Music therapy supervision* (pp. 39–66). Gilsum, NH: Barcelona Publishers.

Farnan, L. A. (2001). Competency-based approach to intern supervision. In M. Forinash (Ed.), *Music therapy supervision* (pp. 117–134). Gilsum, NH: Barcelona Publishers.

Feiner, S. (2001). A journey through internship supervision: Roles, dynamics, and phases of the supervisory relationship. In M. Forinash (Ed.), *Music therapy supervision* (pp. 99–116). Gilsum, NH: Barcelona Publishers.

Forinash, M. (2002). *Looking Beyond the Familiar. Voices* Resources. Retrieved January 15, 2015, from http://testvoices.uib.no/community/?q=fortnightly-columns/2002-looking-beyond-familiar

Foronda, C. (2016). Cultural Humility: A Concept Analysis. *Journal of Transcultural Nursing, 27*(3), 210–217.

Foronda, C. L. (2008). Cultural sensitivity: A concept analysis. *Journal of Transcultural Nursing, 19,* 207–212.

Fuertes, J. N., & Westbrook, F. D. (1996). Using the Social, Attitudinal, Familial, and Environmental (SAFE) Acculturation Stress Scale to assess the adjustment needs of Hispanic college students. *Measurement and Evaluation in Counseling and Development, 29*(2), 67–76.

Garcia, B., Lu, Y., & Maurer, K. (2012). Cultural Empathy. *Field Educator, 2*(2), 1–8.

Garrett, M., Borders, L., Crutchfield, L., Torres Rivera, E., Brotherton, D., & Curtis, R. (2001). Multicultural supervision: A paradigm of cultural responsiveness for supervisors. *Journal of Multicultural Counseling and Development, 29*(2), 147–158.

Gatmon, D., Jackson, D., Koshkarian, L., Martos Perry, N., Molina, A., Patel, N., & Rodolfa, E. (2001). Exploring ethnic, gender, and sexual orientation variables in supervision: Do they really matter? *Journal of Multicultural Counseling and Development, 29*(2), 102–113.

Gay, G. (2000). *Culturally responsive teaching: Theory, research, practice.* New York, NY: Teachers College Press.

Gilboa, A., Bodner, E., & Amir, D. (2006). Emotional communicability in improvised music: The case of music therapists. *Journal of Music Therapy, 33*(3), 198–225.

Gilroy, P. (1993). *The Black Atlantic.* London, UK: Verso.

Hadley, S. (2013). *Experiencing race as a music therapist: personal narratives.* Gilsum, NH: Barcelona Publishers.

Hadley, S., & Norris, M. (2016). Musical Multicultural Competency in Music Therapy: The First Step. *Music Therapy Perspectives, 34*(2), 129–137.

Hall, S. (1996). New Ethnicities. In K. Chen, S. Hall, & D. Morley (Eds.), *Stuart Hall: Critical Dialogues in Cultural Studies* (pp. 442–451). London, UK: Routledge.

Hanser, S. B. (2001). A systems analysis approach to music therapy practica. In M. Forinash (Ed.), *Music therapy supervision* (pp. 87–98). Gilsum, NH: Barcelona Publishers.

Helms, J. (1990). *Black and White Racial Identity: Theory, Research, and Practice.* New York, NY: Greenwood Press.

Hoshmand, L. T. (2006). *Culture, psychotherapy, and counseling: Critical and integrative perspectives.* Thousand Oaks, CA: SAGE.

Hoskins, M. L. (1999). Worlds apart and lives together: Developing cultural attunement. *Child and Youth Care Forum, 28*(2), 73–85.

Hoskyns, S. (2007). "New Night Sky": *Renewing My Music Therapy Culture. Voices* Resources. Retrieved January 12, 2015, from http://testvoices.uib.no/community/?q=colhoskyns070507

Inman, A. G., Hutman, H., Pendse, A., Devdas, L., Luu, L., & Ellis, M. V. (2014). Current trends concerning supervisors, supervisees, and clients in clinical supervision. In C. E. Watkins, Jr., & D. L. Milne (Eds.), *The Wiley international handbook of clinical supervision* (pp. 61–102). Hoboken, NJ: Wiley-Blackwell.

Jenkins, R. (2008). *Rethinking ethnicity.* Thousand Oaks, CA: SAGE.

Kenny, C. (2003). Beyond This Point There Be Dragons: Developing General Theory in Music Therapy. *Voices: A World Forum for Music Therapy, 3*(2). doi:10.15845/voices.v3i2.129

Kenny, C. (2006). *Music and life in the field of play.* Gilsum, NH: Barcelona Publishers.

Kenny, C., & Stige, B. (2002). *Contemporary voices in music therapy: Communication, culture, and community.* Oslo, Norway: Oslo Academic Press.

Kim, S. (2007). *Cross-cultural music therapy Supervision.* Unpublished manuscript, Temple University, Philadelphia.

Kim, S. (2008). The supervisee's experience in cross-cultural music therapy supervision. *Qualitative inquiries in music therapy: A monograph series, 4,* 1–44.

Kim, S. (2011). Predictors of acculturative stress among international music therapy students in the U.S. *Music Therapy Perspectives, 13,* 126–132.

Kim, S. (2013a, April). *Multicultural training for the healthcare professionals and students.* Poster presentation at the Conference of the Mid-Atlantic Region of AMTA, Scranton, PA.

Kim, S. (2013b). Bringing my Asian identity to light through acculturation. In S. Hadley (Ed.), *Experiencing race as a music therapist: personal narratives* (pp. 151–162). Gilsum, NH: Barcelona Publishers.

Kim, S., Sairam, T., Shapiro, N., & Swamy, S. (2012, March). *When a paradigm shifts: Therapeutic applications of music therapy across cultures.* Presentation at the Conference of the Mid-Atlantic Region of AMTA, Baltimore, MD.

Kobayashi, H., & Rinnert, C. (1992). Effects of first language on second-language writing: Translation versus direct composition. *Language Learning, 42,* 183–215.

Marginson, S. (1999). After globalization: emerging politics of education. *Journal of Educational Policy, 14*(1), 19–31.

Marginson, S. (2003). *Markets in Higher Education: National and Global Competition.* ANZARE/AARE Joint Conference, Auckland, New Zealand.

McGoldrick, M., Giordano, J., & Garcia-Preto, N. (Eds.). (2005). *Ethnicity and family therapy.* New York, NY: Guilford Press.

McIntosh, P. (2010). White privilege and male privilege. *The teacher in American society: A critical anthology, 121,* 83–92.

Misra, R., Crist, M., & Burant, C. J. (2003). Relationships among life stress, social support, academic stressors, and reactions to stressors of international students in the United States. *International Journal of Stress Management, 10,* 137–157.

Nagata, A. L. (2004). Promoting self-reflexivity in intercultural education. *Journal of Intercultural Communication, 8,* 139–167.

Ng, R. (2005). Embodied Pedagogy as Transformative Learning: A Critical Reflection. *Canadian Association for the Study of Adult Education: National Conference On-Line Proceedings.* London, Ontario.

Nilsson, J. E. (2007). International students in supervision: Course self-efficacy, stress, and cultural discussions in supervision. *Clinical Supervisor, 26*(1/2), 35–47.

Nilsson, J. E., & Dodds, A. K. (2006). A pilot phase in the development of the international student supervision scale. *Journal of Multicultural Counseling and Development, 34,* 50–62.

Odell-Miller, H., & Krueckeberg, N. (2014). Music therapy supervision with trainees in adult psychiatry. In H. Odell-Miller & E. Richards (Eds.), *Supervision of Music Therapy* (pp. 113–130). London, UK: Routledge.

Oswanski, L., & Donnenwerth, A. (2017). Allies for Social Justice. In A. Whitehead-Pleaux & X. Tan (Eds.), *Cultural Intersections in Music Therapy: Music, Health, and the Person* (pp. 257–270). Dallax, TX: Barcelona Publishers.

Palmer, P. J. (2007). *The courage to teach: Exploring the inner landscape of a teacher's life.* New York, NY: John Wiley & Sons.

Parham, (1989). Cycles of Psychological Nigrescence. *The Counseling Psychologist, 17*(2), 187–226.

Pedersen, P. B., & Pope, M. (2010). Inclusive cultural empathy for successful global leadership. *American Psychologist, 65*(8), 841–854.

Phinney, J. (1990). Ethnic Identity in Adolescents and Adults: A Review of Research. *Psychological Bulletin, 108*(3), 499–514.

Phinney, J. (2005). Ethnic Identity in Late Modern Times: A Response to Rattansi and Phoenix. *Identity: An International Journal of Theory and Research, 5*(2), 187–194.

Phinney, J. S. (1989). Stages of ethnic identity development in minority group adolescents. *The Journal of Early Adolescence, 9*(1–2), 34–49.

Phinney, J. S., & Ong, A. D. (2007). Conceptualization and measurement of ethnic identity: Current status and future directions. *Journal of Counseling Psychology, 54*(3), 271.

Priestley, M. (1994). *Essays on analytical music therapy.* Gilsum, NH: Barcelona Publishers.

Radhakrishnan, R. (2001). Nationalism, Gender, and Identity. In G. Castle (Ed.), *Postcolonial Discourses: An Anthology* (pp. 190–205). Oxford, UK: Blackwell Publishers.

Ramos-Sánchez, L., Esnil, E., Goodwin, A., Riggs, S., Ratanasiripong, P., Touster, L. O., Wright, L. K., & Rodolfa, E. (2002). Negative supervisory events: Effects on supervision and supervisory alliance. *Professional Psychology: Research and Practice, 33*(2), 197.

Rapp, H. (2000). Working with difference: Culturally competent supervision. In C. Feltham & B. Lawton (Eds.), *Taking Supervision Forward: Enquiries and Trends in Counselling and Psychotherapy* (pp. 93–112). London, UK: SAGE.

Rattansi, A., & Phoenix, A. (1997). Rethinking youth identities. Modernist and post-modernist frameworks. In J. Bynner, L. Chisholm, & A. Furlong (Eds.), *Youth, Citizenship, and Social Change in a European Context* (pp. 87–101). London, UK: Ashgate.

Rice, N., & O'Donohue, W. (2002). Cultural sensitivity: A critical examination. *New Ideas in Psychology, 20*(1), 35–48.

Ridley, C. R., & Lingle, D. W. (1996). Cultural empathy in multicultural counseling: A multidimensional process model. In P. B. Pedersen, J. G. Draguns, W. J. Lonner, & J. E. Trimble (Eds.), *Counseling across cultures* (pp. 21–46). Thousand Oaks, CA: SAGE Publications.

Ridley, C. R., Mendoza, D. W., Kanitz, B. E., Angermeier, L., & Zenk, R. (1994). Cultural sensitivity in multicultural counseling: A perceptual schema model. *Journal of Counseling Psychology, 41*(2), 125–136.

Rudmin, F. W. (2003). Critical history of the acculturation psychology of assimilation, separation, integration, and marginalization. *Review of General Psychology, 7,* 3–37.

Sandhu, D. S. (1995). An examination of the psychological needs of the international students: Implications for counseling and psychotherapy. *International Journal for the Advancement of Counseling, 17,* 229–239.

Santamaria, L .J. (2009). Culturally responsive differentiated instruction: Narrowing gaps between best pedagogical practices benefiting all learners. *Teachers College Record, 111*(1), 214–247.

Schwartz, S., Zamboanga, B., Rodriguez, L., & Wang, S. (2007). The Structure of Cultural Identity in an Ethnically Diverse Sample of Emerging Adults. *Basic and Applied Social Psychology, 29*(2), 159–173.

Shulman-Fagen, T. (2001). The creative arts in group supervision. In M. Forinash (Ed.), *Music therapy supervision* (pp. 149–160). Gilsum, NH: Barcelona Publishers.

Stige, B. (2001). The fostering of not-knowing barefoot supervisors. In M. Forinash (Ed.), *Music therapy supervision* (pp. 161–177). Gilsum, NH: Barcelona Publishers.

Stige, B. (2002). *Culture-centered music therapy.* Gilsum, NH: Barcelona Publishers.

Sue, D. W. (2004). Racial-cultural competence: Awareness, knowledge, and skills. In R. T. Carter (Ed.), *Handbook of racial-cultural psychology and counseling, training, and practice.* New York, NY: John Wiley & Sons.

Sue, D. W., Arredondo, P., & McDavis, R. J. (1992). Multicultural competencies/standards: A pressing need. *Journal of Counseling and Development, 70,* 477–486.

Summer, L. (2001). Group supervision in first-time music therapy practicum. In M. Forinash (Ed.), *Music therapy supervision* (pp. 69–86). Gilsum, NH: Barcelona Publishers.

Swamy, S. (2011a). "No, she doesn't seem to know anything about cultural differences!": Culturally centered music therapy supervision. *Music Therapy Perspectives, 29*(2), 133–137.

Swamy, S. (2011b). *Temple of Ancient Knowing: Music Therapy Portraits of Globalized Indian Identity* (Doctoral dissertation). Available from ProQuest Dissertations and Theses database. (UMI No. 3561400).

Swamy, S. (2014). Music Therapy in the Global Age: Three Keys to Successful Culturally Centered Practice. *The New Zealand Journal of Music Therapy, 12,* 34–57.

Swamy, S. (2017). Music Therapy in the South Asian American Diaspora. In A. Whitehead-Pleaux & X. Tan (Eds.), *Cultural Intersections in Music Therapy: Music, Health, and the Person.* Gilsum, NH: Barcelona Publishers.

Tatum, B. (1992). Talking about race, learning about racism: The application of racial identity development theory in the classroom. *Harvard Educational Review, 62*(1), 1–25.

Tatum, B. D. (2001). Defining racism: Can we talk? In P. S. Rothenberg (Ed.), *Race, class, and gender in the United States: An integrated study* (pp. 100–107). New York, NY: Worth Publishers.

Tatum, B. D. (2007). *Why are all the Black kids sitting together in the cafeteria? And other conversations about race.* New York, NY: Basic Books.

Tervalon, M., & Murray-Garcia, J. (1998). Cultural humility versus cultural competence: A critical distinction in defining physician training outcomes in multicultural education. *Journal of health care for the poor and underserved, 9*(2), 117–125.

The Power of International Education. (2017). *Open doors.* Retrieved October, 2017, from http://www.iie.org/opendoors

Toporek, R. L., Ortega Villalobos, L., & Pope Davis, D. B. (2004). Critical incidents in multicultural supervision: Exploring supervisees' and supervisors' experiences. *Journal of Multicultural Counseling and Development, 32*(2), 66–83.

Toppozada, M. A. (1995). Multicultural training for music therapists: An examination of current issues based on a national survey of professional music therapists. *Journal of Music Therapy, 32*(2), 65–90.

Tseng, V. (2004). Family interdependence and academic adjustment in college: Youths from immigrant and U.S.-born families. *Child Development, 75,* 966–983.

United States Department of Education. (2015). *Education and Title VI (ED/OCR 91-27R).* Retrieved from https://www2.ed.gov/about/offices/list/ocr/docs/hq43e4.html

Vandiver, B. J., Fhagen Smith, P. E., Cokley, K. O., Cross, W. E., & Worrell, F. C. (2001). Cross's nigrescence model: From theory to scale to theory. *Journal of multicultural counseling and development, 29*(3), 174–200.

Wang, P., & Machado, C. (2015). Meeting the needs of Chinese English-language learners at writing centers in America: A proposed culturally responsive model. *Journal of International Students, 5*(2), 143–160.

Wheeler, B. L. (2002). Experiences and concerns of students during music therapy practice. *Journal of Music Therapy, 39*(4), 274–304.

Wheeler, B. L. (2005). *Clinical training guide for the student music therapist.* Gilsum, NH: Barcelona Publishers.

Whitehead-Pleaux, A., & Tan, X. (2017). *Cultural intersections in music therapy: Music, health, and the person.* Dallas, TX: Barcelona Publishers.

Young, L. (2009). Multicultural issues encountered in the supervision of music therapy internships in the United States and Canada. *The Arts in Psychotherapy, 36*(4), 191–201.

Zhang, J. (2008). A comprehensive review of studies on second language writing. *HKBU Papers in Applied Language Studies, 12,* 89–123.

Zhang, X., Shi, R., & Hsu, W. (2016). *A collaborative autoethnographic exploration of experiences of three international music therapy interns during their clinical training.* Unpublished master's thesis, State University of New York, New Paltz, NY.

Chapter 15

DISTANCE MUSIC THERAPY SUPERVISION: QUESTIONS, REFLECTIONS, AND PRACTICES

Mary-Carla MacDonald
Christine Routhier
Annette Whitehead-Pleaux

INTRODUCTION

Distance supervision is becoming increasingly prevalent in the field of music therapy for both students and professionals, yet there is very little written on this topic. (Abbott, 2010; Clark & Thompson, 2016; Krout, 2003; Story, 2014; Viega & Keith; 2012). The fields of counseling and education are perhaps the most senior in research and writing regarding online education, but more recently the art therapy and dance therapy communities have also begun forging ahead in this new territory (Beardall et al., 2016; Brandoff & Lombardi, 2012; Orr, 2010). It is essential that the music therapy community follow suit and begin exploring how music therapy distance supervision is being conducted and what specific issues need to be considered.

Distance supervision is supervision in which technology is used to communicate between the supervisee and supervisor, who reside in different locations. Some of the reasons for the growing popularity of music therapy distance supervision include expansion of the educational programs, as well as the growing need for music therapists to get increasingly specialized supervision that may not be available to them in their locale. As more music therapy programs create and expand existing curricula to include distance learning models, educational practices, including supervision, are changing to meet the needs of students living across the country and internationally. In these programs, supervision courses are being created that include both online and in-person components and are called hybrid courses. Similarly, many clinical music therapists find themselves working in areas where there are few or no music therapists within their own city or county. For these rural clinicians, finding an experienced supervisor is a challenge and has often meant traveling great distances or working in isolation and without supervision. In such cases, distance supervision is a viable option that allows the clinician to find a qualified supervisor who has the specific expertise for which they are looking (Brandoff & Lombardi, 2012).

While the numbers of music therapists continue to grow each year, at the time this chapter was written, there were less than 7,000 practicing in the United States of America (CBMT, 2017). As our profession grows and more music therapists are trained, it is clear that qualified music therapy supervisors are increasingly needed both for students and for clinicians across the country. The American Music Therapy Association (AMTA) Standards of Clinical Practice states that "it is the responsibility of the music therapist to seek and participate in supervision on a regular basis" (AMTA, 2015, n.p.). Furthermore, if we hope to increase the diversity in our field to create a music therapy practice that is reflective and receptive of our clientele, we must increasingly expect our professionals to embrace a stance of cultural humility and educational best practices and be adequately supervised. To continue learning and growing, music therapists need to have access to qualified supervisors in specialized areas and must be able to engage in a reflective process with more experienced clinicians or clinicians experienced with cultural differences. Building on the reflective process and seeking out qualified professionals is essential to the growth of the field. Distance supervision is an answer to these needs, yet it comes with concerns and questions.

Some of the challenges concerning distance supervision have included the technology itself, how to maintain confidentiality, how to create a sense of safety between supervisor and supervisees, how to maintain an online presence, how to support the development of well-rounded, empathic, and musically sensitive therapists, and how to work from a place of cultural humility and openness across all formats with students and professionals. The authors of this chapter have been facilitating distance supervision for many years and have amassed experience in a number of areas. This includes working with undergraduate equivalency students and master's-level students doing practicums or internships across the United States and beyond, as well as supervising professionals locally and internationally. The goal of this chapter is to use this collective experience to shed light on these issues, share practical experiences in supervising both students and professionals, and suggest best practices for music therapy distance supervision.

DISTANCE SUPERVISION IN MUSIC THERAPY EDUCATION

Perhaps what concerns music therapy educators the most regarding distance learning is the question, "Is it possible to re-create online the type of cognitive, emotional, empathic, and sensitive learning that needs to take place in a music therapy education setting?" Music therapy programs are developed around experiential learning, the concept Bruscia (2012) defined as self-experiences. This is a pedagogy focused on both active engagement and self-inquiry. Active engagement takes the form of active music therapy practice. This is accomplished through role-playing, developing treatment plans, and learning to manage the therapeutic process by way of giving, receiving, and co-creating music therapy experiences. "Self-inquiry means that the learner, awakened and stirred by active engagement in music therapy, continually develops the capacity for self-awareness in both client and therapist roles" (Bruscia, 2012, p. 12).

The question then becomes, "Can distance education provide the type of self-experiences required to, as Bruscia said, '… develop self-aware music therapists who are effective practitioners'?" (Bruscia, 2012, p. 12). We, as distance clinical supervisors, have the responsibility to ask of our programs, "How do we, as distance supervisors, provide the means, and support the development, of the well-rounded, musically responsive, culturally aware, qualified music therapist who is needed in the field?" Moreover, how do we, as the supervising "gatekeepers," ensure this in distance supervision as we do in in-person supervision?

While there are questions regarding how to best implement distance supervision, the benefits of this educational model are many. One of the biggest benefits is location. The shift in educational practices that allows for learning to happen where the student resides instead of at the hallowed grounds of the educational institution reflects the realities of modern lives. There are times in students' lives when they cannot pick up and move across the country to a college or university when they want or need the higher learning. They have responsibilities to family, financial obligations, and community ties that limit their ability to relocate for the extent of the educational program. In addition, the costs of uprooting and moving to a campus can be great, for this entails not only tuition but also housing and moving after resigning from gainful employment. Finally, many music therapy programs are located in areas that have a high cost of living. While this is manageable for students who are in the upper-middle and upper socio-economic tiers, these costs may be outside of the budget of students who are in the middle and lower socio-economic tiers. When considering the student debt load and the current salaries of music therapists, these concerns are real and substantial. Distance learning allows for students to get the education they desire and can afford along with fulfilling their responsibilities and obligations. Within this distance educational model resides the practicum and clinical supervision courses, often taught in a hybrid format, with both an on-campus and a distance learning component.

Given the hybrid teaching models that are in place today and the careful vetting of students who are accepted into a hybrid program, we do believe it is possible to provide a high-quality music therapy education; however, this requires a careful examination of the essential makeup of a qualified music therapist and how, without cutting corners, this education can be provided both in person and at a distance. We also must know what can be done from afar and what must be done in person so that in planning the curriculum, the most effective strategies are implemented. In effect, we must educate ourselves in how our students learn and process most efficiently. Given the need for cultural responsiveness in education, clinical practice, and supervision, we must make ourselves aware of differing cultural practices and not confuse these with individual learning traits, not only when teaching from a distance, but also with all supervisees with whom we are working.

CULTURAL RESPONSIVENESS IN DISTANCE SUPERVISION

Over the past several years, the focus of the music therapy profession has begun to turn to culturally responsive or culturally sensitive music therapy practice. In her seminal chapter, Estrella (2001) thoroughly described practices for culturally responsive approaches to music therapy supervision (then termed "multicultural" approaches). Since the writing of that chapter, music therapy has grown in its awareness of cultural responsiveness in practice, education, and supervision (Brown, 2002; Chase, 2003; Hadley, 2006; Kim, 2008; Kim & Whitehead-Pleaux, 2015; Swamy, 2011; Wheeler, 2002; Whitehead-Pleaux, Donnenwerth, Robinson, Hardy, Oswanski, Forinash, Hearns, Anderson, & York, 2012; Young, 2009;. Whitehead-Pleaux & Tan, 2017). Despite this growth, there remains much to do to get to a place of cultural responsiveness across the clinical, educational, and supervisory practices of music therapy.

As cultural sensitivity is incorporated into music therapy education, the challenges of and models for this didactic and experiential learning in the classroom are well documented in the fields of psychology, social work, and counseling. In 2008, Kim explored the experiences of cross-cultural supervision with seven music therapists. Common themes of being understood and misunderstood were identified. Young (2009) asked to what extent culturally responsive supervisory practices were being used by music therapy internship supervisors in Canada and the United States. Young found that despite having many supervisees who were from cultures different from that of the supervisor, the majority of supervisors had little or no formal training in multicultural music therapy and that these issues "were not being consistently addressed" (p. 191). Swamy (2011) described a case study of a cross-cultural supervision where they used a culture-centered, strength-based supervision. In 2017, Whitehead-Pleaux and Tan edited the first text for cultural responsiveness education and training in music therapy in North America. While thorough in its exploration of cultures, bias, and oppression, this text's final section on operationalizing these concepts into clinical and educational practices is underdeveloped. Culturally responsive supervision is not even addressed within the text. As a field, music therapy has a need to define our practices of culturally responsive music therapy clinical and educational supervision, explore the effectiveness of these practices, and develop models and theories of culturally responsive music therapy supervision.

Given the paucity of the music therapy literature on culturally responsive supervision, it is not surprising that the topic of culturally responsive distance supervision has not been explored. In fact, research and theory in our sister professions of psychology, social work, art therapy, drama therapy, dance/movement therapy, and counseling about incorporating cultural responsiveness into distance supervision are still young.

In examining educational practices for teaching cultural responsiveness in distance formats, one of the earliest (but still relevant) articles addressed the challenges and benefits of this form of education. Ancis's (1998) study focused on televised education (in practice for over 40 years and consisting of largely receptive experiences of watching an educator teach through a medium like television) and identified elements of cultural competence training: assessing needs, in-class discussions and experientials, skill practicing, and affective processing. Assessing needs often takes the form of assessing the students' "level of awareness, knowledge, and skills" (p. 136). This can be conducted through pre-existing inventories that assess cultural competence. Discussions and experientials help students to identify, express, and change their beliefs, biases, emotions, and thoughts about topics within cultural competence. Skill practice allows students to begin to master the skill needed for culturally responsive practice. Finally, affect processing allows the students to process the affect related to the educational content and their personal self-growth.

Ancis (1998) continued by discussing the strategies for culturally competent distance education, which include humanizing, setting ground rules, active learning, and interdisciplinary teams. Humanizing is creating an environment where the students feel accepted and honored for where they are in the process of learning about cultural responsiveness. Setting ground rules is self-explanatory but essential to attaining the depth of personal involvement required for this form of learning. Active learning is "guiding students through a process of self-initiated learning (that) fosters the self-reflection and critical thinking necessary to becoming culturally competent professionals" (Ancis, 1998, p. 139). Finally, incorporating interdisciplinary teaching teams that are able to address the myriad of topics and needs of students learning cultural competence is necessary. This can include guest lectures from experts or first-person input from minority members.

While Ancis's (1998) work is about distance educational practices, these practices give us guidance for distance supervisory cultural responsiveness practices. In considering assessing needs, discussions, and experientials, skill practicing, and affective processing, distance supervisors (in both educational and clinical practices) can address these within our sessions. A needs assessment is the best strategy for understanding our supervisee's strengths and areas of need within the realm of cultural sensitivity. There are a myriad of pre-existing models and inventories that music therapy supervisors can use to understand the starting point with the supervisees. Many of these can be used to track changes through the supervisory experience. These can be administered in the distance format either asynchronously (as 'homework') or synchronously (during supervisory sessions). SAMHSA.gov (Substance Abuse and Mental Health Services, n.d.) and Transcultural Care Associates (Transcultural Care, 2015) have a multitude of easily accessible assessments.

Discussions and experientials are core components of music therapy supervision, and conversations about cultural sensitivity are easily incorporated into the standard practice within music therapy distance supervision. In distance supervision, our ability to engage in music therapy supervisory experientials can be limited to asynchronous times, but this does not change the depth of their impact or the need for these experientials. Video and audio recordings can allow the supervisor to experience the musical explorations of the supervisee and then explore the expressions of the supervisee more deeply. This deeper processing is essentially Ancis's fourth element, affective processing.

All of this needs to be carefully moderated with an understanding of the supervisee's educational background, knowing that the type of education system from which a supervisee comes influences their perception of the supervisee and supervisor roles, the power divisions, and therefore the nature of one's contributions within the course. I (MacDonald) find this a benefit of the asynchronous model, as I am able to do a little coaching and work with a supervisee behind the scenes if needed. I also note that it is not only educational systems that impact comfort level regarding contribution and argument; many aspects of personality, culture, and experiential development also all naturally impact supervisee/supervisee and supervisee/supervisor interactions.

At Lesley University, graduate students have an entire class that is devoted to "Power, Privilege, and Oppression." This is a hybrid course in which the students begin together, in person, during the summer and continue the course online during the first semester of their studies. This is a luxury for me (MacDonald), as I begin the supervision class after students have completed this course. The students I have are consequently primed to continue the conversation and exploration in diversity. Even so, I sometimes still find myself needing to remember to stop and lead a reflection into patterns that may be emerging at student sites or within our group that could be reflective of unexplored issues of diversity. Recently, a student spoke about feeling "spoken over" and "overlooked" in her on-site group supervision. She had attributed this to there being a larger number of students from a different school of thought, but we felt that we needed to dig a little deeper. The group was engaged in the discussion, and questions such as "What cultures are represented in your group?" and "Were they mostly male or female?" were carefully explored. The conversation was one that could take place online or in person. The ability to encourage and support these conversations has come from a great deal of work on my ownership and understanding of my privilege, even though I acknowledge I have a great deal more to learn. And, if I am honest, I must say that my students have been my greatest inspiration and source of knowledge. By incorporating Ancis's four elements, we can be grounded in a more culturally responsive supervision.

VIDEO- AND TELEPHONE CONFERENCING

Commonly used tools in distance supervision include videoconferencing, email, chats, discussion boards, and phone conversations (Lund & Schultz, 2015). Videoconferencing software allows the supervisor and supervisee to meet face-to-face and includes such platforms as Skype, Skype for Business, Zoom, and Vsee, among others. Videoconferencing and phone conversations are considered synchronous devices because participants communicate in real time, unlike communications such as email, threaded discussions, and file-sharing, which involve a delay in time and are thus asynchronous. A learning management system (LMS) (such as Blackboard, Canvas, Moodle, and others) used by universities offers both asynchronous and synchronous methods and includes such technologies as email, file-sharing, blogs, discussion boards, wikis, journals, and videoconferencing.

A great benefit to distance music therapy group supervision is the ability to schedule the meetings at a time outside of the traditional college and workday hours. Supervision groups are scheduled while taking into consideration everyone's schedules (school, work, and family), and times are chosen that are (as best as possible) convenient for everyone. With students or supervisees living in different time zones, this process is more complicated, but with flexible mind-sets, a time is found. Online poll services like Doodle can be used to find times when everyone can meet. Most of these services adjust the times within the poll to match the time zone of the people responding to the poll. The use of a world clock app with the time zones of each supervisee set up to be easily accessible can be a simple way of dealing with this. When working internationally, the time change becomes an even larger issue, especially at the beginning of the work. Setting up compatible time frames and consistently speaking in terms of the supervisees' time zone is helpful. It is also recommended to have a consistent time to meet from week to week. This eliminates the back-and-forth emails and the possible miscommunications. Supervising internationally, the supervisor can often feel "far away' from the supervisee, especially when there is a continent, let alone an ocean, dividing them. It is helpful to have regular and consistent contact either through videoconferencing or emails or both, thereby decreasing the sense of distance. Being sensitive to both the supervisees' and supervisor's time constraints will have a clear, positive impact on the feelings of mutual respect and will go a long way toward building a sense of trust.

Because most videoconferencing software has been developed for voice exchanges and to filter out "background" sounds, there are challenges to participants attempting to engage in group conversation or music-making in a spontaneous and natural way. Words and sounds cannot overlap, as they cancel each other and a gap is created. Pauses are needed between phrases. This can lead to more stilted and superficial conversations, and time must be given to allow movement beyond this initial discomfort. A musical or vocal warm-up is sometimes helpful for breaking the ice and practicing taking turns speaking or playing. For example, warm-ups that I (MacDonald) have used include passing around a rhythm between students, using a call-and-response song, and even passing a movement from one supervisee to the next. Supervisees and supervisors need to watch and listen for their turn and the space to respond patiently without jumping in, as there can occasionally be a time lag. I start out with warm-ups being individual to individual, allowing the supervisees to habituate to the pacing and feel of the technology. This is a great way to practice working with clients and being aware of the importance of leaving time for responding and not rushing the process. The pace of conversation is also slowed down, which allows for deeper listening and gives time for native and non-native English speakers to formulate more in-depth responses. The students are reminded that they must find a way to work with the technology and find creative solutions to connect in the music and discussion. Recently, a pair of my (Routhier) students discovered that Facetime can be used without canceling the sound. The students were able to successfully improvise together online, hear each other, feel connected, and record the improvisation. New formats (such as JamKazam) coming online are beginning to allow musicians to play face-to-face without experiencing lag time or having the sound cancel out.

Creative thinking can help to overcome technological complications, and music can also be incorporated in an asynchronous manner. I (Whitehead-Pleaux) have asked supervisees to state the title of a song that reflects their experience of a practicum session or one that resonates with their therapeutic identity. Similarly, I have assigned improvisations and songwriting to explore the relationship with their client and had them submit sound files to which the group can listen. These workarounds are beneficial but not as powerful as music shared in the moment for all to hear and/or participate in. To assess and instruct on guitar and piano skill acquisition, I require students to play a song from their practicum during the supervision session. Even this practice can sometimes be challenging due to sound quality and technological difficulties.

Videoconferencing technology is still far from perfect. Sessions are challenged by buffering, software updates, frozen video feed, and distorted or stalled sound. While group members are patient with these challenges, they can impact the group members' willingness or ability to share personal or difficult questions, experiences, and feelings. I (Whitehead-Pleaux) remember a group I supervised a few years ago. These students lived in several states across the United States. The students were a diverse group, with members who were Asian, Latinx, white, and queer. One student shared about a session she observed where a male client had aggressive behaviors toward the female music therapist. As the group members offered her support and I provided education about the reasons for aggression, the video feed began to stutter. The group member could hear parts of words but could not understand anything I was saying. They asked me to repeat, which I did, and still they were unable to hear my words due to the technological trouble. This continued for a few minutes. By the time the video feed was functioning normally again, the student and group were frustrated with the interruptions and difficulty in understanding. The student stated that she understood, and the group moved to another topic. However, in the student's journal, it became apparent that she did not hear and understand what I was sharing. To remedy this, I reached out and spoke with that student via phone to discuss the aggressive behaviors further. In addition, during the next group supervision videoconference, we discussed difficulties with communication and the frustrations everyone had felt and related our experiences to those of our clients. This allowed the group members to have empathy for the clients with whom they worked, as well as to develop strategies for future communication problems within our supervision sessions. Although the technology trouble impacted the group supervision process and created frustration within the group members, limiting the students' ability to take in information and respond in the moment, it also became an opportunity for the students to explore the topic of communication more deeply in subsequent sessions. I (Whitehead-Pleaux) also work for a community music therapy company that serves a large geographical area. It is nearly impossible for the full staff of music therapists to meet in one place for peer supervision. To meet the supervision needs of the staff as well as take into consideration the fact that they are spread across half of the state, the founder created distance peer supervision groups that are conducted over the telephone. The staff meet biweekly via a conference call. These calls are facilitated by a lead music therapist and attended by both staff music therapists and the senior clinical supervisor. Staff complete and submit a preparation form each week a few days prior to the supervision meeting. This form helps the music therapists to consider what they want to bring to the peer supervision session, including celebrations, sessions that were challenging, questions about diagnoses or processes, personal goals for the following weeks, and so forth. There are both challenges in and benefits from hosting group supervision via a telephone conference call.

I have found it can be challenging when connecting a group through the phone, as there is no visual information. The music therapists on the call have different intersecting cultural identities. These differences influence the group members' communication styles. In addition, given that these groups meet via telephone, the group members are further limited because they cannot communicate through nonverbal language. Because of this, the emotional content is difficult at times to understand or is missed. This requires the group members and lead music therapist to be aware of this limitation in communication. When messages are unclear, it is the responsibility of group members and the lead music therapist to ask clarifying questions. The lead music therapist must listen carefully for content that is deeper than the words the group member is stating. Probing questions are needed to bring these nonverbal communications to the realm of words.

As in most videoconferencing, telephone calls are not conducive to music. The sound on conference call lines is not ideal. Phone microphones and speakers are not designed to capture the timbres and subtleties of music. Many phone lines do not allow for two or more lines of sound, so only one line of music is heard. I (Whitehead-Pleaux) will often use workarounds such as asking group members to share or post meaningful music, improvisations, or compositions with other members prior to group supervision.

Despite these challenges, there are many benefits to distance telephone group music therapy supervision. The fact that the staff does not have to drive to the company office or a central location to meet makes the frequency of these meetings possible within everyone's busy schedules. It increases productivity and reduces unproductive time spent driving from location to location. We find attendance and participation in the groups is higher, which benefits the music therapists and the clients. In addition to the benefits of supervision for both the client and music therapist, this model allows for facilitating the team's cohesion and support. The music therapists have adapted to this form of supervision and work within its limitations.

Another aspect of distance telephone group music therapy supervision is both a challenge and a benefit. When speaking to someone over the phone, one can hide their affect. This is a limitation to telephone supervision that is not as possible in traditional in-person group supervision. But the flip side of this is the phenomenon whereby it is easier for some folks to share deeper emotional content because the people on the other end of the telephone cannot see them feeling upset or crying. This distance can help some music therapists, who may be challenged to open up and share more in person. This is a curious phenomenon that warrants further study. As the emotional growth of the beginning music therapist is an essential component of their development into a well-rounded clinician, we would suggest the default for communication technology in educational settings include the visual component.

When using a videoconferencing tool, I (Routhier) am still always pleasantly surprised when the technology does what it is intended to do and both the image and the sound are present without glitches. Losing signal or having a poor connection with pauses in the speech is even more of an issue when videoconferencing internationally. It is important to address this eventuality beforehand and to determine with the supervisee what to do in case the signal is lost or is too intermittent. There are times when the signal cannot be recaptured and other times when it helps to remove the camera and just have voice. Planning these eventualities and the steps to take can be outlined in the initial supervision contract.

When videoconferencing internationally, it is also crucial to hold a stance of cultural humility and remember that English is most likely not our supervisees' first language. It is important to be mindful of this in the communications, as supervisees may not say they did not understand parts of the conversations, so checking in to see what was understood is essential. I (Routhier) have found that with many of these tools which allow only one person to speak at a time, it is helpful to speak more slowly than normal, while remaining animated and natural, and to repeat important statements in a number of different ways. Listening and asking questions for clarification and to deepen the learning is essential. When working with international supervisees, the supervisee is obviously the expert on their culture. As a supervisor, it is important to read articles on culturally responsive supervision and on the specific culture of one's supervisees, as well as to go to trainings in order to educate oneself on the issues at hand, but this still does not make one the expert. The supervisee is the expert with regard to their culture and their music, and we have much to learn from them. It is important to realize that when translating words or phrases from one language to the other, the meaning of the words can change substantially. In working with a supervisee living and working in Hong Kong, I (Routhier) recently learned that in spoken Cantonese, the phrase "How do you feel?" is really interpreted as "What are you thinking?" Knowing this made it easier to understand why it was challenging for this supervisee, and for many of their peers, to ask clients how they were feeling. In this case, the supervisee looked toward facial images and made a list of words describing emotions to help the client to identify their feeling states. When supervising internationally, it is impossible to properly address clinical issues without looking at the culture of both the supervisee and their clients.

CONFIDENTIALITY

The issue of confidentiality is an important one to address in distance supervision. We often forget that our devices are on almost 24 hours a day and updating without our knowledge. As Rousmaniere (2014, p. 207) so aptly reminded us, devices are designed with the intention of sharing data. Smartphones automatically "share" their photos through wireless connections, which increases the risk that confidentiality will be violated. Advances in technology over the past 10 or more years have created questions regarding the safekeeping of documents and information and protecting the client's confidentiality. With Cloud storage and backups, the emailing of case notes, the transmitting of video, and live video interaction, there is a myriad of places for data loss, breaches, and mishandling of information. It is essential that both the supervisor and the supervisee make sure they are using equipment and systems that are set up from the outset to protect client and student information and identification.

We also must be conscious that HIPAA (the federal Health Insurance Portability and Accountability Act), FERPA (the Family Educational Rights and Privacy Act), and AMTA codes of ethics are based on Western empiricist views of privacy that are not necessarily reflective of the cultures of our supervisees. The practices of confidentiality in our regulations are built upon the Western centrality of autonomy and independence and may conflict with supervisees' values of collectivism and family interdependence (Abrahams & Salsizar, 2005, p. 145). We, as supervisors practicing under AMTA and certification board guidelines, must be conscious of the different cultural views possible in our supervision groups, and clarification of group mores and rules must be made explicit. Including a statement of confidentiality in the supervision contract is recommended. A discussion among the group members, when creating the specific group norms, is essential to the development of a sense of trust and understanding among group members. Ground rules create safety that allows us to open up and share our humanity and the glories and failings of our work and our being.

Where supervisees choose to conduct their supervisory meeting varies and can impact not only confidentiality but also boundaries. Students and supervisees are often in their homes, and there is an intimacy which is shared that does not happen in the classroom. The supervisee may be at their kitchen table, a dog might want attention, a cat may walk across the screen, or a child may want to say hello to the person on the screen. The supervisee may be in a public space, as in a coffee house or library, and people may be walking by. Not only do these situations present a challenge to confidentiality and boundaries, but also the sound and movement present can be a distraction to all involved and can impact focus and process. For these reasons, it is ideal whenever possible to conduct a videoconference in one's office or in a professional space, free from distractions and appropriate for conducting supervision (Brandoff & Lombardi, 2012).

All educational institutions that receive any funding from the U.S. Department of Education are under the obligation to follow FERPA. When working with student documentation under FERPA, the supervisor must not improperly disclose any identifiable student information derived from student records. Most private postsecondary institutions receive some funding and are therefore under the auspices of FERPA. Schools that are subject to FERPA should have specific guidelines for the supervisor to follow as an employee or contractor of that school. This is why most universities require that all interaction with students via technology must happen through the university's LMS.

There are national and state regulations of which the music therapist must be aware. The AMTA has provided an introduction to HIPAA for music therapists. It is recommended by AMTA that the clinician follow the HIPAA standards and become educated regarding coverage and compliance regardless of whether they submit files electronically. According to the AMTA Standards of Clinical Practice, "The music therapist providing supervision will be familiar with current federal, state, and local laws, as well as the AMTA Code of Ethics, as they pertain to supervision and confidentiality within supervision" (2015, section 8.2.1). Although there is no specific mention of distance supervision, it is safe to assume at this point that the same requirement applies.[19]

Supervisors should follow the guidelines of the state in which they are "working" as well as HIPAA regulations. Therefore, if a supervisor is providing supervision to a therapist or student in another state, the supervisor and student must follow the statutes from both states involved as well as HIPAA. Video recording that includes the client's face can never be de-identified (have all identifying information removed according to HIPAA standards) and is therefore always considered PHI (protected health information). A data use agreement and proper security measures must be taken to safeguard the confidentiality of ePHI (electronic Protected Health Information). Any healthcare provider who electronically transmits PHI is a "covered entity," meaning they are subject to HIPAA. C.F.R.§164.508(a)(2) lists certain exclusions for the covered entity regarding "psychotherapy notes," including "for its own training"; however, this is not explicitly defined and therefore can lead to some confusion. It is not clear whether audio transmissions could be de-identified and, therefore, it is recommended to treat audio in the same way one would treat a video transmission.

REGULATIONS AND ETHICS

Regarding music therapy supervision, Music Therapist-Board Certified (MT-BC) is a national certification and applies across states, which means a supervisor working with a supervisee in another state would have the proper credential. Additionally, it would be helpful for the supervisor to be aware of the legislative issues regarding music therapy in the state in which the supervisee is working. This information is kept up to date on the CBMT website at http://www.cbmt.org/advocacy/state-task-forces-map. Licensure is a more complicated issue and is regulated by states, with different guidelines across state lines. This has made it challenging for distance learning students working

---

[19] Readers are directed to the resources in the Reference List to familiarize themselves with HIPAA regulations.

toward licensure in the state in which they are residing and doing their internship and studying music therapy and counseling in a different state. Universities offering distance learning have had to tackle this issue, and some states make this more challenging than others. It is important to cross-check state requirements of the supervisor to make sure their credentials are accepted by the licensure board in the state in which the supervisee works. If licensure is required, it is easier if the supervisee and supervisor are in the same state.

Liability insurance is also required when supervising therapists or students. If one is working under the umbrella of an organization or university, the institution usually provides the insurance. It is important that supervisors know that they are covered. Insurance companies will typically cover supervisors nationally, but at the time of this writing, it was discovered that an insurance company that covers many music therapists across the nation does not cover international supervision.

Carlisle et al. (2013) reviewed ethical codes from multiple organizations, including the ACA (American Counseling Association), APA (American Psychological Association), and NASW (National Association of Social Work), and came up with a list of ethical recommendations for distance supervision in the field of human services. We have reviewed these recommendations, and many have been incorporated into the list of "Best Practices" that we outline below.

PRESENCE AND SAFETY

Garrison (2010) outlined three components to successful distance or hybrid teaching—social presence, cognitive presence, and teaching presence. The Community of Inquiry Model (COI) is a framework for conceptualizing online learning that utilizes the interaction of these three elements to establish the environment. Social presence "is the extent to which persons are perceived to be real and are able to be authentically known and connected to others in mediated communication" (Bentley, Secret, & Cummings, 2015, p. 494). It can also be described as the building of open communication and a sense of community or group cohesion. "Social presence has been both conceptually and empirically linked to the quality of online learning, including levels of student participation, satisfaction, and student engagement" (Bentley, Secret, & Cummings, 2015, p. 494). Our experiences have found that social presence in the music therapy supervisory community allows for risk-taking, group cohesion, increased group accountability, motivation, and a sense of safety. Cognitive presence refers to how the participants engage in critical thinking and reflection. Teaching presence is anything that involves the instructor's presence within the course environment, including responsiveness and feedback.

Ancis's (1998) strategies of humanizing, setting ground rules, active learning, and interdisciplinary teams are also relevant to distance music therapy supervision and to the concept of presence. As supervisors, we have to work to create a humanizing environment through the technology. We do not want the supervisee to experience us only as a disembodied voice on their cell phone or grainy video on their computer screen. We want them to experience us as living, breathing humans invested in their professional development. By creating an environment where our humanity is apparent and present, our supervisees are able to be human with us as well. They will open up and share who they are and the areas within cultural responsiveness that are difficult.

In an article outlining a hybrid model of dance therapy education, authors Beardall, Blanc, Cardillo, Karman, and Wyles (2016) felt the need to add another phenomenon they called "embodied presence, which they described as "being both kinesthetically and affectively present" (p. 412). Embodied presence crosses over the three components stated above. For the supervisor, it involves a mindful attention and attuning to the supervisee, to their vocal intonation and rhythm, to their posture, to their music, and, ultimately, to their "self." The supervisor models online presence through focused attention, patience, and listening. In a group context, this modeling allows the supervisees to explore and deepen embodied presence by attending to different experiences of self and other. The time spent synchronously is an essential space for exploring and developing embodied presence, with the supervisor modeling and supporting the supervisees' development of such presence.

Distance supervision often asks of the supervisor to be more present and watchful of the nuances of supervisees' verbal and nonverbal communications. When using videoconferencing, we usually position ourselves in front of the camera in such a way that others can see only our head and shoulders. Often the resolution is not ideal (pixelated, blurry, or without clear definition) and the picture is small. This limits my (Whitehead-Pleaux) ability to see the nonverbal communications of the students whom I supervise. I cannot see if they are sharing something while sitting with a relaxed, rigid posture or fidgeting or moving their arms, legs, or torso. The more subtle facial expressions can be missed because of poor video resolution or the small picture. These limitations require the supervisor to be even more present, watching and listening closely for the nonverbal and vocal cues that convey emotional content as well as asking direct questions about the student's emotional reactions that accompany the content they are sharing. An example of this is when an older cis queer Asian student was discussing her group at a memory care unit. One of the White males in the group used sexist language about her body during that session. As she spoke, I could not see if she was upset because I could not observe her body language. After the student talked about the incident and how she handled it, I asked her to describe her emotional reaction in the moment of the incident and in the present as she shared it with the group. I then asked the group members (a rural White cis straight male, an urban White nonbinary queer person, a rural White cis straight female, and an urban Latinx cis straight female) to describe their emotional reactions to hearing about their peer's experience. As the group members processed this incident and their peer's experience, I had to be aware not only of the transference of some group members who had experienced similar incidents, but also of the cultural differences (heritage, regional, age, generational, gender identity, and sexual orientation) between each member and how this incident could be interpreted differently through each group member's cultural lenses. While these direct questions and processing can slow the flow of the content delivery, they are vital in helping the supervisor to accurately understand all that each student is expressing and for the students to accurately understand each other. Finally, it is vital to deepening the supervision process and group cohesion. Additionally, it became a way for me to teach the group members about cultural differences and how these impact our music therapy practices.

To facilitate better learning in diverse student populations, there is increasing evidence that online courses must also be highly supportive and interactive. Although the nature of online music therapy supervision allows for much more interaction individually and in small groups than the typical online classroom setting, we must remain cognizant that online education tends to benefit those who are "highly confident, highly motivated, and high-achieving students" (Jaggars, 2014, para. 12). There is growing evidence to support findings that "the performance gaps that some demographic groups experience during in-person classrooms become even wider in online courses ..." (Jaggars, 2014, para. 9). Although some recent studies have shown that students who are male, African-American, Hispanic, or on financial aid or who have lower grade point averages require more support with online courses than they do with on-campus courses (Jaggars, 2014), it has also been suggested that the use of asynchronous learning (discussion boards, blogging, etc.) can benefit less assertive group members, introverts, or non-native language users by allowing them time to reflect on and develop their ideas more fully and allowing them space to be heard. As in the in-person environment, it is essential to pay attention to the balance of power in conversations and assist all students in taking their place in both synchronous and asynchronous conversations.

In group supervision, presence is built and maintained by means of both the asynchronous and synchronous platforms. In this way, a kind of potential online space is created, similar in many ways to Winnicott's potential space (Winnicott, 1971). This online space becomes a place where supervisees can explore their skills while at the same time staying connected with each other. If the supervisees are required to post their work and comment on their peers' work asynchronously, in a consistent fashion, a safe and engaging online community is created. In this way, group cohesion can be built and maintained.

The discussion board, an asynchronous tool, is used for reading assignments and comments in an academic setting. A student posts questions about the readings, and the remainder of the class is asked to respond to the questions and comment on a peer's post. In this way, an asynchronous discussion is begun. The asynchrony and written aspect of the assignment, which would not be present in a verbal discussion, allows for students to reflect more deeply on the topic, and often they offer more thoughtful comments (Beardall et al., 2016). This continued dialogue and sharing of reflections maintains a community of inquiry which is important to the students' sense of social presence, thereby decreasing their possible sense of isolation. The way in which I (MacDonald) help to facilitate argument and the deepening of learning in an asynchronous discussion, without stalling the discussion by bringing in my voice directly, is to send side emails and comments to individual members of the discussion, perhaps helping them to form a furthering question, challenge a thought, or develop an idea. Some students will do this naturally, and others need behind-the-scenes coaching. Supervisors must familiarize themselves with techniques and pedagogy that will best facilitate development for all supervisees. Oftentimes, I (MacDonald) will recommend that a student do a video or audio recording of their post rather than type it. This can lend a more immediate feel to a slow medium of discussion and can also ease the challenge for those who find so much writing laborious.

The supervisor needs to keep the supervisee engaged in active learning. If synchronous learning experiences, especially music experiences, are not possible, assigning asynchronous learning experiences and engaging in accountability practices in preparation for the next session will bring depth to the sessions and learning of the supervisee. I (Whitehead-Pleaux) have experienced the benefits of the slowed tempo of processing when working with a music therapist who was changing their work population. This therapist was struggling with this shift in identity. We were meeting by telephone, and as I listened to the experiences and emotions about this struggle, I wanted to engage in the arts to open into the deeper processes and see these struggles from a different perspective. I first asked that they draw this struggle using their preferred medium and send it to me before our next meeting. I viewed the jpeg of the drawing prior to our next meeting, and, when we met, we discussed the drawing and they shared what each color and shape personally meant and how colors interacted. I asked for another improvisation on struggle be done before the next session, using the drawing and recording. This was sent to me, and I listened to the improvisation several times. In our next session, we listened to the improvisation together as thoughts and emotions were shared during each section. The roots of the struggle became apparent, and discomfort with the changes in career eased. This process has many similarities to my in-person professional supervision practice, as well as some key differences. The distance aspect of the supervision did not allow for in-the-moment arts interventions. The interventions became homework for this supervisee to complete prior to the next session. This somewhat slowed the process but did not stall it. In fact, the time we spent (several weeks) focusing on this through art, discussion, music, and final discussion deepened the exploration, allowing for more layers to emerge over time.

Having been trained in the Bonny Method of GIM (Guided Imagery and Music), I (Routhier) often use music and imagery as a tool for self-reflection in supervision. This method involves identifying a focus, listening to prerecorded music that holds the supervisee in their internal experience, and drawing while listening to the music. The music can be played from the supervisor's computer for the supervisee to hear, but the sound quality is better if the supervisee is asked to locate the music on their own computer. This method can be done using Skype, with the supervisor witnessing the supervisee drawing and "holding the space" for the supervisee. The supervisee can then lift their image up to the screen for the supervisor to see, or the camera can be placed in such a way that the supervisor watches the image emerge. Discussion of the image and the feelings associated with the image can lead to deep insights regarding the supervisee's clinical work and countertransferential issues that might be present. Another option is to ask the supervisee to do this exercise for homework and send the drawing and the music to the supervisor before the next meeting. For the prerecorded music needed in music and imagery sessions, Spotify, a music streaming service that allows you access to a huge library of music, is used by many. This makes it possible for therapists, interns, and clients to choose client-preferred music during a session and for supervision groups to share music and create group playlists.

Research has indicated that sharing each other's cultures and social identities within a peer group positively impacts interactions. "This interaction encourages them to write more, to learn more, and to change their attitudes toward the other students' cultures" (McKenna, Zarestky, & Anzlovar, 2018, p. 125). Through the use of synchronous tools and videos, supervisors, supervisees, and peers can be brought into a common work or internship site or office and in the process have the experience of being in the same space. As a supervisor, I (Routhier) often find it helpful to give the supervisee a virtual tour of my office or even a view from the window to build rapport and bridge the gap of distance. This will give the supervisee a sense of the space and what it might be like to be sitting in the room with the supervisor. My (MacDonald) supervisees will often take their peer group into their own microcosm by creating a video of the environment and aspects of everyday life in their part of the world. A required assignment in the supervision courses I teach is giving a virtual tour of their clinical site. This is an example of an assignment from the online curriculum that has become an on-campus assignment as well.

> Community is realized through collaboration, shared interest, interaction, and support. A focus on the participant's creation of community within the online space is essential for a successful experience in distance education. Becoming part of a learning community is achieved through increased involvement. Engagement in online learning communities can increase when identities are formed in the environment. (McKenna, Zarestky, & Anzlovar, 2018, p. 124)

I (MacDonald) have found that students who are not used to sharing personal experiences and processes with others will need some support in developing their ability to safely communicate their experiences with their peers, developing safe boundaries, and not disappearing from the community. Ways to address this can often be easier in online learning than in-person, as there is time to have side conversations, private emails, and communication with the supervisor to help the supervisee to formulate their contributions to the communication.

Identity, a construct that is based on the understanding of "self" in relation to "other," has only begun to be researched with regard to its impact on online learning and development of community. There is much to which to pay attention and understand. The exploration of the questions "Who am I?" and "Who am I in relation to this group?" impact the development of safety, understanding, and therefore cohesion. By (MacDonald) asking the question "Who are you?" and "What do you want me to know about you?," I am laying the foundations of communication and pulling together information I need to begin seeing the supervisee in the light in which they want me to understand them. Carefully facilitating awareness of identity, culture, and the importance of acknowledging our sameness and difference is how we begin to form our own community, one in which we can listen to, open to, and support each other.

In clinical music therapy supervision, I (Whitehead-Pleaux) have experienced group members exploring who they are in relation to the group. When communicating through distance, via either phone or videoconference, it is vital for the supervising music therapist to listen for changes in group dynamics such as the isolation or insulation of individual members, alliances, and the splitting of the group members. Through group discussions of these dynamics when they exist, I have helped groups to process the differences (real or perceived) that were the root of these dynamics and bring the group through these necessary developmental processes. With distance supervision, these dynamics are sometimes harder to see, since the meeting space is virtual and group members are not choosing to sit next to each other or apart from others. The supervisor must maintain an awareness of the interpersonal connections between group members, assessing them through attending to who speaks to whom and who is not a part of the conversations. In addition to being a point of growth within the group and for each member, these dynamics can become an important educational moment to help group members not only to understand the dynamics and their roles within these dynamics of the supervision group but also to learn about group dynamics in general and how these may be playing out in the music therapy groups they facilitate.

We know that a sense of safety is fundamental to teaching and to the supervisory process. Beginning an online or hybrid supervisory course with a few days of in-person time can be a crucial component to building safety and trust. Likewise, it is important when the student moves back to their community for them to know when and how to contact the supervisor, as well as what expectations to have for response times and boundaries. In an online learning experience, to make up for the lack of proximity, the supervisor needs to be available to the student perhaps even more readily than in regular in-person supervision. When a former low-residency student was asked to name a key component of a first-year online clinical supervision class, she stated, "… the sense of safety, of knowing you had our backs …." (S. Young, personal communication, October 6, 2017). We must be careful to remember that Western online learning (which we often mistakenly believe will democratize education and benefit all just because it is online!) has been developed largely on "constructivist tenants and Socratic methods of knowledge acquisition" (McKenna, Zarestky, & Anzlovar, 2018, p. 124). To avoid this outcome, it is important to ask about how online supervision works for our supervisees, what their experience is, what is helpful, and where they see challenges.

In a professional setting, it is also ideal if the supervisor and supervisee have first met in person. Sometimes prior students will reach out after graduation for additional supervision once they have established themselves in their state or country of origin. In this case, the relationship is already established with the supervisor. Meeting at a national conference can also be a way of making that first contact in person. As with working with students, frequent and consistent contact with the supervisee helps to bridge the distance gap. It is also crucial for the supervisor and supervisee to respond to communications in a timely fashion, and the guidelines for this should be written out in the initial supervisory contract. An international supervisee, when asked about the benefits and challenges of distance supervision, replied, "I am living … where [there is] no senior music therapist. I found myself struggling in my job. My confidence was no longer there, because no one understands my job. … However, Skype technology is very helpful for reaching my supervisor. … I can see my supervisor's body language and facial expression. My anxiety is decreased when we have face-to-face conversations. … Online supervision has been helping me to reflect on myself, conceptualize my work, and create professional goals and clinical goals. The most challenging are time zone and Internet reception …" (S. Apisutiporn, personal communication, May 6, 2018).

CLINICAL OBSERVATIONS

Except for the use of videoconferencing tools, the majority of clinical observation formats are found to be asynchronous and based on case reporting. Amerikaner and Rose, in their 2012 study, showed that although supervisors and supervisees would prefer methods allowing for direct observation, supervisors are still largely relying on case report methods for supervision. It is the supervisee who brings in the case material to be discussed, and therefore supervision tends to be directed by the supervisee rather than by a cooperative assessment of need. Although video of sessions can be supervised synchronously and asynchronously, Remote Live Supervision (RLS) is now technically as simple as using a phone stand and a good microphone (not to mention the ethical requirements and scheduling issues). With these simple tools, the supervisor can literally become the fly on the wall in a replication of the old one-way mirror observation room. In fact, I (MacDonald) have literally been the fly on the wall in a clinical session when a student used Velcro to attach the phone out of reach and also out of sight and out of the mind of a young client.

Originally, RLS began through a one-way mirror, with the supervisor communicating with the supervisee via a telephone or walking into the room. With advances in technology came what is commonly known as the "Bug in the Ear" (BITE) technique, whereby the supervisee was fitted with an earpiece that allowed them to receive in-the-moment feedback from the supervisor. RLS has continued to evolve with the use of "Bug in the Eye" interactions through which instead of speaking, the supervisor types or texts to a screen (computer, tablet, phone) that can be viewed by the supervisee and not the client. This can be considered less intrusive than BITE but is also much easier to ignore, which brings up its own set of issues. Regardless of its drawbacks, one can see why this method is being incorporated into distance synchronous supervision. The supervisor no longer needs to be in an adjacent room or even in the same country as the supervisee.

Of course, as with any supervisory method, deciding when and with whom to use RLS needs to be clearly vetted, and all confidentiality, security, informed consent, and supervisory expectations need to be put into place. It also should be noted that the use of RLS with students is not a substitute for appropriate supervision at the clinical site. Should an emergency arise, there needs to be appropriate personnel within helping distance of the supervisee and client. As common sense and teaching methodology would dictate, the supervisor must be careful not to be intrusive, pick their moments to intervene, and be clear and brief so as not to overwhelm the student with demands and directives. I (MacDonald) have not gone so far as to give feedback during the session but prefer to observe and give considered feedback afterward. It is thought-provoking, however, to think of the possibilities of lending some support in a "stuck" moment or an idea here or there to help enhance the learning. This is an area to carefully consider and an aspect that calls for research in music therapy supervision.

Benefits cited for the use of BITE supervision include significant improvement in trainees' clinical skills and enhancement of self-efficacy in the trainee. Also, a study of novice teachers of students with disabilities determined that effective teaching behaviors increased through the use of BITE in-class feedback (Kadushin & Harkness, 2014). It was also found that "the supervisor can call attention to nonverbal communication, which is often missed, to the latent meaning of communication, to which the worker fails to respond, or to significant areas for exploration that have been ignored" (Kadushin & Harkness, 2014, p. 314). It also allows for a direct assessment of the supervisee's ability to respond to supervision.

Studies have shown benefits and cost-effectiveness from increasing access to RLS for underserved rural areas, where access to clinical supervision has traditionally been much more challenging. Schmidt, Gage, Gage, Cox, and McLeskey (2015) addressed technologies that allowed them to provide innovative distance supervision to teacher-interns in rural Florida. They addressed issues such as Internet access, data access, noise-canceling microphones, and wide-angle lenses that would be needed in a larger classroom space. They found RLS to have widespread applications and to be an efficacious method of delivering quality supervision to high-need students in "hard to reach" places (Schmidt, Gage, Gage, Cos, & McLeskey, 2015). As these writers have found, working out the technological kinks well before the session is scheduled to start can lead to a very rewarding and educationally beneficial session.

REFLECTIONS ON BEST PRACTICES

As the above literature review and practical examples suggest, there are still many unanswered questions regarding distance supervision, and more investigation is clearly needed. Our hope is that discussions such as this one can form a basis of knowledge that supervisors and supervisees can use to guide their process. The literature not only suggests an increasing need for distance supervision but also indicates multiple positive outcomes. As more platforms and tools continue to be developed, one can only assume that the technology will become easier and more reliable in supporting the healthy formation of a supervisory relationship. For anyone interested in facilitating or entering distance supervision, it is important to keep up with the technology, as there is always something new to explore. This also means knowing what to use, when, and for what purposes. Some communications are better when asynchronous, for example, as when receiving and commenting on progress notes and case presentations. At other times, synchronous platforms are what is needed, especially when connecting or creating a community is the goal.

In many ways, distance supervision is more demanding than typical in-person supervision and calls for more attention and resilience on the part of the supervisor and the supervisee. As noted above, nonverbal language can be missed, and miscommunications can easily occur in an online space. This makes it very challenging for the supervisor to provide a safe and engaging supervisory relationship, one that builds not only supervisees' clinical skills but also the self-awareness needed to be an effective clinician. The supervisor must be all the more present with the supervisee, asking many questions when the nonverbal cues are not clear, as a means of "compensating" for the physical distance between them and for the fact that the supervisor cannot see on the screen all that the supervisee might be communicating. The supervisee must also maintain a constant level of commitment and an ongoing state of self-reflection if they are to achieve success in the process. With these many considerations in mind, we have developed the beginnings of an outline of best practices for online teaching.

BEST PRACTICES FOR ONLINE TEACHING

Facilitation and Technology

1. Both the supervisor and supervisee must have familiarity with the technology being used—both asynchronous and synchronous delivery methods—and stay up to date on the most current innovations for reducing lag time and facilitating collaborative music-making online.
2. An asynchronous tool (email, discussion thread) should be used for task items such as scheduling, sharing resources discussed in supervision sessions, or deepened deliberation on readings or self-reflection.
3. Synchronous tools should be used for such items as building the supervisory relationship, playing music together, or negotiating professional boundaries (Orr, 2010).
4. It is preferable to use a hard-wired direct Internet connection rather than wifi in order to sustain a better connection.
5. The supervisor and supervisee should discuss backup plans for when the technology fails during supervision. These guidelines should be included in the contract agreement.

Regulations

1. Supervisor and supervisee must understand and comply with applicable laws for the sites (local, county, state/province, and country) at which they are working.
2. Supervisor and supervisee must have liability insurance appropriate for their locality.

Confidentiality

1. The supervisor and supervisee must use equipment and systems that are set up to protect the supervisee and their client information and identification, using systems that are secure and encrypted end to end.
2. Supervisor and supervisee should familiarize themselves with the Safe Harbor method of de-identification and adhere to this method in all communications.
3. The supervisee must be informed of the additional risks to confidentiality of using technological transmissions.
4. The supervisor and supervisee should discuss confidentiality, security, and encryption policies, and these should be written into the contract agreement.
5. Supervisors must be familiar with FERPA and HIPAA guidelines as necessary. This information should be included in the contract agreement, and all federal and state laws must be followed.
6. A consent for consultation with on-site supervisors signed by all parties involved should be used whenever possible.
7. Both supervisor and supervisee should be in a private space free of outside interference when videoconferencing. There needs to be an agreed-upon norm regarding the mindful use of and respect for the supervisory space. This should be stated in the contract.

Creating Presence and Safety

1. The supervisor must maintain a state of embodied presence at all times when videoconferencing with the supervisee.
2. Extra attention from the supervisor is required to create the community space, allowing for listening and holding to take place. Supervisors need to model online presence, focused attention, patience, and listening.
3. It is preferable that the supervisor and supervisee have at least one in-person encounter before engaging in distance supervision in order to meet and get to know each other. It may also be helpful to have the supervisee tour the supervisor's office via videoconferencing.
4. Getting online and checking the technology before the actual beginning of the supervision session is important to avoid potential technological malfunctions. It should be understood that the supervisor and supervisee will be ready to begin at the appointed time.
5. Supervisor and supervisee should discuss how the supervisor should be contacted in case of an emergency and what is the expected response time for both parties.
6. It is highly recommended that the supervisor have the opportunity to "view" the supervisee's work, either live or recorded. The frequency of such viewings is a question to be explored.

Cultural Issues

1. The supervisor should display cultural humility toward the supervisee and have training in working with cultural differences and multicultural supervision.
2. The supervisor and supervisee should discuss cultural and language differences, that is, confidentiality, boundaries, and so on, that may have an impact on distance supervision.

3. The supervisor needs to be aware that, in distance supervision, they are entering into the supervisee's cultural space and that the supervisee remains immersed in their own culture.
4. The supervisor needs to not only map out their own intersectional identities that consider where they have power and privilege, but also ask supervisees to do the same. The supervisor can then use these visuals during calls as a reminder of where their intersectional cultural identities are shared and where they are different. The supervisor can also be aware of cultural power differences within the relationship(s).
5. The supervisor and supervisee need to pay attention to the affect conveyed in written word correspondence and be aware that writing in a non-native language can impact interpretation of the intended meaning.

Educational and Supervisory Pedagogy and Andragogy

1. The supervisor should establish a clear understanding of how distance learning and supervision change the face of traditional supervision and are best facilitated online.

CONCLUSION

It is safe to assume that distance supervision will only become more prominent as online education grows and music therapy continues to develop worldwide. The literature currently indicates that it can be an effective form of supervision if ethical and technical issues continue to be diligently addressed. We know that it reaches out to practitioners who would otherwise be unable to access these services, yet as may have become apparent to the reader, distance supervision is not for everyone. There will be supervisees who will need more support, guidance, and accountability than can be practically provided by a supervisor who lives far away. There are also subtle nonverbal communications that, although important, can be missed when the supervisor and supervisee are not meeting in person. Over time, these breaks in communication can lead to a feeling of not being supported (supervisee) or of not being effective (supervisor). Distance supervision demands a constant monitoring and a strong presence on the part of the supervisor, possibly more so than in the case of in-person supervision. To this end, it is important that the dynamics of distance supervision be more fully examined to better grasp the differences between distance supervision and in-person supervision and to understand the role of the different factors involved. The initial question of whether distance supervision can create a learning environment that provides the type of self-experiences that build self-aware and effective music therapists may not have been completely answered. Further investigation is still needed to better understand the experiences of the supervisors and supervisees and to determine what crucial variables are required for building and sustaining the supervisory relationship and the reflective process necessary for developing effective practitioners at a distance.

As technology continues to change and advance, technological challenges are decreasing; sound latency is improving, video feed provides better and better resolution, multiple lines of sound are becoming allowed, and so forth. Will future videoconference group supervision ever be the same as group supervision in which all participants are in the same room? This answer is unknown, but likely the experience will be different. Do we even want it to be the same? Different doesn't mean less than or not as good as. It means the experience will be different, but just as there can be many trails to the summit of a mountain, there can be many ways to provide clinical supervision to students and professionals. As we continue to grow in our understanding of distance supervision, we will make more informed choices of the what, when, how, and why of online supervision. We will be able to better utilize the benefits of distance supervision in our curriculum development, use the tools to their full power to support the supervisory process, and nurture students and clinicians who, because of distance, socio-economic factors, language, or other barriers to in-person supervision, may not otherwise have the opportunity. We will continue to incorporate into our in-person supervision many of the technologies and techniques that have come from distance supervision and have been invaluable to the work. Potential clients in distant locales, who otherwise wouldn't have access to music therapy, will benefit from the expanded distribution of appropriately supervised music therapists.

In 2010, Wright and Griffiths concluded that research is "urgently needed" (p. 701) to look at how technology affects the supervisory relationship. They remind us that supervision is part of self-care and not only helps to prevent burnout but also helps us to maintain an ethical practice. Distance supervision allows more music therapists to have access to specialized supervision by experienced supervisors, keeping our profession robust and ethically sound. With this in mind, it is also crucial that the music therapy field continue to wrestle with and examine developments in distance supervision in order to contribute our knowledge and understanding to those of related expressive arts therapy, education, and counseling fields. As we venture more into distance supervision, our literature must catch up to what is being practiced. This means combining research, theory, and practice with the needs and desires of our supervisees and our best supervisory judgment. With each of these, we create a sturdy base for the continued growth of distance supervision within the field of music therapy.

REFERENCE LIST

Abbott, E. (2010). The Bonny method: Training innovations at Anna Maria College. *Voices: A World Forum for Music Therapy, 10*(3). doi:10.15845/voices.v10i3.501

Abrahams, S., & Salazar, C. (2005). Potential conflicts between cultural values and the role of confidentiality when counseling South Asian clients: Implications for ethical practice. In G. R. Walz & R. K. Yep (Eds.), VISTAS: *Compelling perspectives on counseling* (pp. 145–148). Alexandria, VA: American Counseling Association.

American Music Therapy Association. (2014). *Code of ethics.* Retrieved from http://www.musictherapy.org/ethics.html

American Music Therapy Association. (2015). *Standards of clinical practice.* Retrieved from https://www.musictherapy.org/about/standards/#general_standard

American Music Therapy Association. (2017). *2017 AMTA member survey and workforce analysis.* Retrieved from www.musictherapy.org

Amerikaner, M., & Rose, T. (2012). Direct observation of psychology supervisees' clinical work: A snapshot of current practice. *The Clinical Supervisor, 31*(1), 61–80. doi:10.1080/07325223.2012.671721

Bentley, K. J., Secret, M. C., & Cummings, C. R. (2015). The centrality of social presence in online teaching and learning in social work. *Journal of Social Work, 51*(3), 494–505. doi:10.1080/10437797.2015.1043199

Beardall, N., Blanc, V., Cardillo, N. J., Karman, S., & Wiles, J. (2016). Creating the online body: Educating dance/movement therapists using a hybrid low-residency model. *American Journal of Dance Therapy, 38*, 407–428. doi:10.1007/s10465-016-9228-y

Berry, R. M., Ashby, K. S., Gnilka, P. B., & Matheny K. B. (2011). A comparison of face-to-face distance coaching practices: Coaches' perceptions of the role of the working alliance in problem resolution. *Consulting Psychology Journal: Practice and Research, 63*(4), 243–253. doi:10.1037/a0026735

Brandoff, R., & Lombardi, R. (2012) Miles apart: Two art therapists' experience of distance supervision. *Art Therapy, 29*(2), 93–96. doi:10.1080/07421656.2012.683729

Brown, J. M. (2002, March). Towards a culturally centered music therapy practice. *Voices: A World Forum for Music Therapy, 2*(1). doi:10.15845/voices.v2i1.72

Bruscia, K. E. (2012). Self-Experiences in the Pedagogy of Music Therapy. In K. E. Bruscia (Ed.), *Self-experiences in Music Therapy Education, Training, and Supervision* (pp. 12–19). Gilsum, NH: Barcelona Publishers.

Carlisle, R. M., Carlisle, K. L., Hill, T., Kirk-Jenkins, A. J., & Polychronopoulos, G. B. (2013). Distance supervision in human services. *Journal of Human Services, 33*(1), 17ff. Retrieved from http://link.galegroup.com/apps/doc/A418982811/AONE?u=9211haea&sid= AONE&xid=003ea177

Chase, K. M. (2003). Multicultural Music Therapy: A Review of Literature. *Music Therapy Perspectives, 21*(2).

Clark, I. N., & Thompson G. A. (2016). Reflections on music training within e-learning education contexts. *Voices: A World Forum for Music Therapy, 16*(1). Retrieved from https://voices.no/index.php/voices/article/view/835

Deane, F. P., Gonsalvez, C., Blackman, R. J., Saoti, D., & Andresen, R. (2015). Issues in the development of e-supervision in professional psychology: A review. *Australian Psychologist, 50*(3), 241–247. Retrieved from http://ro.uow.edu.au/sspapers/1916

Family Educational Rights and Privacy Act (FERPA). (1974). *20 U.S.C. §1232g; 34 CFR Part 99.*

Garrison, D., Cleveland-Innes, M., & Fung, T. S. (2010). Exploring causal relationships among teaching, cognitive, and social presence: Student perceptions of the community of inquiry framework. *The Internet and Higher Education, 13*(1–2), 31–36. doi:10.1016/j.iheduc.2009.10.002

Hadley, S. (Ed.). (2006). *Feminist perspectives in music therapy.* Gilsum, NH: Barcelona Publishers.

Hadley, S., & Norris, M. (2015). Musical multicultural competency in music therapy: The first step. *Music Therapy Perspectives, 34*(2), 129–137. doi:10.1093/mtp/miv045

Jaggars, S. S. (2014). Democratization of education for whom? Online learning and educational equity. *Diversity and Democracy, 17*(1). Retrieved from https://www.aacu.org/ diversitydemocracy/ 2014/winter/jaggars

Kadushin, A., & Harkness, D. (2014*). Supervision in social work.* New York, NY: Columbia University Press.

Kanz, J. E. (2001). Clinical-supervision.com: Issues in the provision of online supervision. *Professional Psychology: Research and Practice, 32*(4), 415–420. doi:10.1037//0735-7028.32.4.415

Kim, S. A. (2008). The supervisee's experience in cross-cultural music therapy supervision. *Qualitative Inquiries in Music Therapy, 4,* 1–44.

Kim, S. A., & Whitehead-Pleaux, A. (2015). Music therapy and cultural diversity. In B. Wheeler (Ed.), *Music Therapy Handbook* (pp. 51–63), New York, NY: Guilford Press.

Krout, R. (2003). A kiwi odyssey: Music therapy training in New Zealand takes flight. *Voices: A World Forum for Music Therapy, 3*(1). Retrieved from https://voices.no/ index.php/voices/article/view/114

Lund, E. M., & Schultz, J. C. (2015). Distance supervision in rehabilitation counseling: Ethical and clinical considerations. *Rehabilitation Research, Policy, and Education, 29*(1). doi:10.1891/2168-6653.29.1.88

McKenna, K., Zarestky, J., & Anzlovar, M. (2018). Culture and communication online: The inclusion of international and non-native language learners. In K. L. Milheim (Ed.), *Cultivating diverse online classrooms through instructional design* (pp. 116–139). Hershey, PA: IGI Global.

Nasiri, F., & Mafakheri, F. (2015). Postgraduate research supervision at a distance: A review of challenges and strategies. *Studies in Higher Education, 40*(10), 1962–1969. doi:10.1080/03075079.2014.914906

Orr, P. P. (2010). Distance supervision: Research, findings, and considerations for art therapy. *The Arts in Psychotherapy, 37,* 106–111. doi:10.1016/j.aip.2010.02.002

Picciano, A. G. (2017). Theories and frameworks for online education: Seeking an integrated model. *Online Learning, 21*(3), 166–190. doi:10.24059/olj.v2

Rousmaniere, F. (2014). Using technology to enhance clinical supervision and training. In C. E. Watkins, Jr., & D. L. Milne (Eds.), *The Wiley International Handbook of Clinical Supervision* (1st ed., pp. 204–237). doi:10.1002/9781118846360.ch9

Rousmaniere, F., Abbass, A., & Frederickson, J. (2014). New developments in technology-assisted supervision and training: A practical overview. *Journal of Clinical Psychology: In Session, 70*(11), 1082–1093. doi:10.1002/jclp.22129

Rousmaniere, F., Abbass, A., Frederickson, J., Henning, I., & Taubner, S. (2014). Videoconferencing for psychotherapy training and supervision: Two case examples. *American Journal of Psychotherapy, 68*(20), 231–250.

Rousmaniere, F., & Frederickson, J. (2013). Internet-based one-way-mirror supervision for advanced psychotherapy training. *The Clinical Supervisor, 32,* 40–55. doi:10.1080/07325223.2013.778683

Samuel, A. (2016). *Faculty perceptions and experiences of "presence" in the online learning environment* (Doctoral dissertation). Retrieved from Theses and Dissertations, 1196.

Schmidt, M., Gage, A. M., Gage, N., Cox, P., & McLeskey, J. (2015). Bringing the Field to the Supervisor: Innovation in Distance Supervision for Field-Based Experiences Using Mobile Technologies. *Rural Special Education Quarterly, 34*(1), 37–43. doi:10.1177/875687051503400108

Story, K. M. (2014). Music therapy and avatars: Reflections on virtual learning environments for music therapy students. *Voices: A World Forum for Music Therapy, 14*(1). Retrieved from https://voices.no/index.php/voices/article/view/722

Substance Abuse and Mental Health Services Administration. (n.d.). Retrieved from https://store.samhsa.gov/facet/Professional-Research-Topics

Swamy, S. (2011). "No, she doesn't seem to know anything about cultural differences!": Culturally centered music therapy supervision. *Music Therapy Perspectives, 29*(2), 133–137.

Transcultural Care Associates. (2015). Retrieved from http://transculturalcare.net/cultural-assessment-tools/

U.S. Department of Health and Human Services. (2015). *Guidance Regarding Methods for De-Identification of Protected Health Information in Accordance with the Health Insurance Portability and Accountability Act (HIPAA) Privacy Rule.* Retrieved from https://www.hhs.gov/hipaa/for-professionals/privacy/special-topics/de-identification/index.html#rationale

U.S. Department of Labor. (2004). *The Health Insurance Portability and Accountability Act (HIPAA).* Washington, DC: U.S. Dept. of Labor, Employee Benefits Security Administration.

Wearne, S. (2005). General practice supervision at a distance: Is it remotely possible? *Australian Family Physician, 34*(12), 31–33.

Wheeler, B. L. (2002). Experiences and concerns of students during music therapy practica. *Journal of Music Therapy, 39*(4), 274–304.

Whitehead-Pleaux, A., Donnenwerth, A., Robinson, B., Hardy, S., Oswanski, L., Forinash, M., & York, E. (2012). Lesbian, gay, bisexual, transgender, and questioning: Best practices in music therapy. *Music Therapy Perspectives, 30*(2), 158.

Whitehead-Pleaux, A., & Tan, X. (2017). *Cultural intersections in music therapy: Music, health, and the person.* Dallas, TX: Barcelona Publishers.

Winnicott, D. W. (1971). *Playing and reality.* New York, NY: Routledge.

Wood, J., Miller, T., & Hargrove, D. S. (2005). Clinical supervision in rural settings: A telehealth model. *Professional Psychology: Research and Practice, 36*(2), 173–179. doi:10.1037/0735-7028.36.2.173

Wright, J., & Griffiths, F. (2010). Reflective practice at a distance: Using technology in counseling supervision. *Reflective Practice, 11*(5), 693–703. doi:10.1080/14623943.2010.516986

Young, L. (2009). Multicultural issues encountered in the supervision of music therapy internships in the United States and Canada. *The Arts in Psychotherapy, 36*(4), 191–201.

Young, L. (2016). Multicultural musical competence in music therapy. *Music Therapy Perspectives, 34.* doi:10.1093/mtp/miw016

Chapter 16

MUSIC-CENTERED SUPERVISION OF CLINICAL IMPROVISATION

Colin Andrew Lee
Kimberly Khare

INTRODUCTION

Every therapeutic meeting between client and therapist should have musical worth. Music therapists make music with and for clients to enhance and fulfill their potential. Whether promoting medical outcomes, facilitating psychodynamic expressions of the self, assisting imagery, or creating communities, it is music that makes music therapy unique. Clinical intent and artistic integrity should go hand-in-hand if music therapy is to truly reflect the potency of its practice. The art of clinical musicianship is central to the belief that musical construction and its intent is central to an understanding of the therapeutic process. Learning practical musical skills and how they are implemented in therapy should be central for all education programs (Lee, 2011, 2015). Alongside this, students should be able to identify, through supervision, the music that is being created and adapted for the client's needs. Once students are able to accurately hear and describe the music they are using, they can then begin to interpret how music aids the therapeutic process and the future aims and objectives of their work.

This chapter will focus on the supervision of improvisation through the music-centered theoretical lens of aesthetic music therapy (AeMT) (Lee, 2003, 2016a).[20] AeMT was developed as a composer's response to the improvised musical dialogue between client and therapist. The seeds of this work began with the publication of a single case study that described the music therapy process with a musician living with AIDS (Lee, 1996, 2016b). AeMT celebrates all that is musical in therapy and focuses on the inspiration of music and its inherent ability to heal. What makes AeMT unique is its emphasis on creating musical building blocks from precomposed compositions and artistic improvisations. These building blocks come from Western art music, popular song, jazz, and World Music. The multiculturalism of music is paramount in finding a musical palette that is truly contemporary and a part of the world in which we now live. By finding standard and new ways of notation, the therapist is able to generate improvisations based on music that has been primarily created for artistic purposes. The links between music as art and music as therapy are central to the development of AeMT. Precomposed works can then act as a catalyst for the musical–therapeutic dialogue. Each style and/or musical structure is chosen specifically for clinical aims and objectives. The therapist then builds a musical library of responses that come from a combination of the therapist's own creative endeavors and the specific musical learning from different improvised styles (Lee & Houde, 2011).

A music-centered approach to supervision as advocated in AeMT can be studied in isolation or in combination with other theoretical approaches that use improvisation as the core to their practices, for example, neurologic music therapy (Thaut & Hoemberg, 2014) and analytic music

---

[20] AeMT considers music therapy from a musical and compositional point of view, looking at theories of music to inform theories of therapy (Lee, 2003).

therapy (AMT) (Eschen, 2002). The use of music in supervision is dependent on the theoretical orientation of the supervisee and the education they have received. The consideration of how and when music is used in supervision is dependent on many factors (Davies & Sloboda, 2009). Some supervisors do not require students to bring audio and/or video examples from sessions. Instead, the process is carried out through verbal recollection and interpretations of the process in relation to the supervisor's interventions, client responses, and their effectiveness in evaluating the therapeutic process. Another approach is to use music as secondary source to color and highlight verbal discourse. In AeMT and music-centered supervision, knowing the music that is being used in each therapeutic exchange is paramount. Its aesthetic content and clinical–musical appropriateness is central to understanding the balance between art and therapy. The musical response to a physical movement can be bland or beautiful and to an emotional outpouring, scattered or artistically balanced. Through music-centered supervision, students can begin to know and understand the interface between the artistry of music and the clinical adaptation of its structural elements necessary for a defined therapeutic process.

The complex structures of music require complex clinical critiques and assessment, balancing musical illuminations alongside clinical understanding. It is not enough to describe musical responses in simple terms. In supervision, music therapists should be able to hear and describe specific musical elements such as chords and their inversions, modulations, melodic development, rhythmic structures, textures, and playing intensities, as they impact the therapeutic–musical dialogue. Developing the accuracy of clinical listening will illuminate clinical awareness, musically, through words, and in silence. The evaluation and research on music and words (Amir, 1999), psychotherapeutic interpretation (Streeter, 1999), and physiological and emotional responses (Iwanaga & Moroki, 1999) continue to play an important role in defining contemporary clinical practice. Taking a music-centered approach to the supervision of clinical improvisation can help supervisees to understand with greater clarity the balance between music, meaning, and clinical intention. Through evaluations of Colin as supervisor and the narratives of Kimberly as supervisee, this chapter will present a balanced view of the supervision relationship and process.

BACKGROUND

Apart from the music-centered theories of Nordoff-Robbins Music Therapy (NRMT) (chapter 21, this volume) and AeMT, literature on the supervision of music in music therapy is scarce. Stephens (1987) described, through the use of experiential music therapy, aspects of music listening that are essential to our understanding and learning of the process: "In order to learn the 'ways' of music in music therapy, the music therapist must experience in an intimate manner not only the elements of music but also the therapy process that emerges through and with them" (p. 169). Describing the integration of verbal and musical work during supervision, Stephens explained that in moving from music to words, "the therapist works from the music and is encouraged to let the music lead to a possible solution" (p. 173). Learning to clinically improvise effectively is also discussed by Oldfield (1992), who wrote: "Even the most skilled improvisers worry at times about whether they should play in one key or another, whether they should use tonal or atonal improvisation, or whether they should improvise around a given tune rather than incenting completely new material" (p. 14). It is these clinical–musical decisions that are at the heart of NRMT and AeMT supervision and practice. Richards (2009) suggested that students must learn to balance their musical skills and allow themselves also to be aware of the therapeutic process that is behind the music itself. It is this precise shift between music and words, musical and nonmusical aims, that makes music-centered supervision so exacting yet ultimately inspiring.

Detailed music-centered supervision and the knowledge of musical structures is essential in Nordoff-Robbins and AeMT education. The essential contents of this chapter and chapter 21 bear testament to the parallels between the two theories. The building of musical resources, clinical musicianship, and clinical listening are all hallmarks of NRMT and AeMT. What separate the two are the emphasis AeMT places on clinical–compositional form and how it impacts the improvisational process. Verney and Ansdell (2010), in their dialogues on NRMT supervision, discuss the precision required by the supervisee to be able to articulate what they hear from a taped recording of a session. Ansdell describes this process of working with Verney:

> I remember well … when you first supervised me, being very surprised at the laser-intensity of your listening—your focus on the music I'd brought along on the tape, and that finger of yours on the stop-button! Nobody before had stopped my tape four times in the first minute! But for me this is a perfect symbol of the process in that you're listening to every note of that work. Detail counts. (p. 76)

Having worked with Rachel Verney (Colin) as my supervisor while practicing as a music therapist in palliative care, this account resonates on many levels. Being able to listen and articulate the intricacies of musical form in supervision is, in many ways, at the heart of this chapter. Rachel's attention to musical detail and the demands it placed on me, as supervisee, was an important part of my growth as a music therapist and later as an educator.

The first edition of this chapter included detailed examples of notated musical analyses and how they were incorporated within the supervision process. For this updated work, we have deleted these passages and instead included more detailed reflections from Kimberly as supervisee. Her voice now becomes integral to this chapter and helps to define the underpinnings of music-centered supervision. These passages will hopefully resonate with students and practicing music therapists alike.

THE SUPERVISORY RELATIONSHIP

AeMT supervision is based on audio recordings taken from either group or individual sessions. The session is normally chosen by the supervisor as part of the ongoing supervision process or by the supervisee when specific help is needed. Supervision is a musically reflective process addressed through audio and/or video recordings and the supervisee's written assessments. Sessions are normally held on a weekly basis and last one hour. Supervisees must come prepared, having listened intently to the music under discussion, after fully indexing the complete session itself (Lee, 2003, 2015).[21] Supervisees may also come with sections of improvisations transcribed into musical notation. These musical notes can act in helping students to identify musical motives that may become important in the therapeutic dialogue and influential in the development of short-term and long-term aims and objectives.

Because AeMT supervision is primarily focused on tapes of sessions, the supervisee may feel musically insecure. The art of clinical improvisation and improvised songs is one that takes many years of dedication and practice. It is normal, therefore, at the beginning for supervisees to feel musically vulnerable. By focusing initially on the musical structures themselves, rather than the quality of improvisational input, the supervisee will begin to gain confidence and feel less musically scrutinized. This being said, there is in an inherent understanding that the therapist's/supervisee's musical input does and will affect the therapeutic process. Apart from musical identification, the supervisor may help in developing musical resources that are pertinent to the client and the ongoing therapeutic process. The supervisor should both musically support and challenge the supervisee to

---

[21] Indexing is a form of evaluation that describes, assesses, and interprets the music therapy dialogue. Listening back to the session, the therapist will stop the tape or video at salient points (the tape counter is noted) and transcribe through words and/or musical transcription the meaning and intent of the segment. Through evaluation and interpretation, indexing provides a detailed map of a session that can be used as assessment data and also be referred to before the following session.

understand the balance between the scientific process of nonclinical aims and how they affect the musical aims and creative responses to the client. Creativity and clinical clarity go hand-in-hand as the supervisee begins to understand the balance between music as "art" and music as "therapy."

STAGES OF SUPERVISION

The four stages of supervision described in this chapter do not necessarily move sequentially but accumulate, each adding and enriching the supervisee's clinical experience and understanding of the unfolding supervision process. There are no limits to the amount of time spent on each stage, the process being ongoing, exacting, and enriching. The first stage, clinical listening, forms the backbone of this approach and can be returned to at any point. Indeed, to return to previous stages only adds to a deeper understanding of the supervisee's individual theory and philosophy and his/her continuing clinical practice.

Central to the descriptions of each stage, Kimberly, the supervisee, adds narrative reflections from both the original version of this chapter and her practice, now some 18 years later. Her words bring a sense of personal reality and searching to the dialogue. Kimberly and I worked together for two years, contributing her voice as supervisee on each of the four stages as they unfolded. Since the original chapter, when Kimberly was working mainly with children, she has developed her practice and focuses now on working with young adults diagnosed with rare genetic disorders, HIV, and cancer. She has developed an original songwriting, recording, and production approach that incorporates the essential stages of music-centered supervision and improvisation as a mainstay in her music therapy method, known as "Song.Studio." Alongside her clinical work, Kimberly has been on faculty in the music therapy department at Berklee College of Music for the past 15 years and infuses her experiential teaching with the tenets and practices of clinical listening, structural repertoire training (concentrations in harmonic repertoire, rhythmic repertoire, melodic repertoire, and lyric/lyrical content repertoire), the study of music styles and genres, clinical music assessment (evaluation, interpretation, and judgment), and clinical improvisation techniques and foundations. The clarity of her musical and clinical questioning illustrates the potency of this music-centered approach to supervision.

The Supervisor Reflects—Colin Andrew Lee

I am a trained classical musician who has a passion for a broad range of musical styles, including jazz, pop, World, and fusion music. My love of J. S. Bach is equal to my love of Frank Zappa and Keith Jarrett. As a child growing up in a white middle-class family in the suburbs of the UK, I was exposed mainly to British pop to go with my growing interest in classical music. I became passionate about was classed as the "avant garde," veraciously hunting for recordings of and scores by composers such as Karlheinz Stockhausen, John Cage, Pierre Boulez, and Luciano Berio. This further led me to discover contemporary jazz and fusion World styles, which to this day provide me with inspirations for developing styles and resources in clinical improvisation. I am also a gay man who has fought to incorporate and acknowledge my identity and how this has impacted my role as a therapist and clinical musician.

As I matured and realized that my professional career would be as a therapist, I soon began to acknowledge that I could draw on being gay as a strength rather than a weakness. As I began to forge music therapy relationships with clients who had profound physical and developmental disabilities, I began to recognize that my understanding of their life situation was different from that of my heterosexual colleagues. I reflected on how our different life experiences affected our responses to clients. For so long I had felt like a second-class citizen, and yet now I understood that perhaps my emotional ability to understand loss placed me in a stronger position. I felt a sense of enlightenment as a gay therapist that brought with it validation and self-worth. Being authentic became central to my developing philosophy as a music therapist (Lee, 2016b, p. 9).

Stage One: Clinical Listening

Clinical listening (Lee, 2003) is central to the music-centered supervision of improvisation. To hear objectively the musical content being examined is a critical first step in the supervision process. Separating what we think we hear from the actuality of sounds themselves can be liberating for the supervisee's music. We may think that to describe in simple terms is enough:

a)   The client improvises/creates a song using simple phrases. The therapist responds with music in a minor key.
b)   A melody develops between client and therapist.
c)   The music/song becomes dissonant.

In AeMT supervision, these descriptions are not enough. More detailed musical structures need to be articulated. The supervisee should bring to the sessions notated transcriptions of the music under discussion.

a)   The client improvises phrases/creates a song based on the intervals of a minor 3rd; the therapist responds with a harmonic progression in C minor (Cm, Fm, B flat, E flat, Dm, G7) using 2nd inversion chords.
b)   A melody develops, using long and extended phrases balanced and focused on small and open intervals.
c)   The music/song becomes dissonant, using scattered melodic ideas, atonal intervals, and harmonies.

Living in the knowing of music can dramatically transform our sense of the process. Music is the starting point for a greater understanding of the process—not words or exterior clinical interpretations, but the pure phenomenon of music itself. Clinical listening is the ability to recognize the actuality of music. "Clinical" is defined here as the identification of music constructs that constitute the musical–therapeutic dialogue. The supervisee must extend their aural skills to describe what they hear without bias—without interpretation. In *clinical listening,* there is a re-examination of the boundaries of knowing and understanding. The supervisee must learn to hear precisely before making therapeutic choices. This stage of supervision is challenging, as supervisees will instinctively feel the need to interpret. Music therapy education is built on knowledge of theory, practice, skills, and interpretation.

At the beginning, the most important segments of the tape to which to listen are the beginning passages of music. Here, the client and therapist explore the musical groundwork from which the ongoing musical dialogue develops. By accurately describing these musical beginnings, the supervisee will begin to understand the importance of clinical listening and responding. These opening moments often contain musical seeds from which the improvisation develops. By identifying the generative musical cells that the client improvises and the beginning dialogue between client and therapist, the supervisee can understand the balance between musical content and therapeutic outcome.

Often, the starting point for clinical listening is the identification and qualities of the tone (Lee, 2015) and its effect on the developing musical structure.[22] Once the opening tone is established, others can be recognized as evolving intervals and harmonies are developed. Returning to the initial tone

---

[22] Tone is described as a single pitch that may also be described in terms of its quality, character, timbre, color, and intensity of playing and/or singing.

will establish a fundamental architectural tonic (Lee, 2016a) that can be important in defining on overall tonic center for the improvisation as a whole. The tone then acts as a musical epicenter that holds the key in understanding the stability between musical identification and the unfolding dialogue between client and therapist.

The Supervisee Reflects—Kimberly Khare

From the first edition:

Music, as emotions, is immediate. I never perceived these experiences as separate. It was during supervision that I first began to understand the clinical implications that my lack of conscious separation was creating. In "clinical listening," the "I feel …" and "I think …" are removed. The clinician's personal and musical biases are stripped away to reveal the musical intention and clinical direction. By directly dealing with the factual experience, what is actually happening musically, rather than one's own perception, the focus is shifted from therapeutic presence to musical presence.

Initially, it is frightening to listen at this level. Feelings of self-doubt and inadequacy are shamelessly experienced. But this is not the purpose of listening in this capacity. To listen "clinically," not perceptually or even therapeutically, is shocking. We have rules and fundamental concepts of the inherent nature of the medium that, when disregarded, can lead to a situation not unlike playing with fire. The aesthetic of music is a combined effort of profound emotions and fundamental clinical aptitude. Knowing the geography of one's instrument can only support knowing the geography of one's emotional landscape. And in supporting a client's growth toward self, we must know the precise application of the music that effects the emotions.

Clinical listening brings you to the basics. What is the timbre of the client's instrument/expression? The pitch? The duration of their tone? What is the attack, the phrasing of their rhythmic/melodic work? Here is where we separate from style. We do not ask the "feel" of the expression, but the precise measurement of it.

The next question for me was not "How can I match the sound?," but rather "How can I meet the sound?" This concept is the key, in that I believe it is what helps the clinician to continue to separate clinical listening from perceptual listening. By "meeting" a client's sound, we remain separate, presenting our own identity, our own voice, which ultimately supports the client but does not impede or step upon their individual voice. By "matching," we tend to "do the same," which neither indicates our intention as clinicians nor provides direction for our clients. Matching can at times simply be repeating, whereas meeting is a conscious choice. Meeting supports co-creating; it motivates independent thinking and awareness of the present, immediate moment.

For this edition:

When asked what has made the difference in my music therapy practice, I answer, "Three very specific things: (1) my clinical listening, (2) my musical theater training, and (3) my clinical listening."

What I understand now is that during my music-centered supervision, I was developing my critical thinking *and* my creative thinking based on the infrastructure of music. These combined abilities are vital to me as a music therapist, as they are the foundation of my clinical thinking—how I focus, assess, form purpose, and determine a course of intentional action with clients.

As a young music therapist, I focused on *my* relating to my clients. Music-centered supervision turned my attention to the relationships inherent in music and how they served the clients' relating——to themselves, their abilities, their challenges, and their possibilities. By fostering this awareness, I was no longer in the way of the music—the therapy agent. I was becoming a facilitator of the music in a compelling and exacting way that provided the optimal environment for the client's growth and personal work.

Specifically, I was learning how to critically think through my creative choices and creatively think through my critical choices. In developing my receptive competence and my attending abilities through acquiring reliable and confident music resources, I became responsible for my awareness, for my clinical choices and actions, by becoming musically accountable to and for my clients. In order to achieve this skill set—critical and creative thinking, responsible awareness and musical accountability—I first had to learn how to listen: how to listen to the music. Accurately. Clinically. I needed to learn what to listen to, without assigning or aligning any other meaning.

For example, I was using the guitar as the harmonic instrument for an improvisation with a client, and I started with a G Major chord. As if muscle memory were my only guide, the next chord that followed was almost always a C Major chord. There was connection to the client's emotional presentation, as I perceived it, through dynamics and tempo—but there was no listening in the making of this musical choice, this clinical choice. Not to the client, not to the music. I was listening to me, to what I was playing or to what was next in the song I had memorized. I was packaging my music therapy into a premade musical meal. My focus in my music therapy training had been on learning the structures of music—but not how to structure music intentionally.

I was not trained to think within the music. I was taught to have a song ready with instruction for the client, driven by the lyric, and to tailor this song to the client's emotional dynamic. My facilitation was determined by my personality and how well the client followed instruction. Ultimately, I was very disappointed in music therapy practice and almost sought another occupation. Fortunately, I was introduced to Nordoff-Robbins music therapy, which set me on my path to learning how to clinically improvise, relate musically, and become music- and client-centered. I am grateful to my Nordoff-Robbins mentors—Clive Robbins, Carol Robbins, and Alan Turry. To this day, I am still learning from all they provided me. And if it were not for them, I would not have met Colin and been given the opportunity to have him guide me in the study of music at its cellular level—coming to understand music's complex and carefully designed structure and its unique ability to create relational infrastructure.

Through the lens of clinical listening were I to be in that session now, I would begin with one tone—perhaps an E. My next choice would be "Listen … create space to hear …," and I would wait with my attention forward, concentrating on the next factual–musical element created. Perhaps the client vocalizes intentionally—or echolaliacally. In that moment, I factor in all aspects on a continuum starting with the music components of the expression. What was the rhythm? What was the tonality—what interval was created? What was the phrasing—the melodic direction? What was the inner current, not the undercurrent, but the musical momentum that their expression provided? And what musical traction can be offered by my accurate listening? How will I be informed by listening to the resource my client contributes? What creative and critical choices are next musically?

Stage Two: Clinical Evaluation

Moving on from the rigor of clinical listening, the supervisee is then ready to assess and evaluate the music therapy dialogue. During this stage, two central areas are covered: the quality of musical resources used and the development of musical assessment skills. The supervisee's use of musical skills in reflecting the client's playing now becomes important as she/he looks to extend their musical palette. Developing music resources is an essential skill needed to be able to practice from a music-centered perspective. Nordoff-Robbins (2007) (Turry, chapter 21) has documented pedagogy for gaining the clinical–musical skills necessary to practice music-centered music therapy. Central to the development of AeMT has been literature devoted to acquiring the ability to improvise in different styles (Lee & Houde, 2011), create songs (Lee & Pun, 2015), and compose themes (Lee, Berends, & Pun, 2015).

During supervision, improvisations and songs taken from audio recordings of sessions can be analyzed for the immediacy of the work under discussion and also for future therapeutic scenarios. By isolating critical sections of the improvisations, the supervisee can examine in more detail the music itself, which in turn will enable them to better understand the client's musical creativity within the therapeutic domain. Once specific musical forms have been isolated and notated, they can also be used for practical explorations between supervisee and supervisor. In the first instance, the supervisor will take the role of *Soloist (S)*, which reflects the role of the client and *Accompanist (A)*, which reflects the role of the therapist (Lee & Houde, 2011). *S* should improvise around the musical ideas of the client, and *A* should respond as the therapist exploring and developing musical forms from the original musical seeds. After recording the music, the supervisor and supervisee should listen back, discussing how new and different responses affect the musical relationship. These concrete explorations help to further the supervisee's developing musical palette.

The supervisee should also be encouraged to begin finding their own unique musical assessments that best suit the needs of the client and the supervisee's theoretical stance. Music-centered assessment in AeMT took its foundation from Lee's research (1992) and subsequent method of analysis (Lee, 2000). It is based on the relationship between music analysis and clinical understanding. The stages—(1) holistic listening, (2) reactions of therapist to music as process, (3) client listening, (4) consultant listening, (5) transcription into notation, (6) segmentation into musical components, (7) verbal description, (8) in-depth analysis, and (9) synthesis—highlight the step-by-step possibilities of detailed musical inquiry and how these apply to the form of improvisations and the balance between music and clinical assessment.

The Supervisee Reflects—Kimberly Khare

From the first edition:

In terms of developing resources, my first resource was realizing I had more concrete concepts that could be applied and that this could guide me in my clinical interventions and choice-making. Up until this point, my understanding was, when faced with a client with whom I was going to improvise, that my choices were either divine intervention or the key of D major! I always began a session by creating a song in a certain "style" or "feel." In essence, I was rushing beyond the client's expression with sound that made me feel certain and competent. By leading with an emotional edge, I was supporting only my own emotional experience. Through supervision, I began to give myself the option of "tone" vs. "chord progression." I began to work intervalically with tones, rather than improvising in a specific key. By challenging my thinking, my listening, on the level of reception vs. response, I began to develop the resource further, from clinical listening, to "meeting" vs. "matching." Reception indicates a taking in and is a step toward integrating. We are to respond to our clients, but not haphazardly. Through my inexperience and naïveté, that was exactly what I was doing.

Clinical listening gave me the ability to develop clinical evaluation. I was no longer evaluating my personal responses to the ambiguities of relationship in music, but developing clinical strategies and awareness that led to clear, justified, clinical evaluations. The relational connections between my music choices and the child's became clearer, more definite, more flexible, and more integrated in our developing relationship. The responsibility for that relationship and meeting was now more conscious for both client and therapist.

My supervisor's guidance was at times direct and then subtle, but always specific. There were times when we listened to the same three seconds over and over again until I began to move through the levels of listening and began grasping the explicit form created. My developing ability to listen had to be mine. Supervision could not just simply point out what I should be listening to because that would impede the development of my judgment. So, painfully and slowly, we moved through entire sessions listening mainly "in between" and "behind" obvious moments of expression and connection. By doing this, I began to hear nuances, subtleties, possibilities, and potential. I began to hear "ahead" of the moment because I was directly aware of the music's intention—what the music was conceiving—and the clinical direction that was to come.

This resource, hearing "behind," "in between," and "ahead," created a fuller spectrum of listening for me. I was now working in the "past," "present," and "future" of the clinical moment. I was in the creative now, living in the immediacy of music within the therapeutic relationship. The emotional implications of this awareness were obvious, but the musical, not as simple. As therapists, we often, I think, start the music and keep going. We don't breathe, pulse, or fluidly move or even stop—yet our clients do. We tend to create a chorus, or a refrain, or a style of song, or a theme that embodies these characteristics. But rarely do we use the architecture of music itself to actualize the moment.

My recognition of pitch, rhythmic expression, phrasing, and timbre dramatically changed. When I heard a cymbal, I no longer played a long pedal tone but actually received and integrated the attack of the mallet, the physical force, the crispness or dullness of the sound. I had more to choose from. By having these choices, I realized that the child had all these choices, too. I could now begin to musically, and therefore truly clinically, assess their decision-making abilities, their processing, awareness, presence, directedness, and so on.

Through the clinical evaluation of learning to separate, I also learned to differentiate. Starting with a tone instead of a chord determines so much more. I could then distinguish other tones and tone colors that would effectively affect the clinical moment.

For this edition:

In my beginning years, I focused my musical development on song repertoire—and from these songs, harmonic repertoire, rhythmic repertoire, and melodic and lyric/lyrical content repertoires. During my early days of music-centered supervision, I knew I had to cultivate my musical abilities more deeply—that just having songs wasn't enough to bolster the listening and relating for which I was responsible.

I started to broaden my musical horizons—listening to styles and genres that I wouldn't regularly have chosen—and in doing this, I created another listening strategy that supported my clinical work. I'd never created my professional music listening outside of songs I needed to learn for my next session—I didn't have a growth plan for my ears. I had my personal preferences musically, which naturally influenced my clinical music resources and offerings. By intensifying my listening studies, I created a way for me to practice listening to new music and develop my abilities in listening to newness, to contributions I hadn't heard before. Knowing that my clients had diverse listening preferences based on their cultural and social backgrounds, I made sure to listen to all forms of music, ranging from Top 40 to Afro-pop, from Thelonius Monk to Tchaikovsky, from Blues to Funk. I remember focusing on vocal music at one point—the works of Bobby McFerrin, Sweet Honey in the Rock, Miriam Makeba, chants, calls, rounds—and then beatboxing! This particular focus helped me to be not only that much more expressive in my voicework, but also that much more receptive toward my clients' voicework. As I branched out, I began to discover themes that led me to more World Music awareness. I listened and learned from Hugh Masekela, Baaba Maal, Ibrahim Ferrer, and Rubén González. I also had an opportunity to travel abroad and work for an expressive art therapy program in Russia. I had a crash course in Euro-Pop, Russian folk songs, and gypsy music. What mattered was that I had a keen understanding of how music worked and that I could readily adapt into any style, particularly when introduced to a new form that was of all importance to a client. This understanding, coupled with my enthusiasm to be introduced to and/or learn any style of music, has served me well as a music therapist. I have always listened to a variety of styles and instrumentations—developing my facility vocally (solo, harmony, and ensemble); on piano, guitar (acoustic and electric), and percussion; arranging and writing. There is such beautiful diversity in music, and it was critical to my development that I expose my listening beyond my personal, social, and cultural preferences.

269

As I did this, I started to keep folders for ideas for each repertoire—rhythmic, melodic, harmonic, and lyric/lyrical content (I refer to these as "the main four"). I would analyze songs and write down their rhythms or hear a theme and work out the melody through ear training, or perhaps I'd hear a new chord progression or intervallic theme. All the while, I was writing them down and mapping out distinct repertoires for each of the main four. My next step was to practice these repertoires—which I did, just like I'd practice a song or composition in piano/voice/guitar lessons. I created exercises for myself and built on several exercises that Colin provided me. Two in particular that were very helpful were practicing "the cell" and practicing "tonal centering" (Lee, 2015). "The cell" was first introduced to me as a melodic practice—the aim was to improvise a short theme (a cell) that would be developed throughout the improvisation, appearing in its initial form, but also within larger melodic phrases, inverted, repeated in another tonal sequence, and so forth. I went on to develop this concept for myself rhythmically as the terms completely are transferable and simply fun to practice. "Tonal centering" was an exercise in choosing and playing one tone—which becomes your "root" tone—and improvising intervals with this tonal center, or against it, or creating chords. Improvising intervals—the practice was in playing tones together or as an arpeggio or ostinato. Playing against the tonal center was about exploring intervallic or chord elements that were "outside the scale" or your typical harmonic practice/training—and it was illuminating! So many colors and textures came into my practice from this exercise. Adding in more chord structures—either with or against the tonal center—took my playing to compositional levels, helping me to develop my abilities in a more focused manner within song structures, but also helping me to go beyond these typical structures. Looking back at this time, I can reflect on how developing these main four repertoires enhanced my accuracy and my acuity musically and led me to study song structure more intentionally.

Stage Three: Clinical Interpretation

Linking musical response to the aims and objectives of sessions is now explored. Musical and clinical interpretations now become merged as the supervisee begins to understand the link between musical response, development, and the therapeutic process. Exploring the supervisee's reactions to the client, the musical dialogue, the stage of the therapeutic process, and the possible links between music as art and music as therapy now become central. During this stage, the supervisee may bring issues of musical and intrapersonal inquiry:

- Why have I chosen to focus on a specific passage of music to analyze?
- What are the musical components and structures?
- How would I interpret the passage musically?
- How would I interpret the passage therapeutically?
- How does an understanding of the musical structures affect my understanding of the stage of therapy and the longer-term focus of aims and objectives?
- What are musical responses to the passage?
- What are my personal responses to the passage?
- What was it about the client's improvising that made me respond musically with specific musical forms?
- What was it about the client's physical presence that made me respond with specific musical forms?
- How do my personal reactions to the passage, the client, and the therapeutic process influence my musical and clinical responses and future direction of work?

These kinds of questions help the supervisee to *begin* to make connections between the musical responses of the client and how they *affect* the therapeutic process.

Interpreting and making sense of the relationship between client and therapist and how this is manifested through clinical improvisations is multifaceted. Music contains a labyrinth of emotional patterns. Merging musical form, the human condition, and the relationship between client and therapist is a complex process. Musical and emotional interpretation of music is highly subjective. Music to which the supervisee responds may not be appropriate for the client. Finding the musical bridge between art and therapy is the key to a truly balanced practice. The supervisee must acknowledge that this path of learning is both musicological and humanistic. At this stage in the supervision process, contentious questions should be raised about the inherent forms of music and how they affect and relate to the therapeutic process.

The Supervisee Reflects—Kimberly Khare

From the first edition:

My value judgments were now musically no longer limited to keys, major or minor, idioms, or chord structures, but were based on tonal relationships, melodic direction, intervals, cell formation, and the development of clinical themes. My activity level when it came to conscious creative thinking increased. The responsibility to clinical music, and the analysis of my reactions to it, became foremost. I reconsidered everything. Is a hello song necessary? What in fact is a hello song and what does it mean to clinically sing hello? What is the transition needed to move into the music work? I realized also that I alone was not responsible for the music-making. I had a partner, the client, and this changed the value of the work greatly. I needed to leave space for the child's ideas and expressions, and I needed to value their receptions of my expressions. I acknowledged to being "met" by the client. It was our work, not my work. Exploring my emotional reactions to this stage of the work was necessary and personally revealing.

I also began to play against and not always on every pulse of a child's musical expression. This was not abandonment but exchange and interchange. I was better able to value the emotional time of clinical music-making, not just the physical obvious time, and what this meant for my personal growth as a music therapist. I was developing judgment and ways to exercise that judgment clinically, emotionally, and musically.

For this edition:

Beginning my "music meaning" studies in Nordoff-Robbins, I initially learned how to link music response to goals and objectives. But as I was still new to being a music therapist, my interpretations were often diagnosis-focused. I recall a parent–therapist meeting for a young boy for whom I was the primary therapist. In sessions, when the music turned to an upbeat tempo, rock-based with full chord voicings, syncopated chords in a measure, and bold melodic choices, this child would start to move quickly about the room with hand and foot gestures, some vocalization, and at varying times a "stop" stance where he would freeze momentarily and then continue on again. I interpreted all of this as a sign that he was anxious and therefore whatever I was providing musically was overstimulating. During the parent–therapist meeting, when we shared a video clip of the moment I just described, his parents became elated, overjoyed even, expressing that this was his happy dance and that it meant so much to them that he was experiencing this in music. I suddenly realized how off my understanding was of this child.

Stage Four: Clinical Judgment

The importance of defining aims and objectives is central to many theories of music therapy. In AeMT, they stem initially from an understanding and assessment of the musical foundations of creative music-making and how this applies to the more nonmusical considerations of outcome. The therapist must recognize the extramusical considerations, such as identified behaviors and desired outcomes that stem from specific aims, objectives, and how they relate to the process and outcome of therapy. The clarity, balance, and understanding between music and nonmusical intent ultimately allows clients a therapeutic process that is reflective of their needs. The therapist's evaluations and understanding of the developing relationship, their professional role in providing the needed musical and clinical skills, and the ability to reflect the client's personal complexities combine to produce a therapeutic essence that is fundamental for potential and growth.

The identification of short-term and long-term aims is congruent to the four stages of music-centered supervision. To understand the complete music therapy picture, the therapist must explore, question, and analyze the countless components that come together to make up the whole. By defining what is essential for the moment, the supervisee will begin to know how detailed musicological and clinical thinking combine to produce a deeper understanding of the therapeutic process. Supervisees should be questioned and challenged in this final stage of supervision:

- What is your understanding of the balance between musical knowing, expertise, and the nonmusical aims for the client's space and growth in the music therapy process?
- What are your long-term musical aims as a therapist?
- What are your long-term aims for developing your own music therapy theory?
- How are these connected?
- How can you continue integrating the art and science of improvisation in your practice?
- How do think musical artistic intention and aesthetic quality affect therapeutic outcome?
- How do you define musical growth?
- How do you define therapeutic growth?
- Do you think it is possible to integrate music-centered practices with nonmusical and scientific ones?
- Do you think it is possible to integrate music-centered practices with the verbal interpretations of psychotherapy?

The Supervisee Reflects—Kimberly Khare

From the first edition:

I now began to differentiate between emotionally forced pathological playing and rhythmic skill development that enables creative freedom—and by discerning this, I could consciously choose which need, which aim to meet. I was able to acknowledge when I'd gone in the wrong direction and change my aims *in* the session, not after. This allowed the child to do the same. I am now more able to clearly determine musical and nonmusical aims and can follow through in meeting these goals. The change in my perception when formulating goals is the difference of "being" in music vs. "doing" in music. Activity does not necessarily determine the effects of the use of clinical music. Direct contact with an instrument comes in many forms, such as actively drumming or playing the piano or actively listening. Children who move away from direct contact and who appear to retreat into idiosyncratic behaviors or speech scripts provide a therapeutic and musical challenge. Here the use of skilfully and surgically appropriate music is a challenge that demands a clear connection between listening, evaluation, interpretation, and judgment. Through exploring my own clinical listening, my understanding of the child's clinical listening changed. Listening for me has been the intellectual and emotional nucleus. Music therapists must listen on many levels and work on many listening levels.

For this edition:

My clinical work is now focused on young adults who are coping with serious medical illness—in treatment, beyond treatment, and/or living with the impacts, such as stigma, anxiety, recurrence, survivorship, loss of abilities, and chronic degeneration. They are all coming of age and need support in determining their self-identity separate from an illness mind-set and more firmly poised in a growth mind-set. As a psychotherapist, my music therapy approach, known as Song.Studio, situates these young adults at the center of envisioning their health narrative (medical, social, emotional, physical, cultural, relational) and supporting them in developing the personal skills that will help them to navigate daily life and a positive future. I use songwriting and recording *as* the music therapy process. At the heart of my facilitation is helping these young adults to develop both their critical and creative thinking so that they can process their experiences and create solutions in challenging moments. By constructing their own original song, they learn how to make critical and creative choices and have complete control over the song's content, musical direction, and structure. Inherent to Song.Studio is recording—the songwriting process as well as the finished song—because of the remarkable personal value the young adults gain by listening to themselves, by listening to their song. Their ability to evaluate, interpret, judge, and determine next steps regarding thematic designs is elevated exponentially by the mere experience of listening to their process—listening to how they think, consider, choose, express, or withhold themselves. As our therapy relationship develops, deeper and more involved analysis is incorporated into the songwriting and recording process—both by me and by them—ensuring the young adult's voice is the primary focus (whether singing, spoken word, rapping, writing, producing, playing, beat-making or designing). Songwriting is an important and enlightening tool, but it is the recording work that is done in Song.Studio that makes the signature, defining, and lasting difference for the young adults in their music therapy work. For me, there is no clearer example of the impact of music-centered supervision on my craft.

REFLECTIONS

Supervision is as complex as the therapeutic process itself. Defining a clinical epistemology and then relating it to the supervisory process requires fine examination and judgment. The supervisor's role is to contain, debate, question, and challenge. That the first stage of supervision described in this chapter is so musically exacting bears witness to the boundaries and clarity of musical form that is needed before interpretation can take place. The four stages of supervision will ultimately uncover the musical and personal vulnerabilities of the supervisee. With this in mind, the supervisor must also be supportive and acknowledge the supervisee's successes and failures as positive steps along a lifelong learning curve of music-centered practice, one that celebrates the artistic advancement of the supervisee and the aesthetic fulfillment of music as a healing force.

What can music-centered supervision add to clinical practice and the future of music therapy? With the recent focus on medicine, community, and psychodynamic assessment, what about the structures and forms of music itself to advance a greater understanding of music and therapy? The challenge to music therapy is that therapists should pay greater attention to, and strive to understand in greater detail, the music in music therapy. Listening is at the heart of music therapy:

- Listening to the client's music, the therapist's music, and the musical relationship
- Listening behind and beyond the music
- Listening to silence
- Listening to the client as personhood and musichood

- Listening as musicians
- Listening as therapists
- Listening as sound and community

If music therapists cannot hear accurately and clinically, then they will never understand the musical eloquence of clients and their potential for growth.

AeMT is an exploration of the dignity and elegance of music and people. This refers not only to the therapeutic relationship and outcome of sessions, but also to every nuance of the balance between music, therapy, identity, and health. The aesthetic potential of resistance and disturbance should be equal to consideration as the expression of the purely beautiful. The balance between personhood and musichood is central to AeMT and a music-centered approach to supervision. This means always returning to the central frame of music as the yardstick and core of understanding. Listening defines music therapists as both artists and clinicians, and it is through music that we offer clients the chance for musical transformation.

The Supervisee Concludes—Kimberly

Clinical listening requires courage within oneself. It is a process of ownership. When you own your musicianship as a music therapist, you can help others come into their own in music and take responsibility for themselves, acknowledge their potential or their insecurities, celebrate their joy, and be present in their losses. You can be genuine and genuinely be. This is the kind of inspired space that is so needed for our client communities.

The Supervisor Concludes—Colin

Supervision challenges supervisees to listen, respond, interpret, and develop their clinical practice through improvisation. Music therapy challenges the therapist to continually define and redefine what makes the bridge between epistemological and emotional thought. A music-centered approach to supervision balances the ever-changing nature of music as a creative force and the clinical exactness of therapy. This approach demands dedication and the desire for musical self-examination. Music-centered supervision should be inspiring and enlightening. As music therapists begin to appreciate the magnitude and dignity of music, their creativity will begin to radiate. Discovering the direct relation between music, people, and communities can be transformative for both clients and therapists. True meeting and listening is a profound experience. Music-centered supervision attempts to facilitate this understanding and the supervisee's path in finding a balance that will nurture individual therapeutic growth and maturity.

Acknowledgments

Colin Andrew Lee
I would like to thank Kimberly Khare for allowing me to guide her through our supervision together and for taking the time to reflect further for the second edition of this chapter. Since the first edition of this book, I have developed the theory of AeMT. Thank you to all of the colleagues and students who have supported and believed in my work and the music-centered values of AeMT.

Kimberly Khare
I have always known that my studies as a Nordoff-Robbins Music therapist and as an aesthetic music therapist have held great sway in who I've become as a professional—but until this writing, I don't

think that I have understood how deeply, wonderfully, and significantly reinforced I have been by my three Cs:

Carol and *Clive*—Thank you so much for empowering me and for showing me the care and compassion that it takes to be a music therapist. My time with you changed me for the better.

Colin—Thank you so much for challenging me to be my higher music self. There is no doubt that my time as a supervisee in music-centered supervision has generated my clinical stance and my music therapy mission. Song.Studio would not be a reality without your vision and your supervision. It has and continues to be an honor and a privilege to have you as a guiding creative force and a mentor. You have made this journey possible.

REFERENCE LIST

Amir, D. (1999). Musical and verbal interventions in music therapy: A qualitative study. *Journal of Music Therapy, 36*(2), 144–175.

Brown, S. (2009). Supervision in context: a balancing act. In H. Odell-Miller & E. Richards (Eds.), *Supervision of music therapy. A theoretical and practical handbook.* London, UK, & New York, NY: Routledge.

Davies, A., & Sloboda, A. (2009). Turbulence at the boundary. In H. Odell-Miller & E. Richards (Eds.), *Supervision of music therapy. A theoretical and practical handbook.* London, UK, & New York, NY: Routledge.

Eschen, J. Th. (2002). *Analytical music therapy.* London, UK, & Philadelphia, PA: Jessica Kingsley Publishers.

Iwanga, M., & Moroki, Y. (1999). Subjective and physiological responses to music stimuli controlled over activity and preference. *Journal of Music Therapy, 36*(1), 26–38.

Lee, C. (1992). *The Analysis of Therapeutic Improvisatory Music with People with the virus HIV and AIDS.* Unpublished PhD thesis, City University, London, UK.

Lee, C. (2000). A method of analyzing improvisations in music therapy. *Journal of Music Therapy, 37*(2), 147–167.

Lee, C. A. (2003). *The Architecture of Aesthetic Music Therapy.* Gilsum, NH: Barcelona Publishers.

Lee, C. A. (2015). Aesthetic Music Therapy and the Role of Music-Centered Education in Contemporary Clinical Practice. In J. Goodman (Ed.), *International Perspectives in Music Therapy Education and Training.* Springfield, IL: Charles C Thomas Publisher.

Lee, C. A. (2016a). Aesthetic Music Therapy. In J. Edwards (Ed.), *The Oxford Handbook of Music Therapy.* Oxford, UK: Oxford University Press.

Lee, C. A. (2016b). *Music at the edge. The music therapy experiences of a musician with AIDS* (2nd ed.). London, UK, & New York, NY: Routledge.

Lee, C. A., Berends, A., & Pun, S. (2015). *Composition and Improvisation Resources for Music Therapists.* Gilsum, NH: Barcelona Publishers.

Lee, C. A., & Houde, M. (2011). *Improvising in Styles. A workbook for music therapists, educators, and musicians.* Gilsum, NH: Barcelona Publishers.

Lee, C. A., & Pun, S. (2015). *Song Resources for Music Therapists.* Gilsum, NH: Barcelona Publishers.

Oldfield, A. (1992). Teaching music therapy students on practical placements—some observations. *Journal of British Music Therapy, 6*(1), 13–17.

Richards, E. (2009). Whose handicap? Issues arising in the supervision of trainee music therapists in their first experience of working with adults with learning disabilities. In H. Odell-Miller & E. Richards (Eds.), *Supervision of music therapy. A theoretical and practical handbook.* London, UK, & New York, NY: Routledge.

Stephens, G. (1987). The experiential music therapy group as a method of training and supervision. In C. Moranto & K. Bruscia (Eds.), *Perspectives on Music Therapy Education and Training.* Philadelphia, PA: Temple University, Esther College of Music.

Streeter, E. (1999). Finding a balance between psychological thinking and musical awareness in music therapy: a psychoanalytic perspective. *British Journal of Music Therapy, 13*(1), 5–20.

Verney, R., & Ansdell, G. (2010). *Conversation on Nordoff-Robbins Music Therapy.* Gilsum, NH: Barcelona Publishers.

Chapter 17

Songwriting and Clinical Identity Formation for Music Therapy Students in Academic Supervision

Michael Viega
Felicity A. Baker

Introduction

Therapeutic songwriting is a method of music therapy that has been used to address a wide range of challenges faced by people across the life span. It has been defined as "the process of creating, notating, and/or recording lyrics and music by the client or clients and therapist within a therapeutic relationship to address psychosocial, emotion, cognitive, and communication needs of the client" (Wigram & Baker, 2005, p. 16). In other words, clients engage in a songwriting experience with the specific purpose of enhancing their well-being. The therapist supports clients as they create lyrics and music, ensuring that the potential for transformation is maximized.

Several methods and models of therapeutic songwriting have emerged in recent years and are presented in detail in Baker's latest monograph (Baker, 2015). She categorizes methods into those that are most focused on lyric creation, those most focused on music creation, and those methods that consider lyrics and music to be more equal partners. For example, song parody is regarded as more of a lyric-focused approach because the music is more or less predetermined and fixed, whereas as song improvisations focus more on creating the music. All methods are regarded as important and have a place in practice; all have their own unique strengths and benefits, but they also inherently have limitations.

Models of songwriting also dictate the way in which a clinician might approach a clinical songwriting experience (Baker, 2015). Some approaches are more outcome-oriented (for example, psychoeducational songwriting, contingency songwriting), whereby the clinician has a predetermined, targeted outcome for the client. Conversely, those songwriting experiences that are framed as an experience-oriented approach (for example, strength-based songwriting, narrative songwriting, insight-oriented songwriting) are more focused on allowing the process to unfold; the songwriting experience could take many unforeseen but clinically important directions as the people creating the songs explore their own experiences and capture the events and associated feelings within a song. Finally, the ecological-oriented songwriting models are often focused on social change and may target changes that go beyond just benefiting the person creating the song.

Songwriting and Identity in Health-Related Contexts

The reasons why songwriting is used in clinical practice are as diverse as the types of clinical contexts from which it is practiced (Baker, Wigram, Stott, & McFerran, 2008, 2009). However, it is its potential as a tool to address issues of identity that has perhaps been the most frequently documented in the music therapy literature (Baker & MacDonald, 2017). A survey of clinicians who regularly use songwriting in their practice (Baker et al., 2008, 2009) found that the most frequent uses were to (1) externalize thoughts, fantasies, and emotions; (2) tell the participant's story; (3) develop a sense of self; and (4) gain insight or clarify thoughts and feelings. All of these processes are important in building a strong sense of self-concept and self-identity.

While an account of how people build, maintain, modify, or reconstruct identity is beyond the scope of this chapter, it is important to note that the concept of self-identity relates to people's sense of "Who am I?," a collection of integrated self-schemas (Markus & Nurius, 1986) that connect the past, present, and possible future selves. Importantly, how people view themselves impacts how they experience the world, how they act, and their mental health and well-being (Byrne, 1996). Those with a disintegrated or unhealthy sense of self tend to have a low self-esteem and are unlikely to takes risks (because they want to avoid failure). The unconscious avoidance of personal challenges may further affect self-esteem and reduce possibilities for personal growth.

As already highlighted, songwriting has been used extensively as a tool for exploring the sense of self, and there are many reasons why songwriting is an enabler of this process. First and foremost, songs are like mirrors of the self—they are a vehicle for expressing who we are through what is communicated in the lyrics and what is communicated in the music. Indeed, the music created is in and of itself a form of identity work (Baker & MacDonald, 2017). The music of a song creates an impression of how we feel at the time of creating the song, and it may reflect our environment, our morals and ethics, and the musical culture to which we may belong. For example, creating a rap song with lyrics describing the events of their local neighborhood (and the songwriters' feelings toward those events) may be an authentic account of their context and an opportunity to communicate their moral beliefs on certain social issues either explicitly or in an implied way. Certainly, for young people, the music they create will often reflect the music they listen to, which, in this sense, reaffirms their identity (McFerran & Hense, 2017).

Songs tell people's stories and contribute to building or rebuilding personal identity. Pennebaker and Seagal (1999) consider that the act of telling one's story enables emotional expression of feelings associated with a person's history, while also bringing the material into conscious awareness for cognitive processing. In doing so, people share who they are with others while gaining new insight or reinforcing existing knowledge about themselves. However, for some people, verbalizing and sharing their story with others can be confronting. For example, talking with family or friends about past traumas may be important in their healing process but also difficult to do when feeling vulnerable. Songs can add an element of distance between the songwriters (our clients) and the audience (family/friends). Creating songs that tell people's stories offers the possibility of presenting their stories in a medium that is appropriate to communicate both facts and emotions and for these to co-exist—even when incongruent. As people create songs, they may explore micro-narratives (stories of a confined period of time; an aspect of a larger story or sense of self), which may contribute to the building of a macro-narrative (Tamplin, Baker, MacDonald, Roddy, & Rickard, 2017).

SONGWRITING AND IDENTITY IN ACADEMIC OR PREPROFESSIONAL CONTEXT

Music therapy education has always considered experiential activities as an essential part of its training. These include training in therapeutic conversations, improvisation, leading music groups, receptive methods of music therapy, and therapeutic songwriting. Indeed, all of these might be present in the training of students during their practicums. Here, a credentialed music therapist might ask students to present their material to the trained therapist for feedback prior to delivering this in real practice. It is through these "quasi" therapeutic experiences, and then in real life experiences, that students learn the skills of the discipline. However, just because one has acquired the skills does not necessarily indicate the student has developed a sense of professional identity. Given that songwriting is a useful medium to assist in the development of identity with clinical patients, it would be reasonable to assume that it could be used to assist music therapy students in reflecting on their journey to becoming a music therapist and on their identity as a music therapist.

The use of songwriting as an experiential learning tool has been explored by Baker and Krout (2011, 2012), who conducted a study with students from the University of Queensland (Australia) and Southern Methodist University (USA) that focused on creating songs about their clinical practicum experiences. In dyads containing a student from Australia and a student from the USA, these students created songs in a quasi-therapeutic context (the students functioned as co-therapists to each other). The songwriting process focused on describing, processing, and resolving feelings that were of concern while on placement. They used the songwriting process to describe fears, inadequacies, feelings of being unsafe, failure, and anxieties about unfamiliar contexts. In addition to identifying these negative experiences, they were encouraged to also consider more positive self-growth experiences, such as the identification of their strengths, feelings of authenticity, and questioning the self when feeling out of their depth. While students at both universities had been in music therapy training for approximately the same length of time, the Australian students had experienced substantially more clinical practicum experiences, compared with the US tradition of offering some clinical experiences with a long internship after training has finished. While these differences existed, it did not seem to impact how the students from each university could work together and tease out their experiences and feelings about clinical training.

The songs created by these students and their written reflections on the process gave the researchers insight into how songwriting can be used as a learning tool for professional skills and as a medium for self-growth. While specific music therapy identity did not emerge organically (which is not surprising, as they were not specifically asked to address it in the songwriting experiences), a number of learnings about being a music therapist emerged from the experiences. They recognized that collaborative songwriting is an effective outlet for humor, venting, and sharing with other—a form of peer supervision. It provided opportunities for them to feel understood by others. They acknowledged that the process allowed them to be open and honest about what they had experienced. Because the songwriting activity was task-focused, it may have enabled the students to feel a bit more comfortable in sharing negative experiences, as songs often contain pain, sadness, and frustrations. Also, as musicians, these young people may have felt more at home when sharing in the musical space than when doing so in the purely verbal space.

DEVELOPMENT OF MUSIC THERAPY IDENTITY DURING MUSIC THERAPY TRAINING

Music therapy training can be a sensitive time period for developing clinical identity. This can be due to the diversity of life experiences, personalities, and readiness for clinical work that each student brings. The role of an academic supervisor is to nurture safety and trust in the group process, helping guide the group through moments of challenge, tension, and growth. In addition, their role is to help navigate the various boundaries within the group dynamic, such as their various roles as an academic advisor, supervisor, examiner, and future colleague. Students navigate their own boundaries between themselves as they learn how to appropriately self-disclose and share within supervision. Our hope, as their academic supervisors, is to help students move into internship with an understanding that clinical identity is the reflexive integration of various selves, including the personal self, the professional self, and the musical self.

Personal Self

Students are often hesitant to share personal issues in clinical supervision related to their clinical training experiences. Didactically, we might help them to understand what supervision is in therapeutic contexts through readings and discussion. Conversely, experiential music-making might be utilized to help to uncover and explore personal feelings, thoughts, and emotions toward their clinical training. However, some students might present as overtly personal, lacking ethical boundaries needed for therapeutic context. Oftentimes, students are guided toward more didactic elements of their course work, and, in some cases, they are referred for counseling if the need arises.

Professional Self

Development of the professional self requires students to learn how to communicate using clinical terminology and to view their work from a theoretical perspective. During clinical training, clarifying clinical decisions based on an individual's health-related goal can be challenging due to a lack of professional language. Toward the end of their training programs, we hope that students can develop treatment plans in a way that is both confident within clinical decision-making and open to feedback from others. Being able to respond to professional feedback in a way that is not personal may be very difficult for many students.

Musical Self

Students come from very diverse musical backgrounds. Oftentimes, they might neglect their musicality, feeling that developing a professional clinical persona is salient. Nurturing a musical self in music therapy requires music competencies, an understanding of the clinical use of music, and being relaxed and confident with one's musicality. The role of music and other creative arts modalities during academic supervision may be to stress the importance of one's musical self in an integrated clinical identity.

During music therapy training, students are just learning to negotiate these boundaries between their professional, personal, and musical selves. This often requires academic advisors to bring a reflexive stance as to their role as a leader, moving between didactic lecture, open listener, co-musician, and conflict mediator. In addition, open cultural and sociopolitical dialogue is nurtured as an important element of ethical development as a therapist. Since this often challenges the group to navigate the various boundaries and components described above, the arts—in this case, songwriting—play an important role in helping to provide a path toward development.

SONGWRITING EXAMPLES

The three songwriters who will be presented in this chapter were graduate music therapy students at the State University of New York (SUNY) at New Paltz.[23] Their songs were written during an early phase of their clinical training. This stage of clinical training occurs over three semesters for a total of 180 direct clinical hours. This is the required number of hours needed by the American Music Therapy Association before a student can enter into a full-time internship. Each semester, students are placed at a different clinical setting to experience a diversity of orientations, populations, music therapy methods, and approaches to treatment.

At SUNY–New Paltz, students attend a once-a-week academic seminar where they progressively learn how to utilize group process toward developing clinical reflexivity and work toward viewing supervision as a process-oriented experience. Here, the academic seminar is seen as a space where students begin to develop their clinical identity. The creative arts are used throughout their development as a primary medium through which to share and experience their growth with peers.

For the students at SUNY, the creative arts play an important role in helping to secure a nonjudgmental space for students to share each week. The students' only directive is to creatively

---

[23] Baker uses songwriting to indirectly contribute to professional identity in her songwriting classes with students. As students practice their skills within the class context, they are encouraged to create songs about their clinical experiences. Baker does not have permission to share these songs; hence, all examples were obtained through Viega's academic context.

explore their weekly experiences and share their creations with the group at the start of each seminar. No restrictions are given toward the creative arts modality. At the start of each seminar, students are provided a moment to share. The group members do not provide feedback. This is to encourage a space where creativity can be expressed without judgment, analysis, or commentary. The hope is that students will deepen their connection to their creative self, trusting it to guide them through their professional and personal growth. After the sharing is complete, the group can later elaborate if the need arises.

Below, three songwriters and their songs will be presented to demonstrate the development of their clinical identity (personal, professional, and musical selves) as they moved forward into their internships. Original songwriting is a medium that many students choose for exploring and processing their experiences each week. However, due to the time-consuming nature of songwriting, students typically do not write a song weekly. Instead, songs appear to be written during important phases of the semester. Therefore, the songs presented below provide us with a developmental glimpse into each student's formation of clinical identity over the course of a semester. A description of the songs and what they reveal about each student's developmental journey in academic supervision will be provided, in addition to a summary of the songs in the songwriters' own words. Each songwriter gave permission to share these songs and presented different methods of music and lyric notation (some come with lyrics and chords, others just lyrics, and others with notations).

Alison[24]: Embracing the Darkness

Alison is a Caucasian woman in her mid-20s whose clinical placement was at an outpatient mental health facility in New York City. There, she worked with a diverse group of people who are experiencing homelessness and face challenges with mental health and trauma. Entering into this placement, Alison expressed that she had unresolved feelings of frustration with her previous clinical training experiences. In addition, she noted anxieties over beginning a new placement in an emotionally demanding facility, as well as about length and cost of her commute into New York City.

Alison wrote four songs over the course of the semester: "Right Now," "Sus," "I'm Good, but Thanks, Anyway," and "The Abyss." Songs 1 and 2 represent a stage of Alison's growth where she was beginning to look inward, finding a space within for trust and stability. It is as if she had anticipated early on that she would have to confront her anxieties during the course of the semester. Song 3 represents a stage where Alison was defensive, which led to tension with her supervisory and peer relationships. However, she noted that this was an act of self-preservation and a way to harness feelings of self-empowerment. This stage led her to a clear and direct expression of her inner "abyss" in song 4, which allowed for her to cathartically confront her insecurities, make peace with them, and nurture them into positive resources moving into internship.

Song 1: "Right Now"

Am   Dm
Take some space,
G   C
Trust yourself,
Am   G   Am
Know it'll all work out somehow.

Am   Dm
Take it easy,

---

[24] Permission was given by each student to use their songs. Pseudonyms have been given to the students.

281

```
G              C
```
There's room to grow,
```
Am             G              Am
```
Don't have to know everything right now.

```
Am            F
```
And if you're worried,
```
C      G
```
Give it time
```
Am                        G
```
To get yourself off the ground.

```
Am            F
```
Patience's a skill
```
C      G
```
I should find,
```
Am            G              Am
```
Don't have to know everything right now.

Alison's description: This was the first song I ever wrote! I think that the beginning of the semester (when this was written) was a tremulous time for me because I was still completing hours from my previous placement and I still hadn't started my current one. I remember feeling very unsure of myself, and I had a lot of feelings about inadequacy. For me, a big part of my training as a music therapist has been trying to balance the dynamic of being a decent student and doing well in class and then wondering how that will translate to a clinical setting. At the time, I often found myself worrying that I would do well on assignments but then struggle in sessions. I think this song served as a reminder to be patient, and there's also some self-reassurance in there as well.

Song 2: "Sus"

Suspicious of the stillness.
What's going on inside?
Too used to being anxious,
Don't have a quiet mind.

Feels like a meditation,
Being still, feeling fine.
Suspicious of the stillness,
Wish it would last this time.

(instrumental)

Bracing for the movement,
Impact coming down the line.

Alison's description: As the semester progressed, I felt like everything was going … OK. And that was suspicious to me! Reflecting back, I think that the stability and experiences that I had at my placement helped me to feel well, stable and experienced. I wasn't used to feeling that way. The lines "Suspicious of the stillness, Wish it would last this time" break my heart when I read them because I remember being very afraid of going back into a place of uncertainty just when things were starting to feel more stable. Also at around this time, I bought an electric guitar and that had a MAJOR impact on my songwriting. I really enjoy playing electric guitar, and I felt more comfortable in branching out in my songwriting. I think that the first song I wrote was mildly out of … spite (sorry!!!!!!!) … or maybe feeling like I HAD to at least try because I gave you [Viega] a hard time about the assignment and I needed to prove that I could do it? Yikes. Anyway, this second song was when I realized I actually like songwriting.

Song 3: "I'm Good, but Thanks, Anyway"

Dm7   G7
I always know when it's not right.
CM7   FM7
Gotta run from the trouble.
Dm7   G7
Causeless permission, oh, that's fine, but
CM7   FM7
I didn't ask you to bother.

Dm7   G7
Finding what I feel inside.
CM7   FM7
There's just so much to discover.
Dm7   G7
But where's my sense of space and time?
CM7   FM7
It's one thing after another.

Dm7   G7
Em7   A
Dm7   G7
CM7
Always after the other.

Alison's description: I've been having trouble remembering what this song is even about, and then I remembered: I went on a shitty date!! It was weird and I was MAD! I wrote another not-for-class song at the time, but I think that it permeated into my in-class material as well. It's hard for me to describe this song, I don't know exactly how to write about it, but I think it has got a sort of snarky tone. It's also me remembering that I'm intelligent and badass, not that I forgot, but maybe asserting it more? I remember starting to feel more sure of myself and confident around this time. I love the line "causeless permission, oh, that's fine, but I didn't ask you to bother." It still gets stuck in my head from time to time.

Song 4: "The Abyss"

Em C G C G C Em

It doesn't quite fit, no it's not quite right,
What I've come to inspect and identify.

This thing inside, the abyss of mine,
Tried to name it, tried to burn it, tried to rectify.

When you've got the grit, when you've got the nerve,
When it doesn't seem to bother you anymore,

I still know it's there, the abyss inside.
I think I've grown to love it over time.

F   C   G (G sus for flavor)
And maybe the abyss lives inside of you.
And it's not quite as bad as it seems.
And maybe I don't have to explain myself.
Maybe it's always been a part of me.

It's easy to climb yourself in and out.
If you don't miscalculate the landing.
I spend so much time trying to explain myself.
Maybe I forgot what's in the heart of me.

MMMMMmm, the abyss.
Mmm, the abyss.

Alison's description: YEAH! My favorite one! I think I embraced the darkness and moved through my rebellious phase while still maintaining parts of it in my identity. My other songs never ended on the tonic, and I realized after I wrote this one that it did, and that felt VERY significant to me. I feel like this song has a bit of a celebratory aspect to it.

Summary of Alison's Songs

Alison's songs integrate personal, professional, and music growth over the course of the semester. Her placement, which provided stability and support within a demanding clinical setting, allowed for her to grow professionally by trusting herself and gaining confidence. During the semester, Alison began to identify strongly with feminist perspectives in music therapy. Values of feminism appear throughout these songs, including connecting her cultural and professional identities. She discovered her preference for the electric guitar as a songwriting resource to express her frustrations and insecurities. It is as if the electric guitar was a symbol of her developing power and strength. By the end of the semester, Alison had discovered new positive resources within herself that she was taking into her next stage of training.

Eric: Building Resources Toward Transition

Eric is a Caucasian male in his mid-20s. His clinical experience was at a long-term residential facility for older adults. Coming into the semester, Eric had experience with songwriting and had already utilized improvisation (voice and guitar) as a means for coping with stress and the rigors of being a student. His songs and improvisations typically involved meditative musical moments that then crescendoed into passionate emotional releases. His general demeanor is polite, compliant, amiable, and nonconfrontational. Eric did not outwardly show his stress, and it was challenging to know how I (Viega), as his academic supervisor, could support his growth in moving into pre-internship.

Eric wrote two songs during the course of the semester, "One Brick at a Time" and "Final Good-bye." Both songs reveal the songwriter's natural resources, including his positive self-coping, thoughtful demeanor, meditative presence, and emotional nature. At the same time, it is clear that Eric is at a crossroads (song 1) and in a period of transition (song 2) of some sorts. His descriptions note that the songs provided a space to cope with the stress of being a student and in his personal life. After attuning to the songs with this knowledge, his harmonic structures and breathy vocal performances hold the tension of a songwriter in transition and a person who is gathering resources to prepare for the challenges of his internship placement.

Song 1: "One Brick at a Time"

What has come knockin' on my door?
They said go plant the special seeds that make you who you are
The plants are green, the trees are free of all that could do harm

One brick at a time I build the hope in my life
One breath at a time I keep my heart intact
One day at a time I realize life goes by fast
Memories they last forever, they last forever

Now it's time to water them down nutrients for the soul
Do it slow, and do it right, connections rich with love
I see the stars up above blooming all around
It's time to sleep to take good care of all those who have passed

One brick at a time I build the hope in my life
One breath at a time I keep my heart intact
One day at a time I realize life goes by fast
Memories they last forever, they last forever

One path leads right, the other left, my mind in the right place
My eyes closed, I can see it now, the city in my dreams
Shining bright and beautiful, and coming to me soon

One brick at a time I build the hope in my life
One breath at a time I keep my heart intact
One day at a time I realize life goes by fast
Memories they last forever, they last forever

Eric's description: The lyrics of this song describe several feelings within my experience at an inpatient assisted living facility for aging adults. At this point in my semester, I was dealing with schoolwork and responsibilities as the Music Therapy Club president and trying to develop meaningful session plans for the residents. The creation of this song brought forth an awareness of how I could deal with my stresses and how I can utilize my thoughts on life and purpose to keep me going. At the same time, I found elements of my work as a student and professional that helped me to do what was needed: passion, hope, love, beauty, health, and connection. This song helped to reflect on my experience within my semester as a student and professional and allowed me to come to a realization of how I can manage my stresses and difficulties: "One brick at a time" (I'm building my future), "One breath at a time, One day at a time" (I prepare myself and do what is needed because this is where I feel I belong; I want to keep myself going and embrace the beauty in my work and in the people I meet). I must embrace all, the wonderful moments and the difficult ones.

Song 2: "Transition"

I can't believe the end is oh so near
Where did the time go?
You all shined so brightly
So beautiful like a rainbow

Transition, transition

Slow and deep I sink now
Into myself into my soul
You all showed and taught me something
About life

Transition, transition

Now it's time to say good-bye
The moments come to close my eyes
Reopen them to a different room
Another door to walk through
A change in pace

Eric's description: This song was created to explore my thoughts and feelings about my fieldwork experience at an inpatient, assisted living facility for aging adults. I aimed to come to terms with my feelings around leaving the facility and having to move on to another experience within my training, internship. In this song, I discovered the importance of self-reflection and personal growth, as both a person and a professional. It became an avenue for self-expression, finding new meaning, and becoming aware. This process also painted a better picture of what I had learned from the residents and staff at the facility. As I discussed and shared a recording of the song with my supervisor, we both agreed that the song should be shared with the residents at the facility. This song became part of closure with the residents in which I shared with them what I had learned from each and every one of them. While I found it difficult to say good-bye after only a semester of providing music therapy, I found contentment in the experience: building rich relationships, learning new skills, and finding greater purpose as a music therapist within the field.

Summary of Eric's Songs
Eric's songs stayed focused on his feelings toward his clinical placement, especially in building a rapport with the people with whom he was working. He used his musical self to express the gratitude and gifts that his placement had revealed to him. Eric's deepening self-awareness and reflexivity demonstrated his deepening cultural understanding of how he, as a young adult, could impact and be impacted by older adults. It appears that he learned something about himself from the people with whom he was working, which was not yet tangible but could be expressed in a song. Eric seemed to be transitioning toward a deeper sense of self-awareness, perhaps moving toward more direct expression of the stress and inadequacies he was experiencing as a student in clinical training. It is as if being with older adults who were losing their independence forced Eric to unconsciously face his own autonomy.

Terry: Toward Mutuality

Terry is a Caucasian male in his early 30s. Terry's placement was at a residential facility for autistic[25] adults. This was a very challenging experience for Terry since there was no formal music therapy program at his facility. Terry received supervision from a local music therapist, who would make observations on-site. Terry had a lot of experience in musical theater and demonstrated attributes of being organized, musical and artistic, and self-expressive. In addition, he was very open about his mental health, positively processing it toward his growth as a music therapist.

Terry wrote four songs during the semester: "The Weigh Down," "Just Fine," "Two Roads Converge," and "The Leaving." The lyrics and the music played an integral role, all meticulously arranged on the piano. Song 1 expressed the feelings of depression and exhaustion Terry was bringing into the semester. These feelings were enhanced by the chaos he experienced at the start of his placement. In song 2, Terry recognized the "good enough" music therapy student within himself. This self-acceptance helped him transition into song 3, which sees Terry in a new, hopeful space, anticipating new journeys ahead. His last piece is a meditative improvisation in which he expressed the tenderness of nurturing both himself and the people he worked with over the course of the semester.

Song 1: "The Weigh Down"

Table 1
"The Weigh Down"

Feet too heavy to get out of bed,
Lids too weak to fight the weight of my head
The weigh down, the weigh down

People yelling and moving about
Have weighed me down so much I'm already done
I thought I would be of sound mind, but I left it behind

Terry's description: This song was written during the second week at my clinical placement. My depression was intense, and I was very fatigued. I entered the sessions thinking about myself, and I was not present for the individuals. It took so much energy to go through an hourlong session. There is a lot of weight and personal baggage that I carried as I entered the session. This song made me

---

[25] Identity-first language is utilized to recognize the neurodiversity community, which has communicated that autism is an integral part of who they are.

recognize that my depression was impacting the sessions and a change was needed. "The Weigh Down" is a whole tone–inspired blues. The right hand is in a whole tone mode, representing the disorderly environment of my placement. The upward and downward chromatic motion of the left hand is a search for grounding. But I cannot rise above. My voice is in a low range and descends even lower when the verses end, reflecting the hopelessness I felt.

Song 2: "Just Fine"

Gm7   EbM   AbM   DbM7

From the lowest low
To the highest high
If they reach, the horn will blow
If they don't, don't bark or bite

It's bright to be bright
And the sun fills the room
It's pathetic to be pathetic
Enter gray skies full of gloom

It's okay to feel down
But save it for the downtime
If you smile, then you won't frown
You don't have to be happy, just fine

Terry's description: This song reflects my growth. I was enjoying my clinical placement much more. I felt I was making an impact, and this changed my attitude and mood. I was able to leave my personal issues at home. I was present, authentic, and enjoying the music experiences. This song fits comfortably in my register, which is similar to the comfort and confidence I was gaining at my placement.

Song 3: "Two Roads Converge"

Table 2
"Two Roads Converge"

Two roads converge
For a moment
Two footprints
One on another

Two roads, two roads
One moment
What happens next?

Song 4: "The Leaving"

Terry's description: I had made a connection with an individual who had made a great deal of progress in two months. I knew we would be together for a short period of time, and then we would part ways. I had accepted that, but I was concerned for his future. Music therapy was very effective, and I worried that he would not be able to receive services after I left. These pieces were a way to process this fear and the bond established during the semester. The melody used in the improvisation was set to the line: "It's not the leaving that's hard, it's the leaving behind." The song begins with a single line, for I started the semester feeling alone. Measures 4 and 5 are similar to my relationship with the individual. The two hands move in contrary motion in measure 4 and then move together in the following measure. He provided support for me as I did for him. The piano is my true voice, and improvisation is the most sincere form of expression for me. My fingers can process what words cannot.

Summary of Terry's Songs

Terry's songs used his innate musicality to express his struggles, making connection within himself and with the people with whom he worked. The development of his songs moved from expressing his depression and exhaustion to developing self-care (being good enough) to, finally, finding mutuality within his interpersonal and intrapersonal relationships. As he prepared to transition to internship, Terry appeared to be both nurturing newfound relationships that he had developed over the semester and having a difficult time in finding resolutions, as noted both in his descriptions and in the unresolved cadences in songs 3 and 4.

THE IMPLICATIONS FOR SONGWRITING IN CLINICAL IDENTITY FORMATION INTEGRATING PERSONAL AND PROFESSIONAL IDENTITIES

Songwriting provided each songwriter presented here with a way to integrate and balance their personal self with their growing professional identity. Often, the personal self was related to their identity as a student, which was rooted in traditional notions of academic success. Alison noted that she was worried about how her work as a student would translate in a professional setting, revealing her insecurities in integrating her student self with her professional self. She also presented personal feelings of anger and frustration, which she feared would get in the way of her professional work. The stability of her placement allowed for her to notice these strong feelings, express them, and develop a new sense of professional confidence. She summarized this by saying, "I think that I embraced the darkness and moved through my rebellious phase while still maintaining parts of it in my identity."

Like Alison, Eric's identity coming into the semester was centered on his role as a student, which seemed to inhibit meaningful connections and professional success at his placement ("At this point in my semester, I was dealing with schoolwork and responsibilities as the Music Therapy Club president and trying to develop meaningful session plans for the residents"). Eric found that songwriting allowed him to find the connections between his student-self and a growing personal identity. This is reflected in his statement about his last song, *Transition:* "I discovered the importance of self-reflection and personal growth, as both a person and a professional."

Whereas Alison and Eric stayed close to their personal identities as students, Terry was more intimate, expressing his depression, fatigue, and struggles with mental health. Terry admitted: "I was not present for the individuals. There is a lot of weight and personal baggage that I carried as I entered the session." Songwriting provided a powerful medium to help Terry to recognize his immediate need for self-care and how it was impacting his sessions.

It appears that by integrating personal and professional identities, new positive resources for each songwriter emerged. Each songwriter viewed these resources as strengths for moving into the next phase of their clinical training, internship. Alison noted that a new sense of stability and empowerment as a clinical training student emerged from her songs. In addition, Alison found ways to express authentic feelings of frustration, which aided in her development. Although Terry's placement was more chaotic, his experience of overcoming adversity toward developing deep connections with the people with whom he worked was empowering. Meanwhile, Eric discovered that "passion, hope, love, beauty, health, and connection" were innate attributes he possessed that bridged his personal and professional identities. Songwriting, as a self-care practice, allowed for positive resources to emerge for each songwriter. The sharing of these songs in a nonjudgmental space helped each songwriter to own and nurture their strengths as they moved into internship.

Using Innate Musicality

Songwriting called for each songwriter to harness their innate musical sensibilities and individuality to express their clinical development. At first, Alison did not trust the songwriting process, perhaps mirroring her feelings of inadequacy at the start of the semester. However, early in the semester she bought an electric guitar, which she said "had a MAJOR impact on my songwriting." It appears that the electric guitar played a pivotal role in the voicing of her insecurities, anger, and fears. This led her to use songwriting as a cathartic release and self-acceptance.

Eric's use of songwriting and improvisation was a natural way for him to mediate and cope with stressors. This was often mirrored by his use of repetitive musical motifs and contemplative lyrics. However, punctuated moments of emotional musical crescendo revealed pent-up frustrations that could be further surveyed. Eric's songs revealed a songwriter in transition, gathering resources in preparation for future explorations.

Meanwhile, Terry had a very strong sense of his musicality, confidently suggesting, "The piano is my true voice, and improvisation is the most sincere form of expression for me. My fingers can process what words cannot." His strong identity in musical theater provided him with a natural ability to use the music and lyrics to tell the story of his development. He was able to express how musical elements of his songs related to his developing clinical identity, such as "this song fits comfortably in my register, which is similar to the comfort and confidence I was gaining at my placement." For all three songwriters, the experience of songwriting allowed them to use their innate musicality to nurture positive resources toward developing clinical identities as music therapists.

Songwriting's Role in the Supervisory Relationship

Being present to the performance of these songs allows the supervisor to hear these songwriters at their natural stage of growth without imposing evaluative measurements or subjective feelings toward each student. The supervisor can listen to their songs with eyes closed, noticing images that might appear and important musical motifs and become more aware of their own thoughts, feelings, and reactions. By listening for both the musical and lyrical content and then integrating the two, a supervisor may gain more empathy for the developmental needs of music therapy students during clinical training.

This was important in several ways. First, the supervisor may discover new attributes and qualities of each songwriter that were not readily presented through verbal discourse or experiential course work. For instance, in the aforementioned case of Alison, there was often tension between Alison and Viega, which is reflective in her comments. "I think that the first song I wrote was mildly out of … spite (sorry!!!!!!!)… or maybe feeling like I HAD to at least try because I gave you [Viega] a hard time about the assignment and I needed to prove that I could do it?" This tension felt unresolved within Viega while listening to her songs. As he attuned to these feelings and owned them as his, he began to hear an empowered, strong woman asserting her independence. From this point forward, he was able to bring that image of her into their relationship, respecting and trusting her as she worked on owning her own strength.

Second, their performances allowed Viega to find patience for their growth, preventing him from pushing them outside of their comfort zones too quickly. For instance, he often felt frustrated with Eric, wishing he would move past niceties and express tension in a more visceral fashion. However, when attuning to the qualities of the music, Viega was able to develop sensitivity to Eric's process, trusting that he needed to take time to accept his natural resources before moving into unknown emotional territory.

Finally, while listening to their songs, Viega often found himself discovering empathy for their struggles and respect for their lived experience. For instance, Terry's vivid musical and lyrical imagery often left him somatically responding to the depth of conflict, depression, and fatigue he was experiencing at the start of the semester. As this shifted during the semester for Terry, Viega was able to experience the benefits of his developing intersubjective growth through the growth of their own supervisory relationship.

CONCLUSION

We offer examples of how songwriting may be used in an academic context to assist music therapy students in developing a professional identity. The personal, professional, and musical selves are all integral to the music therapy identity, and all three have the potential to be explored through songwriting either simultaneously or individually but at different developmental stages. Our experiences are that students' identities can enjoy, be challenged, experience insight, and transform through their song creations. While the cases reported here were of group supervision but enabled individual students to create their own songs, group songwriting experiences also have possibilities for students to explore their developing identities as they co-create songs about their clinical experiences. By identifying what is common about their clinical challenges and constructing lyrics and music to express these, students can experience support and opportunities for self-growth.

REFERENCE LIST

Baker, F., & Krout, R. (2011). Collaborative peer lyric writing during music therapy training: A tool for exploring students' reflections about clinical practicum experiences. *Nordic Journal of Music Therapy, 20*(1), 62–89.

Baker, F., Wigram, T., Stott, D., & McFerran, K. (2008). Therapeutic songwriting in music therapy: Part 1. Who are the therapists, who are the clients, and why is songwriting used? *Nordic Journal of Music Therapy, 17*, 105–123.

Baker, F., Wigram, T., Stott, D., & McFerran, K. (2009). Therapeutic songwriting in music therapy: Comparing the literature with practice across diverse populations. *Nordic Journal of Music Therapy, 18*, 32–56.

Baker, F. A. (2015). *Therapeutic songwriting: Developments in theory, methods, and practice.* London, UK: Palgrave Macmillan.

Baker, F. A., & Krout, R. E. (2012). Turning experience into learning: Educational contributions of collaborative peer songwriting during music therapy training. *International Journal of Music Education, 30*(2), 133–147. doi:10.1177/0255761411427103.

Baker, F. A., & MacDonald, R. A. R. (2017). Shaping identities through therapeutic songwriting. In R. MacDonald, D. Hargreaves, & D. Miell (Eds.), *The Oxford Handbook of Musical Identities* (pp. 436–452). Oxford, UK: Oxford University Press.

Byrne, B. M. (1996). *Measurement and instrumentation in psychology.* Washington, DC: American Psychological Association.

Markus, H., & Nurius, P. (1986). Possible selves. *American Psychologist, 41*(9), 954–969. doi:10.1037/0003-066x.41.9.954

McFerran, K., & Hense, C. (2017). I would die without my music: Relying on musical identities to cope in difficult times. In R. MacDonald, D. J. Hargreaves, & D. Miell (Eds.), *Handbook of Musical Identities* (pp. 668–681). London, UK: Oxford University Press.

Pennebaker, J. W., & Seagal, J. D. (1999). Forming a story: The health benefits of narrative. *Journal of Clinical Psychology, 55*(10), 1243–1254.

Tamplin, J., Baker, F. A., Macdonald, R. A. R., Roddy, C., & Rickard, N. S. (2016). A theoretical framework and therapeutic songwriting protocol to promote integration of self-concept in people with acquired neurological injuries. *Nordic Journal of Music Therapy, 25*(2), 111–133. doi:10.1080/08098131.2015.101120

Viega, M., & Baker, F. A. (2016). What's in a song? Combining Analytica and Arts-based Analyasis for Songs Created by Songwriters with Neurodisabilities. *Nordic Journal of Music Therapy, 26*(3), 235–255. doi:10.1080/08098131.2016.1205651

Viega, M., & Baker, F. A. (2017). Remixing identity: Creating meaning from songs written by patients recovering from a spinal cord injury. *Journal of Applied Arts & Health, 8*(1), 57–73. doi:10.1386/jaah.8.1.57_1

Wigram, T., & Baker, F. (2005). Introduction: Song writing as therapy. In F. Baker & T. Wigram (Eds.), *Song Writing Methods, Techniques, and Clinical Applications for Music Therapy Clinicians, Educators, and Students* (pp. 1–23). London, UK: Jessica Kingsley.

Chapter 18

ADVANCED SUPERVISION

Darlene Brooks

INTRODUCTION

When students complete their clinical internship, they are eager to join the work world, become therapists, and demonstrate their ability to effect change in the lives of their clients. They enter the work world with zest and compassion in sharing those new skills with their clients, with staff, and with the team. They have become Board-Certified Music Therapists (MT-BCs) and are gaining expertise with the population with whom they are working.

After working awhile, however, the demands of the job, the sameness of their routine, the long workdays, the amount of paperwork required by the facility, the fight for recognition, and the heaviness of their client load are some of the issues that lead the therapist to begin questioning their adequacy—and sometimes career choice. The need for supervision looms, yet there is a concern that receiving supervision may confirm a lack of efficiency or qualifications to do their jobs. Yet music therapy is a field in which they believe and that they usually love. Finding the right supervisor, the right group (if applicable), while maintaining their employment and autonomy, is a challenge. Education differences, different theoretical models, the need to find supervisors who understand the population and respect their work, and the necessity of maintaining the professional status of a therapist also add to the complexity of seeking supervision. These issues are further compounded for music therapists who have been working for several years. Who can they find who will respect their expertise and understand the subtle and not so subtle issues they confront? With these concerns in mind, the guidance and feedback offered to the supervisee must be of the nature that the supervisee/therapist is able to employ recommendations offered, feel empowered, and maintain their professionalism.

This chapter presents a model of an advanced supervision course that I feel is beneficial for new and experienced therapists. It provides: (1) an opportunity for therapists to come together while maintaining their jobs; (2) an opportunity for therapists to share their expertise about their population; (3) an opportunity to learn about and consider alternative approaches in treatment; (4) the ability to receive guidance from the supervisor and support from peers, and (5) the ability to develop a network of therapist colleagues with whom they can continue a supervision practice following the course, if they choose. Therapists taking this course are Board-Certified Music Therapists (MT-BC) and are working clinically. Their experience ranges from three months to multiple years as a music therapist. Therapists taking this course may be graduate students or perhaps practicing clinicians who want supervision and see the benefit of this unique group format.

Because this course is also offered as a graduate course, therapists come from different states, regions, countries, theoretical orientations, and experiences with varied populations. This course offers therapists a rich opportunity for growth. In my opinion, successful supervision necessitates some face-to-face interaction between supervisor and supervisee. As most of the participants in this course are working therapists, it was important to design a course that included some in-person interaction, while respecting and supporting that most of the participants work full-time jobs as therapists. To accomplish this, the course was designed to provide two face-to-face eight-hour meetings, spaced out in at least a one- to two-month time period, along with regular distance communication through online forums throughout the semester.

Day 1

At the beginning of class, I introduce myself and provide the supervisees with information on my clinical background and years of supervisory experience. After welcomes, because this is also a graduate course, the course syllabus is presented. The syllabus serves several purposes: The first purpose is to outline what is going to happen in the class, which is often reassuring to the supervisee/therapist coming into this supervision approach for the first time. The second purpose is to present objectives that are resonant with the Board Certification Domain Professional Development (CBMT), and the American Music Therapy Association (AMTA) professional competencies, which specifically address professional supervision. To assist students with preparation for supervision, the syllabus includes the following points:

> Think about your reasons for supervision.
> Think about the client population you are working with.
>
> - What are the positive attributes of this population?
>   - What do you do to maintain those positive attributes in music therapy?
> - What are the challenges with this population?
>   - How have you addressed the challenges in music therapy?
> - How do you determine goals and objectives?
>   - How successful have you been in meeting your goals and objectives?
>   - What has prevented you from achieving your goals and objectives?
> - What multicultural challenges have you encountered in your work?
>   - How have you addressed these challenges?
>   - Do these challenges interfere with your delivery as a music therapist?
> - What music therapy methods do you use with your population?
> - What methods are you most comfortable with?
> - How comfortable are you with the idea of sharing your work with the class?
> - What, if anything, prevents you from sharing?
> - How comfortable are you with sharing aspects of yourself with the class?

While not exhaustive, this list helps students to prepare for the discussion topics that may occur during supervision and allows them to choose a starting point with which they are the most comfortable at the onset of the supervision group.

Supervision requires consent, so an equally important step at the beginning of supervision is the presentation of consent forms. The consent form includes willingness to participate, a request for authentic participation in supervision, and notification that authentic supervision may bring up emotional issues that will be supported but not addressed in depth in this supervision forum. Students must understand that they come into supervision voluntarily and are not coerced into participating. If the student does not consent or feel prepared to undergo the demands of supervision, delayed enrollment is often recommended. Also: What happens in supervision remains in supervision. I consider the supervision space to be a sacred space. There are several reasons I call supervision "sacred." First of all, there is an ethical imperative by the AMTA and CBMT organizations that requires our protection of clients. Even though this is supervision, pseudonyms are used to discuss clients, and only limited information about the client's behavior is shared for the purpose of understanding the issues in music therapy. The need to maintain the confidentiality of the client is of primary importance. Second, supervision is one of the most vulnerable periods for a therapist in professional life. It is important that this vulnerability be honored by providing a respected and nurturing environment that offers safety in sharing. A third factor is that often the work environment is discussed, and in some cases, not in the most positive way. What is discussed is the opinions and projections of the supervisee, and the reality may be different from the experiences of other supervisees who have worked in the same environment. Here again, one of the goals of this sacred space is to allow these occasional descriptions as we work to help the supervisee recognize what is actually occurring in that work environment. This requires a nonjudgmental attitude and a safe space for expression. In order for supervision to work for participants, there must be some assurances that what is revealed is confidential and honored nonjudgmentally. Students should know that what they say in supervision will remain in the room and will not be discussed after the class at any point. Both supervisees and supervisor sign the consent forms; one copy is for the supervisor and one is for the supervisee. Following this business part of supervision, introductions are made. Supervisees introduce themselves and include their length of time practicing as a music therapist.

After introductions, I then ask the supervisees to define supervision. It's important to have people share their perception of supervision. This gives the supervisor an idea of the defenses that might be present before the supervision session begins. There is no attempt to correct anyone's perceptions of supervision at this point in the class. Generally, supervisees will define supervision based on their experience as an intern or new employee with their own judgments and perceptions, based on positive or negative experiences. The supervisor then offers a working definition of supervision for the class. It may resemble something already said or it may be completely different.

After defining supervision, the supervisor leads a discussion on the difference between supervision and criticism and the need to constantly remind supervisees of this distinction. Along the same vein, the importance of receiving and offering feedback nonjudgmentally is discussed. It is important that the supervisor acknowledge the struggle that some supervisees have in receiving feedback because of what feels like an assault on the ego or because of transference/countertransference reactions. Once this business is completed, the heart of supervision begins.

Supervisees are encouraged to share their clinical work with the group—the population with whom they work, the number of sessions done in a day, and the music interventions generally used. Here again, this description is only for sharing the varied environments that may be discussed in supervision. After each supervisee has responded, the supervisor then asks each supervisee to share one of their *most recent positive sessions*. They are asked to share the aspects of their session that affected them and the client and how this indicated progress. This approach is another method to ease supervisees into supervision and serves as a reminder that there are good things that happen in their work. Often, after everyone has shared their positive experience, a referential music improvisation may follow, where the focus is on those positive experiences just described by the supervisees. This is a group improvisation where supervisees choose an instrument that best represents their feelings related to the just described positive experience. There are no rules during this improvisation. Supervisees are encouraged to begin playing whenever they are comfortable, and the improvisation has no time limit but ends organically. Discussion follows the improvisation, where supervisees discuss their use of the instruments, what they were trying to communicate, and the feelings that accompanied the improvisation experience, along with the feelings about playing with other supervisees. There may be some similarities noted by various supervisees or even reflections on their connection with others or lack of connection. An additional discussion may occur on how easy or difficult it was to recall the positive experience from their respective sessions. At this point, the beginning of rapport has been established among supervisees, and the environment becomes more comfortable. Supervisees are encouraged to write a log about the experience they just had. Logs are a continual part of supervision both for immediate responses to experiences and discussions and as a reference at the end of the semester, when they submit their summaries. The focus for this first log is on the positive aspects of being a therapist and sharing that experience with others. At this point, the supervisor is generally not seen as adversarial, waiting to find flaws in their work as therapists, but rather as an ally who has encouraged supervisees to remember the positive impact of their work with clients and the feelings that are evoked in them as a result of these positive experiences.

Supervisees are now ready to examine the *challenges* they face. I prefer to use the word "challenges" rather than "problems." Challenges are things that can be overcome through strategizing, planning, and discussion, whereas problems are often personalized in a way that supervisees often see the problems as flaws within themselves, leading to resistance, defensiveness, and games, which slow down the supervision process. To assist in this next step, a discussion on the music therapy methods most commonly used at the site, the establishment of goals and objectives, group size, and facility demands may be useful in easing supervisees into a discussion of specific challenges they face. Keeping in mind that it is fairly easy for a student to become defensive, I generally ask for only one challenge, not every challenge the population or facility presents. I find that for supervisees who are experiencing their first advanced supervision, this may feel overwhelming, so to ease them into this approach, only one challenge is mentioned, without comment or judgment. This helps the supervisee to narrow their focus to a challenge that more accurately reflects their reason for supervision. By simply having the supervisee name one challenge, we might find that there are similar challenges among other members of the group. As the new supervisee listens to the list, there is an almost palpable breath and a welcomed ability to accept what is occurring in the supervision space.

Another approach, used with supervisees who have had advanced supervision before, is to focus on one person without undo concern that reactions or responses to the challenge will be overwhelming for that supervisee. What is interesting is that I find that the first challenge the supervisee presents is at the core of other challenges in their work environments, both for new and experienced supervisees. For example, an issue that often occurs is how to get clients to focus on the therapy session when the aides are having conversations in the background that are distracting. If this comes up, deeper exploration of these behaviors emerges, and we focus on both multicultural issues and general relationship issues. "Multicultural" in this case refers to the racial and ethnic makeup of the clients and aides and includes the culture of the facility and the particular unit where patients are housed. Relationship issues focus on the rapport or lack thereof that has been established between the supervisee and the aides.

As a supervisor, I use two main approaches in addressing supervision challenges. The first is to engage the group in discussion on strategies that might be employed to deal with the challenge presented by the peer. Supervisees are initially more receptive to peer suggestions than supervisor suggestions because of the perceived difference in hierarchy, that is, being relegated back to the intern status, where the supervisor knows all. I find that having supervisees work together in strategizing bridges the gap between experience levels and provides genuineness, support, and empathy to the receiving supervisee. For instance, in the multicultural issue and general relationship issues presented above, I encourage discussion between supervisees so they are able to help gain personal insights on the racial culture of the staff and clients, the culture of the environment, and the perception of the supervisees that might be generated from both the aides and the clients. The focus here is not on a condemnation of the supervisee or the aides, but on an increased awareness about self in relation to aides, an enhanced understanding of the environmental culture, and strategies for bridging the gap between supervisee, aide, and client so that therapy can take place in an optimal way. There are times when the suggestions of peers are all the supervisee presenting the challenge needs to hear—for example, choosing appropriate music for a client group that closely sounds like the original artist, is recognized by the aides, and stimulates participation by all. Supervisees have a wealth of music at their disposal and readily share how to approach this music in a way that is acceptable to their clients.

The second approach I use is based on Bruscia's (2001) *A Model of Supervision Derived from Apprenticeship Training.* In his model of supervision, Bruscia offers five levels[26] or approaches to supervision that can be used separately, based on what the supervisee presents, or can be used in tandem if that is the need. I often find that when supervisees are offering each other feedback, the *action-oriented approach* is the one they offer. Here, they will tell each other what needs to be done to be successful in dealing with the challenge. I tend to reserve my use of this particular approach until I have had the opportunity to help the supervisee examine in more depth the challenge presented. For example, what does the supervisee understand about the population and music therapy methods utilized with that group? This might lead to a *client-oriented approach,* where the supervisee describes the client during the process of the session, from the onset to the end. Here I'm interested in knowing what it is that the supervisee observes or understands about the client, and the client's behavior (interactions with others, affective state, active or passive involvement in the music session, response to the music and to the supervisee). At this point, I may offer *action-oriented* responses to help the supervisee to focus on the clients and music based on responses to my inquiries. Where needed, I may ask leading questions that will be directed toward supervisee learning or simply provide responses that are educational in nature—a *learning-oriented approach.* Unless a supervisee has experience in supervision, I tend to leave the last two supervision approaches, *experience-oriented* and *countertransference-oriented,* to the second supervision meeting, regardless of the vocal utterances of the supervisee. I find that to introduce these approaches too soon tends to make supervisees more defensive or to respond too quickly that their challenges are all countertransference-oriented. Instead, these are introduced with gentle prodding in the second class, where those "A-ha!" moments are easier to discover and absorb.

To help uncover supervision issues, music is often used. Music goes beyond the verbal representation of the challenges. We will often use music improvisation methods and role-play the challenges in order to amplify them, which in my experience will make it a little easier for the supervisee to see and hear what is happening in the session and will lead to a new awareness about the challenges and the supervisee's approach to addressing them. The role-play process involves a thorough description of the clients, the music experiences, and the goals of the session. Peers are then divided into several sections. Some may serve as observers, while other peers act as the clients described by the supervisee, so that feedback from the supervisee's peers is more authentic to the experience. Supervisees who are presenting the challenges play themselves, leading a mock group. It is during the musical exchanges that I might use more *action-oriented supervision,* by having the supervisee stop action to describe what is happening musically in the interaction with the therapist and other clients. I may give *action*-oriented directions on how to better address the musical interaction, or the supervisee may be asked what they can do to change the interactions. The experience is repeated with these new insights, and, as an added measure, peers offer feedback as clients, providing the supervisee with more information on what transpired in the session. After the second improvisation, peers who served as observers offer their feedback on both experiences, helping the supervisee to look at the challenge from different perspectives. For example, the peers serving as clients may address their feelings during the experience and their responses to the therapist/supervisee. The peers who served as observers offer a broader perspective on interactions between the supervisee/therapist and clients, the music, and missed opportunities, should any have occurred. This exercise is repeated until each supervisee has an opportunity to address their challenges in this mock session format.

Following these experiences, the supervisees are encouraged to log their thoughts, feelings, and discoveries from the experience they witnessed or participated in. The log allows the supervisee to reflect in real time uncensored feelings and thoughts about the experiences. Supervisees do not

---

[26] See chapter 19 for an update on these levels.

have to submit these logs. Instead, they serve as references for the supervisee when they submit periodic logs to the supervisor, summarizing their experiences during and after the supervision group. At the same time, all supervision participants are also asked to reflect on the observed experiences as they may relate to their own clinical challenges, so that they maintain a running dialogue about techniques and strategies they might employ in their respective environments. Following the logs, another opportunity is provided for supervisees to engage in the *learning-oriented approach* to supervision through discussion with the supervisor about choices made, client issues, strategies, and so forth. These approaches to supervision continue until each supervisee has shared their challenge. At the end of the day, each supervisee has had the experience of sharing and receiving feedback from peers and the supervisor on their work as music therapists. A summary of the day's work is highlighted, along with suggestions for implementing various strategies.

Because this model involves only two face-to-face meetings, it is important to maintain some momentum of sharing and addressing positive experiences and challenges. One way to continue this is through some sort of communication thread that is confidential but allows the freedom of expression that was established in the classroom environment. Due to work schedules, time zone differences, and other factors, I set up a discussion board on the university's Canvas site. Here each supervisee has an individual blog site where each can share their progress (or lack thereof) or any new challenges they have encountered since returning to work. As in the class, each supervisee responds to every other supervisee, offering feedback and support. As supervisor, I also respond to Canvas postings, but with less guidance and more thought-provoking questions. The intent here is to encourage the supervisee to use knowledge and skills already learned and reiterated from the peer supervision model that had begun in the class and encourage less dependence on the supervisor. Additionally, once per month, supervisees send a detailed log to the supervisor that provides in-depth analysis of their work, responses to supervision, more personal concerns if any arise, and their ability to deal with the clinical challenges they face. The feedback I offer in these individual log summaries will be more challenging than in my responses on the Canvas postings. Specific issues unique to the supervisee are highlighted in this feedback, with questions and, where appropriate, recommendations for the supervisee to consider.

Day 2

The supervision group meets again approximately one to two months after the first meeting. This gathering of supervisees is relaxed, and emerging relationships are becoming more apparent. Fellow supervisees' length of experience, education level, or other issues around sharing in the first meeting have begun to dissipate through supervisee implementation of strategies discussed in the last class and on Canvas. Supervisees are eager to discuss not only how they benefited from the supervision group, but also how they have somehow managed to rid themselves of most of the challenges they faced. I will generally begin the supervision group with a themed improvisation on their progress since the last supervision group. Supervisees seem happy to begin the supervision this way. They are generally playful, musical, and at ease. Following the improvisation, there is discussion on their playing, instrument choice, and feelings about their work as therapists.

Before beginning discussions on new challenges, I find this is an excellent time to introduce Kadushin's (1967) "Games People Play in Supervision." Supervisees are given the opportunity to read the article on games and are instructed to identify the games that they immediately know they play with the clients, with coworkers, in all forms of supervision, and in their personal relationships. Examples of games often seen in supervision include "Two against the Agency," where the supervisee is dissatisfied with the bureaucracy's demands. Another common game is "Be nice to me because I am nice to you." Here the supervisee flatters the supervisor about her wisdom and insight, avoiding the discomfort of exposure. For many experienced therapists, a favorite game is "If you knew

Dostoyevsky like I know Dostoyevsky." This game is often played when the supervisee instructs the supervisor about their work and their environment, in an effort to reduce the supervisor's power and decrease supervisee anxiety. Supervisees are encouraged to keep a log about the games with which they resonate and that they find themselves playing most often. I do not ask the supervisees to share their games with the class. Instead, I ask that they submit a paper on their games a few weeks after the class has met. The purpose of introducing games at this point is to encourage a more authentic representation of their supervision challenges. I find that supervisees are more thoughtful in presenting their challenges and choose those that more accurately reflect their work issues.

It is during this phase of supervision that I also explore Bruscia's last two levels of supervision, *experience-oriented* and *countertransference-oriented.* This is not to imply that the other levels are abandoned, but rather this additional focus allows more in-depth examination of supervision challenges. At this point in supervision, supervisees are more willing to examine in a more authentic way their own experiences and their feelings about their work, their relationships with clients, their feelings about supervision, and the transference and countertransference issues they encounter. Supervisees are willing to examine their use of games in treatment and how that may impact their work as well. Now, keep in mind that I do not ask supervisees to identify their games to the group, but only to maintain awareness of how their games may impact treatment. However, some of them will willingly state what game they engage in as they describe their challenges. As with the first supervision meeting, challenges are acted out musically through role-play as in Day 1, but with additional music therapy methods and feedback coming from peers as clients and peers as observers. During this second supervision, I am more vocal in response to what the supervisee submits, working to keep defenses to a minimum, while gently nudging the supervisee to be honest in the examination of their work. My focus is on honest representation of who you are as a therapist and increasing awareness of transference and countertransference responses.

Often during this second supervision, the subject of burnout comes up. Supervisees feel they have done everything they can to effect change, with no overt results and a lack of support from their facility leaders. There is a lot of mutual support for these feelings among supervisees, and the supervisor has to be careful in acknowledging the feelings but not letting that acknowledgment serve as an endorsement that allows them to ignore or excuse their role in the challenges they face. I encourage supervisees to take steps to deal with burnout through continued supervision, involvement in music in their personal lives, exercise, and so on, while also enticing them to look at their clients and environment through a different lens. As the supervisor, I carefully weave through the feelings of burnout to seek alternative strategies to overcome the feelings and address the needs of the clients. I intentionally have the supervisee describe in detail the client, the music, the music therapy room, the instruments used, and details about what the supervisee does in the session.

I then suggest another role-play. What is different about this role-play is that the supervisee who has described the issue is now an observer. I assign another supervisee to act as therapist and assign others to serve as clients, while the supervisee and the remaining supervisees are observers. This allows the supervisee who has the described issue the opportunity to observe and assess patient responses from a distance in order to gain a more succinct understanding of what the client is presenting and possible reasons for those behaviors. In this role-play, the music therapy method used is whatever method the supervisee uses in the described session, so it could be improvisation, re-creative, creative, or receptive methods. This generally takes some time because the supervisee often feels exposed and has to work through feelings such as lack of skills, taking on more than is recommended, not understanding the population, weak music skills, not understanding the clients' reactions, and feeling burned out. Gradually through the role-plays, the supervisee begins to see the clients differently and is better able to determine goals and objectives within the client's ability, rather than the supervisee's desired outcome. The supervisee becomes more empowered to perform duties, understands games played by both supervisee and clients, and generally describes this empowerment with more energy. Peers are encouraged to offer feedback during this portion of supervision because often they are able to see the subtle differences in clients as observers that the supervisee misses.

Another challenge that may emerge in supervision has to do with the role that the supervisee has as supervisor of preprofessional music therapy students in training. As more students are pursuing music therapy, many supervisees find themselves in the role of supervisor early in their professional practice. Inevitably, supervisees try to give their preprofessional students everything they didn't get as students. This can be overwhelming for both the preprofessional student and the supervisee as supervisor. What is interesting here is that as a rule, regardless of how the supervisee feels about their environment and population, they are not very tolerant of their preprofessional student's lack of positive response about either the facility or the patients. The preprofessional student's lack of sensitivity brings up negative feelings from the supervisee as supervisor. In addition to these feelings, the supervisee as supervisor begins to question personal adequacy, preparedness, educational differences, the use of appropriate assertiveness with preprofessional students, and issues around diversity.

It is during some of these discussions that I first try to shift the focus back to them. I want to know what their feelings are about diversity in their clients, in the clinical environment, and in their preprofessional students. To address diversity, I will occasionally ask supervisees their feelings about having supervision from me as a Black supervisor, what their feelings are about our different theoretical orientations, and what their feelings are about coming to my university for supervision. This can be an uncomfortable conversation to have because some of the supervisees did their original music therapy training with me and their newer peers are sensitive to this and not sure how to respond. The discussions around me as a supervisor, however, are rarely brought up, and students often overlook my race in favor of my competence and experience as a supervisor. Rather than pursue this avenue further, I simply remind them that the differences exist and that they should be mindful of them, especially when working with preprofessional students who come from different orientations, schools, genders, religions, and races. This direct approach opens the door to discussing deeper feelings that the supervisee might have about their preprofessional supervisee, who may be from a different cultural background and have different life experiences. It is also during this time that I again address the multicultural differences in the clinical site itself, which may include race, gender, educational background, socio-economic differences, and communication skills. This second supervision session is the more difficult of the two, and a level of depth in understanding challenges continues until those of each supervisee have been addressed. I am much more direct in my inquiries on these issues with supervisees because I believe acknowledgment opens the door to better understanding and working through difficulties, and I rarely ask other supervisees to offer opinions during this discussion. At the same time, I begin to shift my approach from being the questioner/confronter to being a curious supporter, to being a guide and then an active supporter of the supervisee. As with the first supervision class, supervisees are encouraged to post their progress and challenges on Canvas and submit a detailed log to the supervisor on issues they have overcome or are still confronting, especially as they relate to multicultural issues and diversity, either with their preprofessional students or clients and staff.

In the supervision class, we spend time reviewing the Bruscia chapter and the levels of supervision he presents, with the focus now on supervisees as supervisors. I also use this as a time to again review the "Games People Play" article (Kadushin, 1967) so that supervisees are aware of the games in which they engage with their preprofessional students. In one case,[27] the supervisee had negative feelings about a preprofessional student who presented as more knowledgeable than the preprofessional student actually was and who appeared to lack sensitivity toward the clients or respect for the supervisor. The supervisee as supervisor used action-oriented and transference-

---

[27] In this example, I did seek the permission of the supervisee to share this information prior to including it in this chapter.

oriented supervision with the preprofessional student rather than any of the other types suggested by Bruscia. Consequently, the preprofessional student was more resistive to supervision, and it was difficult for the supervisee to see anything positive in the work of the preprofessional student. After a lengthy discussion on the differences between the supervisee and the preprofessional student, the transference/countertransference issues around the preprofessional student's attitude of privilege, both ethnically and economically, surfaced. Once the supervisee became more aware of reactions to the preprofessional student and the supervisee's own countertransference issues, the relationship shifted and the supervisee was able to see what games the preprofessional student played to conceal fear or feelings of inadequacy. Additionally, the supervisee was able to engage in learning-oriented supervision with the preprofessional student, which helped the preprofessional student to engage more comfortably, recognize the efforts of clients, and improve relationships with the supervisee. Similar experiences were experienced by other supervisees as supervisors, around issues such as the preprofessional student's musical skills, interpersonal skills, and fears.

At the end of the last supervision class meeting, I discuss the value of continued supervision and point out that during this advanced supervision, supervisees have begun a peer supervision process that enables them to continue meeting without the need for the supervisor so that the work they began in class can continue. Supervisees have learned that regardless of level of experience, there is something to be gained from fellow supervisees. Supervisees are free to share emails, establish times when they might want to meet either with one other person or as a group, or use this experience to engage in supervision with peers who are closer to their home environments. There are social media networks that are private that students may use to continue these forums if they are unable to meet in person. It should be noted, however, that while peer supervision is helpful for many supervisees, it is often impossible to continue with this type of format because of distance or time. Therefore, supervisees are reminded that they already have the skills needed after this course to engage in self-supervision by logging experiences, analyzing these logs, using music to reflect situations they are encountering, and examining strategies they might employ to resolve conflicts. Supervisees are reminded that until the semester comes to an end, interactions between supervisor and supervisees continue on Canvas.

I like to end the advanced supervision class in the way it began. I have students take a few minutes to think about any positive experiences from the class that they had and can take with them. Once they have had a few minutes to think, I suggest they engage in a referential improvisation on these positive experiences. Students choose the instruments that reflect their feelings about their positive experiences during the supervision class and begin to improvise. As with the first music improvisation, there is no defined time limit and improvisation is allowed to end organically.

At semester's end, supervisees submit a paper highlighting their experiences in supervision and their progress in dealing with supervisory issues in their workplace. This type of supervision can occur over one semester or multiple semesters. It is not uncommon for supervisees to come back for supervision as long as three years after the first supervision course, when they are more mature, more experienced, and have more aptitude about their supervisory issues and skills.

CONCLUSION

Music therapy is a journey across rivers, streams, lakes, and oceans. Learning to successfully maneuver through these to bring a good quality of life to clients is filled with both rewards and challenges. Supervision is that road that therapists take to enhance their ability to work with these rewards and challenges. Following internship, to find a supervisor or supervision group in your own field is its own reward. Therapists are more willing to continue this growth process if presented with a model that respects their positions as music therapists and professionals. This chapter offers a way for therapists to engage in advanced supervision in a professional, nonjudgmental manner, where the skills of all involved can optimize each person's learning and growth.

Reference List

Bruscia, K. (2001). *A Model of Supervision Derived from Apprenticeship Training.* In M. Forinash (Ed.), *Music Therapy Supervision.* Gilsum, NH: Barcelona Publishers.

Kadushin, A. (1967). Games People Play in Supervision. *Social Work, 13*(3), 23–32.

Chapter 19

A MODEL OF CLINICAL SUPERVISION IN MUSIC THERAPY

Kenneth E. Bruscia

Music therapy supervision currently takes place in a wide variety of preprofessional and professional settings. In preprofessional settings, it is a required component of the student's practicum and internship training, which may be provided by field and/or academic supervisors. In professional settings, supervision is strongly advised but optional, and it may be provided on the job or privately by more experienced music therapists or in peer groups.

The purpose of this chapter is to present a model of clinical supervision that can be used in diverse settings with students and professionals at different stages of development. The chapter is an expansion of an earlier model derived from apprenticeship training (Bruscia, 2001).

The basic premise is that effective supervision has the same fundamental *aims* across these settings and that differences between them can be addressed using different *levels* of supervision at different *stages* with the same set of *methods* and *techniques*. The level needed depends upon the complexity of the clinical work being supervised and the depth of the intervention needed to guide the supervisee at her level of development. The developmental stage is determined by the complexity of the clinical work and the challenges it poses for supervisees with varying knowledge and skills.

Aims of Supervision

Clinical supervision has two overarching aims. The first is to help the supervisee to develop the knowledge, insights, and skills needed to be an effective clinician. An effective clinician is one who is adept at assessing the client's resources and needs, formulating relevant goals and treatment strategies, evaluating client progress, and monitoring one's own effectiveness. In some cases, this requires applying previous learning, and in others it requires gaining new knowledge and skills.

The second aim is to help the supervisee to develop the reflexivity essential to working effectively when not being supervised.

> Reflexivity is the therapist's efforts to bring into awareness, evaluate, and when necessary modify one's work with a client—before, during, and after each session, as well as at various stages of the therapy process (Bruscia, 2014, p. 54).

These two aims are interdependent. Achieving self-awareness is a prerequisite to becoming an effective clinician, and a clinician cannot be effective without self-awareness. Thus, reflexivity is both the process and outcome of supervision.

Accomplishment of these aims is contingent upon the supervisor's sensitivity to both individual and cultural differences—between supervisee and client as well as supervisee and supervisor.

Methods

Depending on how "method" is defined, one can identify numerous ones employed in music therapy supervision, as evidenced in this book. Here is a categorization of these methods.

Observation is the most fundamental method because it provides the most direct and accurate information on the supervisee's work. It can be done in vivo, through audio and video recordings, or via Skype or streaming. Each type has its own advantages and disadvantages in accommodating the clients being served while also addressing the learning needs of the supervisee. Thus, deciding on the best type of observation is the first and most important decision for the supervisor and supervisee to make. In vivo supervision can be intrusive for the client, especially in individual sessions. The supervisor's presence can be threatening to both the client and the supervisee. On the other hand, seeing and hearing what goes on in the actual clinical setting provides the most comprehensive and accurate picture of the supervisee's work. Although audio and video recordings are less intrusive, audio recordings provide less complete information and video recordings are biased by what the camera person decides to focus on. All require the client's or guardian's consent.

Verbal discussion is another indispensable method. When a supervision is not based on actual observation, supervisor–supervisee conversations are a primary source of data on what transpired between client and supervisee, and when an observation is done, they provide additional information and clarification. Thus, this is a very important method both for gathering data and for then examining them in greater detail. The discussion can take place through individual conferences or group seminars, and it can be implemented in person, in writing (e.g., logs), on the telephone, online, or through Skyping or videoconferencing.

Experiential methods provide rich opportunities for the supervisee to learn about their work through active participation in music therapy in the role of both therapist and client. These may include demonstrations, enactments or re-enactments of specific music therapy scenarios, authentic experiences of music therapy, music-making, and so forth. Homework assignments can also be experiential when students are asked to make music or practice different techniques outside of the work setting.

Collaborative methods are used whenever supervision involves more than one supervisor. For example, in some degree programs, the student is supervised by both a field supervisor and an academic supervisor, thus involving two people who must share responsibilities. In peer supervision, supervisees are supervised by other supervisees, sometimes with the aid of a supervisor.

TECHNIQUES FOR VERBAL DIALOGUES

A variety of verbal techniques can be used with the above methods of supervision. These techniques have been described throughout this book, but for purposes of this chapter, they are best described in broad categories.

Probing

Probing, or asking questions, is the primary way of getting information from the supervisee about her work. Sometimes the supervisor needs new information, and sometimes the supervisor needs to clarify something already observed or in his awareness. Probing is also an important technique to bring something into the supervisee's awareness or to identify a topic that needs further exploration. When used in this way, probing encourages the supervisee to take a meta-perspective on the session and herself and thereby further develop her reflexivity. The questioning leads to self-observation, self-evaluation, and self-correction.

To probe effectively, the supervisor must know when, how, and how much to probe. Usually, probes should occur at the opening of a supervisory session, when trying to establish or change focus during the session, and when introducing one of the levels of supervision. Open-ended questions are usually more fruitful than yes/no questions. Most important, the supervisor must be careful not to probe too much. On the one hand, probing ensures that the supervisee has a voice and is participating in the supervisory process. On the other, probing too much or too intensely can be not only annoying to the supervisee but also ineffective in helping the student to learn.

Focusing

All methods of supervision require a meaningful focus. To *focus,* the supervisor and/or supervisee attempt to pinpoint a topic that requires attention, and when the most relevant topic is identified, the supervisor's job is to sustain their attention for the appropriate amount of time.

Sometimes the supervisee will present a focus, but just as often, the supervisor will need to establish one. Each way has its advantages and disadvantages. The supervisee may or may not identify the most fruitful focus for numerous reasons, most often lack of knowledge and experience or resistance to supervision. Nevertheless, whatever focus the supervisee presents as important must be acknowledged and adequately addressed by the supervisor. Although the supervisor is more likely to identify the most fruitful focus, supervision can fail if the supervisee does not have a voice in expressing her own concerns.

Some supervisors prefer to focus by going through a session or series of sessions from beginning to end and dealing with each issue at it arises in sequence. For example, when an activity therapy session has been observed, the supervisor focuses on how the supervisee led each activity in sequence. The main advantage of this sequential focus is that it can provide a wealth of information on how to work within various types of music experiences and then how to manage the flow of a session. A disadvantage is that such detail can be overwhelming and meaningless to the supervisee, especially if the supervisor does not attempt to consolidate or synthesize what the supervisee should take away from the supervision.

Other supervisors prefer to focus by finding patterns in the way a supervisee works and then dealing with them in a thematic way. In this approach to observing an activity therapy session, the supervisor continually analyzes similarities in the way the supervisee led each activity and then notes themes in the issues that have arisen during the entire session. For example, the supervisor may notice that in more than one activity, the quality of the supervisee's music was inconsistent or her verbal instructions for participating in the music were unclear. Then, after recognizing these issues, the supervisor tries to figure out how they relate to one another. Is there a theme that can explain these two issues? Does the supervisee care enough about the quality of the music or perhaps its value in the therapeutic process? Or maybe the supervisee is unprepared or even lazy.

Affirming

To *affirm* is to acknowledge, praise, or reinforce what the supervisee is doing that was effective, sensitive, well informed, or admirable in any way. It has been differentiated from critiquing, the other side of evaluation, because affirming has two objectives instead of one. The first is to help the supervisee to understand the best way to *work* with clients; the second is to help the supervisee to *recognize her own worth*—as a learner, as a therapist, and as a human being.

In both cases, affirming provides the supervisee with ideals. It provides a foundation for understanding the relationship between positive and negative, that is, it gives a framework for comparing what to do with what not to do and how to be with how not to be. Clinical errors and misjudgments are best understood in relation to the ideal; similarly, negative feelings of self-worth must be interpreted through and balanced with positive self-perceptions and feelings.

Affirming is also the primary way of helping the supervisee to identify and better utilize her professional and personal assets. As with all undertakings, what one does well provides the resources needed to improve what one is not doing so well. Helping the supervisee to identify her own professional and personal strengths is also a way of guiding supervisees in determining how and with whom to practice music therapy most effectively.

Dialoguing

Supervisee and supervisor often bring different sets of information, expertise, and skills to the supervision process. They know different things and have different insights and intuitions about the supervisee's client, the clinical characteristics of the population, the work setting, the most effective music therapy strategies, and even human nature! There are times when the supervisee needs to know what the supervisor knows, and there are also times when the supervisor needs to know what the supervisee knows. On such occasions, questions and answers must flow freely in a dialogue that is best described as a brainstorming session. Many different ideas and suggestions are generated by both parties, and then each is seriously considered for their merit.

Critiquing

To *critique* is to identify and describe what the supervisee is doing that needs to change and how it should be changed. Unfortunately, critiquing is too often used as the main technique in supervision, without sufficient probing, dialoguing, or affirming. Before the supervisor can help the student to address her clinical shortcomings, he must know how the supervisee perceived or felt in the clinical situation, what her intent was, and generally what she was experiencing. The problem may not be what the supervisee did¾—it may just have been how the supervisee was conceptualizing the issue at hand.

Critiquing is also ineffective when it is not accompanied by and related to affirming. Too much critiquing can paralyze the supervisee and impede her ability to correct a behavior. Moreover, affirming is often more effective, that is, the supervisor affirms in order to point out problem areas. Critiquing should always be focused on the supervisee's work and not on the supervisee as a person.

Guiding

To *guide* is to formulate ways for the supervisee to improve her effectiveness or to map out a path for future work with the client. Guiding may involve helping the supervisee to implement an intervention, design a different strategy, or develop a more holistic picture of the client or patterns in the supervisee's work. Thus, the solutions offered when guiding may involve many forms of supervision: changing the supervisee's behavior, providing instruction, giving insights into the client, reframing the supervisee's experience, addressing countertransference issues, and any combination thereof.

The best guiding takes place when the supervisor knows the supervisee well enough to discern patterns, themes, and cause–effect relationships in the way she works. It is also based on using various methods, techniques, and levels of supervision with the same supervisee. Sometimes effective guiding depends upon previous supervision at the action level, or the experience level, and so forth; similarly, sometimes effective guiding depends upon probing techniques, or focusing techniques, and so forth. Adequate preparation for the guiding level of supervision ensures that relevant issues have been addressed and that the supervisee is ready to identify and make the changes independently.

An important variable when guiding is how directive the supervision needs to be. This is determined by who formulates the future course of action: the supervisor, the supervisee, or both together. Thus, directiveness can be described along a continuum from changes formulated primarily:

By the Supervisee——————Jointly——————By the Supervisor

Typically, the most directive level is needed when the supervisee is less experienced and when the specific changes needed are non-negotiable: The supervisee is unknowingly doing something that is inappropriate, unethical, unsafe, or contraindicated, or the supervisee is not doing something to address the client's needs.

The jointly developed level is indicated when the supervisee has the knowledge and experience needed to provide reliable assessments of the clinical situation but still needs help in deciding what to do about it. Here the supervisor depends upon the supervisee for accurate information and the supervisee depends upon the supervisor for help in formulating the best plan of action.

As the supervisee advances further, she is increasingly able not only to assess the clinical situation but also to identify the specific changes in approach needed. This becomes evident when the supervisee can offer possible options for change and provide a solid rationale for choosing the best option. In other words, the supervisee has learned how to be reflexive. The supervisor's role here is to provide information and insights that will help the supervisee to formulate and choose the best and safest plan of action.

LEVELS: AN OVERVIEW

The supervisory process can be broken down into five levels, each with a different focus and outcome. Briefly summarized, they are:

1. *Action-oriented:* What does the supervisee need to do?
2. *Learning-oriented:* What does the supervisee need to know?
3. *Client-oriented:* What does the supervisee need to understand about the client?
4. *Experience-oriented:* How is the supervisee thinking and feeling about the client and her work with him?
5. *Countertransference-oriented:* Whose needs is the supervisee addressing, her own or the client's?

Any level may be used at any time, depending on the nature of the issue presented by the supervisee and her readiness for that level of supervision. Some supervisory sessions may involve a few levels, and others may involve all five. A sequence need not be followed. Eventually, each level becomes part of a more complete supervisory process that integrates all of the levels.

To illustrate how these levels relate to one another, let us consider a particular clinical problem: The supervisee is having trouble with one older adult in a group who continually gets out of his seat and wanders around the room. The supervisor might start by suggesting possible ways of responding to the client's wandering (action-oriented) or by recommending literature on how other music therapists have dealt with this behavior (learning-oriented). Sometimes the supervisee needs to have a better understanding of the client and his condition, and the supervisor will suggest studying the client's records or talking to other team members (client-oriented). If the supervisee seems upset, the supervisor might ask how the supervisee feels when the client wanders and then seek ways to reframe her experience (experience-oriented). Sometimes, it is difficult for the supervisee to reframe her experience of the client's wandering and change her approach to intervening. This may indicate that watching someone wander or failing to stop the wandering is a replication of previous life experiences (countertransference-oriented), wherein the supervisee has felt ignored, abandoned, and powerless.

In this example, it becomes clear that the supervisor must be skilled in identifying at which level to begin the supervisory process, while the supervisee must be developmentally and emotionally ready to open the supervision at that level. The practice works best when the opening level can easily lead into other levels, which sometimes are more relevant and helpful than the initial level. In short, the initial level of supervision must be relevant to the supervisee's needs, while also providing easy access to addressing the issue at another level.

Action-oriented

The first level of supervision is action-oriented: The supervisee needs to change what she is doing or how she is doing it. The aim is to help the supervisee to perform basic tasks or duties, first at a functional level and eventually at a professional level. Action-oriented supervision focuses on how the supervisee should behave to be most effective.

Action-oriented supervision is warranted when the addition, modification, or elimination of a behavior is the most effective way of improving the supervisee's work with a particular client and with other clients as well. It is also the most expedient way to correct any behaviors of the supervisee that are inappropriate, contraindicated, unethical, or unsafe.

An action orientation is contraindicated when it fosters dependency or laziness in the supervisee. This can happen when the supervisor tells the supervisor what to do too often, in too much detail, and/or too directively. The main signal is when the supervisee complains frequently that she does not know what to do or that she needs the supervisor to tell her what to do. Action supervision is also not advisable when the supervisee feels that she does not need or want to be supervised at all. It is least effective when the supervisee is resistant to supervision or the supervisor.

Developmentally, action supervision is most needed in the earliest stages of supervision, when the supervisee is beginning her clinical training. It is also needed later by more experienced clinicians, when learning a new clinical approach or technique, or when beginning to work with a new, possibly culturally diverse client or population. Finally, action supervision is often the last level to use after other levels of supervision and a test of whether the other levels have been effective. For example, delving deep into experience or countertransference issues does not become meaningful until the supervisee understands not only how these issues affect her clinical work, but also what she can do to ameliorate the problem.

Action supervision is best suited when using observational methods and when the supervisor and supervisee share perceptions of what transpired in the session. The supervisor may have more experience in evaluating and interpreting clinical phenomena, but if his perceptions are not shared with the supervisee, it is difficult to show why a certain intervention needs to be corrected or improved. On the other hand, the supervisee has greater knowledge than the supervisor about the client and the clinical environment but may lack the perceptual skills or objectivity needed to evaluate the situation. In short, shared perceptions are better than unilateral ones: "Is this what you did?" is more helpful than "This is what you did."

Action supervision can be implemented using all six verbal techniques. Notice that they all focus on behaviors or procedures of the supervisee. For example:

- *Probing:* asking the supervisee to describe or evaluate her own procedural steps or behaviors during the session; asking how they might be improved or corrected.
- *Focusing:* calling the supervisee's attention to specific behaviors or interventions that need to be addressed.

- *Dialoguing:* brainstorming with the supervisee about how her behaviors or procedural steps might be improved.
- *Affirming:* praising the supervisee for those behaviors or procedural steps that were effective and should be continued.
- *Critiquing:* pointing out behaviors or procedures that were not effective, appropriate, or ethical and therefore require attention.
- *Guiding:* instructing or demonstrating how to improve or change the supervisee's behaviors or procedures.

Learning-oriented

The second level of supervision is learning-oriented: The supervisor helps the supervisee to gain the knowledge, insight, or skill needed to be more efficient or effective. Here the focus is not on what actions or behaviors the supervisee needs to develop or change, but instead on what the supervisee still needs to learn to be more effective. In most cases, this level is focused on gaps in the supervisee's previous training and knowledge or blind spots or distortions in the supervisee's understanding. All of the verbal techniques can be used to address the learning needs implicated in the supervisee's work, not only in the specific situation being supervised but also generally in the entire professional area of endeavor. For example:

- *Probing:* asking the supervisee what she knows about a clinical problem or what skills she has to use a particular intervention; asking whether the supervisee has received instruction or training in addressing a clinical problem; asking the supervisee about the client's culture.
- *Focusing:* identifying patterns in the supervisee's work that demonstrate inadequate knowledge and skill.
- *Dialoguing:* brainstorming with the supervisee about what she needs to learn to work more effectively.
- *Affirming:* complimenting the supervisee on the knowledge and skills she is has demonstrated in her work.
- *Critiquing:* pointing out those aspects of the supervisee's work that indicate a lack of knowledge and skill.
- *Guiding:* providing instruction or informing the supervisee where and how to gain the knowledge and skills.

Learning-oriented supervision is best accomplished through verbal dialogues in individual meetings or group seminars. These settings provide the greatest opportunities to explore the extent of the supervisee's learning needs and when necessary to provide the learning needed within the supervision session.

Learning-oriented supervision has the same pitfalls as the action level. When used too frequently, the supervisee may begin to lose confidence in her own knowledge and skills and then depend entirely too much on the supervisor for further instruction. Conversely, when the supervisee is overly confident, she may reject any suggestion that she needs to learn anything identified by the supervisor as lacking.

Client-oriented

The third level of supervision is client-oriented: The aim is to help the supervisee to gain a deeper understanding of her client(s). An important shift takes place at this level: The focus of supervision shifts from the supervisee to the client. The supervisor becomes less focused on what the *supervisee* needs to do or learn and more focused on who the *client* is and the nature of the client's health condition and needs. Accordingly, there is also a shift from a treatment orientation, which emphasizes inducing change in the client, to an assessment orientation, which emphasizes understanding the client better.

Signs of readiness for this level of supervision are when the supervisee shows increased concern, empathy, and emotional investment in the client. Helping the client becomes equally if not more important than developing one's own clinical skills. The supervisee and client become more attached to one another and begin to develop a closer relationship. With this comes the supervisee's realization of how complex the client and his health condition are, as well as how many factors have contributed to them. At first, there is a need for more specific information about the client himself. Such information can be gathered directly from the client, from the client's health records, and by consultation with significant others, team members, other professionals, and one's supervisor. Notice that all the data concerns a particular client but may have significant implications for others.

This increased interest in a client eventually raises broader and deeper questions that call for a more in-depth form of learning-oriented supervision. What causes health problems? Why do they occur? Of what relevance and value is music therapy? How does any therapy work? What enables human beings to change themselves and their lives? How does anyone overcome health problems? For answers to these questions, the supervisee must go beyond specific data on a client to more general sources of data, starting with theory and research on music therapy, various health conditions, and different client populations.

Observational and experiential methods of supervision are useful in pointing out aspects of the client that the supervisee has not noticed or addressed; however, verbal dialogue is additionally needed to clarify what information or insights need to be gained. Verbal techniques, then, focus on what the supervisee needs to learn about the client, not only to facilitate the therapeutic process but also simply to better understand another human being with health needs. For example:

- *Probing:* asking if the supervisee has certain data on the client; asking for the supervisee's own insights about the client; asking for explanations of how the client responds to any facet of the music therapy process.
- *Focusing:* suggesting that the supervisee may need to gain specific information or insights about the client or the client's culture; suggesting that the supervisee be more aware of her own cultural biases.
- *Dialoguing:* brainstorming on who the client is and the nature of his health and life problems.
- *Affirming:* praising the supervisee for the insights demonstrated when working with a client.
- *Critiquing:* pointing out those aspects of the supervisee's approach that might indicate a lack of sufficient information or insight about the client.
- *Guiding:* instructing the supervisee on identifying and gathering the data and insights needed; giving the supervisee insights about the client that will change her approach.

There are at least two dangers in client-oriented supervision. First, upon gaining a better understanding of the client, the supervisee might become overwhelmed by the complexity of his needs and the difficulties involved in meeting them. This can lead to a fear of working at an appropriate level of therapy and/or implementing the music therapy experiences indicated. The supervisee may begin to keep the sessions superficial, or she may become paralyzed and lose all self-confidence in working at the appropriate depth. Affirming techniques are essential to prevent or ameliorate these kinds of reactions.

The second danger is the opposite. Upon gaining a better understanding of the client, the supervisee might become overconfident and assume that she now knows the best ways to work with the client, when her revised approach to the client demonstrates otherwise. This is a more difficult supervisory problem. Two verbal techniques are contraindicated. Critiquing or guiding supervisees who are so self-assured is rarely easy or effective, and often the supervisee will challenge or reject the supervisor's critique or even his expertise. Both techniques are likely to threaten the supervisory relationship. A better approach is to engage the supervisee in experiential methods where she can empathize with the client or become more aware of how she herself is thinking and feeling. Several such experiences may be necessary before the supervisee is ready for verbal techniques of probing, dialoguing, and even affirming.

Experience-oriented

The fourth level of supervision is experience-oriented: The supervisor helps the supervisee to examine her own perceptions and reactions to the client and their work together. This level is indicated when the supervisor perceives that the supervisee is uncomfortable, inauthentic, or insensitive when working with the client or when the supervisee has lost her self-confidence or motivation. It is also indicated when the supervisee begins to notice that her own personal reactions to the client must be taken into account in understanding the client and knowing how to work effectively with him.

Here again, critiquing and guiding are the least effective verbal techniques, as they do not resolve the supervisee's internal dilemma. Thus, probing and dialoguing should be used to examine how she experiences the client, the client population, particular sessions or clinical events, the work setting, supervisors, and the supervisory process. For example:

- *Probing/Focusing:* How does this client make you feel? What are your perceptions of the client population? How do you react personally when the client behaves in such a way? What are your perceptions and feelings about the client's cultural background?
- *Dialoguing:* Working with this client poses some challenges to the therapist. Let's share your own personal thoughts and perceptions.
- *Affirming:* You seem very comfortable when working with this client in this situation.
- *Critiquing:* You often look tense when working with this client.
- *Guiding:* In your next session, try to take a deep breath every few minutes and remind yourself to relax your body.

These verbal dialogues can explore the supervisee's experiences at the conscious, preconscious, and/or unconscious level; however, the uncovering and projective techniques used by the supervisor should focus only on the supervisee's experiences in the here-now or there-then reactions to a specific client, event, or aspect of the work. The context is limited to supervisee–client interactions, and no effort is made to relate them to the supervisee's personal life (i.e., biographical material from the past). This is a very important distinction to be made between this level of supervision and the next.

Countertransference-oriented

The fifth level of supervision is countertransference-oriented: The supervisor helps the supervisee to recognize how her interactions with the client are replications of the past, of relationships in either the *supervisee's* life or the *client's* life. At this level, the explorations are aimed at unconscious motivations and delve specifically into similarities between the supervisee's past and the client's past. For a complete discussion of the signs of countertransference, see Bruscia (1998).

Signs of readiness for this level are when the supervisee consistently (and sometimes rigidly) works in ways that are irrelevant or even contraindicated to the client's needs and when the supervisee begins projecting her own life and needs onto the client and then begins to work accordingly. Another clear sign is when the supervisor can see a parallel process, that is, the supervisee–supervisor relationship is replicating the client–supervisee relationship.

Notice that the previous level of supervision (experience-oriented) explores the *uniqueness* of each relationship and situation, whereas this level shifts to a focus on *similarities*. It becomes apparent that the supervisee is repeatedly using interactional patterns with the same or different clients and that these patterns are of her own doing rather than dictated by the clinical situation. The common denominator is herself—she seems to be doing the same thing with clients as she does with significant others and in situations in her own life, or she is identifying with significant others and situations in the client's life. Thus, the effectiveness of her work with clients depends upon her working out her own personal issues and needs.

Experiential methods of supervision are the most relevant but must be followed by sensitive and thoughtful verbal dialogues. Probing, focusing, dialoguing, and confirming are most useful; guiding can be too interpretive, and critiquing is to be avoided. Examples include:

- *Probing:* Does this client remind you of anyone in your own life? Do you identify yourself with anyone in the client's life? Where did you learn how to interact with people in this way? How do you know this is what the client needs?
- *Focusing:* There seem to be similarities between you and the client or the client's situation. Can you identify what they are?
- *Dialoguing:* Let's talk about why you tend to interact with this client in this way or why you interact with several clients in this way.
- *Affirming:* You are very nurturing with this client. How did you learn to do that?
- *Critiquing:* You are not responding to the client based on what the client is presenting. It seems like you are perceiving the client as someone else in your life.
- *Guiding:* Try to be more observant of what the client is actually presenting to you, devoid of your experience with anyone else.

This level of supervision is not appropriate for every supervisory situation. Much depends upon the theoretical orientation of the supervisor, the readiness of the supervisee, and the nature of the supervisory contract. The supervisor must be knowledgeable about the psychodynamic orientation and sufficiently skilled in its application; the supervisee must be working with the other person at a deep enough level and using the relationship as a central vehicle in the therapeutic process; and the supervisor–supervisee contract must allow for this exploration of the private life of the supervisee. Ethically, the supervisee must give informed consent to enter into such a supervision contract, not only because personal and biographical material of the supervisee will be brought into the supervisory situation, but also because the supervisee–supervisor relationship may extend into more of a client–therapist relationship. Needless to say, expanding the supervisor relationship in this way is appropriate only when the supervisee is working at a deep level with the client and when the client's progress and safety must be guarded against interference by the supervisee's personal needs.

PARALLEL PROCESSES

The use of "parallel process" has been found helpful by many supervisors, especially those with a psychodynamic orientation, despite the lack of research evidence supporting its effects. The author has used parallel process to guide his own supervisory efforts and has found it quite useful, especially when perplexed by the supervisee. The basic premise is that what is happening in supervision is probably happening in the clinical situation, and vice versa: What is happening in the clinical situation is probably being replicated in the supervisory situation. Most relevant are parallels that can be clearly seen between the needs, problems, and reactions of the supervisee and client and of the supervisee and supervisor—both professional and personal. For example:

The *professional needs* of the supervisee may reflect the *clinical needs* of the client, and vice versa. When the *supervisee* persistently needs more instructions from the supervisor, the *client* may also need more instructions from the supervisee. Conversely, when the *clients* are unable to participate or follow instructions, the *supervisee* may demonstrate the same inabilities in supervision. Both scenarios may indicate that the supervisor needs to give better instructions to the supervisee and/or that the supervisee needs to give better instructions to the client.

The *emotional needs* of the supervisee are likely to be the emotional needs of the client, and vice versa. When the *supervisee* needs continual praise and support from the supervisor, it is worth exploring whether the *client* needs the same from the supervisee. Or, when the *client* needs continual affirmation from the supervisee, the *supervisee* probably needs continual affirmation from the supervisor.

The *supervisory problem* presented by the supervisee may reflect the kind of *clinical problem* presented by the client, and vice versa. When a *supervisee* does not participate very openly or fully in supervision, the *client* may not be participating openly or fully in therapy. This informs the supervisor to explore how the supervisee can better motivate the client's participation. Or, when the *client* is not participating in therapy, the *supervisee* may begin to falter in her participation in supervision. This informs the supervisor to explore why the supervisee is not participating fully in supervision.

The *reactions* induced in the supervisor by the supervisee may reflect the reactions induced in the supervisee by her client. For example, when the *supervisor* begins to feel inadequate in meeting the needs of the *supervisee,* the *supervisee* may also be feeling inadequate when working with the *client,* and the *client* may feel inadequate when working the *supervisee.* This informs the supervisor to explore feelings of inadequacy in both the supervisee and the client.

It is important to realize that these parallels are operating at an unconscious level and therefore require careful exploration before any inferences or conclusions can be drawn. There is always a risk that the supervisor will misinterpret the existence or significance of parallel processes and then uncover unconscious material about the supervisee that is erroneous or harmful, while also going beyond the amount and depth of uncovering that is appropriate to the supervisory contract. At the same time, the client's therapy can also be jeopardized by misinterpretation by the supervisor of the clinical situation and wrongful advice to the supervisee. Only supervisors who have the necessary training and skill in uncovering techniques should rely upon parallel processes (see above).

DEVELOPMENTAL STAGES

The above five levels of intervention fall into three stages of development. The first stage is concerned with the development of the supervisee's *technique.* It includes both action-oriented and learning-oriented levels of supervision, both aimed at helping the supervisee to lead client sessions effectively.

The second stage is concerned with the development of the supervisee's *relationship* with clients. It includes both client-oriented and experience-oriented levels of supervision. In this stage, the supervisee moves from the exterior aspects of the work to interior aspects of those doing the work. It is a shift from efficiency of action and interaction to depth of shared experiences. In addition, the supervisee begins to shift the focus from self as a therapist-in-training to being aware of both client and self as persons interacting within a helping relationship. Of key importance in this stage is the development of empathy for the client, awareness of oneself in relation to the client, and clear boundaries between the two experiences. These are the three hallmarks signaling completion of this stage. Sometimes, however, a supervisee immediately feels a close bond with the client and seems to have an instinctive understanding of him. Although this can be a healthy place at which to begin work with a client, when premature or unwarranted it can also signal negative countertransference issues that are difficult to address early in the supervision process.

The third and final stage is concerned with *internalization*. It consists entirely of the countertransference-oriented level of supervision. Here the various components of the previous stages become parts of the self that can be differentiated, fused, and/or integrated as needed.

INDIVIDUAL AND CULTURAL DIFFERENCES

This entire model has been designed to address individual differences in supervisees. The very aim of a level-stage model is to sensitize the supervisor to the different needs of each supervisee as they unfold developmentally in each unique clinical situation. Thus, rather than imposing the same approach on every supervisee, the supervisor uses these levels and stages in order to gear every intervention to the uniqueness of each supervisory and clinical situation.

Cultural differences, like individual differences, are myriad in number and variety, and there are no fail-safe recipes for guaranteeing that every difference between client, supervisee, and supervisor is respectfully addressed. The challenge is not "managing" the differences through prescribed ways of relating to the other person. Instead, it is maintaining an awareness of oneself and the other person that is respectful of both differences and similarities. Ultimately, cultural differences call for reflexivity before action.

The author has found that there are two interdependent, erroneous assumptions that lead to insensitivities and microaggressions between individuals who have cultural differences. The first is assuming similarities where they do not exist, and the second is assuming differences where they do not exist. An assumption of nonexisting *similarities* can predispose one to overidentification with the other and unfounded and sometimes inauthentic feelings of empathy. An assumption of nonexisting *differences* can predispose one to feelings of uncertainty or alienation about the other and relationships that are distant.

The challenge to these assumptions is to always consider potential similarities and differences together as one integrated process—not as apart—and to find the relationships between them. Similarities must always be qualified by differences in relation to the similarity; conversely, differences must always be qualified by similarities in relation to the difference.

It is the supervisor's responsibility to challenge such erroneous assumptions in the supervisee's clinical role. This can be done by helping the supervisee to recognize both similarities and differences (1) among her clients and (2) between herself and the clients. For example, if all clients in a group have hyperactivity, it is important to notice the different ways in which it is manifested. Similarly, if the supervisee and client belong to the same minority group, it is important to identify differences within that group and between the two of them.

The same challenges must be confronted in the supervisor–supervisee relationship. If the supervisor and supervisee have similar beliefs, it is important to examine in what ways they are different, and if the supervisor and supervisee belong to the same minority, it is important to examine their differences.

Learning when and with whom these efforts are indicated depends to a great extent on the degree of reflexivity in both the supervisee and supervisor. Going into further detail about handling individual vs. cultural differences is beyond the scope of this chapter; however, an important difference among supervisees that warrants discussion is the ways in which they resist the supervisor and the supervision process. Resistance varies widely according to individual and cultural differences.

RESISTANCE PATTERNS

Resistance is commonly understood as any conscious or unconscious effort of the supervisee to reject, foil, contest, ignore, or devalue the supervisor's input. In a levels/stages approach, resistance is a multifaceted phenomenon—one that cannot be understood in terms of a single dynamic or a single theoretical orientation. Within the present model of supervision, resistance is an outgrowth of four supervisory scenarios, as described below.

Intervention at an Ineffectual Level

In this scenario, the supervisor intervenes at a level that does not address the supervisory problems and needs of the supervisee within the clinical situation at hand. For example, the supervisee is experiencing a clinical problem that calls for action supervision (e.g., how to keep the restless client in the room), but the supervisor provides countertransference supervision (e.g., how the client reminds the supervisee of his father). That is, instead of helping the supervisee to figure out what to do, the supervisor jumps into how the problem is similar to the supervisee's past relationships with parents. When confronted with this level of intervention, the supervisee naturally (and justifiably) reacts by trying to redirect or neutralize the supervisor's efforts—and for good reason: A countertransference insight will not help the student in the concrete way that is needed at the time in that particular situation. In the example, examining abandonment issues with the supervisee's father does not address the supervisee's inability to handle the client's wandering within the session. Note that intervening at an ineffectual level is a supervisory error in identifying the nature of the clinical situation and that such an error can happen at any stage of supervision. Sometimes the clinical situation confronted by a beginning supervisee may call for experiential rather than action supervision (a more advanced level); similarly, the problems of an advanced supervisee can call for action supervision instead of countertransference supervision (a less advanced level)—even though the level of supervision is not characteristic of the supervisee's stage of development.

Expectations at an Inappropriate Stage

In this scenario, the supervisor intervenes without sufficient attention to the supervisee's developmental stage. For example, the supervisor may expect a supervisee at the "technique" or first stage to have highly developed "relationships" or a greater degree of "internalization" at the second or third stage; conversely, the supervisor may not trust an advanced supervisee to work out "technique" when there is already a high degree of internalization.

True Resistance

In this scenario, the supervisee has psychological issues that cause defensiveness toward the supervisor and the supervision process. For example, the supervisee may have problems with authority that lead to frequent opposition toward the supervisor or low self-esteem that leads to painful hypersensitivity to every supervisory comment. Within the present model, the supervisor intervenes at the appropriate level, has expectations at the appropriate stage, and is responsive to the supervisee's problems and needs, but the supervisee will not accept the level or stage of intervention. For example: The supervisee does not follow supervisory suggestions on what to do with the client when the supervisee is not responding effectively and needs such direction, or the supervisee refuses to meet expectations at the technique stage when actually ready to do so, or the supervisee does not respond to any level or stage of intervention, regardless of how many methods or orientations to supervision the supervisor takes.

Supervisor Issues

In this scenario, the supervisor has psychological issues and needs or professional biases that are detrimental to the supervisee and/or the supervision process. Here the supervisee may actually resist or only appear to the supervisor as resistant, but the origin of the problem is in the supervisor's own inability to be appropriately responsive to what the supervisee needs. The hallmarks of this scenario include inappropriate boundaries with the supervisee, defensiveness, authoritarianism, unwarranted reactions, insistence on supervising at only one level or only one stage, rigidity of method or style of supervision, and so forth.

What is most important to note about these four resistance scenarios is that three of them implicate the supervisor, while only one implicates the supervisee.

SUMMARY AND CONCLUSIONS

Five levels of supervision were identified, oriented toward action, learning, the client, the supervisee's experience, and countertransference issues. Verbal techniques commonly used in these levels include probing, focusing, dialoguing, affirming, critiquing, and guiding. Three stages of development can be used to describe the course of supervision, with each stage indicating the supervisee's readiness for mastering technique, relationships, and internalization. Upon implementation of this approach, parallel processes may become apparent between supervisor with supervisee and supervisee with client. The supervisee demonstrates the same needs, problems, and reactions to the supervisor as the client demonstrates to the supervisee in therapy, and vice versa. One of the advantages of this levels/stages approach is the recognition and accommodation of individual and cultural differences among supervisees and their work situations. A shared issue, however, is four scenarios of resistance: intervention at an irrelevant level, expectations at an inappropriate stage, true resistance by the supervisee, and issues and biases of the supervisor. An important conclusion is that three of the four problems originate in the supervisor, while only one originates in the supervisee.

REFERENCE LIST

Bruscia, K. (1998). *The dynamics of music psychotherapy.* Dallas, TX: Barcelona Publishers.

Bruscia, K. (2001). A model of supervision derived from apprenticeship training. In M. Forinash (Ed.), *Music therapy supervision* (pp. 281–298). Dallas, TX: Barcelona Publishers.

Bruscia, K. (2014). *Defining music therapy* (3rd ed.). Dallas, TX: Barcelona Publishers.

Part Three:
Institute Supervision

Chapter 20

CONCEPTS USED IN GUIDED IMAGERY AND MUSIC SUPERVISION

Denise Grocke

There is an art to the supervision of Bonny Method GIM trainees that requires the supervisor to balance an approach that encourages and extends, while also being affirming and supporting, so that the trainee comes to the end of training having gained knowledge and expertise and having developed richly as a person in the process. Supervision is first and foremost a relational connection (Martenson-Blom, 2003–2004) between supervisor and supervisee that should extend the supervisor's knowledge as much as the trainee's.

Supervision is a requirement of Bonny Method GIM training. Different supervision strategies may be employed across the various training institutes that now operate throughout the world; however, all trainees must participate in a minimum number of Bonny Method sessions that are supervised by an experienced GIM therapist.

The Bonny Method is also used as a supervision experience in its own right for GIM therapists or other professionals to reflect on practice. Individual GIM sessions may focus on the therapists' conflicts in conducting sessions with a particular client, and group GIM may also be used for therapists who benefit from hearing others' professional stories (Martenson-Blom, 2003–2004).

As the Bonny Method is now practiced throughout the world, there are cultural aspects to take into account, particularly in relation to the music used in the Bonny Method, which predominantly comes from the Western classical tradition. Other cultural aspects important in the supervision of trainees relate to the values, myths, and legends of a particular culture.

QUALITIES OF TRAINEES AND TRAINING STRUCTURE

Trainees are often already qualified therapists when they enter training in the Bonny Method, and they have already experienced supervision of some kind in their primary therapeutic modality. It is often helpful to know what those prior supervisory experiences were like for a trainee and to allow the trainee to work through any unfinished entanglements from previous supervision before commencing a new supervisory relationship.

Trainees who come from a background in music therapy will already have a knowledge of music and its development over periods of history, but they may need to acquire skills in psychotherapy beyond what was taught in music therapy training. Trainees who come from other therapeutic backgrounds sometimes are not musicians at all or may have little formal knowledge of the structure and repertoire of Western classical music, yet they have the knowledge of psychotherapeutic practice. Similarly, trainees who come from previous behavioral training may be challenged by the Bonny Method process, which is largely humanistic and psychodynamic. The supervisor needs to be aware of the background of the trainee in order to best craft the supervision to the trainee's benefit.

Trainees whose therapy practice has been in hospitals, mental health clinics, schools, and other institutions are often faced with the challenge of establishing a private practice for their GIM training.

First, they need to establish an appropriate place to work. There are limitations on practicing GIM at home, where family members or partners may intrude with noises outside the therapy room. Trainees may need to practice in a separate environment such as professional rooms, which necessitates paying for the venue. Trainees may be inexperienced in managing a therapeutic process where they are the sole therapy practitioner and where they must take on responsibility for the mental health of the client. In some countries, there are additional requirements, such as ensuring that professional indemnity insurance is current and that the trainee has a privacy statement in place so that clients are aware of the limitations of confidentiality. For the beginning GIM trainee who is challenged by the early phases of establishing a private practice, consultation may be needed to ensure that everything is in place.

Training in the Bonny Method of GIM is an integrated study experience that requires client sessions, supervisions, and personal sessions. Each component interacts with the others. Skills required in the client sessions are developed from reading the literature and from the experience of personal sessions and receiving supervision comments. Similarly, personal sessions allow the trainee to explore new areas of consciousness so that the trainee can be comfortable in guiding clients to new experiences. When a trainee enters their personal work with commitment and being fully open to experience, it is likely that their guiding of clients will also allow the person to explore openly.

Training Structure

Training standards in the Bonny Method of Guided Imagery are delineated by the Association for Music and Imagery (AMI) in the United States and the European Association for Music and Imagery (EAMI) in Europe. Other associations around the world tend to follow AMI requirements if they have not developed their own. Up until recently, training in the Bonny Method of GIM was structured around three levels: Introductory, Intermediate, and Advanced. *Introductory-level* training is largely experiential, whereby trainees are introduced to altered states of consciousness, dyad work, and Bonny Method music programs in the supportive training environment. In the traditional *Intermediate-level* training, there is further dyad work and more music programs are introduced. The trainee trials 10 Bonny Method sessions with colleagues or friends who do not have mental health conditions, and four personal sessions may also be required. In the traditional *Advanced-level* training, AMI requires that the trainee conduct a minimum 75 sessions with clients, 15 of which are supervised. The majority of client sessions are full-length Bonny Method sessions.

In 2018, AMI introduced more flexibility into the training structure, whereby the Introductory level continues to be an exploratory phase, followed by *Professional Training* that blends the traditional Intermediate level and Advanced level. The requirements of client sessions, supervision, and personal sessions are then combined across Intermediate and Advanced.

A further development in training standards has been the introduction of competencies for the practice of the Bonny Method of Guided Imagery and Music (AMI, 2017).

THE BONNY METHOD SESSION

An advantage of the Bonny Method in its traditional form is that it is practiced similarly throughout the world. The session comprises several elements, which are explained in different ways across the literature. For the purposes of this chapter, the session is delineated into four segments:

1. A preliminary discussion (also referred to as a Prelude, or premusic discussion), which may include biographical information, goal-setting, and exploring current concerns or feelings (AMI, 2017). In some training programs, the preliminary discussion culminates

in a focus or theme for the session, which may be an image or feeling. In other training programs, this is left open for the client to explore the music first.

2. A "transition process" (AMI, 2017), where the therapist provides a relaxation induction for the client, assists the person into an altered state of consciousness, and sometimes culminates with a reminder of the focus/theme for the next phase.

3. The interactive music experience, in which the client listens to a music program chosen by the therapist and reports on imagery, memories, and emotions that the music evokes. The therapist engages in a dialogue process by offering encouragement through reflections or open questions that allow the client to experience the imagery more fully.

4. At the end of the music program, the therapist guides the client back from the altered state of consciousness and there is a process of integration, which may involve drawing a mandala or a verbal discussion of the session.

Bonny stated that GIM involves the client and therapist in "an intense and close interaction" (Bonny, 2002, p. 271), during which the therapist needs to be "open-minded, open-ended, receptive, allowing and caring" (Bonny, 2002, p. 277). Diverse skill is required to conduct a Bonny Method session, including an ability to:

• Collaboratively draw out a theme for the session with the client;
• Provide an effective relaxation induction;
• Choose an appropriate music program;
• Be open in guiding the interactive component;
• Guide the client back from the altered state of consciousness;
• Facilitate the processing of mandala drawings or other creative elements.

It follows that for the beginning trainee, supervision focuses on these diverse skills.

WHAT THE SUPERVISOR LOOKS FOR

The session begins as the client enters the room and the trainee observes energy level, affect, dress, physical appearance, and the first words that the client utters. The trainee is welcoming to the client and establishes rapport for the session by listening attentively and responding empathically to the client.

The trainee must have the room set up for the session in a way that is conducive to an exploration of the client's inner world. There is a space for discussion, a mat or reclining chair and covers for the client, a music system (CD player or iPod/iPad connected to speakers) that is ready to use, transcript paper, and mandala materials (sketchbook-size paper with circle already drawn, high-quality oil pastels).

The Discussion (Prelude. or Premusic)

In the Prelude, the trainee is responsive to the client's emotional and physical state and verbally facilitates the drawing out of salient themes to be explored through the music. Facilitation skills draw on gentle probing for information, paraphrasing to condense material into a coherent focus, and guiding the discussion to a focus for the session. Sometimes a client may bring a dream to the session as a focus. The trainee listens carefully to the content of the dream and helps the client to explore the emotion in the dream. Either an image or an emotion can be the focus for the interactive music and imagery component.

The Relaxation Induction and Focus

The trainee facilitates a transition from the discussion phase to the relaxation phase. The client is encouraged to lie on a mat; some therapists use a reclining chair. The trainee ensures the client is warm enough and comfortable. The trainee then encourages the client into a relaxed state by providing a relaxation induction that matches the client's emotional and physical state. The pace and length of the induction is important, as is the trainee's voice tone (Grocke & Wigram, 2007). The focus may have been decided upon collaboratively with the client during the discussion or it may be left open, for example, "Let the music to take you where you need to go" (Bonny, 2002, p. 273).

Choosing the Music Program

A crucial step in the session is to choose an appropriate music program for the session. Helen Bonny developed 18 music programs of 30 to 45 minutes' duration, drawn predominantly from the repertoire of the classical genre. These programs were compiled along a therapeutic trajectory, for example, there are programs for clients new to GIM all the way through to programs for an experienced traveler. Others were compiled to draw out or support specific emotions, such as the need for nurturing or the expression of anger, while still others engage the body (Grocke, 2002). Bonny crafted her programs according to profiles of affect and intensity, so that each program has integrity. Her programs were also trialed extensively before she made them available to therapists (Bonny, 2002, p. 302).

Over the years, GIM practitioners have also developed new programs, with some 66 available in 2002 (Bruscia & Grocke, 2002, Appendices B–L, pp. 555–591) and possibly more than 100 in current practice. Trainees are required by AMI to know and use at least 12 of the 18 Bonny music programs (AMI, 2017), and training programs often require a knowledge of other specific music compilations. Therapists sometimes spontaneously program music in the traditional model, beginning the session with an established program and then making music choices relative to the client's experience, sometimes cutting across a number of programs. Summer (2009, 2011) has also researched the use of repeated pieces of music to deepen the client's experience.

Guiding the Music and Imagery Component

Probably the most challenging skill required of the trainee in the Bonny Method is nondirective guiding of the imagery experience. The verbal comments or questions are based on identifying key images and emotions for exploration, a sensitivity to the client's emotional state, and matching the modality of the client's experience, for example, whether the imagery is visual, kinesthetic, emotional, or transpersonal in nature. The therapist's quality of voice and sensitivity to the music are paramount. Knowing when to intervene and when to remain silent are critical skills for the GIM therapist. Bonny believed the guiding interventions functioned to:

- Encourage the client with new experiences;
- Help the client confront, assimilate, and deal with images, feelings, symbols, and associations that arise;
- Suggest deepening techniques when the client is stuck in a nonproductive space;
- Help the client, at the conclusion of the music session, review and integrate what has occurred. (Bonny, 2002, p. 276)

Sometimes a client may need further music to bring their imagery experience to a close, and the therapist has a choice of guiding the imagery to a natural close or adding more music to bring closure. The therapist then guides the client back from the altered state of consciousness and facilitates the move into processing the experience.

Processing the Experience

Traditionally, the processing of the music and imagery experience is made through drawing a mandala, or by verbal processing, or by other creative means, as in sculpting clay. The trainee's skill in discussing the mandala with the client depends on whether the trainee has undergone any training in Joan Kellogg's mandala theory (Kellogg, 1978).

At the conclusion of the processing, the trainee facilitates a discussion about the highlights of the imagery, guiding the discussion toward a maximizing of insight into the meaning of the imagery and relevance to the person's life.

Adaptations and Modifications

There are numerous instances where the traditional model of the Bonny Method of GIM calls for adaptation and modification. These include:

1. Sessions conducted within a hospital environment (Gimeno, 2015; Meadows, 2015).
2. Adults who are working through abuse, where each aspect of the session may be modified, including longer or shorter discussion, shorter music programs, incorporating music from a more familiar genre, or using more directed guiding (Goldberg, 1994; Körlin, 2002, 2008; Maack, 2015).
3. Working with palliative care patients, where physical and emotional energy levels may require a short session, with a short piece of music, or the use of predetermined positive images enhanced by music (West, 2015).
4. Working with clients who have poor ego control, where music of a small container is most likely used to contain the experience (Goldberg, 1994).

Sometimes the Bonny Method session requires adaptation due to a client's fragile state. This may occur early on in a trainee's experience, so that adaptations of the method cannot be neatly kept as a topic for later in the training program. Often, they need to be discussed early in training.

TYPES OF SUPERVISION

Little has been published on the skills required of the Bonny Method supervisor; however, Keiser Mardis has stated that the supervisions should be "positive and enriching experiences, carried out with the same spirit of trust and support that is evident in and important to the method itself, thereby providing students with a reliable environment in which to own their strengths, confront their weaknesses, and receive additional motivation to strive for excellence" (cited in Lewis, 2002, p. 509). AMI specifies that the supervisor should be a qualified GIM therapist. EAMI adds that the supervisor must have at least two years' experience.

Supervisors should be trained by the primary trainer of the training program. Training programs usually have their own set of forms to guide the supervision of trainees, and these forms serve to prompt comments on the mechanics of the session, transferences and countertransferences, which skills need development, and what strengths were seen in the session.

Given the complexity of skill require to conduct a Bonny Method session, new trainees can easily be overwhelmed in a supervised session if they feel that every moment is being scrutinized by the supervisor. For this reason, it is often helpful for a trainee to identify a specific component of the session on which they wish the supervisor to focus. This is not only helpful for the supervisor, but also gives the trainee some control over how the supervision will begin.

Various forms of supervision are used currently, including:

1. *On-site.* The supervisor is in situ while the trainee carries out the GIM session. The supervisor has a preliminary discussion with the trainee about the client and the GIM sessions to date. When the client arrives, the supervisor observes the entire session in silence (other than the obligatory social graces of greeting and farewelling the person). Once the client leaves, the supervisor and trainee then discuss the session.

2. *Recorded sessions with Skype/telephone follow-up.* Increasingly, it is difficult to arrange on-site supervisions to take into account the schedule of the client, the trainee, and the supervisor. Recorded sessions can be implemented instead. Audio recording can be sufficient, although some training programs require video recording in order to see the trainee and client interact and monitor changes in the client's body and facial expressions. The trainee sends a copy of the recording to the supervisor, along with notes on the client's background and transcripts or summaries of previous GIM sessions. The Skype/teleconference is arranged and the session reviewed. An advantage of the recorded session supervision is that sections of the session can be replayed so that trainees can reassess decisions that were made.

3. *Consultations* are also recommended by both AMI and EAMI. Consultations can provide an opportunity for the trainee to discuss with the consultant supervisor the overall trajectory of a client's progress or an overview of several clients in one consultation. Variations exist across different trainee programs as to the content of consultations. AMI does not specify the number of consultations required, whereas EAMI requires a minimum five consultations in addition to the 15 supervised sessions.

4. *Group supervisions.* Peer-group supervisions can be conducted during training seminars, where a trainee presents case material that summarizes the GIM given to date and development over time. Peer-group discussion allows opportunities to explore the metaphoric and symbolic meaning of the imagery, options for choice of music programs, and discussion of mandala drawings.

These sessions are particularly interesting when the trainee and GIM clients come from a different culture where the symbolism of the imagery may not be understood by the trainee group. Similarly, there are learning opportunities when trainees work with a client from a different culture where the symbolism of the imagery may need explaining, for example, the appearance of a culturally significant figure in politics or a comedian or film star.

In one group supervision, the trainee, who comes from an Asian culture, was presenting the first session of a client who had repeated images of black—being surrounded by black, seeing black patterns and thoughts of death. There was an interesting discussion about whether GIM was suitable for the male client. The trainee explained that stories of "black magic" are common in her culture, particularly in children's stories, and that blackness may not mean the same thing as in Western cultures. After discussion, the trainee decided that GIM may not be suitable for the client, and that an alternative music therapy approach might be better for him.

Bruscia also included group supervision of his trainees (Brooks, 2002b, p. 527). In a process called "psychodynamic supervision," Bruscia encouraged the group of trainees to engage in projective activities to uncover unconscious feelings and conflicts that may be operating within the trainees' GIM sessions. Traveling to the same music, the group enters into an image that one of the trainees' clients created in a previous session. The group experienced that imagery and then, after the music had concluded, the group members shared their insights into the image (Brooks, 2002b, p. 527).

A Developmental Model of Supervision

One model of supervision for Bonny Method training is based on Hawkins and Shohet's (1994) developmental model. Not all trainees will progress according to these stages, particularly if the trainee is already an experienced therapist. Similarly, not all supervisors will agree that this is the best supervision model. The first three levels are:

1. Trainee-centered

In the early phases of training, it is common for trainees to be dependent on supervisors for affirmation that they are doing the sessions correctly. There is a focus on specific skills:

- Verbal discussion skill (reflecting, paraphrasing, probing, summarizing, drawing out a theme or focus);
- Relaxation inductions (choice of induction, voice tone, pacing and content);
- Choice of music (drawn from knowledge of established programs; the trainee should be able to provide a rationale for the choice);
- Guiding/interventions (matched to the client's modality of experience, not complicated); and
- Processing creative media.

In the early stages of supervision, the trainee often focuses on the verbal interventions and whether these were right or wrong. From the start, it is best to reassure the trainee that there is no correct verbal intervention. It is possible then to brainstorm different interventions. An example would be:

> Client: *The road ahead is dark, I'm not sure I want to go there.*
> Trainee: Where else would you like to go?

The example could indicate countertransference, that is, the trainee may not want to go down the dark road with the client either. But it may also reflect a naïve response by the trainee, who is unsure of how to guide ambiguous imagery. An advanced trainee, on the other hand, might respond "How do you feel as you see the dark road?," which engages the client in the imagery that has been evoked.

It may be difficult for the trainee to see the big picture at this stage, and often the trainee is protective of the client when the supervisor suggests some pattern of behavior or underlying mental health condition evident in the client.

Brooks (2002a) completed the most extensive study of supervision strategies for the Bonny Method of GIM. She conducted interviews with 12 supervisors who were endorsed primary trainers with AMI. Brooks found that there were different expectations according to the level of training. At the Introductory level, supervisors believed the focus was on the basic mechanics of guiding, that is, the ability of the supervisee to implement each segment of the session with basic competence (Brooks, 2002b, p. 521).

2. Client-centered

As the trainee's skill in these fundamentals is established, supervision moves into a different phase around deepening an understanding of the metaphoric and symbolic nature of the client's imagery evoked by the music.

Brooks's (2002a) study confirmed that at the Intermediate level, the expectation shifts to client-centered. Supervisors expected that trainees would be able to draw out an intention for the session with a client/traveler and to choose a music program in relation to the traveler's needs. Additional skill development at the Intermediate level was centered on guiding (verbal interventions) and the ability to respond to the traveler in the modality of the traveler's imagery experience.

In the early phases of Advanced-level training, the trainee is honing the flow of the session from the preliminary discussion to the focus of the session, choosing a relaxation induction and focus image (where appropriate); choosing an appropriate music program; guiding sensitively throughout the interactive component of the session; facilitating the traveler through the processing of the imagery, either through discussion of a drawn mandala or verbal integration; and providing closure to the session.

An example from this level of training relates to the choice of a music program. In a supervised session, the trainee had facilitated an intense discussion about the client's relationship with male figures and had progressed into the relaxation induction. I could see that she was unsure about which music program to use, as there were several CDs lying out but none had been placed in the CD player. The relaxation induction came to an end and the trainee quickly placed a CD into the player and the music began. In the subsequent discussion with the trainee, I asked about her dilemma in choosing the music program. She explained the difficulty well, citing previous sessions with the client where the client had commented that she disliked the stringed instruments, and another session where she disliked female voices. The trainee, recalling all of these facts, was trying to choose a music program that the client might like, as distinct from choosing a music program that might support the client in addressing her relationships with male figures.

3. Process-centered

In later phases of Advanced training, the emphasis shifts to an understanding of the richness of the traveler's imagery process (process-centered). Theoretical underpinnings from Jungian theory (Ward, 2002) or Gestalt theory (Clarkson, 2002) may be incorporated to delve more deeply into the metaphoric meaning of the imagery sequences. An understanding of spiritual experience (Kasayka, 2002) and transpersonal (Abrams, 2002) realms also enhances the depth to which a trainee can comfortably go with a traveler.

In addition, the trainee may be challenged by the life experience of the client. Unresolved material from the client's past may surface, sometimes early in a series of sessions, and this may catapult the trainee into a fast learning curve. Perhaps the most challenging of these is the client's recall of sexual, physical, or emotional abuse as a child. The trainee must be knowledgeable about current theories related to trauma and to avoid retraumatizing when unexpected memories and emotions flood the client's experience.

Transference and Countertransference

As GIM sessions deepen over time, there may be instances of transference to the therapist and countertransference dynamics that influence decisions made by the trainee. It is common to see transference to the therapist in a client's imagery, for example, "I see a woman at the door ... she is opening the door for me to go in." On occasions, the transference may indicate something different, for example, "The woman is behind me and pushing me ahead," which can indicate to the trainee that some aspect of the GIM therapy is moving ahead too quickly.

Countertransferences can occur at any point in the session, and supervision can focus on decisions made by the trainee during the prelude discussion, the choice of music, the guiding interventions, and the postlude discussion. It is helpful to ask the trainee about whether countertransference was evident in the session, as this allows the trainee to reflect first, before the supervisor brings the discussion to elements where countertransference may have been evident. Furthermore, supervisors themselves need to be aware of their own countertransference to the client's material and to the decisions made by the trainee.

CULTURAL DIFFERENCES IN BONNY METHOD PRACTICE AND SUPERVISION

The Bonny Method is now practiced throughout the world, and trainings are well established in Europe, Australia, Korea, Japan, and Southeast Asian countries. When introducing the Bonny Method trainings to a new culture, some immediate questions are:

1. How is the concept of "therapy" understood in this culture?
2. How easily will an altered state of consciousness be understood and accepted?
3. What cultural traditions and folkloric symbolism will be seen in the imagery?
4. How will clients in this culture relate to music of the Western classical genre?
5. What skills will the GIM therapist need to guide clients of this culture?
6. How will the training model be adapted to meet the cultural needs?

Having conducted Bonny Method GIM training in Spain, Korea, and Singapore, I have been part of interesting discussions on the above questions. Perhaps the most enlightening discussion focused on the cultural differences between Asian countries built on collectivist values drawn from Confucian philosophy and Western countries where individualist values are respected.

Collectivistic cultures emphasize the needs and goals of the group as a whole over the needs and wishes of each individual. Identity within a collectivist culture is defined in terms of relationships with others (Ma & Schoeneman, 1997), and there is a selflessness manifested by putting community needs ahead of individual needs and doing what is best for society. Families and communities are more important than individual goals.

In individualistic cultures, the focus is on a clear boundary that separates self from others. Main life goals include being independent of others, realizing one's potential and uniqueness, and self-determination (Ma & Schoeneman, 1997, p. 263).

In relation to GIM practice and training, such differences can be seen in all aspects of the Bonny Method GIM session—in the preliminary discussion, the intention set for the session, and the manner in which the trainee engages the client in the imagery. The supervisor therefore needs to be aware of cultural differences in the guiding, so that a Western bias is not introduced. Consider the following hypothetical difference in a Bonny Method GIM session where the focus is a favorite place:

For the client from an individualist culture:
Therapist: Can you describe your favorite place?
Client: It is a beautiful place in nature.
Therapist: Can you describe this place?
Client: It is so peaceful and quiet.
Therapist: How does it feel to be there?

Client: I can leave all the stress of my work life here. I am alone, my family is somewhere else, and I can be in this place just for myself.
Therapist: Allow yourself to enjoy this experience.

For the client from a collectivist culture:
Therapist: Can you describe your favorite place?
Client: I am in the kitchen—I am preparing the meal.
Therapist: Can you describe it?
Client: I am preparing food for the family. We will eat together.
Therapist: What food are you preparing?
(Client describes.)
Therapist: How does that feel for you?
Client: I am looking forward to seeing them.

For a supervisor from the individualistic culture, the preparing of food may not appear to be addressing any life goals, whereas for a supervisor from a collectivist culture, the imagery is completely in accord with everyday life and values.

Short (2005–2006) also highlights the need for therapists to demonstrate "cultural awareness, cultural sensitivity, and cultural competence within the therapeutic context" (p. 75). In relation to the practice of the Bonny Method, she found that cultural impact was present in (a) language and expression, (b) relationship and context, (c) cultural connotations and icons, (d) cultural values and spirituality, and (e) the role of the music and culture.

Western Classical Music in Non-Western Cultures

One of the questions asked most often about the practice of the Bonny Method of GIM concerns the music of the Western classical tradition. Enquirers ask why classical music is used. And why not other genres? Bonny advocated music of the classical tradition because of its structure and form, capacity to evoke emotion and mood, and multilayered complexity that enables different instrumental voices to add new perspectives (Bonny, 2002, pp. 301–321).

An early study by Hanks (1992) compared imagery experiences of American and Taiwanese participants while listening to music of both the Western classical tradition and Taiwanese culture. Hanks found that the participants tended to respond in similar patterns—personal, cultural, and archetypal. She maintained that there were intracultural patterns evident in the participants' imagery. In one example, when the music of Ch'in was played, all participants experienced somatic or kinesthetic imagery and personified the imagery as a "wise musician/philosopher who lives for his music" (Hanks, 1992, p. 28). Similarly, all participants had imagery of tall mountains during the playing of Brahms's *Symphony #1*. The ontological connection is that Brahms composed the work while holidaying in the European Alps.

A more recent study (Ng, 2015) was based on the development of five Chinese music programs for use with participants from Chinese culture. Ng (2015) explains that Chinese music has a long history and that contemporary Chinese music now incorporates Western music instruments. Ng (2015) noted that Chinese people sometimes do not relate to traditional Chinese music, as it does not relate to the current generation. In the study of Ng's Harvest music program, six clients had diverse imagery experiences and one person responded negatively to the selection titled "Red Detachment of Women," as it raised negative memories from the Cultural Revolution in China. For other participants in the study, imagery pertinent to Chinese culture was evoked, such as temples and music instruments. Most participants concluded their GIM session with imagery of being at home.

THE BONNY METHOD OF GIM AS A METHOD OF SUPERVISION

Various forms of supervision have involved modified individual Bonny Method sessions or group GIM sessions. Participants may be Bonny Method GIM therapists, or they may be other professionals. For GIM therapists, professional supervision is particularly important if they are isolated in their private practice. In addition, by utilizing the same method (Bonny Method GIM) as the supervisory experience, therapists can feel supported by the music.

Bruscia (1998) developed a technique known as Reimaging "to develop a form of experiential self-inquiry to uncover unconscious dynamics operating within the GIM experience and to devise procedures for analyzing the transference and countertransference material unearthed through such a self-inquiry" (Bruscia, 1998, p. 529). He chose fragments from several client sessions, focusing on significant and memorable images that had stayed in his mind. He chose short pieces of music from the Bonny music programs, about 6 to 10 minutes in length, which he associated with the memorable image of each client's session. There followed a typical GIM session with short relaxation induction, a focus imagery of the memorable images of the client, and an interactive dialogue about his re-experience of the client and the imagery. He recalled the images from the session with his client Tom and in the reimaging session engaged in dialogue with Tom, asking him initially "Why don't you get in there and do something? Get into your life." Bruscia (2002, pp. 533–534) poses a five-step process for addressing countertransference by first clarifying the feelings experienced while re-imaging. He then poses a three-step process to analyze the transference from the client (Bruscia, 2002, pp. 544–548, 549–560).

The same technique was used in professional supervision with a GIM practitioner who expressed frustration in the work she was doing with a client (Grocke, 2002). The practitioner described that she frequently tried to rescue the client during the interactive music and imagery phase of the session, for example, asking "Is there someone there to help?" so that the client wouldn't experience further hurt. The GIM practitioner chose music for the supervision session that would best depict the client and her frustration with the client. After a short relaxation induction, the music began. Immediately, the GIM practitioner had imagery of the client as a beetle lying on her back, with her legs moving in the air, unable to flip herself over. The GIM therapist realized this was how the client might feel in GIM when the music and/or imagery was confronting. The supervision discussion then moved to how the GIM therapist might address this in future sessions.

Martenson-Blom (2003–2004) adopted group GIM as a supervision strategy for five social workers (four females and one male). The group experienced eight group GIM sessions, in which there was a discussion of the issues each brought to the session, followed by a relaxation induction and 3 to 7 minutes of music drawn from the Bonny Method music programs. Each person experienced his or her own imagery but then shared that experience with the group after the end of the music.

Martenson-Blom commented that professional therapists "need nourishment and understanding [and] space for reflection and creativity" (2003–2004, p. 97). She believes that group GIM provides a place for "polyvision," or "what you see," as distinct from supervision, which implies an overview of what has happened. In her study, she interviewed each person to gain a sense of how group GIM contributed to their professional work. She found that for one participant, group GIM was "more effective than process supervision" (p. 112). For another, group GIM "strongly connected me to the relationships and working contexts, like setting the stage and then getting up on it" (p. 112). For a third participant, "it meant a lot to listen to the images and experiences of colleagues," and for another, group GIM gave energy "far from the tiredness I came in with." (p. 112). Martenson-Blom reflected that the group participants increased their capacity to be "empathic, caring, and loving toward both their clients and themselves" (p. 115).

In a Korean study, Kang (2007) also chose group GIM as supervision for four music therapists. The four therapists were all female and engaged in GIM training, but at different levels. The intention of the qualitative study was to explore how peer-group supervision could help music therapists with their clinical and personal issues as professionals. Data were sourced from participants' personal journals, the researcher's field notes, video- and audiotapes of supervision sessions, interviews with participants, and mandalas.

Kang (2007) used the four-phase process advocated by Helen Bonny, including the Preliminary Conversation, where each group member shared personal goals for the sessions; the Induction, wherein the group members sat on chairs or lay on the floor and a structured relaxation induction and focus were given that could continue while the music was played; the Music Program, which was a single short piece of music from the classical or popular genre or quiet music listening with voice-over by the therapist; and the Postlude, a return to normal consciousness and group sharing of experiences. The study included 10 group GIM sessions.

In order to analyze the participants' experiences, Kang selected three sessions from each participant representing the beginning, transitions, and ending phases. In the beginning phase, all participants shared their difficulties from personal, professional, and clinical aspects and were ready to explore the source of their difficulties (Kang, 2007, p. 48.) In the transition phase, the participants' experience deepened and psychological traumas from early in life emerged. In the ending phase, the participants began to resolve their conflicts by rehearsing new experiences and replacing past negative ones with new possibilities (Kang, 2007, p. 49).

CONCLUSION

Supervision of the Bonny Method of Guided Imagery and Music takes different forms. For the beginning trainee, supervision most often is focused on the mechanics of the four phases of the session. As training progresses, supervision shifts to an understanding of the symbolic and metaphoric meanings of the client's imagery and emotional, spiritual, and transpersonal experience.

The individual form of the Bonny Method can also be adapted for supervision of GIM therapists and other professionals, and group GIM similarly can be a creative and nourishing way for professionals to address their own personal concerns that may impact their professional lives. In these varied ways, the Bonny Method provides enriching experiences in part due to the intimate way in which participants engage with music and the emotion and imagery evoked.

REFERENCE LIST

Abrams, B. (2002). Transpersonal dimensions of the Bonny Method. In K. E. Bruscia & D. E. Grocke (Eds.), *Guided imagery and music: The Bonny Method and Beyond* (pp. 339–358). Gilsum, NH: Barcelona Publishers.

Association for Music and Imagery. (2017). *Competencies, training program standards, and procedures for the Bonny Method of GIM* (effective January 1, 2018). Retrieved January 12, 2019, from https://ami-bonnymethod.org/members/documents

Bonny, H. L. (2002). Facilitating Guided Imagery and Music (GIM) sessions. In L. Summer (Ed.), *Music Consciousness: The evolution of Guided Imagery and Music*. Gilsum, NH: Barcelona Publishers.

Brooks, D. (2002a). A holistic description of beginning trainee experiences in live observation GIM supervision. *Nordic Journal of Music Therapy, 11*(2), 142–151.

Brooks, D. (2002b). Supervision strategies for the Bonny Method of Guided Imagery and Music. In K. Bruscia & D. Grocke (Eds.), *Guided Imagery and Music: The Bonny Method and Beyond* (pp. 519–532). Gilsum, NH: Barcelona Publishers.

Bruscia, K. E. (1998). Reimaging client images: A technique for exploring transference and countertransference in guided imagery and music. In K. E. Bruscia (Ed.), *The Dynamics of Music Psychotherapy* (pp. 527–548). Gilsum, NH: Barcelona.

Bruscia, K. E. (Ed.). (2013). *Self-experiences in music therapy education, training, and supervision* (1st ed.). Gilsum, NH: Barcelona Publishers.

Bush, C. (1992). Dreams, mandalas, and music imagery: Therapeutic uses in a case study. *Journal of the Association for Music and Imagery, 1,* 33–42.

Clarkson, G. (2002). Combining gestalt dreamwork and the Bonny Method. In K. E. Bruscia & D. E. Grocke (Eds.), *Guided imagery and music: The Bonny Method and Beyond* (pp. 245–256). Gilsum, NH: Barcelona Publishers.

European Association for Music and Imagery (EAMI). (2017). *Standards for Training in Guided Imagery and Music (GIM).* Draft revision.

Fincher, S. (1991). *Creating Mandalas.* Boston, MA: Shambala.

Goldberg, F. (1994). The Bonny Method of Guided Imagery and Music as Individual and Group Treatment in a Short-Term Acute Psychiatric Hospital. *Journal of the Association for Music and Imagery, 3,* 18–34.

Gimeno, M. (2015). MED-GIM: Adaptation of the Bonny Method for medical patients: Individual Sessions. In D. Grocke & T. Moe (Eds.), *Guided imagery & music (GIM) and music imagery methods for individual and group therapy.* London, UK: Jessica Kingsley.

Grocke, D. (2002). Re-imaging in GIM supervision. *Nordic Journal of Music Therapy, 11*(2), 178–181. doi:10.1080/08098130209478061

Hanks, K. (1992). Music, affect, and imagery: A cross-cultural exploration. *Journal of the Association for Music and Imagery, 1,* 19–31.

Hawkins, P., & Shohet, R. (1994). *Supervision in the helping professions.* Bristol, UK: Open University Press.

Kang, H. J. (2007). Peer group supervision for Korean music therapists with Guided Imagery and Music (GIM) Unpublished Master's degree thesis, Michigan: Michigan State University.

Kasayka, R. E. (2002). A spiritual orientation to the Bonny Method: To walk the mystical path on practical feet. In K. E. Bruscia & D. E. Grocke (Eds.), *Guided imagery and music: The Bonny Method and Beyond* (pp. 257–270). Gilsum, NH: Barcelona Publishers.

Kellogg, J. (1978). *Mandala: Path of Beauty.* Clearwater, FL: MARI.

Körlin, D. (2002). A neuropsychological theory of traumatic imagery in the Bonny Method of guided imagery and music (BMGIM). In K. E. Bruscia & D. E. Grocke (Eds.), *Guided imagery and music: The Bonny Method and Beyond* (pp. 379–415). Gilsum, NH: Barcelona Publishers.

Körlin, D. (2008). Music breathing: Breath grounding and modulation of the Bonny Method of Guided Imagery and Music (BMGIM): Theory, method, and consecutive cases. *Journal of the Association for Music & Imagery, 11,* 79–113.

Lewis, K. (2002). The development of training in the Bonny Method of guided imagery and music (BMGIM) from 1975 to 2000. In K. E. Bruscia & D. E. Grocke (Eds.), *Guided imagery and music: The Bonny Method and Beyond* (pp. 497–517). Gilsum, NH: Barcelona Publishers.

Ma, V., & Schoeneman, J. (1997). Individualism versus collectivism: A comparison of Kenyan and American self-concepts. *Basic and Applied Social Psychology, 19*(2), 261–273.

Maack, C. (2015). Adaptations of guided imagery and music in the treatment of trauma-related disorders. In D. Grocke & T. Moe (Eds.), *Guided imagery & music (GIM) and music imagery methods for individual and group therapy.* London, UK: Jessica Kingsley.

Martenson-Blom, K. (2003–2004). Guided imagery and music in supervision: Applications of Guided Imagery and Music (GIM) for Supervision and Professional Development. *Journal of the Association for Music & Imagery, 9,* 97–118.

Meadows, A. (2015). Music and imagery in cancer care. In D. Grocke & T. Moe (Eds.), *Guided imagery & music (GIM) and music imagery methods for individual and group therapy*. London, UK: Jessica Kingsley.

Ng, W. M. (2015). Chinese Music Program "Harvest." In D. Grocke & T. Moe (Eds.), *Guided Imagery and Music (GIM) and Music Imagery Methods for Individual and Group Therapy* (pp. 319–328). London, UK: Jessica Kingsley.

Short, A. (2005–2006). Cultural dimensions of Music and Imagery: Archetypal and Ethnicity in GIM practice. *Journal of the Association for Music & Imagery, 10*, 75–90.

Summer, L. (2002). Group music and imagery therapy. Emergent receptive techniques in music therapy practice. In K. Bruscia & D. Grocke (Eds.), *Guided Imagery and Music: the Bonny Method and Beyond*. Gilsum, NH: Barcelona Publishers.

Summer, L. (2009). *Client perspectives on the music in Guided Imagery and Music* (Doctoral dissertation). Aalborg University, Aalborg, Denmark.

Summer, L. (2011). Client perspectives on the music in Guided Imagery and Music (GIM). In *Qualitative inquiries in music therapy* (Vol. 6). Gilsum, NH: Barcelona Publishers.

Ventre, M. (2001). Supervision in the Bonny Method of Guided Imagery and Music. In M. Forinash (Ed.), *Music Therapy Supervision* (pp. 335–349). Gilsum, NH: Barcelona Publishers.

Ward, K. M. (2002). A Jungian orientation to the Bonny Method. In K. E. Bruscia & D. E. Grocke (Eds.), *Guided imagery and music: The Bonny Method and Beyond* (pp. 207–224). Gilsum, NH: Barcelona Publishers.

West, T. (2015). A spectrum of adaptations for palliative care and end of life. In D. Grocke & T. Moe (Eds.), *Guided imagery & music (GIM) and music imagery methods for individual and group therapy*. London, UK: Jessica Kingsley.

Chapter 21

SUPERVISION IN THE NORDOFF-ROBBINS TRAINING PROGRAM

Alan Turry

OVERVIEW

Nordoff-Robbins music therapy (NRMT) is based on the work of Paul Nordoff, an accomplished composer/improviser, and Clive Robbins, who began the work as a special educator with a musical background. Both therapists are acknowledged as pioneers in the model of live, interactive, music-making with clients that has come to be known as creative music therapy. Robbins spent nearly his entire professional life teaching and researching the creative process in music therapy—what he and Nordoff called the art of music as therapy. NRMT is a model in terms of its comprehensiveness and broad applicability, but calling it a model doesn't imply the presence of guidelines for practice that the term "model" can imply (Aigen, personal communication, January 7, 2019). NRMT is music-centered in that musical processes are viewed as the primary vehicles of change. It is a form of music psychotherapy in that relationship factors are considered, and there is recognition that music affects the psyche. It is a transpersonal discipline in that the approach utilizes music to harness the client's will and recognizes that musical peak experiences can help clients to transcend behavioral or dynamic patterns that impede self-enhancement. Training in this approach is musically advanced, its primary goals being the development of *clinical musicianship* and the release of creativity in the therapist. Instructional resources include much of the original Nordoff-Robbins clinical research, supplemented by the expanding field of exploration by therapists skilled in this approach. Recording and comprehensive documentation of every therapy session is standard practice and provides trainees with a resource for supervision and self-evaluation. Supervision frequently utilizes the recordings of therapy sessions. An advanced (post-master's) training in the United States, it is open to credentialed music therapists who have already utilized improvisation in their clinical work. This chapter will describe the training program and the supervision process during the training.

FOUNDATIONS OF NORDOFF-ROBBINS SUPERVISION

The following graphic representation (Figure 1) was created by Clive Robbins to display and interrelate the various skills and capacities that are recognized in developing *clinical musicianship* in the Nordoff-Robbins trainee. It indicates each area of creative potential as it relates to its mode of clinical application. Drawing on his considerable experience as a clinician and teacher and influenced by a transpersonal worldview that incorporates elements common to many spiritual approaches, Robbins created this model to identify and differentiate the components of creative endeavor and their polarities. The upper part of the model encompasses the artistic qualities needed in the training of the therapist; the lower part references the craft or practical tools—the nuts-and-bolts skills and methods necessary to conduct the therapy. Each category serves as a balance for another; the freedom needed to create musically must be balanced with the clinical responsibility of applying this improvised music as therapy. The top half can be looked at as the transpersonal meeting ground of the client and therapist and considers the inner aspects of creative musical processes. The bottom half of the diagram contains the application of these aspects. By addressing the inner aspects of creative music therapy with trainees, the creative process becomes more understandable and reachable for them. They are thus able to participate in their own development of creative capability with more insight. This approach to training serves to integrate the intrinsic and extrinsic aspects of their training experiences. The gestalt of the model itself emphasizes the integrative, holistic approach inherent in the Nordoff-Robbins practice of music therapy. There is a dynamic, interactive relationship between the categories. There is an art to the understanding of behavior, a science to the construction of chords and progressions; musical and psychological processes are not seen as separate but as synthesizing: All of the subjects that make up the model connect and coordinate.

Just as each quality represented in the diagram has implications for the process of therapy, so too each quality represented has implications for the process of supervision. In many ways, these two processes are parallel, and a full understanding of the terms in the diagram opposite illuminates them both.

Creative Now refers to the potential of the creative moment in which the therapist is open to receive and respond to what the client is presenting—either in active playing or merely in presenting him-/herself in the room—as music. The idea of the *Creative Now* has some similarities to the more common phrase used to describe the therapeutic space conducive to change, the "here and now." The therapist is described as being *Poised in the Creative Now*—this refers to a state of balanced, receptive alertness on the part of the therapist. In this state of readiness, listening is a creative, musical act. There is no script, no game plan, but a willingness on the part of the therapist to act, respond, and enter into a mutual musical relationship with the client.

The *Creative Now* is a place for both therapist and client. Creating music, "creative musicing"[28]—in a mutual fashion with freedom and clinical intention—is potentially in and of itself an agent of change, a transforming experience for both client and therapist. By entering into an active musical relationship, both client and therapist have the possibilities of realizing untapped potentials. In the immediacy of the moment, the musical relationship is in a constant state of forming. The *Creative Now* is a space where resources within the client can begin to be activated, come to expression, and, in the process, initiate changes that are self-enhancing. The therapist has the responsibility—and opportunity—to create this space, observe the process, and undertake to serve its continuing development.

Creative Freedom/Clinical Responsibility

In order to have *creative freedom,* the trainee must inevitably develop faith in the power of music, a readiness to meet the client's needs or circumstances, and trust in his/her own abilities. Belief that music has capabilities to effect change is the underlying motivation for the therapist in creating music. As trainees develop creative freedom, they are increasingly able to improvise responsively and with variety so that the music is uniquely suited for their client. Rachel Verney (2010), a master trainer who studied directly with Paul Nordoff, feels it is important for supervisors to help trainees to become more aware of what brought them into music therapy in the first place. By rekindling his or her "personal flame" to music, she feels each trainee may become a more effective therapist, trusting in music in a genuine way.

A supervisor must recognize that creative freedom in music therapy takes courage. The supervisor is a role model in trusting music. Also, the importance in supervision of respecting individual choices and respecting the uniqueness of each trainee is paramount in developing creative freedom in the trainee. Supervisors communicate that they are learning from trainees, valuing

---

[28] "Musicing," as described by Elliot (1995), denotes the importance of perceiving music as a living, human activity and not merely as a cultural artifact or object.

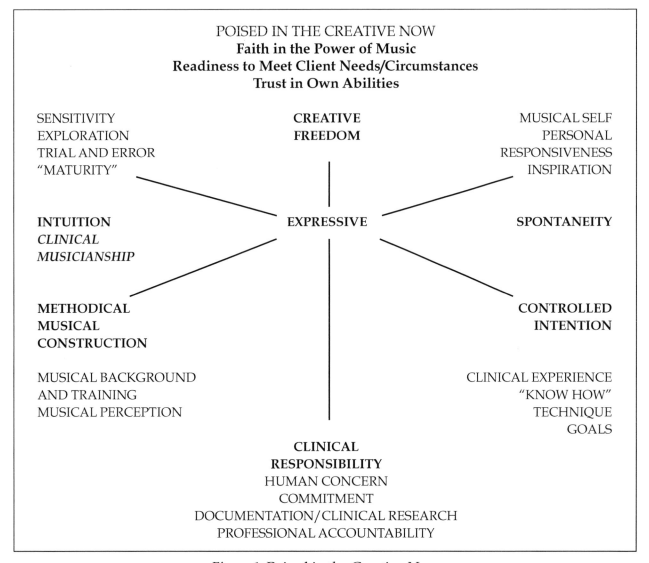

Figure 1. Poised in the Creative Now.

different perspectives, and discovering with them. This helps to cultivate each trainee's trust in his or her own music. It is essential that the supervisor create a safe space for the trainee and respect his/her own individual growth time, helping the trainee to find his/her creative voice.

Creative freedom is balanced by *clinical responsibility*. In order to balance the creative freedom needed in the development of clinical musicianship, the trainee must learn to be professionally accountable for his or her actions. In describing the processes inherent in the Nordoff-Robbins approach in another publication (Turry, 1998), I stated that "becoming too inwardly focused in an effort to be creative can be a defense against problematic dynamics and threatening feelings" (p. 164). A major task for the supervisor is to help the trainee to understand musical/clinical processes in order to move the process forward. The supervisor also helps the trainee to speak with clarity about their clinical work. The supervisor works with the trainee to cultivate a genuine human concern for the client, a commitment to stay in a challenging process, and an ability to document and research the work so that new understandings can feed back into the creative process. The trainee has an obligation to monitor the therapy process and adjust his/her approach to benefit the client.

Expressive Spontaneity/Methodical Musical Construction

Expressive spontaneity allows for genuine, energy-producing interaction. It allows for flexible, dramatic musical interventions that can motivate and engage clients. In order to be personally responsive with expressive spontaneity, the trainee needs to develop a musical identity, a firm musical self from which to draw musical ideas without hesitation.

Expressive spontaneity allows the trainee to act on a musical inspiration with immediacy. This quality allows for moment-to-moment freedom and energy—an ability to shift flexibly and interact with mutuality. The ability to be playful with a client can help to facilitate this kind of spontaneity. Jean Eisler (personal communication, April 1999) suggests that trainees find time to play with infants and toddlers in order to cultivate this playful interactive spontaneity.

Another way to cultivate expressive spontaneity in trainees is to provide a space where they don't need to know or explain; they can simply *be* in music and express themselves freely. Ongoing participation in their own music therapy can be an important part of the training process. This process allows trainees to explore themselves, their relationship to music, and their relationship to others through musical interaction. It is also important for supervisors to bring experiences to trainees that reinforce their love of music. This will allow trainees to utilize music with authentic expression, not merely as a technique.

One cannot be spontaneous without the building blocks of musical thinking, the musical know-how. This is why expressive spontaneity must be directly dependent on the trainee's capacity for methodical musical construction.

Methodical musical construction—the craft of musicing—is vital for the development of clinical musicianship. In order to have the ability to express oneself musically with spontaneity, the trainee must have the musical foundations, the musical background, to tap into. Technical musical training is also important in developing the skills of musical perception. This allows the therapist to listen musically to what is occurring in the session and create with coherent fluidity and form. Trainees need to have technical control over their musical ideas in order to shape them aesthetically. This allows for expressive spontaneity; musical inspirations can be realized.

During the training, new musical resources that may be unfamiliar to the trainee are introduced. These extrinsic experiences become intrinsic when the trainee develops a personal relationship with them. It is only after these new musical structures become meaningful that they are useful; often, this discovery can come in the experience of musicing with the client. Therefore, trainees are encouraged to try out newly learned musical forms in sessions—not in a haphazard sense, but tuned in to what is happening. Musicing is not prescriptive, and because therapy is a mutual process, the meaning comes only after the client and therapist share in the experience.

Intuition/Controlled intention

Intuition can be an immediate perception of reality—a way of knowing that transcends rationalization and also bypasses the usual sensory processes. Developing intuition can allow the trainee to improvise music with a sense of purpose. The trainee must be willing to explore, to try out ideas. Trying out ideas in sessions brings musical experiences to the trainee that help to develop clinical maturity. This maturity feeds back into the intuitive processes. Rather than developing theories or prescriptive strategies about music, the trainee learns principally by doing, by living in the experience of interactive musicing with his/her client. For the trainee, an intuition often originates with an insight into the client, and a completely new musical idea may occur in the moment. There needs to be a willingness to live in uncertainty, mystery, and doubt without anxiously searching for a logical conclusion to the situation. The very fact that the clinical situation is in essence unrehearsed and unprescribed can force trainees to experience living in the creative now. As they continue to enter into this enhancing situation, they grow more confident in coping with its challenges. Their increasing ability to rely on their capacities for intuition and inspiration results in a natural development of clinical perception. This is strongly supported by the close analysis of session recordings.

How can supervision help to develop intuition in the trainee? The supervisor cultivates *sensitivity* in the trainee as well as the *courage* to develop and trust intuition. This can be a highly individualized potential within each trainee. Some are ready to tap into their intuitive faculties without hesitation. Others may struggle. Often, when trainees begin working, they have blocks that prevent them from developing and trusting intuition. The supervisor needs to discern whether the inability to trust intuition is due to the trainee's low self-esteem or some other personal dynamic. Or could it be that they simply do not have sufficient technical ability yet? Have they internalized parental or other authority figures who have discouraged nonrational explorations? Are they afraid they will not be able to explain why they did something? Are they afraid of making a mistake? Talking about these possibilities in supervision may help the trainee to enter more fully into the clinical situation. Exploring the fear of failure by exploring the worst possible scenario of what might happen helps to alleviate anxiety. This search is done to help expand the trainee's awareness and ability to be more fully present in the session, without fear. The less psychic energy that is dedicated to inner concerns, the more receptive the trainee can be to the client, listening closely and picking up on subtle communications which feed into the intuitive process.

Many factors contribute to the intuitive process. Consider a clinical example from the early Nordoff-Robbins work that led to the creation of a song that has subsequently been used with other clients. When Paul Nordoff improvised the phrase "Oh, when you feel like crying, just cry" to help a crying boy in a group feel supported and accepted, he was reacting to a situation about which he personally felt impatience; the classroom teacher was, in Nordoff's view, mocking the boy, not taking his feelings seriously enough.[29] Nordoff impulsively acted to change a situation he felt was unjust. He allowed his personal reaction to trigger his intuitive response, which immediately took the form of a song. In his clinical practice, he often approached the clinical situation with a kind of impatience toward the restrictions of pathology, an urgent readiness to do something to move the client forward, to release him or her into new levels of awareness and capability. The challenge in the training is to help trainees to take this kind of interventional stance without being too demanding or insensitive to the client.

Assessing the condition of the client, and how the restrictions imposed by the condition affect the client's overall functioning, can help provide an orientation in therapy that facilitates the intuitive-creative direction taken by the therapist. Nordoff was particularly adept at perceiving what kind of musical stance to take based on a client's condition. He seems to have wondered, Is the client somehow imprisoned within the confines of the condition? Or are they withdrawing into the protection of the condition? How can the client's will be activated? Did Nordoff need to work *through* the condition, for instance, through matching a perseverative behavior with music? Or could he build upon the potentials not fully displayed? Adopting this stance of perception fed directly into his intuitive process. His approach, not just in improvising but in *perceiving*, was an active one. The concept and diagram of the "music child" and the "condition child"[30] was developed in part to help trainees to acquire this kind of perception.

The development of intuition cannot be directly taught to the trainee in supervision. It needs to be nurtured, like cultivating a plant. By creating an understanding, resonating space for the trainee, the supervisor can create the conditions for him/her to become more intuitive. Gaining experience and expanding awareness by entering into the creative situation with the client is the ultimate source

---

[29] "The Crying Song" by Nordoff and Robbins is in *The Second Book of Children's Play Songs* (1968). New York, NY: Presser.
[30] Originally developed by Nordoff and Robbins and first published in an article by Clive and Carol Robbins titled "Self-Communications in Music Therapy" in Bruscia's *Case Studies in Music Therapy* (1991). Gilsum, NH: Barcelona Publishers.

of developing intuition. The supervisor can help the trainee to reflect on the events that took place in the clinical situation, and these reflections feed back into the intuitive process.

There are times when trainees are so focused on their own feelings that they cannot listen carefully and then take action. Brown (1997) found that it can be helpful to remind trainees to stay focused on their clients when feeling uninspired. By guiding trainees to keep their thoughts and focus on the client, the supervisor is reminding them that they do not have to provide everything in the session—clients are giving input all of the time, even if they are not active. Gentle reminders to listen to the client, feel the client, and find the music that is motivated by this feeling and hearing can help the trainee create music in the session.

In applying intuition through *controlled intention,* the trainee progressively gains a sense of how to proceed. With clinical experience, the trainee begins to develop the "know how," or technique, and formulates fluid, flexible goals that can change adaptively from moment to moment. Having controlled intention provides direction—in the musicing and for the client. Studying archival material and integrating the feedback they receive in supervision build upon the trainee's ability to develop controlled intention.

Understandably, there are times when a trainee has the personal need to gain an overt response from the client or needs a sign that they are liked or are an effective therapist. Acting on this need may lead to ineffective musical interventions—and may result in working to be responded to personally rather than letting the contact come through musical interaction. Awareness of this need, which is natural in all of us, can help trainees maintain controlled intention in their sessions.

It can be helpful for trainees to recognize their personal need for musical expression and to be heard as musicians. For this reason, it can be important for trainees to provide for themselves opportunities outside of their clinical sessions in which they can find release from the demands of controlled intention in the service of their own musical expression. This is another reason why being involved in personal music therapy can be valuable to a trainee. Controlled intention helps to focus and guide the intuitive process.

THE SUPERVISORY RELATIONSHIP

The creative music therapy approach recognizes that people make music. Music played between people creates interpersonal, intrapersonal, and transpersonal experiences. Therefore, it is important to look at intrapsychic processes, the musical relationship, and what this reveals about the therapy process. The supervisory relationship is the microcosm in which these experiences can be addressed. The trainee entering into such a relationship must be prepared to ask, "How can my supervisor help me cultivate my listening skills and perceive how musicing will help my clients? How can I create the optimal conditions to learn from my supervisor? How will I develop in order to do effective therapy?"

Supervision has traditionally been a place to help trainees move past emotional blocks, expand awareness of unconscious processes, and gain insight into their own personal dynamics and how those dynamics influence the therapy situation. It is imperative for trainees to become aware of and more fully understand their motivations, assumptions, and needs in order for them to become more effective therapists. Discovering previously unknown personal qualities can help them to gain insight into the therapy situation. Examining their own music played in the therapeutic relationship can help trainees to gain further insight into themselves and their client.

In the same way that a therapist becomes sensitive to a client's presence, mood, and potential areas of need and strengths, the supervisor gathers this same information from the trainee. In order to feel empathy for the client, the therapist puts himself or herself into an open state. In the therapeutic relationship, the therapist does not approach the situation with the assumption that they have all of the answers or that everything will run smoothly. The therapist understands that it is essentially a musically facilitated adventure in human encounter in which both client and therapist are human and possess human frailties and vulnerabilities. Kornfield (1993), a psychologist who integrated Eastern spiritual teachings into his psychotherapy practice, wrote that "when we let ourselves become vulnerable, new things can be born in us" (p. 49). This approach and process is similar in supervision—supervisors approach the supervisory relationship with gratitude and humility, knowing they too will learn from the experience. They do not have all the answers for their trainees in exactly the same way that therapists do not have all the answers for their clients. As supervisors, we are entering into a creative situation, and we cannot know or anticipate the extent of our abilities to help. We are approaching this situation with openness and a willingness to learn from the trainee. In these important ways, the relationship between a trainee and supervisor is similar to the relationship between a client and therapist.

In Nordoff-Robbins music therapy, important practices for the trainee to implement include the ability to listen carefully with sensitivity, to be spontaneous, to trust the unknown, and to move away from preplanned activities and repertoire in order to responsively improvise in sessions. The supervisor can encourage the trainee's integration of these concepts by approaching supervision in a spontaneous way. Rather than setting up an agenda, the supervisor can be poised in the creative now with the trainee. In this way, the supervisor and trainee are mutually responding to each other, as coactive partners who are growing together, as the client and therapist do. The development of creative freedom, expressive spontaneity, and intuition often blossoms in the trainee when the relationship with the supervisor becomes a trusting one through time and experience. When the trainee has a genuine sense that the supervisor is not a judge but an invested mentor who genuinely wants the trainee to succeed, creativity within the trainee can flourish.

By being poised to respond to what happens *in* the moment, rather than focusing on and planning for the next moment, the supervisor responds to the trainee as a unique individual and does not use the same method or expect the same responses from all trainees. Rather than teaching, the supervisor listens with intention and focus to the trainee, sensing how to move him/her forward in his/her development. The trainee's skills and temperament will affect how supervision proceeds. The supervisor must be open to the trainee's individual mixture of talent and personality.

Barbara Hesser (personal communication, January 2019) developed a method of supervision that distinguishes between what is a technical skill and learning issue for the trainee and what is a personal/insight-oriented issue to work on in supervision. This distinction helps to guide the direction of the supervisory session. She begins by focusing on the skills and knowledge issue first. If the issue still exists, Hesser then explores to see if there are personal issues that need to be addressed.

The amount of experience of the trainee may determine what aspects of the session may be focused on. Is the focus to be insight-oriented or to provide a practical account of what took place in the session? Will techniques need to be focused on? The supervisor needs to take into account the length of the supervisor–trainee relationship and the capacity of the trainee for insight and self-exploration. The focus of the supervision will change as the trainee gains experience.

The timing of these new discoveries for the trainee is important, in that insights can create self-consciousness, which can trigger inhibition. It is important in the supervisory relationship to set a tone of acceptance and help trainees to embrace previously unknown parts of themselves so that they do not come to fear the unknown. They must trust in their unconscious, as this is where intuition begins and triggers musical action. Carl Rogers (1995) has pointed out that only after people accept themselves can they make changes and grow.

Supervision is a developmental process. Susan Feiner (see chapter 10) has described various stages through which the trainee goes during the training process. Moving from a dependent position, trainees learn to be independent, forming their own identity as therapists. There may be a stage when it is important for trainees to disagree, to develop their own way of thinking and working. At a certain point in trainees' development, there can often be a need for challenge, and it can be expected that crisis situations will develop that require resolution in ways that cannot be anticipated. At such a time, the supervisor may need to become more directly interventional in guiding trainees.

Finally, trainees must separate from their supervisor, feeling they can do the work on their own. They have taken in the ideas they believe and discarded the ones they feel are not right for them. This is an important and natural step for trainees. As part of the separation process, they begin to integrate and take away what they have learned from the experience. At the end of the supervisory process, the supervisor and the trainee are on a more equal level, relating more as peers.

The Supervision Process

A supervisor's role is multifaceted. They can function as a coach, enthusiastically supporting trainees' gains; a counselor, sorting out the trainees' feelings that may be impeding their development; a role model, acting in a way they would like the trainee to act; or a teacher, imparting practical techniques. Yet, supervision is different from all of these. At some point, coaching must lessen and the confidence the supervisor has tried to instill must be internalized in the trainee. Supervision is not therapy, and personal issues may need to be explored further in that context. As the relationship changes, the trainee develops the ability to relate to the supervisor as more of a peer than a role model. The process is different from teaching in that it is important to ask trainees what *they* think or feel about the session rather than to just tell them ideas or impart values.

Supervision can arouse feelings of vulnerability in the trainee. It is an experience that the supervisor must treat with sensitivity. The trainee has their own feelings and reactions to the process. It is important for the supervisor to try to understand the trainee's style, perspective, and approach, which helps the trainee to develop his/her own theoretical understanding of their work. The supervisor can build on a trainee's individual potential in the same way that the trainee does with his or her clients.

When listening to trainees, the focus is not on advice-giving but instead on trying to understand what they need in order to take the next step as aspiring therapists. Is there a particular reason why trainees bring certain sessions to supervision? How can their developing beliefs in themselves be cultivated and nurtured? How can the supervisor help them to trust their intuition, their own creativity? As supervisors, we try to understand the essential themes presented through the trainee's choice of *what* to present in the session and *how* they describe it.

In body language, facial expressions, and responsive comments, the supervisor can convey acceptance and an authentic belief in the trainee, as well as respect for their willingness to share and be open. It is crucial that the supervisor have patience and the faith that with time this trainee can be an effective music therapist. Ultimately, the supervisor conveys a genuine caring about the trainee as a person and the conviction that by allowing who they truly are to blossom, they will develop as clinicians.

As we begin to listen to tapes of the trainee's work, we seek to find not what is *wrong* but instead what is *right* in the work, striving to build on that strength or ability. Usually the objective of the supervisor's first comment is to point out and acknowledge a particularly effective intervention. This gesture creates the atmosphere for the ensuing supervision session and can determine the tone of the meeting. However, this kind of praise must be genuine, as a trainee can sense when the supervisor is giving false praise. After the trainee has begun to internalize a positive self-image, the supervisor can build on this by asking what could have been done further. Instead of pointing out what is lacking in a session, ask what can be added to something that is already present.

It can be important for supervisors to become aware of their own personal motivations and attitudes and how they affect the supervisory process. When a supervisor is not conscious of these attitudes or prejudices, it can be detrimental to the supervisory relationship and process. Supervisors sometimes make the mistake of looking for problems in the trainee's work in order to feel that they (the supervisor) are smart, are experts, and have all the answers. To feel superior to the trainee might be a way for supervisors to feel good about themselves and their own clinical work. A supervisor must be aware of the possibility, even if very subtle, of personal motivations to point out mistakes in the trainee's work in order to feel competent. This can create a competitive atmosphere or co-dependence in the supervisory relationship.

The trainee may possess personal characteristics and dynamics that make supervision more difficult for the supervisor. It is important for the supervisor to explore their personal feelings toward the trainee. Does the trainee possess certain qualities that remind the supervisor of themselves, and what kind of response do these similarities arouse in the supervisor? For example, the supervisor may find that they are unusually harsh when a trainee does not leave enough space for the client. With some personal reflection, they realize that this is a personal issue that they themselves had to work on in the past in order to correct this tendency. So, when confronted with a trainee who is struggling with the same issue, the supervisor may have less patience and respond in an insensitive manner. Once the supervisor becomes aware of this dynamic, the supervision can progress in a healthier and more effective way.

Sometimes, events in the supervision session can reveal previously hidden dynamics that are simultaneously occurring in the therapy session. For example, the supervisor may notice that the trainee talks endlessly in the supervision session and the supervisor begins to feel there is not enough space for them to respond. It could be that the trainee's client may be experiencing the same feeling—that there is not enough space for them. In order to help trainees with this problem, it may be important to have them reflect on how they are feeling in the supervisory session. They may feel anxious, which causes them to talk without reflecting or pausing. This same feeling of anxiety may be present in trainees in both supervision and the therapy session. By addressing the issue in supervision and helping to alleviate the anxiety, the supervisor can help them feel less anxious and be more sensitive to leaving space for their client.

One of the most difficult challenges for supervisors is to refrain from immediately reacting when they see the trainee do something that needs to be changed. It is important to not give advice in an impulsive fashion, but to reflect and consider how to most effectively communicate so that the trainee is able to hear what the supervisor is saying. Instead of telling the trainee *what* to do, the supervisor can encourage the trainee to share their own ideas first, and suggest possibilities by asking, "What if you tried ….?" It is possible to encourage the trainee to reflect more deeply on the client by asking guiding questions, such as "What prevents the client from joining in life in a way that is fulfilling? What limitations does the client experience due to the disability? How can you address this in music? What can playing together do for this client?" However, there *are* times in supervision when a supervisor needs to give suggestions or teach a concept. So, when a trainee does something that needs to be changed, it is helpful for the supervisor to view it as a positive opportunity to teach something new and develop alternative approaches.

It is important to learn the way the trainee thinks. Can the trainee explain *why* they are doing/playing what they are doing/playing? Sometimes trainees can focus on the details of a session and lose sight of the big picture. When this happens, the supervisor can ask broad questions aimed to help the trainee reflect on the larger meaning of therapy. For instance, a supervisor might ask, "Why work in a group? What are the benefits of working in a group situation for the clients? Why use music? What are the qualities of musicing with another person that are important for this client? How can you make the musical interaction meaningful? How can you connect the outer activity of music-making to the inner experience of thought and feeling for the client?"

The supervisor can start the supervision by asking trainees what it is they want from supervision. It is helpful to ask them to articulate what they would like the supervisor to focus on and to identify aspects of the session on which they are particularly interested in getting feedback. The supervisor considers how they can raise their awareness. Another approach is to ask about trainees' relationships with the clients. Is there anyone they feel particularly close to or someone with whom they feel a special connection? The supervisor can learn about the trainee through their relationships with various clients. This also helps the trainee to reflect on the qualities of his/her client and what the client needs.

It is helpful to ask trainees what they thought was positive about their session. One task of the supervisor is to help trainees to think in a more accepting and less judgmental way about their work. Asking the trainee to think about it him- or herself can help the trainee more fully integrate the positive aspects of the session. Through the trainee's own process and insight, their awareness of personal strength and ability becomes more solid and they can more fully internalize the gained knowledge. Therapists who embrace the object relations approach talk about the child who internalizes "the good mother" who provides positive feedback. This is a basic developmental task. As the mother provides consistent positive feedback, the child eventually internalizes this praise and positive self-image and becomes able to provide positive feedback to him- or herself. The supervisor–trainee relationship has similar characteristics. Our aim is that the trainee eventually be able to trust in the unknown, in their abilities as a clinical improviser, and to internalize a professional, positive self-image as a music therapist.

MUSICAL SUPERVISION

In another publication (Turry, 1998), I wrote that despite new insights into a situation, a trainee may not be able to make the musical changes necessary for effective therapy to take place, as he/she may not have the skills necessary to play in a new way. More important, they have not had the opportunity to experience a new way of playing. Therefore, it is an important part of the supervisory process in the Nordoff-Robbins approach to bring musical experiences to the trainee—to actively play and teach musical ideas to move the therapy process forward for their clients.

Challenges that often arise for trainees when improvising clinically include a difficulty in developing flexibility in tempo, dynamics, and articulation; awareness of the importance of silence; remembering musical ideas and repeating them to create form; and the ability to enhance, rather than merely imitate, a client's music in order to lead to new developments. Because trainees are struggling to create form in their improvisations, their improvisations are often so complete in and of themselves that the client is not motivated to respond. Often a trainee is trying to activate a client without a clear purpose. He/she may follow every discrete action of the client, and the music thus becomes scattered and unclear. All of these struggles may be due to an underlying sense of not knowing what to do in the session. As the trainee gains experience, development is made naturally. The music becomes more individualized, more uniquely suited to the client. Clients, in the way they respond to the trainee's music, are the best teachers of these skills. Listening closely with their supervisor and playing music together can help trainees develop a wider and more flexible musical response to their clients.

Learning to Listen

Including music in supervision, either by listening or playing, can be an immediate and effective way of working with a trainee. It provides for an experience that parallels that of therapist and client and provides an opportunity for the trainee to develop sensitivity for their client. In addition to talking about the process, it is important to have the experience of relating through music and feeling the freedom to improvise. In her theories of music therapy, Pavlicevic (1997) distinguished actual experience from description: What we say about an experience is essentially different from the experience itself. Music-making in supervision encourages trainees to continue to develop their relationship to music and improvisation and to relate to another through shared music-making. It helps the trainee internalize and integrate an experience of music as a potential agent of change. Rather than having an intellectual theory about musicing, they have an intrinsic knowing of it.

Musicing affects how we think and how we feel, and how we think and feel affects how we music. Musicing is not merely a physical skill. Elliot (1995) described musicing as an act that is thoughtful, that entails acting with intention. In this sense, musicing is a psychological phenomenon: By examining musical events, we can also examine psychological events. One of the paramount tasks of the supervisor is to help the student to integrate psychological and musical understanding. Through careful listening to the session music in supervision, the supervisor guides the trainee in sharpening his/her listening skills in order to discern the more subtle aspects of musical interactions. These dynamics can subsequently be explored by playing in supervision. It can help trainees to discover how they feel about the client and how these feelings are affecting the specific ways in which they are responding to the client musically. Focusing on the trainee's musical response to the client may give the trainee insight into the client. Is the client evoking a musical response from the trainee that reveals something of the client's inner makeup? While these kinds of psychological issues are appreciated, the primary focus is how these dynamics manifest in the music and how music can be utilized to help the client and the relationship between client and trainee move forward.

The ambiguity inherent in the musical experience may initially arouse a natural sense of anxiety for the trainee and provoke him or her to utilize psychological models and jargon in an effort to understand the process and establish a sense of inner control and mastery. The trainee understandably may be trying out how to communicate "like a therapist" by adopting psychological theories. External psychological interpretations can alleviate a trainee's anxiety by providing a context for the therapy process and concretizing specific dynamics by labeling them. However, doing this can also provide a way to avoid the ambiguity and abstract nature of musical interaction. Labeling a musical event in psychological terms may be a way to avoid examining the more fundamental, albeit threatening, components of the music therapy situation: the music, the trainee, and the client. Trying to understand events primarily in psychological terms can devalue the importance of the trainee's playing or the client's music and distract from listening to the events in the session in more *musical* terms. By labeling a musical event in psychological terminology, the trainee may inadvertently be adapting a reductionist stance about musicing, and this is antithetical to how its potentials are seen in this approach.

The supervisor can be a role model for the trainee facing this challenge by letting the discoveries emerge from the music, ensuring that psychological understanding is based on genuine musical events. The art of supervision is to assess what the trainee needs—verbal insight that triggers a more complete understanding or musical experience that creates new musical paths in the session. At times, one experience leads to the other; at others, they happen in concert. It may be important to point out to the trainee that it is not truly possible to know exactly what the experience means for a client. The supervisor helps the trainee to make attempts at understanding by describing musical events, by exploring music, and then by coming to a hypothesis about what it may mean.

Session Listening

A unique aspect of supervision in the Nordoff-Robbins approach is that the supervisor and trainee can listen closely to the session together, since every session is either audio- or videotaped. When trainees feel insecure about their music, they might talk over the recording that they are playing for the supervisor. The supervisor sets the tone that when the session is being played, all auditory focus is on the session.

During the listening sessions, Sandra Brown (personal communication, April 1999) likes to listen quietly and let the tape of the session play for a while in order to get a feeling for the session. She pays attention to who controls what is heard in the supervisory session. Is the trainee holding the controls to the recorder? Does this help them to feel in control of the session and is that important for them? Is this a reflection of the therapy session itself, a parallel process—do they fear losing control in their session?

When she hears that something significant has happened in the music, she asks her trainees why they played what they did. To further this exploration, she asks trainees to describe the music. In the beginning of the student's training, this description can often be challenging, so Brown sometimes asks what the music *isn't*. The aim of this strategy is to help the trainee begin to identify and describe the music that occurred. She asks the trainee to describe the client's music and then explores with the trainee what they were feeling in the session as well as in that particular moment. She might ask, "Where was the connection made? Where was the connection lost? What might help?"

Brown felt that questions are preferable to statements or suggestions by the supervisor. Through questions, a supervisor encourages a trainee to explore different perspectives within a given event rather than trying to find the "correct answer." Instead of telling a trainee what to do, the supervisor can help the trainee to reach their own insights or generate alternative options to a situation. In addition, the questions asked can guide the trainee to consider areas that the supervisor feels are important and bring greater awareness of what is going on in the session. This process encourages trainees to begin to trust their own perceptions and develop their own identity as therapists.

Rachel Verney (2010) also emphasized the need to develop rigorous and precise music-listening skills. Her approach to Nordoff-Robbins supervision is designed to help trainees develop musical intention and begin to formulate their own model about music and music therapy. Like Brown, Verney also asks the trainee questions—"Who can this client be in music? How can you play to facilitate that?"—and closely explores the trainee's musical responses to the client in order to determine their intention in the moment. She affirms that every note is important and helps the trainee to examine their musical responses to the client in a given moment—the musical dynamic, an energy level, or a subtle response from the client. Through these explorations, the trainee can develop a sense of how direct, reflective, supportive, or challenging the music needs to be in order to optimize a client's developmental potential.

In supervision, trainees bring a tape of a session that has already been indexed (analyzed in close detail and documented). In the supervision session, Verney assigns three tasks for the trainee:

- To summarize or characterize the session—to give a musical portrait of the client
- To identify the significant events in the session, particularly in the music
- To articulate why those events were significant

Through the trainee's answers and descriptions, Verney is able to understand more fully their perceptions of the session, how closely they listen to the music, what they hear and don't hear, and how aware they are of the musical subtleties. This process gives the supervisor a sense of the areas of further focus for the trainee.

After the above questions are answered, the tape of the session is played. In this approach, the supervisor stops the tape when the session music does not match the trainee's description. Helping trainees to become aware of the disparity between their a priori description and what they hear while listening in supervision can trigger new directions for them to take in the sessions.

However, Verney assures the trainee that it is a common and normal occurrence to hear things differently during subsequent listening sessions. The context of where and when one listens to a session affects one's perceptions. For example, the trainee can be influenced by how the supervisor listens and begins to hear the music with more objectivity and clarity than previously. On the other hand, supervisory transference issues may interfere with a trainee's ability to objectively listen to the music in the presence of the supervisor, or authority. They may become overly critical of the music and base their listening on distortions they project onto the supervisor. Or, the trainee may conclude that their initial description of what they heard in the session was based on how they felt in the session rather than on what actually occurred. This may or may not be true, and the supervisor needs to help sort this out for the trainee.

This careful kind of listening to moment-to-moment musical interactions can help the trainee develop more clarity. The trainee begins to listen more closely as the supervisor helps them to focus and notice subtle events with greater detail and understanding. This takes time and is often exhausting for a trainee. Endurance and a willingness to expand their listening awareness are required at this juncture. While it is important for the supervisor to challenge and support, it is equally important to maintain a constant belief in the potential of the trainee. It must be understood that the trainee is in the therapy room and has perceptions that cannot be accounted for on the tape.

Live Music in Supervision

As trainees begin to work, because they are unsure of where to lead the client, their music may contain the necessary warmth, comfort, and nurturance but lack vitality, direction, and drive. As they learn that music can be supportive and challenging, indirect yet leading, they begin to create music with a wider emotional and structural framework. Having the experience of this by playing music in supervision can help the trainee trust in music's qualities to both support and challenge, follow and lead.

It is important to meet each week in a room with a piano, even if there is no foreseen agenda to play. The trainee has been playing everywhere else and may feel vulnerable playing in supervision. They may need time to acclimate and develop trust in order to feel safe. Therefore, the supervisor might suggest playing without any agenda to "break the ice."

Playing music in the supervision session can be an effective way to help the trainee to achieve new insights and expressive musical capacities. The experience can help the trainee to feel more empathy for the client, gain more awareness about the client's experience during the sessions, and develop new ways of musically responding to the client. To increase a trainee's musical awareness, Brown often asks the trainee to play the opposite of what they played in the session. At other times, she plays the opposite and asks the trainee to describe the experience.

Often, a struggle with musical technique is connected to an emotional block. One trainee struggled in using the full range of the piano in order to play more dynamically powerful music for a client's drumming. Despite her awareness of and agreement with its importance, she found herself unable to spread her hands at the piano to use both the lower and upper registers. Through supervision, she had the opportunity to explore this experience. As she sat at the piano and played, she had an insight into her fear of spreading her arms apart. The supervisor accepted and acknowledged the trainee's fears as legitimate, although she did not explore the underlying reasons behind this fear, as this was supervision and not therapy. After this supervisory session, the trainee was able to play with more freedom.

Jacqueline Birnbaum (personal communication, September 2018) worked with a trainee who felt comfortable playing with soft or moderate dynamics but uncomfortable playing with greater intensity to challenge or match the energy of her clients. In supervision discussions, the trainee became aware of her tendency to avoid conflict and to "play it safe." In supervision, they played what they called "crazy music" together; Jacqueline encouraged and supported the trainee in taking risks and finding new freedom in her playing. The trainee was then able to bring this creative freedom into her session.

Musical role-playing is common in supervision and can be structured in several ways. One method is to have the trainee role-play the client and play music as the client did in the therapy session. The supervisor role-plays the trainee and plays in a musically similar way to the trainee. The trainee will often gain insight into the experience and new possibilities in creating music in the session simply by trying this exercise. As the supervisory partners continue to role-play in this configuration, the supervisor might make changes in the music to provide a different experience for the trainee. The supervisor may exaggerate a specific component of the music or play in a way that might lead to new potentials for the client. Through this modeling, the supervisor offers new possibilities for the trainee, and through role-playing, the trainee has the opportunity to experience the various options that the supervisor feels are possible.

Another configuration is for the trainee to maintain his/her role as the primary therapist and the supervisor to role-play the client. The supervisor may emphasize specific qualities of the client's music that will help the trainee gain insight into their client's playing. Or, through his or her playing, the supervisor may try to evoke potential qualities within the trainee that have previously remained dormant. For instance, when working with a trainee who plays in a perpetually timid and quiet style, the supervisor might introduce a gradual crescendo or accelerando while role-playing the client on the drum. Through the musical experience, the supervisor leads the trainee into new ways of being with the client, rather than simply talking about the issue or offering the trainee a suggestion to play more loudly.

In general, the supervisor seeks to identify areas in the trainee's playing that are fixed or rigid and tries to develop more fluid mobility in these areas. The more flexible the trainee is with their music, the more they will be able to be musically responsive and sensitive in sessions.

Another goal of using live music in supervision is to help trainees to increase awareness of their attitudes toward a client by addressing their feelings in the moment as they play in the session. Described in a previous publication (Turry, 1998) was the use of music in a supervisory session in which the trainee became aware of feelings that were keeping her from connecting more fully to her client. Through the supervisor's use of musically expressive components that were not present in the trainee's music—that is, rubato, rounded phrasing, a wider use of register—the trainee became aware of previously blocked emotions toward the client. This insight allowed the trainee to become more open and responsive to her client in subsequent sessions.

To begin this kind of exploration, the supervisor may ask the trainee to play their impression of the client or ask the trainee to play how the client makes them feel—their reaction to the client. All of these musicing situations can lead to new ideas for the trainee. Psychological considerations are made by the supervisor in order to unleash the musical power of the trainee. The goal is not necessarily for intellectual insight or emotional catharsis for the trainee, but for new musical paths that can ultimately lead to gains for the client.

One way for the trainee to understand a client's experience might be to adopt the body posture of the client, moving and playing as similarly as possible. It is helpful to ask the trainee to close their eyes to enhance the auditory experience of the moment. This helps the trainee to experience how the music may affect their client. Important questions might include, "What is the music telling me to do? How does the music influence me? What do I want the music to do? How do I feel now that it is over?"

During certification training, a supervisor may assign the trainee music to which to listen and review a case from the Nordoff-Robbins archives that has relevance for their current work. During one course of supervision, Michele Ritholz (personal communication, January 2019) found that her trainee was continually having difficulty in integrating musical feedback regarding a tendency to play "metronomically" in a rigid pulse. Ritholz sensed that only through a musical experience would the supervisee gain greater awareness of this tendency and thus become able to create more expressive opportunities for his client. During one supervision session, she spontaneously brought in a composition that might provide an opportunity for him to play more freely. Ritholz asked him to first listen as she played the piece without pulse. She emphasized the use of *rubato,* leaving space between melodic phrases to help him feel and process the experience of "breath" in music. The quality of this piece—its character and expressive nature—touched him. The experience enabled him to play the piece and, eventually, the music he created with his clients, in a different and more effective way.

Developing Musical Resources

Trainees often have a difficult time in breaking out of their familiar musical styles and habits. Rachel Verney (2010) developed an exercise in order to develop the ability to improvise in a variety of aesthetic forms. The first four measures of a composition are given to trainees. They sight-read it in order to get a sense of the style. In addition, they are asked to identify its qualities: the melodic sequence, articulation, harmonic style, and so forth. Verney then asks trainees to continue to play, improvising in the style of the piece. This exercise is done with a variety of composers and styles over time and helps to expand the trainee's musical resources. They begin to develop the ability to improvise in a wider variety of musical forms.

Church modes, a variety of scales and idioms, are introduced to the trainee as a springboard for improvisation. I have created an exercise that helps the trainee become more fluent in a variety of tonal structures. Using one tone as a tonal home base, the trainee moves through various structures—from Chinese pentatonic to Japanese pentatonic to Middle Eastern, and so on—by making an adjustment of one tone: either adding one or altering one. This helps the trainee understand the qualities of each tonal structure, contrast them, and transition from one to the other.

It is important to help the trainee understand what makes each particular scale or mode unique. Particularly with modes, there is a tendency to play them without bringing out the tones that help to identify them. Pointing out the unique tones in comparison to a major or minor scale can be helpful. This kind of exercise can help the trainee to develop fluidity and direction in their improvisations.

It can be difficult for beginning trainees to play in a wide range of tempos, and they often play with a fixed tempo and pulse. This can be due to a feeling of anxiety and an urgency to create something, stemming from a need for some sense of security. Trainees also demonstrate limited dynamic flexibility and are concerned more with the specific notes they are playing rather than *how* they are playing. The supervisor can try to address this through musicing with the trainee, perhaps leading with a melodic instrument and playing with variety. If the issue continues to challenge the trainee, it may be an indication of an emotional block, and insight into the issue may help the trainee to change his/her playing. One trainee was able to play with a significantly wider tempo flexibility after realizing she was playing in a fast tempo in order to "run away from being judged."

The trainee may not be aware of all of the adjustments that can be made to their music. They may not have control over how they play. Verney devised an exercise in which the trainee improvises a simple phrase and is directed to repeat it, attempting to play it exactly the same way each time. The trainee is then asked to change one aspect of the music—articulation shift from legato to staccato, for example—while keeping everything else exactly the same. This exercise encourages the differentiation of musical elements and a more focused awareness on the part of the trainee. In general, it has been observed that trainees tend to play softer when getting slower and louder when playing faster. This kind of exercise can help to create mobility and differentiation.

Developing a sensitivity to tones, intervals, chord voicings, and inversions and an awareness of the natural directions that melodies take and the creative leaps that are possible are important areas to develop in the trainee. Studying the natural directions that tones take, including intervallically to create melodies, and how chords connect to create progressions can help the student to hear in "chunks"—to hear the potential of an entire musical phrase from one musical action. This is an important skill in developing direction and form while improvising. Paul Nordoff's lectures on the power of tones as dynamic forces, published in *Healing Heritage* (1998), are a vital resource on which to base understandings in this area. The idea is not to memorize, but to be able to hear internally where tones can move—to think musically. By practicing progressions, inversions, various voicings, and scale structures, the fingers begin to acquire a kind of memory. Often the hand moves to a tonal direction before the mind is conscious of where it is going.

Hearing the music of the client as a question or posing a question in their own music by creating an ascending melody or an unresolved harmony can be a way of approaching the musical interaction that helps the trainee to extend and enhance the client's music. Rather than play musical ideas that are complete in and of themselves, the music is mutual and builds upon each person's contributions.

In order to help trainees remember their improvisations, melodies that span a small range and fit within the span of the hand are suggested. This simplifies and limits the choices that can be daunting to a beginner. The small movement helps the player to retain what was played.

Creating intentional silences in the service of the musical relationship can be a challenge for the trainee. In some ways, this is more challenging for the trainee, as they feel responsible for the session and feel compelled to *do* something. The supervisor can help the trainee to live in silence and appreciate the value in it. Silences are active, and there are different types of silences. The quality of the silence will be influenced by what precedes it. Through silence, the therapist can communicate that the client's music is most important.

From a technical perspective, the trainee's ability to generate a variety of musical moods can be expanded in a variety of ways. After an exploration in a mode, ask the trainee to play in an opposing way. Suggesting shapes (e.g., angular) or landscapes (e.g., a desert) can also be a source of inspiration for the trainee when creating a type of musical mood. Suzanne Nowikas (personal communication, September 1998) asked trainees to choose a card that has an emotion written on it. The other trainees do not know what the card says, and the trainee at the piano tries to play in a way that portrays the emotion. The group subsequently discusses the music and identifies what worked in the improvisation and what could have been different. This exercise helps trainees to develop musical ideas as well as to expand their appreciation of how different the experience can be for each person.

Kana Okazaki (personal communication, September 1999) asks trainees to try to create imagery while listening to improvisations. After sharing the image with the group, the trainees together try to identify the specific qualities in the music that helped to create the imagery. This exercise helps to expand awareness to the musical elements and their role in evoking imagery and an emotional response. Sharing these ideas builds trust among the trainees.

In cultures that cultivate learning to play an instrument by improvising, improvisation is taught by the teacher playing phrases in turn with the student, bringing out the character of the music rather than looking at written notation. Reading notation is seen as a potential impediment to progress toward creative expression and aesthetic musicality. Written notation is used in the training as a starting point rather than an end product. Intrinsic learning of the essential qualities of the music is what is valued.

SUPERVISION AS PART OF THE OVERALL TRAINING PROCESS

At this point, the reader will recognize that there are many practical capacities and skills that a supervisor helps the Nordoff-Robbins trainee to cultivate. The supervision takes place within the overall Nordoff-Robbins training. Over the years, much discussion has taken place among Nordoff-Robbins researchers and educators on concretizing a list of competencies. The first published edition of the competencies was included in the first edition of this book. What follows below is a greatly expanded version, entitled *Guiding Principles of Competencies, Working Practices, and Attitudes*. The process of developing them was overseen by the directors of Nordoff-Robbins International under the leadership of Mercédès Pavlicevic in 2016.

Nordoff-Robbins Music Therapy Competencies

Prerequisites to Nordoff-Robbins Training and Practice
1. General Musicianship and Resources
These capacities and skills may or may not pre-exist in qualified music therapists who are seeking to specialize in Nordoff-Robbins music therapy. They may form a part of selection criteria for full NR training.

- Ability to play and sing flexibly and responsively
- Ability to improvise in a wide range of idioms, modes, and styles to capture their essential character and to use them appropriately in clinical applications
- Ability to create a wide variety of moods through improvisation
- Ability to improvise with expressive musicianship—this includes:
  - tempo freedom
  - a variety of articulations/touch
  - varied and mobile dynamics
  - freedom in using the range of the keyboard or guitar fretboard (or other harmonic instruments); playing a variety of registers, hands close together or separated
- Awareness of and sensitivity to tones, intervals, modes, scales, chord voicing, and piano sonorities
- A variety of rhythms and meters
- Awareness of phrasing
- Harmonic variety—simplicity as well as complexity
- Playing with pulse and without pulse
- Utilizing consonance and dissonance, tonality and atonality
- Utilizing a wide range of accompaniment patterns
- Creating and shaping tensions and resolutions
- Playing with compositional awareness and intention
- Ability to arrange pre-existing compositions in a variety of styles (classical, popular, folk) for use in music therapy

Core Nordoff-Robbins Competencies
1. Nordoff-Robbins Specialist Musicianship
Trainees will need to demonstrate the following:

- Ability to listen while playing
- Ability to listen (to self and other), *Poised to listen musically*
- Ability to listen (to self and other) with attention to detail
- Ability to hear all the client's sounds and movements and gestures as music
- Ability to work spontaneously in the immediacy of the present moment—the *Creative Now*
- Ability to co-create with the client
  - To create musical energy and momentum without abandoning the moment to moment focus on the client's process
- Ability to improvise with intentional communicative and relationship focus, leading client into new musical experiences
  - To make the client's responses vital to the ongoing musical process
  - To improvise music that calls out for response from client

- Ability to integrate the client's musical knowledge, interest, and skills in the musical relationship
  - To identify and work with the *developmental threshold* of the client (especially children)
  - To evoke with music
  - To support, enhance, lead, and follow with music
    Ability to sustain the following qualities of musical interaction:
  - To adjust the music accordingly, particularly in tempo and dynamics
  - To be responsive to the client musically
  - To improvise with mutuality: making the client's contribution to the mutually created music a necessary part of it
  - To form the improvisation with the client aesthetically
  - To utilize silences with intent
  - To know when to be direct or indirect musically
  - To know what to play, when to play, and how to play
  - To facilitate new and different musical actions and experiences for the client
  - To intervene musically, on the understanding that to lead, guide, and support client toward musical change, effects personal change in the client
  - To recognize and utilize important musical events
  - To identify and potentiate *clinical themes*—musical/clinical goals—to be worked on from week to week
  - To utilize supervision, indexing, and musical analysis and integrate these into ongoing clinical work
- Ability to compose songs and instrumental compositions in a variety of styles (spontaneously in sessions and/or specifically for use in therapy) that reflect NR. techniques and resources (such as harmonizations, lyric-melodic constructions, chord voicings)

2. Nordoff-Robbins Group Work–Specific Competencies
Trainees will need to demonstrate the following:

- Effective group leadership of precomposed musical materials
- Guiding group instrumental vocal improvisations
- Guiding the development of spontaneous musical structures (songs, motifs, song forms) that relate to in-the-moment concerns of group members and ongoing group process
- Where appropriate and professionally/locally (and economically) possible and relevant:
  - Demonstrate group leading skills as a co-therapist in the following areas:
    - Group leadership of precomposed musical materials
    - Guiding group instrumental/vocal improvisations
    - Guiding the development of spontaneous musical structures (songs, motifs, song forms) that relate to in-the-moment concerns of group members and ongoing group processes
- Where locally appropriate and relevant, demonstrate the ability to facilitate performances, stage musical events, run choirs, etc., in addition to music therapy groups

3. Nordoff-Robbins Planning, Treatment/Practice, Evaluation, Communication
In addition to NR direct work with clients, these competencies include NR-informed planning of work, evaluating, demonstrating NR work directly, and communicating this to colleagues and other audiences:

- To use Nordoff-Robbins knowledge and skills and apply core concepts with a range of clients (age, pathology, ability, well-being) in a range of session formats (individual and group), as follows:
  - To assess the music therapeutic needs and potentials of an individual client/group/communal situation, using verbal and musical means as appropriate to the situation (taking into account psychological, social, cultural, economic, and other factors when doing so)
  - To develop appropriate NR therapeutic strategies (with appropriate time-scales) to address these
  - To demonstrate core reflective music-therapeutic Nordoff-Robbins practice, as described in Core Competencies 2 and 3
  - To articulate core reflective music therapeutic Nordoff-Robbins practice, as described in Core Competencies 2 and 3
  - To link NR core concepts, theory, philosophy, and evaluation scales (where appropriate) in reporting and discussing aspects of the clients' musical and emotional responses and experiences to caregivers, colleagues, and other audiences.

Nordoff-Robbins Working Practices and Professional Attitudes
1. Professional Attitude and Behaviors

- Nordoff-Robbins music therapists demonstrate confidence in, and understanding of, their Nordoff-Robbins professional identity within the work setting and its multidisciplinary and professional teams
- Nordoff-Robbins music therapists demonstrate values and attitudes commensurate with their national, regional, and statutory registration and certification boards and with the relevant professional associations through professional conduct in professional roles, through ethical and safe practices, and through proactive maintenance of personal health and well-being
- Nordoff-Robbins music therapists demonstrate awareness that NR is complementary to, but not subsumed by, other professional models (medical, psychological, psychosocial, educational, etc.)
- Nordoff-Robbins music therapists demonstrate their valuing of co-operation and the exchange of skills and perspectives with members of other professions working within work settings and communities
- Nordoff-Robbins music therapists undertake ongoing improvement and development of musical skills, knowledge, and understanding as part of their personal and professional development

2. Sociocultural-Responsive Engagements

- Nordoff-Robbins music therapists demonstrate a commitment to making NR accessible to all and to practicing in a nondiscriminatory manner that promotes inclusion
- Nordoff-Robbins music therapists demonstrate a professional availability to the setting as a whole, making NR music therapeutic skills available in whatever ways are most responsive to need, while building maximally on the available social-musical resources
- Nordoff-Robbins music therapists demonstrate awareness of the particular contribution that NR can make within a particular setting and community

- Nordoff-Robbins music therapists demonstrate competence in linking Nordoff-Robbins and clients' everyday social musicianship as appropriate to the client's needs and resources, and practice contexts, including:
  - relating Nordoff-Robbins therapeutic process to clients' everyday contexts and resources
  - reflecting on local musical culture and contexts in which Nordoff-Robbins happens
  - making available opportunities for shared musical pathways beyond Nordoff-Robbins, including performances where possible/necessary

Because Nordoff-Robbins certification in the United States is an advanced training in music therapy, the candidate already understands the basic concepts of being a therapist. They already have the ability to talk about therapy processes; now there needs to be a willingness to live in the musical moment without the distancing provided by theorizing. There are a variety of components to the training program to address these needs. Classes are given that contain new information and practical workshop experience about music. Lectures are offered that give the trainee an opportunity to closely analyze archival work that illustrates the effectiveness of clinical improvisation. Improvisation classes that work on developing resources, enhancing clinical awareness, and developing awareness of personal musical characteristics are offered. Methods of analysis—indexing,[31] the relationship scale,[32] and the tempo dynamic schema[33]—are learned in a group setting. The study of archival material, practical musical technique, self-awareness, and the sharing of contemporary clinical experiences are all important components of the classes in the training. Because the classes take place concurrently with clinical work, the experience of the trainee is integrated and what is discussed in classes is related to what is happening in sessions. Trainees then follow up on these teachings in individual supervision.

The Nordoff-Robbins Center for Music Therapy has a wealth of clinical videos that are archived and can be utilized in supervision. On occasion, supervisors have created instructional videos, choosing themes that they feel are challenges in general for trainees, such as the importance of silence or the ability to create musical consistency when a client's playing is fragmented. A variety of therapists' work is used to illustrate learning points. This also helps to emphasize that there are many ways of working and that each therapist will find his/her unique way of utilizing effective musical resources.

At the Nordoff-Robbins Center for Music Therapy, the supervisor has input into what client the trainee will work with, choosing clients that will help the trainee as well as the client grow. It is also important to assess who will best work together as teams. Each trainee will work as both therapist and co-therapist and work with a peer as well as a staff member. Each experience allows the trainee to try out a different role. Some trainees are ready to begin with peers; others need the guidance of a senior staff member. A potential hazard when a trainee works with a senior staff member is that they might abdicate authority in the session, accompanying the action with their music rather than taking leadership in their music. Although this is natural in the beginning of the work, it can become a problem if this reliance on the supervisor continues and is not addressed.

Trainees learn how to be co-therapists as well as primary therapists in the training. Co-therapists need to learn how interventional to be, how to facilitate the musical relationship between the primary therapist and client, and how to work with an understanding of where the primary therapist wants to take the client with their music. The co-therapist is constantly assessing "How close

---

[31] Indexing is the method of analyzing therapy sessions in the Nordoff-Robbins model. It consists of two major aspects: a brief written description of events in the sessions, which are catalogued in real time, and a transcription of the significant musical events in the session for possible use in subsequent sessions. Each session is indexed before the client's next session.

[32] In *Creative Music Therapy* (2007), Part Four: Evaluation, pp. 367–457.

[33] In *Creative Music Therapy* (2007), pp. 317–339.

do I need to be to the client? How much direction do they need? What will help the client to live in the music more deeply?" The experience of being a co-therapist contributes to trainees' developing abilities as primary therapists, as insights gained while being close to clients and listening to music can be internalized and utilized when they are playing in a session.

The supervision of teams is relevant in this approach. It is important for the supervisor to look at the team dynamics and give feedback that does not split the team. At times, it may be necessary to meet with the team together. Nowikas (1994) studied the dynamics of working as a team, and this study is presented to the trainees during the training. This can help to bring awareness of team dynamics and lead to a more supportive and understanding team. This in turn leads to more creative freedom on the part of the trainee.

During the training, trainees are placed together and share their work in a class designed to give trainees feedback on their work. In this situation, two trainees can work together by playing under the supervisor's guidance. While they role-play the client–therapist situation, the supervisor can conduct the pianist, helping them to adjust their music in "Now time."[34]

Indexing is a way to develop perception of what is important in the sessions and to define subsequent directions in the therapy. In this way, the trainee learns how to identify and work with the client's unique musical responses while asking important questions. Is establishing a basic beat important? What is the next musical development that this client may be able to make? Can the client beat the melodic rhythm? Can they hear the punctuation inherent in the phrase? Are they drawn into playing music in the tempo and on the beat? Are they responding to tempo or dynamic changes? What is the quality of the client's playing? Are they moving in a physically free way? Would a different instrument, mallet, or position of the instrument enhance the experience? Would a stick rather than a mallet help for rhythmic clarity? What would happen if the music were composed of a clear melodic idea in octaves rather than a continuous harmonic support? Did the client respond to the change from legato to staccato? Why is it important for the client to be active? Is it more relevant to work on musical mood and match the emotional quality of the client? What motivated the client to play? What triggered the vocalizations? How would one describe the sound being created? Since these are all areas that every trainee needs to understand, they can be discussed as a group. The trainee can choose to share a particular session, handing out their index notes to the group. As part of the indexing process, manuscript paper is used to write down important musical ideas that are brought back in subsequent sessions. As team members, one trainee can write the index, describing the events and qualities of the client's responses and noting their significance, while the other can summarize more broadly what is happening in therapy specifically and the therapy process in general. As the session is played, the supervisor may suggest what can be included in the index and what can be excluded.

In these group learning situations, various group dynamics are activated and at times will need to be addressed in supervision. Issues of belonging, comparison, and competition can be aroused. It is important that the supervisor be alert to these dynamics and allow for the trainee to discuss them in supervision. There is a distinct group process that exists, which includes stages of growth as a group as well as individual growth. It is important to remind trainees that each person learns at his/her own pace and that each therapist will play something differently; there is not one right musical intervention. Each trainee has the opportunity to learn from the others. As the trainees realize that there is room for all of them, that each one is unique and valued, they can begin to trust each other and share in an honest fashion. This sharing builds deeper levels of trust and can enhance the learning process for everyone involved. When anxiety is high, which is often the case in the beginning of the training, feelings of competition surface. By the end of the training, an understanding of how hard each person has worked in their own individual fashion allows for support, camaraderie,

---

[34] From "A Time Paradigm: Time as a Multilevel Phenomenon in Music Therapy" by Robbins and Forinash (1991). Now time, also called Creative time, is "the moment of intuition, of perception, of sudden insight or understanding. It takes place in the creative instant" (p. 53).

and recognition. It is important for supervisors at our Center to communicate to each other about the group process and discuss how to facilitate healthy development for the group as a whole. The more that trainees feel that their true selves can be revealed and integrated into their identity as therapists, the more successful the training will be for them.

Working with their supervisor can stimulate feelings in trainees of being judged, fear of making mistakes, and the need to be perfect. These are all natural reactions that need to be discussed in supervision. One way to counter the supervisor being experienced in this way is to have the trainee work with the supervisor as co-therapist. All of the supervisors at the Center are active clinicians. The trainee is able to see the supervisor with the same challenges that they have. The supervisor, rather than holding on to an authority position, is in a vulnerable position similar to that of the trainee. After allowing trainees to have their initial phase of idealizing the supervisor and the situation, the supervisor can share their own struggles, difficulties, and uncertainties when it is appropriate. This encourages the trainee to assume a more genuine and realistic attitude toward the supervisor.

Nordoff-Robbins Training: Supervising International Students, Utilizing World Music for Improvisation, and Cultivating Cultural Reflexivity

Because the Nordoff-Robbins approach is recognized and practiced throughout the world, many trainees come to the Center from diverse locations such as South Korea, Japan, China, Hong Kong, Malaysia, Switzerland, Argentina, Brazil, Singapore, Italy, Colombia, and Chile. The diverse cultural backgrounds of international trainees create an opportunity for supervisor and supervisee to work together to define basic concepts such as: *What is music? What is therapy? How do people develop and grow? How can music-making help our clients to develop?* The supervisor is open to discovering their own assumptions based on personal culture and to reflect and adjust perspectives in collaboration with the supervisee. These issues are relevant not just for international students, but also for students from the United States who come from a different part of the country to train. East Coast, West Coast, Midwest, urban, rural—the United States is a large and diverse country with many different cultures.

Different learning styles, based on one's cultural background, challenge the supervisor to find sensitive and effective ways to cultivate the ability to improvise music with clinical intention. Creating music outside of the student's cultural experience can be quite liberating for the student. It can also be intimidating. Cultural expectations regarding how much to fit in, to not stand out, can impact a student's ability to develop improvisation skills. Some students flourish with direct instruction and modeling from the supervisor; others prefer to introduce their own ideas privately and can ask for guidance when they decide what is needed. No assumptions as to what works best can be made based on someone's nationality. Like the therapy sessions themselves, each supervisee is unique. Some are attracted to the training because they sense the process will help them develop an individual sense of themselves in another cultural context outside of their home country. For some, improvising music with assertion, particularly when utilizing voice, goes against cultural norms. For others, being active receptively but not actively playing or singing can be difficult. These tendencies may or may not have to do with one's culture.

Embedded in much of the foundational texts utilized in the training is a perspective from the privileged position of the Western musical tradition. Like many classically trained composers, Paul Nordoff was fascinated with music from Eastern traditions. He placed great emphasis on the historical development of music and studied music from a variety of cultures. Tonal scales in his training for students to learn to improvise developed, from his perspective, from what he deemed then as "exotic, far-off locales."[35] Many of the terms he used to describe the music would be seen today as being

---

[35] This phrase is from his writing in the 1960s.

insensitive. Calling a scale Chinese or Middle Eastern and ascribing particular qualities to them without fully understanding the cultural context can be a type of appropriation. It can lead to creating a sense of other and a hierarchy of superior/inferior, more developed/less developed. Despite Nordoff's respectful and serious academic study of World Music, his musical explorations manifest through his classically trained pianism.

Nordoff did truly value World Music and did much to introduce a rich diversity of musical styles, forms, and idioms for music therapists to utilize. In order to truly embrace his idea that music from all cultures has the same potential to be meaningful in a clinical context, current training at the Center includes lectures on music given by those who have lived in the culture of the music. We have had Argentinian musicians teach tango, an expert on Indian music teach ragas using traditional instruments, a trainee from Malaysia with great familiarity with gamelan do a workshop, and a Jordanian music therapy student teach scales on a stringed instrument from his native country, helping to cultivate an understanding of quarter tones. All of these experiences have helped to broaden and widen the trainees' relationship to music and to improvise with more flexibility and awareness, while becoming more sensitive to and respecting music from unfamiliar cultures.

Many current Nordoff-Robbins researchers and educators make a concerted effort when working with trainees to be sensitive to how Nordoff-Robbins resources are taught (Low, personal communication, 2018). The growing cultural reflexivity has helped to encourage international students to value their own music and prepare to utilize music from their own countries when they return home. Ultimately, the universal skill being nurtured in the Nordoff-Robbins trainee is the cultivation of listening and responsive engagement while improvising. These qualities are inherent in clinical musicians wherever their country of origin may be.

Nordoff-Robbins Training As A Spiritual Discipline

Although trainees usually complete their certification process within two years, the continued development of the competencies is a lifelong process. The training is a discipline that demands commitment and focus. Through supervising, supervisors continue to work on these competencies within themselves. The devotion to mastering a discipline such as creative music therapy is, if looked at in the context of spiritual practices, a type of yoga that leads to raised consciousness and an expanded capacity to love, just as do meditation and prayer.

Traditionally, supervision has been based on developmental or psychological concepts. These are important in the cultivation of clinical awareness, creativity, and musicality. The act of being a music therapist brings artistic discipline and sensitivity to the forefront. As supervisors, we are helping trainees to become *arts* therapists, to utilize their art to transform. Artists in the heat of creation produce a state of absorption similar to the mystic rapture described in both Hindu and Buddhist literature. Murphy (1993) states that spiritual practices depend upon a certain amount of trial-and-error, the love of adventure, and improvisation. Kornfield (1993) mentions the importance of "risking the unknown" in order to "gain a sense of life itself" (p. 52). These are all qualities that are cultivated in the training. Aigen (1998) suggested that training include some kind of personal process aimed to expand awareness, including personal therapy or a spiritual practice. It is my contention that the demands inherent in the Nordoff-Robbins training—the expansion of awareness, the application of the will, the focus on creativity, the challenge to live freely in the moment, and the development of a loving attitude—inevitably introduce the trainee to the elements inherent in a spiritual practice.

In trying to cultivate genuine human concern for the client within the trainee, the supervisor is really helping the trainee develop a certain quality of perception. This perception, which nourishes the attitude of the trainee, is one of love—not in the romantic sense of the word, but as an active thinking and doing. In his teachings, Robbins often quoted Herbert Geuter,[36] stating that "love is not just a warm happy feeling, love is perception." This is a way of saying that how we perceive an event or a person is colored by our present underlying attitudes. Practicing love as perception means trying to understand the client, gain insight into the client's needs, and develop a sense of the client's potentials. The trainee may not experience love as the familiar feeling of fondness and protectiveness. In fact, the client can teach the trainee to give up the need to express love in that way. We are trying to teach unconditional love, a love that may be challenging. The trainee may experience this as unsettling, yet it sets the tone for new developments. It is a love that is not possessive or dependent. As aspiring professionals, trainees try not to invest in their clients in order to feel better about themselves, yet it may be from this that they need to start. As they gain clinical maturity, their capacity to love becomes more perceptive and more resourceful. In reality, they are following a path of spiritual learning.

Also to be considered is the unique nature of music itself. This approach recognizes the transpersonal powers of musicing. It considers the living dynamics of musical archetypes. Utilizing the aesthetic energies of musical creation is at the heart of the trainee's task. Musical peak experiences cannot be explained solely by psychoanalytic interpretations such as regression in the service of the ego. They are more than behavioral rewards or stimuli; they are holistic, integrative, often transcending issues of personality.

In this way, then, the commitment to the supervisory process by the trainee and the supervisor can be recognized as a contemporary form of spiritual training. Robbins himself called creative music therapy a transpersonal discipline (1991). This challenges us to see the integration of applied spirituality into the professional practice as a natural consequence of inherently creative work. It requires that we ground our research in the study and comprehensive documentation of clinical phenomena and process.

CONCLUSION

Supervision in the Nordoff-Robbins training program is multifaceted. Its foundations lie in the philosophy inherent in the approach, which includes the cultivation of musical creativity and awareness, personal growth, and technical understanding. The supervisory relationship contains the same elements as the client–therapist relationship, as supervisor and trainee enter the *creative now* with a willingness to learn from each other and develop together. The supervisor has the responsibility to observe the process and discern what steps to take to enhance the trainee's development. Musical supervision is paramount in sharpening listening skills, increasing musical awareness and sensitivity, and deepening insight into the musical relationship. The supervisor helps to enhance the trainee's musical facility by developing their musical resources and helping them to become more musically responsive. The trainee gains confidence in supporting and leading the client while improvising with mutuality. The training program builds cohesion and support among the trainees; this helps them to trust their development, gain a sense of belonging, and establish a professional identity. Ideally, the trainee takes steps that enhance their personal, social, and transpersonal development.

Acknowledgments

I am most grateful to all of the trainees who have taught me how to listen, be patient, leave space in the music, sit in silence, and enjoy the process of discovering notes that I didn't expect to hear.

---

[36] Dr. Herbert Geuter was the director of research at Sunfield Children's homes, where Nordoff and Robbins began their teamwork, and was a guiding influence on their early development. Geuter was well versed in anthroposophy and was invested in updating and extending Rudolph Steiner's teaching, particularly in the areas of ego psychology and therapy practice and process.

APPENDIX 1

Nordoff-Robbins International Guiding Principles:
Competencies, Working Practices and Attitudes

The diagram below illustrates the nesting of NR International Core Competencies within three circles that may differ considerably between countries and continents. Individual and Group Working practices are embedded within Professional attitudes and behaviors that form part of a broader stance of sociocultural-responsive engagements.

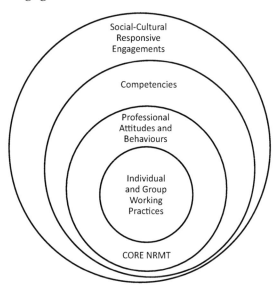

APPENDIX 2

Development of Nordoff-Robbins Competencies

Consultation Process: Phases 1 and 2
The first draft was drawn up from various sources:

- International consultation on NRMT identity, which formed part of the Vision 2020 strategic review carried out by the London HQ in 2013–4;
- Competencies document received from the NR Center for Music Therapy, NYU;
- NRMT alumni survey (of UK-trained NRMTs) completed by London HQ in April 2014;
- NR core principles as identified both in Vision 2020 and also in current Nordoff- Robbins training modules in the UK/US;
- Nordoff-Robbins literature spanning foundational and historical Nordoff-Robbins texts, first -generation and contemporary NR texts.

Phase One
The first consultation (September–November 2015) was with the music therapist directors of Nordoff-Robbins International (Dr. Ken Aigen, Pauline Etkin OBE, Dr. Mercédès Pavlicevic, Dr. Simon Procter,

Dr. Alan Turry and Michele Ritholz), all of whom have substantial experience in training NR music therapists in their home countries and in different continents. This led to a first draft.

Phase Two
The first draft was circulated to experienced and active NR music therapists, researchers, and educators in various parts of the world. They were invited to contribute and comment from their distinctive localities and musical traditions and especially asked to consider the vocabulary in this document, given local and regional diversities. This formed the second draft.

Final Phase
The current draft has been overseen once again by the music therapist directors of Nordoff Robbins International and circulated to the full board of directors of Nordoff-Robbins International.

Grateful thanks go to the NRI music therapist directors and to all Phase Two contributors: Dr. Ken Aigen (US), Dr. David Aldridge (Germany), Dr. Gary Ansdell (UK), Mary Brown (UK), Belinda Burns (Australia), Pauline Etkin, OBE (UK), Sunelle Fouche (South Africa), Janet Halton (UK), Dr. Peter Hoffmann (Germany), Dr. Colin Lee (Canada), Carol Lotter (South Africa), Dr. Lutz Neugebauer (Germany), Kana Okazaki-Sakaue (Japan), Dr. Mercédès Pavlicevic (UK), Dr. Simon Procter (UK), Michele Ritholz (US), Dr. James Robertson (UK), Dr. Suzanne Sorel (US), Dr. Alan Turry (US), and Rachel Verney (UK).

Dr. Mercédès Pavlicevic
London
March 2016

Foundational Nordoff-Robbins Texts
Nordoff, P., & Robbins, C. (1971). *Music Therapy in Special Education.* Gilsum, NH: Barcelona Publishers.

Nordoff, P., Robbins, C., & Britten, B. (1973). *Therapy in Music for Handicapped Children.* London, UK: Gollancz.

Nordoff, P., & Robbins, C. (1977). *Creative Music Therapy: Individualized Treatment for the Handicapped Child.* New York, NY: John Day Co.

Nordoff, P., & Robbins, C. (2007). *Creative Music Therapy: A Guide to Fostering Clinical Musicianship.* Gilsum, NH: Barcelona Publishers.

Robbins, C., & Robbins, C. (Eds.). (1998). *Healing Heritage: Paul Nordoff Exploring the Tonal Language of Music.* Gilsum, NH: Barcelona Publishers.

REFERENCE LIST

Aigen, K. (1998). *Paths of Development in Nordoff-Robbins Music Therapy.* Gilsum, NH: Barcelona Publishers.

Ansdell, G. (1995). *Music for Life.* London, UK: Jessica Kingsley Publishers.

Brown, S. (1997). Supervision in context: A balancing act. *British Journal of Music Therapy, 11*(1).

Elliot, D. (1995). *Music Matters.* Oxford, UK: Oxford University Press.

Kornfield, J. (1993). *A Path with Heart.* New York, NY: Bantam Books.

Low, M. Y. (2017, November 9). *Romanticism in Nordoff-Robbins Music Therapy.* Unpublished manuscript, Drexel University, Philadelphia, PA.

Murphy, M. (1993). *The Future of the Body: Explorations into the Further Evolution of Human Nature.* New York, NY: Putnam Books.

Nordoff, P., & Robbins, C. (1977). *Creative Music Therapy.* New York, NY: John Day Company.

Nordoff, P., & Robbins, C. (2007). *Creative Music Therapy: A Guide to Fostering Clinical Musicianship.* Gilsum, NH: Barcelona Publishers.

Nowikas, S. (1993). *A Qualitative Investigation of Teamwork in Nordoff-Robbins Music Therapy.* Unpublished master's thesis, New York University, New York, NY.

Pavlicevic, M. (1997). *Music Therapy in Context.* London, UK: Jessica Kingsley Publishers.

Robbins, C., & Forinash, M. (1991). A Time Paradigm: Time as a Multilevel Phenomenon in Music Therapy. *Music Therapy, 10*(1), 46–57.

Robbins, C., & Robbins, C. (1991). Self-Communications in Creative Music Therapy. In K. Bruscia (Ed.), *Case Studies in Music Therapy.* Gilsum, NH: Barcelona Publishers.

Rogers, C. (1995). *On Becoming a Person.* Boston, MA: Houghton Mifflin.

Turry, A. (1998). Transference and countertransference in Nordoff-Robbins Music Therapy. In K. Bruscia (Ed.), *The Dynamics of Music Psychotherapy.* Gilsum, NH: Barcelona Publishers.

Verney, R., & Ansdell, G. (2010). *Conversations on Nordoff-Robbins Music Therapy.* Gilsum, NH: Barcelona Publishers.

Chapter 22

FORMING AN IDENTITY AS A MUSIC PSYCHOTHERAPIST THROUGH ANALYTICAL MUSIC THERAPY SUPERVISION

Benedikte B. Scheiby[37]

HISTORY AND OVERVIEW

Analytical music therapy (AMT) is a music therapy model that incorporates an approach to supervision in which the musical and verbal processing of clinical material are essential components. AMT was developed in the 1970s over a two-year period by three pioneers in Great Britain: Mary Priestley, Peter Wright, and Marjorie Wardle. The model was developed through self-experimentation, with the term "analytical music therapy" first used by Peter Wright as a description of the work. Because Mary Priestley took the leading role in describing the model extensively in her 1975 text *Music Therapy in Action*, she is considered to be the founder of the model.

Priestley, the daughter of author J. B. Priestley, was originally a skilled performing violinist. She was educated as a music therapist in a one-year postgraduate diploma course at the Guildhall School of Music and Drama in London and granted the title LGSM, a licenseship granted by the school. Juliette Alvin, who founded the British Society for Music Therapy, directed the training. Priestley also undertook a full course of Kleinian analysis and worked for several years under psychotherapeutic supervision at Saint Bernhard's Hospital in London prior to developing AMT.

According to Priestley (1994), AMT is the "analytically-informed symbolic use of improvised music by the music therapist and client. It is used as a creative tool with which to explore the client's inner life so as to provide the way forward for growth and greater self-knowledge" (p. 3). The term "analytic" refers partly to the psychoanalytic thought behind the approach—incorporating influences such as Freud, Jung, Klein, Adler, and Lowen—and partly to the analysis of the musical and verbal content of the session undertaken jointly by therapist and client.

The approach is in use with a variety of populations, and clinical work has been documented with the following types of individuals: psychiatric patients; neurological rehabilitation clients; geriatric clients; victims of sexual, physical, or emotional abuse; clients with eating disorders and substance abuse problems; developmentally delayed individuals; and clients in forensic settings. Clients who are not able to understand or use language do not profit as much as those who can verbalize their experiences in the musical improvisations, but they can still benefit from the approach.

During her life, Priestley trained over 50 music therapists from 10 different countries in AMT. Many of these practitioners have become trainers themselves, offering courses in AMT in academic settings and as private institute training.

In order to undertake training as an analytical music therapist, one must first possess a master's degree in music therapy. The training consists of four sequential stages oriented to assisting the music therapist in learning how to integrate musical, verbal, relational, aesthetic, intellectual, emotional, psychological, and spiritual content into their music therapy being and, hence, into the

---

[37] This chapter is published posthumously. Thanks to Ken Aigen for providing final edits. I have aimed to keep Benedikte's voice as authentic as possible to honor her memory and her lifelong dedication to music therapy and to analytical music therapy as this is likely her final publication.

clinical work. The first stage comprises self-experience in individual and group music therapy sessions offered by an analytic music therapist. There is a minimum of 48 individual music therapy sessions mandated. The second stage consists of a process called "Intertherap," which comprises a minimum of 15 two-hour sessions in which a dyad of training music therapists alternates being each other's therapist and client, with the entire process taking place under the direct supervision of the AMT trainer. The third stage consists of 48 individual music-centered AMT supervision sessions where the basis is music-centered supervision on the trainee's clinical work undertaken in their job at a facility or in private practice. The fourth stage consists of one year of music-centered AMT group supervision every other week. The trainee is receiving music-centered AMT group supervision where they present their clinical work. The entire training can be completed in three-and-a-half years but may take longer for students who do not have prior experiences in music psychotherapy or psychoanalysis.

The present chapter will focus on stages two, three, and four of the training process because the first stage does not incorporate a supervisory component, as do the other dimensions. This is not to minimize the importance of the first stage, as much of the material that emerges there will be of significant value to the trainee/supervisor during the subsequent stages.

SUPERVISION IN INTER MUSIC THERAPY (IMT): STAGE TWO OF AMT TRAINING, HISTORY AND TRAINING

Mary Priestley introduced Intertherapy in the early 1970s together with her two colleagues, Marjorie Wardle and Peter Wright. The process was first called "Intertherap," then "IMT" for Inter Music Therapy, and then, currently, "intertherapy" (Priestley, 1994)—although the terms are interchangeable. It started as an experiment, the purpose of which was to identify the uses of a variety of music therapy techniques on relatively well, normal, unmedicated human beings. Mary Priestley called it a learning and research enterprise. Each member was a therapist to one and client to another member: Mary was therapist to Peter and client to Marjorie. who was client to Peter and therapist to Mary.

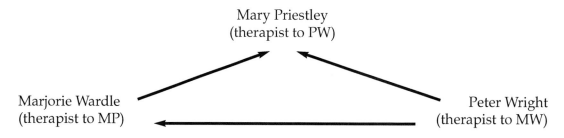

Figure 1. Relationships in Intertherap.

There was no observing supervisor, but occasionally the third member, who documented the process, upon completing the note-taking, would make a comment afterward—thus behaving in an embryonic supervisory role. These situations are well described by Priestley (1975).

Priestley decided to offer Intertherapy as a supplementary training to music therapy students when in the mid-1970s a student in the music therapy program at Guildhall School of Music and Drama, Johannes Eschen from Germany, asked if he could join the IMT (Inter Music Therapy) team. Instead of letting him join the team, Priestley asked him to find a partner and then asked both of them to take a number of individual music therapy sessions with her before she would allow them to experience IMT under her direct supervision. She wrote about the preparation for IMT: "Regarding the dialogue in the therapy, where a trainee has had no experience of longer-term analytical psychotherapy of once weekly or more, he may need anything from 20–120 AMT sessions before he feels ready to start Intertherapy" (Priestley, 1994, p. 298).

The format was such that the two students took turns being a therapist for each other, while at the same time Priestley would take notes. After the ending of the two "therapies," she would make comments to the one who had been the therapist first, then to the one who had been the therapist the second time. The duration of the whole session was two hours, divided as follows: A is a therapist for B for 30 minutes. B is a therapist for A for 30y minutes. Supervisory comments and theory last for 60 minutes, and both A and B would be present during each other's supervisory comments. The Intertherapy is videotaped so that the trainees can listen back to their session and analyze the content at home for further learning. For example, the student can study how the process of transitioning from verbal processing to musical processing and back again to verbal processing was happening, review how the student was asking nondirective questions, or time the interventions.

By 1979, students from seven different countries had completed what is now described as the first two stages of Priestley's AMT training. Some of these students have become AMT trainers and have continued this training practice in their respective countries at academic institutions where music therapy training is taking place.

After Johannes Eschen returned to Germany, he incorporated the IMT supervision with students in the music therapy program at Hochschule für Musik und Darstellende Kunst and later integrated this type of training in music therapy training in Herdecke, Germany, in 1978. The IMT supervision of this time is discussed by Priestley (1994).

This author established an academic master's music therapy program at Aalborg University in Denmark in 1980, together with Prof. Inge N. Pedersen. We integrated IMT as a part of the training program. We changed the design such that during A's supervision, B leaves the room, and during B's supervision, A leaves the room. We also began using videotapes instead of audiotapes to document the practice more in depth, with ability to study bodily behaviors, instrument use, and so forth. The specifics of how this form of supervision is integrated in a university setting are discussed in Scheiby and Pedersen (1999), where there are case examples and a description of evaluation procedures.

Since 1990, I have been developing a private postgraduate AMT training program in which IMT is an essential part of the training. A minimum of 15 IMT sessions are offered to music therapy students who have undergone AMT individual music therapy for at least one year. After the IMT training, the students undergo a whole year of individual AMT supervision sessions and a whole year with AMT group music therapy supervision. Stages three and four can be trained with the help of telehealth Internet videoconferencing tools. This is in order for the trainees not to be dependent upon location to finish the training.

The way IMT training is being conducted with the use of videotaped sessions where the students take turns being a client and a therapist under direct supervision is in use in many music therapy programs as well as counseling graduate training programs in academic settings at this point (2017). This shows the innovativeness of Mary Priestley's AMT training, which started taking form in the mid-1970s. One example is New York University's graduate master of arts program in counseling for mental health and wellness at the Steinhardt School of Culture, Education, and Human Development. Here the department of applied psychology is providing a one-year required training in counseling skills, where this type of videotaped psychotherapy training is in use.

The Format of IMT in Private Training

The AMT supervisor may help to establish the IMT team, which meets once a week or once every second week for two hours. The format is as follows: A is a therapist for B for 30 minutes. B is a therapist for A for 30 minutes. Both sessions are videotaped. A receives individual supervision for 30 minutes while B is not in the room. B receives individual supervision for 30 minutes while A is not in the room. Both supervisions are videotaped. During the session, the supervisor takes notes in a corner of the room. The final IMT session is one hour long so that the student experiences and understands the difference between the half-hour training sessions and the more typical sessions of one hour. In the beginning, the supervisor may serve as a timekeeper and if needed make verbal suggestions.

It is important to emphasize that during IMT, the trainees are not engaged in role-playing. They are not simulating issues with which they want to work. The process is authentic, and they are bringing in material from their lives. The situations described are not imagined or hypothetical. This can be viewed as a natural next step in the student's individuation process and personal growth begun during formal education and pursued in the individual and group music therapy sessions comprising the first stage of AMT training.

The importance of this type of genuine self-experience has received support in the music therapy literature: "A therapeutic training cannot consist only of an enumeration of skills and techniques. A student has to experience the process him-/herself" (Wigram, De Backer, & Van Camp, 1999, p. 289). These authors advocated that students receive music psychotherapeutic self-experiential training during their education to become music therapists. Otherwise, they would not be able to deal with and understand the phenomenon of transference and how it presents itself to the music therapist in clinical situations. They learn from experiencing the presence of their music therapist in their own personal music therapy and how to take up a neutral position musically and verbally so that the client can use him/her for transferring feelings toward central persons and relationships in his/her life. They also learn when and how to help the client to gain insight regarding the content of the transference on the basis of musical content and interactions in the sessions.

My experience has shown that many students are able to continue their personal individuation process when they enter into the position of client in IMT. However, it has sometimes initially been difficult for the student to trust that a fellow student may be experienced enough and have enough authority to conduct the music therapy.

As part of the theoretical training, the student therapist submits to the supervisor notes in which the session is described. The video recording of the session facilitates this task. The following areas must be described in the notes: session number; objective description of session process, both musically and verbally; subjective description of the process, musically, verbally, and bodily; summary of musical/verbal interventions and issues that were addressed; problem areas for the therapist; and potential goals and objectives for the next session.

After all of the sessions have been completed, the student therapist is asked to write a paper that …

- Presents an overview of the process of the whole treatment and identification of goals and objectives;
- Identifies different phases in the process;
- Presents developmental steps expressed musically and verbally;
- Identifies their strengths and weaknesses as a music therapist;
- Discusses their roles as a music therapist in this course of therapy;
- Presents an overview of the developmental process of the music therapist;
- Presents significant countertransference/transference psychodynamics that happened in the course of the 15 sessions.

The student is also asked to make an audiotape with clinical excerpts that demonstrate significant musical dialogues or solos from different phases of the process; significant changes in the client's musical/verbal presence; and examples of musical interventions, techniques, musical countertransference/transference dynamics, and the construction of playing themes.

Areas of Competency in Private IMT Training

In general, this stage of the training is the beginning of the integration of four areas of music therapy competency:

- Personal competency—the ability to be therapeutically relevant (being)
- Technical competency—the ability to act therapeutically relevant (doing)
- Artistic competency—the ability to create therapeutically relevant (creating)
- Theoretical competency—the ability to think therapeutically relevant (thinking)

In the following description, all of these categories are woven into each other, as all levels are practiced at the same time in the session. The area of theoretical competency is particularly focused upon in the supervision session described in detail below, where in addition to the working through of personal issues, theoretical papers and texts are to be read. These papers and texts relate to the topics that emerge from the music therapeutic practice of the student. The addressing of the area on personal competency has been started in the individual AMT sessions of stage one that the student has undergone before beginning the IMT sessions in stage two. When the student has undergone individual and group music therapy supervision, the material from all four content areas should have been learned and integrated. If that has not happened after finishing training, the music therapist is encouraged to receive weekly AMT supervision in order to continue growth in all areas.

Identifying and Developing a Personal Philosophy and Method

Prior to beginning the IMT stage, the trainee's identity as a music therapist is not yet formed. The student often has not settled down to a certain way of working, has not clarified a particular methodological interest, and may not be conscious of a philosophy behind the work. Here, the student can have an opportunity to develop a personalized style of working within an analytical context and can become conscious about how philosophical and ethical issues affect clinical work. This also includes becoming conscious about preferences and avoidances in musical idiom and style, cultural differences with the clients, and the consequences of these in the choice of music. A music therapy professional must have a well-grounded training in clinical improvisation and the use of composed music as well as in the field of psychotherapy, no matter what kind of clients one works with. In IMT, these two fields are integrated. Wigram, De Backer, and Van Camp (1999) support this belief. "The development of the psychotherapeutic identity is as equally important a cornerstone as the development of the musical identity. The way in which music is handled in a therapeutic setting is embedded in a specific therapeutic background" (p. 288).

The fact that a student is being trained in AMT does not mean that they will always be practicing as an AMT music therapist, and it does not mean exclusion of other forms of music therapy. Personally, I received training in the Nordoff-Robbins method as a part of the education curriculum in my training in Germany (Herdecke), and I have incorporated the skills that I was taught in clinical improvisation in my current practice. The AMT training will provide the student with a solid music psychotherapeutic foundation and consciousness, on top of which the student can add musical and therapeutic knowledge. In this setting, one also can test the theoretical framework that one has learned from reading material on music therapy. The trainee learns whether it is possible to transfer to clinical reality particular ideas and practices from the music therapy literature.

In an informal survey of professional music therapists conducted by music therapist Prof. Inge N. Pedersen and the present author regarding how the IMT component of the AMT training had affected their present practice, one person wrote the following:

> When I, as a finished educated music therapist, was entering the real therapy world, I was fumbling for finding an answer to the question: Who am I as a music therapist? Exactly in this development the IMT training has given me the best tools to get closer to my identity as a music therapist. In IMT, there is peace and time to test oneself as a therapist, testing different methods and techniques—and not the least realizing that what one believed to be true in theory did not apply to one's practice, because one's client suddenly was a different place … and what do I do now? [author's translation from Danish]

Permission to Make Mistakes and Experiment

It is important to offer a place for the student to make mistakes without being nervous about harming the client. As a supervisor with over 37 years of experience, I have learned that one will mostly learn from one's mistakes. The fear of making mistakes is a well-known phenomenon among music therapists (performance anxiety) because their working medium is music and because one traditionally has learned to avoid making mistakes in the music in order for the product to sound good. Through supervision, the student will be encouraged not to cover up if they make a mistake and sometimes to admit to the client that they indeed did make a mistake. Nobody is perfect, not even a music therapist, and many clients who may feel like one big mistake themselves may feel a sense of relief when they realize that the music therapist also is struggling with mistakes. When a situation arises with a client where the therapist just doesn't know what to do or say, this will not be a devastating experience because they can identify with it from the training process and learn how to use this in a constructive way. Dealing with and learning to be comfortable in "being in the unknown" is a skill that is very important to accrue as a music therapist. Many clients are in the unknown in terms of their process of recovery and will need the music therapist's empathy and skills to practice that state of being.

Flexibility in Moving Between One's Inner Process and the Client's Process

It is important to offer an opportunity in training where one must quickly move between one's own "inner music" and inner reality as a therapist and the client's inner and outer reality. The fact that the student has to switch so quickly from focusing on the client's needs to focusing on their own needs as a therapist (keeping track of process, overview, which technique/intervention to use, checking potential countertransference) will automatically develop this ability and flexibility. One can compare it with the ability to oscillate between being strictly objective (observing the client) and being subjective (observing myself being a therapist).

In an article about the importance of the psychotherapist's authenticity and about the importance of training this skill, my bioenergetic body psychotherapy trainer Olav Storm Jensen (1998) wrote that "the fact that the therapist is experiencing and is in touch with the process of the client in the given moment it is happening must be a definitive prerequisite for the fact that the theoretical understanding and the technical skills can be brought to relevant use. It can be described as available concentrated presence and attention in an empathic understanding of the process of the client" (1998, p. 275) [author's translation from Danish].

One professional music therapist who took the IMT training wrote the following about her learning experiences of IMT:

I think IMT is a good training method in terms of teaching the therapist to be empathetic with and understand the therapy from the client's point of view. The ability to be able to switch between being aware of oneself and the client. To train this sensitivity toward the client is a very essential part of this music therapeutic method. [author's translation from Danish]

Another professional music therapist who took IMT wrote:

IMT has been training me in the ability to be 100% involved in the process of the client and at the same time keeping an overview—looking at the process from the outside. At the same time, it has been teaching me the ability to protect myself and let myself become involved without being too much pulled into the process of the client. I also have a feeling that this has sharpened my ability to adapt to quick changes in the therapy work. In the work with the triad of client, interpreter, and therapist, it has helped me to maintain a clear consciousness about the different channels of communication and an ability to make quick changes between these. [author's translation from Danish]

These comments attest to the value of developing the ability to have therapeutic presence. As my supervisor for 26 years, Prof. Arthur Robbins (1998), wrote in his book on this topic: "I am being present, in the presence of my client. In so doing, I temporarily suspend my boundaries and let the full force of the client enter my inside. Yet at the same time, I am separating out my feelings and giving them shape and form" (p. 21).

The student is trained in identifying the flow and pattern of not only the rhythms that develop in the musical interactions with the client, but also those that develop outside the musical contact. This occurs in the movement for the therapist from a more interactive stance in identifying with the conflicts of the client to a more cognitively separate one, structuring of the offered material. The student will be able to get in touch with the dissonances and resonances that are created when the client meets the therapist in and outside of the music.

Transition Management

The fact that there is such a rapid change between being a client and being a therapist in the Intertherapy practice can help the student to better manage the transitions inside and outside the sessions in future work situations. This helps develop the ability to change focus quickly and the ability to stay as neutral as possible in the musical and verbal realms. This will also help the music therapist working in an institution who must meet with many clients consecutively without breaks or a transition time in between.

In the beginning of the IMT process, some students complain about having difficulty in making such a quick change between being a client and being a therapist. In my own experience as an AMT trainee and later as a professional music therapist, it has been very helpful to develop my ability to quickly put my own immediate needs aside and be able to focus completely on the needs of the client.

Mary Priestley (1994) commented on this aspect of the training:

It is not a bad idea for a student to realize that he is capable of this change of role, for as a working therapist he will be vulnerable to life's bruises outside therapy and will have to walk into the workroom and put his own troubles behind him until his working day is finished. Until he has tried it, he will not realize his strength in focusing his mind firmly in one direction toward another human being in trouble. (p. 305)

Transitions from verbal to music or music to verbal interactions will be invented and explored. Particularly important will be discovering how silence can give space and honor the musical statements and, as such, function as transition to and from musical interaction.

Time Management

The relative brevity of the sessions (30 minutes for work of an individual and in-depth nature) forces the therapist not to waste time and to be economical with time management. Many verbal clients spend a large amount of session time talking and often end up playing music briefly. The short time frame makes it even more urgent to either help the client identify the issue rather quickly or find a way to initiate playing/singing and get to creating and processing musically before the session is over. In some institutions, there is only half an hour available for sessions, so the time limit is not that unrealistic.

The student therapist will learn how to help the client to stop inside and outside the music when the session has ended. Many clients will continue to play or talk, even though there is no time left in the session. The student will learn how to prepare the client for the end, either musically or verbally.

Management of Key Phenomena in AMT

The student can become familiar with key concepts in AMT, such as musical transference, musical countertransference, musical resistance, defenses, regression, symbiosis, separation, and developmental stages in the music and learn how to deal with such phenomena in music and words. The following are the types of questions to which students will develop their own answers: How do I determine if the music is transferential? How do I deal with musical resistance? Do I go with it or do I break it? Do I encourage playing mutually or do I encourage playing dialogically and separate? How do I pull a client out of a musical regression? Which aspects of the client's music are eliciting musical countertransference (intersubjective countertransference)? Is there any intrasubjective countertransference? What are the developmental aspects of the music? How can I facilitate or bring the client to the next developmental stage?

Management of Musical Interventions

I define a musical intervention as a focused musically expressed action with the intentional purpose of making a change in the client's inner and outer music. The student will get an understanding of when to accompany and when not to accompany the client's playing or singing. Initially, students tend to automatically accompany the client, but there might not be a clinical rationale for this intervention in the particular situation. As an example, when the trainee can identify whether the focus is on intrapersonal or interpersonal work, then the decision can be made as to whether the playing should be separate or together.

In terms of timing, when is it appropriate to offer a musical structure through rhythm, melody, or harmony or in the form of a style such as blues, gospel, pentatonic, or Middle Eastern? The student will learn by trial-and-error and by getting to know the musical being of the student client. The student will be trained in creating clear musical beginnings and endings and help the client learn phrasing. Some clients stop abruptly in their music and do not know how to create an organic musical phrase.

As the sessions will be videotaped, the student will be able to use listening to the taped music as an intervention in sessions where the client cannot remember what he/she played/sang. The student therapist will also be asked to listen for and "vacuum clean" redundant tones in his/her music. In the beginning of one's training, there seems to be a tendency to play more tones than needed.

There are tones that seem to have no intention and direction and are there just there to fill up the space. The student will be encouraged to make the music simple—it does not have to be very complicated in order to have an effect.

The student will be asked to become familiar with the musical identity of the client and become able to reproduce the musical and vocal expression of the client. This is done in order to examine how it feels to have such a musical identity and in order to be able to mirror the person musically, when needed. The student will be helped to identify when improvisation, songwriting, song singing, and composition is appropriate to use and when not.

The student will receive training in transforming verbal questions into music. Students are often very verbal in the beginning of the training and get trapped in a very verbal student client's "verbality." They will become exposed to musical interventions that can help the student therapist and the student client to communicate more efficiently with each other through the music.

Consider this example of a very verbal student client. He began a session wanting to work with a dream. He told the content of the dream in lengthy detail and reflected over the meaning of several symbols. The student therapist got drawn into the verbal process of working with the dream, and when the two of them had decided how to work with the dream in music, the session was almost over, so they had to stop and break up the organic flow of the musical processing. In the following supervision session, the student therapist learned to ask the student therapist not to tell the dream first, but to communicate its content in music first, and then in the end there would be some time if needed to process verbally what was significant for the student client.

Because I consider silence to be an important part of the music and as such can be used as an intervention, the students are trained to endure the long pauses that there may be, where seemingly "nothing happens"—where one listens to one's own breathing and "inner music" or where one is recentering oneself.

Students will receive training in trusting musical intuition, which means that they play spontaneously without filtering from the thought process. The student will learn to get an overall consciousness of the session by viewing it and conducting it as a piece of music: tuning in—beginning—middle—closure.

They can, for example, try out different ways of being for each of these sections of the session—tuning in: listening to and staying with the silence or listening to and focusing on the rhythm of the breath of the student client and attuning themselves to that; beginning: listening closely to the beginning music of the client and which instruments/how voice is being used; middle: letting happen what needs to happen in an organic flow; closure: musical guidance through slowing the tempo and toning down the dynamic and intensity.

The student will get used to experiencing musical interventions that turn out to have unknown, mysterious qualities that are unexplainable and should remain like that. They will develop awareness that not everything can or should be explained or verbalized.

Amir (1999) interviewed six music therapists about their musical and verbal interventions, and she concluded her article with the actual words of one of the therapists interviewed. "I allow myself to 'not know,' to make mistakes, to learn. I never know that my interventions are right. Sometimes they are right, sometimes they are wrong, and sometimes they are proven to be unimportant" (p. 173).

Verbal Interventions and Interactions

I will define a verbal intervention as a focused verbally expressed action made with the intention of effecting a change in the client's inner and outer music. Students are likely to be working with both verbal and nonverbal clients when they have finished their training. Therefore, it is necessary to be trained in handling the possible verbal parts—verbal interventions and interactions—of the music therapy session. The IMT training is an ideal place to start practicing verbal skills because the client is verbal and one can get a direct response from the client if the verbal communication is not clear.

The student will be trained in how to help the client to form an improvisation title that can serve as an entrance or invitation to the music-making. The title is often an essence of what the client has expressed verbally or bodily in the communication before the music.

Here are some examples of titles from my own IMT experiences as a student client:

- Improvisation A: I am manipulating
- Improvisation B: I am becoming manipulated

I was encouraged to express in music how it felt to be manipulated and how it felt to manipulate, in order to explore what the underlying emotions may be. In another session, the verbal focal point was:

- Improvisation C: being surrounded by a wall
- Improvisation D: being without the wall

I arranged the instruments in C so they surrounded me and explored what that felt like. In D, I played without having the instrumental wall and explored musically how that felt.

Mary Priestley wrote about the role of the title: "This title may focus the therapy in a vital direction for the work, or it may turn away from this important aim and make the music into a defensive and vapid note-patting" (1994, p. 301).

Students will also gain knowledge in how to handle the verbal parts of the session that occur before and after the improvisation(s). In my own training with Mary Priestley, she emphasized the importance of listening to the client's words and vocal dynamics as music. Examples of training areas:

- Ask nonleading and nonmanipulative questions.
- Avoid asking questions that tend to put the client in a defensive position.
- Do not give advice.
- Sometimes repeat essential words mentioned by the student client.

Another area that will be explored is how to integrate the verbal part with the musical part. Words do not always have to be used before or after an improvisation. Only in those situations where material needs to be brought into the conscious are verbal communications needed and the words can function as a bridge between the unconscious and the conscious.

During verbal interactions, trainees will learn to listen to the body language of the client. Is the client saying one thing with the body and another with the words? How does the client make me feel in my body? How can I reflect that back in the music?

The reason that body awareness and expression are part of the training is that as a music therapist, one will often be working with populations of nonverbal individuals, with whom reading body communication together with the music can be an effective diagnostic tool.

Mary Priestley included in her training a dimension called *psychodynamic movement.* She referred to Alexander Lowen's training, *bioenergetic body psychotherapy,* and his body of literature and terminology. This psychodynamic movement discipline was further developed by Prof. Inge N. Pedersen and the author as we taught the discipline at two master' programs in Europe, at Aalborg University in Denmark and the Hochschule für Musik und Darstellende Kunst in Hamburg, Germany (Pedersen, 2002; Scheiby & Pedersen, 1989).

Inspired by Priestley's training, I took a three-year training in bioenergetic body psychotherapy when I started working with schizophrenic adults, psychotic adolescents, and autistic children.

At the beginning of treatment, these clients often are afraid of touching the instruments for a long period of time—yet they are expressing and communicating through their body all the time. It can be difficult to understand what is going on in the client without body-reading, analysis, and communication skills. The IMT offers a particularly ideal situation in terms of identifying body language, because the supervisor is present and is observing both partners' body communications. It may be a little challenging in the later AMT individual and group supervision training module for the student therapist to reflect to the supervisor exactly what the body communication was.

It takes some time before the student therapist is able to relax and allow images and symbols to emerge in the consciousness driven from the verbal and nonverbal presence of the client. These images and symbols may or may not be appropriate for the student therapist to share. In the individual supervision right after the IMT, these images and symbols will be taken into consideration and discussed in terms of how the material might be related to the client's process.

The student will learn how to distinguish between when words are needed and when they are not. In terms of music and meaning, the student will be taught how to help the client to develop his/her own interpretive world unique to each person.

Instrumental, Vocal, and Body Language

In AMT, it is the understanding that instruments can function as a vehicle of meaning in terms of symbolic representation and a vehicle for imagination of objects or situations. Therefore, the student must be trained in having awareness about the following: Which instruments are the clients picking in relation to which theme? How does the client arrange the instruments? How does the client play the instruments? How does the client sit with or hold the instruments during the verbal part of the session? Which ones are preferred and which ones are avoided? Which instruments does the student therapist tend to choose? When should the student therapist choose instruments that are like the ones the student client chooses and when should the instruments be contrasting?

Vocal music psychotherapy techniques will be explored and examined, and if the student therapist has problems in using the voice as an instrument in a dynamic and expressive way, this will be worked with in supervision. The student will also be trained in observing the body language of the client while he/she is playing/singing.

The Contract

The students will learn to adhere to the rule of analytical confidentiality. They are not supposed to discuss the content of their sessions outside the sessions. The taped sessions are not supposed to be played in other contexts unless the client and the therapist have given consent. The student will get an understanding of the function of having a contract. As a rule, the time and day of the week of the session are kept the same, and the student therapist cancels only when ill. This creates stability and consistency in the relationship and a trust in the fact that the relationship has an inner rhythm that is maintained.

Tuning In to Communication Through the Unconscious or Subconscious

In AMT, one makes use of the fact that music can open up contact with the unconscious. Sometimes the spontaneous improvisations are direct communications of what is going on in the unconscious, taking on somewhat the same function as our nightly dreams. Music can for the client function as a bridge or a channel to contact the unconscious. Consequently, one of the tasks of the student therapist in IMT is to learn to be available for connecting with the unconscious of the client. This can be taught by helping the student therapist to tune himself/herself as an instrument and resonator, either just before the session is to be conducted or in the beginning of the session. The student therapist focuses on breathing, grounding, centering, and hearing. The trainee starts listening to the sounds of the client, the rhythm of the breathing, the body feeling and movements, and their own overall psychological tempo as well as that of the client. Sometimes when one is working with a client, a certain song may be coming up in the therapist's mind. This song may either be an unconscious communication from the client or contain essential material that is related to the client's issues in the here-and-now. This type of openness is trained in IMT.

Model for Analysis of the Musical Material

The student is encouraged to develop his/her own model of analysis of the musical material that emerges in the sessions. In addition, I offer a basic model that can be a helpful starting point for catching the essence or the significance of the music.

Figure 2 represents a variety of categories that are involved in and have to be taken into consideration when one analyzes improvisations.

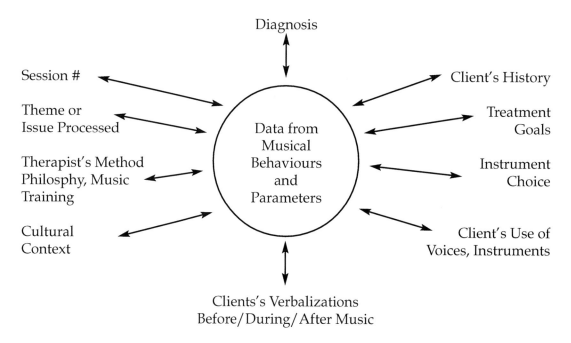

Figure 2. Categories in the analysis of improvisations.

Listening categories

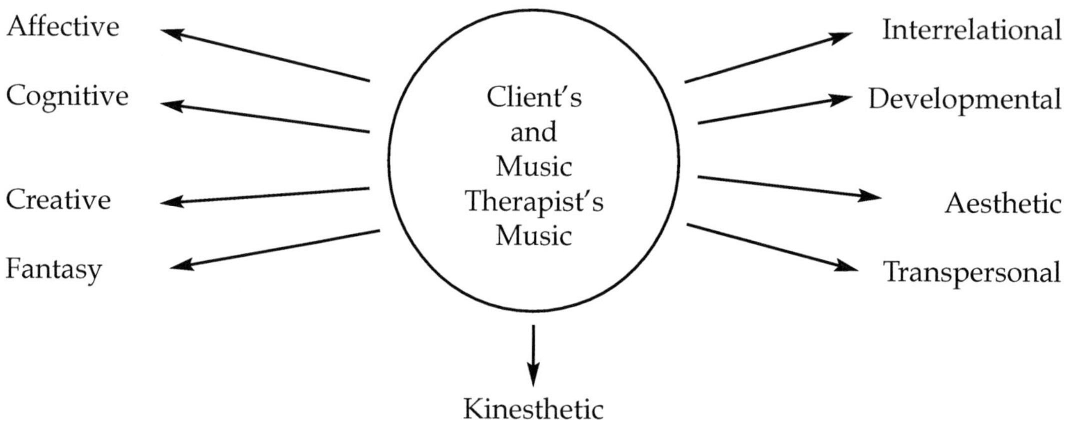

Figure 3. A variety of listening categories of which one needs to be aware.

Table 1 describes a variety of types of information that one may gain through making use of the different listening categories. As all of the sessions are videotaped, the student can analyze from the taped version of the music in case it cannot be remembered.

Table 1
Examples of Possible Information Derived from Videotaped Sessions Leading to Clinical Data

Affective Information: Emotional qualities, musical transference, musical countertransference
Interrelational Information: Style of connecting
Cognitive Information: Level of organization, structural components
Developmental Information: Ego function, drives, defenses, differentiation between self and others, authenticity, level of integration/chaos/dissociation
Released Fantasies and Images Information: Images, gestalts, mirroring significant experience in past and present
Transpersonal Information: Spiritual quality, meditative quality, altered state of consciousness
Aesthetic Information: Quality of beauty
Kinesthetic Information: Body expressions/sensations released by the music
Creativity Information: Absence/presence of ideas that develop, playfulness

I developed this model of analysis on the basis of the following considerations:

- Mary Priestley's referential position: Music can refer to something else—for example, emotions and unconscious content. It may not always be sufficient with the musical experience per se.
- My experiences working with AMT with a variety of verbal populations. When asked what the meaning of the music was for them, they would refer to at least one of the categories in the figure.
- My experiences in my private supervision, where co-supervisees and my supervisor would listen to tapes from my sessions with patients and interpret what the significance of the music might be.
- My own experiences as a client in individual and group music therapy analysis.
- My IMT training with Mary Priestley, in which the student client's music was analyzed by Mary and me as the student therapist. Mary Priestley was providing direct supervision on the work.

Containment, Timing, and Pacing

The student will be trained in the musical ability to contain emotional states that are unmanageable or unbearable for the client in the moment. The student learns to hold the client's emotions until they are ready to be owned. Perhaps the therapist needs to develop a musical form for the stressful material that is modified and seems more manageable to the client. By trial-and-error, the student will learn about musical and verbal timing. When do I musically reflect this feeling of tremendous frustration or anger? When is the client ready to reflect upon this feeling? How can I "de-poison" the music of the client so it doesn't seem so toxic to the client? When do I address certain phenomena that I hear in the client's music and when not?

The student will learn about the importance of pacing the session in order for the tempo not to become too intense, hectic, or unbearably slow. Trainees will learn to observe the pace of the client and how this might affect the pace of the student therapist.

Supervisor's Function While Observing the Dyad

Music therapy supervision can focus on client-oriented or therapist-oriented supervision. In the following, I am occupied with the part that is focused on the therapist.

I see my function as a helper for the student therapist with anything that creates problems in the therapy process. Every person has a unique way of expressing themselves musically, verbally, and bodily and of being in the world. Does the therapeutic presence stand in the way of the clinical work? We have to identify areas together that have to be worked on and changed. Every student has a different pace in his or her individuation process as a music therapist and that has to be respected by the supervisor.

During the observation, the supervisor takes notes while sitting quietly in the background, not interrupting the session. The presence of the supervisor should be as neutral as possible in order for the student therapist to be allowed to find his/her own way to make contact with the student client and to develop his/her own relational music together. Mary Priestley wrote about the presence of the supervisor: "The supervisor empathically feels himself into the inner music of the therapeutic couple and remains observant and silent for as long as he can. While the therapy is moving, even stammering, silent or raging, he can leave them to themselves and take up any points afterwards" (1994, p. 299).

Often, timekeeping may be a problem for the student therapist, and it can be helpful in the beginning for the supervisor to indicate when there are five minutes remaining in the session. Mary Priestley suggested that the supervisor also may want to make a suggestion if the student therapist has trouble deciding upon a title for the improvisation. I personally do not do that, but if the title seemed not to be effective, I will address this in supervision. The long-term goal is for the couple to get rid of the supervisor, so it is important to create as little dependency as possible. One can compare the position of the observing supervisor to that of *a receptive and empathic container* and *radar* that records the strengths and weaknesses of the student therapist in terms of being, doing, creating, and thinking.

I pay particularly close attention to the following questions during my observation. Is the student able to give space inside and outside the music to the client? Can they be nondirective and directive inside and outside the music at appropriate times? Is the student handling the verbal part in an appropriate way? Is the student clear in her verbal part? Were the musical interventions working? Is the student self-presenting in an emotionally neutral position so that the student client can use him/her for transference? How is the pace of the student therapist compared to that of the student client? Is the student able to contain musically and verbally? Is the music of the student therapist creative and flowing naturally or is it stiff and nonorganic? Does the student therapist project the singing voice in the music? Is there intentionality in the musical interventions of the student therapist? How does the student handle silences? Do the verbal, body, and musical languages complement or contradict each other? Are the musical parameters used appropriately? Does the student therapist tend to get stuck in the use of a certain parameter, such as displaying little flexibility in tempo or rhythm? Is the student therapist physically as well as mentally grounded in his/her presence? Is the student therapist operating from a centered place or from an overly intellectualized position?

As a supervisor, I use my own feelings in two different ways during the observation. I tend to oscillate between empathizing with the student client and with the student therapist in order to detect possible transference and countertransference that is going on inside and outside the music. Am I getting bored? If I am, there will be a high likelihood that the process is stuck or moving in circles. Is the student merging with the client in the music, or can the student keep a separate musical identity?

376

Does the student give a clear message about the therapeutic role before the music (e.g., reinforcer, companion, mirror, a certain defined role in a musical psychodrama, supporter)? Does the student make sure that it is clear what the verbal starting point is or the rules for the improvisation are? Did the student notice what went on in the first five minutes of the session? This is important, because the first five minutes of the session often reflect in a condensed form the issues with which the client is struggling. Was there any obvious musical or extramusical countertransference?

What kind of presence is the client calling for in the therapist? What does this indicate diagnostically about the client? It can sometimes be a difficult job for the supervisor to be the third, excluded part of the triangle. Mary Priestley wrote about this subject: "First of all, this can stir up feelings from earlier periods in his life when he was an excluded third party, possibly in a trio of mother and father against him, or mother and sister against him. This may arouse in him an impulse to interject at all costs, or it may cause his interest in the intimate scene revealed before him to mysteriously die away. If he understands these possibilities, he will be able to withstand the feelings better and to act from this understanding rather than from blind impulse" (1994, p. 303).

Individual Supervision in the IMT Context

The half-hour individual supervision that follows immediately after the therapies can be viewed as a condensed form of what the student will receive in the third stage of the training, where the individual supervision session lasts one hour. In general, it is the student's responsibility to bring up areas of concern and to discern where help is needed. However, I will bring up things that I noticed if I believe that this is important to the learning process of the student. Because this may represent the first opportunity that the student has to experience the offer of assistance in relation to her clinical expertise, I pay close attention to see whether the student can allow himself/herself to receive help or has difficulty in requesting assistance.

Usually, the supervision follows five steps within one session:

- Identification of musical/verbal phenomena that the student therapist was not able to handle
- Identification of the issue(s) with which the student wants to work
- Working through the issue(s) in music if possible
- Verbal integration and clarification
- Identification of possible parallel process (aspects of what happened in the discussed session being reflected in the supervision session)

The Role of the Supervisor

First and foremost, the supervisor must be able to function as a container for the student therapist in the sense that Bion uses the term: "It is the creation of a psychic space in which each and every communication, however confused and painful, is received by the therapist, retained, and mentally digested with the aim of removing any unbearable qualities from the client's feelings" (1962, p. 306).

The student therapist will often be overwhelmed by feelings of incompetence, inner critiques, impotence, failure, feelings of having to rescue the client, feelings of not knowing enough or not being good enough, feeling stuck, and mixed emotions released by the previous session. The supervisor has to be able to receive, retain, and sit with these feelings and eventually help the student to express them in music and accompany and give shape to the expressions, so that the student does not feel alone with this and feels accepted. After the musical expression, the supervisor can help the supervisee to gain insight from the music.

The second role of the supervisor is to help the student to develop a personal musical identity. In case this already has been formed, one's role may be to challenge and encourage the student to learn new ways of musical expression, such as how to incorporate atonal language in the improvisations or to incorporate particular songs or musical styles that may relate to the issues that are brought up by the client.

The third important role of the supervisor is to help the student to develop a personal interpretation universe and help the student to see that there are no correct or wrong recipes and that the client is the one with the knowledge of the meaning of the music. The student can develop an ability to help the client discover his/her unique interpretation universe.

In the following, I will mention areas that I often bring to the attention of the student therapist.

It is important to look at the student's *verbal skills*. Often, students feel responsible for giving answers to client questions. They need to learn to help the client to find his/her own answers. Advice-giving and too much questioning are not helpful for the client. It seems hard for the student therapist to stay neutral in the first IMT sessions, and often I will suggest that the student therapist make an improvisation in which the person explores where the tendency to give advice and questioning is coming from.

It is important to clarify with the client what *the improvisation theme* is, and in cases where a particular intervention calls for more than one title, deciding which *improvisation title* is played first. It is also important to clarify *the role of the student therapist* in the music before the music starts. It is important to try to remember to *create connections,* if there are any, between the previous sessions and the present one. A musical/verbal/emotional theme may reoccur or a dream may be connected to what was processed in a former session.

Sometimes I find a *missing resonance* on the part of the student therapist. The student might not be able to co-respond to the client's reality or to let himself/herself become touched by the client's being.

At times, I find that *authenticity* is missing from the student therapist. In the beginning, the student therapist may be copying the style of previous therapists or supervisors and not daring to be himself/herself.

The supervisor is charged with responsibility for *uncovering unconscious material* inside and outside the music of the student therapist and the student client. This includes becoming aware of phenomena such as transference, countertransference, and/or repressed material or resistance and bringing these to the attention of the student therapist.

The overly represented *"doing"* mode of the student therapist may also be a focus. Often in the beginning of the therapy course, the student is doing too much and almost taking away from the client the responsibility to work.

The presence of *artistic creativity* may be missing. The creativity of the student seems to be dead or missing. In this case, we will identify whether the student therapist is sufficiently stimulated creatively outside of the therapy room. Are they playing or singing in any other context? Is she receiving instruction or musical nurturing and inspiration on her instrument/voice? Are they listening to music or going to concerts? If not, this may be the reason for the stuckness or the deadness of the music.

The *awareness about the process* in the session as such and in the whole course of sessions may be missing. In the beginning of the training, the student may not be aware of what process means, so I will often ask the student to describe the process that just unfolded in the previous session. How does this process relate to the rest of the sessions, and where are we in the overall course of the treatment—beginning, middle, or end? How can one start a music therapy process, and how can one terminate a music therapy process?

Supervisory Techniques and Common Student Therapist Challenges

Depending on what has to be accomplished, one can develop a repertoire of techniques that can be helpful in giving the student therapist personal and technical insight.

- *Musical role-playing.* The student therapist plays the client in music. The supervisor takes the role of the student therapist. This technique will help the student therapist to be able to better resonate with the client.
- *Musical release.* Sometimes the student therapist has been building up tension during the earlier session, but the student cannot localize the source(s) of it. The student is supported in experiencing and expressing the tension on a musically symbolic level. Verbalization of such a release can lead to insights about which conflicts are evoking the tensions.
- *Theme identification.* If it is obvious that the student therapist is identifying with the client, one can suggest that the student therapist improvise over the same theme they had asked the client to improvise over. This will reveal some of the identification pitfalls that the student therapist may have.
- *Closure solutions.* If the student has problems finding a natural closure, I sometimes suggest improvising over titles like "Important Good-byes," "Endings," "Boundaries," and "Separation" to detect the more unconscious reasons for this difficulty.
- *Doing/being problems.* In cases of the student therapist being too much in the doing mode, I suggest improvising over titles such as: "Playing As Little as Possible," "Improv. A: Doing, Improv B: Being," "Improvise Over a Situation Where You Just 'Are'" (could be lying in the sun on a beach, or meditating, or other images that facilitate this state of being), "Being Out of Control" or "Being in Control." Unconscious reasons and traumas may come up to the surface and cause the student to have the urgency to act.
- *Authenticity problems.* As performing therapy is dealing with our relational reality, issues of the ability or lacking the ability to be authentic in stressed situations are activated. If the student therapist has trouble in being authentic inside and outside the music, I suggest improvisation a title such as "Accepting the Needs of My Inner Child," or I may suggest that the student think about the earliest situation in life where authenticity was not allowed and then improvise over that situation.
- *Controlled musical regression.* There may be several reasons, often unconscious, that hinder the student therapist in listening and empathizing with the client. Depending on what the issue was in the previous session that the student therapist conducted, the starting point of an improvisation could be "The First Time I Remember Being Accepted for Who I Am."
- *Dream exploration.* Often, the student therapist has dreams that are related to the sessions that are conducted. If these dreams are brought in, they can be musically explored in a variety of ways. Symbols from the dream can be the focus of improvisations. One can play the dream through chronologically, one can play the emotions that the dreamer had during the dream, and one can play the emotions that the dream evoked after waking up. This work with dreams can give the student guidance in working with the client's dreams.
- *Listening attitudes.* As the IMT sessions are recorded, the supervisor and the student therapist can listen to the musical and verbal parts of the session together. The supervisor can help the student to develop a way of listening that is reverent and uses intuition. During listening to the music together, the student can relax the usual superego function and let the music resonate inside without having to focus on anything specific. Every preconception and personal interpretation can be put aside so that anything that is being played and/or sung

can be fully taken in by the student therapist. It may be compared with the situation of a parent holding a child so that it can be able to take in the sounds around it in a safe atmosphere. This listening attitude may then be transferred to when the student therapist is working with the client.

- *Facilitation of musical self-acceptance.* In the beginning stages of becoming a practicing music therapist, students often experience performance anxiety or discomfort with their own musical expressive language. There may be an academic or formal quality to the musical language. When I notice this phenomenon, I often have the student play music with me right after the session. My role in the music is a holding and dialogical attitude, just like the mother or father vocalizing and holding a baby. This may facilitate development of the student's own musicality, musical identity, and growth. This is of importance because the client will sense, consciously or unconsciously, if the music therapist is unhappy with his/her own music. It will be hard for the client to find his/her musical self if this is the case.
- *Dialogical playing/singing.* In the beginning of the IMT training, I often encounter students who have a preference for playing simultaneously with the client. When one plays dialogically, one is more exposed and cannot hide or merge with the music of the client. Perhaps there is a natural fear of being too exposed in one's actions in the beginning of the training. When I notice this avoidance, I offer myself as a musical partner in the supervision. In this dialogical playing, one can train functions of organizing and timing the switch from one player to another and develop skills in musical timing, which include when to pause and the appropriate duration of musical statements.
- *Types of accompaniment.* Sometimes a student therapist is not aware of when to accompany in unison, harmonize, mirror, reinforce, or oppose. If it is not clear to the student when to do what, I improvise with the student therapist, letting him or her be in the client position and notice what the different accompaniment relations feel like. A musical unison can be experienced by clients as being held in a symbiotic or merging state. When the therapist is accompanying with harmonies to the client's music, it can be experienced as being held, but at the same time as having independence or freedom to separate (the client can make dissonance when he/she wants distance). Mirroring can be experienced by clients as encouraging, a strengthening of the self, recognizing, and validating. In cases where a client has difficulties in sensing his/her emotions or is defensive in his/her expression, reinforcement of the client's sounds can help the person to acknowledge or identify the emotional or defensive content of the expression. For clients who need to have something or somebody to go up against or to rebel against, it can be helpful to accompany in an opposing style—for example, tonal vs. atonal, major vs. minor.

Evaluation

When the whole course of the IMT sessions has been completed (the clinical part, the theoretical part, the videotaped excerpts), the students will be asked to do a self-evaluation and the trainer will evaluate them. The evaluation covers the four areas of music therapy competency: personal, technical, artistic, and theoretical. If the student is missing skills in any of the areas, recommendations are made depending on which areas are not fulfilled. If the student has obtained the necessary skills, he/she will be asked to receive a year of weekly individual AMT supervision and after that or at the same time a year of weekly group AMT supervision. These supervision sessions last for one hour each.

MUSIC-CENTERED INDIVIDUAL AND GROUP SUPERVISION: STAGE THREE OF AMT TRAINING

As the AMT model can be adapted to most populations—even clients without verbal skills or with moderate degrees of developmental delay—it is up to the student to choose with which population they want to be supervised. The student will need an entire year of individual supervision and possibly more, depending upon the level of the student at the beginning of the training.

Because the supervision sessions in this part of the training last one hour, there will be more time to focus on various needs and issues that the student brings up. What has been previously discussed regarding skills that are taught in the IMT can also be said about the individual and group supervision. We fine-tune and continue to grow in areas that have been addressed in the IMT.

The role of the supervisor is multifaceted and less active than in the IMT supervision, and I experience myself as fluctuating between using my skills as a music therapist and using my skills as a teacher.

The student is expected to take more responsibility for what is happening or not happening in the supervision sessions. I make it clear that it is a shared responsibility that we finish on time.

In this form of supervision, there will be sessions that straddle the gray area between clinical music therapy and clinical supervision because countertransference, among other phenomena, related to the clinical material will be processed inside and outside the music in order to facilitate insight and professional growth. It is the job of the supervisor to stop at the point of realization or recognition of possible intrasubjective/intersubjective countertransference issues. The supervisor does not encourage further exploration of the relational experiences in the past that may have led to the behavior of the supervisee. One may suggest that the issues be brought to personal therapy for further exploration.

Dvorkin wrote about her experiences in this area: "The boundary between supervision and therapy can be very thin, due to the similarity in techniques and the enormous effect the therapist's own unresolved issues can have on the clinical work" (1999, p. 278).

Arthur Robbins, an experienced therapist, trainer, teacher, and supervisor in the creative arts therapies, wrote about the importance of training creative arts therapist students in processing transference and countertransference communications: "The study of transference and countertransference cannot be put aside until the student enters a later stage of professional development. The fundamentals of treatment technique are often compromised by highly charged emotional reactions on the part of the therapist. When opportunities are presented for processing these reactions through artwork, blocks toward learning are often lifted, leading the artist/therapist to a deeper comprehension of therapeutic process" (1994, p. xii).

The intersubjective/intrasubjective countertransference reactions from the music therapist are processed in music as well as verbally in the supervision, if the countertransference stands in the way of the treatment of the client.

In the supervision sessions, we are entering a process that is characterized by a constant oscillation between primary and secondary process thinking. Primary process thinking is handled by the right hemisphere of the brain and governed by the laws of the preconscious; this happens mostly in the musical parts of the session. Secondary process thinking is handled by the left hemisphere and governed by more rational and conscious thinking; this happens mostly in the verbal parts of the session.

The goal is to achieve an integration of both sides of the brain. This also reflects the process that we go through with our clients in the sessions.

The steps of the supervision often take the following form:

- *Identification of the issue(s) with which the supervisee wants to work.* This can be verbalized or expressed in music. If the supervisee is unprepared or has no idea where to start, I suggest that the supervisee improvise alone or together with me and see what comes up. If the supervisee is prepared, they will be presenting videotaped or audiotaped material in this part of the supervision. Certain demographic information may be communicated to me, such as diagnosis of client, age, history, goals, objectives, number of sessions, and number of clients. In this part comes clarification of whether the focus is on the client or on the supervisee or on both. We may start verbally, if the focus is on the client(s), to identify which approach may be appropriate according to the needs and the goals of the client. Questions may come up, such as: Will there be a need to focus on the self (mirroring, self-affirmation), or on the drives (control/out of control), or on behavioral modification, or on a spiritual dimension, or on an actual physical skill (speech, movement), or will an object relations approach be more appropriate? At which developmental stage is the client? Which physical/psychological need does the client have right now?
- *Musical facilitation and exploration of issues/techniques* which were brought up in the previous step.
- *Verbal integration and clarification* of what was brought up in the previous *step.*
- *Identification of possible parallel process* inside and outside the music in the session (the client's behavior with the music therapist is often reenacted in the music therapist's behavior with the supervisor).

The Role of the Music

The music can play a variety of roles in the individual supervision. First and foremost, the music can be used as a tool of clarification and insight into aspects of the presented issue.

- It can be used to clarify musical countertransference, defenses, resistance, projective identification, musical transference, whether the supervisee is able to reproduce musically, what the client(s) sang/played in the presented session.
- It can be used to mirror how a supervisee connects with themselves in the interaction with the client.
- It can be used to improve the musical repertoire or improvisational reservoir of the supervisee.
- It can be used to help the supervisee to connect with their creativity.
- It can be used for the purpose of stress reduction in situations where the supervisee is in danger of burning out.
- It can be used to establish connection between supervisee and supervisor, if the communication for some reason is blocked or unclear.
- It can be used to identify parallel process that is occurring in the session.
- It can be used, in general, to bring unconscious associations to a conscious level, when there is a need for that. (This way of using the music can be very helpful when there is resistance on the client's or the music therapist's part, e.g., resistance toward playing/singing.)

Stages in the Process of Individual Supervision

A supervision process can be compared, in a condensed form, with the individuation process of a person growing up.

Stage I: Tuning In and Getting to Know Each Other

The supervisor and supervisee are starting to form a relationship through verbal and musical relating, getting to know each other, and getting to know the content of the contract. Assessment of the student's strengths and weaknesses musically, verbally, and theoretically is done here, and goals and objectives are set for the future. The supervisee gets into a routine and learns to receive supervision and to present material. The role of the supervisor often seems to be like that of a parent or authority, and the need for structure and direction surfaces often. Didactic instruction and support are key words. The supervisee often experiences and expects a certain degree of dependency on the supervisor. The supervisor often carries a function of being a holding container while the supervisee is learning about basic concepts of AMT.

Stage II: Working on the Improvement of Skills and Personal Growth

The supervisee works on musical and verbal skills. Often the verbal skills are in great need of improvement because many music therapy students have not been trained in verbal skills related to musical communication and interaction. Work is also being done on integrating musical, verbal, and theoretical skills. Relationship issues between supervisor and supervisee may surface and may be processed musically and verbally. This indicates the beginning of work and knowledge achievement in the area of transference, countertransference, resistance, projection, and resonance. The stance of the supervisee is less dependent than in Stage I. Often the supervisee has fluctuating needs in moving between polarities of being active and passive. The seeds are getting planted for a beginning music therapeutic AMT identity and style. The supervisor is "giving permission" to make mistakes and learn from these.

Stage III: Establishing AMT Identity and Personal Style—Beginning Separation

An identity and style will now emerge in bits and pieces, and the supervisor will facilitate growth and confidence for the supervisee. The supervisor is letting go more of the supervisee and he/she is often at this stage working on issues of integrating his/her own authority into the work. The relationship between supervisor and supervisee may be tested, conflicts may arise, and transference and countertransference between each other may be identified and worked on. The supervisee's work is starting to demonstrate the fundamental basics of AMT practice. Goals of skill development and personal development are re-evaluated. The supervisor is constantly evaluating the progress or areas of need at this point. The supervisor ensures that the supervisee is exposed to a variety of musical and verbal techniques in the supervision sessions. The supervisor is taking a more challenging stance in the supervision.

Stage IV: Consolidating AMT Identity and Style—Termination

In this stage, the supervisee may often reject the ideas and values of the supervisor (like the teenager who is challenging the parent), and power struggles may occur in the sessions. The supervisor supports the supervisee's autonomy and feels moments of being peers instead of being in a purely supervisor/supervisee relationship. A thorough termination process is being worked through musically, verbally, and emotionally. A theoretical case study on an individual client and on a group is being produced with appropriate video- and/or audiotaped material. At the end of this stage, the supervisee will have reached a grounded and centered sense of professional music therapeutic identity and the goals of technical skills and personal growth have been met. The supervisor and supervisee will evaluate the whole supervision process. The quality of the relationship will be more like that of peers and of a collegial nature. The supervisee has developed his/her own "internal supervisor."

Clinical Supervisory Example: "Sometimes I Feel Like a Motherless Child"

Background of Supervisee

A supervisee, S., 29 years old, was working with developmentally delayed blind children, ages three to seven, within a school context and had been doing this for one-and-a-half years. Before the session subsequently described, she was dealing with the recurring problem of feeling stuck in the approach to her clients. We role-played being the blind children through music and came up with a variety of techniques that could be applied.

Another theme involved feelings of insecurity in terms of musical efficacy when S. was being observed by others (teachers, interns, helpers, and parents), which we also dealt with musically. Meanwhile, this did not prevent her from having some episodes of feeling stuck, so I suspected that some deeper underlying professional and personal issues might have been at the root of the recurring phenomena. At the same time, I was puzzled by the fact that in positive moments, the supervisee reported that the children were improving, the school psychologist was very impressed with the work of the supervisee, and the school that provided the internship to the supervisee was more than satisfied. When the issue of feeling stuck came up in the following session, I suggested that we explore more directly the emotional underlying issues connected to this complex issue.

She started the session by saying that she had fallen into her old pattern of depression, which she related to feeling frustrated in her music therapy work with the children. She had very little help in the classroom and felt that her techniques did not work or that she was stuck when it came to improvisation skills and management of the children who were out of control. She had had a very chaotic session where nothing seemed to work. She stated, "The session was horrible." She felt very alone in the institution; she was the only music therapist there and received little support from the staff, which was mostly teachers. Nobody listened to her. This made her feel that she was at an entry level and not a skilled master's-level clinician. She said, "Perhaps I am just a little stuck."

She also felt stuck in her marriage. I suggested that she improvise over the title "Being Stuck Together" and that I would be reinforcing and supportive in the music when needed. I encouraged her to stay as long as she could in the stuckness and not try to consciously find a way out. I also encouraged her to use her voice. She said: "I feel that the defenses are up—it's going to be hard for me!"

The Music

S. chooses to play the piano. The tonality moves between tonal and atonal language. The tones do not seem to be very related to each other; it is as if they are not listening to each other. She uses the whole register of tones. The rhythm is the structural component that holds the music together in a march-like 1-2 walking rhythm. It sounds as if it is a marching robot— on the spot, with no specific direction. She looks like a child playing on a piano with pleasure in making the tones clash. The tempo is rather quick, and there is not much variation in the dynamic, which is medium loud.

I underline the rhythm-playing on a high-hat cymbal (mirroring). While I am playing, I get in touch with feeling like marching in an army, not knowing the direction that I am going. I feel restricted and stuck in this position.

After a while, S. moves down in the bass register and stays there for a long time, still keeping the monotone rhythm, I sing to S.: "Where are you now?" (checking in). She sings back: "I feel so alone, I feel like I don't have peers to talk to. I feel so alone." I sing back in the same tonality and melody: "I feel so alone" (mirroring).

She makes an explosive atonal and arrhythmical dramatic outbreak in a loud volume (anger?). I support her volume and intensity. Then it slowly quiets down in tempo and dynamics and she stops playing. There is a five-minute-long pause.

In the pause, I get the sense of sitting with a little girl who is angry, lost, and stuck. I ask her what she would do when she was a little girl and was alone and stuck (verbal intervention). S. answers: "Take a doll."

I then ask: "Is there any way you can hold and comfort yourself in music?" (musical intervention). After a little pause, S. walks over to the client chair, sits down, and starts to hum by herself in pianissimo volume, playing with little melody pieces in a minor mode.

I take the guitar and start accompanying her with playing on single strings, one at a time, fitting the tones into the tonality of the melodic fragments (musical intervention). S. sings in a blues-like fashion, and a sad blues song grows out of our music. S. sings: "I feel so alone." Her voice slides down in glissandi several times. Out of this grows a line that she sings half-crying: "Sometimes I feel like a motherless child, sometimes I feel like a motherless child, alone, alone, alone, away from home." She sings a variation of the well-known song "Sometimes I Feel Like a Motherless Child," adding some of her own text. I am accompanying her gently with minor accords on the guitar until she stops singing.

In the verbal processing of the music, S. talks about the loneliness in her work situation and the transference of the loneliness and anger of the blind children, which reinforces her personal loneliness and anger. She mentions feelings of loneliness in her relationship and feelings of not being understood by her family. Her feelings of being insecure and not skilled enough are being dismissed, and even I, as a supervisor, do it sometimes (parallel process), which we talk about. I am happy that she finally expresses some negative feelings toward me, because I sense that she has been hiding her anger from me in previous sessions. In the improvisation, there was a short passage with explosive material, and perhaps this part of the music gave her permission to let some steam out. S. starts talking about feelings of being disconnected that were released during the improvisation. These feelings are well known in relation to her family.

I point out to her that maybe these feelings of being stuck and depressed were released every time she felt disconnected from the children. Then she would be reminded of her areas of disconnection in her past and present life, and this may make her feel stuck.

She realized in the end that she needed to nurture and stimulate herself musically, perhaps taking a summer course in improvisation, and make her needs be heard and listened to better by the staff at work, her husband, her family, and me. She also talked about feeling underpaid when compared to other work contexts. She seemed relieved when she left.

Reflection on the Musical Process

In the next supervision session, S. made comments about how amazing it was that this song ("Sometimes I Feel Like a Motherless Child") had just come flowing out of her mouth from the unconscious. She seemed to be in a more flowing process during that session. She mentioned that she had asked for a raise at her work and if they would not agree to that, she would ask to have fewer hours per day for the same amount of money that they were paying her, thereby improving her work conditions.

The music helped in the supervision to "de-mask" what was behind or underneath the feelings of being stuck. We sat in the stuckness (the intra- and intersubjective countertransferential reaction to the clients) together until the "motherless child" theme emerged from the unconscious. It has to be added that this supervisee mentioned in earlier sessions that her mother did not seem to be able to give her a good mothering experience while she was growing up.

Concerning the choice of the music instruments and the accompaniment of the supervisor: I chose to accompany S. in the first improvisation on the high-hat cymbal, underlining the rhythm, the volume, and the energy level in order to reflect and mirror this back to the supervisee. The music did seem to be stuck, but not completely without movement, which was important to reflect to her. There was an underlying quality of repressed anger that may have had the potential to surface, which it did in the end for a short while.

In the second improvisation, I chose to accompany her on the guitar, which is S.'s main instrument and one that she uses primarily with her voice in her clinical work. I thought that this might make her feel heard and held, but not intruded upon. I made the accompaniment simple, on open strings, so that enough space for S. to explore vocally would be offered.

We may have come to the insights through talking, but my experience is that the music facilitates the process of gaining insight in a creative way, which touches and sometimes surprises oneself, and it seems as if it is easier to take in the knowledge when it emerges from an artistic process that is not guided in a purely cerebral way.

Indirectly, the supervisee is being taught music therapeutic techniques through the supervisor's musical and verbal interventions, as illustrated in this session.

Description and Format of Music-Centered AMT Group Supervision

The group supervision session consists of four or five supervisees and lasts for one-and-a-half hours. The group is led by an experienced AMT group supervisor. The student receives group supervision for at least one year. At the end of the year, the student will be evaluated by the group supervisor, by the group members, and by self-evaluation.

It is up to each individual group member to decide what they want to work with and how they want to work with the presented material musically. The supervisor may decide to play or not to play during the musical part of the sessions. There is no rule about who has to present at any given time. The group senses who has the biggest need if there is not clearly a person who has brought in clinical material. Sometimes the group or a group member starts playing without any verbal contact. The verbal processing then takes place after the improvisation. The model describing the different phases in the actual session in individual supervision is the same for the group supervision.

One of the purposes of the group supervision is to explore, exchange, and investigate a variety of theoretical and affective issues, approaches, and methods that each group member represents. Each person may handle a problem differently and use music therapeutic techniques that the other members do not know about. An important part of the process is the emotional and cognitive feedback from the group.

The training is, in general, focused on the supervisee's professional, personal, and social competence. The training of the musical (e.g., improvisational flexibility, meaning within the music) and the verbal skills of the music therapist takes up much space in supervision.

The Role of the Supervisor

The supervisor has a variety of roles in this work:

- To promote a warm, nonjudgmental, accepting atmosphere where the supervisees can learn from each other and the supervisor and grow and improve. Key areas in this supervisory growth matrix are varied and include the following: empathy; emotional support; a place to try out new techniques; realization of insight and meaning; connectedness; resonance; training of listening skills and observational skills; reloading of the creative batteries; consolidation of one's own music therapeutic identity; networking; experiencing allies; experiencing strengths and limitations; emotional expressivity; inspiration to read, practice, and write; a place to hear a variety of types of music; support of self-promotion; support of

well-being (to avoid burnout); training of openness to preconscious as well as conscious presented material; and group leadership skills.
- To be the group leader and facilitator of the group process. Among others, to assess what is going on with the group process and relate this to the actual presented material.
- To be responsible for time management.
- To pick up on possible resistance toward learning and address it.
- To facilitate that the presented material is processed in music in one way or another. This may include help with formulation of improvisation themes or rules.
- To facilitate integration between musical and verbal processing.
- To provide support with identification of the issue(s), if this is unclear to the group members.
- To help to maintain the goal of supervision rather than treatment or therapy for the supervisees.
- To be a musical facilitator in the improvisations.
- To help out in analyzing the music that is being played and examined (audiotape/videotape improvised music in the session).

The role of such a group is basically that of a safe container or holding environment, where material can be presented and explored creatively through musical, bodily, and verbal interactions.

Robbins (1988) wrote about supervision groups for creative arts therapists. He articulates a concept of the group as container that is congruent with how it is used in AMT supervision: "The group becomes a 'container,' as members support the presenter's attempts to expand his ability to project, externalize, and investigate the myriad of affects that arise in transference/countertransference reactions. This 'holding' helps to neutralize the anxiety associated with the enormous strain under which a therapist works in grappling with a client's primitive emotional states" (p. 17). It is often experienced in such groups that over time, the group members develop strong bonds with each other.

The Role of the Music

In addition to the roles of music described earlier, we can add the following:

- It can help each supervisee to experience a wide variety of types of musical expressivity and improvisational flexibility in terms of listening to the music of the supervisees and to the music of the clients of the supervisees. This can help the supervisee to not become stuck in his/her musical language and expressivity.
- Listening to the analysis of the music of the clients and the other supervisees can help the supervisee to expand his/her understanding of multiple or specific meanings of the music. The music is contextualized and interpreted in relation to the informed musical analysis.
- By listening to the musical presentations, the supervisee can acquire a reservoir of techniques for responding to a client's music.
- Through the other supervisees' responses to the music played in a session of one supervisee, she/he can receive feedback from group members about what she/he is carrying as unconscious musical luggage, both instrumentally and vocally.
- In cases where precomposed music is presented or used, the supervisee can extend his/her musical repertoire.
- The fact that the group members are playing music together as a processing tool creates cohesiveness, authenticity, and a deep level of intimacy among the group members.

- If there are problems between the group members, the music can be used to facilitate problem solution.

Techniques

Besides training in employing the AMT techniques mentioned previously, the supervisee will indirectly experience group music improvisation techniques that will be helpful in facilitating knowledge and insight about presented issues.

After one person has presented an issue or a problem, discussion will center on how the group can help through music. There are many techniques that can be used, depending on the need:

- The presenter plays a musical portrait of a client with whom the presenter has difficulties. The rest of the group members take turns in trying to act as music therapists.
- The presenter explores his/her countertransference musically, and the group musically supports the expression and exploration.
- The presenter plays a tape with the music of a client. After having listened to the tape, the group responds in music to the client's music either individually or together.
- A group member presents a problem, theme, or issue with a client. The rest of the group members may be able to identify the same problem, theme, or issue in their own clinical reality. The group starts out in an improvisation together, and when everybody is ready, each member improvises a solo piece over their specific problem, theme, or issue, thinking about a particular client with whom it arises. In this way, the presenter does not feel alone with the problematic situation and can experience different ways of relating to the same problem, theme, or issue.
- The group starts playing music without verbalizing beforehand and sees what material comes to the surface from the improvisation.

Clinical Supervisory Example: Group Description

The group to be discussed consisted of four supervisees, one male, A, and three females, B, C, and D, of varying levels of clinical experience. The group had been together for half a year, seeing each other weekly. All of the group members were highly intellectual, and the group frequently spent much time verbalizing before they started playing.

Supervisee A was presenting about not knowing how to approach an issue brought up by a client with whom he was working. The client was a 21-year-old shooting victim who was paralyzed in both legs. In the session, the client was bringing up this issue: How can I be a sexually attractive man when I am paralyzed and not able to please a woman? This issue had come to the surface at a point when the client was about to end the relationship with his girlfriend. The supervisee felt the trauma of the client inside but chose to comfort the client by telling him that his legs were just a vehicle to transport him around and that there was more to him than his legs. This did not seem to be a satisfying answer to either the supervisee or to the client.

Another supervisee, B, who was from Japan, empathized by starting to talk about a male Asiatic client of hers who also had had a physical trauma. The client kept asking the supervisee if she thought he would get back to normal again and whether she would go back with him to his home country. She did not know how to react to the client, particularly also because in this Asiatic culture, it was not appropriate to talk about feelings or show them directly. A couple of group members said to B that perhaps her client had expressed to her that he was in love with her. She said, "No! No! No! No!," and it was obvious that she did not feel comfortable in talking about that subject.

A third supervisee, C, who frequently took on the role of therapist in the group, asked B what she felt about being asked such a question by the client. She couldn't answer, and she seemed even more uncomfortable.

As supervisor, I sensed three things at this point. First, that the group could go on at an intellectual level and spend a long time discussing approaches, as it had a habit of doing if not interrupted by an intervention that would allow them to get into the music. Second, that some of the group members had a need to explore feelings evoked when they were working with physically traumatized clients. Third, that it was important to relieve the pressure on B of having to talk about feelings.

Therefore, I suggested that each group member, after a common musical entrance, express and explore in solo instrumentally and vocally what feelings, images, and music were evoked in them when they thought about a particular physically traumatized client in their work. In this way, they might be able to detect possible countertransference and also possible ways to empathize.

The group found this suggestion a good idea. Each person identified a client on whom they would improvise. I defined my role as a musical supporter, if needed.

The Music

The male supervisee, A, chose a drum set and a djembe drum; B chose a violin; C chose a frame drum and a horn; and D chose the piano. I chose a cymbal and an accordion.

Beginning phase: Each person seemed to experiment with musical expressions, as if they were finding their way to the variety of feeling qualities. A was dominating the sound picture rather quickly with heavy drumming, which forced the rest of the group members to become louder so they could hear themselves better. I chose to play in the background in a very soft and quiet way with melody on the accordion to harmonize with the energy and dynamic of B's developing violin melody. I indicated my connection with the rest of the group by bashing the cymbal in the rhythm of A's and C's music.

The participants seemed to find a communal ending rather quickly. There was a short pause. Then B started a violin solo that sounded like a structured Eastern folk song in a major tonality in a rather slow tempo. The emotional quality seemed to be hopeful and reaching out. The music had a high degree of aesthetic beauty.

A followed after B with loud outbreaks on djembe and drum set, first at a slow tempo but quickly accelerating in tempo and loudness. There was a clear sense of rhythmical structure in the beginning of the solo, which changed at the end to where the rhythm seemed more chaotic.

Supervisee D followed with a solo on the piano with one hand in F major. The music seemed a little stiff and arrhythmic but communicated a sense of a strong and sturdy identity through medium-loud volume, the particular chosen harmonic progressions, and clear direction and intentionality in the music.

Supervisee C followed after, with blowing and vocalizing on a horn in a way that sounded like musical sighs and resignation. This was followed by an outbreak of loud, uncontrollable drumming. She ended with swinging a rattle, which gave off a wrenching noise like an old wagon wheel that was almost falling apart. All of the music of C was musically arrhythmic and was carried by a strong expressive quality in the melody, dynamic, and timbre.

All of the solos seemed rather condensed and short. After the end of C's music, there was a short pause. Supervisee D initiated the verbal process by talking about what she had come in touch with through playing like her client, who could use only one hand. She talked about what she had in common with this client—among other things, that they both played by ear and the pros and cons of that ability and that they had both taught themselves how to play. She also got in touch with this client's assertiveness and need to be independent by playing with firm tonal direction, F major, the client's preferred tonality and style of playing. She was surprised that she had found a freedom in this type of playing and not the frustration she had expected. This corresponded to her client's character, which seemed to deal with his physical trauma in a positive, "survivor" way: How can I get the best out of the situation that I am in?

Supervisee B took over and asked if she could just play a Japanese song on her violin. It seemed to resemble what she played in her solo in the former improvisation, but there seemed to be a longing, emotional quality to the tune. After the playing, she said that she felt very nervous in playing this song, but she did not know why. I asked her what this song symbolized for her, and she said that it was a song that came from the town that both she and her client came from. She then talked about her strong empathy with her client, being from such a different Eastern culture, and the trauma she and he had in common in having to face adapting to a Western culture. She also got in touch with missing her country, just like he did.

Supervisee A spoke about getting in touch through playing the drums with a deep frustration and anger that he could feel by imagining being in his client's situation. The group talked about the therapeutic value of the music therapist being able to empathize with this feeling and communicate this to the client, who indeed did have a problem with anger management, which had to be addressed by A in future sessions.

Supervisee C said that she was empathizing with a client who had multiple sclerosis in the end stage and with whom she currently felt stuck. Through the playing, she got in touch with a variety of feelings: the endlessness and hopelessness expressed on the horn, the anger and stubbornness expressed on the drum, and the weakness and feeling of almost giving up and abandonment by playing the rattle in the way she did. Together with C, the group identified these feelings as partly possible transference from the client, partly countertransference from C. The supervisee felt helpless because she was not getting any direct verbal or nonverbal response from the client. Identifying the musical transference and countertransference dynamic together as a group seemed to help C to not feel so stuck and alone with the client. She got some ideas about how to possibly reflect back musically some of the possible transferential feelings through playing and singing songs and improvisations containing those emotional qualities to the client in the future. She also realized how her countertransference, being stuck, could be partly a source of information about what the client might go through as a result of being in her particular physical condition (being abandoned by the body functions and feeling angry about the illness). Time had run out, and we ended the session at that place.

Reflection on the Musical Process

The role of the music seemed to help each group member empathize with their physically traumatized clients, each in their own way. Aspects of musical transference and countertransference were identified and shared for one group member.

The main role of the supervisor in this session was to help the group to get into the musical processing. I chose to suggest that each group member think about a physically traumatized client, which seemed to be the theme for two of the group members. This was done in order to spread the work out to all group members, so A and B would not feel so much in the spotlight.

I chose the timing of suggesting the improvisation when one group member asked B how she felt about her client asking her these difficult and intimate questions. B had in former sessions expressed discomfort in expressing feelings verbally to group members, which indeed is inappropriate following a Japanese cultural code. I thought that getting into the music might make B feel more comfortable and facilitate expression of her emotions and her connection with her client. I also wanted to prevent some group members from feeling tempted to play therapist for another group member. I consider this phenomenon to promote a resistance toward learning.

My role in the verbal part was minimal in this session. This often seems to be the case because the music opens up to experiences at an emotional and cognitive level as well. The group process flowed naturally both verbally and musically. The level of intensity was high due to the theme of physical and psychological trauma.

My role in the musical part seemed to be minimal except for showing my support to B through harmonizing with her violin playing. I took the musical backseat, as I could hear in the music that everybody was fully engaged in his or her process internally and externally. At this point in the group process, I had other reasons for not being very active and directive: I was indirectly encouraging the group members to take leadership so that they could start to become less dependent on me and enter into a more autonomous state of functioning.

COMPLETING AMT TRAINING

If the student finishes all of the training modules of the AMT training, including individual music therapy, group music therapy, IMT, individual supervision, and group music therapy supervision, he/she receives a certificate that indicates that he/she is a trained AMT music therapist who is granted permission to practice AMT.

Each student is doing the training at his/her own pace, and some students may need more training in each of the areas, depending on their level of skills in the four areas mentioned earlier in this chapter: personal competency, technical competency, artistic competency, and theoretical competency.

After having received an AMT certificate, the AMT music therapist is expected to continue to receive weekly music therapy supervision. The character of this type of supervision is more focused on process according to the need of the moment, oscillating between the concrete content of the session and taking wider factors into consideration. Audiotaped or videotaped material from cases is also presented.

CODA: FINAL WORDS ON SUPERVISORY PRESENCE

From my own experience as a supervisee for 37 years, I would like to sum up some essential qualities that an AMT music therapy supervisor who trains supervisees must present as a professional:

- To show respect to the supervisee's own learning process;
- To be able to adapt style and focus to the musical/verbal style and developmental stage of the supervisee;
- To be consistent;
- To have clear boundaries;
- To exert disciplined subjectivity in analysis of the musical/verbal presented material;
- To be able to listen clinically and to listen to his/her own inner and outer music;
- To be willing to receive professional supervision and being taught himself/herself;
- To trust the process of the student and not push;
- To be able to serve as a musical and verbal container;
- To be able to empathize musically and verbally;
- To be able to admit mistakes;
- To avoid idealization and omnipotence;
- To love his/her work;
- To be committed;
- To be nonjudgmental;
- To have a broad experience working with a variety of populations.

Let me end this article by repeating what my own supervisor for the last 26 years has said on many occasions: "Do not forget: A supervisor is not God."

REFERENCE LIST

Amir, D. *(1999).* Musical and verbal interventions in music therapy: A qualitative study. *Journal of Music Therapy, 36*(2), 144–175.

Bion, W. R. (1962). A theory of thinking. *International Journal of Psychoanalysis, 43,* 306–310.

Dvorkin, J. (1999). Psychoanalytically oriented music therapy supervision. In T. Wigram & J. De Backer (Eds.), *Clinical applications of music therapy in developmental disability, Pediatrics and Neurology* (pp. 272–281). London, UK: Jessica Kingsley Publishers.

Frohne-Hagemann, I. (1999). Integrative supervision for music therapists. In T. Wigram & J. De Backer (Eds.), *Clinical applications of music therapy in developmental disability, Pediatrics, and Neurology* (pp. 249–271). London, UK: Jessica Kingsley Publishers.

Jensen, O. S. (1998). Psykoterapeutens autencitet—terapiens afgoerende led. *Psyke & Logos, 19*(1), 271–286.

Pedersen, I. N. (2002). Psychodynamic Movement: A basic training methodology for music therapists. In J. Th. Eschen (Ed.), *Analytical Music Therapy* (pp. 190–216). London, UK: Jessica Kingsley Publishers.

Priestley, M. (1975). *Music therapy in action.* London, UK: Constable.

Priestley, M. (1994). *Essays on analytical music therapy.* Gilsum, NH: Barcelona Publishers.

Robbins, A. (1988). *Between therapists.* New York, NY: Human Sciences Press.

Robbins, A. (1994). *A multi-modal approach to creative art therapy.* London, UK: Jessica Kingsley Publishers.

Robbins, A. (1998). *Therapeutic presence.* London, UK: Jessica Kingsley Publishers.

Scheiby, B. B., & Pedersen, I. N. (1989). Psychodynamische Bewegung innerhalb eines musiktherapeutischen Konzepts. In H. Decker-Voigt (Ed.), *Dipl.-Aufbaustudium Musiktherapie, 3* (pp. 70–74). Lilienthal/Bremen, Germany: Eres Edition.

Scheiby, B. B., & Pedersen, I. N. (1999). Intermusic therapy in the training music therapy students. *Nordic Journal of Music Therapy, 8*(1), 59–72.

Wigram, T., De Backer, J., & Van Camp, J. (1999). Music therapy training. In T. Wigram & J. De Backer (Eds.), *Clinical applications of music therapy in developmental disability, pediatrics, and neurology* (pp. 282–297). London, UK: Jessica Kingsley Publishers.

Chapter 23

AN ANALYTICAL MUSIC THERAPY–ORIENTED SUPERVISION (AMTOS) MODEL TO DEVELOP EXPRESSIVENESS, CREATIVITY, AND FLUIDITY IN MUSIC THERAPISTS

Seung-A Kim

OVERVIEW

With heightened awareness of the need for culturally informed music therapy practice over the past few years, demand for various more accessible forms of music therapy supervision have increased both nationally and globally (Kim, 2011a, 2017). In response to this demand, I developed Analytical Music Therapy–Oriented Supervision (AMTOS). The goal of the AMTOS model is to meet the individual needs of professional music therapists and to reinforce the importance of supervision. It is rooted in analytical music therapy (AMT) principles and techniques relevant to clinical supervision and also has flexibility in applying these principles to address supervisees' specific individual needs. Supervision can be done in person, by telephone, or via the Internet, depending on geographic or scheduling needs.

AMTOS is designed to help supervisees to continually grow. It increases self-awareness, nurtures their inner music, and frees their creative energy. It also helps supervisees to manage culture-related countertransference and maintain *psychohygiene* (Jahn-Langenberg, 2001), as well as demonstrates how music heals.

Music therapy supervision can be defined as "an act of co-creation, or a process of shared composition about musical and therapeutic experiences in which the [client] is absent. Supervision is a triangular relationship, involving the supervisor, supervisee, and the music within a clinical context" (Sutton & De Backer, 2014, p. 317). It is a space where supervisees' cases and relevant professional work are discussed and analyzed. In AMTOS, transference, countertransference, resistance, and other psychodynamic concepts are identified, explored, and worked through musically and verbally. When supervisees openly share their clinical work, supervisors help supervisees identify the challenges and strengths of their work, demonstrate a variety of ways of working, offer suggestions, and use the actual cases as opportunities to teach effective techniques. Also, supervisors stress supervisees' self-care and continued professional development. Due to the nature of the work, it can bring out supervisees' personal issues that affect the therapeutic process as well as the supervision process because the supervisory relationship has "therapy-like" and "parent-like" qualities (Dileo, 2001). This requires supervisors to "be aware of these qualities and be prepared to safeguard and maintain the boundaries between supervision and therapy" (Lang, McInerney, Monaghan, & Sutton, 2002, p. 212). When supervisors and supervisees foster an effective supervisory relationship that is defined by safety and professionalism, the supervision will take place as both personal and professional exploration and enhancement, leading to opportunities for transformation (Watkins, 1997, 2013, 2014).

In this section, I discuss the needs for a variety of supervision models for professional music therapists in music therapy and introduce the benefits of AMTOS. Music therapy supervision is currently offered in a variety of settings: academic, clinical, and private, for both professional music therapists and students still in training (Forinash, 2001; McClain, 2001). Students have mandatory supervision during their education and training during both practicum and internship. At the professional level, supervision may be offered in a variety of formats: peer supervision, private supervision, supervision in academic and/or clinical settings, and institutional supervision. These opportunities are not available, however, to many music therapists around the country. Such opportunities depend on clinical setting, geographical location, and the financial resources of the music therapist. For example, while music therapists working in a clinical agency or institution often receive supervision of some kind, those in private practice must seek out and pay for private supervision. A second issue regarding music therapy supervision is the need for supervisors to receive the necessary training (Forinash, 2001; Kim, 2008). As Forinash (2001) pointed out, "the preprofessional supervisors are the backbone of our profession" (p. 4) because they are responsible for the training of music therapy students in clinical sites. However, there seems to be a lack of resources for supervision training at conferences or university settings. At the professional level, supervisor expertise can vary greatly, depending on whether an individual supervisor has had sufficient advanced training in both music therapy and supervision.

Forinash (2001) also noted that there are still important questions to answer regarding the efficacy of various approaches: What is the best method of supervision? Should it be action-oriented or person-oriented? When personal issues arise in the course of supervision, do we need to address these issues? If so, what would be the best way to address them? As creative arts therapists, do we integrate music or other creative mediums in supervision? How much do we use music in supervision? To what extent should we encourage supervisees to find their own voice in clinical work? In addition to these questions, issues of multicultural supervision and ethics should be considered: What are the most important considerations in cross-cultural supervision? What are the most effective ways to supervise a person whose culture differs from that of the supervisor? How can we handle racial issues that may arise in multicultural supervision? What boundary issues arise during supervision? How do we ensure ethical behaviors in supervision? How do we monitor supervisors' inherent power in supervision?

Due to the unique nature of each case in music therapy, the work of a music therapist requires ongoing development that ought to include a variety of supervision models, all of which can offer some benefits. There are several benefits to receiving adequate supervision: continued development of their knowledge and skill set, increased sense of self-awareness, early detection of feelings of stress or burnout, and development of management strategies. According to Langdon (2001), "as the music therapist continues on, day by day, the isolation and the seeming repetitiveness of the work may lead to burnout" (p. 216). Some of the strategies that are helpful in preventing burnout can be accomplished within supervision: keeping in touch with other music therapists, developing and documenting goals in order to see personal progress, and continuing education (Fowler, 2006). Another important factor to consider is that music therapy professionals are motivated to look for supervision for more practical reasons, such as attaining graduate degrees, continuing education or postgraduate institute training, exploring new areas and models of specialization, seeking greater quality of care, and personal exploration (McClain, 2001). With different models of supervision available, music therapists can choose which one or combination of models would best meet their personal and professional needs. Therefore, the model presented in this chapter is my model, AMTOS. AMTOS is one such model that allows music therapists to reap the benefits of supervision more fully.

ANALYTICAL MUSIC THERAPY–ORIENTED SUPERVISION (AMTOS)

The purpose of the AMTOS model is to meet the individual needs of professional music therapists and to reinforce the importance of supervision in general. The ultimate purpose of AMTOS is to serve clients better. To do this, AMTOS has been designed:

- to provide a support system;
- to meet the need for continued growth on the part of supervisees;
- to further develop music therapy techniques;
- to continue to develop a professional identity as a music psychotherapist;
- to identify personal issues early in their training; and
- to prevent any occupational stress and burnout.

One of the strengths of this AMTOS model is its flexibility; the format of the supervision can be customized depending on the needs and current knowledge of analytical music therapy (AMT) that the supervisees have. This model can be offered through two avenues: online supervision as well as in-person sessions. Educational technology tools can be employed to engage supervisees in experiential exercises through music and verbal discussions. Since supervisees can be supervised regardless of where they reside, AMTOS may even foster international bonds by providing an opportunity for international supervisees to experience the potential benefits of AMTOS. Beyond its flexibility, there are four main reasons that AMTOS can be beneficial for music therapists, with some being unique to this model.

First, like other models, it teaches music therapists essential skills needed to experience a deeper level of therapy. According to Pedersen (2002a) …

> Whatever method you use in music therapy, a basic tool is your own presence and mental preparedness as a therapist. Sensitive and clear musical and verbal communication with clients is another fundamental requirement … it offers training in learning not only to listen in order to analyze the client or the client's music, but also to listen to oneself listening to the client. (p. 170)

Second, AMTOS's emphasis is on the importance of including the musical process in music therapy supervision because it includes both verbal and musical processes. It is ironic that although the main tool for music therapists is music, we often rely more on verbal processes in music therapy supervision.

Third, AMTOS supervisors are knowledgeable in helping supervisees to explore their inner child and to connect music and emotions in a balanced way.

Fourth, the emphasis given to transference and countertransference and other key psychodynamic concepts in AMTOS provides supervisees an opportunity to develop their professional identity as music psychotherapists (Bruscia, 1998; Scheiby, 2001, 2002).

Through experiential methods and exploration of countertransference, the AMTOS model offers an opportunity for music therapists to enhance their expressiveness, creativity, and cognitive-emotional flexibility while also promoting cultural well-being (Kim, 2011b, 2013a, 2017). This model also focuses on increasing therapists' awareness of transference and countertransference and ability to manage their own stress that may affect sessions. While this model is widely applicable to many music therapists, it may be most effective in training music therapists whose verbal and musical expressions are inadequate or those who struggle to identify their internal strengths and transform them into creative energy. This model is particularly effective in training culturally conditioned music therapists who must adapt to be culturally responsive when working with a music therapy client who is from a different culture. Finally, music therapists who wish to continue to grow both as a person and as a professional are ideal candidates for AMTOS because they become more creative, expressive music therapists and improve their ability to express emotions outwardly. To describe the salient points in my supervision model, it is important to discuss the underlying philosophy of this model.

Philosophical Basis

The AMTOS model was greatly influenced by the analytical music therapy (AMT) approach (Priestley, 1975, 1994; Scheiby & Pedersen, 1999) and my training with analytical music therapy supervisor Benedikte Scheiby. In addition, my experiences of being supervised and supervising in both clinical and academic roles over many years has helped me to build this AMTOS model. Further, as a bicultural music therapy supervisor and educator, culturally responsive supervision (see chapter 14) and flexible learning models (Al-Qahtani & Higgins, 2012) have influenced me and given me a new way of thinking.

Analytical Music Therapy (AMT)

In the 1970s, Mary Priestley, Marjorie Wardel, and Peter Wright in Great Britain developed analytical music therapy (AMT) based on 96 experimental sessions, which were later dubbed "Intertherapy" by Mary Priestley. Wardel and Wright took on the roles of client and therapist while a third person observed and documented the sessions to provide commentary. During the Intertherapy phase, they explored new techniques and interventions that became the basis of AMT (Scheiby, 2017). Since AMT developed using a peer-supervision model, Priestley (1994) discussed the purpose of supervision, role of the supervisor, use of improvisation, and Intertherapy as a training model throughout her career. Later, Priestley implemented Intertherapy for music therapy students at the Guildhall School of Music and Drama. In order to remain creative as a therapist, Priestley (1994) suggested continuing Intertherpy with colleagues as a form of peer supervision.

AMT training has developed further since then in Europe and the United States. Eschen (2002) brought the concept to Germany, and Pedersen (2002a, 2002b) and Scheiby (2001, 2017), Priestley's first trainees, piloted experiential training in music therapy (ETMT) as a method of teaching music therapy to students at Aalborg University in Denmark in the 1990s. They believed that the experiential component of AMT training was beneficial and created a five-year music therapy training program that employed this philosophy (Scheiby & Pedersen, 1999; Wigram, Pedersen, & Bonde, 2002). In addition, they also explored *psychodynamic movement* techniques based on Priestley's method. After Scheiby moved to the United States in the early 1990s, Pedersen continued to further expand these programs with a colleague, Susanne Metzner, in Europe. Scheiby continued to develop AMT training in New York (Cohen, 2018; Scheiby, 2017).

Related Paradigms

In addition to the AMT approach, I often use Adler's (1959), Bruscia's (1995, 1998) and Kenny's (2006) theories about supervision goals and fluidity as my supervision framework because I strongly believe that their paradigms are highly applicable when supervising music therapists. As music therapists, we should continue to strive for significance and higher levels of development. I try to keep in mind when Bruscia and Kenny said that we should have fluidity: "If we can be fluid in our consciousness, then we have the richest potential for conceiving what is" (Bruscia, 1995, p. 86). We should be able to develop our own principles and values relevant to our clinical work, while being capable of being open-minded to a variety of views. If not, we may become rigid and limited in understanding other approaches or techniques that may be effective in treating our clients (Kenny, 2006) because creativity can counter rigidity.

The characteristics of creative individuals include a particularly rich fantasy life that "could tolerate ambiguity, capable of very complex symbolic identification; had more fluid and permeable outer and inner ego boundaries with a strong ego core, requiring less unconscious defensive maneuvers" (Gordon, cited in Kenny, 2006, p. 15). When we are open-minded, the awareness of our consciousness can be directed toward a more well-balanced being, and we are better able to utilize our creativity and musicality effectively. I have noticed that some supervisees have difficulty in reaching their full potential creatively and musically because they are unyielding. As a supervisor, I aim to foster creativity, musicality, and the ability to be expressive in AMTOS by helping supervisees identify what blocks their abilities so that they can grow in their self-awareness and move on to the next phase of their training. Additionally, I believe music experiences during supervision are extremely important, as supervisees are often placed in new and unfamiliar situations, which help them further develop these talents. This can be challenging if the dynamic nature of therapy is not actively addressed.

SALIENT FEATURES

The five key concepts within the AMTOS model are the supervisory relationship; the use of musical countertransference, promoting the cultural well-being of supervisees; experience-oriented supervision; nurturing supervisees' inner child (Priestley, 1994); and maintenance of psychohygiene (Jahn-Langenberg, 2001). To address these, I often utilize music-centered techniques adapted from analytical music therapy (AMT) techniques such as improvisation and psychodynamic movement.

Supervisory Relationship

Exploring the supervisory relationship between supervisees and supervisors is essential for AMTOS because it can make room for the supervisees' growth (Bernard & Goodyear, 2014; Dvorkin, 1999). To do this, supervisors must first establish a strong supervisory relationship with their supervisees and confidentiality must clearly be established. In AMTOS, this supervisory relationship is explored and strengthened over time through musical and verbal processing. Often supervisees' needs are identified during musical processing followed by the verbal processing. Supervisees' emotional reactions may be intense, particularly if they become resistant to the supervision process. Supervisors may touch on sensitive personal issues of which supervisees are not aware. Supervisees can grow if they take this opportunity to work with their supervisors to resolve these problems. It may be necessary for them to make some immediate changes so that they can serve their clients in more effectively:

> While there could be a component of acting-out in such instances, the supervisory relationship has to be robust enough to work through such enactments. This robustness of supervisory relationship has a bearing because it is important for the student supervisee to develop an ability for negative capacity, which can be thought of as having the ability not to understand. In addition, the supervisor should not shy away from difficulty areas. (Sutton & De Backer, 2014, p. 314)

Some of the common issues that supervisors experience are how much feedback to give, what to address in supervision and when, how to work with these issues, and how many musical or verbal processes should take place. Improvisation helps supervisees to process their issues and makes the nature of them more apparent by bringing them to the surface.

Musical Countertransference

AMTOS as a countertransference-oriented supervision model that emphasizes facilitating supervisees in uncovering unconscious feelings and issues that interfere with their relationships with their clients, co-therapists, and supervisors, as well as with the therapeutic and/or supervisory process. AMTOS helps supervisees become better aware of their own feelings and thoughts that may affect their sessions. In addition, supervisees learn to manage their own countertransference reactions in future sessions.

The manifestation of transference and countertransference in supervision is complex because there are multiple layers of the phenomenon. Supervisees consciously and unconsciously interact with their clients or clinical situations based on their own past experiences instead of responding to the client, or they react from a physically or psychologically ungrounded place. As an example of a parallel process, transference and countertransference can also manifest in sessions when supervisees "identify the emotions being repressed by the original client as well as [their] own reaction and avoidance of the suppressed feelings" (Young & Aigen, 2010, p. 126). In addition, e-countertransference (emotional echoes) (Priestley, 1994) can manifest in supervisees physical and emotional reactions toward their clients that originated from their clients.

Countertransference can be detrimental to the therapeutic relationship when supervisees are unaware of it or unable to manage it appropriately. In addition, supervisors' countertransference reactions are also important and can be utilized to facilitate supervisees' growth (Maroda, 1994; Pedersen, 2006). Therefore, these instances should be identified and be utilized effectively to help supervisees to work through these experiences, reframe them, and move forward. It is also important that the AMTOS supervisors also receive clinical supervision, since this type of work requires continual understanding about life, clients, and themselves (Robbins, 2008a, p. 17).

How do we determine if there is countertransference? Using music with supervisees often triggers musical countertransference and can help the supervisor to determine whether it is present (Scheiby, 1998, 2002, 2005). There are a variety of cues that supervisors can use to determine whether music is manifesting countertransference. If they can accurately analyze their own musical responses to supervisees' music, they can monitor, adjust, and use these reactions to guide subsequent interventions in the session. Listening to improvisations that are recorded to monitor sessions, either in a supervision context or alone, can be used to detect countertransferential music:

> From experience, we know that, when the supervisee improvises with the supervisor, the countertransference becomes "hear-able" when the supervisor has enough insight and experience to make a differentiation between the transference and the countertransference. This gives the supervisee an understanding of the [patient's] inner conflicts, personality, and defense mechanisms; it is the task of the supervisor to give the supervisee the possibility of exploring musically how he is listening, acting, and reacting in his relationship with the patient. Transference and countertransference are thus an important aspect of music therapy supervision. (Sutton & De Backer, 2014, p. 316)

Culture-Related Countertransference

Personal, social, cultural, organizational, and professional factors can influence therapeutic relationships with our clients in music therapy (Scheiby & Kim, 2005). For example, perfectionism is an area that supervisees from the Sinosphere struggle with in their learning process. Perfectionism can be regarded as a virtue in these cultures; for them, acceptance of making mistakes was necessary to explore diverse options for their clients in sessions. As Kenny (2006) eloquently described ...

> We are all in the human condition. Who would deny that? This condition can be used as we choose. It brings us home to paradox. ... We are prisoners of our conditions— limited and bound. Yet conditions are also paradoxically what allow us to grow, expand, and change. ... Conditions are part of beauty. (p. 98)

The discrepancy that exists between the culture of Western music therapy and Eastern cultures can interfere with supervisees' growth because they tend to inhibit themselves to pursue perfection in their work. They tend to be reserved and have difficulty in taking risks. This phenomenon can be further complicated when the client, supervisor, and supervisee all have different cultural backgrounds, which can often be the case. For example, a white supervisor noticed that her supervisee came from the Sinosphere, had grown up outside the U.S., and often utilized a sentimental mood of music in her improvisation when working with her clients who come from South Africa. The supervisor was speculating on whether this was clinically effective. Apparently, strong reactions toward this music were brought up by both supervisee and supervisor. By learning more about cultural and personal history and about the supervisee and client, the supervisor was able to help the supervisee to better understand what she was doing and the reasons why she often played this with this client in sessions. Often, significant work is required to explore culture-related countertransference in AMTOS supervision.

Experience-Oriented Supervision

Based on their presenting case issues, supervisees have an opportunity to work on these countertransference issues that have arisen in their work by engaging in music experientials. Experience-oriented supervision emphasizes using the supervisee's personal experiences during their sessions. The experiential component of this supervision "… focuses on the presence and function of the music therapist being with clients, and can be seen as a basic training for all music therapists irrespective of the area in which they are working" (Pedersen, 2002b, p. 171). In role-plays, supervisees participate in experiential exercises during supervision sessions, taking on the role of therapist, client, or colleague. Role-plays are a particularly effective method of helping supervisees learn better ways of working with clients (Murphy, 2007; Murphy & Wheeler, 2005; Young & Aigen, 2010) and can also be used to resolve a conflict that a supervisee may have with a colleague. Supervisees will gain new insight about themselves or others, regardless of which role supervisees play. For example, asking supervisees to take the role of themselves while the supervisor takes the role of the colleague who is in conflict, or vice versa, to explore what would come up in improvisation can be helpful. Music usually brings out the blind spots for supervisees and others.

Nurturing the Supervisee's Inner Child

As Priestley (1994) asserted, regardless of our chronological age, we have an inner child who needs to be nurtured so that our inborn creativity can help us grow as a person and a music therapist. She explains how important it is for the therapist to recognize our "inner child" when working with a client, as …

> … the knowledge and healing of [our] inner child through the unfreezing of its traumatized emotion, are an essential part of his inner preparation for work. In this way, he will make sure of treating the patients as separate individuals without causing them to express the emotions of their unconscious and projected damaged inner child instead. (p. 214)

I have observed that some supervisees have trouble with utilizing their creativity and musicality. They are emotionally frozen and disconnected from themselves and what goes on during their sessions at times, or they may not even be aware of their state of mind. As a result, they cannot optimally use their creativity and musicality. Some may be able to be more expressive when playing alone than when playing music with their clients in sessions. In some cases, they have difficulty in expressing their empathy to clients musically or verbally. For example, I worked with a supervisee who initially was very defensive and unable to utilize her voice therapeutically in her sessions. Voice was her primary instrument, and she had relatively good technique and control of her voice as a classical singer. Through improvisation during supervision, she explored ways in which her inner child may have affected her sessions. She explored her voice in a vocal improvisation titled "My Voice," while I provided a holding space with a steady ostinato vocalization. At first she felt awkward in doing so, but as time passed, the music helped her to focus better. She shared with me that she remembered her critical mother during vocalization, which prevented her from freely vocalizing. She was able to identify the issue in supervision and felt the need to work through it further in personal therapy. Incorporating preverbal vocalization and constructive feedback about her therapeutic voice throughout supervision helped her increase her self-awareness and become more comfortable with her voice. Austin (2002) supports this idea:

> The act of singing is empowering: sensing the life force flowing through the body; feelings one's strength in the ability to produce strong and prolonged tones; experiencing one's creativity in the process of making something beautiful; having the ability to move oneself and others; and hearing one's own voice mirroring back the undeniable confirmation of existence. Owning one's voice is owning one's authority and ending a cycle of victimization. (p. 236)

Sometimes, a supervisee's personal issues related to past experiences arise. For example, childhood relationships so profoundly affect us that we "reply" to them over and over again: "... the past is not over and done with, but lives on in the present person, affecting every mood and every decision and every relationship" (Priestley, 1994, p. 207). Therefore, it is very important that supervisees understand and analyze the messages from their inner child.

Using the AMTOS techniques, I explored a supervisee's discomfort when working with adolescents through an improvisation titled "Feeling of Discomfort with My Client, M." During the role-play, I played the role of the client, M., and the supervisee played as M.'s therapist. We engaged in improvisation. He chose to play some percussion instruments such as the wooden block, small gongs, and sticks, while I vocalized and played a djembe. His music was rather inconsistent, often changing tempo, and he made a lot of crashing percussion sounds. I had a hard time connecting with him and his music. I felt that he was not willing to hear or respond to my voice and music. He ended his music abruptly and then would go silent for a moment. Eventually, he shared that he had been bullied when he was young. Also, he did not remember whether anyone in his family had provided a solid structure and set boundaries in his childhood. His experience of being bullied and lack of consistency and structure were brought out through supervision, and he became aware that he needed to work on these problems in personal therapy. The primary purpose of identifying parts of supervisees' inner child is to determine when it is causing trouble and affecting the therapeutic relationship with clients. Once these unconscious conflicts are brought out in supervision, supervisees must work through the challenges more in personal therapy. Self-awareness will help therapists to engage in supervision more deeply; however, "the ability to maintain the boundary between supervision and therapy is a central requisite skill in the registration scheme for specialist clinical supervisors ..." (Lang, McInerney, Monaghan, & Sutton, 2002, p. 212).

Maintenance of Psychohygiene

Since we, as music therapists, are helping professionals, the nature of our job as a caretaker may consume a lot of energy. Self-care is very important to ensure the quality of service that we provide to our clients (Jahn-Langenberg, 2001; Kim, 2008; Robbins, 2008a), as well as to maintain own health. In AMTOS, maintaining supervisees' "psychohygiene" (Jahn-Langenberg, 2001) is emphasized in every supervision session. Maintaining psychohygiene, or emotional cleanliness, increases the ability to be fully present in sessions:

The desired psychoanalytic perceptual attitude of balanced-floating attentiveness, an openness for the events of the inner world, is described as the optimal centering of the therapist on his/her own person … to be used as living instruments of perception—this optimal attitude remains a posture to be continually reacquired and practiced. (Jahn-Langenberg, 2001, p. 275)

Supervisees often share that they need to manage their stress well to be more grounded in sessions. In the AMTOS model, supervisors sensitively detect supervisees' emotional status to help them develop strategies to manage work-related stress. Their stress management skills need to be addressed in supervision so that supervisees can manage their stress better and view their daily stress in a more positive way: "times of stress, viewed as opportunities for maturation, can produce in both therapist and patient the incentive to struggle and grow" (Priestley, 1994, p. 198).

Music is a powerful and effective tool for maintaining one's psychohygiene. Music can help to explore one's emotional life and also bring more awareness about one's current state of mind. Improvisation or other creative modalities can be used to lower supervisees' stress levels (Kim, 2011a, 2011b). For example, I often use chanting to liberate the stress of supervisees. Below is an example of a chanting experience that can be used in supervision. More exercises are described in my chapter in *Guidelines for Music Therapy Practice in Mental Health* (2013).

Chanting to Liberate Stress

Supervisees create a sound or chants based on a personal affirmation, a prayer, or a line of a song and sing it repeatedly to release stress. The goals are to release tension, to build a stronger identity, and to create harmony between mind, body, and spirit. Repetitive chanting may deepen brain wave activity, increase warmth in the hands, and create a feeling of being centered. Supervisees with tensed muscles or who are fatigued or are depressed may benefit from this method. Some supervisees may be reluctant to try chanting due to unfamiliarity with this method or due to religious beliefs. The supervisor begins with *music-assisted breathing* to center the clients. She asks the clients to choose an affirmation or word based on personal need—for example, "I can do it" or "I love myself"—or to use a phrase from a prayer or a meaningful song. They then close their eyes, find a tone, and sing the word or phrase, using a simple melody and repeating it. The supervisor can add gentle and nonintrusive instrumental accompaniment or provide a soft, steady beat on a drum. Self-produced repeated sounds are most effective for relaxation. If a supervisee cannot think of a word or phrase, the supervisor may demonstrate a sound and ask supervisees to repeat it. For example, the "M" sound is a connector—"Om" can move one from the objective world to the inner world; "Aum" can be sung for a closure. Humming a melody is soothing and can help them relax. Chants and words can be sung in call-and-response, with the supervisees repeating the chant after they sing. Singing or playing spiritual songs (e.g., "Down by the Riverside," "Nobody Knows the Trouble I've Seen") or their favorite songs can also be used for liberating stress (Kim, 2013, pp. 823–824).

Some supervisees have difficulty in achieving a balance between doing and being in sessions. This may be because they have a very hectic daily schedule or be a sign of their resistance toward looking at themselves:

It is one of the great pleasures in life to be able to occasionally just "hang out" and do nothing. The ability to do this is part of being "nice" to oneself. It is also a sign of having some degree of "inner peace." It is a pity that so many of us really cannot "relax." It can also be a sign that these people have "lost touch" with themselves. (Rauchway, 1985, p. 80)

AMTOS Techniques

Use of Improvisation

Stemming from the psychoanalytic approach (Freud, 1949; Winnicott, 1971) that hypothesized that the three parts of one's personality (the id, ego, and superego) are constantly battling inside of us, our mind works with a large number of hidden ideas—especially our fantasies, unfulfilled wishes, traumas, and conflicts. These unconscious components of our psyches can often be uncovered through free improvisation in AMTOS (Priestley, 1974). For the supervision sessions, "as one might expect, such things as music can become either parental or sibling figures and can easily shift back and forth between these vertical and horizontal types of relationships" (Bruscia, 1998, p. 27). Therefore, improvisation is an important medium for AMTOS. There are several reasons to use free improvisation:

- To uncover issues while role-playing based upon the clinical cases;
- To deepen understanding of therapeutic processes;
- To nurture the inner child through improvisation;
- To explore aspects of one's self;
- To enhance creativity and spontaneity in improvisation (Gilboa, Bodner, & Amir, 2006; Priestley, 1994); and
- To manage stress (Fowler, 2006; Kim, 2011b, 2013b; Pelletier, 2004).

Improvisation can provide supervisees with an opportunity to identify their blind spots that affected sessions and better prepare them to react authentically to clients and music. Particularly when supervisees experience atypical and strong reactions toward their clients, co-therapists, caregivers, or music, exploring the phenomenon of their countertransference and transference through free improvisation can bring their unknown issues to the surface by moving from unconscious to conscious. By doing so, unpleasant and uncomfortable feelings may arise and these feelings need to be addressed, regardless of whether supervisees are willing, if therapeutic relationships are affected. Sometimes, supervisees have difficulty in expressing their unpleasant emotions due to their personal issues or culture. It is important for supervisees to understand that unpleasant feelings are also a part of their own emotions, and if the sound is authentic and meaningful, they should give themselves permission to express their state of mind in the moment. Also, for some of them, expressing their unpleasant emotions through improvisation may be easier than verbalizing them. Finally, improvisations in AMTOS do not always have to be verbalized, as supervisees often benefit from engaging in the free nature of improvisation.

Supervisees' resistance toward the therapeutic process can also be identified and worked through improvisation. For example, when reviewing a session video with my supervisee, I noticed that she had a tendency to sound very organized and harmonious, even when her client seemed to need different sounds. When I shared my observation with her, she expressed that she has difficulty in creating certain sounds, for example, loud, dissonant, "ugly" sounds, in music. We discussed what "ugly" sounds are and what these sounds mean to her. She then agreed to play "ugly" music with my support. She was playing on the piano, making sounds tentatively while I expressed how her music influenced me by playing on another piano that sounded similar to hers. After this, while we were listening to the audio recording together, she noticed that her sounds were not what she had thought she was playing. I asked her possible reasons for the discrepancy between what she was playing and what she thought she was playing. Then, I asked her to play an "ugly" sound again on the cymbal and drum, which she do not use often. At this time, I asked her to permit herself to play "ugly" sounds on these instruments and see what would come up during improvisation. This time, I noticed that her posture was more open and a bit more relaxed, and she seemed to be more connected to her playing.

I also encouraged her to make any sounds she wanted. She tried vocalizing but was unable to fully engage in it. After this, she shared with me that the ugly sounds were not as uncomfortable as she had previously thought. Rather, she felt more relieved and her playing was more communicative within herself. She was working on a part of herself into which she had not yet tapped.

Furthermore, a supervisee expressed that she was angry at her on-site supervisor who had co-led a session with her. She felt that her on-site supervisor was controlling and critical of her teenage client and her. Apparently, this impacted the therapeutic process in sessions and she was unable to discuss this with her in a professional manner. Instead, the supervisee was experiencing somatic symptoms whenever working with this client. When we engaged in an improvisation titled "I Am Angry at You," I took the role of her supervisor. She chose to play the piano and made rather a mild sound, while I played a dominating role on the drum. After we completed the improvisation, I shared with her what I heard in the music. She responded that she did not like to sound angry because having angry feelings made her feel guilty due to her upbringing. She asked me why playing "angry" music is necessary. She felt that her supervisor was an authority, and she needed to listen to her, blaming herself if she did not. I explained to her that she looked very tense, which would affect her therapeutic relationship with her clients if the cause were not explored properly. Then, she shared with me that her supervisor reminded her of her own mother, who was controlling and critical. Once this was processed musically and verbally to provide her with an outlet so she could release the strong emotions, she appeared to be more assertive and relaxed. We rehearsed communicating with her on-site supervisor to let her know that she has feelings toward her in a professional way. I discussed ways to deal with her anger and to set limits with the supervisor, drawing on advice from Rauchway (1985):

> Emotionally mature [supervisors] are open to all their feelings, fantasies, and thoughts. They do not judge or condemn any of these aspects of their inner world. They are well aware that all feelings, fantasies, and thoughts are simply human and, as such, need simply to be accepted by the individual experiencing them. In essence, a person's inner world can only hurt this individual if he does not accept it or tries to divide feelings into being either "good" or "bad." (p. 3)

A major function of music in AMTOS is rooted in the concept of the inner child and examines our unconscious as proposed by Mary Priestley (1994). In AMTOS, music can be used as "a musical representation of a fantasy of reliving a moment in the acoustic-mirror stage poised right between complete union with the voice of the mother and a recognition of acoustic difference between one's own voice and the voices of the mother and the father" (Schwarz, 1997, p. 82). Music often breaks down defenses and is a bridge between unconscious and conscious. Using the ATMOS approach with my supervisee helped her to process the difficulties of her past and unleash her inner child.

Improvising with supervisees helps them to express what happens during their sessions and to re-create their true emotions (Ahonen-Eerikäinen, 2007). Supervisees may have difficulty in connecting themselves into music as well as their clients. This may result in a lack of empathy toward their clients. During supervision sessions, some supervisees are unable to fully explain what happened in sessions or interpret their sessions by themselves, which is another sign of resistance. I usually ask supervisees to play an improvisation to describe their cases and clinical problems before describing them in words. At times, it is difficult for supervisees to think of a phrase and give a title to improvisations before actually improvising. When this happens, we decide to play and see what comes up in the music. However, oftentimes the music finishes and has done the intended job without a title. Consequently, supervisees became more expressive verbally and musically and have an opportunity to experience emotional release and less anxiety.

At times, supervisees may experience unexpected or anticipated stress, so they need to develop proper coping strategies. For example, a supervisee expressed that recently he was sad, occasionally depressed, and generally felt helpless. His world had been turned upside down by his personal circumstances, which had been aggravated by his concerns about his personal and professional issues. While improvising with him, I provided a holding space, utilized a rubato, and created a soundscape. Different parts of his personality came out in music. His musical expression became strong and firm and his music could be described as abrupt—interruptions, with quick changes that were driven by frustration. My countertransference was, "I am frustrated because I am not able to do what I usually do." I felt pressured to take care of him all the time. Here was a young boy who wanted Mother to do everything. It seemed that I was experiencing what this supervisee may go through every day. It was clear that expressing his feelings in music was easier than expressing them in words. At first, he was unable to elaborate on his thoughts and feelings or discuss his problems with me, but we were able to communicate on an emotional level through improvised music. As I was aware of both my supervisee's transference and my countertransference, I was able to better understand his emotional life, guide the therapy direction, facilitate this musical process, and support him. After we finished the improvisation, we discussed what we experienced, and the supervisee was able to come up with a theme: "I Ran Out of My Resources!" This supervisee learned that it is OK to seek help, even as a music therapist.

Free improvisation can be a challenge for some supervisees. They often think a lot while playing it, so there is a lack of spontaneity. This is not limited to those who need technical and functional skills, but also is seen among those who have received good formal musical training. Their perfectionism may get in the way. They may take some time to learn to accept themselves. Priestley (1994) claimed that "it is impossible to teach a trainee AMT how to improvise with a patient. The only thing that one can do is to help him to teach himself" (p. 143). She did, however, offer a few guidelines for learning, which include to: (1) learn to improvise by oneself, (2) continue to develop musical relationships with oneself, (3) develop a dual sensitivity to inner and outer stimuli from the client, (4) develop the ability to understand what is in the music that is not in the words, (5) develop a sensitivity to the healing music of the client, and (6) learn to judge when to respond to a stimulus and when to hold back.

Creative Arts Forms

Besides improvisation, utilizing a variety of modalities (e.g., art, dance, drama) as a primary source in AMTOS can help supervisees to process their clinical work better and often be an effective way to enhance their therapeutic skills. As music therapists, we are accustomed to utilizing creative forms to process our work, and we seem to respond to creative modalities more effectively. For example, supervisors can incorporate different modalities into supervisory work by asking supervisees to play music, draw, move, or write creatively to reflect on their thoughts and feelings about clients (Kim, 2017; Ko, 2016; Robbins, 2008b).

Psychodynamic Movement

One of the salient points in AMTOS is to emphasize bodily movement as a way of communicating with one another, as "… the nature of the human mind is largely determined by the form of the human body, putting forward the idea of an embodied cognition and an embodied mind … knowing can happen in the body, in an unconscious, preconscious, and or nonlanguaged way" (Panhofer, Payne, Meekums, & Parke, 2010, p. 12). Developed by Priestley and modified by Pedersen and Scheiby, improvised movement to improvised music (Pedersen, 2002b) is particularly useful in training students to gain greater insight into their entire selves. While one or more supervisees are engaged in improvised movement on an agreed upon topic, other supervisees follow and interpret the movement in a parallel instrumental or vocal improvisation (p. 191). In doing this, supervisees have an opportunity to explore their kinetic melodies—"a chain of isolated motor impulses which, upon repetition, become stored in the body" (Panhofer et al., 2010, p. 12).

For example, supervisees improvise movements based on their experiences of stress while the supervisor provides a grounding accompaniment and interprets the movements musically. They may also vocalize while moving. This method (improvised movement to improvised music) is adapted from Priestley (1975). Priestley claims that communicating with one's own body is "the most primitive and natural form: expressive movement" (Priestley, 1975, p. 78). It is important that supervisors address supervisees' self-awareness as a whole when targeting stress reduction. This includes the supervisee's body, mind, and spirit. Being aware of them, as a whole, will help make the music more effective when combined with other modalities. Through moving, speaking, and relaxing to music, one learns to relax different kinds of tension. One also learns to be aware of tense shoulders and thighs and of feelings of anger and jealousy and to investigate their causes and try to do something about them (p. 84). The goals are to release tension, to develop coping skills, and to improve connections with one's mind and body.

AMTOS OBJECTIVES

Analytical Music Therapy–Oriented Supervision (AMTOS) offers an opportunity to:

- Continue to develop personal and professional growth
- Discover and work with the supervisee's inner child
- Identify and alleviate any conflicts and further develop one's integrity
- Better manage countertransference issues that may arise in sessions
- Identify culture-related countertransference
- Promote cultural well-being
- Become freer in musical expression
- Develop strategies for managing stress
- Relieve somatic symptoms
- Obtain professional information

Competency Objectives

Supervisees work toward meeting personal, technical, artistic, and theoretical competencies. These competencies have been developed based on the advanced AMTA competencies, as well as Scheiby's AMT training competencies (2001, 2017):

Technical Competency

- Build therapeutic presence
- Work on mental preparedness
- Establish an effective working alliance
- Be able to relate to the client authentically
- Develop assessment, goals, objectives, and evaluation skills
- Develop advanced clinical listening skills
- Identify therapeutic themes
- Integrate between music and words
- Utilize group dynamics
- Understand the dynamics of client, music, and music therapist
- Manage the possible recurrent countertransference reactions in the future sessions
- Communicate clearly bodily
- Keep appropriate boundaries

- Sit with silence
- Conduct termination responsibly and creatively
- Develop effective documentation skills
- Facilitation of integration between music and words
- Explore psychodynamic phenomena: transference, resistance, projection, regression, internalization in/outside the music
- Develop strategies for managing occupational stress and self-care

Theoretical Competency

- Identify developmental stages
- Understand therapeutic relationship and psychodynamic concepts
- Read the most current literature regarding music psychotherapy and supervision
- Understand and effectively utilize countertransference and transference, resistance, ego defenses, splitting, projection, unconscious phenomena in and outside the music

Artistic Competency

- Utilize a symbolic use of instruments
- Utilize improvisation analytically in supervision
- Use metaphors in and outside the music to facilitate supervision process
- Continue to develop free improvisation skills
- Learn advanced improvisation techniques
- Explore unpleasant emotions through free improvisation
- Analytically utilize and analyze an improvisation
- Utilize AMT musical interventions and verbal interventions
- Choose instruments and musical interventions conducive to the therapeutic process

Personal Competency

- Explore interpersonal skills
- Continue to develop the trainee's own musical self
- Develop an ability to manage transference and countertransference and use oneself effectively
- Understand the AMT supervision methods
- Explore the supervisee's own cultural background and how it affects others in supervision
- Increase self-awareness
- Discover and work with the supervisee's inner child
- Work with the trainee's strengths, resources, challenges, emotions, dreams, and images
- Explore the supervisee's own cultural background and how it affects others in sessions
- Identify the supervisee's strengths, resources, and challenges as a student therapist
- Explore an individuation process as a student therapist
- Explore the trainee's musical self

SUPERVISION FORMAT

AMTOS can be done in person, via telephone, or via Internet meeting applications such as Skype, Zoom, Google Hangouts, or Canvas. Ideally, supervisees will be placed either in individual or group supervision sessions, with a maximum of five supervisees in a group session. The ideal length of weekly sessions is an hour for individual sessions and one-and-a-half hours to two hours for group sessions.

Procedure

At the initial supervision session, supervisors will ask supervisees to play an improvisation that expresses themselves. Using Priestley's (1994) Emotional Spectrum, supervisors assess supervisees' flexibility, readiness for music psychotherapy, and creativity with a series of titled improvisations. Discussion aimed at assessing supervisees' strengths and challenges as a music therapist follows. The supervision schedule, goals, and consent forms are then discussed, based on the assessment and interview. Supervision sessions are provided according to the following guidelines. It should be noted that the procedure of the sessions is flexible and depends on supervisees' needs.

Identification of Themes for Exploration

Supervisees will propose a topic to be discussed in supervision that day. For example, a session description or an excerpt from a recording of a session may be used, or supervisees can suggest professional issues such as preparing presentations, relationships with colleagues, or professional identity. Depending on the topic, the supervisor may suggest role-plays, demonstrations, or further discussions. Often the sessions start with an opening improvisation to clarify presenting problems and issues. Supervisors ask them to think about a case client or group on which they want to work in that session and improvise on the case without telling supervisors. This technique is especially helpful when supervisees have difficulty in articulating the supervision topics.

Improvisations: Role-Plays, Demonstrations, Free Improvisations

Supervisors and supervisees will decide their roles to improvise. When the issues are not clear, the supervisee may play alone and supervisors can take an active role as a listener, or they take roles as therapist and client to further identify issues and find a way to work through them. Also, supervisors demonstrate and use aforementioned music therapy supervision techniques. On other occasions, supervisees may need to make free improvisations in order to energize and enhance creativity. In this case, it is the supervisee's choice to determine the supervisor's improvisational role. Supervisees will have an opportunity to evaluate their state of being and practice stress management, as well as learn techniques and strategies that can be helpful in taking care of themselves.

Discussion

At this stage, the supervisee and supervisor improvise together and then analyze their music. This leads to new insight about supervisees' clinical work and their relationships with their clients, co-therapists, and related professionals and caregivers. Other role-plays and demonstrations may help them to integrate their learning. In addition, pertinent reading and professional information will be given to the supervisee. Supervision sessions are video- or audio-recorded. During this stage, they listen to the recordings and clarify which parts they perceive differently. Often, this can lead to another improvisation. Countertransference can be shared if supervisees are ready to accept it and if the comments could be helpful. Supervisors begin with what they heard in the music or their imagery experiences. Then they ask supervisees to comment to help link their past experiences with the music, if relevant.

Closure

The supervisor and supervisee will summarize what they have learned from the particular session and develop strategies for the supervisee to follow. If necessary, homework assignments will be given to the supervisee. These might include, for example, improvising every day, assigning related articles, and written homework.

QUALIFICATIONS AND ROLE OF SUPERVISOR

Supervisors must successfully complete advanced AMT training. A minimum of five years of clinical and supervisory experience is required. In addition, supervisors should continue to receive supervision from a more experienced AMT supervisor and be actively involved in continuing education. Supervisors must adhere to the AMTA code of ethics and participate in professional activities to promote the music therapy profession.

Teaching, supervising, and music therapy all depend on empathetic understanding (Bruscia, personal communication, May, 2010). When working with supervisees, empathy is key to building an effective supervisory relationship between the supervisee and supervisor. Eschen (2002) claimed that "... empathy is one of the preconditions for understanding. Having been understood (by mother, father, therapist, and so on) is one of the preconditions to understanding oneself and developing self-esteem and sense of identity" (p. 18).

Supervisors are effective when they take the initiative to make and maintain meaningful and genuine connections with each supervisee. Without this understanding, it is difficult to build an effective supervisory relationship between the two parties. This responsibility becomes essential when training music therapists. Supervisors have a professional responsibility under which they are accountable for guiding and advising supervisees who work with emotionally vulnerable clients. Supervisors encourage supervisees to foster empathic attitudes, become more open-minded, and have a better cultural understanding of their clients.

As a supervisor, I have noticed that supervisees are more motivated when they feel understood, encouraged, and valued (Kim, 2008). From the very start of the supervision process, supervisees know that I genuinely care for them and that I will support them in whatever capacity I can. Even with more challenging supervisees who act out during supervision, I find that it is more effective to find their strengths first and acknowledge them, instead of targeting their challenges for correction. This is even more important for supervisees who grew up in a culture where "making a mistake" was seen as a failure. For example, a supervisee was devastated when she was notified that she did not pass her board certification exam. This was unacceptable within her cultural upbringing. Her supervisor explained to her that this could happen to native-born music therapy students as well, and that this did not mean that she was incapable of doing music therapy in the near future or that she had let her family down. Building on supervisees' strengths allows valuable opportunities to inspire passion and empower students to improve on their professional and personal skills.

The AMTOS supervisor takes on the role of a container, resonator, supporter, and nurturer. Scheiby (2001) noted that "first and foremost, the supervisor must be able to function as a *container* for the student therapist ... the supervisor has to be able to receive, retain, and sit with these feelings, and eventually help the supervisee to express them in music ...." (p. 315). In this role, the supervisor displays a nonjudgmental attitude and believes in the supervisee's utmost potential. The supervisor also functions as a resonator for supervisees. As a supporter, the supervisor uses empathy to become a part of the supervisee's musical and verbal worlds. The supervisor also serves as a mentor. A supervisor observes the supervisee's emotional world and provides guidance in cultivating freer expressiveness, as well as a balanced emotional world. Nurturers are concerned with both the intellect and the emotions of the supervisee, providing professional information and guidance. It is important for supervisors to share their own principles and values relevant to supervisees' clinical work, while being capable of being open-minded. If they are not open, they may become rigid and limited in understanding other approaches or techniques that may be effective in supervising supervisees from diverse cultures. Moreover, this inflexibility will adversely affect their supervisory relationship with their supervisees.

CONFIDENTIALITY

Prior to the first supervision session, the prospective supervisee and supervisor will have an interview session to discuss each other's expectations about the supervision, including goals, guidelines, and payment. The supervisee will sign a consent form that covers confidentiality and professional ethics (Dileo, 2001). Occasionally, personal issues may surface in the course of discussion in unanticipated ways. The supervision sessions are limited to educational learning purposes and are not personal therapy. Any supervisee who needs further exploration of personal issues will be referred to appropriate resources.

Note that all personally identifiable information (e.g., medical services—spoken, written, printed, photographic, and electronic) are *kept confidential,* except when the supervisor deems it necessary to share with the appropriate faculty or college personnel to protect the well-being of the client, supervisee, or others. This is in accordance with the AMTA Code of Ethics (2017). Supervisors periodically discuss and monitor supervisees' progress as a team, sharing only the information necessary to provide a better learning experience, safeguard the health and well-being of the supervisees, and protect the quality of care for the client while maintaining confidentiality. Anticipating authentic participation, session attendance and cancellation policies and payment methods are addressed on the form.

SUMMARY

AMTOS, by expanding on Priestley's model (1975, 1994) and Scheiby and Pedersen's training model (1999), provides supervisees with an opportunity to increase awareness of the transference and countertransference that may arise in sessions. They can become more centered as a music therapist, experience less occupational stress, and develop cultural competency by using AMTOS. In AMTOS, I have witnessed and experienced how clinical supervision can be a transformative experience that encourages growth for both the supervisee and the supervisor through effective supervisory relationships.

Every supervisory relationship is unique. To facilitate growth, supervisors establish a strong and effective relationship and show genuine concern for supervisees' evolution, and thus they become receptive. This results in positive outcomes. When I work with my supervisees in AMTOS by utilizing music and creative mediums to perform case analysis, discussion, teaching, or engaging improvisation or when demonstrating music therapy strategies and techniques, vibrant interactions happen. Improvisation is vital to both increasing the awareness of and bringing to the surface the unconscious in each supervisee's music therapy sessions. It can also help supervisees to analyze their progress in supervision sessions. When supervisors and supervisees together become fluid, the awareness of their consciousness can be expanded toward a well-balanced being and "we have the richest potential for conceiving what is" (Bruscia, 1995, p. 86). Ultimately, supervisees will become more open, creative, and musical when working with their clients. The goal of the AMTOS model is to provide an opportunity to explore a supervisee's own professional identity as a music psychotherapist as well as to motivate and develop music therapists who seek further advanced training.

REFERENCE LIST

Adler, A. (1959). *Understanding human nature*. New York, NY: Premier Books.

Ahonen-Eerikäinen, H. (2007). *Group analytic music therapy*. Gilsum, NH: Barcelona Publishers.

Al-Qahtani, A. A. Y., & Higgins, S. E. (2012). Effects of traditional, blended and e-learning on students' achievement in higher education. *Journal of Computer-Assisted Learning, 29*(3), 220–234.

American Music Therapy Association (AMTA). (2017). *AMTA Code of Ethics*. Retrieved November 11, 2017, from http://www.musictherapy.org/about/competencies/

Austin, D. (2002). The voice of trauma: a wounded healer's perspective. In J. P. Sutton (Ed.), *Music, music therapy, and trauma: International perspectives* (pp. 231–259). London, UK: Jessica Kingsley Publishers.

Bernard, J. M., & Goodyear, R. K. (2014). *Fundamentals of clinical supervision* (5th ed.). Upper Saddle River, NJ: Pearson.

Bruscia, K. (1995). Modes of consciousness in guided imagery and music (GIM: A therapist's experience of the guiding process. In C. Kenny (Ed.), *Listening, playing, creating. Essays on the power of sound*. Albany, NY: State University of New York.

Bruscia, K. (Ed.). (1998). *The dynamics of music psychotherapy*. Gilsum, NH: Barcelona Publishers.

Cohen, N. S. (2018). *Advanced methods of music therapy practice*. London, UK: Jessica Kingsley Publishers.

Dileo, C. (2001). Ethical issues in supervision. In M. Forinash (Ed.), *Music therapy supervision* (pp. 19–38). Gilsum, NH: Barcelona Publishers.

Dvorkin, J. (1999). Psychoanalytically oriented music therapy supervision. In T. Wigram & J. De Backer (Eds.), *Clinical applications of music therapy in developmental disability, pediatrics, and neurology*. London, UK: Jessica Kingsley Publishers.

Eschen, J. (Ed.). (2002). *Analytical music therapy*. London, UK: Jessica Kingsley Publishers.

Forinash, M. (Ed.). (2001). *Music therapy supervision*. Gilsum, NH: Barcelona Publishers.

Fowler, K. L. (2006). The relations between personality characteristics, work environment, and the professional well-being of music therapists. *Journal of Music Therapy, 33*(3), 174–197.

Freud, S. (1949). *An outline of psychoanalysis*. New York, NY: Norton.

Gilboa, A., Bodner, E., & Amir, D. (2006). Emotional communicability in improvised music: The case of music therapists. *Journal of Music Therapy, 33*(3), 198–225.

Jahn-Langenberg, M. (2001). Psychodynamic perspectives in professional supervision. In M. Forinash (Ed.), *Music therapy supervision* (pp. 271–280). Gilsum, NH: Barcelona Publishers.

Kenny, C. (2006). *Music and life in the field of play: An anthology*. Gilsum, NH: Barcelona Publishers.

Kim, S. (2008). The supervisee's experience in cross-cultural music therapy supervision. In S. Hadley (Ed.), *Qualitative inquiries in music therapy: A monograph series* (Vol. 4, pp. 1–44). Gilsum, NH: Barcelona Publishers.

Kim, S. (2011a). Analytical Music Therapy–oriented supervision (AMTOS) examined within the context of Asian cultures. *Proceedings of the 13th World Congress of Music Therapy*, Korea.

Kim, S. (2011b). Predictors of acculturative stress among international music therapy students in the U.S. *Music Therapy Perspectives, 13*, 126–132.

Kim, S. (2013a). The Cultural Integrity of a Music Therapist in Analytical Music Therapy–Oriented Supervision (AMTOS). *Voices: A World Forum for Music Therapy*. Retrieved June 10, 2013, from http://testvoices.uib.no/?q=fortnightly-columns/2013-cultural-integrity-music-therapist-analytical-music-therapy-oriented-superv

Kim, S. (2013b). Stress reduction and wellness. In L. Eyre (Ed.), *Guidelines for Music Therapy Practice in Mental Health: A Four-Volume Series* (pp. 797–839). Gilsum, NH: Barcelona Publishers.

Kim, S. (2017). The transformative applications of Analytical Music Therapy techniques in music therapy wellness. *Proceedings of the 15th World Congress of Music Therapy*, Japan.

Ko, K. (2016). Using bodily movement in supervision for expressive arts therapy students: a case study. *The Arts in Psychotherapy, 48,* 8–18.

Lang, L., Mclnerney, U., Monaghan, R., & Sutton, J. P. (2002). In J. P. Sutton (Ed.), *Music, music therapy, and trauma: International perspectives* (pp. 231–259). London, UK: Jessica Kingsley Publishers.

Langdon, G. S. (2001). Experiential music therapy group as a method of professional supervision. In M. Forinash (Ed.), *Music therapy supervision* (pp. 211–218). Gilsum, NH: Barcelona Publishers.

Maroda, K. J. (1994). *The power of countertransference.* Northvale, NJ: J. Aronson, Inc.

McClain, F. J. (2001). Music therapy supervision: A review of the literature. In M. Forinash (Ed.), *Music therapy supervision* (pp. 9–18). Gilsum, NH: Barcelona Publishers.

Murphy, K. (2007). Experiential learning in music therapy: Faculty and student perspectives. In A. Meadows (Ed.), *Qualitative inquiries in music therapy: A monograph series* (Vol. 3, pp. 31–61). Phoenixville, PA: Barcelona Publishers.

Murphy, K., & Wheeler, B. L. (2005). Symposium on experiential learning in music therapy. Report of the symposium sponsored by the World Federation of Music Therapy commission on education, training, and accreditation. *Music Therapy Perspectives, 23*(2), 59–84.

Panhofer, H., Payne, H., Meekums, B., & Parke, T. (2010). Dancing, moving, and writing in clinical supervision? Employing embodied practices in psychotherapy supervision. *The Arts in Psychotherapy, 38*(1), 9–16.

Pedersen, I. N. (2002a). Self-experience for music therapy students—Experiential Training in music therapy as methodology—A mandatory part of the music therapy programme at Aalborg University. In J. Th. Eschen (Ed.), *Analytical Music Therapy* (pp. 168–189). London, UK, & Philadelphia, PA: Jessica Kingsley Publishers.

Pedersen, I. N. (2002b). Psychodynamic movement—A basic training methodology for music therapists. In J. Th. Eschen (Ed.), *Analytical Music Therapy* (pp. 190–215). London, UK, & Philadelphia, PA: Jessica Kingsley Publishers.

Pedersen, I. N. (2006). *Countertransference in music therapy* (Doctoral dissertation). Aalborg University, Aalborg, Denmark.

Pelletier, C. L. (2004). The effect of music on decreasing arousal due to stress: A meta-analysis. *Journal of Music Therapy, 41*(3), 192–214.

Priestley, M. (1975). *Music therapy in action.* London, UK: Constable.

Priestley, M. (1994). *Essays on analytical music therapy.* Phoenixville, PA: Barcelona Publishers.

Rauchway, A. G. (1985). *Relating: reflections of a psychologist.* Wayne, NJ: Avery Publishing Group, Inc.

Robbins, A. (2008a). A healing space for mental health professionals. *Psychoanalytic Review, 95*(1), 17–44.

Robbins, A. (2008b). The play space of supervision. In A. A. Drewes & J. A. Mullen (Eds), *Supervision can be playful: Techniques for child and play therapist supervisors* (pp. 191–210). Lanham, MD: The Rowman & Littlefield Publishers, Inc.

Scheiby, B. B. (1998). The role of musical countertransference in Analytical Music Therapy. In K. E. Bruscia (Ed.), *The dynamics of music psychotherapy therapy* (pp. 213–247). Gilsum, NH: Barcelona Publishers.

Scheiby, B. B. (2001). Forming an identity as a music psychotherapist through analytical music therapy supervision. In M. Forinash (Ed.), *Music therapy supervision* (pp. 299–334). Gilsum, NH: Barcelona Publishers.

Scheiby, B. B. (2002). Improvisation as a musical healing tool and life approach: Theoretical and clinical applications of analytical music therapy (AMT) in a short- and long-term rehabilitation facility. In J. Th. Eschen (Ed.), *Analytical Music Therapy* (pp. 115–153). London, UK, & Philadelphia, PA: Jessica Kingsley Publishers.

Scheiby, B. B. (2005). An intersubjective approach to music therapy: identification and processing of musical countertransference in a music psychotherapeutic context. *Music Therapy Perspectives, 23,* 8–17.

Scheiby, B. B. (2017). Analytical music therapy. In B. Wheeler (Ed), *Music therapy handbook* (pp. 206–219). New York, NY: The Guilford Press.

Scheiby, B. B., & Kim, S. (2005). 분석적 음악치료(Analytical Music Therapy)—방법, 훈련 그리고 동양 문화권에서의 적용 [Analytical Music Therapy—method, training, and application to an Asian context]. In H. J. Chong (Ed.), *Techniques, Methods, and Models in Music Therapy* (pp. 409–441). Seoul, Korea: Hakjisa.

Scheiby, B. B., & Pedersen, I. N. (1999). Inter music therapy in the training of music therapy students. *Nordic Journal of Music Therapy, 8*(1), 59–72.

Schwarz, D. (1997). *Listening subjects: Music, psychoanalysis, culture.* Durham, NC: Duke University Press.

Stephens, G. (1984). Group supervision in music therapy. *Music Therapy, 4*(1), 29–38.

Sutton, J. P., & De Backer, J. (2014). Supervision in music therapy. In J. De Backer & J. P. Sutton (Eds.), *The Music in Music Therapy. Psychodynamic music therapy in Europe: Clinical, theoretical and research approaches* (pp. 300–319). London, UK: Jessica Kingsley Publishers.

Watkins, C. E. (2013). The contemporary practice of effective psychoanalytic supervision. *Psychoanalytic Psychology, 30*(2), 300–328.

Watkins, C. E. (2014). On psychoanalytic supervision as signature pedagogy. *Psychoanalytic Review, 101*(2), 175–195.

Watkins, E., Jr. (Ed.). (1997). *Handbook of psychotherapy supervision.* New York, NY: John Wiley.

Wigram, T., Pedersen, I. N., & Bonde, L. O. (Eds.). (2002). Music therapy training—A European bachelor's/master's model. In T. Wigram, I. N. Pedersen, & L. O. Bonde (Eds.), *A Comprehensive Guide to Music Therapy. Theory, Clinical Practice, Research, and Training* (pp. 267–292). London, UK: Jessica Kingsley Publishers.

Winnicott, D. W. (1971*). Playing and reality.* London, UK: Tavistock Publications Ltd.

Young, L., & Aigen, K. (2010). Supervising the supervisor: The use of live music and identification of parallel process. *The Arts in Psychotherapy, 37*(2), 125–134.

Part 4:
Doctoral Supervision

Chapter 24

DOCTORAL EDUCATION IN THE CREATIVE ARTS THERAPIES: "PREPARING STEWARDS OF THE PROFESSIONS"[38]

Robyn Flaum Cruz
Michele Forinash

We began working together on doctoral education for expressive therapists in 2006 at Lesley University. Over the years, we have worked together in a constant dialogue, closely examining curriculum, benchmarks in the doctoral journey, doctoral competencies, and dissertation standards. We have developed models to counteract attrition, encourage engagement, and develop students' scholarship skills. With the support of our doctoral faculty committee and other groups at the university, we have engaged in continual review and revision of the program over time to enact a low-residency model of program delivery and to keep the model up to date to correspond to changes in the field and technology.

Specific doctoral education programs in creative arts therapies are still relatively rare and present a range of challenges both practically and theoretically for this group of professions that continue rapidly developing but are still not mainstream pursuits. Our own educations reflect the differences in availability of doctoral education for creative arts therapists, as one of us holds a doctor of arts specific to music therapy and one of us holds a doctor of philosophy in educational psychology because no doctoral program in dance/movement therapy or creative arts therapy was available in the early 1990s. The necessity to study "outside" one's arts therapy specialization at the doctoral level is one that many faced, and it frequently involved rejection or less than total acceptance of one's arts therapy background.

We both feel quite fortunate to have had doctoral experiences with excellent doctoral instructors and mentors. Thus, one of our goals has always been to pay it forward and give our students the supportive doctoral experience that we had so that they also pay it forward and help the arts therapies professions grow. To us, doctoral education is about the excitement of giving back to the arts therapies professions and keeping them vital through our students and our students' students. We take singular pleasure in tracking our doctoral graduates' successes as they move into academic positions, become executive directors, and make contributions to the research literature. For example, we are excited to examine tables of contents of prestigious professional journals and see contributions from our former students who are now colleagues. We confess that we also feel especially fortunate to witness the growth that happens over the four to seven years that we typically work with our doctoral students. Watching the changes and growth that take place also sets the stage for the rewards and enjoyment that we reap in working collegially and collaborating on research and professional writing with our former students.

Our engagement with doctoral education and the mentoring models we ourselves experienced also keep us going, even in times when we face organizational and other challenges that are part of full-time work in universities. Before delving further into creative arts therapies doctoral education, we will give a general overview of doctoral education in other disciplines.

---

[38] "Stewards of the Discipline" is the phrase used in the Carnegie Foundation publication *Envisioning the Future of Doctoral Education* (2006).

The Development of Doctoral Education

Historically, the first doctoral degree (Doctor of Philosophy, or PhD) was granted in 1150, in Paris. The PhD degree did not arrive in the US until the 1800s, when the first degree was awarded in 1861 at Yale University (Golde, 2006). The Council of Graduate Schools' (CGS) September 2016 report indicated that between 75,000 and 100,000 doctoral degrees have been awarded annually since 2006. It is estimated that about 2% of the US population has a doctoral degree.

Criticisms of Doctoral Education

Doctoral education has been criticized from several different perspectives. Briefly, doctoral programs have been accused of being territorial and not recognizing or educating students in the benefits of interdisciplinary collaboration. Doctoral education has also been criticized for not preparing students for the real world of business, education, and public policy. General trends indicate that a majority of doctoral graduates actually do not become academics working in colleges and universities but instead end up working in settings where interdisciplinary collaboration is expected. Another major criticism of doctoral programs in the US is that around 50% of students who begin doctoral programs never graduate, with most of these never completing the dissertation (Council of Graduate Schools, 2008). Some of the reasons cited for students not completing doctoral studies are the expense, the demands of doctoral study, and loss of passion for the area of study (Damrosch, 2006; Prewitt, 2006; Taylor, 2006). Van der Linden et al. (2018) studied doctoral persistence, grounding two studies in self-determination theory across doctoral students from social sciences, science and technology, and health sciences. They found that autonomy predicted persistence for social sciences students but not for science, technology, and health sciences students and attributed the difference to the lack of time spent with colleagues in the lab. Rockinson-Szapkiw, Spaulding, and Spaulding (2016) also extended understanding of doctoral persistence, specifically for students in largely online programs, finding that the connectedness between students and faculty, open communication with the dissertation advisor, and feeling confident in faculty and family support were more important predictors in persistence than economic factors. These studies help to create a more accurate and updated picture of persistence that can be used to fashion program features to enhance this important characteristic.

Further criticisms of doctoral education from academics involved in doctoral education revolve around the sense of turning inward that can happen during one's education. Doctoral students may have to answer to only two or three faculty advisors, creating an insular environment in which they are not encouraged to explore research or ideas that cross over to other disciplines (Golde, 2006). In arts therapies, this can mean not crossing over and getting the benefits of knowledge that have accumulated in other related disciplines. Other discipline-specific issues can impact the learning environment. Goodman (2015) explored doctoral education in social work, where learning is confounded by a long-standing division in the profession around practice vs. research or scientific inquiry. Certainly, other professional education models struggle with similar challenges, in addition to that of creating more open interdisciplinary learning environments in doctoral education. An additional issue in these learning environments is that clear assessment of learning is also limited in doctoral education, although criteria and models of assessment of learning outcomes have been developed (Maki & Borkowski, 2006).

Criticisms aside, the majority of doctoral graduates across disciplines do not end up working in academia, and programs likely need to take the approach of better preparing students for the world outside the teaching and research that characterize academia. From our experience with doctoral expressive therapies students, many do in fact seek jobs in academia, which is likely due to the developing and expanding nature of arts therapies education and revised requirements at universities for master's teaching that require doctoral-level instructors.

The Importance of Relationship

Alvin Kwiram (2006) wrote about doctoral education and discussed mentoring using the ideal of the master and the student. This stems from the dialogue between Aristotle and Alexander in which knowledge is passed through discussion and debate. So doctoral education "is first and foremost an apprenticeship—an apprenticeship in the art of discovery" (p. 141). When this works, it is beautiful and creates a wonderful, often very close, relationship that can last well past graduation. When it has not worked, it has led not just to high rates of dropping out, but also to extremes such as murder and suicide. As recently as 2016, a former doctoral student in engineering at UCLA returned to the university and killed his faculty advisor before turning the gun on himself (Mather, Winton, Branson-Potts, & Hamilton, 2016; Woodyard, Krantz, & Keveney, 2016).

Often in academia, the term "mentoring" comes to define someone who advises students on courses or requires students to contribute to the mentor's research. Some of the issue and difficulty with mentoring for doctoral students is the "implicit assumption among university leaders that people with PhDs or other advanced degrees intuitively know how to mentor" (Palmer, 2019, p. 51). Mentoring in which doctoral students and junior faculty are purposely teamed up with a senior faculty member can be rewarding when attention is paid to mentoring skills such as establishing clarity about the mentoring relationship, devoting time to the relationship to listen to and learn from the mentee, modeling key behaviors, and offering support and focusing on a few other skills (Palmer, 2019). Accessible and approachable faculty was reported by students as a key component in doctoral persistence in the research by Robinson-Szapkiw et al. (2016). It seems that a relationship has to be mindfully and knowledgeably fostered. For creative arts therapists who spend significant time in studying how to establish relationships with clients, this might seem like a simple task.

Kwiram (2006) wrote about problem areas in doctoral education and suggested 12 specific topics that graduating doctoral students who plan to teach in the academy should be learning via their relationships with faculty, but likely are not learning. While he wrote specifically for doctoral education in chemistry, the application of these 12 topics resonates across disciplines. These topics are understanding "education as a profession"; having an "apprenticeship in teaching"; knowing the "history of the discipline"; having "exposure to other disciplines"; understanding "management and personnel skills"; understanding "institutional structure and governance"; understanding "tenure and the tenure clock"; receiving "ethics, conflict of interest, and sensitivity training"; becoming proactive in the "importance of diversity"; developing "leadership skills"; learning about "grant writing"; and, finally, understanding "regulatory and compliance issues" (pp. 153–157). After studying Kwiram, we took time to look at our curriculum to introduce topics into existing courses and create new courses. The introduction of these topics into the regular curriculum for doctoral education seems to be a reasonable solution but can be difficult, given the necessary density of existing curricula. However, convening ad hoc seminars and workshops to address topics like grant writing, working practical assignments like curriculum development and ethics explorations into courses, and the pursuit of other creative solutions abound when faculty are intent on addressing these important topics. In addition, clearly documenting some of the expectations for faculty advisor and student communications can also assist in addressing relationship.

Developmental Stages

Susan Gardner (2009) discussed doctoral education in three developmental phases. In the first phase, the student is entering the admission process, making decisions about where to attend, and, once accepted, acclimating to the demands of coursework and learning how to balance demands on time from the university with family and friends. The second phase includes completing coursework, preparing for and passing benchmark examinations, and forming deeper bonds with fellow students and the faculty advisor. The final phase is when the student has achieved candidacy and is steadfastly working on the dissertation. We propose that these stages correspond to the development of relationships and phases of relationships with colleagues, instructors, mentors, and research topics. While colleagues and instructors can be vital in supporting students, the relationship with the research topic that will be used to culminate one's doctoral education should not be underestimated. Selecting a topic that continues to be engaging without becoming overwhelming is challenging indeed. The extensive amount of time devoted to learning about and understanding this topic to be able to pose a research question about it has the quality of requiring one to be "all in." Once this happens, sustaining interest in the topic may have a serious impact on the student's ability to complete the doctorate. But this is an important consideration related to successfully mastering the developmental stages of doctoral education.

When we revised our program from an on-campus program to a low-residency format for doctoral education, we realized that students would need more help not only with developing solidly sustaining topics but also with developing connections—connections not only with faculty and advisors, but also with colleagues in order to sustain and persist in their doctoral research journeys at a distance from faculty and from each other. We focused time and energy on creating ways for cohorts of students to create a self-sustaining sense of community. This seemed to be a simple goal originally, but we found that we had successes and failures in the first few years and had to devote more time to analyzing and developing the right structures for students to use to connect and stay connected. These efforts paid off as the cohorts began to consistently function supportively in the ways that students need. By focusing on creating cohort connections in the first year of doctoral study, we have found that these connections work well in supporting the ensuing developmental stages of doctoral study. Students both build on their early relationships and develop further relationships as they continue in different stages. Of course, at the same time that cohorts are developing to establish peer relationships, multiple interactions with instructors in different pedagogic formats and advisors also take place to establish mentoring relationships. For us, it is our roles as faculty and advisors in ongoing contact with students as they achieve different stages of doctoral development and witnessing their ensuing growth as scholars that make doctoral teaching rewarding.

Stewards of the Discipline

The Carnegie Foundation for the Advancement of Teaching began an initiative in 2001 that was called the Carnegie Initiative on the Doctorate. From this have come several publications, including a book titled *Envisioning the Future of Doctoral Education: Preparing Stewards of the Discipline* (Golde & Walker, 2006). In this book, doctoral students are described as preparing to become "stewards of the discipline" (Gold, 2006, p. 5). Lee S. Shulman, then president of the Carnegie Foundation for the Advancement of Teaching, wrote:

> We view the doctorate as a degree that exists at the junction of the intellectual and moral. The PhD is expected to serve as a steward of her [sic] discipline or profession, dedicated to the integrity of its work in the generation, critique, transformation, transmission, and use of its knowledge. (Golde, 2006, p. 3)

Golde went on to write that a steward takes on "… a role that transcends a collection of accomplishments and skill. It has ethical and moral dimensions" (p. 12). To further develop this idea, she wrote …

> … we intend to convey the sense of purpose that guides action. … Adopting as a touchstone the care of the discipline and understanding that one has been entrusted with that care by those in the field, on behalf of those in and beyond the discipline, the individual steward embraces a larger sense of purpose. (Golde, 2006, p. 13)

In this formulation, stewards are people who are forward-thinking and willing to take calculated risks to advance their field. They are people who can preserve the best of the past and also envision the future, and individuals who have a sense of purpose that is larger than themselves.

According to Golde (2006), a steward is able to generate new knowledge, and one can do that only if one has a solid understanding of the intellectual history of the field. Stewards must know the history of the field, as well as the current best practices.

The "stewardship" described here echoes many of Kwiram's (2006) suggestions cited earlier about the relationship of faculty and student and doctoral education as an apprenticeship. In this endeavor, understanding the history of the field and how it impacts current questions, understanding the need for diversity, engaging in ethical practice, understanding the importance of leadership, and being familiar with neighboring disciplines are all important elements.

Tasks of a Steward

According to Golde, (2006), there are three tasks that stewards need to take on. These are generation, conservation, and the transformation of knowledge. A steward …

> … should be capable of *generating* new knowledge and defending knowledge claims against challenges and criticism, *conserving* the most important ideas and findings that are a legacy of past and current work and *transforming* knowledge that has been generated and conserved by explaining and connecting it to ideas from other fields [emphasis in the original]. (p. 10)

The generation of knowledge is generally what we think of when we think of doctoral education, producing research that results in new knowledge. Generation also includes developing appropriate research methods to address research questions. The questions need to be meaningful to the field as a whole, not just to the person designing the study. These questions also need to include a diversity of voices within the field, not just the dominant narrative. The person must be competent in data collection and data analysis and have the ability to make sense of the results. Conservation of knowledge means not only holding on to ideas from the past, but also being able to overturn or refute previous knowledge and thus discard some ideas from the past. It also refers to understanding what counts as knowledge and how this changes over time. Transformation of knowledge has to do with taking what we know, putting it out into the world, and making it available and accessible to others, both within the discipline as well as across disciplines.

The conservation of knowledge is the second task. This task involves constantly re-evaluating knowledge over time to see if it still holds up as true and useful and understanding the historical context of the times in which the knowledge was created. As disciplines grow and change, there needs to be both stability as well as evolution. There needs to be a pruning of knowledge as new research replaces old ideas and theories. One need think only of the Copernican Revolution to remember that people originally thought that Earth was the center of the universe and that the Sun revolved around Earth. Copernicus showed that this was not true. Hence the prior assumed knowledge was overturned and no longer conserved. For music therapy and other arts therapies, conservation is keenly focused on understanding what makes effective services for people in need and provides a clear motivation for doctoral students and faculty.

Transformation of knowledge is the final task. This has to do with taking the results of research and making them explicit and applicable. "*Transformation* encompasses teaching in the broadest sense of the word" (Golde, 2006, p. 11). This can include communicating findings relevant to communities who might benefit from or be impacted by the results of research. Transformation also requires an awareness of what is happening in neighboring disciplines, so an interdisciplinary focus is vital. Specifically in music therapy, with its range of practitioner education levels and so many different consumers, developing skills in the clear communication of research results and their implications is important. In addition, as many as 60% of doctoral graduates can end up in community service work rather than academia, so the need for their skill in communicating the impact of research becomes expanded to the community, where it directly affects consumers and policy makers.

Doctoral Education in Music Therapy

The following paragraph is from the American Music Therapy Association Standards for Education and Clinical Training (https://www.musicherapy.org/members/edctstan/).

5.0 STANDARD FOR DOCTORAL DEGREES

The doctoral degree shall impart advanced competence in research, theory development, clinical practice, supervision, college teaching, and/or clinical administration, depending on the title and purpose of the program. Requirements for the doctoral degree must remain flexible to ensure growth and development of the profession. The academic and clinical components of each doctoral degree must be formulated by the institution according to student need and demand, emerging needs of the profession, faculty expertise, educational mission of the institution, and the resources available. Admission of candidates for doctoral degrees in music therapy should require at least three years of full-time clinical experience in music therapy or its equivalent in part-time work. Doctoral students who have less than five years full-time clinical experience in music therapy or the equivalent in part-time experience should be encouraged to acquire additional experience during the course of the doctoral program. AMTA and NASM will work together in the delineation of the doctoral degree in music therapy.

By design, this standard is decidedly vague in content. Forinash was part of the commission that during the unification process of forming the AMTA was charged by the NAMT and AAMT with articulating standards of education and clinical training at the bachelor's, master's, and doctoral levels. The commission wrestled with doctoral-level standards and chose to keep them flexible and open, as doctoral education was just beginning in music therapy and the commission did not want to make too many demands because the direction that the field might take was unknown. The commission did envision that the AMTA and the National Association of Schools of Music (NASM) would work together to further describe doctoral education; however, these standards were passed in 2000. A revision to the entire set of standards, including bachelor's and master's, was done in 2017, yet no revision was made for doctoral standards and no further work is scheduled.

This is similar to what has happened in other disciplines and prompted Prewitt (2006) to write, "The genius of doctoral training in American higher education is that *no one is in charge*" (p. 23, italics in the original).

Developing Doctoral Education

In our experience, it has been difficult to find specific information on how to teach doctoral students—and we have searched repeatedly. To some extent, this may be because such education is frequently envisioned as "seminars" in which the discussion of ideas rather the than introduction of specific content is the main method of delivery. Many traditional PhD programs offer the same courses to MA and PhD students. The PhD students simply take more courses than the MA students, so there is little distinction between MA and PhD teaching. Often, academic departments also have a track of MA students who are accepted to complete the MA first and then continue to the PhD by taking more courses and writing a dissertation. This is particularly common in psychology programs.

In some programs, such as our own, PhD students are typically more mature and more dedicated to their learning experience because they have had the MA for several years and are already professionals in the field. This can make a noticeable difference between our PhD and our MA students. It also necessitates differences in how we approach them. We focus more on mastery in the PhD, with the understanding that through the process of their doctoral education, students will become "experts" in their specific area of research. Mastery of specific content and skills, such as research methods and writing, are emphasized. Comprehension and critical thinking skills are also important, as we want doctoral students to become expert at comparing and contrasting evidence as well as agreement and disagreement in the literature and analyzing levels of evidence that are located in the literature while thinking of these hierarchically with respect to theory.

In many doctoral programs—even in colleges of education or formal education departments—students may not ever receive any doctoral coursework on teaching. Thus, few instructors teaching at the MA or PhD level in the expressive therapies have actually been prepared for teaching in their own doctoral work. In the future, more of our doctoral programs might include some instruction on teaching for our doctoral students. Recent political changes in the US alone inspire some core revisions useful to our students in uncovering underrepresented voices in academia and reviewing course resources with an eye to including those voices. Some university libraries are already thinking about this and providing resources to faculty that could be useful in teaching doctoral students how to teach. For example, our university library has new resources for faculty on "Including Underrepresented Perspectives in Your Course" that can be used as part of an assignment for doctoral students on teaching.

The PhD degree for expressive arts therapies in the US is not a practice degree, for the very practical reason that it cannot be used to obtain any licensing advantages beyond what are available to MA graduates. Instead, it is most typically a research degree and thus aims at producing research competency and pragmatism, in addition to methodological pluralism in students. In most programs, regardless of specialization, students will obviously develop the most comfort with the methods that they use in their pilot and dissertation research, but faculty should intentionally work to steer them to research questions rather than toward research methods, for the simple reason that questions always dictate methods.

Especially in expressive therapies doctoral education as opposed to MA education, doctoral teaching is not about therapy techniques and thus not about students' affective responses. Experiential learning techniques common in the MA teaching of learning about therapy do not translate to the PhD. The focus is different for the PhD, and students' cognitions and ways of thinking are more important for PhD learning than affective responses. PhD teaching requires switching gears from MA teaching techniques. Using social interaction and collaboration can be very useful in PhD teaching, but students need to be graded on individual products. Group work or social learning can be an important and required part of preparing, but this type of collaboration is only a means to an end in which each student produces independent work. The goal of PhD teaching is to give students the tools to create knowledge, not merely to transfer knowledge to them. To this end, didactic and inductive or experiential methods can be usefully combined. As per Landy (1982), students need to wrestle with theory and data. We believe doctoral teaching should, as much as possible, set up situations where students are required to engage with material in an iterative "struggle."

As we work with our doctoral students, we have several areas in which we focus. We often joke with them in the beginning of the program that we are going to help them to "rewire their brains." The development of analytic and scholarly skills, as well as productive and ethical habits of scholarship, are indeed important. So, too, is learning to think like a researcher rather than a clinician. This is an area with which many students struggle sometimes up until the dissertation. Understanding when to take off the clinical hat and put on the researcher hat is critical. Students often reference our prediction of "rewiring" at commencement, and they talk about how differently they see the world as compared to when they began their doctoral studies.

The Future of Doctoral Education

Doctoral education is continuing to develop in the arts therapies. As we envision the future of doctoral education, we offer perspectives that are important for moving forward, building on the work of several previously mentioned authors of the Carnegie essays (Damrosch, 2006; Golde, 2006; Prewitt, 2006; Richardson, 2006;).

Understanding the history of research, and specifically the history of research in our field, is vital for students to create context for embracing the future. Indeed, there are rhythms to the fluctuations in methods and the epistemologies they demonstrate. In music therapy, as in most scholarly disciplines, there has been an epistemological revolution of sorts. After years of accepting only quantitative research, the profession has begun to embrace and appreciate research conducted with qualitative methods. It is exactly this appreciation of the continuum of methods and their associated ontologies and epistemologies that will push developments forward in music therapy and the other creative arts therapies (Cruz, 2018). Students frequently arrive at doctoral study with the unrecognized baggage of a society that has long privileged only specific types of research. Exposing our own epistemologies, sharing them as well as challenging them and our students', is an important part of the modeling process that we undertake as we teach students to be scholars and researchers.

There is a need to examine current emerging areas of research as well as look at areas that have been neglected in the past. Paying attention to voices and perspectives that have been omitted or marginalized in prior research is crucial. To fully understand what has been omitted or marginalized, students must understand their own sociocultural perspectives. These sociocultural perspectives impact the research questions students ask and help them to enact a commitment to understanding and respectfully researching marginalized voices without appropriation by adopting noncolonizing methods (Smith, 2012). The fact that our students represent an international community with many diverse backgrounds that necessitate privileging voices not previously privileged underscores this necessity for us. Incorporating these perspectives into the "habits of heart and mind" (Elkana, 2006, p. 65) of doctoral students so that this notion becomes a permanent feature of how students think long after they have graduated is important to the doctoral teaching mission. This is a major contribution of doctoral study to the individual and society.

Fostering an understanding of our interdisciplinary neighbors and their research questions is a value that needs to be strongly conveyed. Theory and research in the other arts therapy modalities matters and informs across the creative arts therapies. In addition, theory and research in psychology, neuroscience, education, nursing, and other disciplines with which we intersect also has impact and import for our research questions. Students must be able to easily converse with colleagues in other disciplines, and knowing their research questions, theory, and lexicon is crucial.

The balance of supporting risk-taking along with precision and rigor is central. We need to encourage thinking outside of the box and to question authority. In my (Forinash) doctoral education, along with Ken Aigen, Dorit Amir, and others following in the footsteps of Carolyn Kenny, we began to challenge the primacy of quantitative research in the late 1980s. What did we have to lose? We were students and didn't have academic jobs; we saw the world differently and could challenge the status quo. Upheaval happens in all disciplines from time to time. It is important to support this creativity and the passion and true idealism that accompany it.

At the same time, precision and rigor are key in doctoral student development. There is no room for sloppiness and ambiguity. While we support openness to new ideas, we do so with healthy skepticism. Over the course of their studies, students have learned how to think theoretically and critically (Richardson, 2006). They need to be able to apply this thinking as they interact with new ideas. Students also need to be able to situate their research within the current literature, while working to provide new perspectives.

Students need to become researchers and experts in their own right, and faculty should not try to clone themselves in their students. The goal is to move to a collegial relationship, extending the mutual respect from the student–faculty relationship while also accepting differences.

Finally, we need to help students to learn to set aside time for reflection and integration. It takes time to metabolize new ideas, new theory, and new research trends. Students need to grow into thoughtful professionals who have taken the time to process. Creating and supporting community is also important. Those who go into academia may find themselves isolated. Finding a way to stay connected to others keeps ideas flowing and encourages collaboration. We have found that some of our cohorts have stayed connected through quarterly teleconferences or ongoing chats in various social media. The bond that doctoral students form with each other and with their advisors is like no other.

CONCLUSION

We have maintained relationships with our former students. Sometimes this manifests as continued mentoring as our students apply to various positions, evaluate positions that they are offered, and contend with challenges related to the type of work they are doing. At other times, the relationship transitions to one of collaboration, where we publish or present with our former students (Einstein & Forinash, 2013; Hahna & Forinash, in press; Kawano, Cruz, & Tan, 2018; Whitehead-Pleaux et al., 2012; Whitehead-Pleaux et al., 2013). We find that just like teaching and advising, these ongoing contacts with our former students and new colleagues are rich and engaging for us and often present us with new learning. What could be more enjoyable?

REFERENCE LIST

Council of Graduate Schools. (2016, March). *Data Sources: Key Takeaways from the 2014 Survey of Earned Doctorates.* https://cgsnet.org/data-sources-key-takeaways-2014-survey-earned-doctorates-0

Cruz, R. F. (2018). Marian Chace Lecture, 2017: Rhythms of research and dance/movement therapy. *American Journal of Dance Therapy, 40(1),* 142–154. doi:10.1007/s10465-018-9267-7

Damrousch D. (2006). Vectors of change. In C. M. Golde & G. E. Walker (Eds.), *Envisioning the future of doctoral education: Preparing stewards of the discipline. Carnegie essays on the doctorate* (pp. 34–45). San Francisco, CA: Jossey-Bass.

Einstein, T., & Forinash, M. (2013). Art as a mother tongue: Staying true to an innate language of knowing. *Journal of Applied Arts & Health, 4(1),* 77–85. doi:10.1386/jaah.4.1.77_1

Elkana, Y. (2006). Unmasking uncertainties and embracing contradictions: Graduate education in the sciences. In C. M. Golde & G. E. Walker (Eds.), *Envisioning the future of doctoral education: Preparing stewards of the discipline. Carnegie essays on the doctorate* (pp. 65–96). San Francisco, CA: Jossey-Bass.

Gardner, S. K. (2009). The development of doctoral students: Phases of challenge and support. *ASHE Higher Education Report, 34(6),* 1–127.

Golde, C. M. (2006). Preparing stewards of the discipline. In C. M. Golde & G. E. Walker (Eds.), *Envisioning the future of doctoral education: Preparing stewards of the discipline. Carnegie essays on the doctorate* (pp. 3–22). San Francisco, CA: Jossey-Bass.

Woodyard, C., Krantz, M., & Keveney, B. (2016, June 2). Gunman in UCLA murder-suicide was victim's former student. *USA Today.* https:www.usatoday.com/story/news/2016/06/01/police-check-reports-shooter-ucla/85245782/

Chapter 25

DOCTORAL SUPERVISION: A SPECTRUM OF SUPERVISOR ROLES AND POSITIONS DURING THE DOCTORAL JOURNEY

Lars Ole Bonde
Hanne Mette Ridder

INTRODUCTION

If only research were a journey from starting point A to a well-known end point B, we could easily prepare the journey and get it done! The researcher having accomplished the successful expedition would receive the degree of PhD and would perhaps even benefit from some kind of acknowledgment such as a promotion or a higher salary. There would probably be a good enough end product in the form of a thesis. Our worry is that this straightforward A-to-B thesis most probably would entail nothing new and surprising, but only confirm what was expected. The researcher would not be able to tell of something unexpected that led to new important insight. In our view, research is not a linear A-to-B journey. There are detours, stopovers, and sojourns with the discovery of potential new directions, and the awaited end point could be altered or even found to be at a different position. We can close our eyes and pretend that the research journey was straightforward, or we can accept the complex reality and instead welcome the unexpected—although in a format where it is carefully and systematically integrated.

Without the learned lessons integrated in the journey, nothing unexpected has been allowed for. This understanding of the research journey demands at the least the personal qualities of curiosity, motivation, and sense of accomplishment in the research traveler. Without these to permit a journey into the unknown, research would diminish to the *search* for what we already know—mere reproduction of knowledge—and not *re-search* that allows for taking a reflective step back and being open to discovering what we do not know. We therefore see the ontology of research as the construction of knowledge in a context of multiple realities, in contrast to the production of "the truth answer."

Keeping the journey metaphor in the understanding of the learning process of becoming a researcher, we assume that it is fairly easy for a supervisor to guide a PhD student to travel from A to B. A supervisor, who has traversed the same or a similar path can give clear directions, and the student can be well prepared. From a constructivist and realist perspective, where the research process is understood to be a journey from a starting point full of questions and assumptions to an unknown end point that might even provide more questions, an enormous effort is required of the PhD student. Therefore, the supervisee must have the competencies to pin down the essentials from start to end and be prepared to embark on a voyage into the wilderness.

The researcher has to do the traveling all alone, but what if one or more "guides" could help in preparing the journey as well as piloting, guiding, pushing, leading, pointing at, and calling? What if there was a "travel agency" to assist and a group of "fellow travelers" with whom it were possible to share experiences in spite of traveling across different landscapes and distances? Well, there is! If a researcher wants to learn how to do research and to be accompanied in the process, it is possible to enroll as a PhD student at a doctoral program. This allows for engaging in a research milieu and for being guided by one or more supervisors.

Our focus for this chapter is on the supervision of PhD students. We will describe the context of a PhD program and the role of the PhD student and specifically put focus on the role of PhD supervision. Thus, where all chapters but three in this book focus on clinical supervision, this chapter is about academic supervision, a distinctly different professional and educational role.

Our background for giving this perspective on PhD supervision is our own experience first of all as supervisees and further as co-supervisors, primary supervisors, supervisors of supervisors, and doctoral program managers. We both have supervised numerous MA research theses, have accompanied several successful PhD students on their journeys (Bonde: 13, Ridder: 6), and are engaged in ongoing supervision and doctoral program management.

We both have worked closely together with the late Prof. Tony Wigram. For 13 years, he was head of the doctoral program in music therapy at Aalborg University. The program started as a trans-Nordic research network. With Wigram's enthusiastic management and collaborative competencies, the program grew and developed into an internal research community. Wigram emphasized quality supervision, and in several presentations on PhD supervision, he referred to the three general principles of supervision:

- A PhD study is a training to be a researcher.
- A PhD study is a discipline where the "student" changes from "student researcher" to "qualified researcher."
- A PhD study is isolating and lonely, and there should be a milieu within which there is support and critique. (Wigram, 2009, p. 174)

These three principles are integrated into our understanding of doctoral supervision that we will present in the following. We will come back to each of the three principles, but in reverse order, starting with the importance of a research milieu.

THE CONTEXT: THE DOCTORAL PROGRAM

Each country around the world builds on their own national education systems. Wishing to harmonize higher education systems in Europe, two cycles of degrees were formulated in 1999, with the bachelor's degree as the entry requirement for the master's. In 2003, a third cycle, the doctor of philosophy (PhD), was added to the European system (Keeling, 2006). This development was continued, with a focus on the research milieu. In 2009, the intertwining of education, research, and innovation was emphasized by the European Union through its request for (1) increased research competencies, (2) better integration of research within doctoral programs, and (3) career development of researchers (EU, 2009; Ridder, 2015). In the USA, a similar process was led by a combination of the federal government and national foundations and organizations (Humphrey, Marshall, & Leonardo, 2012).

In his general principles of supervision, Wigram described PhD study as isolating and lonely and emphasized a milieu within which there was support and critique. By 2009, the Aalborg PhD program was already well established and had the capacity to serve as an excellent model for how to integrate research within doctoral programs. Its progression from a research network to an international high-quality program was steady and convincing. The first directors, Inge Nygaard Pedersen (1993–1995) and Lars Ole Bonde (1995–1997), continued to assist Wigram, who was head of the program from 1997–2011, with Hanne Mette Ridder serving from 2010 to the present. The program has continued to grow (Bonde, 2011), and in 2017, a team of nine professors was engaged as lecturers and supervisors, along with adjunct professors and a number of external supervisors. The first two PhD theses were successfully defended in 1998; thesis number 50 was defended in 2018.

Only a few programs around the world offer PhD degrees in music therapy, and music therapy researchers may therefore be enrolled in doctoral programs in related fields such as musicology, music education, expressive therapies, creative arts therapy, psychology, and so forth (see Goodman, 2015). However, with more MA trainings in music therapy, we may also expect more PhD programs in the field—for example, the European Music Therapy Confederation now links to 10 doctoral programs on their website, while also stating that the list is still incomplete (EMTC, 2017).[39]

We assume that this will advance music therapy research with research programs specifically focused on the music therapy field, but we are also aware that PhD programs in other fields with a high level of collaboration between various professions equally have advantages. As an example, if a music therapy researcher does his data collection in a medical hospital, he may benefit from support and knowledge from the professions in a medical research program. The PhD student is more explicitly forced to formulate the research in a language understood by medical professions, in contrast to the case of a program with focus on music therapy. The advantage of a field-specific program is that a more field-specific discourse is integrated. This is what we encourage at the music therapy program in Aalborg, where the biannual research courses play an important role in bringing together PhD students with supervisors, the research team, and invited guest researchers. It is important for the student not only to present his own research, but also to engage in dialogue with the other participants in the course about how core aspects of research (ontology, epistemology, methodology, and axiology) are integrated into a realistic and well-structured setup (Ridder, 2015).

The eventual problems of isolation and loneliness for the PhD student, mentioned by Wigram, can occur in whatever context the study is carried out. It is a matter of being offered learning possibilities and social networks where the student has the possibility to engage with professionals and peers who are able to address the problems with which the student is dealing and help him to take relevant measures. It is the task of the research program management to build up a constructive and enriching learning environment for each of the enrolled PhD students, but it is the responsibility of the student himself to engage in these activities and to let others know when the loneliness of travelling becomes too much of a challenge. For this, certain competencies are expected from a PhD student.

THE DOCTORAL STUDENT

Many heavy tasks and advanced competencies are demanded of the PhD student. With the PhD journey understood in a constructivist and realist perspective vs. a straightforward A-to-B one, the task of the student is not only to be aware of the opportunities given by the research milieu around him, but also to nurture his own drive and motivation, to learn from each step, and to explore, dissect, scrutinize, sort out, systematize, and structure all of the relevant data and knowledge streaming in. The student must be able to balance between independently taking responsibility and making decisions on the one hand and being able to follow advice and be challenged on the other. This means a balance between being an expert and being a student.

According to the Quality Code for Higher Education, the demands on and expectations of PhD students are extremely high. Doctoral students should have the capacity not only to structure and learn but also to engage and communicate and should be able to "think critically about problems to produce innovative solutions and create new knowledge" (QAA, 2015, pp. 4–5).

As stated before, Wigram understood PhD study as a *training* to be a researcher; therefore, the role as a *student* is imperative. With music therapy as a young discipline, most of the students enrolled during the first 20 years of the Aalborg program were developers of the music therapy profession or art-based research and most had many years of expertise in clinical practice and/or teaching. Having such an expert or teacher position can make the shift to a student role quite challenging, but sometimes

---

[39] We were able to find a similar list on the American Music Therapy Association website.

it is also much easier, considering the high expectations of doctoral students. It certainly becomes easier to shift between an expert role and a student role if the student is aware of what she knows combined with knowing which areas of knowledge are missing. To accept gaps in your own knowledge and to see yourself in a learning position is a challenging necessity.

With students from 17 nations, the cultural diversity at the Aalborg program has been large, sometimes reflecting huge differences in approaches to the clinical use of music and to academic learning and sometimes with surprising agreements across very different contexts. Such diversity helps students in defining their own standpoints and in seeing their clinical and academic work in a larger perspective. This is fruitful when it comes to describing the theoretical framework of a study and linking it to methodological considerations.

THE DOCTORAL SUPERVISOR

The third principle mentioned by Wigram was that doctoral research is a discipline where the student changes from being a student researcher to being a *qualified researcher*. To allow for and help to facilitate this change to being a qualified researcher, the PhD supervisor plays an important role. Being highly inspired by Trafford and Leshem's (2008) conceptual model of "doctorateness," we understand a qualified researcher as someone who demonstrates doctorateness. Among other qualities, doctorateness demands advanced scholarship and, the ability to understand a substantial body of knowledge and to "conceptualize, design, and implement a project for the generation of new knowledge, applications, or understanding at the forefront of the discipline" (Green & Powell, 2005, p. 37). In short, this is about creating synergy between relevant elements. Trafford and Leshem (2008, 2009) describe the most frequently occurring elements of doctoral level research, such as dealing with knowledge, concepts, argumentation, theory, methodology, and precise presentation. The student demonstrates doctorateness by creating synergy between these elements.

We want to emphasize that doctorateness is also about being able to see ethical dilemmas and carefully handle them. Researchers are required to apply for ethical approval; however; rather than be restricted to rule-based judgment, ethics should instead be integrated into the entire research in a reflexive process (Stige, Malterud, & Midtgarden, 2009).

In a review of the literature, Chiang (2011) analyzed multiple realities that underline doctoral education, resulting in a distinction between various theoretical positions—for example, suggesting an epistemological position with focus on (a) the knowledge of the discipline, (b) the research object as such, and (c) the fundamental structure of research training. In the latter position, Chiang distinguishes between teamwork and individualist research. Teamwork is when student and supervisor work together on the same research project, and individualist research, when the student is working on his own individual project. Although there are major disciplinary variations between academic cultures and the intercultural facilitation of research, teamwork and group interaction seem to foster a better research understanding and a more positive student attitude toward the supervisor's knowledge (Chiang, 2011). In addition, when the supervisor works together with the student, this leads to a less heavy "student load" (p. 260). For the student, opportunities for intellectual debate with the supervisor are important, as well as debate and exchange with peers and members of the research group (Blaj-Ward, 2011).

A PhD student needs a competent and empathic primary supervisor. However, not so clear is what this pretty obvious statement means in practice. PhD supervisors have different backgrounds, qualifications, and competencies. PhD training programs have very different profiles, which is related to the recruitment of supervisors (internal and external). Sometimes co-supervisors and/or consultants can be appointed, sometimes not. The primary supervisor needs to know all of the formal rules and regulations of the specific program; however, the most important competency of the supervisor, as we see it, is a reflective stance, a self-monitoring awareness of the many roles or positions a supervisor can have and will have as a pilot guiding the student through the often rough landscapes of the voyage. In contrast to such personal qualities, the literature on doctoral supervision has mainly focused on the functions to be carried out by the supervisor (Lee, 2008). In addition to dealing with functional management, Lee found four other approaches to supervision. These approaches deal with encouraging critical thinking, enculturation, emancipation, and, finally, developing a quality relationship (Lee, 2007, 2008).

We are inspired by the various approaches to supervision described in the literature and also from participating in a supervisors' course organized by Wigram, Trafford, and Leshem in Denmark in 2008. Further, we are informed by many years of teaching according to the principles of problem-based learning, PBL (see Ridder, 2015). Aalborg University is dedicated to PBL and holds the Danish UNESCO chair in PBL. The pedagogical principles of this approach to learning come to the foreground when the role of the supervisor is that of a facilitator of learning, when the student takes responsibility for his own self-directed and self-regulated learning process, and, finally, with the ability to analyze what has been learned from working with a problem formulation (Savery, 2006; Savery & Duffy, 1995). With these perspectives and understandings, we have developed "A Spectrum of Supervision" (Figure 1) to illustrate at least some of the many potential roles, supervision styles and positions of the supervisor.

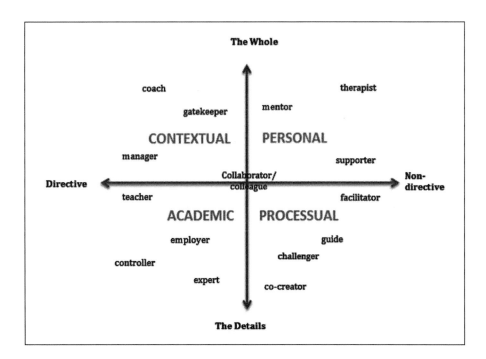

Figure 1. A Spectrum of Supervision.

A Spectrum of Supervision illustrates various roles and positions a supervisor may take during the supervision process. The overall themes of each of the four quadrants in Figure 1 are CONTEXTUAL (upper left), PERSONAL (upper right), ACADEMIC (lower left), and PROCESSUAL (lower right). The roles and positions are flexible and not fixed to a specific place in the model. A supervisor may have a favorite role/placement in the spectrum; however, the engaged supervisor will also place him-/herself differently from case to case—and certainly from phase to phase in the research process—attuned to the student's changing needs and growing skills and knowledge. An optimal situation is when two supervisors with different areas of expertise (and maybe also different preferred roles) agree to supervise a student together, based on an open exchange of ideas and points of view related to the student's project description. In this situation, it is possible to include meta-reflection in the supervision. If the student is able to accept different opinions and to engage at a more abstract level, he or she will always benefit from this, especially when the meta-perspective is made explicit.

We will now characterize each of the roles/positions in a few words. All roles/positions have advantages and disadvantages; there is no "correct position," and we understand them as metaphors rather than fixed labels. In addition, the supervisor may adopt her "teacher" or "supporter" position differently according to the horizontal degree of direction that we suggest in Figure 1. The vertical continuum illustrating a gradual shift from the Whole (overall meta-perspectives, a personal, contextual, ethical understanding,) to the Details (the academic expert knowledge about a specific topic, methodologies, techniques, and learning methods) is similarly not to pinpoint at a fixed location, but to be seen more flexibly. Further, one or more roles may often be merged. Thus, what we suggest is quite a floating model; however, as you will see, the position of the "collaborator/colleague" is fixed to the center and has special advantages.

Contextual

The Manager
The *manager* immediately sees the potential of the project in a future clinical reality and supports the student in contextual maneuvers to strengthen the evidence of the research project. The disadvantage of this position is that the student may be pushed in a direction that is not identical with her/his true aspirations and that genuine problems in the project (methodological, theoretical, or clinical) may be minimized in the interest of music therapy as a profession.

The Coach
The *coach* is directed more toward the development of specific skills or ambitions that the student explicitly wants to develop or fulfill. In contrast to the therapist, the coach will direct the student toward effective ways to achieve such skills or ambitions. The problem in this position may be that the skills or ambitions are not necessarily focused on the research project and its needs. For example, if the student's ambition is to apply for a certain position, some skills can be more relevant than others as related to that goal; however, many other skills may be more relevant on the journey.

The Gatekeeper
The *gatekeeper* is the well-established and renowned professor or manager who is in a position to invite the PhD student into attractive research milieus or settings to which it is otherwise difficult to gain access. The gatekeeper is a door-opener to important events and networks and may offer the student the opportunity to participate as a co-author or research assistant in important research milieus. This gives the student unique possibilities to be introduced to relevant researchers and thus have his career boosted. The disadvantage is that the student can be overwhelmed with tasks and duties that do not move the research forward or is left alone to sort out the details of the research process that this prominent supervisor has no time to deal with or no interest in.

Personal

The Supporter
There is often a need for support—whether psychological or practical—when the student is facing difficulties. Typical problems are recruitment worries; delayed or missing ethical approval; blocks in collaboration with institutions, hospitals, and staff members; dealing with peer review feedback; and, of course, also worries of a more personal nature. Sometimes the supervisor can contribute actively

to solve the problems, but often the main role is to "be there for the student," always remembering and reminding that these problems are a part of the journey, just as they will be later in life: All researchers have to deal with many kinds of problems in their projects. The downside of the *supporter* role arises when the supervisor tries to fix the problems for the student without leaving room for him to come up with solutions himself or resists challenging the student.

The Therapist

The *therapist* may take over from the *supporter* when problems seem to originate in the student's personal life and not in the context of the surroundings as such. Music therapy (academic) supervisors are often trained as (music) psychotherapists, and this can be an advantage if the student does not believe in his own competencies or has unrealistic expectations about the project outcome. However, the therapist position should not be mixed with the supervisor role. The supervisor may use her therapeutic insight and may also suggest personal therapy independent of the supervision, but she should not engage in a therapeutic relation with the student. It can be extremely helpful for the student if the supervisor addresses the student's personal problems and suggests ways to solve them, but the supervisor needs to act professionally and be attentive to her role and her competencies. The disadvantage is that the academic supervision can become mixed with personal therapeutic processes, blurring expectations of the research process and creating an unclear mutual dependency.

The Mentor

The *mentor* is a typical role for the older and experienced supervisor of a younger, less experienced but clearly talented student. Mentor support is not only focused on or related to specific periods, problems or challenges; it is stable and even throughout the whole project period, because the main goal of the mentor is to help the student find their own way and trust their own personal talents. The project is not the true goal; it is the discovery of the student's potential and identity as a researcher. The mentor's experience—be it as a researcher or/and as a clinician—is also related to a firmly rooted knowledge of learning processes and how students develop and mature, a deep trust in the process of learning how to manage a complex project from beginning to end. The mentor role often continues after the PhD journey is finished, if the process and the relationship has been rewarding for the student. Potential disadvantages can be that the mentor overestimates the student's competencies, underestimates the project's complexity, or is clinging to the mentor role without acknowledging the development of the student.

Academic

The Expert

The *expert* knows the field of study, the clinical context, and/or the research methodology in detail. The advantage of this position is that the supervisor can give the student authoritative advice, directions, and clear answers to many basic as well as subtle questions. Expert knowledge is based on detailed knowledge, but there are also those experts who are knowledgeable on the epistemological and methodological aspects of the PhD topic and PhD journey, so therefore the knowledge can also be at an overall meta-level. Such an expert supervisor could be placed in the upper left quadrant. The disadvantage here is that the expert may not support the student's development of independence, curiosity, and confidence in finding his own way and own expertise.

The Teacher

That of the *teacher* is a very well-known role, comfortable for many supervisors who are already teaching in academia. They may even have taught the PhD student earlier in their training. The advantage is that the good teacher-supervisor knows which literature, exercises, and methods to recommend and how to teach the student more or less advanced methods and techniques, for example, in literature searches or transcription. The disadvantage and potential ethical problem with the teacher—especially in a previously established teacher–student relationship—is that this may be a hindrance to the student's development of independence as a researcher. It is necessary that the supervisor leave the teacher position and set the student free to explore the field.

The Controller

The *controller* is also a teacher type. Both primary and co-supervisors want to be sure that tests are performed correctly, the right measures selected, and statistical calculations made and especially that the written output—articles, book chapters, monographs—is subject to special scrutiny from the supervisor's side. In most cases, the student will benefit a lot from this detailed and directive function; however, the disadvantage appears when a supervisor acts as an "examiner" or dictates to the student what to do. This hinders the student in finding a personal voice.

The Employer

The *employer* is a supervisor who is interested only in the advantages the role gives her, such as bringing her own research forward and letting the supervisee do extra or unacknowledged work. PhD positions are difficult to get, and sometimes students are assigned to this type of supervisor as the only possibility to be enrolled in a PhD program. Even if the employer may be able to provide a job, we see many disadvantages from an academic point of view with this supervisor type, unless the student is strong enough and manages to stop such an exploiting culture in order to succeed in the journey.

Processual

The Co-Creator

This is a favorite position of many supervisors. Together, the student and the supervisor can enter into an inspiring work flow in which they develop the student's ideas and the study's potential beyond what they would be able to do individually. They can work together at a detailed level on, for example, new methodology, new questionnaires and tests, and/or creative mixtures of presenting quantitative and qualitative data. The problematic dark side of this innovative position can be that the supervisor loses the overview and forgets the more educational and formal aspects of the journey or even turns the student's project into her own.

The Challenger

The challenger is a special type of teacher who—often or in certain phases—questions the choices, ambitions, and moves of the student in a critical way, in order to raise the student's awareness of the process and promote reflexivity in general. When done in a straightforward and empathic manner, such challenges can be very productive and transformative. However, challenges at the wrong time or of the wrong type can be harmful to the student's process.

The Guide

The *guide* can be more or less directive. A directive guide is an expert type who shows the student where to go through the vast landscape and points to hindrances and bypass options along the way. However, there may be other routes and views that the guide does not know. A nondirective guide will let the project "take the student where he needs to go" (this is a paraphrase of the classical GIM guide position), pointing out whatever important comes up on the way as an option for development of skills and insights. The role of a guide is the essence of the supervisor role, and this role may be combined with several other roles. As mentioned in the introduction, we distinguish between *clinical* and *academic* supervision. This chapter is about the latter. We see the two as very different professional and educational roles, but indeed with many overlaps. This is probably advantageous only with a guide or supervisor who also has profound insight into clinical techniques and methods. The difference between discussing clinical issues and formally giving clinical supervision can be unclear. When guidance develops into an invisible therapeutic or clinical supervisory process, several underlying processes between supervisor and supervisee are left uncovered. This sometimes pushes the supervisor into an idealized and superior role, which can rupture the relationship with the PhD student in an unconstructive manner.

The Facilitator

This position uses a student-focused way of learning so that the student takes responsibility for his own learning. The supervisor does not give directions but uses various learning methods that enable the student to pick up relevant methods and theories for the research. The disadvantage can arise when the student misses important details or is not able to see the research in a broader perspective, unless the supervisor is able to facilitate learning is this direction as well.

The Collaborator/Colleague

The *collaborator/colleague* often knows the student and his talents well. It may be as the student's former teacher (from the BA/MA program), or it may be as a former colleague in the clinical field. If the supervisor is a staff member of the BA/MA program, the main incentive in the recruitment and supervision of PhD students may be that the student could become a future colleague. This point can be illustrated with facts from the Aalborg program: Bonde was appointed associate professor in 1995, and over the years, four of his former PhD students have become colleagues. Ridder graduated in 1989, returned to Aalborg in 2000 as a PhD fellow, and is now a colleague with one of her supervisors and two of her former PhD students. From this position, the supervisor guides the student with the awareness of the student as a potential colleague or collaborator in future research projects. A disadvantage of this can be that the supervisor's convictions about the student's potential and talent are too set in stone and she does not see the student's limitations or incomplete competencies.

Examples

We will now illustrate the spectrum model with two examples. Both are realistic and based on problems that we and our colleagues have experienced; the first is related to the project design, while the second is related to the student–supervisor relationship.

Example One: Recruitment Problems Affect the Study Design and Timetable

PhD students (and supervisors) are often very ambitious. They want to do excellent (and, if possible, groundbreaking) research. RCTs are perfect examples of ambitious research designs; however, when it comes to real life, the estimated time to recruit participants (enough participants to meet the demands of a statistical power calculation) is seldom sufficient. Then, when, for example, a year has passed and only 40% of the estimated participants needed have been recruited, both student and supervisor face a serious problem. The expert and the manager supervisor types may force the student to stay with the design and endure the painful and problematic extra recruitment time. The coach or the guide may help the student either to live with a smaller sample (and power) or even to find a different and more realistic topic/target group and design. The pragmatic collaborator will look at all possibilities and help the student to make the best decision on the given premises: Is it possible to prolong the data collection period? Is it preferable to downsize the project (e.g., from an RCT to a feasibility study)? Or should the student redefine the project, find a new clinical target group, and develop a more modest but realistic research design?

Example Two: The Student Does Not Meet Deadlines

Many students are not able to work as efficiently as they want to or think they can. They may not be realistic about other obligations in their professional and private lives. What the supervisor then experiences is that deadlines and other agreements are not met or respected. The manager and the controller will have difficulty in handling this and will perhaps issue serious letters of warning, while the supporter or the facilitator will try to understand the student's situation and perhaps extend the deadlines. From the more balanced position of the collaborator, it may be accepted as natural in the early phase of the research journey that the student is not yet realistic about meeting time-related obligations. The collaborator believes that there will be time to adjust. If the problems continue, the supervisor will be worried and may confront the student more directly (e.g., as a controller or a manager). This may transform the relationship and teach the student something important about academic collaboration. If the problem continues, the relationship will probably be compromised or even broken; it is not likely that the student becomes a future colleague, even if very talented.

Discussion: The Interplay Between Student and Supervisor

In suggesting a spectrum of supervisory roles, we have described highly beneficial positions for learning but also pointed out numerous traps and risks. This emphasizes how the relationship between PhD student and supervisor is dependent on advanced competencies in both parties. Considering the immense personal and academic pressure that often accompanies the research process, the saying that a supervisor easily "can make or break a PhD student" (Lee, 2008) is thought-provoking. In order to progress safely through the PhD journey, good advice and directions are presented in *A Survival Kit for Doctoral Students and Their Supervisors* (Tanggaard & Wegener, 2016). This hands-on guide is aimed at supporting both students and supervisors on the doctoral journey, not only in order to avoid its pitfalls, but also to help in traveling the landscape of research in such a way that it becomes something enjoyable as well as productive. In a practical guide for research in the arts therapies, Ansdell and Pavlicevic (2001) give advice for "managing your supervisor (and yourself)" (p. 158). They suggest that supervisors ideally are wise, neutral, and unthreatening but they are also human, and thus supervision is a two-way process wherein both participants share the responsibility of making the research supervision successful.

In order to form the basis of a constructive and enriching interplay between student and supervisor, Halse and Malfroy (2010) suggest a learning alliance. The doctoral learning alliance is described as an agreement between supervisor and student to work on a common goal, namely the production of a high-quality doctorate, based on responsibility and relationships and grounded in concrete circumstances (Halse & Malfroy, 2010). Key features of the alliance are defined as mutual respect, flexibility in accommodating each other, commitment to collaborate, clear communication, and explicit strategies for progressing toward the common goal. Apart from the learning alliance, doctoral supervision comprises, according to Halse and Malfroy, four other facets: habits of mind, scholarly expertise, *technê* (craftsmanship), and contextual expertise. These are about the ability to responsively engage in constructive response, continuous and fruitful production of knowledge, competence and skills in craft knowledge, and, finally, the knowledge of the institutional and disciplinary context of doctoral study. These facets underline how complex supervision is and that it is necessary to develop ways of supervisory learning (Halse & Malfory, 2010).

PhD students will always bring in their distinct and individual expectations for specific learning styles, not least in multicultural contexts. It is highly challenging for a student who comes from a learning environment where the reproduction of knowledge is central to deal with a supervisor from, for example, a PBL background. This supervisor will ask the PhD student to seek the good questions, not give the right answers. Further, the supervisor will expect the student to be explicit about—or even to present—ongoing and unfinished research in progress. For a student who is used to being told precisely what to read and what guidelines to follow, it may be very difficult to share doubts and be explicit about problems and topics the student has still not fully understood. If the supervisor and PhD student are not aware of such unspoken expectations, the learning alliance is threatened. Unspoken expectations differ from person to person but are highly influenced by cultural beliefs and habits—for example, expectations related to gender, socio-economic status, and ethnicity. Roles in which one is expected to know and the other is thought not to know may turn into matters of power. In unfortunate circumstances, power struggles may lead to misunderstandings, misuse, or even abuse.

Not knowing is mainly very confusing and is a mental state that we mostly want to avoid, but in doctoral research, *not knowing* might be the catalyst to learning. Therefore, learning catalysts should be carefully supported in the learning alliance and not hindered by power struggles. Working in this way—with the construction of knowledge as the common aim of the research—is a delicate discipline, and our reactions to the lack of knowledge can be more destructive than constructive. As an example, if a supervisor mechanically responds to the student's insecurity or panic as the controller or the teacher, the problem may be fixed, but the supervisor may not have considered bringing other, more appropriate supervisor roles into play. Maybe the student could have been guided, challenged, or facilitated in exploring his own understandings and misunderstanding and ended up with new insight. Without awareness of why a certain supervisor role and position is beneficial in a certain situation, fruitful exchange and critical thinking are lacking. If such reactions are repeated over and over, we might have a student who succeeds in the traveling but does not have the ability to reflect at a meta-level and take ownership of the learning process.

Supervisors who are aware of their strengths and weaknesses will also develop as supervisors and have better chances for enjoying the rewards of doctoral supervision (Lee, 2008). In his concluding comment about the supervision of doctoral research, Wigram (2009) reminds us that the way in which supervision is carried out and the level of trust that is built up in the interplay with the PhD student will be transferred to the next generation of supervisors. The model of supervision a PhD student has experienced will most probably be brought forward when this student later engages as a supervisor. We therefore see training in PhD supervision, including supervision of supervision, as necessary for bringing the researcher learning process to the forefront.

CONCLUSION

We have used the journey metaphor to illustrate the PhD process. If it is commonly acknowledged that the PhD journey is a traveling into the unknown wilderness, the student researcher, supervisor, and research milieu will accept the bewilderment of the student. Instead of seeing bewilderment and confusion as something that hinders the research process, the need to understand and explore the unknown is integrated as a prerequisite competency for a *re-searcher*. We will see a competent and qualified researcher who goes beyond the mere reproduction of knowledge. This researcher is motivated by his own curiosity about a defined subject and is able to bring theory and data together in an analysis before finally disseminating the results in a relevant and comprehensive way. With this understanding of the research process and the competencies of the researcher come many expectations of the supervisor. We have suggested a range of supervisor roles/positions and described their advantages as well as their disadvantages. Supervision is understood to be a learning process that goes on in a complementary, dynamic process in the interplay between PhD student, supervisor, and other phenomena. By being explicit about and aware of the supervisor's role and position (e.g., by using the spectrum of supervision in a reflective process), it is our hope that we have enabled colleagues to have greater clarity on the interplay between supervisor and PhD student so that they are better able to ease the journey—and maybe even make it more enjoyable and enriching for all involved.

Reference List

Ansdell, G., & Pavlicevic, M. (2001). *Beginning research in the arts therapies. A practical guide.* London, UK: Jessica Kingsley Publishers.

Blaj-Ward, L. (2011). Skills versus pedagogy? Doctoral research training in the UK Arts and Humanities. *Higher Education Research & Development, 30,* 697–708.

Bonde, L. O. (2011). Postgraduate Training in Music Therapy Research in Aalborg University: An International Enterprise : A tribute to Tony Wigram. *Voices, 13*(1). Retrieved from http://vbn.aau.dk/ws/files/66643745/Training_of_music_therapists_as_researchers_AAU _Voices.doc

Chiang, K. H. (2011). The Experience of Doctoral Studies in the UK and France: Differences in epistemology, research objects, and training. *European Journal of Education, 46*(2), 257–270.

EMTC. (2017). *Doctoral music therapy research programmes in the European countries.* Retrieved August 8, 2017, from http://www.emtc-eu.com/doctoral-programmes/

EU. (2009). *The Bologna Process 2020—The European Higher Education Area in the new decade.* Leuven, Belgium. Retrieved from https://www.eurashe.eu/library/modernising-phe/ Bologna_2009_Leuven-Communique.pdf

Goodman, K. D. (Ed.). (2015). *International perspectives in music therapy education and training.* Springfield, IL: Charles C Thomas Publisher.

Green, H., & Powel, S. (2005). *Doctoral study in contemporary higher education.* Glasgow, UK: Society for Research into Higher Education & Open University Press.

Halse, C., & Malfroy, J. (2010). Retheorizing doctoral supervision as professional work. *Studies in Higher Education, 35*(1), 79–92.

Humphrey, R., Marshall, N., & Leonardo, L. (2012). The impact of research training and research codes of practice on submission of doctoral degrees: An exploratory cohort study. *Higher Education Quarterly, 66*(1), 47–64.

Keeling, R. (2006). The Bologna Process and the Lisbon Research Agenda: the European Commission's expanding role in higher education discourse. *European Journal of Education, 41*(2), 203–223.

Lee, A. M. (2007). Developing effective supervisors : Concepts of research supervision. *South African Journal of Higher Education, 21*(4), 680–693.

Lee, A. M. (2008). How are doctoral students supervised? Concepts of doctoral research supervision. *Studies in Higher Education, 33*(3), 267–281.

QAA. (2015). *Characteristics Statement. Doctoral Degree.* Southgate House, Southgate Street, Gloucester, UK. Quality Code for Higher Education, Part A: Setting and maintaining academic standards. Retrieved from http://www.qaa.ac.uk/en/Publications/Documents/Doctoral-Degree-Characteristics-15.pdf

Ridder, H. M. (2015). Doctoral education: a model of problem-based learning. In K. D. Goodman (Ed.), *International perspectives in music therapy education and training* (pp. 75–100). Springfield, IL: Charles C Thomas Publisher.

Savery, J. R. (2006). Overview of problem-based learning. *Interdisciplinary Journal of Problem-Based Learning, 1*(1), 9–20.

Savery, J. R., & Duffy, T. M. (1995). Problem-based learning: An instructional model and its constructivist framework. *Educational Technology, 35*(5), 31–38.

Stige, B., Malterud, K., & Midtgarden, T. (2009). Toward an agenda for evaluation of qualitative research. *Qualitative Health Research, 19*(10), 1504–1516.

Tanggaard, L., & Wegener, C. (2016). *A survival kit for doctoral students and their supervisors: Traveling the landscape of research.* London, UK: SAGE Publications.

Trafford, V., & Leshem, S. (2008). *Stepping stones to achieving your doctorate. By focusing on your viva from the start.* Berkshire, UK: Open University Press.

Trafford, V., & Leshem, S. (2009). Doctorateness as a threshold concept. *Innovations in Education and Teaching International, 46*(3), 305–316.

Wigram, T. (2009). Supervision of PhD doctoral research. In H. Odell-Miller & E. Richards (Eds.), *Supervision of music therapy. a theoretical and practical handbook* (pp. 173–191). East Sussex, UK: Routledge.

Chapter 26

SUPERVISING DOCTORAL STUDENTS AND DISSERTATIONS IN MUSIC THERAPY

Kenneth E. Bruscia

CLARIFICATION OF TERMS

Helping students to do doctoral dissertations has been referred to interchangeably as supervising, advising, and mentoring. In some countries and academic institutions, professors *supervise;* in others, they *advise*. Ideally, they all *mentor* to some degree. Standard dictionary definitions reveal that there are differences between the terms; however, only when taken together do they adequately cover the full gamut of responsibilities involved in guiding a dissertation.

- *Advise:* to suggest, recommend, inform, caution, or consult
- *Supervise:* to take responsibility for, to observe and direct
- *Mentor:* to serve as trusted counselor, to guide

Given the title of this book, and for the sake of brevity, "supervise" will be used throughout this chapter to refer to any or all these responsibilities, and "supervisor" will be used to refer to the professor assuming these responsibilities.

In the dissertation process, the supervisor may focus on the student or the dissertation, the process or the product; he may serve in the roles of researcher, educator, dissertation supervisor, or mentor. In assuming these roles, the supervisor may be imparting specific skills, providing general knowledge about research or the student's major field, helping the student to do research and write the dissertation, and counseling the student about how to achieve her educational and career goals.

Another responsibility is chairing the dissertation committee. In most universities, each student has a committee of professors who assist the chair in guiding the student's research and, in addition, an examining committee that, upon completion of the dissertation, evaluates whether the dissertation meets scholarly and institutional standards. The chair of the committee coordinates the efforts of all parties involved and ultimately ushers the dissertation through completion, approval, and graduation.

STATUS OF THE LITERATURE

For many decades, music therapists could pursue doctoral degrees only in other disciplines (e.g., music, music education, counseling) and only at those institutions willing to adapt their program to include music therapy studies and dissertations. True doctorates in music therapy, that is, doctorates with music therapy courses and dissertations as the core requirements, have appeared only during the past 20 years. It is not surprising, then, to find that literature on doctoral dissertations in music therapy is sparse. Only two examples were found. Wigram (2009) outlined the steps in doing a music therapy dissertation in Europe, based on the various sections of the dissertation, and Merrill (2010) reported on case study research examining the mentorship practices of professional music therapists.

This chapter is based on research and writings in other disciplines, mostly counseling and psychology, that in the author's opinion are quite relevant to dissertations in music therapy. It is also based on the author's experience as a chair, committee member, and examiner of doctoral dissertations and master's theses. The chapter is based on dissertation practices in the USA.

GOALS

Dissertation supervision has several overlapping goals. Most would agree that a fundamental one is to help the student make a significant, scholarly contribution to the literature. In addition, as an educator, the supervisor has an equally important priority: to provide opportunities for the student to gain the research and writing skills needed to conduct research independently and to develop the ethical and personal integrity needed to be a scholar.

The supervisor must also consider the student's career goals. Supervision of students who plan to be clinicians should help them better understand how research and practice can be efficiently and effectively integrated. Supervision of those who plan to be researchers should prepare them to use a wide spectrum of paradigms, epistemologies, and designs. Supervision of those who plan to be educators should help them understand the myriad facets of scholarship and how they are most effectively utilized in the education of students at all levels.

Very few, if any, of these goals can be achieved if the dissertation experience is not a positive one. Despite the many trials and tribulations of doing research, supervisors should strive to help the student find the dissertation a rewarding and enjoyable experience. Students may derive fulfillment and enjoyment from many different aspects of the dissertation process, such as data collection, analysis, interpretation, and/or preparation of the final document. But, of these myriad aspects, students can find their relationship with their supervisor to be their greatest source of inspiration and comradery, sometimes for many years after completion of the dissertation. In these instances, the supervisors do become mentors in the fullest meaning of the word.

Unfortunately, a significant problem in doctoral education is attrition. Many students complete all degree requirements but the dissertation (ABD) because they lose interest, self-confidence, or the motivation needed to persevere. Thus, another necessary goal of supervision is to provide the continual motivation and support that students need to complete the dissertation.

INDIVIDUAL AND CULTURAL DIFFERENCES

A major topic in the research literatures is how various student groups differ in their experience of the dissertation process, such as because of differences in gender, age, developmental maturity, ethnicity, race, culture, and language. An equally important topic is how individual and cultural differences between the student and supervisor are best addressed.

Gender plays a factor both in student satisfaction and in successful degree completion. Men tend to be more satisfied than women with their overall dissertation experience, and particularly with the time spent with their supervisor. Perhaps this is because supervisors tend to insist on more regular discussions and meetings with men than women (Benkin, Beazley, Jordan, & California University, L.D., 2000). Women tend to be more forthcoming than men on their feelings about the dissertation, their perceptions of barriers, and their expectations of support from the university (Pullen, 2004). Some research shows that there is a bias against women in the supervision and evaluation of their dissertations (Vallejo, Torralbo, & Fernando-Cano, 2016). The gender of the chair may be implicated. Women are more likely to complete the degree when their supervisor is a woman (Main, 2014). When women mentor other women, the relationship often develops into a professional friendship; however, nonmentoring supervisory relationships with other women in the program are not always positive

(Heinrich, 1995). Finally, gender and sexual orientation may be implicated when they lead to friendships and romantic relationships that impede the dissertation process.

Differences in age among students and between student and supervisor are important to consider. Dissertation students benefit in many ways from maintaining active, positive relationships with their peers. When age differences detract from these relationships, the student may experience unnecessary difficulties. Significant age differences with the supervisor in either direction can also create difficulties.

Along with age, maturity is implicated. Students at later stages of psychosocial development are better able to maintain positive relationships with their supervisor and to successfully avoid or manage conflicts that may arise. Psychosocial development is also predictive of the ability to persevere and successfully complete both the dissertation and the degree program in the estimated time frame (Goldman & Goodboy, 2017).

Doctoral students who are in ethnic or racial minorities can often feel marginalized and neglected during the dissertation process, and, instead of seeking the necessary support from their peers or supervisor, they look to their personal family and friends (Sanders, 2017). This is less likely to happen when the student and supervisor are of the same ethnicity or race. In this scenario, supervisors are more likely to develop an empathic and emotional bond with students in the same minority (Brown, 2009), and this bond contributes greatly to a positive dissertation experience.

Finally, differences in culture and language can be very influential in shaping the dissertation experience. They can have direct effects on the quality of the student–supervisor relationship, the student's satisfaction with the dissertation experience, and degree completion. Corner and Pio (2017) provide a comprehensive description of the myriad tensions experienced when undertaking doctoral study in another country, and although this is written in reference to management education, all the tensions cited are clearly recognizable in other fields, including music therapy. As can be expected, international students often begin their studies in culture shock, mostly unaware of social conventions and academic cultures in the study country. This makes it very difficult for them to develop the kinds of relationships that are so essential for success in doctoral study. Although many pass the language examination required for admissions to universities in the study country, they may still be ill-prepared to read, speak, and write at the level of proficiency required for doctoral study, much to the consternation of the student. There can also be cognitive differences between the two cultures in how ideas are organized in scholarly writings, as well as about what rules must be followed when using the ideas and words of others. These difficulties in language and scholarly writing can overwhelm and exhaust the student because of the many additional hours of translation, study, and adaptation required for them to complete assigned tasks. Aside from providing the necessary instruction, the most effective means of helping international students is to be sensitive to their resources and needs and to ensure that they have the relational support from professors and peers that they need to succeed (Corner & Pio, 2017).

Special attention must be given to avoid tokenism, described by Corner and Pio (2017) as three common perceptions the majority has about minorities: visibility, contrast, and assimilation. Because minorities are often *visibly* different, they are unable to recede into the background; as a result, they are often scrutinized more intensely and frequently than the majority. To make matters worse, the majority tends to *contrast* or even exaggerate these differences. This leaves minority individuals with two unacceptable choices: Either stay distant and isolated or denigrate those aspects of themselves that are different so that they can fade into the background. Contrasting differences leads to a third distortion, *assimilation*. When the minority tries to assimilate, the majority distorts their efforts by fitting the person into stereotypes of the minority. For example, when the majority assumes that African-Americans have a better sense of rhythm than Caucasians, their expectations of rhythmic ability are likely to be higher and their perception of any deficiencies becomes overblown. Such stereotypes are very difficult for minorities to overcome, especially in close relationships such as a student and supervisor.

Cultural differences, like individual differences, are myriad in number and variety, and there are no fail-safe recipes for guaranteeing that every difference between student and supervisor is respectfully addressed. The challenge for the supervisor is not "managing" the differences through prescribed ways of relating to the student. Instead, it is maintaining an awareness of oneself and the student that is respectful of both differences and similarities. Ultimately, individual and cultural differences call for reflexivity before action.

The author has found that there are two interdependent, erroneous assumptions that lead to insensitivities and microaggressions between individuals who have cultural differences. The first is assuming similarities where they do not exist, and the second is assuming differences where they do not exist. An assumption of nonexisting *similarities* can predispose one to overidentification with the other and unfounded and sometimes inauthentic feelings of empathy. An assumption of nonexisting *differences* can predispose one to feelings of uncertainty or alienation about the other and relationships that are distant.

The challenge to these assumptions is to always consider potential similarities and differences together as one integrated—not separate—process, thereby finding the relationships between them. Similarities must always be qualified by differences in relation to the similarities; conversely, differences must always be qualified by similarities in relation to the differences. Two melodies, for example, can be the same in pitch sequence but different in rhythm. Both are of equal significance and meaning.

The supervisor's responsibilities are multilevel. First, he must help the student to be reflexive about similarities and differences in any research participants who might be involved, as well as between the student researcher and the participants. The same reflexivity is also needed in the supervisor–student relationship. If dissertation students have the same needs, it is important to recognize how differently they will be expressed and addressed by each student. If the supervisor and supervisee have similar beliefs about music therapy research, it is important to examine in what ways they are different; if the supervisor and supervisee belong to the same minority, it is important to examine differences within that group and between the two of them.

Learning when and with whom these efforts are indicated depends to a great extent on the degree of reflexivity in both the supervisee and the student. Going into further detail about handling individual vs. cultural differences is beyond the scope of this chapter, but an important difference among supervisees that warrants discussion is the ways in which they resist the supervisor and the supervision process. Resistance varies widely according to individual and cultural differences.

THE RELATIONSHIP

The relationship between dissertation student and supervisor is unique; it is not like any other in academe. It is an extended, one-to-one, private relationship that can last several years during and after the dissertation. It often develops into a close professional relationship, mentorship, or personal friendship. During the dissertation, however, it is a helping relationship—the supervisor helps the student by giving the guidance and support needed by the student to complete the dissertation, graduate, and eventually find a place in the professional community.

Disparity in Expertise and Power

The student–supervisor relationship can be experienced as more or less hierarchical because of several unavoidable disparities (Rosenberg & Heimberg, 2009). First, the supervisor is assumed to have more knowledge, skill, and experience than the student, at least in those areas pertinent to the student's dissertation and field of study. This can bring both advantages and disadvantages. When the supervisor is perceived as having more expertise, the student can feel safer and less vulnerable. The supervisor can be trusted to prevent scholarly problems and mistakes in the research process and thereby ensure the acceptability of the dissertation. However, when the disparity in expertise is perceived as too large, the student can easily be intimidated by the supervisor's stature. When this happens, the student may become uncomfortable in sharing or valuing his own ideas and working independently.

Yet another disparity is in the opposite direction, when the student perceives the supervisor as not having sufficient or relevant expertise. This is a stickier problem for the student because bringing it to the supervisor's attention might jeopardize their relationship and requesting another supervisor might have catastrophic political consequences. Usually, the best recourse is for the student to consult another member of her dissertation committee or another trusted professor on how to handle the problem. Another way is for the student to ask the supervisor if she can work with other professors for very specific reasons. The supervisor should be alert to the potential need for outside consultation when mapping out the dissertation process in the early stages of their work together and then be humble enough to accept that the student does not want to work with him. The students must always be given viable and safe alternatives, and responsibility for doing so ultimately rests with the supervisor and the entire doctoral faculty.

Second, there is a disparity of power and influence. Ultimately, the supervisor has power over the student's grades, program status, and dissertation approval. Moreover, after the student graduates, the supervisor may have the power to enhance or impede the student's entire professional future (Rosenberg & Heimberg, 2009). Some supervisors are more inclined than others to wield this power, and this determines how vulnerable the student will be.

The supervisor also has more influence as an advocate. He can protect the student from unfair criticism by the examining committee while also helping the committee to recognize the value of the student's dissertation. Equally important, the supervisor can usher the student through the complicated maze of dissertation approval and degree completion. Carrying the completed dissertation through the academic system can be quite daunting, and even when power is not an issue, the supervisor's influence and advocacy are of utmost importance to the student's success.

Ultimately, student perceptions determine how power and influence disparities will help or impede their efforts. When students overestimate the supervisor, they may depend more on the supervisor rather than themselves to produce an approvable dissertation. The first sign of this is when the student shows little concern over the quality of her work as well as overconfidence in the approvability of her dissertation. Here, too, much trust in the supervisor leads to dependency and overconfidence rather than self-reliance.

On the other hand, there is always the possibility that the supervisor in fact does not have the essential powers or influences or that the student perceives him as not having them. Naturally, the student will feel vulnerable and insecure and, because of this lack of trust, is likely to become more self-reliant and less dependent on the supervisor. Then problems are likely to arise in the supervision process. The supervisor might interpret the student's self-reliance as resistance and then become more directive unnecessarily. The student is left in a double bind, not allowed to be self-reliant and afraid of complying with the supervisor's directives.

Compatibility

Students and supervisors are bound to have professional differences, but this should not be problematic if the two are compatible along the most relevant dimensions of dissertation work. In music therapy, it is ideal for students to work with supervisors who are compatible in any of the following:

- Research interests (e.g., objectivist or interpretivist research, topics in the field)

- Career path (e.g., educator, clinician, researcher)
- Theoretical orientation (e.g., behavioral, psychodynamic, humanistic)
- Method (e.g., improvisation, listening)
- Medium (e.g., vocal, instrumental)

Personality may also be important to consider. Some research has been done on how compatibility in personality traits may affect the student–supervisor relationship and the likelihood of student burnout. Agreeableness, extraversion, and neuroticism were found to be the most important traits (Kosh, 2014).

Incompatibility along any dimension can lead to communication or relationship problems that disrupt dissertation work. For example, if they are incompatible in research interests, students may have difficulty in selecting a dissertation topic and design of interest and significance to them rather than the supervisor. If they are incompatible in method or medium, students may dismiss the supervisor's advice too readily, causing the supervisor to withdraw his support. All such unresolved incompatibilities make meetings between the two both unpleasant and unproductive.

The best way to prevent problematic differences is to allow the student to select her own dissertation supervisor and committee. Students who select their own supervisors have greater overall satisfaction with their dissertation experience than those who were assigned a supervisor (Neale-McFall, 2012; Schlosser, Knox, Moscovitz, & Hill, 2003). It is interesting to see what students report as the most important criteria in deciding on a supervisor, for example:

- the supervisor's usual behaviors (Neale-McFall, 2012)
- the supervisor's openness to collaboration (Neale-McFall, 2012)
- similarities in work style (Neale-McFall, 2012)
- degree of personal connection the student feels with the supervisor (Neale-McFall, 2012)
- the student's beliefs about the supervisor's opinion of her research capabilities (Morrison & Lent, 2014)
- the supervisor's research method preferences (Carpenter, Makhadmeh, & Thornton, 2015)
- the supervisor's recent productivity as a researcher (Carpenter, Makhadmeh, & Thornton, 2015)
- the supervisor's academic rank (Carpenter, Makhadmeh, & Thornton, 2015)

Students are most likely to select the most suitable supervisor when they have taken courses taught by the supervisor or when they have been supervised previously by the supervisor. Such experiences can apprise students of their compatibility with the supervisor and the potential for a positive working relationship.

Professional Mutuality

Professional mutuality is a key ingredient in the student–supervisor relationship. It fosters growth, and, as it increases in time, it leads to a developmental shift that enables the student to take more ownership of her work, while also recognizing the value of input from the supervisor. As this occurs, disparities in the relationship become mutually empowering (McMillan-Roberts, 2015). In this context, professional mutuality is not the same as interpersonal reciprocity—one party does not reciprocate in kind what the other party provides. In professional mutuality, each party contributes to the other party, but within their appropriate role parameters, to different degrees, and in different ways.

Trust

Trust is essential in professional mutuality. Ideally, the student trusts the supervisor and the supervisor trusts the student, although in different areas and in different ways. The student needs to trust that the supervisor will use his expertise, power, and influence to ensure the student's success, while also providing the academic and personal support needed. Dissertation supervisors typically establish trust through the kinds of feedback they give to the student, the consistency of their behaviors, and their personal connection to the student (Rademaker, O'Connor, Wetzler, & Zaikina-Montgomery, 2016). And, of course, students can only trust supervisors who meet all of their responsibilities in a professional way.

In return, the supervisor needs to trust that the student will recognize when he is acting in her best interests. Moreover, when the necessary guidance and support are provided, the supervisor trusts that student will do her best to think and act autonomously as a researcher (i.e., gain research self-efficacy) (Overall, Deane, & Peterson, 2011). When it is agreed that the student should perform a certain task or handle it in a certain way, the supervisor needs to trust that the student has either done so or honestly reported otherwise.

Role Expectations

Trust is impossible if even one party has inappropriate role expectations of the other. The supervisor must faithfully carry out his responsibilities to the student within appropriate role boundaries, and the student must do the same. Otherwise, it is impossible to have reliable role expectations. One party cannot predict what the other will do, and the other party will not understand why it is inappropriate. Without accurate role expectations, there can be no mutuality in trust. A department-wide contract between student and supervisor can be very helpful in avoiding these kinds of problems.

Open, Honest Communication

Professional mutuality requires open communication and honesty. The student and supervisor must expect each other to be honest with one another. Whenever either party senses a problem in the relationship or encounters an obstacle in the dissertation process, there must be timely and honest communication with the other party. For example, when the student is frightened or annoyed with the supervisor's style of guiding, it is more helpful to talk openly with the supervisor instead of letting the negative reactions remain unaddressed. Similarly, when the supervisor senses that the student is avoiding or resisting his guidance, it is more helpful for the supervisor to talk openly with the student rather than let this pattern obstruct their work together.

Personal Connection

Although not often discussed openly in academic circles, professional mutuality depends greatly upon the supervisor and student having a personal connection, which in turn depends upon having a basic affinity for one another. If they are to have a productive and enjoyable relationship, they have to at least like each other or have the possibility of doing so. Also, if they have been in a previous disagreement or confrontation, residual anger and resentment cannot be carried forward into the relationship without serious consequences.

Confidentiality

The student–supervisor relationship is confidential; it can flourish only if the student knows with certainty that whatever she shares with the supervisor and whatever the supervisor learns about her during the supervision process will not be revealed to others without her express permission. This includes both personal and professional information. It is advisable to clarify from the very beginning the kinds of information that must be kept confidential and with whom. This can be done either through informal, verbal agreements or through a signed contract.

Notwithstanding the importance of confidentiality, valuable learning opportunities can be gained by group meetings and seminars involving students and supervisors. When dissertation students meet together for any form of dissertation supervision, the very first meeting must include a discussion of what student and supervisor can expect of one another in terms of confidentiality.

Autonomy and Support

An important goal of the dissertation is to develop the student's "research self-efficacy." This is the term used to describe the student's ability to do research autonomously upon completion of the dissertation and to do so with the necessary self-confidence. To develop research self-efficacy in the student, the supervisor has to find the right balance between encouraging the student to work autonomously and providing the necessary support to do so. Research has shown that students who receive higher levels of autonomy and support from their supervisor are more likely to develop greater research self-efficacy than those who receive lower levels. Research efficacy is developed by helping students find and develop their own voice as researchers, while simultaneously providing the guidance and encouragement needed to successfully complete all the tasks involved in doing research (Overall, Deane, & Peterson, 2011).

This demanding yet supportive style of supervision brings many benefits to students. It helps the student develop higher levels of cognitive, affective, and professional skills; it increases the student's productivity; and it leads to the highest levels of student satisfaction. Noteworthy is that such high levels of demandingness and responsiveness are the essential qualities of parent–child communications that optimize child development (Ni, 2017).

Transference and Countertransference

Not all supervisors subscribe to psychodynamic thinking; nonetheless, transference and counter-transference are phenomena that pervade the dissertation process and the student–supervisor relationship. In a transference, the student relives a past relationship with a significant other with the supervisor. The nature and object of the transference depends greatly upon the degrees of autonomy and support experienced with the significant others as compared to the supervisor. Also implicated are the many feelings experienced in the supervisory relationship that may be associated with significant others, such as vulnerability, fear, insecurity, and so forth.

The solution depends upon whether the feelings aroused in the student are positive or negative. When the transference is negative, the supervisor should help the student to pay attention to the unique aspects of their own relationship as it is unfolding in the present. In addition, the supervisor must adjust the work and relationship so that similarities between the significant other and the supervisor can be minimized. The similarities that need to be minimized could range from the autonomy/support continuum to the feelings engendered in the student by the supervisor. Depending on the student and the field of study, the supervisor can discuss the transference with the student; if this is inappropriate, the supervisor should discuss any adjustments he would like to make in their work.

Positive transferences, that is, when the student projects positive feelings onto the supervisor, can be beneficial to the supervisory relationship; however, they may be detrimental if the feelings are too intense or distorted. Once again, the solution lies in adjusting the degrees of autonomy and support and engendering feelings that are less intense and distorted.

Countertransference occurs when the supervisor relives past relationships with significant others in the client's life or in his own life. When reliving the student's past, the supervisor accepts the student's projections and adopts interactional patterns that the student has created to match those with her significant other. When reliving his own past, the supervisor projects feelings and interaction patterns from his own personal past onto the student. Here, negative countertransference occurs when reliving the past relationship is destructive, and positive occurs when the past relationship is helpful to the dissertation process. Reflexivity is the best remedy.

Dual Relationships

Dual relationships between student and supervisor may be romantic or nonromantic, avoidable or unavoidable, and problematic or unproblematic. They can develop before, during, or after the dissertation. They become unethical when "there is the potential for loss of objectivity by either party or exploitation of the student by the supervisor" (Rosenberg & Heimberg, 2009, p. 181). This occurs when the supervisor intentionally or unintentionally misuses his rank, status, or power to the detriment of the relationship and the dissertation (Rosenberg & Heimberg, 2009) or when the student uses their personal relationship to benefit completion and approval of the dissertation.

Romantic relationships become harmful when student and supervisor have incompatible expectations with respect to roles and responsibilities and, as a result, have significant difficulty in carrying them out. Mixing different kinds of power with romance is both difficult and unethical. Important questions arise. To what extent can the supervisor be directive or authoritative? How accurately can the supervisor evaluate the student's work? What kinds of reciprocity are inappropriate? Is the relationship truly consensual? Who is the supposed beneficiary of this relationship? Can the student act in her own interests?

Dual relationships affect more than the student and supervisor. They also affect other doctoral students, the integrity of the degree program, and even the reputation of the university. They discredit "the guarantees of professionalism and equal treatment expected by the larger learning community" (Rosenberg & Heimberg, 2009, p. 184).

Nonromantic dual relationships with friends or colleagues are often unavoidable. It is not unusual for students to pursue doctoral degrees in programs where friends or colleagues teach. And, as mentioned before, it is not unusual for student and supervisor to develop a personal bond as mentor and mentee. Dual relationships bring confusion over the goals and expectations of each relationship. The issues and questions are the same as those cited above for romantic dual relationships. Nevertheless, nonromantic dual relationships are usually easier to manage than romantic ones, and they are not necessarily problematic.

One other dual relationship can occur, which is when a student–supervisor relationship is also an employee–employer relationship. Here there is a power differential in both relationships, and money rather than love is the contaminating variable (Rosenberg & Heimberg, 2009). The same problems and remedies apply. The supervisor and student must maintain clear boundaries and role expectations for each relationship, and both have to communicate whenever objectivity is lost and there is a possibility for exploitation of either party.

BARRIERS, BLOCKS, AND IMPASSES

O'Connor (2017) identified three types of problems commonly encountered by students in the dissertation process: barriers, blocks, and impasses. They can occur alone or together, and often one problem leads to another. The following discussion is the author's elaborations of O'Connor's thoughts as applied more specifically to music therapy.

Barriers

A *barrier* "is a largely non-negotiable reality, internal and/or external, which limits a student's ability to enter into this work at a sufficiently developed level" (O'Connor, 2017, p. 3). Included are any practical limitations or obstacles that cannot be overcome by student or supervisor but instead must be accommodated. Barriers can be found in the academic environment, the student, the student's family, the supervisor, the relationship, and/or the dissertation itself.

The barriers most often encountered are student disabilities, such as a medical illness, psychiatric disorder, sensory or physical disability, or learning disability. Some of these are more visible than others, thus requiring the supervisor to be extra sensitive to such problems. More often than expected, doctoral students may have a learning disability that affects reading abilities, the organization of ideas, the ability to write, and so forth. Such disabilities must be recognized, and then ways of getting around them must be developed by both student and supervisor, ideally with the help of the university's disability office.

Demographic variables (e.g., gender, race, ethnicity, and culture) can also be perceived as barriers that cannot be changed. These have already been discussed above.

Blocks

A *block* is an emotional reaction the student has to the dissertation process that prevents her from making any progress. Vulnerability is one of the worst reactions. Aside from the emotional hurt felt by the student, it strains the supervisory relationship and disrupts the dissertation work itself. Vulnerability often stems from exaggerated disparities between student and supervisor that predispose the student to feel inferior, powerless, and at risk. All three feelings intersect. When the student feels inferior, she feels powerless to do the dissertation work adequately and then feels the risk of failure. Compounding the problem, the student does not want to reveal her dilemma to the supervisor or share any personal information that would expose other weaknesses (Rademake, O'Connor, Wetzler, & Zaikina-Montgomery, 2016).

Vulnerability may also result when the supervisor gives the student too much autonomy and not enough support. The student is left to make major decisions and perform important tasks without the supervisor's guidance and support, once again predisposing the student to feeling inferior, powerless, and at risk.

Fear and anxiety are also common blocks in dissertation work. Students may fear that the dissertation is not meaningful or representative of themselves or that the dissertation will be rejected by the examining committee. They may also fear that others will perceive them as incompetent or that their supervisor will be disappointed or displeased with their work. The ultimate terror is that the student's self-esteem will be shattered and that her illusions about her own capacities will be debunked (O'Connor, 2017).

Students need the supervisor's help to prevent and overcome these feelings. The supervisor's availability and dependability are key factors (Inman, Schlosser, Ladany, Howard, Boyd, et al., 2011), along with a good amount of praise and encouragement.

Sometimes the supervisor is unable or unqualified to address these blocks directly or prevent them from interfering with the dissertation. Referring the student to a counselor or therapist is advisable. Some universities or departments provide supportive therapy groups for dissertation students, and these can be very beneficial. One clinical study showed that, through the group process, students were able to counter their feelings of isolation and gain a sense of connection and community with their peers. It also showed that students were able to develop new perspectives on themselves, supervisors, and the dissertation process, and this helped them to forge ahead with their work. (Pauley, 2004).

Impasses

Impasses are stalemates in the student–supervisor relationship that prevent or inhibit working together collaboratively and productively (O'Connor, 2017). The student and supervisor consciously and/or unconsciously collude to create a dynamic that halts or adversely affects progress. Dual relationships are especially susceptible to impasses. Since an impasse involves both parties, the supervisor is unable to deal with it on any level. Unfortunately, depending on the severity and scope of the impasse, the only solution might be a change of supervisor. Mediation by a third party might help in some situations, but it may also exacerbate the impasse.

UNHELPFUL SUPERVISION

Students are not the only ones to present problems that impede dissertation work. Supervisors also cause several problems for the student. Rosenberg and Heimberg (2009) propose that the supervisor is very unhelpful when he:

1. Is absent, unavailable, or undependable;
2. Fails to provide reliable, informed, or helpful feedback;
3. Is punitive and hypercritical;
4. Interferes with the student's funding through the department.

Undoubtedly there are many other forms of unhelpful supervision, and these are examined in other parts of this chapter, primarily in terms of what supervisors should do to prevent problems rather than what they should not do.

THE PROCESS

Dissertation research usually requires the student to proceed in stages based on how sections of a dissertation are sequenced. These stages do not necessarily include how the actual supervisory process unfolds. Here the process is described in terms of what the supervisor must do at different times throughout the dissertation work.

Identifying Prerequisites

Potential dissertation topics must be considered when advising the student from the very beginning of the degree program. Certainly, the student needs courses in different types and methods of research as well as courses on content areas that are likely to become dissertation topics. In addition, the doctoral student should be involved in positive research experiences prior to the dissertation. This not only prepares students for the academic and supervisory requirements of the dissertation, but also lessens the usual threats of doing a dissertation (Bridgmon, 2007).

Establishing Rapport

In the first or second meeting, the supervisor's main concern is establishing a rapport with the student. Establishing *personal* rapport can begin with friendly, relaxed dialogues on any topic that will bring out each other's personality. Humor is often helpful. Establishing *professional* rapport usually begins with an open-ended discussion of professional interests and experiences of the student, with follow-up comments from the supervisor. Potential topics for the dissertation may be explored, but no effort should be made to select a topic yet.

Underlying these discussions are some basic questions for both student and supervisor. Is there the possibility of us working together productively and enjoyably? Can I collaborate with this person? Are we sufficiently compatible personality-wise? How comfortable am I with the disparities I perceive between us?

Mapping Out the Dissertation Process

In meeting two or meeting three, the supervisor should lay out the entire dissertation process so that the student has an overview of what needs to be done. This is an essential part of the dissertation in the early stages (Tengberg, 2015) because doctoral students often do not understand dissertation requirements or processes prior to beginning the dissertation. The map should include:

- Steps in doing the dissertation
- Required sections and format of the dissertation
- Communication plan for student and supervisor and for student and dissertation committee
- Role responsibilities of each party
- Course work needed, if any
- Support system to be provided
- Requirements for ethical approval
- Process of writing and editing the document
- Approval process
- Oral defense

Developing a Topic

The student can develop a topic with the help of the supervisor, other students and professors, or other members of the committee, usually starting with the supervisor. No matter who provides guidance, the student has ultimate responsibility for selecting the topic of the dissertation. A topic must not be imposed by the supervisor or any other person in authority.

Often the most efficient and effective way of committing to a topic is to sketch out statements of the research problem on that topic. This will help to determine whether the topic lends itself to quantitative or qualitative data collection and analysis. The student's comfort with objectivist and interpretivist epistemologies can greatly affect topic selection, so this should be considered at the very beginning of the process.

Students can change their minds easily, not only because they are afraid to commit to one topic, but also because upon further exploration, the topic may pose too many problems. Certainly, the amount of time and work required to research each topic should be considered. Changes in topic should not be discouraged unless they happen too many times.

Establishing a Support System

Contact with one's supervisor through regular meetings or discussions is the most important part of the support system for the dissertation student. A meta-synthesis of 118 research studies showed that the frequency and quality of contact between the student and supervisor during dissertation work is the strongest predictor of successful degree completion (Main, 2014; Neale-McFall, 2012). The contact must take place regularly and dependably, more often in the beginning, when the student needs support, and less often when the student is able to work autonomously. Contacts must be positive experiences. Supervisors should continually acknowledge, praise, and encourage the student whenever the student implements a task well, tries to perform a difficult task, or meets a challenge.

Peer groups are a valuable way of providing support to dissertation students. The groups need not meet often, as long as they are scheduled regularly (e.g., twice a semester). Preferably, the group consists of students in the same degree program working with the same supervisor. When this is not possible, students can work with students and supervisors in other related degree programs. Sharing their dissertation work with other students is usually a supportive and helpful experience; however, sharing it with another supervisor may present problems. If the student receives criticism or different advice from another supervisor, she may become worried and upset that she is not doing the dissertation correctly. This in turn brings up whether her own supervisor knows what he is doing. Both consequences make the student vulnerable and frightened, while also disrupting her relationship with the supervisor.

Two special models of peer support have been reported. The first is the "Collaborative Cohort Model," or "buddy system" (Burnett, 1999). In this model, doctoral students stay in pairs and help each other through the entire dissertation process. The pairs form a cohort of buddies who meet and communicate regularly under the leadership of the supervisor. The supervisor also trains each pair on how to edit and critique each other's dissertation, while also providing the necessary personal support.

The second model is a retreat format, wherein dissertation students come together for two to four days for an "intensive, focused, distraction-free, supervised, writing time" (Carter-Veale, Tull, Rutledge, & Joseph, 2016, p. 1). The retreat includes at least five hours of writing each day, learning exercises, and various methods of sharing each other's dissertation. The retreat is led by a "dissertation coach" who meets with students individually and provides guidance and support.

Another part of the support system is comprised of professors who are on the student's dissertation committee. Hopefully, the student and supervisor have carefully chosen as members of the committee academics who have expertise in areas needed. The supervisor cannot be expected to have the expertise on every topic or aspect of the dissertation, so outside support is often necessary.

Designing the Research

Once a topic has been finalized, the student must do a review of the literature, not only to determine the significance and need of the topic, but also to examine the various design options that might be relevant. The supervisor plays a significant role in guiding the literature search and in evaluating with the student the relevance of the design options identified. Ultimately, the student takes responsibility for making the final decisions about the research design but usually needs considerable guidance from the supervisor. The amount of supervisory help provided should not exceed the limits required to give clear and full ownership to the student.

Studying

Studying lays the foundation for dissertation supervision. It is difficult to imagine any dissertation that does not require independent study by the supervisor. Notwithstanding how much expertise a supervisor may have, there will always be gaps in his knowledge about the topic, the research design, the methods of data collection and analysis, ethical issues, and so forth.

Studying serves to complement the student's knowledge in all areas of the dissertation and to ensure that there are no significant omissions or errors in the student's work. For example, it is advisable for the supervisor to do his own literature search to ensure that the student has included all relevant writings. When a student's dissertation requires a particular design or statistical test, the supervisor must understand them at least as well as the student—otherwise, the results may be interpreted incorrectly. When the dissertation is a qualitative study, the supervisor must understand the epistemology associated with the type of research.

Supervising the Dissertation Process

At various times in the dissertation process, the student will need different levels of supervision. The author describes these in detail in another chapter of this book. Briefly, the levels are:

1. *Action supervision:* What does the student need to do? This is the most directive, behavioral approach, best used when the student needs a yes/no answer or needs to do something immediately. For example, the supervisor gives a deadline or tells the student to proof whatever she submits to the supervisor.
2. *Learning supervision:* What does the student need to learn? Depending on the research courses taken previously, the student may need to do readings that will go deeper into the dissertation topic, design, statistics, and so forth. Here the supervisor must be careful not to teach what the student should be learning in outside courses or independently.
3. *Data supervision:* What does the student need to understand about the participants and/or the data gathered? This is the first meta-reflection, dealing with the research process. The student has to step out of his usual mind-set as a doer and take a third-person perspective on any or all aspects of the dissertation work. What transpired during data collection? Did the participants provide the desired data? Which data are most meaningful? Am I approaching analysis and interpretation appropriately? What am I forgetting?
4. *Experience supervision:* What is the student experiencing to work in this way? This level is a second meta-reflection. It is a student self-inquiry of her personal feelings and their implications for dissertation work and the supervisory relationship. The feelings are shared and discussed with the supervisor. Frustration is commonly reported, along with the different forms of vulnerability described above.
5. *Reflexivity supervision:* What personal issues of the supervisee are affecting the student's work? This is a third meta-reflection, dealing with the student's world. This is an opportunity for the student to give the supervisor information about herself or her life situation that is impeding her work. When the student relates her situation or feelings to the past, transference and student countertransference issues are surfacing and the supervisor must assess whether he is qualified to manage them.

Editing

Editing a dissertation is very different from editing a scholarly publication. Dissertation editing is about teaching the student while also ensuring that the document is scholarly and clearly written. The aims are both educational and scholarly. It is a form of supervision that has many layers.

Editing is concerned with writing up decisions that have already been made through the supervisory process. The writing proceeds in stages as decisions are made about each phase of the research. Dissertation editing can be delineated into two layers, content revision and supervisory editing. Content revision takes place when the supervisor adds, deletes, or amends what the student has written, using his own ideas and judgments. This is only an acceptable practice when the supervisor is referenced as the source and the student accepts the modification. The document must make it clear which ideas and statements belong to the student and which to the supervisor. Content revision as defined here may give the supervisor ownership rights not to the dissertation itself, but only to the idea or statement inserted.

Supervisory editing can include any of the following:

1. Guiding the student to make decisions about the topic and design of the dissertation.
2. Ensuring that the layout and format of the document are correct.
3. Informing the student when the document contains statements that are unfounded, erroneous, contradictory, or lacking in sufficient breadth and depth or pointing out that the document lacks certain content.
4. Helping the student to rethink any part of the dissertation or process and then guiding her to find her own solutions to any problems.
5. Evaluating how the student has organized ideas into paragraphs and sections of the document.
6. Pointing out errors in wording, grammar, and spelling.

The first four layers require direct, live communication between student and supervisor through face-to-face meetings, telephone calls, or Skypes. It is important that this be a dialogue. The supervisor may have the expertise to spot scholarly problems, but the student most likely knows more about the actual content and what potential solutions are. Thus, the dialogue must be a scholarly negotiation between student and supervisor, and both parties must agree to any modifications made to the document.

Having poor writing skills is a problem for many dissertation students, and often developing or remediating these skills requires more than a supervisor can provide. Whenever students can learn basic writing skills elsewhere, that is where it should be done. Ideally, the student can get help from writing programs offered by the university or, when financially possible, from a private tutor or editor; however, when such help is not available, the supervisor faces a real challenge.

How much to edit is a complicated issue. On the one hand, the student can learn much from what the supervisor includes in his edits; on the other hand, too much editing can bring some dangers. Students can lose self-confidence in their writing ability and sometimes come to doubt their capabilities as a professional. They can also become lax and dependent on the supervisor. One way of addressing these dangers is to wean the student off edits, not only by gradually editing less and less, but also by editing with less detail. Practically speaking, if using "Track Changes," instead of making corrections in the document itself, provide comments on the side of the document telling the student what needs to be revised, first in some detail and then with less and less.

Authorship

Authorship is a controversial issue in dissertation research. Some dissertation supervisors assert that if they have spent an enormous amount of time in supervising both the student and the dissertation process, they have some right of ownership. Several codes of ethics for the helping professions state that the supervisor may not claim authorship unless he has made a significant and substantive contribution to the dissertation that goes above and beyond his responsibilities as a faculty advisor or dissertation committee member. Authorship always depends upon the relative scientific or professional contributions of student vs. supervisor and identification of the appropriate role responsibilities of each party. It is not tied to the amount of time a supervisor spends with the student.

There is a conundrum here, for if the supervisor has made significant and substantive contributions to the dissertation, it is unethical to submit the dissertation to the university under the student's name and subsequently recommend that the university grant the degree to the student. If the supervisor owns part of the dissertation, this raises the question of whether it is the student who is actually meeting the degree requirements.

Going even further, if the dissertation supervisor is working under contract with the university, the supervisor is being remunerated for his efforts and time. Thus, when the supervisor claims ownership, it is a nullification of the purpose of that contract. Noteworthy is that the university grants copyright ownership to the student and not the supervisor—notwithstanding any ownership claims by the supervisor.

Finally, supervision of a dissertation is an educational undertaking—the student is the intended beneficiary, and rightly so. Dissertations are not made degree requirements to enhance the supervisor's research record. Thus, adding the supervisor as a beneficiary is likely to distort the very nature of the supervisory process as well as its educational benefits for the student.

Supervisors who feel they deserve ownership usually want to serve as second author if the student publishes the dissertation. This seems warranted when the published version contains sufficient contribution to its content from the supervisor, but once again, ownership requirements must be defined in ethical terms.

Preparing for the Defense

The more a student prepares for the oral defense of her dissertation, the less anxious she is likely to be when the time comes. If there are other students in the same doctoral program, it is highly recommended that every dissertation student attend the oral defenses of their peers. Students should be prompted to observe what makes for the clearest presentation and how the method of presentation can lead to various kinds of questions and discussions by the committee. A follow-up meeting with the supervisor is very helpful.

As soon as the first draft of the dissertation has been approved, the student should prepare a slide presentation that gives a clear overview of the dissertation. Once approved by the supervisor, the student should present the dissertation to various groups of students on different levels, both within and outside the field. Practicing the presentation alone and with family and friends is also helpful. All of these presentations help the student to identify parts of the presentation that need to be simplified, as well as parts of the dissertation itself that are difficult for people to understand. It also helps the student to learn how to speak clearly and smoothly and to time the presentation to fit within the limits provided.

Reflexivity

In the context of dissertation supervision, reflexivity is the supervisor's continual efforts to bring into awareness, evaluate, and adjust the way he is supervising, based not only on accepted scholarly, ethical, and supervisory practices, but also on how the student is reacting to his supervision. (Bruscia, 2014). It is self-contradictory to encourage the student to be reflexive without the supervisor also practicing it. Questions to ensure reflexivity for the supervisor may be (Bruscia, 2014):

- Do I have the appropriate goals to help the student learn how to complete a dissertation?
- Am I supervising in ways that will address these goals?
- Is the student learning and progressing with the dissertation?
- Are my own issues and needs contaminating the dissertation process?
- Am I sufficiently aware of similarities and differences between the client and me, so that these can be used to the student's advantage?
- Do I know enough about the dissertation topic and the research methods used?
- Am I supervising in an ethical way?
- Am I practicing reflexivity enough?

IMPLICATIONS

A dissertation is more than the last degree requirement or the final hurdle for graduation. It is a scholarly internship, the culmination of all learning experiences of doctoral study. By implication, dissertation supervision is the final opportunity to help the student integrate her learning, and this calls upon all the supervisor's abilities as an educator and scholar.

Quality dissertation supervision involves more than teaching in the classroom and meeting the responsibilities described above. It requires a deep commitment to the student, which, in turn, depends upon the generosity of the supervisor. The supervisor must be generous with himself, his time, his expertise, and his concern for the student and the student's learning. Without such commitment and generosity, the student's educational experience will be incomplete. Professors, beware. If providing that generosity is not possible, advise the student to seek supervision elsewhere.

REFERENCE LIST

Benkin, E., Beazley, J. A., Jordan, P., & California Univ., L. D. (2000, February). Doctoral recipients rate their dissertation chairs: analysis by gender. *Graduate Focus: Issues in Graduate Education at UCLA.*

Bridgmon, K. D. (2007). All-but-dissertation stress among counseling and clinical psychology students. *Dissertation Abstracts International, Section A, 68,* 872.

Brown, S. K. (2009, January 1). Race and color-blind racial attitudes in supervision: implications for the supervisory relationship. *ProQuest LLC.* Available from ERIC, Ipswich, MA. Accessed August 27, 2017.

Bruscia, K. (2014). *Defining music therapy* (3rd ed.). Dallas TX: Barcelona Publishers.

Burnett, P. C. (1999). The supervision of doctoral dissertations using a Collaborative Cohort Model. *Counselor Education and Supervision, 39*(1), 46–52. doi:10.1002/j.1556-6978.1999.tb01789.x

Carpenter, S., Makhadmeh, N., & Thornton, L. (2015). Mentorship on the doctoral level: an examination of communication faculty mentors' traits and functions. *Communication Education, 64*(3), 366–384. doi:10.1080/03634523.2015.1041997

Carter-Veale, W. Y., Tull, R. G., Rutledge, J. C., & Joseph, L. N. (2016). The Dissertation House Model: doctoral student experiences coping and writing in a shared knowledge community. *CBE Life Sciences Education, 15*(3). doi:10.1187/cbe.16-01-0081

Goldman, Z. W., & Goodboy, A. K. (2017). Explaining doctoral students' relational maintenance with their advisor: a psychosocial development perspective. *Communication Education, 66*(1), 70–89. doi:10.1080/03634523.2016.1202996

Heinrich, K. T. (1995). Doctoral advisement relationships between women. *Journal of Higher Education, 66*(4), 447–469.

Inman, A. G., Schlosser, L. Z., Ladany, N., Howard, E. E., Boyd, D. L., Altman, A. N., & Stein, E. P. (2011). Advisee nondisclosures in doctoral-level advising relationships. *Training and Education in Professional Psychology, 5*(3), 149–159. doi:10.1037/a0024022

Kosh, E. P. (2014). The moderating effect of personality traits on advisor relationships in predicting doctoral student burnout. *Dissertation Abstracts International, 75.* Available from ERIC, Ipswich, MA. Accessed August 27, 2017.

Main, J. B. (2014). Gender homophily, PhD completion, and time to degree in the humanities and humanistic social sciences. *Review of Higher Education: Journal of the Association for the Study of Higher Education, 37*(3), 349–375. doi:10.1353/rhe.2014.0019

McMillian-Roberts, K. D. (2015). The impact of mutuality in doctoral students and faculty mentoring relationships. *Dissertation Abstracts International, Section A, 75.* Available from ERIC, Ipswich, MA. Accessed August 27, 2017.

Merrill, T. R. (2010). The music therapist as mentor: Two portraits of positive mentoring relationships. *Dissertation Abstracts International, Section A, 70,* 3788.

Morrison, M. A., & Lent, R. W. (2014). The advisory working alliance and research training: test of a relational efficacy model. *Journal of Counseling Psychology, 61*(4), 549–559. doi:10.1037/cou0000030

Neale-McFall, C. W. (2012). Perceived satisfaction of counseling doctoral students with their dissertation chairperson: examining selection criteria and chairperson behaviors. *Dissertation Abstracts International, Section A, 73,* 1304.

Ni, C. (2017). Are scientometric profiles hereditary? Analyzing scholarly practices of doctoral advisors and advisees in the social sciences. *Dissertation Abstracts International, Section A, 77.* Available from PsycINFO, Ipswich, MA. Accessed August 27, 2017.

O'Connor, J. (2017). Inhibition in the dissertation writing process: barrier, block, and impasse. *Psychoanalytic Psychology, 34*(4), 516–523. doi:10.1037/pap0000132

Overall, N., Deane, K., & Peterson, E. (2011). Promoting doctoral students' research self-efficacy: combining academic guidance with autonomy support. *Higher Education Research and Development, 30*(6), 791–805. doi:10.1080/07294360.2010.535508

Pauley, D. (2004). Group therapy for dissertation-writers: the right modality for a struggling population. *Journal of College Student Psychotherapy, 18*(4), 25–43. doi:10.1300/j035v18n04_04

Pullen, F. J. (2004). Perfectionism, procrastination, and other self-reported barriers to completing the doctoral dissertation. *Dissertation Abstracts International, 64*(12B), 6339.

Rademaker, L. L., Duffy, J. O., Wetzler, E., & Zaikina-Montgomery, H. (2016). Chair perceptions of trust between mentor and mentee in online doctoral dissertation mentoring. *Online Learning, 20*(1), 57–69.

Rosenberg, A., & Heimberg, R. G. (2009). Ethical issues in mentoring doctoral students in clinical psychology. *Cognitive and Behavioral Practice, 16*(2), 181–190. doi:10.1016/j.cbpra.2008.09.008

Sanders, D. R. (2017). Mentoring experiences of African-American doctoral students at historically black and historically white colleges and universities. *Dissertation Abstracts International, Section A: Humanities and Social Sciences, 78*(1-A).

Schlosser, L. Z., Knox, S., Moskovitz, A. R., & Hill, C. E. (2003). A qualitative examination of graduate advising relationships: the advisee perspective. *Journal of Counseling Psychology, 50*(2), 178–188. doi:10.1037/0022-0167.50.2.178

Tengberg, L. (2015). The agile approach with doctoral dissertation supervision. *International Education Studies, 8*(11).

Vallejo, M., Torralbo, M., & Fernández-Cano, A. (2016). Gender bias in higher education. *Journal of Hispanic Higher Education, 15*(3), 205–220. doi:10.1177/1538192715592927

Wigram, T. (2009). Supervision of PhD doctoral research. In H. Odell-Miller & E. Richards (Eds.), *Supervision of music therapy: A theoretical and practical handbook* (pp. 173–191). New York, NY: Routledge/Taylor & Francis Group.

INDEX

T

technology, 146, 239–40, 243–48, 253–57, 259–60, 415–16

theoretical approaches to supervision, 4, 11, 13, 15, 17, 19, 21, 23, 25

therapeutic relationship, 18, 30–32, 34, 103–5, 112–13, 120–21, 129–30, 132–33, 135–37, 143–44, 153–54, 340, 398, 400, 402–3

transference and countertransference, 177, 185, 189, 195, 328, 333, 361, 376, 381, 383, 395, 398, 406, 409, 448

transgender, 47, 57–58, 60, 77–78, 80–84, 88, 90–91, 93, 96–100, 176, 259, 424

transgender clients, 80, 92–94, 183

transitioning, 83, 206–7, 214, 286, 365

trauma, viii–x, xii, 20, 158, 163, 165–67, 174, 193, 281, 328, 379, 388, 390, 402, 410–11

V

verbal interventions, 232, 275, 327–28, 366, 371, 385–86, 392, 406

verbal skills, 146, 378, 381, 383, 386

verbal techniques, 16, 137, 143, 148, 306, 310–13, 318, 383

W

white supervisees, 103, 113, 116, 119–20, 125

white supervisors, 103–4, 111, 113–16, 119, 121–22, 220, 225, 399